THE ABANDONMENT OF THE JEWS

ALSO BY DAVID S. WYMAN

*Paper Walls: America and the Refugee Crisis,
1938–1941*

THE ABANDONMENT OF THE JEWS

America and the Holocaust,
1941–1945

David S. Wyman

Pantheon Books, New York

All rights reserved under International and Pan-American Copy-
right Conventions. Published in the United States by Pantheon
Books, a division of Random House, Inc., New York, and simultaneously in Canada by Random House of Canada Limited,
Toronto.

Much of Chapter 15 originally appeared in *Commentary* in May
1978. The author is grateful to *Commentary* for permission to
reprint excerpts from that essay.

Library of Congress Cataloging in Publication Data

Wyman, David S.
The Abandonment of the Jews.
Bibliography: p.
Includes index.
1. Holocaust, Jewish (1939–1945). 2. World War, 1939–
1945—United States. 3. World War, 1939–1945—Jews—
Rescue—United States. 4. United States—Emigration and
immigration. 5. United States. War Refugee Board. I. Title.
D810.J4W95 1984 940.53'15'03924 84-42711
ISBN 0-394-42813-7

BOOK DESIGN BY GINA DAVIS

Manufactured in the United States of America

68975

FOR MIDGIE

*because of
the smell of summer earth after the rain,
roses by the study gate,
the magic of the shooting star,
and all the rest.*

FOR MIDGIE

*because of
the smell of summer earth after the rain,
roses by the study gate,
the magic of the shooting star,
and all the rest.*

*"Our only hope will lie in the frail
web of understanding of one person
for the pain of another."*

JOHN DOS PASSOS
December 1940

CONTENTS

PREFACE

This book has been difficult to research and to write. One does not wish to believe the facts revealed by the documents on which it is based. America, the land of refuge, offered little succor. American Christians forgot about the Good Samaritan. Even American Jews lacked the unquenchable sense of urgency the crisis demanded. The Nazis were the murderers, but we were the all too passive accomplices.

Between June 1941 and May 1945, five to six million Jews perished at the hands of the Nazis and their collaborators. Germany's control over most of Europe meant that even a determined Allied rescue campaign probably could not have saved as many as a third of those who died. But a substantial commitment to rescue almost certainly could have saved several hundred thousand of them, and done so without compromising the war effort. The record clearly shows, though, that such a campaign would have taken place only if the United States had seized the initiative for it. But America did not act at all until late in the war, and even then, though it had some success, the effort was a very limited one.

This book is a report on America's response to the Nazi assault on the European Jews. It is not a new subject; others have written on it already, as have I, in my earlier book *Paper Walls: America and the Refugee Crisis, 1938–1941.* What is new about the present volume is that it brings out much information not previously published; and it offers several new answers to the key question: Why did America fail to carry out the kind of rescue effort that it could have?

In summary form, these are the findings that I regard as most significant:

1. The American State Department and the British Foreign Office had no intention of rescuing large numbers of European Jews. On the contrary, they continually feared that Germany or other Axis nations might release tens of thousands of Jews into Allied hands. Any such exodus would have placed intense pressure on Britain to open Palestine and on the United States to take in more Jewish refugees, a situation the two great powers did not want to face. Consequently, their policies aimed at obstructing rescue possibilities and dampening public pressures for government action.

2. Authenticated information that the Nazis were systematically exterminating European Jewry was made public in the United States in November 1942. President Roosevelt did nothing about the mass murder for fourteen months, then moved only because he was confronted with political pressures he could not avoid and because his administration stood on the brink of a nasty scandal over its rescue policies.

3. The War Refugee Board, which the President then established to save Jews and other victims of the Nazis, received little power, almost no cooperation from Roosevelt or his administration, and grossly inadequate government funding. (Contributions from Jewish organizations, which were necessarily limited, covered 90 percent of the WRB's costs.) Through dedicated work by a relatively small number of people, the WRB managed to help save approximately 200,000 Jews and at least 20,000 non-Jews.

4. Because of State Department administrative policies, only 21,000 refugees were allowed to enter the United States during the three and one-half years the nation was at war with Germany. That amounted to 10 percent of the number who could have been legally admitted under the immigration quotas during that period.

5. Strong popular pressure for action would have brought a much fuller government commitment to rescue and would have produced it sooner. Several factors hampered the growth of public pressure. Among them were anti-Semitism and anti-immigration attitudes, both widespread in American society in that era and both entrenched in

Congress; the mass media's failure to publicize Holocaust news, even though the wire services and other news sources made most of the information available to them; the near silence of the Christian churches and almost all of their leadership; the indifference of most of the nation's political and intellectual leaders; and the President's failure to speak out on the issue.

6. American Jewish leaders worked to publicize the European Jewish situation and pressed for government rescue steps. But their effectiveness was importantly diminished by their inability to mount a sustained or unified drive for government action, by diversion of energies into fighting among the several organizations, and by failure to assign top priority to the rescue issue.

7. In 1944 the United States War Department rejected several appeals to bomb the Auschwitz gas chambers and the railroads leading to Auschwitz, claiming that such actions would divert essential airpower from decisive operations elsewhere. Yet in the very months that it was turning down the pleas, numerous massive American bombing raids were taking place within fifty miles of Auschwitz. Twice during that time large fleets of American heavy bombers struck industrial targets in the Auschwitz complex itself, not five miles from the gas chambers.

8. Analysis of the main rescue proposals put forward at the time, but brushed aside by government officials, yields convincing evidence that much more could have been done to rescue Jews, if a real effort had been made. The record also reveals that the reasons repeatedly invoked by government officials for not being able to rescue Jews could be put aside when it came to other Europeans who needed help.

9. Franklin Roosevelt's indifference to so momentous an historical event as the systematic annihilation of European Jewry emerges as the worst failure of his presidency.

10. Poor though it was, the American rescue record was better than that of Great Britain, Russia, or the other Allied nations. This was the case because of the work of the War Refugee Board, the fact that American Jewish organizations were willing to provide most of the WRB's funding, and the overseas rescue operations of several Jewish organizations.

Parts of this book are critical of the American Jewish leadership in the Holocaust era. The policies of Zionist leaders are particularly questioned, in part because their movement held the greatest potential for effective Jewish action. This criticism is made reluctantly. Yet it must be included if the report is to be honest and objective. Several of those leaders have since criticized their own failures in the face of the catastrophe.[1]

I have written not as an insider. I am a Christian, a Protestant of Yankee and Swedish descent. But I have advocated a Jewish state for a very long time, and I would undoubtedly have backed the Zionist movement during the World War II era had I been old enough to be involved in political affairs. Today I remain strongly pro-Zionist and I am a resolute supporter of the state of Israel. My commitment to Zionism and to Israel has been confirmed and increased by years of study of the Holocaust. I look upon Israel as the most important line of defense against anti-Semitism in the world. Had there been a Jewish state in the 1933 to 1945 era, it would be much less painful today for all of us to confront the history of European Jewry during World War II.

A final comment; then a question. The Holocaust was certainly a Jewish tragedy. But it was not *only* a Jewish tragedy. It was also a Christian tragedy, a tragedy for Western civilization, and a tragedy for all humankind. The killing was done by people, to other people, while still other people stood by. The perpetrators, where they were not actually Christians, arose from a Christian culture. The bystanders most capable of helping were Christians. The point should have been obvious. Yet comparatively few American non-Jews recognized that the plight of the European Jews was their plight too. Most were either unaware, did not care, or saw the European Jewish catastrophe as a Jewish problem, one for Jews to deal with. That explains, in part, why the United States did so little to help.

Would the reaction be different today? Would Americans be more sensitive, less self-centered, more willing to make sacrifices, less afraid of differences now than they were then?

ACKNOWLEDGMENTS

I gratefully acknowledge the valuable help provided by these institutions and their staffs: American Friends Service Committee Archives, American Jewish Committee Archives and Library, American Jewish Historical Society, American Jewish Joint Distribution Committee Archives, Center for Migration Studies, Division of Special Collections of Columbia University Library, Columbia University Oral History Research Office, Herbert Lehman Papers at Columbia University School of International Affairs, Special Collections Division of Georgetown University Library, Manuscript Division of the Library of Congress, Interlibrary Loan Department of University of Massachusetts at Amherst, National Archives and Records Service (Legislative, Judicial, and Diplomatic Branch; Modern Military Branch; Social and Economic Branch), National Council of the Churches of Christ, New York Public Library, Franklin D. Roosevelt Library, Albert F. Simpson Historical Research Center, Swarthmore College Peace Collection, George Arents Research Library at Syracuse University, The Temple (Abba Hillel Silver Papers), Travelers Aid International Social Service of America, Unitarian Universalist Service Committee Records at Tufts University,

Manuscripts and Archives Division of Yale University Library, Yeshiva University Library, YIVO Institute for Jewish Research, Zionist Archives and Library.

For the funds that freed me from teaching during the semester in which I began research for this book, I wish to thank the Social Science Research Council and Harvard University's Charles Warren Center for Studies in American History. My work was also assisted at that stage by the American Council of Learned Societies.

I am especially grateful to Eliyho Matz and Aaron Berman for allowing me to use source materials which they uncovered in their own research and which have been of critical importance to this book.

Very many other people helped in the making of this book, many of them in several ways. An attempt to acknowledge that help properly would far overrun the space that is available. I have concluded, regretfully, that the only practical procedure is to set their names down in a list and trust that each person will realize that my gratitude is deep and sincere and that it is not through any lack of warmth that I do not express it in a more personal way.

Those people are: Harry Alderman, Dean Alfange, Claire Barker, James Barker, Leora Baron, Felicity Barringer, Yitshaq Ben-Ami, Jay Berkovitz, Winfred Bernhard, Shmuel Bolozky, Jean Bowman, Randolph Braham, Irving Bunim, Henry and Lydia Cadbury, Emanuel Celler, John Conway, David Culbert, Lucy Dawidowicz, Dorothy Detzer Denny, Josiah DuBois, Ira Eaker, Alfred Eckes, Eileen Egan, Edith and Leonard Ehrlich, Barbara and Donald Einfurer, Helen Fein, Henry Feingold, Marcia Feinstein, Jerome Finster, Frank Freidel, Haim Genizi, Morris Golden, Harold J. Gordon, Jr., Arthur Goren, Marian Greenberg, Robert Griffith, Alex Grobman, Hester Grover, William Harrison, Jerry Hess, Raul Hilberg, Ira Hirschmann, Laura Z. Hobson, R. H. Hodges, Laurence Jarvik, Irene Jones, Robert E. Jones, Herbert Katzki, Warren Kimball, Rose Klepfisz, Arthur Kogan, Hillel Kook, Joseph and Mary Kovner, David Kranzler, Emil Lang, Henry Lea, Elenore Lester, Archibald Lewis, Guenter Lewy, Dwight Macdonald, Edward Mainzer, Charles Markels, Lucille and Phillip Marsh, Joseph Marshall, Barbara Matz, Roswell McClelland, Samuel Merlin, Sybil Milton, Morton Mintz, Amy Mittelman, Juanita and Wallace Nelson, Emanuel Neumann, Jeanne Nieuwejaar, Paul O'Dwyer, James E. O'Neill, Eleanor and Perry Ostroff, Robert Parks, Claiborne Pell, Mary Penxa, Claude Pepper, Jules Piccus, David Pierce, Robert Poirier, Justine Wise Polier, Jacob Price, Howard Quint, Edward Reese, Gerhart Riegner, Max Rosenberg, Halina and Robert Rothstein, Roland Sarti, Dore Schary, André Schiffrin, Eva Schlesinger, Shlomo Shafir, Sherry

Shamash, Fred Shuster, Lawrence Suid, Jack Sutters, Marvin Swartz, Arlo and Polly Tatum, John Taylor, Ted Thackrey, Laszlo Tikos, S. M. Tomasi, Carl Hermann Voss, Rudolf Vrba, Bernard Wax, Robert Wolfe. And last, my mother and father, Midge, Jim and Norah, Teresa, Laura, and old Twig.

·Part One·

BACKGROUND

‖ 1 ‖

THE SETTING: EUROPE AND AMERICA

In Europe: The "Final Solution"

During the spring of 1941, while planning the invasion of Russia, the Nazis made the decision to annihilate the Jews in the territories to be taken from the USSR. On June 22, before dawn, the German army opened its drive against the Soviet forces. Following directly behind the frontline troops were special mobile units (*Einsatzgruppen*) that rounded up Jews and killed them in mass shootings. Typical of these scenes of horror is an eyewitness report by a German construction engineer:

> I saw one family of about six, all already stripped naked and waiting for the order to get down into the grave. Next to the father was a boy of ten or twelve years old. He placed a hand on the boy's head and pointed the other towards heaven and said something to the boy, who, I could see, was trying to keep back his tears. The man's wife was standing near an old woman with snow-white hair, either her mother or the mother of her husband, who held a baby in her arms, singing softly to it and stroking it. Then came the order, "Next ten!" and the family started moving round the mound of earth to climb into the grave. . . .

Then the next were called out to make themselves ready, that is, to take off their clothes. And then I heard shooting and believed that everything was over. . . . I then walked round the grave and saw a few people still moving. Not all the shots had killed. An S.S. man sat on the edge of the grave, with one leg crossed over the other. . . . I called out to the S.S. man, "Look, they're not all dead!" to which he replied, "Ach! Tonight the grave will be filled up with rubbish and so it'll all be finished!" [1]

Between June and December 1941, the *Einsatzgruppen* and associated support units murdered some 500,000 Jews in what had been eastern Poland and Russia. A second sweep through the occupied territory, lasting from fall 1941 through 1942, annihilated close to 900,000 more.[2]

Meanwhile, Hitler had ordered the systematic extermination of all Jews in the Nazi grip. The directive, issued on July 31, 1941, by Reich Marshal Hermann Goering, instructed Reinhard Heydrich, chief of the Reich Security Main Office, to organize "a complete solution of the Jewish question in the German sphere of influence in Europe." Heydrich, who was already in charge of the mobile killing operations in Russia, began preparations for collecting the Jews in the rest of the Nazi domain and deporting them to eastern Europe. The organization of the deportations was assigned to Adolf Eichmann.[3]

Advanced planning for the extermination of the Jews took place in Berlin on January 20, 1942, at the Wannsee Conference. There Heydrich outlined the basic program to a group of German officials whose agencies would collaborate in carrying out what the conference minutes called "the final solution of the Jewish question." In the interval between Goering's directive to Heydrich and the Wannsee Conference, the Nazis had acted to hem in their victims. From October 1941 on, Jews were forbidden exit from German-held territory.[4]

Most of the slaughter of Jews by the *Einsatzgruppen* in the East in 1941 and 1942 involved mass shooting at large grave sites. For the rest of Europe's Jews, the Germans established six extermination centers in Poland. The first of these, at Chelmno, began its work in late 1941, with gassing vans as the instrument of murder. The victims, packed into the enclosed trucks, were suffocated by carbon monoxide from the vehicles' exhaust systems. Mass annihilation at most of the other locations (Belzec, Majdanek, Treblinka, Sobibor, Auschwitz) was well under way in the spring and summer of 1942. There gas-chamber buildings and crematoria were constructed. Gassing was by carbon monoxide fumes produced by stationary engines, except at Auschwitz, where the crystalline Zyklon B (hydrogen cyanide, or prussic acid) was used. Country by country, Jews from most parts of Europe were crowded into freight cars and carried to these assembly lines of death throughout 1942, 1943, and 1944. Nearly three million were murdered in the six killing centers.* [5]

The Nazis assigned very high priority to the annihilation of European Jewry. Locked in a world conflict, in which the very existence of their nation was at stake, Germany's leaders diverted significant amounts of war potential into the genocide program. *Einsatzgruppen* activities absorbed ammunition and able manpower. At several points in the march of murder, gasoline was used to burn the bodies of victims. The extermination process strained the overburdened German administrative machinery. But the heaviest costs were paid in transportation and labor. [7]

Moving millions of Jews across Europe to the death factories in Poland overloaded a railroad system that was hard put to meet essential transportation of troops and war material. Most important, despite a constant labor shortage, one that reached four million by 1944, the Nazis wiped out a capable work force of two to three million Jews. Even skilled Jews employed in war-related industries were deported to the gas chambers. And this occurred despite the recognition that Jewish labor productivity was frequently well above the norm, because Jews saw their best hope for survival in making themselves economically valuable. [8]

To kill the Jews, the Nazis were willing to weaken their capacity to fight the war. The United States and its allies, however, were willing to attempt almost nothing to save them.

In America: Barriers to Rescue

Until the Nazis blocked the exits in the fall of 1941, the oppressed Jews of Europe might have fled to safety. But relatively few got out, mainly because the rest of the world would not take them in. The United States, which had lowered its barriers a little in early 1938, began raising them again in autumn 1939. Two years later, immigration was even

* Of the approximately 5.5 million Jews killed by the Nazis, close to 3.0 million were slaughtered in the extermination centers and almost 1.5 million were massacred in the mobile killing actions. Most of the rest died in other mass shootings, or on the deportation trains, or from the lethal conditions that prevailed in the ghettos (starvation, cold, disease, and crowding). [6]

more tightly restricted than before 1938. In fact, starting in July 1941, America's gates were nearly shut. The best chance to save the European Jews had passed.[9]

After 1941, with the Holocaust under way, the need for help became acute. By then, though, saving Jews was much more difficult, for open doors in the outside world, while essential, would not be enough. Determined rescue efforts would also be needed to salvage even a segment of European Jewry. But the United States did not take rescue action until January 1944, and even then the attempt was limited. Nor were America's nearly closed doors opened. Immigration was held to about 10 percent of the already small quota limits.* Thus the second—and last—chance to help the Jews of Europe came and went.[10]

In the years before Pearl Harbor, the United States had reacted to the European Jewish crisis with concern but had refused to permit any sizable immigration of refugees. Although Congress and the Roosevelt administration had shaped this policy, it grew out of three important aspects of American society in the 1930s: unemployment, nativistic restrictionism, and anti-Semitism.[11]

After Pearl Harbor, the war itself narrowed the possibilities for saving Jews. In addition, the mass media's failure to draw attention to Holocaust developments undercut efforts to create public pressure for government rescue action. But the deeper causes for the lateness and weakness of America's attempts at rescue, and for its unwillingness to take in more than a tiny trickle of fleeing Jews, were essentially the same ones that had determined the nation's reaction to the refugee crisis before Pearl Harbor.

American Restrictionism   From 1933 to 1941, opponents of refugee immigration had built their case around the high unemployment of the Great Depression. Restrictionists persistently asserted that refugees who came to the United States usurped jobs that rightfully belonged to unemployed American workers. Their viewpoint was widely accepted. The counterargument, that refugees were consumers as well as workers and thus provided as many jobs as they took, made little headway.[12]

Economic pressures against immigration had been reinforced by

---

* The quotas, established in the 1920s, set specific limits on the number who could immigrate to the United States in any given year from any given foreign country. Eligibility was based on country of birth. There was, for example, a German quota, a British quota, and so on. The total of all quotas was 154,000. Almost 84,000 of this was assigned to the British and Irish, peoples who had no need to flee.

strong currents of nativism or "100 percent Americanism." These xeno-phobic feelings, which had run very high in the aftermath of World War I, had combined with economic forces during the 1920s to install the quota system, the nation's first broad restriction of immigration. Then, during the 1930s, anti-alien attitudes had played a major part in keeping refugee immigration at low levels. American nativism contin-ued strong throughout World War II.[13]

Wartime prosperity did not dissolve the economic argument against immigration. Fear was widespread that the depression would return with the end of hostilities. Millions believed that demobilization of the armed forces and reconversion to a peacetime economy would bring, at the very least, an extended period of large-scale unemployment.[14]

Veterans' organizations were especially forceful in insisting on the protection of employment rights for returning servicemen. In their view, every foreigner allowed into the country meant unwarranted job competition. Accordingly, throughout the war, the American Legion called for a virtual ban on immigration, to last well into the postwar period. The Veterans of Foreign Wars demanded similarly tough re-strictions. By August 1944, the VFW was urging a stop to all immigra-tion for the next ten years. In the early 1940s, American Legion membership exceeded 1.2 million and included 28 senators and 150 congressmen. Enrollment in the VFW stood at nearly one million. In addition, a large array of patriotic groups actively backed the veterans' organizations in the drive to cut off immigration. In the forefront were the influential Daughters of the American Revolution and the American Coalition of Patriotic Societies, a body that represented the legislative interests of 115 different organizations with combined memberships of some 2.5 million.[15]

The anti-immigration forces wielded substantial political power. Moreover, a large number of congressmen were staunchly restrictionist, a reflection of their own views as well as of attitudes that were popular in their home districts. Many of them, typified by Senator Robert Rey-nolds (Dem., N.C.), Senator Rufus Holman (Rep., Oreg.), and Repre-sentative William Elmer (Rep., Mo.), embraced an intense anti-alienism that shaded into anti-Semitism.[16]

Holman, who introduced a bill in 1942 to end all immigration (ex-cept temporary visits), constantly kept an eye open for attempts to weaken the barriers that kept aliens out. He once blocked legislation in the Senate simply because it aroused his suspicion "that it relaxes the immigration laws," though he openly admitted, "I know nothing about this bill." It did not concern immigration. Elmer, equally distrustful, warned the House in October 1943 of "a determined and well-financed movement . . . to admit all the oppressed, Hitler-persecuted people of Germany and other European countries into our country." [17]

Even lawmakers as far removed from Reynolds, Holman, and Elmer as Senator Harold Burton (Rep., Ohio) lined up on the restrictionist side. Burton, a committed internationalist and a liberal-minded Unitarian, believed the United States should channel refugees "toward areas other than our own." He maintained that "there are many other places in the world where there is much more room for their reception than there is here." [18]

During the war, hundreds of bills were introduced in Congress to decrease immigration. Among the most important—and the most typical—were three put forward in the House. Leonard Allen (Dem., La.) initiated two of them. One would have suspended all immigration until the end of hostilities; the other called for terminating immigration when the war was over. Edward Rees (Rep., Kan.) sponsored a more moderate proposal: to cut the quotas in half for a ten-year period. [19]

The tendency in Congress was clear, and it frightened the leadership of several refugee-aid and social-service organizations. On the basis of their own information sources throughout the country, they were convinced by fall 1943 that a rising tide of public opinion, along with the anti-refugee mood in Congress, endangered the entire quota system. In response, these organizations began to plan an educational and lobbying effort to head off legislation for a "drastic curtailment of immigration." Their campaign probably helped preserve the quota system and avoid a complete stoppage of immigration; none of the many restrictionist bills were enacted. But it did not succeed in widening America's virtually closed doors during the war, even to the extent of increasing the tiny percentage of the quotas that was being made available. [20]

America's limited willingness to share the refugee burden showed clearly in national opinion polls. In 1938, a year when the Nazis had sharply stepped up their persecution of Jews, four separate polls indicated that from 71 to 85 percent of the American public opposed increasing the quotas to help refugees. And 67 percent wanted refugees kept out altogether. In a survey taken in early 1939, 66 percent even objected to a one-time exception to allow 10,000 refugee children to enter outside the quota limits. [21]

Five years later, in the middle of the war, attitudes were no different. Asked in January 1943 whether "it would be a good idea or a bad idea to let more immigrants come into this country after the war," 78 percent of those polled thought it would be a bad idea. At the end of 1945, when the terrible conditions facing European displaced persons were widely known, only 5 percent of the respondents thought the United

States should "permit more persons from Europe to come to this country each year than we did before the war." (Thirty-two percent believed the same number should be allowed in as before, 37 percent wanted fewer to enter, and 14 percent called for closing the doors entirely.)[22]

American Anti-Semitism While it is obvious that many who opposed refugee immigration felt no antipathy against Jews, much restrictionist and anti-refugee sentiment was closely linked to anti-Semitism. The plain truth is that many Americans were prejudiced against Jews and were unlikely to support measures to help them. Anti-Semitism had been a significant determinant of America's ungenerous response to the refugee plight before Pearl Harbor. During the war years, it became an important factor in the nation's reaction to the Holocaust.[23]

American anti-Semitism, which had climbed to very high levels in the late 1930s, continued to rise in the first part of the 1940s. It reached its historic peak in 1944. By spring 1942, sociologist David Riesman was describing it as "slightly below the boiling point." Three years later, public-opinion expert Elmo Roper warned that "anti-Semitism has spread all over the nation and is particularly virulent in urban centers."[24]

During the decade before Pearl Harbor, more than a hundred anti-Semitic organizations had pumped hate propaganda throughout American society. At the head of the band were Father Charles E. Coughlin and his Social Justice movement, William Dudley Pelley's Silver Shirts, the German-American Bund, and the Reverend Gerald B. Winrod's Protestant fundamentalist Defenders of the Christian Faith. Within a few months of America's entry into the war, these four forces were effectively silenced, along with many of the lesser anti-Semitic leaders and their followings. Coughlin, stilled by his archbishop, also saw his *Social Justice* tabloid banned from the mails. Pelley received a fifteen-year prison sentence for sedition. The German-American Bund disintegrated; some members were jailed and several others were interned as dangerous enemy aliens. Winrod, under indictment for sedition during much of the war, continued to publish his *Defender Magazine,* but its contents moderated noticeably.[25]

Organized anti-Semitism had been set back, but by no means did it go under. During the war, several of the minor demagogues remained vocal and new ones came forward. Father Edward Lodge Curran, president of the International Catholic Truth Society, worked to maintain the momentum of the Christian Front, a militant Coughlinite group. And in 1942 the fundamentalist preacher Gerald L. K. Smith came into his own as a front-ranking anti-Semitic agitator. That was the year Smith launched his magazine, *The Cross and the Flag,* inaugurated the Committee of One Million, and achieved a reasonably strong showing in the Republican primary for U.S. senator from Michigan. The next year, he formed the America First party, an isolationist, anti–New Deal venture. From his various platforms, Smith spread anti-refugee and anti-Semitic propaganda, along with attacks on internationalism, Communism, and the New Deal.[26]

It was during the war, too, that anti-Jewish hatreds that had been sown and nurtured for years ripened into some extremely bitter fruits. Epidemics of serious anti-Semitic actions erupted in several parts of the United States, especially the urban Northeast. Most often, youth gangs were the perpetrators. Jewish cemeteries were vandalized, synagogues were damaged as well as defaced with swastikas and anti-Semitic slogans, anti-Jewish markings were scrawled on sidewalks and Jewish stores, and anti-Semitic literature was widely distributed. Most upsetting of all, in scores of instances bands of teenagers beat Jewish schoolchildren—sometimes severely, as when three Jewish boys in Boston were attacked by twenty of their classmates. In another incident, in a midwestern city, young hoodlums stripped a twelve-year-old Jewish boy to the waist and painted a Star of David and the word *Jude* on his chest.[27]

The worst outbreaks occurred in New York City and Boston. In New York, the incidents began in 1941 and continued at least through 1944. They spread throughout the metropolis but hit hardest in Washington Heights, where almost every synagogue was desecrated and where attacks on Jewish youngsters were the most widespread. In the fall of 1942, the city's commissioner of investigation, William B. Herlands, started a formal inquiry into the situation. His comprehensive report, released to the press in January 1944, analyzed thirty-one of the cases of anti-Semitic violence and vandalism and examined the backgrounds of fifty-four of the offenders. The Herlands Report criticized the city police for laxity and inaction in 70 percent of the cases. As for the perpetrators, the investigation found them to be typically in their middle to late teens, from poor and troubled home situations, and with records of low achievement in school. All had been influenced by anti-Semitic propaganda and indoctrination, received mostly at home, at school, and through pamphlets.[28]

In Boston, three years of sporadic property damage, cemetery desecrations, and beatings turned into almost daily occurrences in 1943. Most flagrant were the violent attacks on Jewish children by teenage gangs, particularly in the Dorchester, Mattapan, and Roxbury sections.

In October, pressure from citizens' groups and exposure of the situation by the New York newspaper *PM* impelled Governor Leverett Saltonstall to act. An official investigation that cited police negligence led to the replacement of the police commissioner. The situation improved rapidly, although some beatings did occur well into 1944. Major factors igniting the trouble were the flood of anti-Semitic literature circulating in Boston and inflammatory oratory and other provocative actions by local Coughlinite Christian Front groups.[29]

Throughout the nation, a particularly pernicious kind of anti-Semitism circulated in handbills, pamphlets, posters, and as jokes and jingles. The wide currency of this material was indicative of the extent to which anti-Jewish attitudes had spread through American society. These vehicles of hatred turned up in buses, subway stations, industrial plants, public buildings, army camps, schools, and numerous other places. The most recurrent theme involved the widely disseminated slander that Jews shirked military service, stayed home, and prospered, while Christian boys were sent off to fight and die.* Here are two of the most extensively circulated items. The first parodied the Marines' Hymn.

> *From the shores of Coney Island,*
> *Looking out into the sea,*
> *Stands a kosher air-raid warden,*
> *Wearing V for victory,*
>   *who chants:*
> *Let those Christian saps, go fight the Japs,*
> *In the uniforms we've made.*
>
> . . . .
>
> *So it's onward into battle,*
> *Let us send the Christian slobs.*
> *When the war is done and Victory won,*
> *All us Jews will have their jobs.*[30]

The following piece, with minor variations, surfaced in all parts of the country, in oral and written form. It was called "The First American." No version mentioned that the bombardier who died on the same mission that claimed Colin Kelly's life was Meyer Levin, a Jew.

First American killed in Pearl Harbor—*John J. Hennessy*
First American to sink a Jap ship—*Colin P. Kelly*

---

* In reality, the proportion of Jews in the armed forces was at least as great as the proportion of Jews in the American population.[31]

First American to sink a Jap ship with torpedo—*John P. Buckley*
Greatest American air hero—*"Butch" O'Hare*
First American killed at Guadalcanal—*John J. O'Brien*
First American to get four new tires—*Abraham Lipshitz* [32]

Symptomatic of even more deeply negative attitudes was a small but noticeable flow of hate-filled letters to government officials and members of Congress objecting to Jewish refugees. These three excerpts are typical:

> I am writing to you to protest against the entry of Jewish refugees into this country. . . . Their lack of common decency, gross ignorance and unbelievable gall stamps them as undesirables even if they could be assimilated into a common society, which they can't.

> I see from the papers that 200,000 Refugee Jews in Hungary will not live through the next few weeks. Thats too Dam Bad what in the Hell do we care about the Jews in Hungary.
> What we want is the Refugee Jews brought to this country returned where they come from.

> Are we to harbor all the riff raff of Europe. . . . The Jews take over everything here. [33]

Ugly and bitter though it was, the coarse, mostly overt anti-Semitism of the demagogues, the street gangs, the snide leaflets, and the poison-pen letters represented only the surface of the phenomenon. Negative attitudes toward Jews penetrated all sectors of wartime America. A more subtle social and economic discrimination against Jews was accepted and practiced by millions of respectable Americans. Many millions more were not anti-Semitic in the usual sense of the term. They would not personally have mistreated a Jew. Beneath the surface, however, were uncrystallized but negative feelings about Jews. In ordinary times, this "passive anti-Semitism" would have worked little damage. But in the Holocaust crisis it meant that a large body of decent and normally considerate people was predisposed not to care about European Jews nor to care whether the government did anything to help save them. [34]

The quieter strains of wartime anti-Semitism were more difficult to gauge than the blatant, overt type. But the fact that they reached serious levels can be established from anecdotal evidence as well as from results of opinion polling.

In the middle of the war, the British government sent Freya Stark, a pro-Arab archaeologist and author, on an extensive lecture tour of the United States. Her mission was to build American support for British policies, especially for those regarding Palestine. Miss Stark, a non-Jew, was impressed by the amount of anti-Semitism she ran across among well-to-do, well-educated Americans. Dr. L. M. Birkhead, a Protestant clergyman and close observer of anti-Semitic trends, traveled through the Midwest in 1943. He found vicious anti-Jewish attitudes rampant not only among extremist groups but also in the "best circles." The respectable elements, he thought, would probably not support violence, but neither would they oppose it. The following year, in its annual review, the American Civil Liberties Union pointed out that reports from across the nation carried "an almost unanimous verdict that race tensions are increasing, affecting Negroes, Jews, and Japanese Americans. Some even described the situation as 'explosive' or 'potentially dangerous.' "[35]

Nor were the armed forces exempt. In a letter to a Jewish magazine, a Marine corporal, two years in the service, expressed frustration about attitudes that were not uncommon in the military:

I am the only Jewish boy in this detachment. I am confronted with anti-Semitism on all sides. Sorry I got into this outfit.[36]

Anti-Semitism ran through the upper ranks as well, as illustrated by the experience of an American Red Cross staff member who was working alongside the liberating Allied armies following V-E Day. One morning she set out to visit Jews at a displaced persons' center near Magdeburg, Germany. About 2,700 of them had survived Bergen-Belsen and then ten days locked in a train before American Army units found and freed them. The Red Cross worker stopped at the American Military Government office in Magdeburg to ask directions to the DP center. The officers she saw were not aware that she was Jewish. This is what happened:

Major A said to me, "Oh, you want to visit our kikes; be careful or they'll take everything you've got," and turned to the senior officer and said "Major M, Miss N wants to visit our Brooklyn kikes. Can you tell her how to get there?" . . . Major S . . . then [spoke up and] with an accent said, "So you want to visit our long-noses," pulling his nose. "Maybe you can cut down their noses to the size of some of the parts the Nazis cut off."

This incident was only one of several in which she encountered anti-Semitism in the American Military Government.[37]

Anti-Semitism was no stranger on Capitol Hill either. It was, in fact, an important ingredient in the sharp hostility to refugee immigration that existed in Congress. In early 1943, government officials and friendly members of Congress cautioned refugee-aid organizations about pushing too hard on immigration-related issues because of "the prevalence of anti-Semitic feeling in Congress." A leader of one of the aid organizations described this attitude as an "unprecedented and disturbing element throughout Congress." Several members of Congress—for example, Senators Claude Pepper (Dem., Fla.) and James Murray (Dem., Mont.)—sought to turn back these currents of prejudice, but without much success.[38]

For the most part, congressional anti-Semitism was not expressed openly, though a few legislators had no compunction about putting their anti-Jewish views on record. The most shameless anti-Semite in Congress was Representative John Rankin (Dem., Miss.), who regularly used his considerable oratorical talent to lash out at Jews. In June 1941, one of his verbal assaults contributed to the death of Congressman M. Michael Edelstein of New York. Edelstein collapsed and died of a heart attack in the House lobby shortly after rising to point out the unfairness of Rankin's comments. Undeterred, Rankin kept on with his diatribes. Speaking in the House in 1944, he referred to a Jewish news columnist as "that little kike." He was even petty enough to block special legislation, unanimously approved by the normally restrictionist House Immigration Committee, to allow a Jewish refugee couple and their daughter to come to the United States. The family's two sons, aged twenty-two and nineteen, were already in the United States, had joined the Army, and were about to be sent overseas.[39]

The pervasiveness of anti-Semitism in the United States during the late 1930s and the war years was confirmed by national public-opinion polls. A series of polls from 1938 to 1946 dealt with the images Americans had of Jews. The results indicated that over half the American population perceived Jews as greedy and dishonest and that about one-third considered them overly aggressive.[40]

A set of surveys extending from 1938 through 1941 showed that between one-third and one-half of the public believed that Jews had "too much power in the United States." During the war years, a continuation of the survey saw the proportion rise to 56 percent. According to these and other polls, this supposed Jewish power was located mainly in "business and commerce" and in "finance." From late 1942 into the spring of 1945, significant Jewish power was also thought to exist in "politics and government." * [41]

Other surveys from August 1940 on through the war found that from 15 to 24 percent of the respondents looked on Jews as "a menace to America." Jews were consistently seen as more of a threat than such other groups in the United States as Negroes, Catholics, Germans, or Japanese (except during 1942, when Japanese and Germans were rated more dangerous). [43]

If a threat actually existed, however, it was not from Jews, but to them. An alarming set of polls taken between 1938 and 1945 revealed that roughly 15 percent of those surveyed would have supported an anti-Jewish campaign. Another 20 to 25 percent would have sympathized with such a movement. Approximately 30 percent indicated that they would have actively opposed it. In sum, then, as much as 35 to 40 percent of the population was prepared to approve an anti-Jewish campaign, some 30 percent would have stood up against it, and the rest would have remained indifferent. The threat never crystallized into organized action. But even allowing ample room for inadequacies in the survey data, the seriousness of American anti-Semitism in those years is evident. [44]

These attitudes raised formidable barriers to the development of an American initiative to save European Jews. Yet the need was critical: an entire people was being systematically eliminated by America's principal enemy. And pressures against extending help were not the only forces on the scene. Other important factors in American society created the potential for a positive response. America was a generous nation, a land of immigrants, led by a national administration known for its humanitarian sympathies. Most Americans embraced Christianity, a faith committed to helping the helpless. The country had an articulate and organized Jewish population that could play a vital role in arousing those positive forces. A truly concerned leadership in the government and in the Christian churches could have turned that potential into a powerful influence for effective action.

---

* The view that Jews had too much power in government may have reflected the widely circulated assertion that Jews exerted excessive influence in the Roosevelt administration, a notion summarized in the term *Jew Deal.* The belief that Jews wielded substantial power in government declined sharply in the polls directly after Truman succeeded Roosevelt. [42]

· Part Two ·

"A PLAN TO EXTERMINATE ALL JEWS"

|| 2 ||

THE NEWS FILTERS OUT

The First Reports and Their Impact

The perpetrators of annihilation sought to conceal their operations. Even in secret communications, they used code words such as *final solution* (for systematic extermination) and *special treatment* (for gassing). They told Jews destined for the death factories in Poland that they were going to labor camps in the East. From time to time, the Germans forced Jews arriving at killing centers to write postdated cards assuring friends and relatives that they were working and living under reasonably good conditions. The efforts at secrecy, along with the location of the killing centers deep inside Nazi-held territory, kept clear information about the annihilation process from reaching the outside world for many months.[1]

But so extensive and sensational a campaign could obviously not be hidden indefinitely. Initially, reports on the massacres were few, like the first spits of snow that hint at what the winter air holds in store. With time, they increased in number and clarity. Even so, throughout the war the regular American newspapers published comparatively few of these disclosures and nearly always relegated them to the inner pages.[2]

Almost from the start, intimations of the bloody swaths cut by the *Einsatzgruppen* reached the American Jewish press via the Jewish Telegraphic Agency, a news bureau with extensive foreign contacts. For instance, in July 1941 the New York Yiddish dailies revealed that hundreds of Jewish civilians had been massacred by Nazi soldiers in Minsk, Brest-Litovsk, Lvov, and other places, all within the first thrust of the German attack on Russia. The same papers relayed an August broadcast from Moscow that made essentially the same charges. Several weeks later, to cite only one other example, they carried a summary from the Polish government-in-exile in London telling of the machine-gunning of thousands of Jews in eastern Poland and the Ukraine. In late October 1941, a similar report appeared in a small article inside the *New York Times.* The story, based on unspecified "reliable sources," drew on eyewitness accounts from Hungarian army officers who had returned to Hungary from Galicia. It included estimates of ten to fifteen thousand Jews killed in Galicia.[3]

During the first half of 1942, disclosures of slaughter on the Russian front continued to reach the United States, along with more and more reports of deportations of Jews to Poland from Slovakia, Germany, and elsewhere. These accounts, many of them taken from Swedish and other neutral newspapers, received wide coverage in the Yiddish and English-language Jewish press and occasionally appeared in major American newspapers.[4]

An extremely trustworthy source of information, used by the *New York Times* as well as by several Jewish publications, was a New York press conference held by S. Bertrand Jacobson in mid-March 1942. Jacobson was back from Budapest after two years as chief representative in eastern Europe for the relief activities of the American Jewish Joint Distribution Committee. He based much of his report on eyewitness statements. Estimating that the Nazis had already massacred 240,000 Jews in the Ukraine alone, Jacobson stated that the killing in eastern Europe was continuing in full fury. Among the most horrifying relevations to appear in the United States until that time (but omitted from the *Times*'s account) was a description by a Hungarian soldier who had seen a vast burial site near Kiev. Seven thousand Jews, some shot dead but others wounded and still alive, had been thrown into the shallow grave and covered thinly with dirt. Burned into the soldier's memory was the sight of that field, "heaving like a living sea."[5]

In discussing the despair that enveloped East European Jews, Jacobson noted that the Jews of Slovakia had already been crowded into concentration centers, most likely a harbinger of wholesale deportation to Poland. In fact, two weeks after he spoke, the deportations began. By June 1942, this forced evacuation would carry away 52,000 of Slovakia's 90,000 Jews. Most went to Auschwitz. A terse message in March from the Slovakian capital to an American relief agency summarized the situation from another perspective: "Bratislava will require no matzoth for Passover this year."[6]

On May 18, the *New York Times* published a report by Glen Stadler, a UP correspondent caught in Germany when the United States entered the war. In Lisbon with a group of American citizens who had been exchanged for Axis nationals, Stadler revealed reports that German gunners had killed more than 100,000 Jews in the Baltic states, nearly that many in Poland, and over twice as many in western Russia.[7]

Sometime that same May, the Jewish Labor Bund in Poland compiled a summary of verified massacres and succeeded in transmitting it, along with an anguished plea for action, to the Polish government in London. The persistence of the two Jewish members of the Polish National Council in London—Szmul Zygielbojm, of the Bund, and Dr. Ignacy Schwarzbart, of the Zionist group—forced British and American government officials and news media to take notice. The Bund report became the decisive factor in the first breakthrough of extermination news.[8]

In their message, the Jews in Poland traced the path of murder through their country, city by city, region by region, month by month. They described the Chelmno killing center, including the gas vans: "For gassing a special vehicle (gas chamber) was used in which 90 people were loaded at a time. . . . On the average, 1,000 people were gassed every day." They estimated the number of Polish Jewish victims to be 700,000 already. Their conclusions: Germany had set out to "annihilate all the Jews in Europe" and millions of Polish Jews faced imminent death. To save the remaining Polish Jews, they called on the London Polish government to press the Allies for a policy of immediate retaliation against German citizens living in their countries.[9]

One of the very earliest rescue proposals, the retaliation entreaty seemed plausible to the desperate and despairing Jews in Poland. But it was not feasible. The Germans would have responded with counterthreats against Allied nationals under their control. Furthermore, even had the plan offered some hope of effectiveness, it is inconceivable that the American and British legal systems could have sanctioned the execution of individuals who were not themselves involved in Nazi crimes.[10]

On June 2, shortly after the Bund report reached England, the BBC broadcast its essence, including the estimate of 700,000 Jews killed. But the broadcast did not emphasize the conclusion that an extermination program was under way. A week afterward, the Polish National Council officially informed the Allied governments of the report's contents. On June 25, Zygielbojm released the full document to the press and on the following day broadcast a summary over the BBC. As the month ended, the British section of the World Jewish Congress held a press conference in London to which Schwarzbart brought further information on Jewish deaths. He also emphasized the impending extermination of all the European Jews. These efforts brought no reaction from the Allied governments, so the Polish National Council, on July 8, repeated its earlier notice to the Allies and added that it had new evidence of planned destruction of masses of Poles, both Jews and non-Jews.[11]

As the Allied governments marked time, newspapers slowly began to publish the information. Indicative of the early confusion was a UP report from London on June 1. In striking contrast to the figure of 700,000 slain *Polish* Jews that the BBC would broadcast the next day, it declared that the Nazis had killed 200,000 Jews in Russia, Poland, and the Baltic states. The *Seattle Times* chose this report for its top story on June 1; the paper's main headline read, "JEWS SLAIN TOTAL 200,000!" (It was one of the very few times during World War II when a Holocaust event received a front-page headline in an American metropolitan daily.)[12]

Probably the first American newspaper to carry information on the Bund report was the *Boston Globe,* in its morning edition of June 26. Relegated to the bottom of page 12, the *Globe* story was nonetheless noticeable because of its three-column headline: "Mass Murders of Jews in Poland Pass 700,000 Mark." Wired from London by the Overseas News Agency, the dispatch minced no words: "A systematic campaign for the extermination of the Jews in Poland has resulted in the murder of more than 700,000 in the past year." That evening, the *Seattle Times* published much the same information, on page 30, under a tiny headline, "700,000 Jews Reported Slain." Originating in London with the Chicago Daily News service, this article characterized the Bund report as "new evidence" of "the systematic extermination of the Jewish population." Polish sources, it stated, spoke of portable gas chambers at Chelmno.

The *New York Times* devoted two inches to the Bund report on June 27. It had picked up the information from CBS in New York, which had recorded Zygielbojm's BBC broadcast the preceding day. The *Times*'s brief account noted that 700,000 Polish Jews had been slain, and it quoted the broadcast's disclosure that "to accomplish this, probably the greatest mass slaughter in history, every death-dealing method was employed—machine-gun bullets, hand grenades, gas chambers, concentration camps, whipping, torture instruments and starvation." Not until July 2 did the *Times* publish (on page 6) a thorough summary of the Bund report, including details on the mobile gas chambers at Chelmno.[13]

The World Jewish Congress (WJC) press conference, held in London on June 29, generated additional information. Combining the Bund report with other evidence received from the Continent, the WJC compiled a country-by-country summary of the Nazi assault on the Jews. The WJC estimated that the Nazis had already killed over a million Jews, mostly in Poland, Lithuania, Russia, and Rumania. (The estimates were low as measured against today's knowledge.) In the words of WJC spokesmen, the Germans had turned eastern Europe into a "vast slaughterhouse for Jews." From Germany, Austria, Czechoslovakia, and the Netherlands, Jews had been deported en masse to Poland to be shot in large groups. All of it, the WJC claimed, was part of a Nazi policy to exterminate the Jews.[14]

Full reports on the WJC press conference were carried on both the AP and the UP wires from London. But few American daily papers printed more than brief notices to the effect that the World Jewish Congress had charged the Germans with killing over one million Jews.[15]

Soon afterward, two authoritative voices in Great Britain reinforced the Bund disclosure of mass murder. In a press conference, the British minister of information, Brendan Bracken, announced that "700,000 Jews alone have been murdered in Poland." He declared in the strongest terms that when the war ended the United Nations would bring to speedy and severe punishment the persons responsible for the war crimes committed in Poland against Jews and against other Poles as well.* [16]

And in a special broadcast Arthur Cardinal Hinsley, the seventy-six-year-old archbishop of Westminster and Britain's leading Roman Catholic prelate, stated that "in Poland alone the Nazis have massacred 700,000 Jews." To those who might doubt the charges of Nazi mass atrocities against both Jews and Christians in Poland, Cardinal Hinsley pointed out that some people "reject offhand anything and everything that does not directly touch their own noses" and that others "dismiss even the clearest evidence with the sneer, 'Oh! British propaganda!' " "But," the Cardinal maintained, "mighty is the truth; murder will out."

---

* The term *United Nations* was beginning to be used by early 1942 to refer to the countries allied in the war against the Axis.

The outspoken Hinsley persisted in decrying the Western world's failure to respond to the slaughter of the Jews until death took him, in March 1943.[17]

Only in early July 1942 did the State Department begin to inquire into the massacres of Jews in eastern Europe. In response, the American minister to Sweden sent information to Washington indicating that at least 284,000 Jews had been executed by the Nazis in areas wrested from the Russians since mid-1941. One Estonian officer who had been with the German occupation forces in the Baltic states reported seeing an SS firing squad force 400 Jews to dig their own graves and then shoot them. Another source cited similar executions elsewhere in the Baltic area and in Kiev. From the American representative to the London Polish government, the State Department received a statement by Schwarzbart based on the Bund report as well as other sources smuggled from Poland.[18]

The flow of news about the European Jewish situation, which had surfaced here and there in the regular newspapers, flooded the American Jewish press. It set off calls for mass protests and for American and United Nations action. The American Jewish Congress, the B'nai B'rith, and the Jewish Labor Committee (later joined by the American Jewish Committee) organized a mass demonstration in New York City, where Americans could express their grief and indignation over the massacres.[19]

On the evening of July 21—one day before the eve of Tisha b'Ab, the commemoration of the destruction of the Temple at Jerusalem—20,000 people crowded Madison Square Garden, while thousands more stood outside, to protest the Nazi atrocities. Among the main speakers were Rabbi Stephen Wise, Governor Herbert Lehman, Mayor Fiorello La Guardia, the Methodist bishop Francis McConnell, and William Green, president of the American Federation of Labor.[20]

President Roosevelt sent a message in which he expressed the sorrow of all Americans and declared that the American people "will hold the perpetrators of these crimes to strict accountability in a day of reckoning which will surely come." Repeatedly during the evening, the mention of Roosevelt's name set off ovations. A companion message from Prime Minister Winston Churchill noted that "the Jews were Hitler's first victims." Churchill reminded listeners that he and Roosevelt had spoken out on Nazi atrocities nine months earlier and had then resolved "to place retribution for these crimes among major purposes of this war."[21]

The assembly adopted a declaration that hailed the heroic spirit of the trapped Jews and called on the United Nations to take public notice of the Jewish tragedy and to express their determination to bring the Nazis to justice. It pledged that American Jewry would "make every sacrifice to support the United Nations in their struggle for freedom and human decency."[22]

American Jewish organizations expressed satisfaction with the results of the mass meeting, particularly with the strong public assurances from the highest levels that those responsible for the monstrous crimes would be brought to justice. But neither Roosevelt nor Churchill, nor the declaration adopted by the assembly, nor any of the speakers had proposed measures to rescue the Jews still alive in Hitler's Europe. Rabbi Wise even asserted that "the salvation of our people and all peoples who would be free can only come under God through a victory speedy and complete of the United Nations."[23]

Did Stephen Wise and the others who said nothing of rescue operations that night really mean that the *only way* to save Jews from the Nazis was to win the war? Could the trapped Jews look for no efforts to help them throughout the months and years that lay between the summer of 1942 and the Allied victory? Who among them would be alive to see that victory? After many more months and several more shocks, American Jewish leaders would respond to these questions by pressing a program of rescue on the American government. But then other questions would develop: How high a priority would these Jewish leaders place on rescue? What part of their energies and resources would they commit to it?

In July 1942, Jewish leaders may well have been in a state of shock at learning of the huge and still rising Jewish death toll in Europe. They also were sorely worried about the threat to the Jewish settlement in Palestine resulting from the German drive across Africa and toward Suez that summer. Initially, when the war was running heavily in the Germans' favor, the obstacles to mounting potentially effective programs of aid must have seemed insurmountable. Clarification and reassessment could be expected.

Other observances followed the Madison Square Garden demonstration. The Synagogue Council of America called upon all Jewish congregations to make July 23, Tisha b'Ab, a day of memorial to the victims of the Nazis, and the chaplain of the U.S. House of Representatives opened that day's session with a prayer for the murdered Jews. The Federal Council of Churches and the Church Peace Union sent messages of sympathy to the Synagogue Council. The Union of Orthodox Rabbis of the United States and Canada proclaimed August 12 a day of prayer and fasting.[24]

Other mass meetings were organized to protest the murderous Nazi assault on the Jews. Ten thousand people attended the one held in the Chicago Coliseum, and smaller demonstrations took place in Los Angeles, Milwaukee, Cincinnati, Hartford, and other cities. At these meetings, mayors, governors, congressmen, labor leaders, and spokesmen for Christian churches joined Jews in expressing sorrow and indignation. In Cincinnati, more than one hundred Protestant ministers endorsed a public statement to the Jews of their community declaring, "We of the Christian ministry cannot and will not remain silent before the spectacle of mass murder suffered by Jews of Nazi-controlled Europe." Expressing insights that should have been obvious, but which seem to have gone widely unrecognized in American Christian circles during World War II, the Cincinnati ministers pointed out:

> This is the tragedy of your European Jewish brethren but it is also our Christian tragedy. This is an evil suffered by those of Jewish faith but it is also an evil perpetuated by men of Christian names and Christian pretension.[25]

The mass meetings undoubtedly had some effect on the American public's hitherto nearly complete ignorance about the Jewish catastrophe in Europe. Yet, although well covered in the daily press, the demonstrations fell far short of realizing their full potential for publicizing the disastrous situation. The *New York Times,* for instance, placed a sizable part of its report on the Madison Square Garden meeting in the middle of page 1. But nothing on that page indicated that hundreds of thousands of Jews had been murdered. In fact, Jews were barely mentioned, and the event came across as no more than a "mass demonstration against Hitler atrocities." The *Chicago Tribune* provided substantial publicity prior to the Chicago mass meeting, but its report on the demonstration itself, while comprehensive, offered little understanding of what had caused the meeting. The *Los Angeles Times,* on the other hand, publicized the demonstration in Los Angeles for more than a week and made it clear throughout that the issue was "the terrible mass murders of Jews in Nazi-controlled Europe."[26]

How deeply did the disclosures about annihilation of the Jews penetrate? Obviously, the answer would differ from individual to individual and from group to group. The extent to which the information spread in the United States, and the related matter of how much credence people actually gave it, crucially influenced the American response to the Holocaust. Those who were concerned that the United States do what was possible to rescue the Jews encountered difficulties on both counts, not only in 1942, when hard evidence first appeared, but throughout the war, and this despite the increasing confirmation that came out of Europe as time passed.

By May 1943, for instance, extensive news had appeared regarding the destruction of European Jewry. Yet Dorothy Day, the leader of the Catholic Worker movement, recalled speaking at a meeting that month at which "a member of the audience arose to protest defense of the Jews and to state emphatically that she did not believe the stories of atrocities. . . . She was applauded by the several hundred present." "Against such astounding unbelief," Day reflected, "the mind is stunned."[27]

The tendency to discount the extermination reports arose mainly from two causes. First, many people simply could not believe them. They refused to accept the fact that civilized people would commit such barbaric acts. Schwarzbart and Zygielbojm, the men who vouched most strongly for the accuracy of the Jewish Labor Bund's report from Poland, recognized the problem. At a press conference in July 1942, Zygielbojm stated that he realized that the facts "are so horrifying that one may ask if human beings can be degraded to such a brutality." Schwarzbart granted that "it is difficult to grasp that a human being could fall so low as has the contemporary German, educated by Hitlerism. It is difficult to believe these facts—and yet they are true."[28]

Skepticism about the annihilation reports also stemmed from the abuse of the public's trust by British propagandists during World War I. The British historian A. J. P. Taylor has noted that some of the atrocity charges leveled at Germany in World War I were true but most were inflated; "the violated nuns and babies with their hands cut off were never found." Yet "nearly everyone believed the stories."[29]

During the late 1920s and the 1930s, historians had laid bare the falsity of Britain's World War I atrocity propaganda. By the late 1930s, these exposures had worked their way into the popular mind, and atrocity stories in the first stages of World War II consequently met with much skepticism. As the war ground on, however, and as an increasing volume of information on Nazi crimes against occupied populations issued from numerous trusted sources, and as hatreds built, most Americans came to believe much of the news. Nevertheless, a tendency to see the atrocity reports as at least partly exaggerated persisted throughout the war and weakened the impact of the disclosures.[30]

Besides the problem of the credibility of the reports, two additional factors regarding the flow of information impaired the growth of American concern for rescue. For one thing, only a limited amount of news about the murder of the European Jews reached the American public. The mass media reported it only sporadically and almost always without emphasis. Newspapers printed comparatively little of the available knowledge and commonly buried it in inner pages. Radio seems to have offered even less information. Government-sponsored and independently produced films alike gave almost no hint of the attempt to exterminate the Jews. Mass circulation magazines hardly noticed it.[31]

Of course, Jewish magazines and weekly newspapers and the Yiddish daily press provided thorough coverage of the catastrophe. A few limited-circulation periodicals, such as the *Nation* and the *New Republic,* also made readers aware of the issue. But most Christian publications, both Protestant and Catholic, had little or nothing to say. Only a few Christian church leaders tried to inform their constituencies of the Jewish situation in Europe. Except for a small number of voices, those who spoke with the authority of government either kept silent or very infrequently referred to the Jewish disaster. The main American channels for publicizing events did not entirely black out the extermination news, but they did little to bring it to the attention of the public.[32]

The impact of Holocaust information was further diluted by the background against which it appeared. Throughout World War II, reports of Nazi terror against civilian populations in occupied countries repeatedly made the news. Accounts of German reprisals, mass killings of hostages, executions of suspected anti-Nazis, and other atrocities were regular features in newspapers and news magazines. These war crimes most often were related to the Nazi tactic of terror to control populations and to counter sabotage and assassinations.

Several times, disclosures of Nazi mass killing of Jews appeared within stories of the more general German crimes against civilian populations. News services frequently provided summaries of Nazi repression, country by country. Incorporated into these dispatches were accounts of mass executions of Jews. Even when massacres of the Jews were reported separately, they blended into the background of Nazi terror against civilians all across Europe. Thus, quite by chance, widespread Nazi repression of all subject peoples obscured the fact that a distinct program of systematic extermination of Jews was in progress.[33]

In mid-1942, an especially virulent wave of Nazi terrorism swept over Europe. Mass killings of Poles, both Jews and non-Jews, had increased since SS Chief Heinrich Himmler had visited Poland in the spring. Other reports of severe repression came steadily from all across the Continent. In June, the world was stunned to learn that the Germans had obliterated the small Czech mining village of Lidice in reprisal for supposed complicity in the assassination of Heydrich. (The 190 men of Lidice were shot, the women deported, mostly to the Ravensbrück concentration camp, and the children dispersed among German families.)[34]

In response to the campaign of intensified terror, and at the initiative of General Wladyslaw Sikorski, prime minister of the Polish government-in-exile, the leaders of nine occupied European countries urged President Roosevelt to retaliate for the atrocities. Following State Department advice, Roosevelt rejected the appeal, as well as Sikorski's specific proposal to bomb German cities in reprisal for the mass executions, especially those of Polish Jews. According to the Polish ambassador in Washington, Roosevelt explained that the Allies had not yet attained full air strength and that, furthermore, Germany might respond with an even higher level of terror.[35]

Actually, the Allies were already bombing German cities as a war measure and surely would not have ceased if massacres of the Jews had stopped. In addition, German Propaganda Minister Josef Goebbels had preempted the issue some weeks before. In mid-June, he had publicly declared that American and British Jews were responsible for the bombing of German cities and that the German people were suffering intensely from the attacks. Germany, said Goebbels, would repay "blow by blow," by "mass extermination of Jews in reprisal for the Allied air bombings of German cities." The Sikorski proposal had reached a standoff. Extermination of the Jews had been going on for a year. Little hope for stopping it could be placed in a tactic already in use against Germany and in response to which a top Nazi promised to exterminate the Jews.[36]

Although Roosevelt did not agree to the call for retaliation against Germany, he again warned the Axis, on August 21, 1942, that perpetrators of war crimes would be tried after Germany's defeat and face "fearful retribution." During the rest of the year, American and British officials worked on plans to set up a United Nations commission to investigate war crimes. In October, in the midst of these negotiations, Roosevelt once more spoke out about war crimes, declaring that those responsible would receive "just and sure punishment." But he also announced that mass Allied reprisals would not take place. Neither in this statement nor in the one the President had issued in August did he refer to Jewish victims. During the same months, efforts by the United States and other governments to persuade the Vatican to voice public condemnation of Nazi atrocities against civilians came to nothing.[37]

By the time of the July 21 Madison Square Garden mass meeting, American Jewish leaders and much of the Jewish public recognized that the European Jews were suffering terrible losses. They probably did not realize, however, that Nazi barbarism had actually gone as far as the most horrifying reports indicated. And despite increasing use of the term *systematic extermination,* none quite understood then that a planned, step-by-step program to annihilate all of European Jewry was in progress. The outlines of that hideous scheme were only vaguely coming into sight.

Destination Unknown

Within a few days of the July demonstrations, another important dimension of the "final solution" began to become apparent. From the Nazi perspective, this development was an obvious part of the extermination plan, but it could not yet be recognized as such from the outside. It was a massive deportation of Jews from western Europe to "an unknown destination" in the East. Labor service was the announced purpose. But in reality these evacuations were part of the Europe-wide transportation of Jews to the still-secret killing centers already in operation in Poland.[38]

The deportations from France in 1942, especially those from the Vichy, or Unoccupied, Zone, were more fully exposed to the scrutiny of the outside world than any other Holocaust development. At work were the usual European news outposts in Switzerland, England, and Sweden. Beyond that, the peculiar status of Vichy France, which was partially autonomous and maintained diplomatic relations with the United States, meant that American newsmen could operate in the Unoccupied Zone, yet bypass Vichy censorship by dispatching their reports from Switzerland. Even closer to the deportation events were Americans and others who had been assisting some of the many thousand Jewish refugees who had earlier fled to France to escape Nazi persecution. These relief workers were in touch with their agencies in other countries and could thus transmit to the outside world detailed information on events in the Unoccupied Zone.

The relief organizations had been active in southern France for some time, helping refugees in applying for visas to countries abroad and in arranging the necessary transportation. After mid-1940, emigration became more and more difficult as overseas nations, the United States included, all but closed their doors to immigration. Accordingly, the relief agencies had increasingly concentrated on supplying food, clothing, and other assistance to the refugees caught in France. By the time the deportations struck, two years of hard work had raised conditions to a barely livable level in the squalid detention camps in which the Vichy government had incarcerated thousands of the fugitives.[39]

Whatever stability Jewish refugees had attained in France was smashed by a series of ruthless roundups that began in mid-July 1942 in the Occupied Zone. Lacking sufficient forces to carry out mass seizures, the Nazis had to secure the collaboration of the Vichy government and the French police. The price of that cooperation was the exemption of French-born Jews from deportation, at least temporarily. Left vulnerable were 75,000 Jewish men, women, and children, most of whom had already endured a variety of hells in their attempts to escape the Nazis.[40]

At four o'clock on the morning of July 16, the trap was sprung in Paris. French police dragnets swept up 13,000 refugee Jews amid scenes of anguish and terror. Buses backed up to apartment buildings and were filled with screaming, crying people. Hospital beds were emptied. A cancer patient operated on the previous day was carried away. One woman gave birth while police waited to haul off mother and baby. Younger children were permitted to be left behind, and many parents desperately accepted that choice in the hope that neighbors or orphanages would take them in. Family groups, comprising some 9,000 people (half of them children), were funneled into the winter sports arena (Vélodrome d'Hiver) and penned up like animals. Water and food were scarce; some infants died for lack of milk. Since only ten latrines were available, people stood in line for hours to use the toilet. After five days of this nightmare, adults and children were separated and transferred to different deportation centers to await shipment to Poland.[41]

Relief organizations in the Unoccupied Zone learned later what had become of the children left behind in Paris. Many were hidden. But French police gathered up thousands of others who were found in apartments, wandering the streets, or crying at locked doors of houses. Nearly 4,000 of them, aged two to fourteen, were sent to "unknown destinations," packed into windowless boxcars without adult escort, without food, water, or hygienic provisions, without so much as straw to lie on. They were even without identification. The Nazis had destroyed their papers.[42]

Close to 50,000 refugee Jews were deported to Auschwitz from the Occupied Zone, mostly from Paris, before France was liberated in 1944. More than half of them were seized in the roundups of July, August, and September 1942.[43]

Early in August, the Vichy chief of government, Pierre Laval, began the evacuations from the Unoccupied Zone. The Vichy police started with refugees who had already undergone misery and degradation in the internment camps of southern France. In the words of an American relief worker, they were now exposed "like fowl in a chicken pen with a hawk circling overhead, only here very few, if any, escape."[44]

In rapid order, 3,600 Jews were collected from the camps and dispatched to the Occupied Zone for transshipment to Poland. The first train pulled out of the camp at Gurs on August 6, carrying a thousand refugees into the night. Within four days, two more trains swallowed the rest from Les Milles, Rivesaltes, Vernet, and other camps which, though their names had come to mean wretchedness, had not killed all hope of survival.[45]

A French citizen who witnessed a deportation recorded what he saw:

> We were at the Camp des Milles the day the last train left. The spectacle was indescribably painful to behold. All the internees had been lined up with their pitifully battered valises tied together with bits of string. Most of them were in rags, pale, thin, worn out with the strain. . . . Many of them were quietly weeping. . . . Their faces showed only hopeless despair.

The YMCA's Donald Lowrie, an American relief worker, described the evacuation:

> The actual deportation was as bad as could be imagined: men and women pushed like cattle into box-cars, thirty to a car, whose only furniture was a bit of straw on the floor, one iron pail for all toilet purposes, and a police guard. The journey, we were told, would take a fortnight or eighteen days. . . . All of us were curtly refused permission to accompany the trains or even to organize a service of hot drinks and refreshments at the frontier where they passed into German occupied territory.[46]

In the first stage of the deportations from Unoccupied France, refugee parents were allowed to leave children under eighteen behind. Fearing the worst from their return into German hands, most chose separation. After watching the leave-taking, relief workers felt they could "never forget the moment when these truck loads of children left the camps, with parents trying in one last gaze to fix an image to last an eternity." Later in August, however, the powers in Vichy betrayed both children and parents with an order requiring deportation of all refugee youngsters. "We are solving the problem humanely," lied the Vichy spokesman. "We want children to go with their parents." Many whose parents had already been carried away were now deported. The others remained in constant danger of evacuation.[47]

After clearing the camps, the Vichy government moved to hunt down the thousands of foreign Jews who had managed to avoid detention or had gained release from the camps before the deportations had commenced. Houses and hotels were searched before dawn. Mass arrests took place. Frantic parents, hearing of the raids, besieged the relief groups, begging them to hide their children. But French police had also started tracking down children who were in orphanages and care homes throughout Vichy France. These roundups of children, frequent in the summer and fall of 1942, continued sporadically throughout the war. This firsthand account is typical:

> There was the first raid on the nursery at 4 o'clock in the morning with two trucks. There were similar raids in all of L——— that same night. The big trucks were to be seen everywhere. . . . Within a quarter of an hour the children [some as young as three years] had to be awakened, dressed and their belongings packed.[48]

The great tide of Vichy roundups outside the camps lasted from late August until mid-September 1942. It swept another 7,000 Jews onto trains to Occupied France and then to Auschwitz. These large-scale deportations from the Unoccupied Zone in August and September carried away about 10,600 Jews. Before the Germans were driven from France, nearly 4,000 more were transported to Auschwitz, making a total of over 14,000 delivered to the Nazis from the southern sector of the country.[49]

Shock waves from the calamity that struck in the Unoccupied Zone quickly registered in the offices of relief organizations in the United States. As early as August 10, Donald Lowrie traveled to Geneva to send the first in a series of thorough reports to the YMCA in New York. The New York headquarters of the American Jewish Joint Distribution Committee began receiving detailed information by cablegram from its Lisbon office by August 13. Many starkly brief messages of despair were dispatched from Marseilles to the American Friends Service Committee office in Philadelphia. These telegrams reported on people for whom the Quakers had been trying to arrange immigration to the United States. Filed away a generation and a half ago, they may stand as the only epitaphs that scores of Jews ever received. These three are representative:

A——— L——— DEPARTED CAMP RIVESALTES UNKNOWN DESTINATION

MOTHER DEPARTED UNKNOWN DESTINATION

[*to an uncle on Long Island*] PARENTS DEPARTED UNKNOWN DESTINATION SITUATION DIFFICULT[50]

The deportations were devastating on the personal level, even before people realized that evacuation meant murder by gas. A family that had done everything possible to escape from the Nazi grasp offers an example. The fragments of information that remain show that the S____ family had fled German territory some time before and had made its way to southern France. It succeeded in moving one young son into safekeeping in Switzerland. And a second boy, C____ , had been lucky enough to reach the United States earlier in 1942. But the parents had to remain in France, even though the relevant American immigration quotas were 90 percent unfilled at the time. The manner in which U.S. immigration laws were administered during World War II kept most refugees out.[51]

After reaching the United States, C____ wrote to his parents several times. He became increasingly concerned when he received no response. The explanation came in November in a letter from C____ 's sponsoring agency in New York to his case worker in the city where he lived with his new foster parents. Enclosed was one of C____ 's letters to his father. The agency worker wrote:

> What we feared would happen has actually taken place. C____ 's father was deported, because the enclosed letter, as you will note, came back with the famous stamp "parti sans addresse."[52]

Several other children who reached the United States from southern France in July 1942 sent postcards to their parents. Most of the cards came back marked "DEPARTED—DESTINATION UNKNOWN."[53]

In France, the deportations brought a barrage of denunciation. Several Roman Catholic prelates, including the archbishops of Paris, Lyon, and Toulouse, protested vigorously. The cardinals and archbishops of the Occupied Zone united in condemnation.*[54]

A statement by Bishop Pierre Theas, of Montauban, read in all the churches of his diocese, was representative of the attitude of the Catholic leadership:

> Hereby I make known to the world the indignant protest of Christian conscience, and I proclaim that all men, whether Aryan or non-Aryan, are brothers because they were created by the same God; and that all men, whatever their race or religion, have a right to respect from individuals as well as from States.[56]

---

* At the time, the American press reported that the Pope protested to the Vichy government three times during August. But apparently this did not happen, for no confirmation of it has been found.[55]

Pastor Marc Boegner, leader of the Protestant Federation of France, assailed the Vichy government for its collaboration in the roundups and the deportations. With the explicit support of the archbishop of Lyon, Pastor Boegner insisted on an audience with Laval in September in a last, unsuccessful attempt to halt the evacuations.[57]

The outrage of church leaders was shared by many others in the French population. It broke out even within the ranks of the police, many of whom resigned or accepted dismissal rather than round up Jews. The military governor of Lyon was removed because he refused to send his troops to hunt out Jews.[58]

Although the protests failed to stop the evacuations, they may have contributed to the fact that the Nazis never undertook large-scale removal of France's native-born Jews. Moreover, the denunciations voiced by church leaders and spread by local clergy shattered the secrecy that the Vichy regime tried to impose by banning the news from the French press and radio. Several religious leaders sent out pastoral letters calling on church members to help Jews. Many French families took in Jews and hid them. Children, especially, could be concealed, and, despite some betrayals and disasters, about 8,000 were saved by the combined efforts of Jewish organizations, private families, schools, youth groups, and Catholic convents and monasteries.[59]

Interfaith cooperation flourished. The head of the Jewish Boy Scouts in France came to the leader of a Protestant youth federation and simply stated, "Mademoiselle, I have 600 foreign Boy Scouts to be hidden from the police." They were hidden. Le Chambon-sur-Lignon, a Protestant village, successfully concealed scores of Jews, despite persistent police searches as well as government threats to reduce the town's food rations. Again, a force of Protestant and Catholic social workers broke into a prison in Lyon and "kidnapped" ninety children who were being held there with their parents for deportation. The parents signed releases placing their children under the care of a Christian organization, with the assurance that it was simply acting as a protecting cover. The parents were deported the next day; the children were hidden in convents. When Pierre Cardinal Gerlier, archbishop of Lyon, refused an order to surrender the children, Laval struck back by arresting Father Pierre Chaillet, a member of the cardinal's staff. Cardinal Gerlier responded by again instructing the priests in his diocese to conceal Jews. His personal commitment and prestige enabled him to face down Laval; the children remained hidden and Father Chaillet was released.[60]

Americans also spoke out vigorously against the deportations. As soon as they learned of the crisis, American relief workers in France alerted the news agencies and moved to press the issue with the Vichy government. Early in August, Donald Lowrie, a spokesman for several of the relief agencies, and Father Arnou, a special representative of Cardinal Gerlier, saw the chief of state, Marshal Henri Pétain. The aged leader, who seemed barely aware of the developments, agreed that the matter was regrettable but indicated that he was helpless to change it. "You know our situation with regard to the Germans," he said. That same day, Roswell McClelland and Lindsley Noble, of the American Friends Service Committee, had a conference with Laval in which he offered no hope of moderation. Instead, he broke into a long tirade against the Jews generally and the damage Jewish refugees allegedly had caused to France. During their visit to Vichy, the American relief workers gave the U.S. embassy its first detailed information about the round-ups and evacuations.[61]

Following an exchange of communications with the State Department, Pinkney Tuck, chargé d'affaires at the embassy, saw Laval and registered an extremely sharp protest against the "revolting" and "inhuman" treatment of the Jews. In fact, Tuck's deeply felt vehemence disturbed middle-level policymakers in the State Department who complained to Undersecretary of State Sumner Welles that Tuck had exceeded his instructions. Tuck, in fact, was even in advance of the leadership of the main American Jewish organizations, which on August 27 submitted a joint letter to the State Department calling on the United States to protest to the Vichy government. Welles replied that the American embassy in Vichy, "in compliance with instructions sent by the Department," had already made "the most vigorous representations possible."[62]

Some two weeks later, Secretary of State Cordell Hull followed up by personally delivering a blunt condemnation of the "revolting and fiendish" deportations to the Vichy ambassador to the United States, Gaston Henry-Haye. (The next day, Henry-Haye privately expressed his own disgust, with respect both to his rough handling by American officials and to the situation in France. He reportedly told a visitor that his ambition when he went back to France was to become a farmer "so that his dealings will be with animals instead of people. He feels that his dealings with people have spoiled his enjoyment of their society.")[63]

While in Vichy to see Pétain and Laval, Lowrie and the two American Friends workers had asked the Vichy leaders and the American embassy about the possibility of permitting some of the Jewish refugee children to leave for safety in the United States. Laval offered almost no hope but did not refuse outright. At the suggestion of American relief workers in France, their organizations' home offices appealed to the State Department for 1,000 immigration visas for Jewish children stranded in France. Actively aided by Eleanor Roosevelt and the President's Advisory Committee on Political Refugees, the plea was successful. On September 18, the State Department cabled its consuls in France authorizing the 1,000 visas and instructing the consuls to waive virtually all the usual red tape involved in visa issuance in order to hasten the process. Because of increasingly dire reports from France, the American relief agencies soon asked Washington to raise the number to 5,000. By the end of September, the State Department had complied.[64]

But the great difficulty was extracting exit visas from the Vichy regime. While the children were being collected and readied, a sleight-of-hand game was played out in Vichy. On September 30, Tuck sought Laval's cooperation. Laval replied that he agreed "in principle" to the exodus of the children, adding, as Tuck reported it, "that he would be only too glad to be rid of them." But when it came to arranging the details with Laval's underlings, it turned out that a combination of German pressure and Vichy recalcitrance had shifted the ground.[65]

Throughout October, the Vichy government stalled on releasing the children, falling back on sham arguments to drag out discussions. Some religious groups, asserted the secretary-general of police, had illegally hidden children. For the government now to allow those children to emigrate would be to justify illegal acts and encourage such conduct in the future. Vichy officials hypocritically spoke of their government's great concern about separating families and its belief that eventual reunion was more likely if the children remained on the same continent as the parents.[66]

Tuck's constant pressure finally wrenched out of Laval a promise of 500 visas. It was then the end of October, and before a convoy of children could be assembled, moved through the documentation process, and placed on a train for Lisbon, the entire project ended precipitously. On November 8, Allied forces landed in French North Africa. The Vichy government severed diplomatic ties with the United States the next day. By then a group of a hundred children with the precious exit visas had reached Marseilles and needed only their U.S. visas. But the American consulate was closed. On November 11, the Germans occupied the southern sector of France and demolished the chances of salvaging anything from the project. Until spring 1944, diplomatic efforts were made, chiefly by the Swiss government, to persuade the Vichy regime to allow at least the promised 500 to leave. These attempts were fruitless.[67]

American newspaper readers in the summer of 1942 could follow the main configurations of the Jewish tragedy in France. Most metropolitan dailies provided fairly thorough coverage of the mass arrests of mid-July in Paris. The fearful and chaotic conditions connected with those roundups appeared in many of the major newspapers, and some of them carried partial descriptions of the Vélodrome d'Hiver episode. Almost none reported the barbaric shoving of 4,000 children into box-cars for shipment across the Continent without the necessities of life and without adult escort. But the UP did reveal that outrage, and the *Los Angeles Times,* for one, ran the dispatch.[68]

The deportations from the camps in southern France and the round-ups in the Unoccupied Zone received widespread notice. Nothing spe-cific appeared, however, concerning conditions on the deportation trains. But the protests raised by the French archbishops and other members of the clergy drew repeated coverage. Accounts of the church's role in hiding children and the Vichy government's challenge to the church by arresting a priest also ran in most major newspapers.

Much of the French deportation story thus appeared in the American press. But it was almost never featured. For instance, the *New York Times* published some twenty-five items but placed only two on the front page. Those reports reached page 1 apparently because they in-volved leaders of the Catholic church. Even so, each story received only a few inches of type at the foot of the page. One told very little, the other nothing, about what was actually happening to the Jews. Other major newspapers generally conformed to the same pattern. They printed considerable information, but almost always on inner pages, and even there it was often barely noticeable.[69]

In sum, the American daily press carried fuller information on the calamity of the refugee Jews in France than it did on any other devel-opment in the Nazi extermination program. As with all news about the Holocaust, though, American newspapers gave this information very limited emphasis.

The disaster that struck France in the summer of 1942 was the most noticeable part of a large wave of deportations from western Europe to the gas chambers in the second half of that year. Though the Nether-lands, Belgium, and Norway were nearly walled off from the Allied world, bits of information filtered out about the mass arrests and evac-uations there. In July a roundup of 60,000 Jews began in Amsterdam. Convoys rolled to the East, despite the protests of Dutch Protestant and Catholic church leaders. Popular demonstrations against the de-portations, urged on by broadcasts from the Dutch government-in-exile in England, obliged the Germans to reschedule train deportations for the middle of the night. But the transports continued to move. (The first of the trains to reach Auschwitz from Holland arrived while SS

Chief Heinrich Himmler was there on an inspection tour. Himmler observed the whole murder process, from opening the railway cars to removal of the bodies from the gas chamber.)[70]

The few accounts to break out of Belgium mentioned nighttime roundups and mass deportations. Isolated reports from Norway told of the arrest and later removal by ocean freighter of many members of that country's tiny Jewish population.[71]

The massive deportations from western Europe in 1942 were one step in the still-secret program of genocide. The Nazi explanation— labor service at an unnamed destination in the East—seemed plausible at the time. It especially appeared to make sense in view of the poor response to the Vichy government's effort to recruit 150,000 French workers to go to Germany to help fill the labor shortage there. News reports concerning the deported Jews regularly referred to "forced labor" and "slave labor" as their fate, a view that was generally accepted. But some observers, especially those close enough to witness the events, had doubts.[72]

Commenting in August on the announcement that the Jews were being sent to a labor area in Poland, Donald Lowrie pointed out certain inconsistencies:

> Since children, the aged and ill (we know some cases of epileptics, palsied, insane and even bedridden put into the corral for deportation) are taken, and since their destination is uniformly reported (by Laval, Pétain, the Police) as the Jewish reservation in Poland, the need for labor does not totally explain this action. In view of the present transport difficulties in Germany it is hard to understand a German *desire* to have these unfortunates.

Two months later Lowrie was still suspicious, although he did not speculate on what was actually happening:

> By no stretch of the imagination, however, can the majority of the unfortunate Jews thus delivered to the Germans be considered as capable of labour service. Of one convoy totalling 700, not more than 60 were in physical condition to do any useful work.[73]

A Jewish refugee physician working at the Unitarian Service Committee's medical facility in Marseilles had just about figured it out. Months of hoping for a favorable decision on his application for a visa to the United States had run out. Shortly before being forced onto the deportation train, he said, "I waited for the help that was promised.

Now it is too late. We know that nobody returns from the East. Thanks for what all of you have done—alas in vain."[74]

In the midst of the disclosures from France came news from the London Polish government concerning the hundreds of thousands of Jews who had been crowded into the Warsaw ghetto since late 1940. The report revealed that the ghetto mayor, Adam Czerniakow, had committed suicide rather than obey orders to prepare deportation lists that would help the Nazis in their announced plan to evacuate 100,000 Jews to "an undisclosed place in Eastern Europe." (The real destination was death in the killing centers, principally Treblinka. Deportation of the 380,000 Warsaw Jews began on July 22; by the end of 1942, over 310,000 were gone. The remnant included those who would ignite the Warsaw ghetto revolt of April 1943.)[75]

During the summer of 1942, another shocking report was smuggled from Poland by the Jewish Labor Bund, the group that had sent word in May of the murder of 700,000 Polish Jews. A gruesome account of the mass-gassing process at Chelmno, it was the first thorough description of a German killing center to reach the West. The victims, told to undress for a bath, were led down a hallway and suddenly forced into a large truck. Shut and sealed, the truck drove to a deep ditch in a nearby wood, where it became an execution chamber. Exhaust gases killed those trapped inside. A squad of Jewish gravediggers unloaded the bodies. After German workers stripped rings, gold teeth, and other valuables from the corpses, the gravediggers buried the dead Jews in layers in the ditch. Six to nine truckloads were murdered in this way daily. The gravediggers themselves were killed after a time, but three escaped in late January 1942. They succeeded in reporting their experiences to the Polish Jewish underground, which was already aware that thousands of Jews sent to the Chelmno area had disappeared without a trace.[76]

The American affiliate of the Jewish Labor Bund printed the gravediggers' account on August 5, 1942, in a special issue of its publication *The Ghetto Speaks.* A month later, a closely allied journal, the *Workmen's Circle Call,* carried the same report, as did the *Jewish Frontier.*

The American mass media did not mention the gravediggers' revelations. Nor did most of the Jewish press, apparently because the story seemed so incredible. The quandary of the Jewish leadership is illustrated by the case of the *Jewish Frontier,* an important American labor Zionist monthly. Its editors could not believe the report. (We were then "psychologically unschooled for the new era of mass carnage," explained one of them a quarter of a century later. "Such things did not happen in the twentieth century.") But they hesitated to ignore an account that came from a most dependable underground source. So they compromised by printing the story in small type in the back of the September issue. There it appeared, placed with unintended irony among advertisements bearing New Year's greetings from commercial enterprises. This decision, taken by a conscientious and deeply concerned segment of the American Jewish leadership, was not, as one of the editors later termed it, "gross stupidity." Rather it was a reflection of the confusion that gripped American Jewish leaders when first confronted with explicit descriptions of such unprecedented barbarism.[77]

The summer of 1942 revealed disaster after disaster for European Jewry. It was also a time when the war was still running against the United States and its allies. The Germans continued to advance in Russia. The Wehrmacht swept to the Don River early in July and opened the assault on Stalingrad in August. Other forces took Rostov late in July and began to move on the Caucasus oil fields. Rommel's drive across North Africa toward the Suez lifeline and the Mideast reached El Alamein as July opened. Though the Germans were stopped there, the struggle, only 200 miles from the Suez Canal, remained in doubt well into the fall. In the Pacific, the Japanese outward thrust was not halted until June, in the naval battle of Midway. It was August before a limited American offensive, the landings on Guadalcanal and Tulagi, planted the earliest small footholds on the long road back across the Pacific.

But the turning point was approaching. The Russian winter, an ominous threat to the Germans with their overextended supply lines, was approaching. At the start of November, the British would shatter Rommel's forces at El Alamein and Allied troops would storm ashore in northwest Africa. Six months later, the two Allied drives would force the Axis out of Africa. The fight in the Pacific, where the United States applied only 15 percent of its war resources until V-E Day, would be halting and very costly, but the balance was beginning to shift there too.

As the autumn of 1942 unfolded, the situation for America and its allies was becoming more hopeful. For American Jews, though, even more terrible news about the fate of their people in Europe was soon to hit.

3

THE WORST IS
CONFIRMED

_____

News of the existence of a plan for the systematic extermination of Europe's Jews reached the United States in August 1942. Sent from Switzerland, the shocking revelation circumvented State Department roadblocks and came into the hands of American Jewish leaders. They found it credible. State Department officials, however, were skeptical. They asked the Jews not to publicize the disclosure until the government had time to confirm it. Not until late November was the news, along with corroborating evidence, released to the press.

During the first days of August, as desperate Jews were being forced onto deportation trains in France, in Warsaw, and elsewhere, a message from a prominent German industrialist reached Dr. Gerhart Riegner, the representative of the World Jewish Congress in Geneva. This industrialist, whose position in the German war economy gave him access to confidential Nazi sources, had arrived in Switzerland from Berlin at the end of July. He carried news of a Nazi plan to kill all the Jews of Europe. The German revealed the information to a Jewish friend who brought it to the attention of a Swiss Jewish leader, Dr. Benjamin Sagalowitz. Sagalowitz, who conveyed the report to Riegner, also checked into the reliability of the industrialist and found him completely trustworthy.[1]

Riegner, thirty years old and trained for a career in international law, was himself a refugee from Germany. On Saturday morning, August 8, he took the information to the American consulate in Geneva. There he talked with Vice-Consul Howard Elting, Jr., whose summary of the discussion noted that Riegner had come to him "in great agitation" with a report from an apparently thoroughly reliable source

> to the effect that there has been and is being considered in Hitler's headquarters a plan to exterminate all Jews from Germany and German controlled areas in Europe after they have been concentrated in the east (presumably Poland). The number involved is said to be between three-and-a-half and four millions and the object is to permanently settle the Jewish question in Europe.[2]

When Elting mentioned that the report seemed fantastic, Riegner replied that it had looked that way to him at first, but it did mesh exactly with the recent mass deportations from France, Holland, and other countries. He handed Elting a summary of the message and asked that it be telegraphed to Washington and the other Allied governments and to Rabbi Stephen Wise in New York. Elting immediately sent Riegner's information to the American legation in Bern, along with his endorsement of Riegner as "a serious and balanced individual," and his recommendation that the report be dispatched to the State Department.[3]

The American legation telegraphed Riegner's message to Washington on August 11, adding that it had no information to confirm the report, which it characterized as having the "earmarks of war rumor inspired by fear." The recipients, middle-level officials in the State Department's Division of European Affairs, dismissed Riegner's disclosures as totally unbelievable. They were convinced that Jews were being deported for labor purposes. The only disagreement within the State Department was on the question of whether the message should be delivered to Rabbi Wise.[4]

Paul T. Culbertson, who could see no justification for the Bern legation "to have put this thing in a telegram," nonetheless spoke for releasing it to Wise on the grounds of caution:

> I don't like the idea of sending this on to Wise but if the Rabbi hears later that we had the message and didn't let him in on it he might put up a kick. Why not send it on and add that the Legation has no information to confirm the story.

Elbridge Durbrow, another official in the Division of European Affairs, thought it inadvisable to transmit the dispatch to Wise, citing as reasons "the Legation's comments, the fantastic nature of the allegation, and the impossibility of our being of any assistance if such action were taken." Durbrow's view prevailed.[5]

Durbrow also wanted to instruct the Bern legation to refuse to send any more such messages "for possible transmission to third parties unless, after thorough investigation, there is reason to believe that such a fantastic report has in the opinion of the Legation some foundation or unless the report involves definite American interests." This suggestion, however, was not implemented, and the information channels from Switzerland remained open. But the idea had been planted. Six months later, State Department officials would attempt to cut off the flow of extermination news from Switzerland.[6]

To the State Department's experts on European affairs, the German industrialist's disclosure was only another war rumor, a "fantastic" one at that. They saw it in isolation from numerous other reports that had reached the department concerning the Jewish calamity. Riegner, relating the new information to earlier accounts, recognized it as the key. It brought into focus the previously hazy picture of what was befalling the Jews in Nazi-occupied Europe. The information would have the same impact on American Jewish leaders, because it revealed an overall pattern that explained the terrible events reported by the Polish Jewish Labor Bund, the other accounts of large-scale killings, and the ongoing mass deportations "to the East."

Despite the Division of European Affairs, Riegner's message reached Wise, but not until late August. Riegner had given the British consulate in Geneva a summary identical to the one he delivered to Elting. He asked that it be telegraphed to the Foreign Office in London and passed on to Samuel Sydney Silverman, a member of Parliament and chairman of the British section of the World Jewish Congress. Riegner had prudently added one line to the version he took to the British: "Please inform and consult New York."[7]

Riegner's message reached London on August 10. The Foreign Office hesitated for a week, then delivered it to Silverman, but advised him that "we have no information bearing on or confirming this story." Silverman cabled the report to the United States on August 28. Addressed directly to Wise, Silverman's telegram apparently did not attract the attention of the Division of European Affairs, for the War and State departments both cleared it, and it went on to Wise.[8]

Unaware that the State Department already had the Riegner report, Wise sent Silverman's cable to Undersecretary of State Sumner Welles

on September 2. In his covering letter, Wise vouched for Riegner as "a scholar of entire reliability" and "not an alarmist but a conservative and equable person." He asked Welles to have the American minister in Bern confer with Riegner to find out what added substantiation he might provide. Wise also suggested that the information be brought to President Roosevelt's attention.[9]

Shortly after receiving the message, Welles phoned Wise. The undersecretary seems to have been unwilling to take Riegner's report to Roosevelt, for the next day Wise wrote Supreme Court Justice Felix Frankfurter suggesting that he inform the President. Wise also told Frankfurter that Welles had tried to be reassuring: "He seems to think that the real purpose of the Nazi government is to use Jews in connection with war work both in Nazi Germany and in Nazi Poland and Russia." Welles had also asked Wise not to release the Riegner information until the State Department had a chance to confirm it.[10]

Meanwhile, the Division of European Affairs suppressed another telegram to Wise, this one from the World Jewish Congress in London. It called for urgent steps in response to Riegner's report: a press conference, a public declaration by political and religious leaders of the democratic nations, and appeals for action to the Vatican and the United Nations.[11]

In the midst of the developments connected with Riegner's message, another bombshell exploded in the faces of the Jewish leaders. On September 3, Jacob Rosenheim of New York, president of the Agudath Israel World Organization, received a telegram from Isaac Sternbuch, the Orthodox group's representative in Switzerland:

> According to numerous authentic informations from Poland German authorities have recently evacuated Warsaw ghetto and bestially murdered about one hundred thousand Jews. These mass murders are continuing. The corpses of the murdered victims are used for the manufacturing of soap and artificial fertilizers. Similar fate is awaiting the Jews deported to Poland from other occupied territories. Suppose that only energetical steps from America may stop these persecutions. Do whatever you can to cause an American reaction to halt these persecutions.[12]

Rosenheim did try to "cause an American reaction," although he was "physically broken down from this harrowing cable." That same day, he telegraphed Sternbuch's message to Franklin Roosevelt. Much of the following day, Rosenheim and other Orthodox Jewish leaders conferred in New York with James G. McDonald, chairman of the President's Advisory Committee on Political Refugees. McDonald, who was on good terms with Eleanor Roosevelt, sent a copy of Sternbuch's telegram to her, along with a message saying that he did not know what could be done, but felt she should be informed. No reaction from Franklin or Eleanor Roosevelt is recorded.[13]

Rosenheim also notified Wise and other Jewish leaders. These men met to exchange views. Wise gave the others the Riegner information, but expressed some hesitation about the credibility of Sternbuch's report, even though he did see it as circumstantial confirmation of Riegner's disclosure. The group decided to send a delegation to the State Department to ask that American intelligence check into what had happened at Warsaw. Welles received the Jewish leaders on September 10 and agreed to have an investigation made. Within a few weeks, most of Sternbuch's disclosures were authenticated by further reports from Poland.*[14]

A sidelight on Sternbuch's message is that it reached Rosenheim through two independent telegraphic channels. The cablegram that came on September 3 was transmitted through the coded facilities of the Polish government-in-exile. The same dispatch arrived soon afterward through a conventional route, from the American legation in Bern to the State Department and then to Rosenheim. Use of the Polish channel for such communications was illegal. But Polish diplomats in New York and Bern relayed messages to and from Europe for Agudath Israel and related Orthodox rescue committees. Although this process sometimes involved delays, it avoided censorship, especially that of the very stringent American censor. Sternbuch, the Orthodox representative in Switzerland, had underground communication lines into much of Axis Europe. From mid-1942 until the end of the war, use of the Polish facilities between Bern and New York enabled him to transmit messages secretly between sources in Nazi-controlled Europe and Jewish leaders in the United States.[16]

In accord with Welles's request, Wise kept the Riegner information out of the press. During September and October, though, he revealed both the Riegner and the Sternbuch disclosures to several individuals —to government and Jewish leaders, as part of a desperate behind-the-scenes effort to develop some sort of action to help the doomed Jews, and also to a few close friends to ease his own psychological burden. Among the latter was the prominent Protestant clergyman John Haynes Holmes, to whom Wise confided, "I am almost demented over my people's grief."[17]

---

* Production of soap from human remains, however, was not definitely established. But rumors to that effect circulated in various parts of Axis Europe.[15]

Wise's attempts to devise some means for countering the extermination plan began with his steps in early September to alert Washington (his approach to Welles and his appeal to Frankfurter to inform Roosevelt). After Rosenheim showed him Sternbuch's report, Wise took the lead in forming a temporary committee of Jewish leaders to seek ways to help the European Jews. Shortly afterward, he met in New York with the President's Advisory Committee on Political Refugees, a small, quasi-governmental organization formed in 1938 to counsel Roosevelt on refugee matters. He urged Myron C. Taylor, the President's personal representative to the Vatican, to appeal to the Pope to intervene. And during September and October he journeyed to Washington several times.[18]

On one such trip, he showed the terrible telegrams to Vice-President Henry Wallace and Assistant Secretary of State Dean Acheson in an effort to obtain support for allowing food shipments to Jews in Poland. In October, he carried the same news to a very sympathetic Harold Ickes, secretary of the interior, and asked him to attempt to convince the President to open the Virgin Islands as a temporary haven of safety for perhaps 2,000 refugee Jews.[19]

Throughout those weeks, Wise was pessimistic about achieving any results. In Washington, he found many officials unable to perceive the deportations from Warsaw and from western Europe as anything other than part of a forced-labor program. He felt uncertain whether Pius XII could wield any real authority and doubted that he would even try. During this highly depressing time, Wise believed that even Roosevelt could not intervene effectively.[20]

As Wise had feared, his overtures to prominent officials brought meager results; only a few reacted at all. Ickes, whose Interior Department administered the Virgin Islands, did write to the President asking whether he would be willing to consider using the islands as a small-scale refuge. Roosevelt turned this request down. The State Department offered to approve a very limited program for sending individual food parcels, but not bulk shipments, from Portugal to people in German-occupied countries, including Jews in the Polish ghettos. Under this arrangement, $12,000 worth of food bought in Portugal could go to Polish Jews each month, an amount privately described by one high State Department official as "infinitesimal." Ironically, Dean Acheson, the official Wise had thought most approachable on the issue, was the only one in the State Department who opposed this feeble gesture.[21]

Meanwhile, as the autumn of 1942 unfolded, more signs of a campaign of planned extermination appeared. In late September, the New York Yiddish-language *Jewish Morning Journal* published information derived from a Swedish businessman who had traveled through Poland, stopping at Warsaw, Lodz, Krakow, and Lvov. He had learned that half the Jews in those ghettos had been killed. Relying on an entirely different source, the Jewish Telegraphic Agency reported in early October that "in Lodz thousands of Jewish families are taken away from the ghetto systematically and nobody ever hears from them again. They are poisoned by gas." [22]

Before October ended, observations from two widely dissimilar quarters indicated that people who followed European developments very closely were about to piece together the puzzle of genocide. *National Jewish Monthly,* the B'nai B'rith magazine, asked in its October issue why the Nazis were clearing western Europe of Jews and moving them to Poland. This step, maintained the editors, "doesn't make sense, even from the Nazi point of view," because Hitler's war industry badly needs labor in Germany. Even granting that masses of Jews in Poland might be moving into occupied Russia to carry out German construction projects, the writers could not break loose from the enigma: "but they still need workers in Germany." Furthermore, they pointed out, Soviet guerrilla forces report no Jews in all of Nazi-controlled White Russia, including Minsk and Vitebsk, formerly large centers of Jewish population. Then where are they? Not in Germany, because news dispatches from there declare that Germany is "Jew-free," except for some technical workers. Are they all in the Polish ghettos? Apparently not, for another report points out that 300,000 Jews have disappeared without a trace from the Warsaw ghetto. This analysis forced the *National Jewish Monthly* to the very edge of the appalling reality: "it is feared that the Nazis may be resorting to wholesale slaughter, preferring to kill all Jews rather than use their labor." [23]

In England, the archbishop of Canterbury, unconvinced by the "forced labor" explanation for the mass deportations from France, was quoted in the press as being almost certain that planned annihilation was under way. Speaking in late October to a London mass meeting to protest Nazi persecution of the Jews, William Temple declared that it is "hard to resist the conclusion that there is a settled purpose to exterminate the Jewish people if it can be done." [24]

Only days later, another voice declared with no hesitation whatever that Europe's Jews were being systematically wiped out. The editors of *Jewish Frontier,* whose earlier uncertainty had led them to place the gravediggers' account of the Chelmno gassings at the back of their September issue, had been apprised of Riegner's disclosures. Convinced that planned annihilation of the Jews was indeed in progress, they omitted their October issue to put full effort into collecting all the trustworthy documentation they could find for a special edition on the mass murder of the Jews. Printed with black borders, the *Jewish Frontier* for November 1942 declared:

> In the occupied countries of Europe a policy is now being put into effect, whose avowed object is the extermination of a whole people. It is a policy of systematic murder of innocent civilians which in its dimensions, its ferocity and its organization is unique in the history of mankind.[25]

Realizing that people would find the information hard to accept, the editors had worked cautiously. Their estimate of one million Jews killed "through massacre and deliberate starvation" represented a conservative reading of reports then available. And they carefully avoided the use of "material whose authenticity was in any way doubtful." Even so, the documentation that they printed definitely pointed to extermination. Viewed against that evidence, the *Jewish Frontier* maintained, "the deportation of Jews from France and Poland to unknown destinations allows of only the most sinister explanation."[26]

The *Jewish Frontier*'s main editorial closed with a call to the Allied governments "to do whatever may be done to prevent the fulfillment of this horror." The vagueness of the appeal testified to the state of mind that prevailed among American Jewish leaders in the last part of 1942. Stunned by the dimensions of the disaster now revealed to them, they seemed unable for a time to devise concrete proposals for action.[27]

Rabbi Wise, who had been wrestling since late August with the problem of developing practical action, continued to work under the additional handicap of having to withhold his information from the public. Although Sumner Welles had agreed on September 10 to initiate attempts to confirm the Riegner and the Sternbuch disclosures, the State Department did not notify Wise of its progress until late November.

Neither Welles nor others in the State Department pursued the inquiry with much energy. On September 23, a request for information that might authenticate the reports was sent on its way to the Vatican. An unsigned, informal response from the Holy See arrived in Washington three weeks afterward. The Vatican stated that it, too, had reports of "severe measures" taken against the Jews, but that verification had not been possible. (Near the end of November, the Vatican did send Washington a message it had from Warsaw with explicit verification of much of the worst that previously had been asserted, including killing in specially built gas chambers.)[28]

By October 5, a day when Wise saw Welles and pointed out that reports of mass murder in eastern Europe were continuing to reach

American Jewish leaders, the only corroborative information received at the State Department was a brief message that Jews in Warsaw and other ghettos in Poland had been "shipped east" in lots of five to ten thousand. Their whereabouts and fate were unknown. This news had been relayed to Washington by Leland Harrison, the American minister to Switzerland, who had obtained it from the Polish exile government's mission in Switzerland.[29]

Right after this discussion with Wise, Welles wired Harrison asking him to make contact with Riegner and telegraph back whatever additional information he could supply. Harrison delayed for more than two weeks, then relayed his findings in two slow-moving letters.[30]

Before Harrison's letters arrived in the United States, other evidence of extermination reached the State Department. Late in September, Riegner, on his own initiative, conferred with Paul C. Squire, the American consul at Geneva. He handed Squire photostats of two letters that had recently reached him. They offered persuasive evidence that the Jews of the Warsaw ghetto were being deported and exterminated in vast numbers. The letters were written in German and enclosed in envelopes bearing the marks of the German censor. They had been sent to Switzerland from a Jew in Warsaw on September 4 and 12. Innocuous on the surface and thus able to pass German censorship, the letters were actually written in a semicode. A literal translation of part of the September 4 letter follows. The meanings of the coded words, as interpreted to Squire, are in brackets.

> I spoke to Mr. Jäger [hunter, thus the Germans]. He told me that he will invite all relatives of the family Achenu [our brethren, thus the Jews], with the exception of Miss Eisenzweig [apparently ironworkers, thus heavy-industry workers], from Warsaw, to his countryside dwelling Kewer [tomb]. I am alone here; I feel lonely. . . . Uncle Gerusch [deportation] works also in Warsaw; he is a very capable worker. His friend Miso [death] works together with him. Please pray for me.

Wholesale extermination was reiterated in the letter of September 12, which began, "I too was in sorrow, for I am now so lonely. Uncle Achenu has died."[31]

Squire forwarded photostats of the Warsaw letters to Washington on September 28. Sent via the diplomatic airmail pouch, the material reached the State Department only on October 23. It was not brought to Welles's attention until much of November had passed.[32]

By that time, Welles had received Harrison's two letters from Bern. When supplemented by a follow-up telegram that Harrison sent on

November 23, they revealed that a prominent non-Jewish Swiss had disclosed to Squire, "privately and not for publication," that he, too, had learned, through two separate high government contacts in Berlin, that an order had been issued in Hitler's headquarters for the physical elimination of the Jews. The Swiss informant was Dr. Carl Burckhardt, a high official of the International Red Cross and an unimpeachable source.[33]

The materials from Squire and Harrison, weighed with other reports sent that autumn from Europe to American Jewish leaders, convinced Welles. On Tuesday, November 24, he telegraphed Wise to come at once to the State Department. Late that day, Wise arrived at Welles's office.[34]

As Welles handed the rabbi several documents sent from the American legation in Switzerland, he conveyed the terrible news: "I regret to tell you, Dr. Wise, that these confirm and justify your deepest fears." Welles added, "There is no exaggeration. These documents are evidently correct." As for releasing the information to the news media, Welles stated, "For reasons you will understand, I cannot give these to the press, but there is no reason why you should not. It might even help if you did." * [35]

That same evening, while still in Washington, Wise called a press conference. He told reporters that through sources confirmed by the State Department he had learned that two million Jews had been killed in an "extermination campaign" aimed at wiping out all the Jews in Nazi Europe. He disclosed that only about 100,000 of the 500,000 Jews formerly in Warsaw were still there and that the Nazis were moving Jews from all over Europe to Poland for mass killing.[37]

Wise returned to New York the same night. The following day, he met with a committee of Jewish leaders. By then, he had independent confirmation of Welles's news from Myron C. Taylor, Roosevelt's special representative to the Vatican. That afternoon, Wise held another press conference, at which he spoke as a representative for most of the leading American Jewish organizations. He announced that the Jewish groups were convinced, on the basis of the State Department documentation, that Hitler had ordered the annihilation of all Jews in areas under Nazi control. The purpose in publicizing the extermination information, he stated, was "to win the support of a Christian world so

---

* This paragraph is based on Wise's account of his meeting with Welles. Officials in the Division of European Affairs maintained for months afterward that the State Department had never confirmed the extermination reports. But all the evidence indicates that Wise's description of the meeting was accurate.[36]

that its leaders may intervene and protest the horrible treatment of Jews in Hitler Europe."[38]

Just as Wise was revealing the annihilation plan to the world, additional evidence of genocide was appearing in Jerusalem and London. On November 23, the Jewish press in Palestine published black-bordered reports of systematic extermination brought from Poland by Jews who had recently been exchanged for German citizens from British-controlled territories. The following day, information released in Jerusalem included an account of concrete gas-chamber buildings in eastern Europe and a report that trains were carrying Jewish adults and children "to great crematoriums at Oswiecim, near Cracow." (Although mass murder of Jews at Oswiecim, the Polish name for Auschwitz, had been under way since mid-1942, this was one of the first indications of it to reach the outside world.)[39]

In London, dire reports were again coming to the Polish government-in-exile from underground sources in Poland. On the same day that Wise received the documents from Welles, the London Polish government asserted that Heinrich Himmler had ordered half of the three million Jews of Poland destroyed by the end of 1942 as the first step in their complete annihilation. The Polish statement included graphic descriptions of Jews packed into freight cars and deported to "special camps" at Treblinka, Belzec, and Sobibor. Many died of suffocation or lack of water en route; the rest were murdered at the camps. "Under the guise of resettlement in the east," advised the Polish authorities, "the mass murder of the Jewish population is taking place."[40]

The very next day, Ignacy Schwarzbart, a Jewish member of the Polish government, informed the press that one million Polish Jews had perished since the war began. They had been killed by shooting, gassing, and the intentional creation of ghetto conditions characterized by starvation, crowding, and disease. Two days later, in New York, Henryk Strasburger, the Polish minister of finance, announced that "at least a million Polish Jews have been killed." At about the same time, a Catholic underground organization reported from Poland that "the total of Jews murdered already exceeds one million."[41]

German documents seized after the war reveal that almost 1.5 million Polish Jews had been deported to killing centers by December 31, 1942. In addition, hundreds of thousands of Polish Jews had perished either through starvation and ghetto conditions or at the hands of the *Einsatz-gruppen* in what had been pre-war eastern Poland. It turns out that the statistics dispatched by Polish underground sources were cautiously compiled indeed. It is also apparent that Wise's estimate of two million Jewish dead in all of Europe was long out of date by November 1942.[42]

The emerging picture of the Jewish catastrophe was not well defined in its particulars. It could not be. Reports that filtered out were at times confusing and contradictory. Only after the war did a definite understanding of the six killing centers and their operations crystallize. Even Auschwitz was not widely recognized as the pivotal installation that it was until 1944. But after November 24, 1942, it was evident that the reports were basically correct. A hideous and unprecedented mass murder program was in progress. Hitler had been serious when he addressed the German nation from the Berlin Sports Palace in September 1942. Referring to a speech delivered in 1939, he asserted that he had then warned that

> if Jewry should plot another world war in order to exterminate the Aryan peoples of Europe, it would not be the Aryan peoples which would be exterminated, but Jewry.

Now, in 1942, he threatened:

> At one time, the Jews of Germany laughed about my prophecies. I do not know whether they are still laughing or whether they have already lost all desire to laugh. But right now I can only repeat: they will stop laughing everywhere, and I shall be right also in that prophecy.[43]

The events traced so far throw light on two questions which have been raised frequently since World War II; one concerns Gerhart Riegner's August report, and the other Stephen Wise's handling of it. The first asks why Riegner's information from the German industrialist proved to be the key to decisive recognition that the Jews were undergoing systematic extermination. Why not one of the earlier revelations?

One authority has maintained that the Jewish Labor Bund document that reached England from Poland near the start of June 1942 "should have been far more effective [than Riegner's report] in awakening both the Jewish and the non-Jewish worlds to what was going on." After all, it not only listed specific killing actions and provided an estimate of 700,000 Polish Jews dead but also pointed out that the Germans had determined to "annihilate all the Jews in Europe." In fact, the Bund report and the publicity it received *were* of pivotal importance in the emergence of a coherent view of what was happening to the Jews in Nazi Europe. And it was effective in starting to break down the barriers of disbelief that tended to wall extermination information out of people's minds. It was also instrumental in setting off mass protest demonstrations in the United States.[44]

As it worked out, the Bund report, the other accounts of Jewish slaughter, the mass meetings, and the deportation news from France all combined to form a milieu that made Riegner's information credible—"fantastic" though it may have seemed to State Department functionaries. The disclosure that an authoritative person had knowledge of a specific *plan* of annihilation made a vital difference. It not only fit into the previous knowledge but crystallized it all into a meaningful pattern. The deportations from the West, the accounts of killing sites in the East, the mass slaughter of Polish Jews came into focus around a Hitler order. It was equally significant that the source of the report was Berlin. Events outside Berlin could be used to *infer* a campaign of total extermination, but evidence that an actual plan existed in the decision center was compelling. Moreover, the fact that Riegner's report was finally released through the American State Department endowed it with an important stamp of authenticity.

The other question revolves around Wise's acquiescence in Welles's request not to release the Riegner information until the State Department had confirmed it. Wise has been criticized on the ground that his silence cost three irretrievable months desperately needed to build pressure on Washington. True, time was already short by September 1942 and the Roosevelt administration needed strong prodding before it would act. But three points need to be considered before this burden is placed on Wise.[45]

For one thing, there was strategic advantage in awaiting State Department confirmation. The Riegner report might have been discounted if based only on Jewish authorities. Government verification made it far more credible. (The State Department, of course, could have moved much more expeditiously to confirm the information.)

More important, Wise had no viable choice in the matter. The State Department was responsible for American rescue policy. Had Wise contravened Welles's request, he would have alienated the department of government whose cooperation was essential in the effort to help the European Jews.

And finally, if Wise is to be criticized in this instance, numerous others should be also. The British section of the World Jewish Congress had the Riegner report, as well as the British Foreign Office's permission to publicize it. Moreover, it might have used the House of Commons as a forum, since its chairman, Samuel Silverman, was a Labour MP. In addition, Wise showed Riegner's information to many Americans, including the temporary committee of Jewish leaders that formed in New York in early September and the distinguished members of the President's Advisory Committee on Political Refugees, as well as Felix

Frankfurter, Myron C. Taylor, Dean Acheson, Henry Wallace, and Harold Ickes. Any one of more than twenty prominent Americans could have called a press conference and broken the news.[46]

November 1942 was a pivotal month in World War II. During its opening week, the British broke Rommel's line at El Alamein and began the chase westward, reaching Benghazi two weeks later. On the eighth, Eisenhower landed forces in French North Africa; by the end of the month, they had driven nearly to Tunis. And in mid-November the great Russian counteroffensive at Stalingrad began to encircle and isolate an army of a quarter-million Germans. The war was still far from over, but the Germans were clearly in serious trouble.

November 1942 was also crucial in the American response to the Holocaust. The month closed with Rabbi Wise's shattering announcement of confirmed reports that the Nazis were carrying out a plan to annihilate all Jews under their control. November had opened with another development, far less momentous, but nonetheless potentially harmful to prospects for helping European Jewry. That was the sizable gain registered by conservatives in the American congressional elections of 1942.

Although liberal congressmen, both Democratic and Republican, had generally sympathized with the persecuted Jews throughout the Hitler years, few had been willing to press for increased immigration or other measures to aid them. But liberals had not attempted to block the few small steps that the President had taken. Southern Democrats and conservative Republicans, on the other hand, had consistently resisted Roosevelt's moves to help Jewish refugees.[47]

Illustrative of the power of congressional conservatives to thwart proposals to help European Jews, and of the failure of liberals to challenge that power, was the fate of legislation introduced into the House in September 1942 by Emanuel Celler, a Democrat from New York. Appalled by press reports of the mass deportations from France, Celler, a Jew, hoped to convert the widespread indignation aroused by that news into practical action. His bill called for opening America's doors to refugees in France who could prove they were facing roundup, internment, or religious persecution at the hands of the Nazis or the Vichy authorities.[48]

Celler's measure went to the House Committee on Immigration, where it languished almost unnoticed while the great crisis in France passed. A handful of Jewish organizations and the Yiddish press spoke out for it; otherwise silence prevailed. Congressman Samuel Dickstein, another Jew and a New York Democrat, was chairman of the House Immigration Committee. He agreed to hold hearings on the bill, but only *after* the elections. The hearings were never held, however, and the bill died in committee. Dr. Samuel Margoshes, a columnist for the *Day,* a New York Yiddish newspaper, explained that Jewish leaders had not launched a campaign for Celler's proposal because the question of large-scale immigration was an "extremely delicate" one.[49]

The heavy Republican gains in the 1942 elections surprised even the most optimistic GOP leaders. And conservative Democrats from the South retained their near monopoly on that region's seats. Although the Democrats continued to control Congress, the conservative coalition of southern Democrats and right-wing northern Republicans was the main force on Capitol Hill. A liberal victory in the off-year elections would not have meant a sustained American effort to help European Jewry. But the decisive conservative gains signaled that even limited steps in that direction would probably encounter stubborn opposition.[50]

Bolstered by the election's results, conservatives did not wait for the convening of the new Congress to display their new resolve. Almost immediately, they smashed the President's Third War Powers Bill, legislation that he had requested at the beginning of November. The response to this measure provided a barometer not only of anti-Roosevelt sentiment in Congress but also of anti-refugee and anti-immigration strength on Capitol Hill.[51]

The bill would have given the President the power, during the war, to suspend laws that were hampering "the free movement of persons, property and information into and out of the United States." Roosevelt wanted to bypass the maze of complicated forms and procedures required by the tariff, customs, and immigration laws.[52]

These requirements were hindering the war effort in various ways. For instance, for secrecy's sake, citizens of Allied nations flown to the United States for military or industrial consultation frequently landed away from the ports of entry where immigration officials were available. To comply with the law, such persons then had to travel to a port of entry, slowing their missions and increasing the risks to their confidentiality. Again, prisoners of war, even those shipped through New York under full guard en route to Canada, had to be processed individually and inspected like any aliens entering the United States. The tariff and customs laws, for their part, were delaying deliveries of imported materials essential to war production. It was not the fees that were at issue, for the government ultimately paid these to itself. Rather, it was the precious time and manpower that the legally required paperwork was absorbing.[53]

The President's proposal, though a reasonable step to facilitate war production, set off a furor in Congress. Conservatives saw it as yet another Roosevelt attempt to grasp more power and as a thinly disguised device for sneaking open the gates to let in thousands of European refugees. Republican Roy Woodruff (Mich.), a member of the House Ways and Means Committee, spoke for many of his colleagues when he asserted that the legislation would "make the President a virtual dictator." Norwegian-born Harold Knutson (Rep., Minn.) voiced another anxiety abroad in Congress: "As I read it, you throw the door wide open on immigration." The conservative press took up the cry, led by the *Chicago Tribune,* which expressed "shock" (along with geographical confusion) at finding politicians attempting "to flood this nation with refugee immigration from Europe and other nations."[54]

The Ways and Means Committee tabled the original legislation by a vote of twenty-four to nothing. A subcommittee redrafted the measure, deleting the word *persons* from it, thus removing the immigration aspect. But even then opponents stalled the bill until the session ended, thereby killing it. They correctly foresaw that in the new, more conservative Congress the proposal would have no chance.[55]

The centrality of the refugee issue in the uproar over the Third War Powers Bill was noted by an insider, Assistant Secretary of State Breckinridge Long, who testified before the Ways and Means Committee. Long, the architect of the State Department's extremely stringent immigration policy, steadfastly opposed any increase in the small numbers of refugees then entering the United States. And he realized that Roosevelt had no intention whatever of using the proposed legislation to increase that trickle. But he recognized what the problem was and recorded it in his office diary:

> The entire trouble and the cause of the whole opposition, which apparently was coming from *every* member of the committee present, was simply because of the word "persons"—for that meant immigration and that meant that the President *could* (but he would not) throw open the doors.[56]

Long was convinced that if the bill that first came to the committee had not involved immigration, it would have sped through Congress. *Newsweek* magazine, which saw the refugee problem as a mostly *Jewish* refugee problem (as indeed it was), made the point more explicitly:

> The ugly truth is that anti-Semitism was a definite factor in the bitter opposition to the President's request for power to suspend immigration laws for the duration.[57]

With a more conservative Congress due in Washington in January 1943, prospects for congressional support to help the stricken Jews of Europe were bleak. Furthermore, in the face of the shift to the right, Roosevelt, reluctant in the past to run political risks to aid the persecuted Jews, would be very slow to respond to appeals for rescue action.[58]

Seventeen months of systematic, cold-blooded murder ran their course between the time the *Einsatzgruppen* were turned loose on the Russian front, in June 1941, and the day in late November 1942 when the extermination plan was confirmed to the world. The Nazis perpetrated their genocide program for nearly a year before the Jewish Labor Bund in Poland recognized what was happening and managed to send an alarm to the outside. Two months later, at a time when approximately 1.5 million Jews had already perished, Gerhart Riegner transmitted solid proof that planned annihilation was in motion. Three more months of calamity for European Jewry then passed before Western officialdom accepted the facts. In those three months, about one million more Jews were killed. The second sweep of the *Einsatzgruppen* was operating at full speed, and train after train rolled from the Polish ghettos and from western Europe, through the suffocating heat of summer, the chill autumn nights, and the numbing cold of November to meet the timetables of death.[59]

Delays in gaining the attention of the world were costly for the European Jews. Although much of that critical time may have been unavoidably lost, some of it had been dissipated by bureaucratic inertia and the indifference of government leaders. Even more tragic, fourteen *additional* months of mass murder were to pass before President Roosevelt and his administration, although fully cognizant of the ongoing genocide, could be persuaded to act. And when they did act, it was only in response to pressures that could no longer be disregarded.

·*Part Three*·

FOURTEEN
LOST MONTHS

|| 4 ||

FIRST STEPS

November 24, 1942, marked a turning point in Holocaust history. From then on, the news of Hitler's plan to annihilate the Jews was available to everyone in the democratic world who cared to know. But those not especially concerned were hardly confronted with the problem, because the news media gave it little prominence.

American metropolitan newspapers did a mediocre job of informing their readers of Rabbi Wise's disclosures. His November 24 press conference in Washington was widely reported, but it was not a major story anywhere.* The news conference he held in New York the next day received even less exposure.†

---

* Analysis of nineteen important newspapers throughout the United States shows that only five placed the story on page 1, none of them prominently. Two of the nineteen did not carry the report at all.

That same day, virtually all the newspapers found room on the front page for essentially frivolous "human interest" stories. This was also the case on the many other occasions when important news of the Holocaust appeared on inner pages or was omitted altogether.[1]

† Of the nineteen newspapers, only ten reported Wise's November 25 press conference at all, and then mostly inconspicuously on inside pages.

This early pattern of minor press coverage became the rule. During the next month, there were several additional developments concerning the Holocaust. They included a nationwide Day of Mourning and Prayer, a meeting between President Roosevelt and Jewish leaders, a United Nations declaration condemning the extermination program, and an extensive UN report on the mass killing. Most newspapers published something about these events, but none consistently featured that news.[2]

The *New York Times* printed considerable extermination-related information during late November and December 1942. But, except for a front-page report on the UN declaration, it relegated that news to inside pages. Moreover, during the five Sundays of late November and December the paper's weekly ten-page "News of the Week in Review" section included only one brief notice about the European Jewish tragedy. Yet the *Times* provided by far the most complete American press coverage of Holocaust events.[3]

Lack of solid press coverage in the weeks immediately following the November 24 announcement muffled the historic news at the outset. The press's failure to arouse public interest and indignation thus handicapped efforts to build pressure for government action to aid the Jews. Proponents of rescue were soon driven to seek alternative ways to bring the information before the public.

Two or three clear statements from Franklin Roosevelt would have moved this news into public view and kept it there for some time. But the President was not so inclined, nor did Washington reporters press him. In retrospect, it seems almost unbelievable that in Roosevelt's press conferences (normally held twice a week) not one word was spoken about the mass killing of European Jews until almost a year later. The President had nothing to say to reporters on the matter, and no correspondent asked him about it.[4]

Understandably, the American Jewish press focused strongly on the news of the Nazi annihilation program. One analyst has observed that the coverage in the Yiddish dailies was "enormous" compared with that of regular American newspapers. In New York, the *Day,* the *Forward,* and the *Jewish Morning Journal* published accounts, often under main front-page headlines, throughout late November and all of December.[5]

The English-language Jewish press likewise informed its readers of the terrible news. The Anglo-Jewish weeklies, newspapers of general Jewish interest published in many cities across the United States, spread the basic information, mainly through syndicated news columns and Jewish Telegraphic Agency dispatches.[6]

Fuller coverage and a great amount of editorial comment reached American Jews through dozens of English-language periodicals issued by the many political, religious, fraternal, and other Jewish organizations. For instance, a leader among these publications, *Congress Weekly,* brought out its December 4, 1942, issue in a funereal black cover, while the magazine itself was given over largely to documentary evidence of the mass killing.

Throughout December and on into 1943, Jewish publications reported the continuing Jewish tragedy. They called on Americans of other faiths to join them in protest and appealed to the United States and its allies to act to stop the mass murder.[7]

The plea for non-Jewish support went largely unanswered. Exceptions were the liberal periodicals *Nation* and *New Republic,* which publicized and decried the "Murder of a People," as the *Nation* termed it. Throughout the war, both journals continued to speak out on the issue and to demand government rescue action.[8]

The *American Mercury* also confronted readers with the agony of the European Jews through a powerful article by Ben Hecht, a prominent playwright and Hollywood scriptwriter. Hecht's essay reached a much wider audience when the *Reader's Digest* published a condensed version in early 1943. But the *American Mercury* and the *Reader's Digest* were alone among mass-circulation magazines in bringing the extermination issue to public attention in the weeks following the revelations of late November 1942. Except for a few inconspicuous words on the UN declaration, such news magazines as *Time, Life,* and *Newsweek* overlooked the systematic murder of millions of helpless Jews.[9]

Leaders of the American labor movement protested Germany's extermination program. In late November, AFL vice-president Matt Woll, addressing a Jewish labor group, declared, "I speak to you as a Christian and a trade unionist. There are no words in the lexicon of the human race to express the horror." AFL president William Green and CIO president Philip Murray both denounced the slaughter of the Jews in Christmas messages.[10]

A few other prominent non-Jews reacted to the Nazi horror. In the forefront was the noted news columnist Dorothy Thompson. In December, she planned a series of moves designed to stir resistance in Germany itself to the mass murders and concomitantly to bring the annihilation issue to the American public. She proposed two appeals to the German people, one from Americans of German descent and another from American Protestant churches. She also conceived of a special Christmas prayer by the Protestant churches for the stricken Jews of Europe, and a visit to President Roosevelt by a delegation of German

Americans to request that he and Winston Churchill broadcast a direct appeal to the German people.[11]

Dorothy Thompson was able to find support only for the first of her proposals. A full-page advertisement, published in ten metropolitan newspapers, was the sole fruit of her efforts. Yet this minor step marked the high point for months to come of American non-Jewish action to help Europe's Jews.[12]

The advertisement was a "Christmas Declaration" signed by fifty prominent Americans of German descent. They included theologian Reinhold Niebuhr, news correspondent William L. Shirer, George Herman ("Babe") Ruth, and orchestra conductor Walter Damrosch. The statement denounced the "cold-blooded extermination of the Jews" as well as the atrocities against other conquered peoples. It called on Germans to overthrow the Nazi regime. The declaration actually placed little emphasis on the Jewish catastrophe; there is evidence that it had to be toned down in order to obtain the fifty names. Miss Thompson, in fact, had to turn to the American Jewish Congress to cover the costs of the advertisements. Whatever its shortcomings, the declaration was widely disseminated. Newspapers reported it as a news story, and it was broadcast over all major American radio networks. The Office of War Information beamed it to the U.S. armed forces and to Axis Europe as well.[13]

The Jewish appeal to non-Jews for help was frequently addressed to the Christian church leadership. Since Christianity is a religion committed to succoring the helpless, the Christian churches might have been expected to rise to the challenge. In England they did respond positively. But in the United States both the Protestant and the Catholic churches remained nearly silent and seemingly indifferent in the face of this crisis in Western and Christian civilization.

Commonweal, a liberal Catholic weekly, was among the few American Christian voices to speak. Before Pearl Harbor, its editors had stood in the sparse ranks of those who called for widening the nation's gates for Jewish refugees. Now, in December 1942, *Commonweal* pointed with horror at the "policy of complete extermination." It recognized the unfolding tragedy as a "crisis ... not only for the Jewish people, but for all peoples everywhere."[14]

Another outpost of Christian care for Jewish victims was the Church Peace Union, whose general secretary, Dr. Henry A. Atkinson, urged that the churches of America "in the name of our Lord, our religion and suffering humanity ... denounce these crimes against the Jews as major crimes against our common humanity." Atkinson called on the churches to insist that the United States, England, and other countries open their doors at once to those Jews who could get out of Hitler's grasp.[15]

The Federal Council of the Churches of Christ in America, an organization through which twenty-five Protestant denominations cooperated on programs of common concern, began late in 1942 to consider practical aid to the Jews. Out of its biennial meeting in December came an official declaration that the reports on Jewish extermination had stirred Christian Americans to "deepest sympathy and indignation." The Federal Council resolved to do its "full part in establishing conditions in which such treatment of the Jews shall end." In discussions with Jewish leaders soon afterward, the council promised to launch a movement to involve its tens of thousands of local congregations in a Sunday of services focused on the tragedy of Europe's Jews. This "Day of Compassion" did not take place, however, until May 1943.[16]

While most American Christian institutions took little or no notice of the extermination disclosures of late 1942, the nondenominational Protestant weekly *Christian Century* reacted immediately. The very day that word of Stephen Wise's Washington press conference appeared in the newspapers, the *Christian Century* telegraphed the State Department asking whether it actually had, as Wise claimed, confirmed the information he had given out.[17]

The State Department evasively replied that it had no statement for publication regarding Wise's disclosures, since its role had been only "to facilitate the efforts of his Committee in getting at the truth." Thus all questions about the material should be put to Wise. Although the State Department's response neither affirmed nor denied Wise's statements, the *Christian Century* chose to view it as a denial.* [18]

The editors decided to challenge Wise's disclosures, a move that, whether intended or not, spread skepticism and dampened pressures for rescue action. The *Christian Century*'s editorial, entitled "Horror Stories from Poland," conceded that "beyond doubt, horrible things are happening to the Jews in Poland" and "it is even probable" that the Nazis are moving all the European Jews to Poland "with the deliberate intention of exterminating them there." But the writer questioned whether "any good purpose is served by the publication of such charges

---

* When questioned on this point, the editors explained in print that they had asked the State Department whether it had authorized Wise's statements. The State Department had responded, the *Christian Century* wrote, but would not permit its answer to be published. "We have that reply in our files; it does not support Dr. Wise's contention." It did not *deny* Wise's contention either, but the *Christian Century* left that fact unmentioned.[19]

as Dr. Stephen S. Wise gave to the press last week." The editorial went
on to discredit Wise's disclosures and to argue that he had greatly
exaggerated the numbers of Jews killed.[20]

Three weeks later, reacting to the United Nations statement condemning the annihilation of the Jews, the *Christian Century* granted
that "extermination of a race has seldom, if ever, been so systemically
[*sic*] practiced on a grand scale as in the present mass murder of Polish
Jews by the nazi power." But the editorial pointedly noted that the UN
declaration had ventured no definite statistical estimate of the dead.
The *Christian Century* commended the UN statement, especially its
"rhetorical restraint" and "calm tone." These signified, it said,

> a cold determination not to expend in vain outcry one unit of emotional
> energy which can be better employed in bringing the war to such a conclu-
> sion that this gigantic crime can be stopped and the criminals punished.
> The right response to the Polish horror is a few straight words to say that it
> has been entered in the books, and then redoubled action on the Tunisian,
> Russian, Italian and German fronts and on the production lines.[21]

The *Christian Century* had spelled out an argument that people both
inside and outside of government would raise throughout the war: the
only effective way to save European Jews was to win the war as soon as
possible. This assertion also implied that pressure for direct rescue
action was in effect unpatriotic, since it would entail some diversion of
the war effort. Both positions were false. Many possibilities existed
while the war was in progress to save Jews who were still alive in Nazi
Europe, and most could have been acted upon without hampering the
war effort. Proof of this came in 1944 when the Roosevelt administration finally made a commitment to rescue Jews through a specially
created War Refugee Board.

In line with its own advice that "the right response" to extermination
was "a few straight words to say that it has been entered in the books"
and then harder work for victory, the *Christian Century* spoke out for
rescue action only four or five times in the two and one-half years that
passed before Hitler's defeat. It thereby defaulted on an opportunity to
serve the Christian conscience as well as the needs of the desperate
Jews. This was all the more tragic since the journal was highly influential
among liberal, social-action-oriented Protestant clergymen and lay leaders. Because of its social sensitivity, that constituency might have become a leading edge of Protestant-backed pressure for rescue action. It
did not.[22]

The reasons for the *Christian Century*'s attack on Wise's credibility are not clear. Probably the most important factor was Wise's position as the foremost leader of the American Zionist movement. The *Christian Century* had a strong record of anti-Zionism.[23]

Once freed to release the confirmed news of extermination, Jewish leaders were anxious to spread the information as effectively as they could. They sought to build the public support that would be necessary to move the American and other Allied governments to rescue efforts.[24]

The group that charted a basic course of joint action during late 1942 (and again in spring 1943) was a rather loose council of representatives of the major American Jewish organizations. Essentially, it was a continuation of the committee of Jewish leaders that had formed around Stephen Wise and Jacob Rosenheim in early September and had met sporadically thereafter to discuss information coming from Europe as well as possible ways to respond to it. Before March 1943, when the council was reorganized as the Joint Emergency Committee on European Jewish Affairs, it was usually referred to as the Temporary Committee. This was the body that Wise called together on November 25, the day after his meeting with Welles, to decide on an initial plan of action.[25]

To lessen confusion about the numerous Jewish organizations involved in the American response to the Holocaust, it may be helpful to describe the seven groups represented on the Temporary Committee. The first four were the major defense organizations then active in American Jewish life; they worked to protect the religious and civil rights of Jews in the United States and throughout the world.

American Jewish Committee.   Formed in 1906, the committee was still dominated in the early 1940s by wealthy, older-stock (German-background) Jews. Although its membership was small, it possessed substantial prestige and influence, had entry to some high levels of government and American society, and controlled considerable funds. Because it shunned overt political action and mass demonstrations and was non-Zionist, it was usually reluctant to participate in joint projects, especially with activist Zionist organizations.[26]

American Jewish Congress.   Established in 1922, the congress was a mass-membership body built largely on a middle- and lower-middle-class constituency that was mainly of East European origin. Activist in approach and Zionist in outlook, it was the most politically involved of the major Jewish organizations.

Jewish Labor Committee.   This committee was created in 1934 to represent the organized-labor side of American Jewish life in the struggle against Nazism and fascism. Membership consisted of national and local units of its affiliated bodies, including the Workmen's Circle, the International Ladies Garment Workers Union, the Amalgamated Clothing Workers of America, and other labor unions and Jewish socialist groups. The Labor Committee indirectly represented a constituency of half a million; in addition, it could call on some support from the American Federation of Labor because of its close ties with that organization. Oriented toward democratic socialism, the Jewish Labor Committee was for the most part anti-Zionist.

B'nai B'rith.   Founded as a Jewish fraternal and service organization in 1843, B'nai B'rith had come to combine those functions with educational work and defense of Jewish rights. Formation of its Anti-Defamation League in 1913 added to its capability in the latter area. A mass-membership organization, it had over 150,000 men, women, and youth on its rolls in 1942. B'nai B'rith aimed for neutrality in political affairs, but a trend toward Zionism was gathering strength in its ranks during World War II.

World Jewish Congress.   This worldwide organization was established in 1936 to deal with attacks on Jewish political and economic rights. Zionist oriented, it was based on mass-membership affiliates, including the American Jewish Congress, the British section of the World Jewish Congress, and Jewish organizations in several other countries. During World War II, its world executive moved from Geneva to New York, where it added special committees of Jewish leaders from the occupied European nations.

The following two religious groups were also part of the Temporary Committee:

Synagogue Council of America.   Organized in 1925, the council was made up of delegates from rabbinical and lay organizations of the Orthodox, Conservative, and Reform branches of American Jewry. It provided a means for united action to forward the common religious interests of its constituent bodies. Many government agencies as well as Catholic and Protestant organizations recognized the Synagogue Council as their main religious liaison with American Jewry.

Agudath Israel of America.   This organization of nearly 30,000 members had been established in 1921 to assist and maintain the spiritual life of Orthodox Jews throughout the world. Closely aligned with the

Union of Orthodox Rabbis of the United States and Canada, it represented the ultra-Orthodox wing of American Jewry, a segment not connected with the Synagogue Council of America. Agudath Israel was anti-Zionist on religious grounds.

Before tracing the actions undertaken by the Temporary Committee, it might be well to take a closer look at Dr. Stephen S. Wise, the foremost American Jewish leader of the 1930s and 1940s. Reform rabbi and longtime Zionist, Wise had been in the front ranks of the American social-justice movement since the turn of the century. Working closely with Christian reform leaders, he had battled for such causes as free speech, workers' rights and labor unions, black rights, and honest city government. During the Great Depression of the 1930s, he had spoken out early for adequate relief and for unemployment insurance. This was the background out of which he developed a relationship with Franklin Roosevelt, whom he supported for governor of New York in 1928 even though the Republican candidate was Jewish. ("I never voted as a Jew," Wise declared in his autobiography, "but always as an American.") Despite the GOP avalanche of 1928, Roosevelt won the governorship by a very thin margin. He was no doubt helped by Jewish voters influenced by Wise.[27]

In 1932, however, Wise refused to back Roosevelt for President because of his evasive stance on the Tammany regime in New York City. But in 1933 Wise moved back into the Roosevelt camp. ("He rewon my unstinted admiration, and I spoke of him everywhere I went with boundless enthusiasm.") From then on, Wise was strong and vocal in his support of the President, coming out wholeheartedly for him in the 1936 election, remaining loyal through the Supreme Court debacle of 1937, and never wavering afterward.[28]

Wise's autobiography, completed shortly before he died, shows that Roosevelt remained his hero until the end. It also leaves the clear impression that after about 1935 Wise was unable to be critical of, or even objective about, the President. He was convinced that FDR was personally anxious to help the persecuted European Jews in the 1930s, that he wanted to do everything possible to rescue Jews during the Holocaust years, and that he fully, though quietly, supported the Zionist movement. These assessments were wide of the mark and should have been recognized as such at the time. In retrospect, in view of Wise's position as the foremost Jewish leader, his total trust in Roosevelt was not an asset to American or European Jews.[29]

Wise's myriad responsibilities, which attested to his importance in American Jewish life, may also have hampered his effectiveness. During the Holocaust years, he was simultaneously director of, or a high officer in, over a dozen Jewish organizations.* Sixty-eight years old in 1942, Wise was not in good physical condition. He wrote to an associate that year, "I am far from being well and have a chronic ailment [he had polycythemia, an enlarged spleen, and an inoperable double hernia] which necessitates X-ray treatment rather frequently." Yet Wise pushed himself hard and undertook an immense amount of travel, mostly by train (his condition ruled out flying). Despite Wise's willingness to drive himself, one has to question whether his health permitted him to deal effectively with his host of responsibilities. Reason indicates, and some observers at the time suggested, that he should have passed some of them on to others.[30]

Wise was imposing in appearance, his strong, craggy profile set off against swept-back hair. His oratory was superb. His letters, which carry touches of humor, reflect a person warm and close to family and friends.

As to the seven organizations represented on the Temporary Committee, disputes and even sharp conflict normally marked their interrelationships. Despite this volatility, they briefly achieved a fair degree of cooperation in the wake of Wise's important conference with Welles. At the meeting that Wise convened on November 25, agreement was reached on five actions.[32]

The first, to announce to the press the newly confirmed facts of genocide, was carried out that afternoon when Wise held a news conference to supplement the one he had called the preceding evening in Washington. Press coverage, however, was disappointing.[33]

A second step was to dispatch telegrams to over 500 newspapers requesting them to publish editorials on the issue. Comparatively few did so.†[34]

The third move was to telegraph a few hundred important non-Jews to invite them to make statements regarding the Jewish situation in Europe. Several responses were printed in the *Congress Weekly,* but nothing more appears to have come of the project.[36]

---

* To name only his most important posts, he was president of the American Jewish Congress, the World Jewish Congress, and the Jewish Institute of Religion (a theological college), chairman of the American Emergency Committee for Zionist Affairs, vice-president of the Zionist Organization of America, and co-chairman of the American Jewish Conference. He edited *Opinion* magazine and was a force in the journal *Congress Weekly.* He was also rabbi of the large Free Synagogue of New York City, though for part of the war he relinquished much of his work there.[31]

† The *Washington Post,* which did not print such an editorial, carried five editorials during late November and December on the terrible Coconut Grove nightclub fire in Boston, which claimed more than 400 lives. Horror closer at hand had an impact.[35]

Each of the other two actions taken by the Temporary Committee precipitated a brief flurry of national publicity about the European Jewish catastrophe. These were the sponsorship of a Day of Mourning and Prayer and a meeting of Jewish leaders with President Roosevelt.

The Day of Mourning and Prayer, held on December 2, was observed in twenty-nine foreign lands and throughout the United States. Because of its large Jewish population, New York City, summoned to prayer by Mayor Fiorello La Guardia, was the center of the day's solemn activities. Yiddish newspapers came out with black borders. Several radio stations were silent for two minutes. During the morning, half a million Jewish union laborers, joined by non-Jewish fellow workers, halted production for ten minutes.* At noon, a one-hour radio program was broadcast. And special services were held at five o'clock in synagogues throughout the city.[37]

In many other American cities, the Day of Mourning was marked by religious services and local radio programs. Late in the afternoon, NBC broadcast a special quarter-hour memorial service across the nation.[39]

In addition to the religious values and the feelings of solidarity that were generated, the commemorations on the Day of Mourning offered emotional release. The *Dallas Morning News,* for instance, commented on the impressive ceremony held in that city but seemed most deeply affected by the sobbing heard at the service. Another important outcome of the special day was that it focused some public attention on the disastrous situation of the European Jews. A little radio time was devoted to the issue. And many newspapers reported the day's events and their significance, though for the most part inconspicuously.[40]

Soon afterward, a delegation from the Temporary Committee succeeded in meeting with President Roosevelt despite a definite reluctance on his part. A letter that Wise addressed to "Dear Boss" may have overcome the President's disinclination to confer with the Jewish leaders. The rabbi wrote that "the most overwhelming disaster of Jewish history," Hitler's extermination program, had been confirmed through the State Department, and that a few people from his committee would like to talk with the President about it. Wise assured Roosevelt, "I do not wish to add an atom to the awful burden which you are bearing with magic and, as I believe, heaven-inspired strength at this time." But, he added, "it would be gravely misunderstood if, despite your overwhelming preoccupation, you did not make it possible to receive

---

* A one-hour shutdown had been considered, but the leadership decided against it out of concern that Jews would be accused of hampering the war effort. The ten-minute stoppage was the result of worker pressure; the time was made up the following day.[38]

our delegation and to utter what I am sure will be your heartening and consoling reply." He concluded with the plea: "As your old friend, I beg you will somehow arrange to do this."[41]

The half-hour conference with Roosevelt took place at noon on December 8; it included Wise, Henry Monsky (B'nai B'rith), Rabbi Israel Rosenberg (Union of Orthodox Rabbis), Maurice Wertheim (American Jewish Committee), and Adolph Held (Jewish Labor Committee). Held's notes provide a thorough description of this interview, the only one concerning the Holocaust that FDR ever granted to a group of Jewish leaders.[42]

The President received the delegation very cordially and immediately launched into a semihumorous story about his plans for postwar Germany. Wise then read aloud a two-page letter from the Temporary Committee which stressed that "unless action is taken immediately, the Jews of Hitler Europe are doomed."[43]

The only action proposed in the letter, however, was the issuance of warnings about war crimes. The message asked Roosevelt "to warn the Nazis that they will be held to strict accountability for their crimes." It also urged formation of a commission to collect the evidence of Nazi barbarism against civilians and to report it to the world.[44]

As he finished reading the message, Wise handed Roosevelt a twenty-page condensation of the extermination data and appealed to him "to do all in your power to bring this to the attention of the world and to do all in your power to make an effort to stop it."[45]

Roosevelt's reply was significant because it showed beyond doubt that by December 1942 he was fully aware of the extermination program. Thus his subsequent reluctance to act for rescue cannot be attributed to lack of knowledge or disbelief that the destruction of the European Jews was in progress. Held's notes quote the President:

> The government of the United States is very well acquainted with most of the facts you are now bringing to our attention. Unfortunately we have received confirmation from many sources. Representatives of the United States government in Switzerland and other neutral countries have given us proof that confirms the horrors discussed by you.[46]

Roosevelt readily agreed to issue the war-crimes warning. He then asked for other recommendations. The Jewish leaders had little to add; this part of the conversation lasted only one or two minutes. The President then opened a monologue on topics unrelated to the Jewish disaster in Europe. He continued until an aide entered, signaling the end of the conference.[47]

As the group left, Roosevelt, referring to the war-crimes warning, said, "Gentlemen, you can prepare the statement. I am sure that you will put the words into it that express my thoughts." As he shook hands with the Jewish leaders, he remarked, "we shall do all in our power to be of service to your people in this tragic moment." According to Held's estimate, Roosevelt had talked 80 percent of the time.[48]

After clearing the group's press release with the White House, Wise informed reporters that Roosevelt had authorized him to say "that he was profoundly shocked to learn that two million Jews had perished as a result of Nazi rule and crimes" and that "the American people will hold the perpetrators of these crimes to strict accountability in a day of reckoning which will surely come." Wise also furnished the press with copies of the delegation's letter to Roosevelt and the twenty-page summary of extermination data.[49]

News reports of this press conference emphasized that two million Jews had been killed and five million more faced extermination. And some data from the twenty-page summary were published. But the coverage of this event was spotty, and most newspapers that did report it gave it little prominence. The *New York Times,* for instance, provided a very thorough account, but it appeared on page 20, unusually deep in the paper for any news directly concerning the President. The *Washington Post* printed only a small report and placed it far inside the paper.[50]

The meeting with the President completed the five-part plan undertaken by the Temporary Committee. On the initiative of Wise and the American Jewish Congress, the committee was dissolved, ending this two-week venture in united Jewish action.[51]

Soon after the White House visit, the Jewish leaders' hope for a stern war-crimes warning materialized. The statement did not arise from the meeting with Roosevelt, however. The British government was already pressing it on the United States and the Soviet Union when Wise and his colleagues talked with the President. British public feeling and hard work by the British section of the World Jewish Congress had pushed the British government into action. The American State Department cooperated with great reluctance.[52]

The limited publicity about extermination that American Jewish efforts had achieved had already gone too far for some functionaries in the State Department. Soon after the Day of Mourning, R. Borden Reams, who was the specialist on Jewish issues for the Division of European Affairs, suggested that higher officials seek to persuade Wise

to call off, or at least to tone down, the present world-wide publicity campaign concerning "mass murders" and particularly to ask Dr. Wise to avoid any implications that the State Department furnished him with official documentary proof of these stories.[53]

Reams was somewhat more cautious, though, when Congressman Hamilton Fish (Rep., N.Y.) phoned to ask whether the State Department had official verification of the reports of the mass murders. Reams replied that the whole matter was "under consideration," but the reports were to the best of his knowledge "as yet unconfirmed." He suggested an inquiry to Cordell Hull or another top-level departmental official. Only two days before, one of those high officials, Assistant Secretary of State Adolf A. Berle, Jr., had shown, in another context, that he had no doubt whatever about the situation. Speaking to the representative of the Finnish government, Berle strongly advised against handing over to the Germans any Jewish refugees then in Finnish territory. That, warned Berle, "was the equivalent in most cases of condemnation to a horrible death."[54]

When the British government sent its proposed war-crimes declaration to Washington, it went to Reams for evaluation. He informed the heads of his division:

> I have grave doubts in regard to the desirability or advisability of issuing a statement of this nature. In the first place, these reports are unconfirmed and emanate to a great extent from the Riegner letter to Rabbi Wise. . . . The statement . . . will be taken as additional confirmation of these stories and will support Rabbi Wise's contention of official confirmation from State Department sources. The way will then be open for further pressure from interested groups for action which might affect the war effort.[55]

The next day, W. G. Hayter, first secretary of the British embassy, conferred with Reams. Hayter stated the British belief that the declaration would do neither good nor harm. However, the British government was anxious to release it soon because of extreme pressure coming from several quarters, including the House of Commons.[56]

Reams warned Hayter that the British statement

> was extremely strong and definite. Its issuance would be accepted by the Jewish communities of the world as complete proof of the stories which are now being spread about. . . . In addition the various Governments of the United Nations would expose themselves to increased pressure from all sides to do something more specific in order to aid these people.[57]

Reams informed his division chiefs that the best course would be simply to have the United Nations issue another general statement that war criminals would be punished. If the declaration proposed by the British were accepted, however, the phrase "reports from Europe which leave no room for doubt" (that extermination of the Jews is in progress) should be replaced with "numerous and trustworthy reports from Europe." Officials higher in the State Department decided to endorse the British proposal, but weakened the wording even more than Reams had suggested. In the final version, the line read "numerous reports from Europe."[58]

The UN declaration, signed by the three main Allies and the governments of eight occupied countries, was issued on December 17. It pointed specifically at the German government's "intention to exterminate the Jewish people in Europe," and it condemned "in the strongest possible terms this bestial policy of cold-blooded extermination." It affirmed that "the necessary practical measures" would be taken to insure that those responsible for the crimes would be brought to retribution. Despite the State Department's weakening modification, it remained a forceful statement, the strongest concerning atrocities against Jews to be issued by the Allied powers during World War II. Furthermore, it committed the United States, Britain, and the Soviet Union for the first time to postwar prosecution of those responsible for crimes against the European Jews.[59]

When the declaration was read in the House of Commons, everyone there rose simultaneously and stood in silence for two minutes, a demonstration of sympathy reported as unprecedented in Parliament's history. The Vatican's silence was also impressive. Asked by the American representative to the Holy See whether the Pope could make a similar declaration on the extermination of the Jews, the papal secretary of state replied that the Vatican could not condemn particular atrocities publicly but that it had frequently denounced atrocities in general.[60]

The UN declaration was better publicized in the American press than most developments connected with the Holocaust. Most newspapers reported on it, and several ran the story on the front page. The joint warning thus helped spread the facts of genocide. So, to a lesser degree, did a development that occurred shortly afterward.[61]

On December 19, the United Nations Information Office in New York released a report that once again authenticated the accounts of genocide. It was a comprehensive summary of the most telling data then available, including evidence concerning the killing centers at Chelmno and Belzec and a country-by-country analysis of the fate of the Jews, which proved the "continent-wide consistency" of the Nazi campaign of annihilation. Poland, the bulletin declared, had become "one vast center for murdering Jews." Released on a Saturday, the new report received wide coverage and fairly prominent exposure in the Sunday press.[62]

The UN declaration of December 17 brought a small measure of hope to American Jews; at last the powers had taken public notice of the European Jewish agony and seemed concerned about it. Stephen Wise considered it an additional gain that "the declaration places the official stamp of authenticity on the reports which have shocked the world." An editorial in the *New York Times* bore him out: the joint statement, it noted, is "based on officially established facts; it is an official indictment." Reams's fear that the declaration would be seen as confirmation of the extermination reports was realized. But his other concern, that the governments "would expose themselves to increased pressure . . . to do something . . . to aid these people," was only slowly becoming a reality.[63]

The same *Times* editorial expressed a view frequently heard during the Holocaust years: "The most tragic aspect of the situation is the world's helplessness to stop the horror while the war is going on. The most it can do is to denounce the perpetrators and promise them individual and separate retribution." A complete halt to the mass murder was indeed virtually impossible short of victory over the Nazis. Proponents of rescue recognized that. But they rejected the view that nothing could be done except to denounce the perpetrators. Inability to halt the entire genocide machine was no valid argument against attempting to rescue those who might be saved. Wise, reacting to the UN declaration, asserted that, important as it was, other steps "to save those still alive" were essential and possible. That viewpoint gained strength steadily during December among those concerned for the stricken European Jews. Before the month ended, several rescue proposals had emerged.[64]

One frequent suggestion called for providing havens of refuge for Jews who might succeed in getting out of Axis territory. England, the United States, and the other Allies should open their doors and the British should remove restrictions on immigration to Palestine. In addition, the United Nations should encourage neutrals such as Turkey, Switzerland, and Sweden to accept Jewish refugees by agreeing to share maintenance costs and to move them elsewhere after the war. Another plan called for sending food and medical supplies, under proper safeguards against Nazi confiscation, to the starving Jews in Axis Europe. Yet another suggested an appeal from the United Nations to the people in the occupied countries to aid and shelter Jews and to help them with escape efforts.[65]

One other recommendation, first voiced by the Committee for a

Jewish Army of Stateless and Palestinian Jews, called for the establishment of an "American Commission of military and governmental experts" charged vaguely with finding "a way to stop this wholesale murder." With time, it became increasingly clear that a special government rescue agency offered the best hope for saving significant numbers of Jews.[66]

Throughout December 1942, the organization most active in developing rescue proposals and seeking support for them was the Zionist-oriented American Jewish Congress, aided by its affiliate, the World Jewish Congress. A special Planning Committee was formed that designed an ambitious campaign to arouse public opinion. Effective pressure could then be brought on the government to induce it to act.[67]

Plans called for marches of hundred of thousands of Jews through the streets of New York and other large cities. Jewish children were to leave school to join the processions. Appeals were to go out to Americans of Polish, Czech, Yugoslav, and other national backgrounds to join the processions or hold parallel demonstrations. On the day of the marches, Jewish stores were to close, and a work stoppage was to be arranged through the cooperation of the AFL and the CIO. And, as an offshoot of the processions, Jewish mass delegations were to travel to Washington and appeal to Congress.[68]

Another project looked to the Christian churches to hold Days of Mourning and to explain the facts of the extermination at church services. Additional plans called for enlisting the support of newspaper editors, radio broadcasters, educators' and women's organizations, liberal groups, congressmen, and other political leaders.[69]

The Planning Committee also tried to persuade the Office of War Information (OWI) to publicize the extermination news. But the OWI director, Elmer Davis, insisted that his agency's function was to transmit statements that represented government policy. If the State Department had issued the extermination statements, Davis pointed out, it would have been comparatively easy for the OWI to publicize them. He advised Wise and his colleagues to persuade the State Department to release the information officially. Such an effort, of course, was doomed to fail.[70]

The OWI's reluctance to act without State Department authorization eliminated another promising project. The Advertising Council was an association set up to mobilize advertising in support of the war effort. Its director believed the chances were excellent for getting national advertisers to finance a publicity campaign focusing on the Nazi massacres of civilians, including Jews, and calling for rescue measures. If the OWI had supported the plan, the Advertising Council and the nation's leading advertisers unquestionably would have cooperated. But the OWI would not, without State Department endorsement, and that ended the proposal.[71]

In the end, the American Jewish Congress carried out very few of its plans. Why? For one thing, cooperation from non-Jews was meager. In addition, some Planning Committee members had reservations about marches and other mass-action projects, fearing they "might make the wrong kind of impression on the non-Jewish community." Probably most important, the American Jewish Congress was trying to do too many things with too few capable people and with resources that were too limited. The Planning Committee did not work steadily at its task, and its leaders were heavily occupied with numerous other matters.[72]

There is no way to assess the potential of the unfulfilled projects. But mass processions in several cities and a mass delegation in Washington would at least have brought the issue to the public's attention. And they might conceivably have forwarded the cause of rescue considerably more than that. The mere threat of a march on Washington by 50,000 to 100,000 blacks in 1941 had extracted an executive order from President Roosevelt that helped increase employment opportunities for black Americans. In January 1944, when pressures finally became great enough, FDR agreed to an executive order establishing an agency to rescue European Jews. A massive demonstration of concern in late 1942 or early 1943 might have influenced him to take action many months sooner than he did.[73]

During the last weeks of 1942, several Zionists, among them Wise and other members of the Planning Committee, applied part of their energies to the rescue problem. Most Zionist resources, however, continued to be concentrated on the postwar goal of a Jewish state in Palestine. In 1943, the pattern persisted, as rescue remained a secondary priority. Even so, the Zionists of the American Jewish Congress and the World Jewish Congress were more active and effective in pressing the rescue issue in the United States than any of the other major Jewish organizations. None of them, the American Jewish Congress included, managed the dramatic change in course that would have been necessary to wage an all-out rescue campaign.[74]

Nevertheless, by the end of 1942, concrete rescue proposals had begun to appear and the first steps had been taken to arouse public opinion. Along with continued advances in those areas, 1943 would bring a marked increase in pressures on the United States government to act.

|| 5 ||

STRUGGLE FOR ACTION

Almost none of the numerous opinion surveys conducted during World War II dealt with the impact that the mass killing of the European Jews had on the American public. But one Gallup poll (January 7, 1943) provided some information. It included the following inquiry: "It is said that two million Jews have been killed in Europe since the war began. Do you think this is true or just a rumor?" Forty-seven percent of the respondents considered it true, 29 percent thought it rumor, and 24 percent had no opinion. Unfortunately, this finding does not tell what proportion of Americans was aware of the extermination news. But it suggests that during the preceding six weeks Jewish organizations had made important strides in getting the information before the public. The plausibility of such a conclusion is strengthened when one considers the lack of cooperation from the State Department and the Office of War Information as well as the limited interest of most of the mass media.[1]

The American Jewish Congress hoped that public opinion had become sufficiently aroused to bring government action. Its representatives approached the State Department week after week in early 1943,

79

but received, in the words of one Jewish leader, "nothing but a run-around." Discussions with Sumner Welles, Adolf Berle, Breckinridge Long, and officials in the Division of European Affairs were all to no avail.[2]

In contrast to December, during January and much of February Jewish organizations were relatively quiescent; the extermination issue received limited public attention. During those weeks, however, shocking news reports from Europe began to reactivate the campaign for rescue. A courier from the non-Jewish Polish underground reached England in December with further confirmation of the systematic murder of the Polish Jews. He also brought an account of the hideous conditions on the deportation trains bound for the Belzec killing center. It was based on his own observations, for he had infiltrated a Nazi-controlled Polish police force. In Warsaw, he had seen some of the few "fortunate" Jews, children who had escaped from the ghetto and were attempting to survive in the city streets. He described them:

> I shall never forget them. They look less human than like monsters, dirty, ragged, with eyes that will haunt me forever—eyes of little beasts in the last anguish of death. They trust no one and expect only the worst from human beings. They slide along the walls of houses looking about them in mortal fear. No one knows where they sleep. From time to time they knock at the door of a Pole and beg for something to eat.[3]

The greatest shock of early 1943 was another telegram from Gerhart Riegner in Switzerland, written in collaboration with Richard Lichtheim, an official of the Jewish Agency for Palestine. It disclosed an intensification of the systematic killing that Riegner had previously reported. Six thousand Jews were being killed *per day* at a single location in Poland. Vienna had been nearly emptied of Jews, and more deportations were going forward from Berlin and Prague. The condition of the Jews in Rumania was desperate. Of 130,000 Rumanian Jews deported to the Transnistria region in 1941, 60,000 were dead. The other 70,000 were destitute, sleeping in crowded, unheated rooms, prey to diseases, and dying of starvation.[4]

The State Department relayed a copy of the telegram to Stephen Wise on February 9, along with a letter signed by Welles which admonished that "the Department of State cannot assume any official responsibility for the information contained in these reports, since the data is not based on investigations conducted by any of its representatives abroad." The letter also applied the disclaimer retroactively to the documents given to Wise in November.[5]

The disavowal was undoubtedly engineered by the same group in the State Department's Division of European Affairs that had been trying for months to check the spread of information about the fate of the European Jews. For one thing, the Division of European Affairs had persistently sought to disassociate the State Department from Wise's public disclosures of mass murder. Furthermore, the day after forwarding the Riegner-Lichtheim telegram to Wise, the State Department dispatched the following instruction to its Bern legation. The obvious intent was to cut off such messages at their source.

Telegram 354, February 10
Your 482, January 21 *

In the future we would suggest that you do not accept reports submitted to you to be transmitted to private persons in the United States unless such action is advisable because of extraordinary circumstances. Such private messages circumvent neutral countries' censorship and it is felt that by sending them we risk the possibility that steps would necessarily be taken by the neutral countries to curtail or forbid our means of communication for confidential official matter.†

HULL
(SW)[6]

As the signature indicated, Welles had approved the telegram. Almost certainly, however, he had simply initialed it in routine fashion. As the message crossed his desk, it would have attracted his attention only in the unlikely event that he had recalled what 482 from Bern actually was. The authors of the telegram undoubtedly assumed that he would not. Those responsible for telegram 354 were State Department adviser on political relations James C. Dunn and three officials from the Division of European Affairs—the acting chief, Ray Atherton, the assistant chief, John D. Hickerson, and Elbridge Durbrow.[8]

The ban on information from Switzerland ended two months later, as unforeseen developments upset the scheme. But that is part of another story, one that did not become clear until December 1943.[9]

Shortly after receiving the Riegner-Lichtheim message, Wise and his associates at the American Jewish Congress gave it to the press, along with three recently received eyewitness reports from Poland. The press

---

* This referred to the telegram that had transmitted the Riegner-Lichtheim report from Bern to Washington. It carried the number 482.

† Actually, throughout the war the State Department relayed hundreds of private messages from Switzerland to American business firms.[7]

release, timed to make the Sunday papers, had little impact. The *New York Times,* for instance, reported it unobtrusively on page 37.[10]

On February 13, one day before the Riegner-Lichtheim information came out in the press, a report of great interest to those concerned about the European Jews appeared in the *New York Times.* By coincidence, it exactly meshed with the Riegner-Lichtheim description of the dreadful condition of the 70,000 Rumanian Jews still alive in Transnistria, and it threw a ray of hope into that darkness. A dispatch from C. L. Sulzberger in London disclosed that the Rumanian government had offered to cooperate in moving 70,000 Jews from Transnistria to any place of refuge chosen by the Allies. The Rumanians suggested Palestine and offered to provide Rumanian ships for the voyage. In return, Rumania asked to be paid transportation and related expenses amounting to 20,000 Rumanian lei (about $130) per refugee, along with additional funds should Rumanian ships be utilized.[11]

An opportunity to rescue a large number of European Jews seemed to have materialized. Rumania's collaboration with the German war effort had been opportunistic. It now seemed unsure of an Axis victory and evidently was attempting a gradual shift into the good graces of the Allies in the hope of easing the coming terms of peace. If so, the Bucharest government was badly mistaken in assuming that the Allies would consider the release of 70,000 Jews an ingratiating gesture. In fact, as subsequent events showed, the American and British governments looked upon any release of large numbers of Jews as a threat, not an opportunity.

Secretary of the Treasury Henry Morgenthau, Jr. immediately brought the Sulzberger article to Roosevelt's attention. The President said he knew nothing about the matter and suggested that Morgenthau see Welles. Welles, also unaware of the proposal, agreed to look into it. He learned from the British Foreign Office that a representative of the Jewish Agency for Palestine had informed the British government a month earlier that Rumanian officials had made such an offer to the Jewish Agency. The Foreign Office characterized the plan as blackmail, though it did believe it might be an effort by "certain Rumanian circles" to show disapproval of the Nazi extermination of Jews. The Foreign Office also stated that weeks earlier it had asked the British embassy in Washington to inform the State Department of the proposal. Apparently, the State Department simply shelved the matter.[12]

An inquiry from Welles to the American embassy in Ankara brought some clarification. According to a representative of the Jewish Agency, a Dutch businessman, resident in Rumania, had called on him in Istanbul in early December carrying a proposal from top Rumanian officials.

They were ready to permit the departure of the 72,000 Jews still alive in Transnistria and offered to provide ships to move them to Palestine or another Allied port. The Dutchman also stated that the Catholic bishop of Bucharest was prepared to permit the use of the Vatican flag on the ships.[13]

On February 24, Welles passed the information from London and Ankara on to Morgenthau, with a message that the investigation was continuing. But only two weeks later the State Department was responding to inquiries about the Rumanian proposal with stock letters signed by Welles. "This story," the letters asserted,

> is without foundation. It originated from an unofficial non-Rumanian resident of Bucharest who was visiting Istanbul. The probable actual source is the German propaganda machine which is always ready to use the miseries of the people of occupied Europe in order to attempt to create confusion and doubt within the United Nations.[14]

Clearly, the State Department's investigation had been superficial. Any careful consideration would have had to include inquiries sent to the Rumanian government through neutral governments or the Red Cross. Such indirect contacts with Axis governments were not uncommon during World War II; they were even made occasionally to protest persecution of European Jews. Instead of looking into it fully, the State Department had rejected the proposition out of hand.[15]

The Rumanian proposal might not have been workable. Quite likely it would have involved an element of bribery in addition to the actual costs of removing the imperiled Jews. But it most certainly was not a story "without foundation." Nor had it "originated from an unofficial non-Rumanian resident of Bucharest." German Foreign Office correspondence assembled for the Nuremberg trials revealed that the proposal originated at the very top level of the Rumanian government and was seriously meant. The price asked may have been excessive, but it might have been reduced by negotiations. Even the problem of sending large amounts of money into an enemy nation had a solution. It was a procedure that the U.S. government agreed to many months later in connection with a program to buy food inside Rumania to send to the Jews in Transnistria. In that instance, Rumanian holders of Rumanian currency were willing to provide substantial funds in exchange for dollars or Swiss francs that would be kept in blocked bank accounts for them until the war ended. In that way, no foreign currency would have become available to the Axis.[16]

The main issue is not whether the plan might have worked. The crucial point is that, against a backdrop of full knowledge of the ongoing extermination program, the American and British governments almost cursorily dismissed this first major potential rescue opportunity.[17]

Not everyone, however, was willing to let the Rumanian proposal pass by in silence. On February 16, three days after it published Sulzberger's dispatch, the *New York Times* carried a three-quarter-page advertisement with the large headline "FOR SALE to Humanity 70,000 Jews." Its sponsor was the Committee for a Jewish Army of Stateless and Palestinian Jews, an organization formed in 1941 to exert pressure on the U.S. government, and through it on the British government, to permit the establishment of a separate Jewish army. According to the committee's plan, this independent force, based in Palestine, would fight side by side with the other Allied armies under the supreme Allied command. Its ranks would include Palestinian Jews, stateless Jewish refugees from Nazi Europe, and Jews from nonbelligerent nations. Jews from America, Britain, or other Allied countries were expected to join the forces of their own nations.* [18]

An independent Jewish army would offer Jews, the people most victimized by Hitler, an opportunity to fight back in their own units, under their own flag and leadership. In late 1941 and for much of 1942, the threat of German North African forces to Suez and the nearby Jewish Palestine settlement underscored both the appeal and the logic of the proposal. Such a Jewish army would be immediately valuable in holding the Middle East; it could also permit transfer of some Allied troops from that region to other fronts.†

The campaign mounted in 1941 and pressed through 1942 by the Committee for a Jewish Army (CJA) had attracted substantial support from several quarters, Jewish and non-Jewish. The driving force within the CJA was a group of ten young Palestinian Jews who had come to the United States in 1939 and 1940. They were Zionists, committed to a Jewish state in Palestine. But they were heavily influenced by the

* Great Britain did allow Palestinian Jews to volunteer for the British army, but in limited numbers.[19]
† Zionist circles widely supported the idea of a Jewish army. Obviously, such a fighting force would greatly increase the chances for the emergence of a Jewish state in Palestine after the war. It would give Zionists a sound basis for pressing their claims at the peace table and at the same time leave a trained and equipped Jewish army available to insist on Jewish postwar interests in Palestine. These factors were, of course, also recognized by the plan's main opponents, the British government and the Arab powers.
    Late in the war (in September 1944), the British government relented and formed a token Jewish brigade within the British army. Members of the Jewish brigade still in Europe after the war played an important role in the "illegal" movement of Jewish survivors through Europe and onto ships headed for Palestine.[20]

thought of Vladimir Jabotinsky, whose Revisionist Zionism called for a more militant policy toward British control in Palestine and aimed at the immediate establishment of a Jewish state there.[21]

These Palestinians were not associated with the New Zionist Organization of America, which was the Revisionist Zionist body in the United States. Most of them, in fact, were secretly members of the Irgun (Irgun Zvai Leumi), a Jewish armed underground in Palestine. While these men constituted a tiny, American-based wing of the Irgun, they did not conduct underground activities in the United States. During the war, they were almost completely isolated from the Irgun in Palestine.[22]

At the group's core were Hillel Kook and Samuel Merlin. Merlin, a journalist, had earlier served as Jabotinsky's personal secretary. Kook was descended from a noted rabbinical line. In the United States, he adopted the name Peter H. Bergson in order to keep his political activities from reflecting on the name of his late uncle, the former chief rabbi of Palestine, Abraham Isaac Kook. Quick and intense, Bergson was a dynamic speaker and the group's leader. Consequently, the Palestinians and the movements they initiated were referred to as the Bergsonites.[23]

The main Zionist movement harbored a deep-seated animosity toward the Irgun and thus the Bergsonites. At the root of this attitude were three factors. Regular Zionists viewed Jabotinsky and his followers as militaristic and virtually fascist. They strongly disagreed with the Irgun's use of violence in Palestine, in part because they believed it could damage the moral stature of Zionism and thus seriously hurt the Zionist cause.* Perhaps most important, they resented and feared the break in world Zionist discipline initiated by Jabotinsky and perpetuated by the Irgun.[24]

Operating first as American Friends of a Jewish Palestine, the young Palestinians' original purpose in the United States had been to raise money to supply arms to the Irgun and to finance its program of moving refugees from Europe to Palestine, in violation of British restrictions on Jewish immigration. In 1940, the expanding war had halted Irgun activities in Europe and severed communications between Palestine and the group in the United States. The Bergsonites had then shifted their focus to the Jewish army idea.[26]

In December 1941, American Friends of a Jewish Palestine was superseded by the newly organized Committee for a Jewish Army. The campaign for a Jewish army, which peaked in 1942, started to flag when

---

* The Irgun had earlier used terror tactics to retaliate for Arab attacks on Jews. In 1944 it reinstituted the use of violence, this time against the British in Palestine.[25]

the German threat to Suez and Palestine was broken later that year. When the news of systematic annihilation became known, in late November, the Army Committee changed its emphasis.[27]

The new approach was evident ten days later in the committee's large advertisement in the *New York Times,* written by the popular author Pierre van Paassen. Its first objective was to dramatize and spread as widely as possible the recently released extermination reports. The second was to press for rescue action. The seed of an important idea, a commission of military and government experts to try to help the European Jews, appeared along with other tentative proposals.* [28]

By February, when the next advertisement appeared, the commission of experts had become "our primordial demand." Within a week, the CJA announced its decision to open a rescue campaign centered on pressure for an intergovernmental commission of experts to seek out ways to counter the Nazi program of genocide. Although the Jewish-army goal remained, the rescue issue now claimed top priority.[30]

The point was underscored again in the large advertisement of February 16: "The principal demand . . . is that the United Nations immediately appoint an inter-governmental committee" to formulate ways to stop the extermination. The call for a rescue agency was not, however, the most striking aspect of the advertisement. Under the startling headlines

FOR SALE TO HUMANITY
70,000 JEWS
GUARANTEED HUMAN BEINGS AT $50 A PIECE

the advertisement aimed to rivet attention on the disastrous situation of the Jews in Transnistria and build popular pressure for rapid government steps to save them.† [31]

"Roumania is tired of killing Jews," announced Ben Hecht, whose signature appeared on the ad. "It has killed one hundred thousand of them in two years. Roumania will now give Jews away practically for nothing." Hecht then lashed out: "Seventy Thousand Jews Are Waiting Death In Roumanian Concentration Camps . . . Roumania Offers to

---

* A major instrument of the various Bergson groups was the large display advertisement placed in leading metropolitan newspapers. A series of these ads produced during 1942 saw Merlin develop that medium into an effective form of propaganda, which drew on such skilled writers as van Paassen and Hollywood dramatist Ben Hecht.[29]
† Fifty dollars per refugee was the CJA's estimate of the value of the 20,000 lei cost mentioned in Sulzberger's article.

Deliver These 70,000 Alive to Palestine . . . The Doors of Roumania Are Open! Act Now!"

The CJA, the advertisement continued, had launched an intensive drive "to demand that something be done NOW, WHILE THERE IS STILL TIME." It invited readers to join the fight by informing friends, by writing congressmen, and by sending contributions "for the further distribution of messages like these." "In this way," stated the CJA, "you can help save European Jewry!"

Immediately, a barrage of protest came from the established Jewish organizations and press. They angrily charged the CJA with deliberately and deceptively implying that each $50 contribution would save a Rumanian Jew. Jewish spokesmen castigated the CJA as irresponsible, unethical, and willing to edge "very close to fraud" in order to raise funds.[32]

Undaunted, the Committee for a Jewish Army pushed ahead with its publicity campaign. Six days after the Ben Hecht plea, an advertisement in the *New York Herald Tribune* signed by Senator Edwin C. Johnson of Colorado repeated the demand for United Nations action on the Rumanian proposal. And it, too, called for an intergovernmental rescue commission. Both advertisements soon appeared in other major newspapers.[33]

Even before the February denunciations, much of the American Jewish leadership had decried the Committee for a Jewish Army, accusing it of recklessness and sensationalism as well as gross effrontery in presuming to speak for an American constituency. Concern now arose that the Bergsonites would seize the leadership of the languishing effort for rescue. The inertia of the preceding several weeks dissolved rapidly. Aware of the CJA's plan to hold a demonstration at Madison Square Garden on March 9, Wise and the American Jewish Congress scheduled a March 1 mass meeting at the same location.* To complete this display of disunity and rivalry, the Jewish Labor Committee in late February held many smaller meetings of its own throughout the New York metropolitan area.[34]

The American Jewish Congress's "Stop Hitler Now" demonstration of March 1 set off another wave of publicity and activity on the rescue question. This mass meeting was co-sponsored by the two giants of the

---

* The American Jewish Congress had been planning since December to hold a mass demonstration at Madison Square Garden. First set for January, then early February, it had been continually postponed. It and similar rallies projected in other cities were the only remnants of the Planning Committee's original program of nationwide mass processions and demonstrations in Washington.[35]

American trade union movement, the AFL and the CIO, and by two tiny voices of Christianity and liberalism, the Church Peace Union and the Free World Association. Nearly thirty other Jewish organizations also lent support. As the meeting date neared, a full-page advertisement in the *New York Times* urged the public to attend and to insist that "America Must Act Now!"[36]

The public did come, in the tens of thousands. Twenty thousand jammed Madison Square Garden, while 10,000 others milled around outside in the winter cold and listened to the speeches through amplifiers. Still thousands more had dispersed after being turned away from the Garden. Police estimates indicated that, in all, 75,000 had come to the rally.[37]

The meeting opened with brief patriotic and religious exercises. Under lowered lights and amid audible weeping, a cantor chanted El Mole Rachamim, the Hebrew prayer for the dead. AFL president William Green, New York mayor Fiorello La Guardia, and several other prominent non-Jews addressed the meeting, as did Stephen Wise and world-famous scientist and Zionist leader Chaim Weizmann. Messages were sent to the gathering by Wendell Willkie, by New York governor Thomas Dewey, and by England's foremost churchmen, the archbishop of Canterbury and Arthur Cardinal Hinsley.[38]

Indicative of the progress made since the December conference with Roosevelt was a comprehensive list of specific rescue proposals approved by the mass meeting and forwarded to the President. Because the question arose both then and afterward as to what practical rescue actions might have been undertaken during that time of total war, the proposals merit attention here. The eleven-point program called for:

1. Approaches through neutral channels to Germany and the satellite governments to secure agreement for the Jews to emigrate.

2. Swift establishment of havens of refuge by Allied and neutral nations.

3. Revision of U.S. immigration procedures to permit full use of the quotas.

4. Agreement by Great Britain to take in a reasonable proportion of Jewish refugees.

5. Agreement by the Latin American nations to modify their extremely tight immigration regulations and provide temporary havens of refuge.

6. Consent by England to open the gates of Palestine to Jews.

7. A United Nations program to transfer Jewish refugees rapidly out of neutral countries bordering Nazi territory and to encourage those countries to accept additional refugees by guaranteeing financial support and eventual evacuation.

8. Organization by the United Nations, through neutral agencies such as

the International Red Cross, of a system for feeding Jews remaining in Axis territory.

9. Provision by the United Nations of the financial guarantees required to implement this rescue program.

10. Formation by the United Nations of an agency empowered to carry out the program.

11. Appointment, without further delay, of a commission to assemble evidence for war-crimes trials and to determine the procedures for them.[39]

New York newspapers were impressed by the demonstration. Columnist Anne O'Hare McCormick wrote in the *Times* that "the shame of the world filled the Garden Monday night." If the non-Jewish community did not support the rescue proposals "to the utmost," she declared, they would forever compromise "the principles for which we are pouring out blood and wealth and toil."[40]

The mass meeting modified the *Times*'s earlier editorial view that the world was helpless "to stop the horror while the war is going on." A new *Times* editorial commended the rescue plans and asserted that "the United Nations governments have no right to spare any efforts that will save lives." Editorial support for the proposals also appeared in the *New York Post,* the *Sun,* and the *Herald Tribune.*[41]

The mass meeting and the favorable press response that followed forced a reaction of sorts from the Roosevelt administration. Two days after the demonstration, the State Department released previously secret information disclosing that the United States and Britain were planning a diplomatic conference to deal with the refugee problem. A close reading of the State Department release, however, revealed that conference plans called only for a "preliminary exploration" of the question.[42]

Seeking to utilize the momentum generated by the mass meeting, Wise sent letters to President Roosevelt, Secretary of State Hull, all members of the House and the Senate, and many newspaper editors. These letters described the proceedings at the rally and listed the eleven rescue proposals. The White House simply shunted Wise's letter over to the State Department, where a reply was prepared. Signed by the President, it vaguely asserted that "this Government has moved and continues to move, so far as the burden of the war permits, to help the victims of the Nazi doctrines of racial, religious and political oppression."[43]

Meanwhile, in a biting editorial entitled "While the Jews Die," the *Nation* reminded readers that Hitler was carrying out a program of total extermination of Europe's Jews and charged that "in this country, you and I and the President and the Congress and the State Department are accessories to the crime and share Hitler's guilt." "What," asked the *Nation,* "has come over the minds of ordinary men and women that makes it seem normal and indeed inevitable that this country should stolidly stand by and do nothing in the face of one of the world's greatest tragedies?" The editorial printed and strongly endorsed the eleven-point rescue program.[44]

On the evening of March 9, another outpouring of concern and anguish over the European Jewish catastrophe occurred at Madison Square Garden. That night the Committee for a Jewish Army presented a pageant called "We Will Never Die," a memorial to the murdered Jews of Europe. It drew on some of the nation's foremost theatrical talent. Ben Hecht wrote the script, Billy Rose produced and Moss Hart directed the drama, and Kurt Weill created an original score for it. The large cast included Paul Muni and Edward G. Robinson, who occupied center stage as the narrators.[45]

Two weeks prior to the pageant, Billy Rose sought a brief statement of encouragement from President Roosevelt that could be read at the meeting. The White House staff was in a quandary; it did not like to turn down Billy Rose, because of his frequent cooperation with some of Roosevelt's pet charitable projects, but neither did it want to issue any such statement from the President. On request from the White House, the OWI produced an innocuous reply regarding the savage tyranny of the Nazi regime. It did not mention the extermination of the Jews; it did not even mention Jews. Yet, apparently, the statement was still too strong for David Niles and Stephen Early of the White House staff. They decided that no message be sent.[46]

The Committee for a Jewish Army had equally scant success in its attempts to attract unified Jewish support for the pageant. Meeting in January with representatives of several Jewish organizations, Hecht and Bergson volunteered to withdraw the CJA's formal sponsorship of the project if that would bring about its endorsement by the established Jewish organizations. The CJA, however, would quietly contribute to the work involved. The plan was not accepted.[47]

Later, when the American Jewish Congress announced its Madison Square Garden rally for the week before the presentation of "We Will Never Die," the CJA offered to stage the pageant as a joint project and to cooperate with the congress in its mass demonstration. The pageant's script was delivered to the congress to be examined for possibly unacceptable material. The congress rejected the proposal.[48]

"We Will Never Die" drew an audience of 40,000, setting an attendance record for Madison Square Garden. The record was the result of a decision to repeat the performance late that same night. Other thousands remained in the chilly streets hoping that a third showing might take place. The event was also broadcast by radio.[49]

The pageant was performed against a background dominated by two forty-foot tablets engraved with the Ten Commandments. Suspended over them was an illuminated Star of David. In the darkened hall, the stark scenes, dramatized by sharp beams of light and contrasting shadows, concentrated on three themes: Jewish contributions to civilization from Moses to Einstein; the role of Jews in the Allied armed forces; and a vision of the postwar peace conference at which groups of Jewish dead told of their extinction at the hands of the Nazis and pleaded, "Remember us."[50]

No formal addresses were made, but the pageant's final passages dealt pointedly with the inertia and silence of the non-Jewish world:

> The corpse of a people lies on the steps of civilization. Behold it. Here it is! And no voice is heard to cry halt to the slaughter, no government speaks to bid the murder of human millions end.

The ninety-minute memorial closed with the choir and twenty aged refugee rabbis singing the Kaddish for the dead Jews of Europe.[51]

Press and newsreel coverage in New York and across the nation was extensive. With hopes of awakening America to the European Jewish tragedy, the Committee for a Jewish Army pressed forward with plans to present "We Will Never Die" in dozens of other cities. Highly successful performances took place in Washington, Philadelphia, Chicago, Boston, and Hollywood. Over 100,000 Americans witnessed the drama. Present at the Washington performance were Eleanor Roosevelt, six Supreme Court justices, members of the Cabinet, some 300 senators and congressmen, numerous military officials, and foreign diplomats. As in New York, the event was broadcast by radio in the other five cities where it played. Each performance set off a new ground swell of publicity.[52]

In her "My Day" column, Eleanor Roosevelt described "We Will Never Die" as

> one of the most impressive and moving pageants I have ever seen. No one who heard each group come forward and give the story of what had happened to it at the hands of a ruthless German military, will ever forget those haunting words: "Remember us."

Mrs. Roosevelt pointed to the great dangers of intolerance and cruelty, but as to the need for action to help the trapped Jews of Europe she wrote nothing.[53]

"We Will Never Die" had won acclaim throughout the United States. Yet it had drawn almost no support from the established Jewish leadership. Coverage of the pageant in Anglo-Jewish weekly newspapers was widespread but generally less enthusiastic than in the regular daily press. The New York Yiddish newspapers tended to be critical. Most English-language Jewish magazines failed even to report the event.[54]

Far more devastating were steps taken by some Jewish groups to prevent further presentations of the pageant. Because the CJA had little money, it had to depend on ticket sales in order to pay the heavy expenses involved. (The New York showing cost $25,000.) But since a considerable part of the expenses had to be met before the performances occurred, sizable advances of money were needed. To obtain such funds, the CJA organized local sponsoring committees in each city.[55]

This system worked effectively in the first six cities. After that, however, the American Jewish Congress and other Jewish organizations managed to block the Bergsonites. Pressures on prominent sponsors and telephone and letter campaigns vilifying the CJA led many, if not most, local backers to withdraw their support. In Baltimore, Buffalo, Kingston (New York), and Gary (Indiana), the CJA was arranging to present the pageant when the American Jewish Congress and allied groups intervened locally and brought the process to a halt. Plans to take "We Will Never Die" to several other cities similarly came to nothing. The consequence of this bitter conflict, as one observer pointed out, was that "the most powerful single weapon yet produced to awaken the conscience of America" was stopped in its tracks.[56]

What lay behind this strife? The Bergson group was anathema to most of the established American Jewish leadership. The Bergson organizations, opponents insisted, had no legitimate mandate to speak for American Jews, since they represented no constituency in American Jewish life. They were interlopers who had intruded into areas of action that were the province of the established Jewish organizations. Opponents also accused the Bergsonites of irresponsibility, both in their sensational methods (such as the Hecht advertisement) and in their use of the sizable amounts of money they solicited. They were charged, in addition, with injecting into already complicated Jewish issues an element of confusion that made understanding not only more difficult for many Jews but nearly impossible for most non-Jews.[57]

· · ·

The success of the American Jewish Congress's "Stop Hitler Now!" demonstration had, in the meantime, given rise to another series of developments. In November 1942, as has been noted, seven major American Jewish organizations had formed a coordinating council (called the Temporary Committee) to carry out a series of projects aimed at stimulating action to save European Jews. In December, soon after the group had sent a delegation to meet with President Roosevelt, Stephen Wise had dissolved this council because it had completed the tasks it had originally undertaken.

By mid-February 1943, however, Wise was moving to reconstitute the committee. Most likely, he was activated by the shocking information from Riegner and Lichtheim in Switzerland and by the startling report that Rumania had offered to release 70,000 Jews. Shortly after the mass demonstration of March 1, leaders of eight major Jewish organizations began meeting; on March 15 they officially organized the Joint Emergency Committee on European Jewish Affairs (JEC). Carried over from the earlier council were the American Jewish Committee, the American Jewish Congress, B'nai B'rith, the Jewish Labor Committee, the Synagogue Council of America, and Agudath Israel of America. Newly added were Agudath Israel's close associate, the Union of Orthodox Rabbis, and the American Emergency Committee for Zionist Affairs, a political-action agency representing several Zionist organizations. Not included on the Joint Emergency Committee was the Committee for a Jewish Army, though it had asked to join.[58]

The Joint Emergency Committee immediately commenced efforts to influence the upcoming British-American refugee conference, set for late April in Bermuda. One early step was to initiate mass meetings throughout the United States patterned after the American Jewish Congress's Madison Square Garden demonstration. Through the meetings themselves and subsequent press and radio publicity, the JEC hoped to inform Americans of the Holocaust and to mobilize public opinion behind the eleven-point rescue program. During spring 1943, forty such rallies were held in twenty states. They were conducted by local Jewish community organizations with help from the Joint Emergency Committee and the local branches of its eight constituent bodies. In many instances, Christian church groups and local units of the AFL and the CIO cooperated. The national office of the Federal Council of Churches endorsed the entire project.[59]

The rallies held at smaller auditoriums drew capacity audiences in the low thousands, while crowds of more than twenty thousand were recorded in some larger cities. The main speakers at these meetings were nationally known Jewish leaders, important regional Catholic and Protestant clergy, representatives of the AFL and the CIO, and prominent political figures. Although JEC personnel estimated that two-thirds of the mass meetings generated "very good" or "good" overall publicity, they expressed disappointment with the generally sparse amount of editorial comment relating to them.[60]

An interesting aspect of the JEC's campaign (and a sign of the terrible urgency of the European Jewish situation) was the full collaboration of the American Jewish Committee. Through the years, the committee had almost never encouraged mass demonstrations. It wished to keep Jewish issues out of public attention while quietly working to protect Jewish rights through negotiations with high government officials and other powerful persons. The committee's president, Judge Joseph M. Proskauer, had opposed holding the "Stop Hitler Now!" mass meeting. But the dignified manner in which the demonstration was handled ("it was decently conducted; it was addressed by prominent speakers; it was not flamboyant or vulgar") and its joint support by labor and Christian organizations had convinced him and his administrative council that similar demonstrations could help influence American opinion "in a decent and decorous way."[61]

A second objective of the Joint Emergency Committee was to induce the U.S. Congress to go on record in support of rescue action. In January, congressional leaders had assured representatives of the American Jewish Congress that such a resolution would be passed. But weeks of follow-up discussions had proved fruitless.[62]

In mid-February, Rabbi Meyer Berlin went to Washington to speak with congressional leaders. Berlin, a resident of Palestine, was then visiting in the United States under the auspices of the Mizrachi Organization of America (Zionism's Orthodox wing). In a conversation with Senate majority leader Alben W. Barkley, Berlin noted that nothing had thus far been heard in either the House or the Senate about the mass murder of European Jews. Barkley replied that he had already discussed a proposed congressional resolution with Rabbi Wise and Congressman Emanuel Celler. Barkley also said that he personally supported the resolution, but thought it important for the proposal to gain a broad cross-section of support in Congress. Consequently, he was seeking, but had not yet obtained, the backing of the Republican leadership.[63]

In another conversation, Berlin declared bitterly to Senator Robert F. Wagner (Dem., N.Y.) "that if horses were being slaughtered as are the Jews of Poland, there would by now be a loud demand for organized action against such cruelty to animals."* Though clearly sympathetic, Wagner saw little hope for any practical help from Congress.

Rabbi Berlin next went to Congressman Joseph W. Martin, Jr. (Rep., Mass.), the House minority leader, and frankly told him that he had learned from Senator Barkley that the Republican leadership was keeping Congress from taking a stand on the Jewish catastrophe. According to Berlin's report of the interview, Martin stated that he was familiar with the resolution but "not at all posted on the broader aspects of the question." He did agree to do what he could to hasten action on this measure.

Two weeks later, Barkley introduced the resolution into the Senate. It declared that "the American people view with indignation the atrocities inflicted upon the civilian population in the Nazi-occupied countries, and especially the mass murder of Jewish men, women, and children." It then resolved that "these brutal and indefensible outrages . . . are hereby condemned" and "it is the sense of this Congress that those guilty . . . shall be held accountable and punished." The resolution said nothing about rescue. It was simply another general condemnation of Nazi atrocities, another call for the eventual punishment of those responsible.[65]

The Joint Emergency Committee dispatched two delegates to Washington to persuade congressional leaders to add a paragraph urging both the United States and the United Nations to act immediately to rescue the Jews of Europe. But their effort failed. On March 9, Barkley's resolution, in its original form, passed the Senate unanimously. The next week, the House approved the same resolution without dissent.[66]

As the JEC had feared, Barkley's resolution was so insignificant that it received little publicity. For example, when the Senate acted on the resolution, the *New York Times* devoted less than two and a half inches to the story, on page 12. Later, when the House passed the measure, the *Times* carried a similarly brief report on page 11. In both instances, the tiny headlines omitted any reference to Jews.[67]

The project on which the Joint Emergency Committee placed its greatest hope was a conference it sought to arrange between top State Department officials and a delegation of Jewish leaders accompanied by representatives of the AFL, CIO, Church Peace Union, and Federal

* In fact, near the end of the war, an American Army tank unit went out of its way to rescue a herd of valuable Lipizzaner horses. The Germans had seized the horses in Vienna and transported them to Czechoslovakia. The U.S. Senate later cited the unit for its "heroic efforts" in saving the horses.[64]

Council of Churches. The plan depended largely on the cooperation of Myron C. Taylor, President Roosevelt's personal representative to the Vatican. Taylor, formerly chairman of the board of U.S. Steel, had been the chief American representative at the Evian Conference on refugees in 1938. He continued to be involved in refugee matters in succeeding years and to maintain close connections with the State Department. Despite his assignment in Rome, Taylor was in the United States during much of the war. He had access to both Roosevelt and Welles; equally important, he was willing to cooperate unhesitatingly with the Jewish leadership. Taylor, it was hoped, could open the way for a meaningful hearing at the State Department.[68]

The strategy was for Taylor to conduct preliminary discussions with Welles and other State Department officials. These talks were to be based on the JEC's specific rescue proposals, a program that closely followed the eleven-point list that came out of the March 1 Madison Square Garden mass meeting. But the day before Taylor was to begin his discussions, a meeting of the Joint Emergency Committee learned of more alarming reports just received from overseas. One carried information from Geneva:

> Massacres now reaching catastrophic climax particularly Poland also deportations Bulgarian Rumanian Jews already begun. European Jewry disappearing while no single organized rescue measure yet taken.

Another cablegram disclosed that 8,000 Bulgarian Jews had already been deported. Every message stressed the absolute need for rapid and extraordinary action.[69]

This turn of events impelled the JEC to revise its strategy. Time was too short for Taylor to negotiate with the slow-moving State Department on the whole list of proposals. Instead, especially since British Foreign Secretary Anthony Eden was then in the United States, the time had come to go directly to Welles and press for immediate American and British action on the two most imperative proposals. One called for approaches to Germany and its satellites to obtain release of the Jews. The other asked for organization of a program to feed Nazi victims unable to get out of occupied Europe. If the two powers would agree to these steps, the JEC believed, the other points could be acted upon in a less urgent manner by the intergovernmental rescue agency that it was hoped would emerge from the forthcoming conference at Bermuda.[70]

Taylor succeeded in arranging for Wise and Proskauer to see both Eden and Welles, separately, on March 27. The meeting with Eden was most discouraging and presaged the outcome of the Bermuda Conference. Opening the discussion, Proskauer stressed the request that Britain and the United States call on Germany to permit the Jews to leave occupied Europe. Eden rejected that plan outright, declaring it "fantastically impossible." Nor was he taken by the proposal to send food to European Jews. To a suggestion that Britain help in removing Jews from Bulgaria, Eden responded icily, "Turkey does not want any more of your people." Any such effort, furthermore, would require the Allies to ship additional goods to Turkey, and that would be difficult. All in all, Eden offered no reasonable hope of action. Shortly afterward, Wise and Proskauer met with Welles, who stated that he would do what he could concerning the JEC's proposals.[71]

The meeting with Eden dealt a crushing blow to the American Jewish leadership, as is reflected in the following description of the reaction of the Joint Emergency Committee when Wise and Proskauer reported back to it:

> Over the entire meeting hung the pall of Mr. Eden's attitude toward helping to save the Jews in occupied Europe. Without expressing it, the people at the meeting felt that there was little use in continuing to agitate for a demand [for action] on the part of the United Nations by the Jews of America.[72]

Incredible though it may sound, what lay behind Eden's adamant opposition to the plea that the Allies call on Germany to release the Jews was the fear that such an effort might in fact succeed. Later during the same day on which Eden spoke with Proskauer and Wise, he met with Roosevelt, Hull, Welles, and the British ambassador to the United States, Lord Halifax. Also present were a British Foreign Office official and Harry Hopkins, Roosevelt's special assistant. Hull raised the issue of the 60,000 to 70,000 Jews in Bulgaria who were threatened with extermination unless the British and Americans could get them out. He pressed Eden for a solution. According to Hopkins's notes, Eden replied

> that the whole problem of the Jews in Europe is very difficult and that we should move very cautiously about offering to take all Jews out of a country like Bulgaria. If we do that, then the Jews of the world will be wanting us to make similar offers in Poland and Germany. Hitler might well take us up on any such offer and there simply are not enough ships and means of transportation in the world to handle them.[73]

Nothing in Hopkins's notes indicates that anything was said questioning, let alone objecting to, this brutal statement. In a group that included all of the foremost statesmen of the democratic world except Winston Churchill—a group that was well aware of what was happening to the Jews of Poland and Germany—no one expressed any qualms about Eden's callousness. Nor did anyone challenge the contrived reason Eden gave for advising care lest Hitler be encouraged to release the Jews.

Even if one accepts Eden's contention that transportation was not available, can anyone doubt that Jews would have *walked,* if necessary, across the Balkans and out through Turkey? The hard fact of the matter is that, despite the excuse used constantly throughout World War II that the rescue of Jews was impossible because of the shortage of transportation, shipping and other resources were somehow found for non-military purposes when the Allied leadership so desired. Illustrations of that fact will appear in a later chapter. For now, let it be noted that ten days after Eden's discussion with Roosevelt and the other statesmen, the British government announced plans to take 21,000 non-Jewish Polish refugees to East Africa. They were some of the 100,000 non-Jewish Polish, Yugoslav, and Greek refugees whom the Allies moved to sanctuaries in the Middle East and Africa during World War II.[74]

The real problem as far as Eden and the British were concerned was not ships. It was the immense pressure that the release of thousands of Jews from Europe would place on the British policy of placating the Arabs by strictly limiting Jewish immigration into Palestine. Placed in its broader context, this was part of the fundamental problem of where Jews could be put if they *were* rescued. No country wanted to take them in, as had been proved between 1933 and 1941 when persecuted Jews had been free to leave Nazi Europe. American Jewish groups had been correct in devising several proposals for havens of refuge for those who could get out. Unwillingness to offer refuge was a central cause for the Western world's inadequate response to the Holocaust.

Eden's fear that the Axis powers might agree to send the Jews to the Allies instead of to the killing centers was by no means unique. For instance, in December 1943 the British government opposed a plan for evacuating Jews from France and Rumania because "the Foreign Office are concerned with the difficulties of disposing of any considerable number of Jews should they be rescued from enemy occupied territory. . . . They foresee that it is likely to prove almost if not quite impossible to deal with anything like the number of 70,000 refugees whose rescue is envisaged." Six months later, the British War Cabinet's Committee on Refugees declined to pursue a possible arrangement for the exodus of large numbers of Jews from Nazi Europe, partly because it could "lead to an offer to unload an even greater number of Jews on our hands." [75]

The same callousness prevailed on the American side. In November 1941, in the midst of months of mass terror against Jews in Rumania, Cavendish W. Cannon of the State Department's Division of European Affairs spelled out the reasons why the United States should not support a proposal to move 300,000 Jews out of Rumania to safety in Syria or Palestine. He specified, among other problems, that "endorsement of such a plan [was] likely to bring about new pressure for an asylum in the western hemisphere" and that, because atrocities were also under way in Hungary, "a migration of the Rumanian Jews would therefore open the question of similar treatment for Jews in Hungary and, by extension, all countries where there has been intense persecution." Cannon added, "So far as I know we are not ready to tackle the whole Jewish problem." In May 1943, Robert C. Alexander of the State Department's Visa Division described rescue proposals as moves that would "take the burden and the curse off Hitler." [76]

Similarly, R. Borden Reams of the Division of European Affairs, referring to efforts in the spring of 1943 to persuade the Allies to negotiate with Germany for the release of the Jews, spoke of the potential "danger" of such action:

> While in theory any approach to the German Government would have met with a blank refusal, there was always the danger that the German Government might agree to turn over to the United States and to Great Britain a large number of Jewish refugees at some designated place for immediate transportation tc areas under the control of the United Nations. Neither the military nor the shipping situation would have permitted such action on the part of the United Nations. In the event of our admission of inability to take care of these people the onus for their continued persecution would have been largely transferred from the German Government to the United Nations.* [77]

Since policymakers in both the State Department and the British government viewed the escape of Jews from sure annihilation as a "burden," or a "danger," it is hardly surprising that they looked upon the rescue of Jews as something to avoid rather than to strive for. Seen from this perspective, such State Department decisions as the failure to fol-

---

* Reams did not explain why the German government would have insisted on *immediate* transportation of all the freed Jews or why such an unlikely requirement could not have been modified by further negotiations.

low up the Rumanian proposal to release 70,000 Jews and the attempt to shut off the flow of extermination information take on a certain grim logic.

Even after the disheartening encounter with Eden, the Joint Emergency Committee pushed ahead, continuing to place its hopes in Taylor and Welles. But by early April the committee was reasonably convinced that neither the State Department nor the British would seek to effect a rescue program at Bermuda. If anything significant were to occur at the conference, it would have to come at the insistence of President Roosevelt.[78]

Accordingly, Wise telegraphed the White House asking that a few JEC leaders be granted the opportunity to talk with the President as soon as possible regarding the fate of millions of European Jews. Although the committee expected to have no trouble seeing Roosevelt, Wise's request got them nowhere. The White House simply relayed it to the State Department for acknowledgment. Five days later, Hull signed a letter informing Wise that such a meeting could not be arranged. He suggested that the committee convey its information in a memorandum for the President and the delegates to the conference.[79]

Meanwhile, on April 1, the seven Jewish members of the House of Representatives, led by Emanuel Celler, did succeed in talking with Roosevelt.* Although Celler had kept in close touch with the Joint Emergency Committee, the Jewish congressmen did not press its rescue proposals on the President or place much emphasis on the Bermuda Conference. Rather, they concentrated on criticism of the State Department's complex and stringent screening process, which was keeping refugee immigration into the United States at less than 10 percent of the legally established quotas. The congressmen asked for simplification of the procedures.[80]

Although simplification would certainly have been a help, the failure of the congressmen to focus on the major policy issues enabled Roosevelt to avoid the pressure they might otherwise have been able to put on him. The emphasis on immigration procedures opened the way for him to sidetrack the group to Breckinridge Long, the assistant secretary in the State Department who supervised immigration regulations. He could be depended upon to respond courteously to the congressmen, to offer to consider whatever suggestions they would submit, and perhaps eventually to make a few superficial modifications. In that way,

---

* Besides Celler, the Jewish congressmen were Sol Bloom (Dem., N.Y.), Samuel Dickstein (Dem., N.Y.), Daniel Ellison (Rep., Md.), Arthur G. Klein (Dem., N.Y.), Adolph J. Sabath (Dem., Ill.), and Samuel A. Weiss (Dem., Pa.).

Long could largely neutralize their potential for forcing the administration to make any real policy changes regarding the rescue of Jews.[81]

During the first months of 1943, while some Americans were asking why their government was doing nothing to help the European Jews, others were wondering about the near silence of the American Christian churches. *Jewish Frontier* pointed out that although information on the annihilation of the Jews was widely enough known to elicit a Christian reaction, none had been forthcoming. *Congress Weekly* voiced the same dismay. It asserted that a declaration from leading American churchmen expressing their horror and their readiness to act would arouse public opinion and help bring a response from the government.[82]

On an individual level, Rabbi Israel Goldstein, president of the Synagogue Council of America, wrote to his friend Dr. Everett R. Clinchy, a Presbyterian minister and president of the National Conference of Christians and Jews. Goldstein was concerned about the National Conference's apparent inaction and asked, "How can an organization whose program is brotherhood, exclude from its sphere of concern . . . the dying gasp of European Jewry?"[83]

Clinchy replied that the National Conference was already working on the extermination issue. It had publicized the situation through its Religious News Service, which reached both the religious and general press. It also hoped to sponsor sometime in the spring a nationwide exchange between churches and synagogues that would feature appeals for action. Clinchy had shown that the National Conference was not entirely inactive. It was probably doing more than most non-Jewish organizations. But, in truth, it had attempted very little, and Clinchy did not indicate that it would do much more.[84]

A handful of minor Christian and interfaith movements did urge rescue action. But none of the great American Protestant denominations took a stand during these critical months—or later in the war, for that matter. The American Roman Catholic church also was virtually silent. Neither its bishops nor other prominent church leaders pressed the issue.[85]

The American Christian organization that was most active in the campaign for rescue was the Protestant interdenominational Federal Council of Churches. But even it did not do much. The New York office occasionally assisted the Joint Emergency Committee and other Jewish groups. In mid-March, the Federal Council's executive committee called on the government to offer financial help for refugees who reached neutral European nations and to provide havens outside Europe to which refugees could be sent until the end of the war. At the same time, the executive committee urged American Christians to support steps for rescue. And it designated Sunday, May 2, a nationwide Day of Compassion for the Jews of Europe, recommending that church services that day concentrate on the Jewish tragedy.[86]

In preparation for the Day of Compassion, the Federal Council distributed worship suggestions and other materials to church leaders. And it devoted one of its weekly *Information Service* bulletins to a carefully documented summary of evidence of the ongoing "elimination of the Jews in Nazi-controlled Europe." This bulletin, prepared with the help of the Joint Emergency Committee, was mailed to 70,000 Protestant ministers. The JEC assisted in several other ways with arrangements for the Day of Compassion, even to the extent of compiling and paying for some of the printed matter.[87]

The Federal Council hoped that tens of thousands of local churches would focus the attention of their congregations on the terrible plight of Europe's Jews and thus create a favorable public opinion for action in their behalf. The outcome of this effort cannot be fully determined, but available evidence indicates that the impact was slight.

In Boston, for instance, the Joint Emergency Committee and the American Jewish Committee, with cooperation from some Protestant clergymen, made thorough preparations for the Day of Compassion. Publicity was conducted through mailings, subway posters, newspaper advertisements, press releases, and editorials in the Boston daily newspapers. Sympathetic ministers were supplied with materials from the Federal Council and other sources. An honorary committee of sponsors included the mayor of Boston, the governors of Massachusetts, Rhode Island, and New Hampshire, members of Congress, and many church leaders. But Boston's Protestant churches hardly responded. By the eve of the Day of Compassion, only eight Boston-area clergymen had agreed to center services around its theme.[88]

In New York City, the outcome appears to have been even more meager. Several city church services were summarized in the next day's *Times.* In only one instance was the observance of the Day of Compassion mentioned. In Pittsburgh the results were minimal. A Jewish organization there set out to write a story on the Day of Compassion for release to Pittsburgh newspapers. But phone calls to the leading churches affiliated with the Federal Council found that none of them had planned anything connected with the occasion. The most positive response came from a minister who thought his church might do something next year.[89]

Perhaps more significant in retrospect than the slight impact of the Day of Compassion is the fact that this modest effort turned out to be the Christian church's main attempt during the entire war to arouse an

American response to the Holocaust. And even it came only after months of prodding by Jewish friends of the Federal Council's leaders.[90]

Momentous developments had occurred in Europe and North Africa in the months between the emergence of the extermination news in late November 1942 and the solidification of plans for the conference at Bermuda the following April. The Allies had seized the initiative in the war and clearly were on the road to victory, while the German slaughter of the Jews had continued relentlessly. At Auschwitz, four huge new gas chamber–crematorium installations had come into operation, increasing the already high rate of mass killing to a capacity estimated at 6,000 to 12,000 murders and cremations per day.

During those same months, the patterns of the American government's response to the ongoing annihilation of the Jews became evident. The State Department had shown itself to be entirely callous. Most members of Congress seemed to know little and care less. And the President, who was well aware of the catastrophic situation, was indifferent, even to the point of unwillingness to talk about the issue with the leaders of five million Jewish Americans.

The months had seen a variety of efforts by American Jews, aided by a comparatively small number of non-Jews, to stir the conscience of America and its government and thereby bring about some first steps toward trying to save European Jewry. The main Jewish organizations had managed for a time to subdue the chronic fighting among themselves and join in a united operation to press for government action. The results so far had been depressing. But the upcoming Bermuda Conference offered a little hope that something positive might develop.

|| 6 ||

BERMUDA

The Bermuda Conference grew out of the public reaction in Britain to the reports that the European Jews were being exterminated. Publicity about the Holocaust was more widespread and cries for action more forceful in England than in the United States. Pressure on the British government rose rapidly in late 1942 and continued to increase well into 1943. The main impetus came from Christian church leaders and from members of Parliament.[1]

To quiet the pressures, the British government initiated the steps that led to the United Nations war-crimes declaration of December 17, 1942. The declaration, however, did little to moderate the demands for action. In January the archbishops of Canterbury, York, and Wales, speaking for the entire Anglican Episcopate, called on the government to move immediately to save the Jews and to provide sanctuary for all who could get out of Nazi Europe. A similar appeal was issued jointly by Arthur Cardinal Hinsley, Britain's foremost Roman Catholic prelate, Dr. J. H. Hertz, the nation's chief rabbi, and John Whale, moderator of the Free Church Federal Council. A delegation representing all parties and both houses of Parliament met with the leaders of the Cabinet to press for rapid action.[2]

The clamor reached a high point when William Temple, the archbishop of Canterbury, addressed the House of Lords on March 23. He deplored the months already lost, pleaded for immediate rescue steps, and warned, "We at this moment have upon us a tremendous responsibility. We stand at the bar of history, of humanity and of God."[3]

In the meantime, in another move calculated to temper the public outcry, the Foreign Office had sent a memorandum to the American State Department. It proposed an "informal United Nations conference" to consider the possibilities of removing "a proportion" of the thousands of refugees who had reached neutral European countries. This could encourage those countries to allow more refugees in from Nazi territory.[4]

The Foreign Office pointed out, however, that "certain complicating factors" made the problem very difficult. For one thing, the refugee issue could not be handled as "a wholly Jewish problem," because many refugees were not Jewish and "Allied criticism would probably result if any marked preference were shown in removing Jews." Furthermore, there was "the distinct danger" that anti-Semitism would be stimulated in areas to which "an excessive number of foreign Jews" was transferred. The real "complicating factor" for the British was also revealed in cold words:

> There is a possibility that the Germans or their satellites *may change over from the policy of extermination to one of extrusion,* and aim as they did before the war at embarrassing other countries by flooding them with alien immigrants. (Emphasis added)

The memorandum spelled out the supposedly heavy contributions that Great Britain and the empire were already making in accommodating refugees. It also noted the "generous" response of the United States in that regard. The Foreign Office suggested, however, that if the United States and Britain could agree to take in some more, "the way would be open" to approach other governments to find out what they would do.

In Washington, the responsibility for dealing with the British overture fell to Breckinridge Long, one of four assistant secretaries of state.*

---

* During 1940, Long had become the Roosevelt administration's chief policymaker in matters concerning European refugees. This had occurred not through design but because the Visa Division, the arm of the State Department then most involved in

While the Foreign Office grew increasingly anxious because of rising public pressures, Long and his subordinates studied the British proposal for nearly five weeks. Their lengthy reply, signed by Hull, was essentially an attempt to sidestep the issue. As Long boasted in his diary:

> Their note of January 20 (or thereabouts) was a plain effort to embarrass us by dumping the international aspects of that question plumb on our lap. I picked up the ball and by our February 25 reply put the baby very uncomfortably back on their laps.[5]

The American response consisted mainly of examples to prove that the U.S. government "has been and is making every endeavor to relieve the oppressed and persecuted peoples." Because this assertion was not true, nearly all the examples involved gross exaggeration or distortion. For instance, one of the "measures of assistance" was the "application of the immigration laws of the United States in the utmost liberal and humane spirit of those laws." This claim was flagrantly false.* Another item gave the impression that the United States had taken in half a million refugees from Nazism since 1933. Actually, less than half that number had come. A further example of the heavy burdens Americans were supposedly shouldering was the internment in the United States of large numbers of prisoners of war. Even the "relocation centers where approximately 110,000 persons of the Japanese race are being housed and maintained at public expense" were cited to illustrate American sacrifices.†[6]

Ignoring the British proposal for a United Nations refugee conference in London, the State Department asserted that the best approach would be to work through the already existing Intergovernmental Committee on Refugees (ICR). Accordingly, it recommended a British-

---

refugee affairs, was within his administrative jurisdiction. Starting in 1942, as information about the massive destruction of Jews came out of Europe, the State Department's Division of European Affairs was drawn into the refugee issue. Although not under Long's authority, it worked closely with him in determining the American government's response to the Holocaust.

* Its inaccuracy is proven in my book *Paper Walls: America and the Refugee Crisis, 1938–1941,* especially chapters 8 and 9, and in chapter 7 of this book.

† The reference to the internment of prisoners of war had been urged by Wallace Murray, a State Department adviser on political relations. Murray also suggested that American public opinion "be rallied to provide support for the Government in resisting a deluge of refugees which, added to the number of internees now being supported, would aggravate the already critical food situation." (In fact, despite the rationing of some goods, food was abundant in the United States during World War II.)[7]

American meeting at Ottawa for a "preliminary exploration" of ways to strengthen the ICR.[8]

The Intergovernmental Committee, the ineffectual creation of the Evian Conference on refugees of 1938, had been moribund since the war began. Its twenty-nine member nations had never supported it; it had seldom been possible even to convene representatives of the few states that composed its executive committee. While the Nazis methodically murdered thousands of Jews each day, America's leaders offered a "preliminary exploration" of ways to revive a proven failure.[9]

In one respect the State Department note registered full agreement with the British: "The refugee problem should not be considered as being confined to persons of any particular race or faith." Thus the high principle of nonpreferential treatment was employed to avoid the main issue, the total annihilation of one particular people.[10]

The apparent motivation, as with the British, was concern about the possible release of hundreds of thousands of Jews. A subsidiary factor was undoubtedly fear within the Roosevelt administration that special steps to help the Jews would encourage anti-Semitic and anti-Roosevelt forces to attack the administration as pro-Jewish. Roosevelt's appointments of a few Jews to important posts, coupled with strong Jewish support for him, had for years drawn charges that he was operating a "Jew Deal." With anti-Semitism widespread in the United States, such attacks were taken seriously.[11]

State Department officials had been content to procrastinate for weeks while the British government felt the heat. But when confronted with similar pressures, they quickly saw the value of the conference. Less than forty-eight hours after the Madison Square Garden demonstration of March 1, the State Department moved to offset this display of public concern by releasing to the press the message it had sent the British. This constituted an extraordinary breach of diplomatic practice, not only because the confidential negotiations were still in process, but also because the American note, published by itself, conveyed the false impression that the United States had initiated the plans for a conference.[12]

The British angrily countered with a protest to the State Department and a press release detailing *their* claims of extensive aid to refugees. The Canadian government was also upset, for the State Department had failed to inform it of the proposed conference at Ottawa. Moreover, it did not wish to find itself facing possible pressure to modify its own stringent limits on refugee immigration.[13]

The British acceded to the American plan of a "preliminary two-power discussion on the refugee problem" and revival of the Intergovernmental Committee on Refugees, but asked for a change of location. They apparently feared that a meeting in Canada would be vulnerable to the fast-rising pressures in England. They suggested Washington, but Breckinridge Long persuaded Hull and Welles to block that. Long wrote in his office diary:

> I thought that over and decided it would not be in our best interest; that to talk here would put *us* in a bad position with [the archbishop of] Canterbury giving publicity in the press and all the pressure which would be coming from the locally organized groups in this country.

Agreement finally came on Bermuda, a location that would shield the conferees from public opinion, the press, and Jewish organizations because wartime regulations restricted all access to the island.[14]

Selecting a chairman for the American delegation presented difficulties. Myron Taylor was the obvious choice. The central figure at the Evian Conference, he had been associated with the Intergovernmental Committee on Refugees since its formation. But Taylor declined, pleading heavy involvement in his work on postwar planning. The deeper cause, however, was his belief that the conference would achieve nothing. He tried unsuccessfully to convince the State Department of the necessity for prior agreement on what the two great allies were willing to do. An effective program, in his view, required both powers to take refugees in, pay their transportation costs, and guarantee postwar evacuation from other nations willing to act as temporary havens.[15]

Associate Justice Owen J. Roberts of the Supreme Court also refused the post. Court business required his attention until early June. Dr. Charles Seymour, president of Yale University, accepted but later withdrew because his trustees objected. It was not a good spring for finding distinguished Americans who could devote time to the tragedy of the Jews of Europe. Finally, a week before the conference opened, Princeton University's president, Dr. Harold W. Dodds, agreed to serve as chairman.[16]

The State Department also chose two members of Congress for the American delegation, Senator Scott Lucas (Dem., Ill.) and Representative Sol Bloom (Dem., N.Y.). It suggested that the President select additional delegates, but he took no action. Roosevelt showed minimal interest in the Bermuda Conference in other respects as well. Two weeks after plans for the conference were made public, he asked Hull what it was about. Hull referred him to Long, who explained that it "was to be simply a preliminary meeting to put in motion the Executive Committee of the Intergovernmental Committee on Political Refugees."

Long also told Roosevelt that the conference site had been rearranged to sidestep public pressures that would be unavoidable in London or Washington. Roosevelt replied that he agreed completely.* [17]

The President had almost nothing more to do with the conference, although he tried to persuade Justice Roberts to serve as chairman. Roosevelt apparently saw no urgency in the matter, as his note of April 10 to Roberts indicated:

> I fully understand but I am truly sorry that you cannot go to Bermuda—especially at the time of the Easter lilies! After my talk with you, the State Department evidently decided (under British pressure) that the meeting should be held at once instead of waiting until June.

Shortly afterward the public announcement came: the conference would open on April 19, just three months after the initial British proposal.[19]

The long delays, the diplomatic sparring, and the controlled format of the conference did not hearten concerned Americans. *Congress Weekly* wondered in mid-March why the Intergovernmental Committee on Refugees, "which was created in 1938 and which presumably has had this responsibility all along, is now to await the results of a 'preliminary exploration.'" Two weeks later it concluded that shifting the meeting to Bermuda was a ploy "to keep the proceedings veiled in." The *New Republic* expressed similar misgivings:

> No Jewish organizations are represented and the conference is purely exploratory, can make no decisions and must submit whatever recommendations it may have to the executive committee of the Intergovernmental Committee on Refugees. Meanwhile the hourly slaughter of the Jews goes on.[20]

The isolation of the conference troubled the Joint Emergency Committee on European Jewish Affairs. After failing in its attempt to discuss the conference with President Roosevelt, the JEC tried to arrange for a small delegation to be heard at Bermuda. This was also frustrated. The Jewish congressmen who saw the President on April 1 raised the question. But Roosevelt rejected the idea. A week later, Joseph Proskauer asked Sumner Welles about it. Welles said it was impossible, but invited Proskauer to recommend three people to go to the conference as technical experts.[21]

---

* In May, after approving its final recommendations, Roosevelt again asked Hull about the background and purpose of the conference.[18]

After consultation with the JEC, Proskauer suggested George L. Warren, executive secretary of the President's Advisory Committee on Political Refugees, Dr. Joseph Schwartz, European director for the American Jewish Joint Distribution Committee, and Herman Shulman, a highly regarded New York lawyer. Only Warren was chosen, and he had already been selected—a fact unknown to Proskauer—because of his longstanding role as adviser to the State Department on refugee affairs. Schwartz, temporarily home after nineteen months of refugee-relief work in Europe, was more knowledgeable than any of the five experts who were sent, except Warren.[22]

Efforts were made to persuade Congressman Sol Bloom to battle for the JEC proposals. The State Department's choice of Bloom as a delegate had been a shrewd move. His position as chairman of the House Foreign Affairs Committee appeared to qualify him particularly well for the task. At the same time, many people would see him as capable of upholding Jewish interests at the conference. But no one connected with the Joint Emergency Committee had confidence in Bloom. In his many years on the Foreign Affairs Committee, he had consistently followed the State Department's lead. Celler even considered protesting his appointment as a delegate, and Nahum Goldmann characterized the selection of Bloom as "an alibi." Nevertheless, four people from the JEC spoke with Bloom about the group's rescue proposals, and Proskauer wrote to him.* [23]

In a last-ditch effort to influence the conference, the Joint Emergency Committee sent its list of rescue proposals to Welles along with an appendix of specific suggestions for implementing the program. An accompanying letter formally requested that a small group from the JEC be invited to Bermuda to explain the proposals. It closed with an appeal to Welles personally, asking him to use his influence to turn the conference into an instrument for "rescuing a defenseless people who are otherwise doomed to complete annihilation." [25]

By the eve of the conference, the Joint Emergency Committee had received no response. Angered at their inability to make any impact on goverment policymakers, these foremost leaders of American Jewry briefly considered militant action. But they settled for a press confer-

---

* Congressman Samuel Dickstein would have been as logical a choice as Bloom. Dickstein had long been chairman of the House Committee on Immigration and had a thorough knowledge of American and world immigration issues. But Dickstein was not subservient to the State Department. He offered his services as delegate or observer, but was turned down.[24]

ence to expose the government's indifference. It had a negligible impact.[26]

Welles never replied to the Joint Emergency Committee's appeal. An answer came from Breckinridge Long, after the conference had started. He wrote that he had forwarded the committee's material to the American delegation. Long did not mention the JEC's formal request to be heard at Bermuda.[27]

Others who submitted proposals to the Bermuda Conference included the President's Advisory Committee on Political Refugees. It especially addressed the problem of havens to which refugees who had reached neutral nations could be evacuated, thus facilitating a continuing flow out of Axis-controlled territory. The committee particularly urged consideration of the Western Hemisphere and specifically recommended British Honduras, where land and buildings owned by an American refugee-relief organization were available.[28]

Assistant Secretary of State Adolf Berle suggested another war-crimes warning, this time combined with intimations to Hungary, Rumania, and Bulgaria that they might gain more lenient postwar treatment if they would protect their Jews and facilitate their escape. He also recommended Cyrenaica (the eastern hump of Libya) as a sanctuary for as many as 100,000 Jews for the rest of the war. Long dismissed the first suggestion. The Cyrenaica idea, already on the docket for Bermuda and frequently discussed later, never materialized.[29]

Senator Edwin Johnson, national chairman of the Committee for a Jewish Army, introduced a resolution calling on the conferees at Bermuda to take swift action to save the remaining European Jews. It did not reach the Senate floor. As the conference opened, the Army Committee published a large advertisement in the *Washington Post* addressed "TO THE GENTLEMEN AT BERMUDA." It demanded the immediate formation of a United Nations rescue agency. "ACTION is called for," cried the CJA. "ACTION—not 'exploratory' words."[30]

Before the Bermuda Conference convened, the director of the Intergovernmental Committee on Refugees, Sir Herbert Emerson, evaluated the possibilities for rescue. Since the State Department and the Foreign Office had recently decided that the ICR was the proper mechanism for handling the refugee problem, Emerson's views offered an indication of the prospects for Europe's Jews. He emphasized that "the cardinal test" of all rescue proposals was that they "should not be inconsistent with the efficient waging of the war." No one had recommended otherwise, but Emerson interpreted this requirement very narrowly. For instance, concerning proposals that the Allies approach the Axis powers and offer to take in as many victims of persecution as they would release, Emerson believed that, "in their extreme form, it may be assumed that these will be dismissed as not conforming to the above test." He did not explain why. He did concede, though, that "there is a point at which the rescue of limited numbers with the consent or acquiescence of the Government concerned is practicable." His illustrations, involving a few thousand children in the Balkans and France, showed that his idea of "limited numbers" was *very* limited, as was his entire concept of rescue.[31]

Emerson's specific proposals dealt mostly with increasing the refugee flow out of Spain until it equaled the flow coming in. This would head off any Spanish inclination to limit further entry. Though important, this was a minor part of the overall problem. Even for that, all Emerson could suggest was the establishment of an emergency camp in North Africa, provided it was not ruled out by "military and political considerations, in which I include racial difficulties."[32]

Neither Emerson nor the conveners of the Bermuda Conference had large-scale action in mind. When Proskauer asked Welles for his assessment ten days before the conference opened,

> Mr. Welles replied that if one considers the relation between the results one can expect and the magnitude of the problem, then one would be pessimistic. But forgetting this disproportion, he would say that he is optimistic. He hopes that the question of evacuating the Bulgarian Jews and sending them to Egypt and Turkey will be solved. He is confident that the Spanish refugees will be taken out of that country soon. . . .
>   Mr. Welles stated finally that he wants Bermuda to be a success and he would consider it as such if as a result of it 50,000 people could be saved.

As it turned out, 50,000 was wildly optimistic.[33]

For twelve days, the diplomats lived and worked at The Horizons, an oceanside resort set among hibiscus and oleander and lily fields in bloom for Easter. The American delegates, Dodds, Bloom, and Lucas, were assisted by a secretary and five technical experts. The support staff was crucially important because none of the delegates was familiar with the subject of the conference. Lucas, for instance, told the press he was not acquainted with the refugee problem but intended to study it carefully.[34]

The secretary, R. Borden Reams, had persistently sought to stifle publicity about the extermination of the Jews and had tried to cripple the United Nations war-crimes declaration of December 1942. Robert C. Alexander, assistant chief of the State Department's Visa Division, served as one of the technical experts. He was convinced that the Nazis, "for their own ulterior motives," had created some of the Jewish organizations and that Hitler was "really behind the [Jewish] pressure groups."[35]

The other technical experts were George Backer, George Warren, Lloyd Lewis, and Julian Foster. Foster, who served as shipping adviser, was a career State Department official. Lewis was a friend of Senator Lucas. Warren, of the President's Advisory Committee, was competent and greatly concerned about the refugee problem. His views were nonetheless influenced by his close relationship with the State Department. Backer headed the Jewish Telegraphic Agency as well as American ORT, an organization devoted to training Jews of Europe and the Americas in technical trades and agriculture.[36]

The British delegates were experienced, high-level Cabinet officials. And four of their five technical experts were drawn from Cabinet offices relevant to the issues under discussion. The delegates were Richard Law, son of a former prime minister and parliamentary undersecretary of state for foreign affairs; Osbert Peake of the Home Office; and George Hall from the Admiralty. An American journalist at the conference was troubled by the glaring disparity between the two delegations.[37]

Only five news correspondents were allowed to go to Bermuda. They represented the various wire services; no individual newspapers were permitted to send reporters.[38]

A great number of proposals had been submitted to the conference. For the Americans, though, the State Department simplified the task of evaluation. It defined the positive objectives, listed specific prohibitions, and required that all other issues be cleared with Washington.[39]

The positive objectives were three. First, to devise steps to encourage neutral European nations to accept more escaped refugees. Second, to seek temporary havens in United Nations territories in Europe and Africa and to locate transportation to them. Third, to call an early meeting of the Intergovernmental Committee on Refugees to implement the decisions reached at Bermuda.

Strictly prohibited was any special emphasis on Jews. And no steps were to be taken exclusively for Jews. State Department officials also imposed a three-part directive obviously calculated to keep refugees out of the United States. "No commitment regarding trans-Atlantic shipping space for refugees can be made." Such arrangements could delay unpredictable, but urgent, plans for moving Axis prisoners of war and wounded American soldiers across the ocean.* Furthermore, "even if shipping space could be found," it would be unnecessary and impractical to move refugees to America when they could be placed in sanctuaries in or near Europe. Finally, delegates were cautioned that the administration had "no power to relax or rescind [the immigration] laws." (Unmentioned was the fact that the administration *did* have the power to allow the legal quotas, then almost untouched, to be filled.) Clearly, the State Department had rationalized a prior decision to permit no increase in the trickle of refugees then entering the United States.

The British imposed additional limitations. Law characterized as "fantastic" the proposals that the United Nations approach Germany for the release of the Jews and that food be sent to persecuted people in Europe. The American delegates agreed that these suggestions were "impossible and outside the scope of the Conference," but only after having silenced Bloom, who fought tenaciously, if briefly, for negotiations for the release of Jews. The conference's minutes reveal once more the deep fear the two powers shared that a large exodus of Jews might take place.[41]

Law warned

> that if Hitler accepted a proposal to release perhaps millions of unwanted persons, we might find ourselves in a very difficult position. For one thing, Hitler might send a large number of picked agents which we would be forced to take into our own countries. On the other hand, he might say, "Alright, take a million or two million." Then because of the shipping problem, we should be made to look exceedingly foolish.
>
> Mr. Bloom then expressed the thought that we should at least negotiate and see what could be done. . . . Mr. Bloom offered the suggestion that we propose that Hitler release each month the number of refugees that we find it possible to handle. . . .
>
> There then occurred an extended conversation between Dr. Dodds and Mr. Bloom, Dodds pointing out that Mr. Bloom's proposal was completely against the policy of our Government and that we were on record against negotiating on any terms with Nazi Germany. Bloom then began to recede from his former rather uncompromising position.
>
> A member of the British Delegation [Peake] then suggested that the question of potential refugees should be thoroughly discussed. Many of the potential refugees are empty mouths for which Hitler has no use. . . . It

---

* Evacuation of refugees could have been suspended when ships were needed for the wounded or POWs. Most ships that moved military forces and supplies across the Atlantic returned to the United States empty. And neutral shipping, especially by Portuguese and Spanish lines, was available throughout the war.[40]

would be relieving Hitler of an obligation to take care of these useless people. If Hitler would agree to release a large number of old people and children, we should be placed in a ridiculous position because we could only take between 500 and 1,000 a month. . . .

Mr. Bloom then remarked that all he wanted was to somehow not close the door. . . .

Mr. Reams then interposed to say that there was no doubt whatever that the Department of State would oppose any negotiations with Germany.* [42]

Approaches to the satellite Axis countries were not discussed at all. Yet this had been an important part of the proposals sent by the Jewish groups. They believed such negotiations were especially promising now that the tide of war had turned and some satellites were seeking to placate the Allies. [44]

The proposal to send food to the starving victims of the Nazis received no support. The conferees concurred that food shipments into Axis Europe fell under the authority of Allied blockade officials and outside the purview of the conference. Dodds advised, furthermore, that lend-lease supplies would not be available for refugees. [45]

On British insistence, another key issue was excluded from the agenda. Britain's Palestine policy would not be discussed at the conference. [46]

Working, then, under guidelines that precluded large-scale rescue, the diplomats addressed peripheral problems. Most effort focused on refugees who had fled to Spain. If they could be moved out, a channel for a continuous flow of new escapees from Axis territory might be opened. [47]

According to the delegates' information, Spain harbored 6,000 to 8,000 Jewish refugees. (Actually, this was an overestimate.) Most had fled the mass roundups and deportations that began in France in the summer of 1942. The conferees learned that 3,000 of them were capable of military service or war-related work for the Allies. The British and American diplomatic missions in Spain were already moving them to North Africa. The main issue addressed at the Bermuda Conference thus came down to the evacuation of 5,000 Jews from Spain. [48]

The problem of transportation was tackled first. The State Department shipping expert advised that all United Nations shipping was needed to move supplies and troops and to carry prisoners of war and

* Both the State Department and the British had negotiated with Germany and continued to do so throughout the war. They discussed a variety of issues, including exchanges of prisoners of war, exchanges of civilian nationals caught in enemy territory, and even attempts to arrange safe-conduct for refugee-evacuation ships. [43]

wounded soldiers to the United States. Neutral shipping offered the only possibility for refugee transport. Despite a lack of clear information, the delegates decided that four or five Portuguese liners, each with a capacity of 600 persons, could be obtained.* [49]

No effort was made to devise ways that United Nations ships might help, even though thousands of troopships and lend-lease and other cargo vessels were returning to the United States empty or in ballast. The delegates did discuss use of that empty space. But they concluded that diversion of ships to unscheduled ports to pick up refugees would delay their war-related missions. Could refugees be assembled at the ports where troops and supplies were unloaded? The conferees found an answer for that too. The concentration of refugees might interfere with military operations or pose a security risk. [51]

The delegates also wrestled with the question of where the 5,000 refugees could go. Entry certificates for Palestine were available for 3,000, but there appeared to be no way of moving them there. The delegates talked at length about transferring 2,000 people to Angola. Then it occurred to them that no one had asked the Portuguese about using their colony. The British delegates thought Jamaica might possibly accept 500 refugees. But it was most unlikely that British colonies in East Africa could accommodate any. Nothing, it seemed, could be done to open Latin America or Canada. [52]

The Cyrenaican region of Libya looked promising, but not for the Jews in Spain. The delegates decided it would be a good location for non-Jewish refugees, probably Greeks. This suggestion would enable the conference to "create a very good impression" by showing that it was not acting only for Jews. Lucas, who thought this particularly important, emphasized "the existing reaction in Congress against confining the problem just to the Jewish refugees." The delegates agreed to recommend Cyrenaica as a refugee haven. [53]

Late in the deliberations, the British delegation maneuvered the Americans into recommending that the United States admit 1,000 to 1,500 of the refugees in Spain. In reality, America's extremely tight immigration procedures meant that nothing like that number of visas would be granted. But the conferees, eager for results, at least on paper, entered this proposal in their list of recommendations. [54]

The Bermuda Conference also called for establishment of a reception camp in North Africa to accommodate 3,000 people. Refugees could be moved to the camp and held there pending arrangements for migration overseas. Meanwhile, with those refugees gone, Spain could permit

---

* Actually, far more neutral shipping was available than this. [50]

entry of new escapees. The British delegation initiated the proposal, frankly admitting it was needed to placate the public clamor for concrete action.[55]

At first the Americans, especially Bloom, strenuously opposed it. They argued that such a camp could disrupt military operations in North Africa and might incur the hostility of the Arabs. But the American delegation was soon convinced that the plan was "one of the few definitely affirmative steps" the conference could make to "allay some of the criticism" leveled at the two governments. Dodds telegraphed the State Department asking quick approval of the proposal. He pointedly mentioned that American resistance to it placed the British in "an advantageous position so far as the record is concerned."[56]

The idea made Breckinridge Long uneasy, but he saw the force of Dodds's argument. He submitted the plan to the military. The War Department and the Joint Chiefs of Staff strongly opposed it. They maintained that an influx of Jewish refugees might stir up the Arab population and require military action to keep order. The leaders in the area itself, General Dwight Eisenhower and French General Henri Giraud, raised no such objection. They approved the plan, but advised that the removal of the Jewish refugees would have to wait, probably for months, until 15,000 young Frenchmen who had also escaped to Spain had been transferred to North Africa to join the Allied forces.[57]

Since the military did not provide a clear decision, the Bermuda delegates recommended the camp plan, "subject to military considerations." A month later, Roosevelt's ambiguous message to the State Department left the question unresolved:

> I agree that North Africa may be used as a depot for those refugees. . . .
> I know, in fact, that there is plenty of room for them in North Africa but I
> raise the question of sending large numbers of Jews there. That would be
> extremely unwise.

Only in July, following further discussions with the British, did Roosevelt accede to the establishment of the camp.*[58]

Seemingly, the diplomats had solved the comparatively minor problem of the 5,000 Jewish refugees in Spain. But fewer than 2,000 were in fact evacuated, most of them not until a year after the Bermuda Confer-

---

* Almost another year passed before the camp went into operation. Ultimately, it provided a haven for only 630 refugees. As a Quaker relief worker noted, it "hardly made a ripple" on the problem in Spain. Yet, in the end, the camp constituted the Bermuda Conference's only concrete contribution to the rescue of Jews.[59]

ence. The theory that the expeditious removal of the refugees might open a pipeline for continuing escapes from Nazi territory never received a trial.[60]

The Bermuda Conference considered problems other than that of Spain, but not many and not in much depth. Seeking ways to encourage neutral European countries to accept escaping refugees, the delegates discussed the question of providing food and funds for their maintenance. But they made no recommendations. They did draft a declaration to be issued jointly by the Allied nations, including the governments-in-exile. It assured neutral states that each of the signatories would readmit its citizens at the end of the war. The joint declaration also stipulated that refugees who were former citizens of Axis nations would be enabled to return to their countries of origin. The conferees pointed out that the statement's effectiveness depended on its being issued "in the near future." More than a year later, though, the necessary endorsements still had not been obtained. Procrastination, State Department blunders, quibbling over wording, and Russian stalling all contributed to the failure of this plan.[61]

The Bermuda delegates also recommended reorganization and strengthening of the Intergovernmental Committee on Refugees. They proposed several changes. The ICR's pre-war mandate to negotiate with Germany for an orderly exodus of refugees from the Reich would have to be altered to apply to *all* European refugees. The power to deal with Germany had to be rescinded. (The new mandate should provide for "negotiations with Allied and neutral governments but not, of course, with enemy governments.") The ICR's membership should be broadened to include Russia, Poland, Greece, Yugoslavia, and possibly Spain, Portugal, and other nations. In addition, greatly increased funding was essential. Previously, most financing of refugee rescue and maintenance had come from private organizations; governments had contributed little more than the ICR's paltry administrative expenses. For the Intergovernmental Committee to expand its role, the member governments would have to assume the additional costs. Finally, the staff, which consisted of an unpaid director and one secretary, would have to be enlarged.[62]

Convinced of the necessity for "early and decisive action," the conferees urged that the ICR's reorganization be carried out by telegraph. This was a workable suggestion, for its executive committee could make all the changes, and only three nations were on it besides Britain and the United States.[63]

In the end, the ICR accepted the recommendations with only minor modifications. But the picayune analysis and leisurely pace of the State

Department and the Foreign Office slowed the process for months. Instead of telegraphic negotiations, a meeting of the ICR's executive committee was called. It did not take place until August. Implementation of the changes then dragged on for another five months. The delays were not the only reason the Intergovernmental Committee never became an effective agency, but they reflected the basic cause for its failure —the very shallow commitment of the American and British governments to rescuing the victims of Nazi terror.[64]

As the Bermuda Conference neared adjournment, the delegations prepared a joint report for their governments. Their list of recommendations included little more than (1) the admonition "that no approach be made to Hitler for the release of potential refugees," (2) the proposal that the two governments act immediately to obtain neutral shipping to transport refugees, (3) the request that the British consider admitting refugees into Cyrenaica, (4) suggestions for moving refugees out of Spain, (5) the proposal for a joint Allied declaration on the postwar repatriation of refugees, and (6) the plan for the reorganization of the Intergovernmental Committee.[65]

Perhaps out of embarrassment at the poverty of results, the conferees decided to keep the report and the recommendations secret.* They released a one-page bulletin to the press, which stated only that they had carefully analyzed all possibilities of alleviating the refugee problem and were submitting "a number of concrete recommendations" to their governments. Since the recommendations involved other governments and "military considerations," they would have to remain confidential.[66]

American press coverage of the Bermuda Conference was negligible. Ten major metropolitan newspapers across the country paid only casual attention to it. All ten reported on the keynote speeches by Law and Dodds. Beyond that, only the *New York Times* did a fairly thorough job, running stories concerning eleven of the conference's twelve days. But several of the articles were tiny and inconspicuous, and the one report that reached the *Times*'s front page rated only four inches of print there. None of the other nine papers even approached adequate coverage.[68]

The poor performance of the press was consistent with the American mass media's general failure to treat the extermination of the European Jews as significant news. An additional factor regarding the Bermuda Conference was the close governmental control of information. The few

---

* They took no chances on this score. They showed the report to the American technical expert George Backer only after he had signed an oath of secrecy. (Concerning Backer, see appendix A.)[67]

correspondents allowed at the conference were excluded from its deliberations. Forced to rely on guesswork, rumor, and a few official statements, they termed the meeting a "no news conference." [69]

Despite their secretiveness about specific information, the delegates
made it evident that the conference would not produce significant action. At the start, Dodds stressed that "the solution to the refugee
problem is to win the war," a conclusion that he and Law publicly
reemphasized soon afterward. Time and again, conferees advised that
they saw little chance for immediate help. One explained it to reporters
this way: "Suppose he [Hitler] did let 2,000,000 or so Jews out of
Europe, what would we do with them?" As the days passed, bits of
information surfaced intimating that most proposals submitted to the
conference had been rejected or referred without recommendation to
the Intergovernmental Committee.[70]

The miniature headlines above the tiny newspaper reports from Bermuda recorded the failure:

Refugee Conference Delegate Warns Of False Hopes For Aid (*April 19*)
Refugees Are Warned To Wait (*April 19*)
Conference Says Large Scale Rescue Not Possible Now (*April 22*)
Bermuda Parley Decides Most Plans Unfeasible (*April 23*)
Scant Hope Seen For Axis Victims (*April 25*)
Refugee Removal Called Impossible (*April 30, end of conference*) [71]

American Jewish leaders, organizations, and publications denounced
the proceedings at Bermuda. *Jewish Frontier* accused the delegates of
having approached their mission "in the spirit of undertakers." Stephen
Wise described the conference as "sad and sordid," while *Opinion*
magazine termed it a "woeful failure." The Committee for a Jewish
Army headlined a three-quarter page advertisement in the *New York
Times*: "To 5,000,000 Jews in the Nazi Death-Trap Bermuda Was a
Cruel Mockery.' " [72]

Beneath the torrent of outrage flowed a deeper current of despon-
dency. It was evident, for example, in *Jewish Outlook,* an Orthodox
Zionist monthly, which declared that the conference had "revealed the
hardness of heart" of the democracies and had "destroy[ed] every
hope." Despair also overran the Joint Emergency Committee on European Jewish Affairs. Its vitality was sapped by the unmistakable demonstration of indifference by the two great democracies.[73]

The JEC did not meet for a month after Bermuda. When it did
reconvene, it was clear that demoralization had set in. Jacob Rosenheim
of the Agudath Israel World Organization described the mood as

"more than desperate. The Bermuda Conference has crushed any chance of hope for the rescue of our unhappy brethren and sisters doomed to death by Hitler." Lillie Shultz of the American Jewish Congress felt almost completely frustrated about what might be attempted next, given the stark "indifference of the world." The JEC, a once-hopeful initiative in unified Jewish action, never recovered from the shattering impact of Bermuda.[74]

Jews were not alone in their distress over the Bermuda Conference. Dr. Frank Kingdon, a prominent Christian educator, denounced it and its ill-informed delegates as "a shame and a disgrace." CIO president Philip Murray publicly assailed the "closed-door policy" that kept his union's leaders from being heard at Bermuda. Among several other protesters were Socialist party leader Norman Thomas, who decried "the small and sorry results of the Refugee Conference," and a group of distinguished Christian churchmen led by Reinhold Niebuhr and Daniel Poling.[75]

In the House of Representatives, Samuel Dickstein deplored the proceedings at Bermuda: "Not even the pessimists among us expected such sterility." More angrily outspoken was Emanuel Celler, who condemned the conference as an exercise in "diplomatic tight-rope walking." His attack grew into a long-term assault on State Department refugee policies. Celler also tried to interest Stephen Wise in convening "an unofficial conclave of Representatives and Senators sympathetic to active and genuine rescue." The purpose was to put "extreme pressure" on the administration to save Jews. But the plan was not pursued.[76]

Sol Bloom found himself in the eye of the storm a few weeks after the conference when he stated, "No one can criticize what we did in Bermuda without knowing what we did. But I as a Jew am perfectly satisfied with the results." He also warned the Jewish organizations that were pressing for rescue, "The security of winning the war is our first step. We as Jews must keep this in mind." Wise angrily accused him of falling back on "cheap and theatrical emotionalism" and added that Bloom should have chosen "the grace of silence with respect to the ineptitude and worse of Bermuda." Celler was equally harsh.[77]

Bloom appeared surprised at the criticism. He informed a friend that "the Jews have been attacking me because they seem to be dissatisfied with what we did at the Bermuda Conference. . . . I personally believe we did everything we possibly could do and some day when the facts are known, they may think differently." Yet, he later told Celler that "I was helpless" at Bermuda.[78]

In historical perspective, what were the results of the Bermuda Conference? For the stricken Jews of Europe, only the belated establishment of a small camp in North Africa. But help for the Jews was not, after all, the objective of the diplomacy at Bermuda. Its purpose was to dampen the growing pressures for rescue. Richard Law freely acknowledged this many years later: the process was no more than "a facade for inaction." [79]

While the conference was still in session, Rabbi Israel Goldstein publicly exposed the strategem: "The job of the Bermuda Conference apparently was not to rescue victims of Nazi terror, but to rescue our State Department and the British Foreign Office." Goldstein was no hothead, and his organization, the Synagogue Council of America, was a model of respectability. He stood on firm ground when he charged that the "victims are not being rescued because the democracies do not want them." [80]

The Bermuda Conference was executed according to plan. Thereafter, when the State Department received appeals for action to save Jews, it issued this stock answer:

> I assure you that the plight of the unfortunate victims of Axis tyranny is a matter which has been, and is, receiving the careful and sympathetic attention of this Government. In addition the Conference at Bermuda has examined in detail every possibility for the relief of the sufferings of the persecuted people of occupied Europe. Steps are now being taken to put into effect the recommendations made by the Conference.[81]

This ruse undoubtedly lessened public pressure to some extent. But another result of the Bermuda Conference, one not planned by the diplomats, hurt the rescue cause much more severely. In late June, Breckinridge Long observed that "the refugee question has calmed down" and "the pressure groups have temporarily withdrawn from the assertion of pressure." He concluded that the conference's pretense at careful consideration of all possibilities for action had quieted the clamor for rescue. But he was wrong. Proponents of rescue were not deceived by that trick. What had subdued them was the Anglo-American demonstration of utter callousness. It had smashed hope and made continued efforts seem futile. The calm was that of despair.[82]

Reinhold Niebuhr and other Christian leaders warned President Roosevelt of the "deep pessimism" that had taken hold among "wise and well informed" Jewish leaders. Rabbi Abba Hillel Silver, national chairman of the United Palestine Appeal and a foremost Zionist, observed that "our fortunes were never so low." Morris D. Waldman, a leader of the American Jewish Committee and an active participant in the Joint Emergency Committee, wrote in despair that "nothing will stop the

Nazis except their destruction. The Jews of Europe are doomed whether we do or don't."[83]

Although one cannot calculate the number of Jewish victims of the Bermuda Conference's inaction, one death was clearly related to that event. Szmul Zygielbojm, a Jewish Socialist member of the Polish National Council, committed suicide in London two weeks after the conference ended. In June 1942, Zygielbojm had attempted to focus worldwide attention on the Jewish Labor Bund report from Poland, the first alarm to signal the annihilation of Europe's Jews. In the months that followed, he had persisted in pressing the Allied governments to act. Despondent over the failure of his own efforts and the inaction at Bermuda, he took his own life. In one of his final letters, he wrote:

> The responsibility for this crime of murdering the entire Jewish population of Poland falls in the first instance on the perpetrators, but indirectly it is also a burden on the whole of humanity, the people and the governments of the Allied States which thus far have made no effort toward concrete action for the purpose of curtailing this crime.
>
> By the passive observation of the murder of defenseless millions and of the maltreatment of children, women, and old men, these countries have become the criminals' accomplices. . . .
>
> As I was unable to do anything during my life, perhaps by my death I shall contribute to breaking down that indifference.[84]

As Zygielbojm wrote, the Nazi campaign to extinguish the Jewish revolt in Warsaw neared its end. The Warsaw ghetto had erupted on April 19, the day the Bermuda Conference began. Two days later, a secret Polish transmitter flashed news of the ghetto battle. But it was cut off after four sentences, ending with the words "Save us." Monitored in Stockholm, the appeal was radioed around the world. It reached London and Washington but was barely noticed. It was certainly not heard in Bermuda.[85]

Not long afterward, *Jewish Frontier* searched for the meaning of the three events, the ghetto revolt, the suicide, and the Bermuda Conference: "The Warsaw ghetto has been 'liquidated.' Leaders of Polish Jewry are dead by their own hand. And the world which looks on passively is, in its way, dead too."[86]

(For additional information on the Bermuda Conference, see appendix A.)

|| 7 ||

PAPER WALLS
AND PAPER PLANS

State Department policymakers planned the Bermuda Conference in part to help check pressures for increased immigration to the United States. They also intended it to inject enough life into the Intergovernmental Committee to make it appear capable of taking over responsibility for the refugee problem. What were the State Department's immigration policies? What roles did the Intergovernmental Committee assume? Both questions are important to understanding America's response to the Holocaust.

Paper Walls: American Visa Policies

In 1938, increased German persecution of the Jews led President Roosevelt to ease the extremely restrictive immigration policy of the Great Depression and open the European quotas for full use. This step did not, however, set off mass migration to the United States, for the combined quotas of the affected countries amounted to under 40,000 per year. Furthermore, in mid-1940 the policy was reversed. Claiming the

124

Nazis were infiltrating secret agents into the refugee stream and forcing some authentic refugees to spy for Germany, Breckinridge Long, with the cooperation of the Visa Division, suddenly tightened the requirements for entry. This step slashed admissions by half.[1]

In July 1941, refugee immigration was cut again, to about 25 percent of the relevant quotas. Behind this decline was the "relatives rule," a State Department regulation stipulating that any applicant with a parent, child, spouse, or sibling remaining in German, Italian, or Russian territory had to pass an extremely strict security test to obtain a visa. The State Department explained that cases had come to light of Nazi and Soviet agents pressuring refugees to engage in espionage under threat of retaliation against their relatives.[2]

Another innovation in July 1941 required a systematic security review of *all* immigration applications by special interdepartmental committees. (Each committee included representatives of the Visa Division, the Immigration and Naturalization Service, the FBI, Army Intelligence, and Naval Intelligence.) Applications that received unfavorable recommendations from the special committees were rejected. For favorably recommended cases, the State Department sent "advisory approvals" to its visa-issuing consuls abroad. Normally, the consuls then granted the visas. But they were not required to do so; legally, the final decision was theirs.[3]

The President's Advisory Committee on Political Refugees met with Roosevelt to protest the sweeping new policies. It requested substantial modification of the "relatives rule" and the establishment of a review board to reevaluate cases rejected by the interdepartmental committees. No meaningful change was made in the "relatives rule," but a complex appeal process was instituted in December 1941.[4]

Under the new system, cases turned down by the interdepartmental committees were considered by Review Committees consisting of higher officials from the same five agencies represented on the original committees. The applicants' American sponsors were permitted to testify in person before the Review Committees. Cases rejected by the Review Committees went to the Board of Appeals, which consisted of two private citizens appointed by the President. If a Review Committee or the Board of Appeals ruled favorably, the State Department dispatched advisory approval to the consul nearest the applicant.[5]

After Pearl Harbor, visa procedures were even more stringently tightened for a large category of refugees, those who had been born in enemy countries or had been longtime residents there. Visa applications for these "enemy aliens" had to pass through all three security-screening levels. In addition, no enemy alien could receive a visa without proof that his admission would bring "positive benefit" to the United States.*[6]

Strict enforcement of these regulations led to severe difficulties for many refugees. A mother and her twelve-year-old daughter were stranded in Vichy France. The father, an Austrian, was in Cairo with the Allied military forces. The mother was an American citizen and wanted to take the daughter to safety in the United States. But the girl could not obtain a visa because her Austrian birth made her an enemy alien.[8]

Another incident involved a German refugee in France, who was sent to Auschwitz in the great deportations of 1942. Her visa had been approved in Washington in November 1941. But before she received it, the United States entered the war, and as an enemy alien she had to begin the procedure all over again. In October 1942, a Unitarian Service Committee report noted, "In spite of what seemed to be a favorable reception of her case when it was presented by her niece in Washington, the visa was refused and this meant her case could not be reopened for six months. There was nothing we could do. A few days ago came word of her deportation."[9]

By early 1942, private refugee-aid organizations had recognized that State Department stringency regarding visa issuance far surpassed legitimate concern for protecting the nation from subversion. Their observations were summarized by George Warren of the President's Advisory Committee, who described the immigration process as "one of incredible obstruction to any possible securing of a visa." He had earlier disclosed the source of arbitrary exclusion of refugees as "a group in the State Department . . . which of itself sets up new tests for immigration visas." †[10]

During 1943, it became clear to the private agencies, through their day-to-day contacts with the Visa Division concerning refugee cases, that the State Department had gone beyond the law in blocking immigration. The agencies did not publicize the point, for that would have ended their effectiveness in dealing with the State Department. They did press quietly, but unsuccessfully, for modification. And they recorded the situation in numerous documents still in their archives. In

---

* At about the same time, the State Department persuaded Latin American governments to halt nearly all immigration from Europe. The reason given was the need to safeguard hemispheric security. Yet the department's information sources had no reports of Nazi agents or subversive activities among refugees in Latin America.[7]

† Warren, who worked closely with several of the private organizations, also held a post in the State Department. He was a person of measured opinions who normally gave the State Department the benefit of the doubt.

January, Warren pointed to a persistent effort to shut the doors, which he attributed to anti-alien attitudes in the State Department. He noted that "conditions are becoming tougher all the time" for obtaining American visas, especially for refugees in Spain. (At that time, German occupation of Spain looked quite possible.) Four months later, Warren confirmed that State Department opposition to refugee entry remained strong. By December 1943, he saw nearly no hope for much further immigration. He described it as "almost a frozen situation." A representative of the American Friends Service Committee reported a discussion he had with top officials of the Visa Division: "Everybody was very polite, but the resistance to be overcome is evidently enormous." The records of the National Refugee Service, a leading Jewish aid agency, reveal continual anxiety about "the anti-immigration attitude of the State Department."[11]

Alongside official regulations such as the "relatives rule" and the special requirements for enemy aliens, the State Department raised additional obstacles. One was the unnecessarily long time, usually around nine months, required to move applications through the screening machinery. For those in the enemy-alien category, the wait was longer and approval unlikely. Furthermore, even when an applicant faced immediate danger, the State Department would not expedite the case.[12]

Another bureaucratic wall was the visa application form put into effect in July 1943. More than *four feet* long, it had to be filled out on both sides by one of the refugee's sponsors (or a refugee-aid agency), sworn under penalty of perjury, and submitted in six copies. It required detailed information not only about the refugee but also about the two American sponsors who were needed to testify that he would present no danger to the United States. Each sponsor had to list his own residences and employers for the preceding ten years and submit character references from two reputable American citizens whose own past activities could be readily checked.[13]

Two entirely arbitrary barriers were added in the fall of 1943. The presumption that a refugee was "not in acute danger" began to enter into visa refusals. Persons who had reached Spain, Portugal, and North Africa were considered to be in that category. This arrangement permitted the State Department to close the doors at will. Where Jews *were* in acute danger, in Axis-held territory, there were no American consuls to issue visas. But those who escaped to countries where consuls continued to operate were "not in acute danger" and for that reason could be kept out of the United States.[14]

After agreement was reached to establish a refugee camp in North

Africa (but many months before it opened), the State Department attached a new restriction to some advisory approvals sent to consuls in Spain. It stipulated that a visa would be granted, but only if the refugee could not be included with those going to the camp. A Quaker representative in Lisbon reported that this step "practically suspended the granting of visas" to refugees in Spain.[15]

The State Department also plugged any holes the refugee-aid organizations might find in the barricades. In 1943, Quaker and HIAS* personnel in Casablanca attempted to open a refugee outlet through that port. Despite the State Department's unremitting insistence that American ships were totally occupied in the war effort and could not possibly assist in moving refugees, the relief workers discovered that the military authorities in Casablanca thought otherwise. They were willing to take refugees on ships returning empty to the United States, provided they had visas and quota numbers. The American consulate in Casablanca agreed to cooperate. Fourteen refugees reached New York via military transport. Then the State Department's Visa Division halted this apparent breakthrough by refusing to dispatch quota numbers for people in North Africa until after they had assurance of transportation. The military in North Africa would not assure transportation until the refugees had their quota numbers. "So there we are," concluded a frustrated relief worker in Casablanca.[16]

Another tactic was used to hamper the prospects of reactivated visa cases. Unsuccessful visa applications were eligible for reconsideration six months after rejection. But the State Department would never give reasons for the original refusals. Sponsors and refugee-aid agencies were thus left to guess at how to revise the applications. Should one or both of the sponsors be changed? Were the financial guarantees insufficient? Or was the difficulty something unalterable, such as the applicant's birth in Germany? The private agencies expended considerable effort —with little success—trying to fathom State Department reasoning and to adapt reapplications to it.[17]

A constant obstacle to refugee admission was prejudice on the part of many members of the security-screening committees. The Review Committees openly displayed biased attitudes in the hearings they were required to grant to applicants' sponsors. An official of the National Refugee Service described these interviews as "a pretty bad experience, as some are very strictly prejudiced about letting anyone in." The Friends Committee learned that, frequently,

* Hebrew Sheltering and Immigrant Aid Society, a foremost Jewish migrant-assistance agency.

time is consumed heckling and questioning the affiant [sponsor] on his own personal affairs, his habits, the books he reads, his activities and friends, while the Board fails to learn the important facts regarding the prospective immigrant.

The Review Committees also concentrated excessively on possible Communist or other leftist connections of the sponsors.[18]

Reliable people who testified before Review Committees as sponsors of refugees reported being asked:

> Are you Jewish by race and faith?
> Do you belong to any political group or organization in this country?
> Have you read Tolstoy?
> Did the Social Democratic Party want to change the government?
> Would you call yourself a socialist?
> What are your political convictions now?

Some questions astonished the sponsors, as in this incident reported by Dorothy Detzer, executive secretary of the Women's International League for Peace and Freedom:

> There was a Czech soldier who was at Dunkirk. His wife was in Southern France. When the British evacuated, he went with them and is now in England. His mother-in-law is in the United States and is trying to get a visa for her daughter who is still in France, and the military man on the committee asked: "Well, when your son-in-law left Dunkirk with the English, why didn't he get his wife to come up from Southern France to go with him?"[19]

The private agencies concluded that several members of the screening committees were "making absurd interpretations of facts in individual cases." The President's Advisory Committee checked and found that representatives of the FBI and Army and Navy intelligence were especially difficult, seemingly following a "policy of excluding all the aliens that they can." But repeated efforts both to rectify this bias and to improve the conduct of the hearings achieved nothing.[20]

One moderating influence in the visa-screening system was the Board of Appeals. Its original members were Dr. Frederick P. Keppel, formerly president of the Carnegie Corporation, and Robert J. Bulkley, previously a senator from Ohio. Keppel, especially, worked hard to move the visa system away from excessive suspiciousness and toward the tradition of America as a haven for the oppressed. But the possibilities were limited, as Keppel noted in a memorandum regarding such talented refugees as scientists, writers, artists, scholars, and dramatists:

> Case after case comes to our Board, with the unanimous recommendation of the Interdepartmental Review Committee, to exclude an applicant of the type I have in mind on the basis of vague and unsubstantiated charges of communistic, or less often, Nazi sympathies on the part of the applicant or his sponsors. We can and do reverse some of these recommendations, . . . but we are naturally reluctant to run our percentage of reversals too high.

The Board of Appeals overruled about one-quarter of the negative recommendations made by the Review Committees.[21]

Case notes left by the Board of Appeals reveal some of the reasoning behind Review Committee decisions. One person was disapproved because he was born in Germany, although he had not been there for thirty years. A Socialist was rejected because a Review Committee saw an important similarity between Socialists and Communists. Another applicant was turned down because of a negative security report on a sponsor; but the sponsor was working for the Office of Strategic Services.[22]

The Board of Appeals managed to remove one obstacle from the path of visa applicants. Regulations stated that no enemy alien could be admitted without proof that his presence would be of "positive benefit" to the United States. Keppel and Bulkley opened the way for virtually any upright refugee to pass this test. They ruled that "the Board found benefit in maintaining the traditional American policy of providing a haven of refuge for decent people who are in distress and peril." Until his death, in September 1943, Keppel persisted in efforts to offset the anti-immigration bias that prevailed in the visa decision machinery.[23]

In mid-1944, visa procedures were simplified a little. In May, the State Department set up a new committee to screen the cases of applicants who were not enemy aliens. If a file contained "no derogatory information" and the new committee made a favorable recommendation, an advisory approval went directly to the consul, bypassing all three regular review committees. In July, a briefer application form was instituted. These changes expedited visa decisions. But refugee immigration did not increase. The modifications, though they made the procedure less onerous, were superficial.[24]

In justifying its stringent restrictions, the State Department stressed the necessity of keeping subversive elements out of the United States. The nation's security was, of course, essential. But the problem as it related to refugees was greatly exaggerated.

Nazi agents infiltrated among the refugees would have been found out and exposed by the many anti-Nazis who accompanied them. This did not have to be left to chance either. It was suggested at the time that applicants could be screened by committees of refugees, either overseas or in American detention centers. Questionable cases would go through more complete investigation. The Unitarian Service Committee, in fact, did this on its own in Lisbon. Refugees who came to the Unitarians for help in reaching the United States were screened by two Germans who, as former prisoners of the Nazis, were familiar with Gestapo methods.[25]

The other danger cited by the State Department was that the Nazis would force genuine refugees to spy for Germany under threat of harm to close relatives still in Axis territory. Keppel, Bulkley, and their legal adviser, Dean F. D. G. Ribble of the University of Virginia Law School, exposed the fallacy of that argument:

It does not seem likely that hostage pressure can be used as an effective means of compelling anti-Nazis in the United States actively to serve the Nazi cause. The reason lies in the simple fact that such service ordinarily would necessitate collaboration on the part of Nazi agents. That collaboration, even though it might not completely reveal the identity of a Nazi agent, would necessarily give a clue to his identity. The anti-Nazi subjected to pressure and necessarily filled with hate of the Nazi power might readily turn his knowledge over to the proper American authorities. In other words, the chance that Nazi agents will disclose themselves by their use of hostage pressure to make persons in the United States cooperate in Nazi plans seems so great that a realistic appraisal indicates such methods would scarcely be used.[26]

It is not possible to analyze the information that government agencies collected about refugees suspected of subversive intentions. Intelligence records concerning private individuals are not available for research. But the examples that appear in State Department and other sources are exceedingly few and not convincing.[27]

In one celebrated case, a Jewish refugee arrested in Cuba possessed plans of a U.S. air base near Havana. The Cuban court, however, declared the plans valueless and found no connection with German operatives. Occasionally, American military intelligence abroad sent back reports of Axis agents disguised as refugees. But in the instances found in the records, all impostors were detected and dealt with overseas.[28]

Two German brothers, refugees who reached North Africa, applied for American visas. Despite the endorsement of American officials in the area, the support of the Quakers and the Joint Distribution Committee, and a clean report from American military intelligence in North Africa, the applications were turned down in Washington. The difficulty was a statement by the French administration in North Africa that the two might possibly be spies. This suspicion had arisen because a person with a grudge against one of the brothers had denounced them to French authorities. On such evidence, people were judged dangerous and kept out of the United States.[29]

A report by the U.S. Office of Censorship regarding three highly reputable Jewish refugee-aid organizations—the Joint Distribution Committee, HIAS, and HICEM (the European affiliate of HIAS)—reveals some of the ignorance and dubious logic that fed State Department suspicions. The Censorship Office disclosed that "it is reliably reported" that HICEM "is extensively used by the Germans as a medium through which agents can be placed in any part of the world." This unsubstantiated assertion was contravened in the same report by a statement that British intelligence in Bermuda, which closely monitored HICEM-HIAS messages, was not suspicious. Yet the writer concluded that, because the Joint Distribution Committee and HIAS had close ties with HICEM, "it necessarily follows" that they "have been used in the same manner" and should be viewed "with no less suspicion."[30]

The chance that a refugee, or a Nazi agent disguised as a refugee, could have successfully carried out subversive activities once in the United States was extremely small. The American government was highly effective in controlling Nazi espionage and sabotage during World War II. In the famous case of the eight saboteurs landed by U-boats on Long Island and the Florida coast in June 1942, detection and capture came shortly after their arrival. The Nazis had no more success with the spy Herbert Bahr, an American citizen whom they sent to the United States on the exchange ship *Drottningholm*. Planted among other Americans being repatriated from Germany, Bahr was arrested before he left the ship. Throughout the war, reports by the attorney general and the FBI emphasized that no instance of foreign-directed sabotage had occurred in the United States and that enemy espionage was effectively throttled.[31]

The conclusion is that a legitimate need, guarding the nation against subversion, was used as a device for keeping refugee entry to a minimum. Many thousands were turned away who could have come in without risk to the war effort. When Treasury Department lawyers covertly looked into State Department immigration procedures during 1943, they were led to make the following conclusions:

Under the pretext of security reasons so many difficulties have been placed in the way of refugees obtaining visas that it is no wonder that the admission of refugees to this country does not come anywhere near the quota. . . .

If anyone were to attempt to work out a set of restrictions specifically designed to prevent Jewish refugees from entering this country it is difficult to conceive of how more effective restrictions could have been imposed than have already been imposed on grounds of "security.". . .

These restrictions are not essential for security reasons. Thus refugees upon arriving in this country could be placed in interment camps similar to those used for the Japanese on the West Coast and released only after a satisfactory investigation. Furthermore, even if we took these refugees and treated them as prisoners of war it would be better than letting them die.[32]

One positive note in the State Department's response to the Holocaust was its permission in September 1942 for 5,000 Jewish children trapped in France to enter the United States. This offer, made at the time of mass deportations from France, was obtained through pressure by Eleanor Roosevelt, the President's Advisory Committee, and the refugee-aid agencies. The project failed, as we have seen, because of stalling by the Vichy government.[33]

Among the Jews who evaded deportation by fleeing across the Pyrenees were perhaps 200 children. Most were in Spain; some were in Portugal. American refugee-aid organizations feared German occupation of the two countries and a repetition of the events in France. They were also disturbed because Spain's policy of interning these illegal refugees in prisons applied to children as well as adults. The private agencies and the President's Advisory Committee therefore appealed to the State Department to assign 200 of the 5,000 visas to these children and to expedite their evacuation by instructing American consuls to waive the red tape usually involved in visa issuance.[34]

Sumner Welles agreed in December 1942 to do so. He also offered to include the children's mothers. But this generous impulse was undermined before any visas were granted. The State Department ruled that the mothers would have to go through the regular visa-approval process. That meant they had very little chance of reaching the United States, for even though the quotas were already far undersubscribed, 1943 saw further severe tightening of immigration restrictions. And so it happened, to cite but one example, that fourteen-month-old Max reached America in the care of his sisters, nine and twelve years old. His mother, who had somehow smuggled her baby boy and her daughters over the Pyrenees after her husband was deported, remained in Spain.[35]

Even the agreement to bring the children out ran into trouble. The Visa Division tried to restrict the program to children whose parents had both been deported, but backed down following protests from the private agencies. Then it stalled on dispatching the necessary instructions to the American consulates; and when it did send them, they were confusing and vague. Almost immediately after clarified directions finally arrived at the Lisbon consulate, thirty-one children sailed to a new life in the United States. A second group of twenty-one followed a · few weeks later, completing the Portuguese side of the project.[36]

The American consulates in Spain took no such expeditious action. After receiving workable instructions, the Barcelona consulate delayed for two months by insisting on technicalities supposedly waived for the children. For instance, some were required to produce unavailable French passports. Then, in the midst of the processing, the consul sought to postpone the project again because other demands on his time had arisen.[37]

When the first group of thirty-five children from Spain finally sailed, it included twenty-one with visas issued in Barcelona. But an equal number had been turned down there. A frustrated JDC representative wrote to New York that the consulate in Barcelona "instead of facilitating the project apparently is doing everything possible to limit its scope."[38]

The President's Advisory Committee and the private agencies urged the Visa Division to remedy the situation in Spain, but nothing changed. In May, Eleanor Roosevelt pressed Sumner Welles about the children. His reply was entirely noncommittal. A month later, the Quakers reported a continued "lack of action on the part of Barcelona." In September, Madrid was a center of difficulty. The consulate there, by raising technical barriers, had stopped the visas of three of the thirteen children who had been readied for departure. Two of them, a brother and sister whose father was dead and whose mother's whereabouts were unknown, got out two months later. Apparently the other, an orphaned boy of fourteen, did not.[39]

In all, about 125 children left Spain and Portugal for the United States during 1943 under the special program. Another dozen followed before the war ended in Europe. At no time was shipping a problem. Portuguese passenger vessels were sailing regularly to the United States only partially booked.[40]

In Lisbon, the American consulate's cooperative approach toward the children's project also characterized its dealings with adult refugees. Quaker relief workers described the American vice-consul in Lisbon as "splendid and cooperative" and the rest of the consulate—and the legation, too—as very helpful.[41]

No such sensitivity was found in Madrid or Barcelona. Consuls there not only resisted the children's project, but did what they could to stifle adult immigration to the United States. Their interference was crucial; after November 1942, Spain and Portugal were the only countries in continental Europe where American consuls still issued visas. Jewish refugees had encountered obstructionism at Barcelona since the fall of 1941. But in 1943 the difficulties reached extremes, as consuls held back the visas of a substantial number of refugees who had been cleared by the screening process in Washington.[42]

In June 1943, Howard K. Travers, chief of the Visa Division, admitted to a Friends representative that the Madrid and Barcelona consulates were withholding visas from refugees who had advisory approvals. The Quaker pointed out that Spanish officials were disturbed that refugees were not moving on; Travers agreed to press the consulates for an explanation. Six weeks later, Travers said he had received no response but would try again. Two more weeks passed without any word. At that point, in August, the available record runs out. Some of the visas in question had been approved in Washington as far back as February; yet none had been granted, and no explanation could be obtained. It is difficult to believe that in eight weeks the State Department could not get an answer from subordinate personnel overseas. One has to suspect that the Visa Division was a party to this subversion of the visa process.[43]

Two documents will suffice to illustrate attitudes current among American diplomats in Spain. The first, a June 1943 report by Robert Brandin, a middle-level official at the embassy in Madrid, sharply criticized the Joint Distribution Committee for its efforts to help Jewish refugees immigrate to the United States. Furthermore, from Brandin's standpoint, a refugee who obtained advisory approval from Washington had won "only half the fight since the individual consul still has the final say." Proof appeared in Brandin's report: only 64 percent of the advisory approvals sent to Madrid that year had resulted in the issuance of visas.* [44]

The second document is a record of a conversation in April 1944 between a Quaker representative and Mary Evelyn Hayes, the wife of

---

* Statistics in Brandin's report sharply contradicted the State Department's continual insistence that the refugee problem was not essentially a Jewish one. Of 117 advisory approvals, noted Brandin, 114 were for Jews. In Washington, the visa Board of Appeals, drawing on other evidence, made the same point in a report to the President.[45]

Carlton J. H. Hayes, the American ambassador to Spain. Mrs. Hayes mentioned that the ambassador was antagonistic toward the Joint Distribution Committee. She also said the consuls in Madrid were very annoyed that "the Jews always seem to know more than anyone else." The consuls' complaint actually grew out of the JDC's use of cablegrams to inform refugees of their visa status, while the State Department relayed the same data to the consulate by much slower airgrams. The animosity was also unquestionably fueled by the JDC's occasional success in persuading the Visa Division to put pressure on the consuls to issue visas.[46]

Only the close of the war in Europe brought an end to Washington's complex security-screening machinery. On July 1, 1945, the visa system reverted to pre-war procedures.[47]

What were the quantitative results of America's wartime immigration policy? Between Pearl Harbor and the end of the war in Europe, approximately 21,000 refugees, most of them Jewish, entered the United States.* That number constituted 10 percent of the quota places legally available to people from Axis-controlled European countries in those years. Thus 90 percent of those quotas—nearly 190,000 openings—went unused while the mass murder of European Jewry ran its course.†[48]

The quota limits were mandated by law. But the severe restraints that the State Department clamped on immigration were not. They took the form of administrative regulations and, at times, purely arbitrary State Department innovations. President Roosevelt had the legal power at any time to modify the restrictions and open the quotas to full use. He did not do so, possibly out of concern that restrictionists in Congress might lash back and enact the restrictions into law. More likely, he was

---

* A sizable proportion of them were people who had already reached safety in the Western Hemisphere and had waited there for over a year for an opportunity to move on to the United States. Exact statistics are not available, but in late 1942 and in 1943 about 40 percent of the refugees admitted to the United States were in that category.[49]
† The year-by-year numbers follow, based on fiscal years that ended on June 30. The figures for fiscal 1941 are presented for purposes of comparison; that year closed just as the stringent immigration restrictions of July 1941 were imposed. The first five months of fiscal 1942 preceded America's entry into the war, so immigration in those months is not included in the overall wartime total of 21,000.

Fiscal year	1941	1942	1943	1944	1945
Refugee immigration	28,927	11,702	5,944	5,606	4,793
Percentage of quotas used	47.5	19.2	9.8	9.2	7.9

(refers to quotas assigned to countries of Axis-dominated Europe)

just not interested and found it convenient to leave immigration policy to Breckinridge Long and his associates.[50]

Late in 1945, a *New York Times* writer summarized the effect of America's wartime immigration policies: "The United States, once the haven of refuge for the oppressed peoples of Europe, has been almost as inaccessible as Tibet." He was, of course, exaggerating—but not by much.[51]

Paper Plans:
The Intergovernmental Committee

While the tradition of America as a shelter for the oppressed dissolved, another hope, the reorganized Intergovernmental Committee on Refugees, amounted to little more than a cover for Allied inaction. As Breckinridge Long had intended when he urged its renovation in early 1943, the ICR took on the appearance of a capable international organization, the logical body to assume responsibility for the refugee problem. The State Department then used it as a byway to which it could divert rescue proposals with full confidence that little or nothing would come of them.

Ironically, Long had done his best two years earlier to extinguish the Intergovernmental Committee. At Myron Taylor's initiative, Robert T. Pell had been handling State Department activities connected with the ICR.* In March 1941, Pell angrily resigned. He informed Taylor that "Long apparently made up his mind some months ago that he was not going to have any Intergovernmental Committee around this Department. He has since that time indulged in an unrelenting attack on the work and the officers . . . connected with it. There is just no use going on."[52]

Long's assault came on three fronts. He fired Pell's assistant, Alfred Wagg, despite his excellent service as acting secretary of the ICR. Wagg's work, Long explained, was being discontinued. Long then issued orders barring Pell from almost all refugee matters and shifting his former responsibilities to the anti-refugee European Division and Visa Division. Finally, Long did not ask Congress to renew the $26,000 annual appropriation for the work of the Intergovernmental Committee.[53]

---

* Taylor was the official American delegate to the ICR; Pell was his alternate.

Despite Long's attack, the ICR survived—but only in suspended animation. Wagg's dismissal raised enough press protest that Long continued the post of ICR acting secretary, staffing it with a low-ranking State Department functionary. And, following a year's lapse, Taylor forced the reinstatement of the tiny budget item for the ICR.[54]

The affair dampened Taylor's interest in State Department refugee policies and in the Intergovernmental Committee. He was unwilling to participate in the Bermuda Conference, knowing beforehand that it would not be permitted to recommend realistic solutions. After the conference, he privately condemned it.* Taylor did, however, help plan the renovation of the Intergovernmental Committee during 1943. He intended then to quit as the American delegate to the ICR, but acceded to Roosevelt's plea that he stay on. Taylor and Pell, who was again appointed his alternate, worked sporadically with the revived ICR until both resigned in June 1944. From then until spring 1945, the United States had no delegate to the committee.[55]

In the meantime, the Bermuda Conference's recommendations for reorganizing the ICR had bounced back and forth between the State Department and the Foreign Office for months. The ICR's executive committee had finally met in London in August 1943 and approved the proposed changes. The new mandate specifically empowered the ICR to take all steps necessary "to preserve, maintain and transport" European refugees. The organization also moved to expand its twenty-nine-nation membership by inviting nineteen other states to join. (Only seven did so by spring 1945.) The ICR's minute staff was increased. Sir Herbert Emerson continued as director. An American, Patrick Malin, accepted the new post of vice-director. Plans were made to appoint a secretary and additional support personnel.† Finally, funding arrangements, previously nearly nonexistent, were thoroughly restructured. Administrative expenses were apportioned among all member states. But the costs of actual operations such as relief and transportation would be covered by the United States and Great Britain on a fifty-fifty basis.[57]

The agreement on British-American funding of major projects was the result of pressure from Myron Taylor, with backing from Churchill and Roosevelt. Bold ICR leadership and prompt allocation of the funds

---

* Taylor bluntly wrote to Hull, Welles, and Long, "The Bermuda Conference was wholly ineffective, as I view it, and we knew it would be."[56]

† Malin was experienced in refugee affairs, having worked as American director of the International Migration Service. John Sillem, a Dutch citizen, became ICR secretary soon after the August meeting. Gustave Kullmann, a Swiss who was associated with the League of Nations, served as honorary assistant director of the ICR.[58]

might have saved many victims of Nazi terror. But, although each of the two powers pledged $2 million for the first year (mid-1943 through mid-1944), none of the money was forthcoming until well into 1944.[59]

Despite the ICR's reorganization, its leaders never expected it to accomplish much. Right after the August meeting, Emerson informed Taylor that "one of our troubles is going to be the extravagant hopes that have been raised by irresponsible zealots, mainly in this country." (He was referring to the many religious and parliamentary leaders who were demanding rescue.) Emerson saw three goals for the ICR: to use the "very limited" existing opportunities to help refugees, to develop new opportunities when possible, and, "most important, to play a big part in the solution of post war problems." *[60]

During a visit to the United States in April 1944, Emerson and Malin again emphasized the modest roles envisioned for the ICR. Malin informed private refugee-aid agencies, "We hope to operate as little as possible." "There is very little," he explained, "that can be done with regard to rescue." Rather, the ICR was negotiating with various governments concerning such refugee problems as lack of citizenship, retraining, employment, and migration. Otherwise, Malin pointed out, the main tasks of the ICR were to provide relief for refugees where neither the Allied military nor UNRRA was doing so and to work on emigration or postwar repatriation plans for them.†[62]

The revived Intergovernmental Committee did not compile an impressive record. An attempt to persuade Switzerland to admit more refugees foundered because the ICR could not induce Anglo-American blockade authorities to let the necessary relief supplies go through. Protracted negotiations persuaded UNRRA to take over the maintenance of refugees in areas where it operated. UNRRA also agreed to handle the postwar repatriation of refugees willing to return to their former homelands. But by April 1944, eight months after its reorganization, the Intergovernmental Committee had done nothing else con-

---

* Since 1939, Emerson had kept busy working out plans to cope with the population-displacement problems that would inevitably confront Europe following the war. After the ICR's reorganization, the postwar refugee issue continued to command much of the organization's attention.[61]

† One factor behind the ICR's limited aspirations was its failure to perceive Palestine as an important haven. Given the strong British influence in the ICR and Emerson's own anti-Zionism, ICR pressure on the British government to open Palestine was most unlikely. Malin confirmed the organization's lack of interest in Palestine when he visited there and concluded, without allowing for the Jewish community's capacity for sacrifice, that housing and food shortages made large-scale immigration an absolute impossibility.[63]

crete. Steps were under way, though, to place ICR representatives in strategic locations for initiating refugee-aid programs. This potentially valuable plan called for offices in North Africa, Italy, Portugal, Spain, and Turkey. Very little came of it, however.[64]

For one thing, the first office did not open until early May 1944; the second started in late June. For another, representatives were never sent to the most crucial locations—Turkey, Spain, and Portugal.* Furthermore, the main field representatives were almost entirely unqualified for their posts.[65]

Sir Clifford Heathcote-Smith, assigned to Italy, was well-meaning, but a poor administrator who did not work well with others and had no background for complex refugee problems. His office oversaw valuable, though small-scale, relief operations in southern Italy, and it helped with the overseas emigration of 1,500 Jews. But Heathcote-Smith actually had little to do with these projects. They were planned and carried out virtually independently by a few relief workers sent to Italy by the American Friends Service Committee and the American Jewish Joint Distribution Committee.[67]

Only recently made aware of the dimensions of the European Jewish catastrophe, Heathcote-Smith was anxious to help. But he dissipated much time in planning unrealistic rescue schemes. Most damaging, refugees and relief workers alike felt that Heathcote-Smith, though apparently unaware of it himself, was anti-Semitic. This attitude evidently stemmed from his long career in the British foreign service in the Middle East. Whatever the cause, a senior AFSC worker noted not only that he was "not friendly to the Jews," but that his condescending manner toward them "takes from the refugees whatever shred of personal security they may have left." Despite his shortcomings, Heathcote-Smith did at least press the Vatican to try to save Jews, and he traveled to Switzerland in an unsuccessful attempt to arrange the evacuation of Jews from German-occupied Italy to neutral and safe Switzerland.[68]

If Heathcote-Smith was a poor choice for the post he held, Victor Valentin-Smith, a French colonial governor, was even less satisfactory as the ICR representative in Algiers. A Quaker relief worker recorded one problem: "As far as we could ascertain, V-S (the IGCR seems to go in for hyphenated Smiths) has even less idea what the IGCR is all

---

* By late summer 1944, the ICR had offices in Rome, Paris (transferred from Algiers after a brief stint), and Cairo. In addition, a person in Washington who managed ICR liaison with American governmental and private relief agencies used space in UNRRA's offices but lacked even stenographic assistance.[66]

about than H-S had when he started." Valentin-Smith soon made it clear that refugee assistance was not his interest. One of his first steps was to ask the ICR in London to press for the immediate termination of the recently opened refugee camp in North Africa and to arrange to remove its inhabitants from French territory. The French had been uneasy about the camp all along; they feared they would be left after the war with numbers of refugees who could not find permanent homes. American authorities, however, insisted on keeping the camp in operation. Once Valentin-Smith's objective in North Africa was thwarted, the French government persuaded the ICR to shift his office to liberated Paris.[69]

In the summer of 1944, with sizable funds finally in hand, the Intergovernmental Committee undertook its only substantial project of the Holocaust years. It granted hundreds of thousands of dollars to the Joint Distribution Committee. The JDC, working through the underground, used the money to support groups engaged in hiding Jews, providing them with supplies and helping some to escape from Axis territory. Before the war ended, the ICR had transferred $1.28 million to the JDC for such projects in France, Rumania, Hungary, and northern Italy.[70]

Despite this valuable assistance, the overall record of the reorganized Intergovernmental Committee was one of failure. It did little more than carry out a few peripheral relief projects and attempt to find small-scale emigration opportunities. The ICR's lethargic pace, "lack of imagination," and very limited effectiveness had convinced leaders of American relief agencies that there was "little if any hopeful outlook for the Committee." Their assessment was confirmed by a high official who was partly responsible for the course the ICR took. Shortly after the war, Sumner Welles evaluated the Intergovernmental Committee: "The final results amounted to little more than zero. The Government of the United States itself permitted the committee to become a nullity." * [71]

But the purpose in reviving the Intergovernmental Committee had not been to rescue Jews. The State Department intended the renovated ICR to be a detour down which it could divert—and stall—pressures and proposals for rescue. As such, it played a pivotal role in the State Department's response to the Holocaust.

---

* After Germany's defeat, the Intergovernmental Committee continued to carry responsibility for a few groups of refugees, providing relief and seeking emigration possibilities for them. But it remained a weak organization, poorly supported by its member states. In mid-1947, the International Refugee Organization took over its work.[72]

. . .

The spring of 1943 slipped northward across Europe bringing the annual rebirth of life and hope. Summer gradually followed, through the mountains and into the foothills and plains and valleys of the Continent's north slope. Farmers planted and tilled. The promise of harvest and replenishment again radiated from the land. An ocean away, the Bermuda Conference came and went, blighting hope. In America and Britain, important officials planned insignificant plans. And the stifling, unending death trains lurched and rattled across Europe.

As 1942 ended, Allied military forces had seized the momentum of war. Through the spring and summer of 1943, they pressed forward toward the still-distant but increasingly sure victory. After the German collapse at Stalingrad, in February, the Russians began the slow reconquest of the Ukraine. Simultaneously, they started pushing the enemy back along the front in the north. In July, they broke a major German offensive in a week, then regained their forward motion. As summer ended, the Red Army captured Smolensk, reached the Dnieper River at several other places, and threatened Kiev.

In mid-May, the Axis capitulated in North Africa. The Mediterranean was open to Allied shipping and the way cleared for the invasions of Sicily and Italy. Sicily fell in mid-August, after a short campaign. Anglo-American forces penetrated the mainland in early September, just as the Italian government surrendered. Although the Germans took over in Italy and dug in for a long struggle, Allied advances were substantial in September. An American-British stronghold had at last been established on the Continent.

In the Pacific, February saw the end of the struggle for Guadalcanal. The summer brought further Allied advances in the Solomon Islands and New Guinea. Although progress was agonizingly slow, Japan was by then entirely on the defensive.

As the spring and summer passed, people in the Allied nations grew more and more certain of the conflict's outcome. To the conquered populations of Europe, the summer's air carried the hope and anticipation of restored freedom. But for the Jews still alive in Axis Europe, no help was yet in sight.

8

THE EMERGENCY COMMITTEE

Eleven days after the Bermuda Conference, William Langer of North Dakota warned the Senate that "2,000,000 Jews in Europe have been killed off already and another 5,000,000 Jews are awaiting the same fate unless they are saved immediately. Every day, every hour, every minute that passes, thousands of them are being exterminated." He called on his colleagues to press for action or ultimately face "the moral responsibility of being passive bystanders." Langer's appeal was part of a minor debate that was, despite its brevity, the fullest airing the issue of Jewish extermination received in Congress during World War II.[1]

The discussion had been sparked by a large advertisement in the *New York Times* assailing the Bermuda Conference as "a mockery and a cruel jest" perpetrated on the "wretched, doomed victims of Hitler's tyranny." The advertisement, sponsored by the Bergsonite Committee for a Jewish Army, named no one. But Scott Lucas took the criticism personally and made it an issue on the Senate floor. Half a dozen senators rose in his support. Harry Truman, a member of the CJA's national committee, angrily quit the organization.[2]

But Langer, an independent-minded Republican, blasted the Bermuda Conference and Lucas's role in it. Reacting to Lucas's promise to inform the Senate very soon about the achievements at Bermuda, Langer caustically remarked, "I am looking forward to this address with the greatest impatience." It never took place.[3]

Besides venting its anger, the Committee for a Jewish Army responded to the Bermuda Conference by convening another conference. Its announced aim was to do what the earlier conference should have done—bring experts together to seek all possible ways to save European Jews.[4]

The Emergency Conference to Save the Jewish People of Europe was held in New York City in July 1943. Before it took place, however, other Jewish organizations tried to undermine it. A World Jewish Congress staff member who got hold of secret minutes of the Bergson group's planning sessions asked Stephen Wise "whether anything can be done to prevent this proposed Conference from stealing the thunder of the Joint Emergency Committee." Wise attempted to persuade Episcopal Bishop Henry St. George Tucker, who had agreed to play a prominent part in the conference, to withdraw.[5]

Tucker did not. But the influence of Jewish leaders kept the Committee for a Jewish Army from obtaining the help of Myron Taylor or Sumner Welles. When Taylor was asked to participate, he turned to Welles for counsel. Welles replied that he had refused a similar invitation because "not only the more conservative Jewish organizations and leaders but also such leaders as Rabbi Wise . . . are strongly opposed to the holding of this conference [and] have done everything they could to prevent it." Clarence Pickett of the American Friends Service Committee stayed away on the advice of a friend associated with the Joint Distribution Committee.[6]

Jewish Communists, as well, opposed the Emergency Conference. The *Daily Worker* and *Freiheit* (a Yiddish daily) attacked it because, along with people of the proper sort, the conference had the backing of such unacceptable persons as Herbert Hoover and newspaper baron William Randolph Hearst. Echoing Soviet demands, these papers insisted on an all-out Allied invasion of western Europe. This, they argued, would hasten Hitler's defeat, and that was the only way to rescue the European Jews.[7]

In any event, the Committee for a Jewish Army assembled an imposing list of conference participants. But efforts to obtain the endorsement of top American leaders achieved only mixed results. Dr. Max Lerner, journalist, author, and educator, telegraphed the President and Secretary of State Hull, asking each to send a message of hope to the conference. The appeal to Roosevelt was shunted to the State Department. There Adolf Berle, R. Borden Reams, and James Dunn first fashioned a noncommittal response for Hull to sign. It made the usual claim that the State Department was already doing all that was possible. (Reams privately described it as "not exactly a reply," but use of an opportunity "to restate the Department's position on refugee matters.") They then composed a companion message, which Roosevelt signed, that did little more than express "full concurrence" in Hull's letter. In contrast, clear statements of support reached the CJA from Secretary of the Treasury Henry Morgenthau, Jr., and the 1940 Republican presidential candidate, Wendell Willkie.[8]

Eleanor Roosevelt's initial response to a plea for cooperation was negative. In June, she sent a one-sentence reply to author Louis Bromfield's appeal to her to participate in the Emergency Conference's search for rescue plans. "I have your telegram," she wrote, "and can not see what can be done until we win the war."[9]

Michael Potter, a prominent lawyer and chairman of the conference's organizing committee, answered that he was certain that much could be done before the war ended. "The fact is that very little has been attempted and the United Nations seem to have given up before even trying." He asked her to reexamine the question.[10]

On the eve of the conference, the organizing committee recognized there was no chance that Eleanor Roosevelt would take part. Lerner then telegraphed to request a message of support for the gathering. Six days later, at the conference's midpoint, her reply arrived. She conveyed "every good wish," then stated her position:

> It is hard to say what can be done at the present time, but if you are able to formulate a program of action I am quite sure that the people of this country who have been shocked and horrified by the attitude of the Axis powers toward Jewish people will be more than glad to do all that they can to alleviate the sufferings of these people in Europe and to help them reestablish themselves in other parts of the world if it is possible to evacuate them.[11]

The day after the Emergency Conference ended, Eleanor Roosevelt responded to Michael Potter's letter. She remained unconvinced that practical action was possible, but expressed a willingness to cooperate:

> I think perhaps mass meetings may be of help and the expressions of the feelings that people have may penetrate into the Nazi countries so I do hope that all the agitation possible will go on. I do not see beyond the statements which the President has made, what more emphatically could be said. I will

be glad to say anything or help in any way but I do not think it wise for me to formally go on any committee.[12]

Despite its preliminary problems, the Emergency Conference succeeded beyond most expectations. Fifteen hundred people attended the sessions, held July 20–25 at the Hotel Commodore. An impressive group of participants, many of them non-Jews, met in panels that dealt with such topics as transportation, diplomatic negotiations, military affairs, publicity, and the role of the church. Through three hot days, the panelists worked out rescue plans. Evening sessions, open to the public, featured prominent speakers, including Mayor Fiorello La Guardia, Dean Alfange of the American Labor party, writer Dorothy Parker, and (by radio) Herbert Hoover.[13]

Among others associated with the conference were Harold Ickes, Senators Guy Gillette, Edwin Johnson, William Langer, and Elbert Thomas, labor leaders William Green and Philip Murray, and journalists William Randolph Hearst and William Allen White. Plainly, people of greatly diverging views and backgrounds had come together to try to do something about the European Jewish tragedy.[14]

The Emergency Conference concluded that much could be achieved without hindering the military effort. The key step was formation of a U.S. governmental agency charged specifically with rescuing Jews. Beyond that, the conference called for several types of action. Pressure should be exerted on Axis countries to permit Jews to emigrate. Where emigration did not take place, Axis governments should be pushed to provide Jews with sufficient food and other basic necessities. If need be, the United Nations should furnish the supplies for distribution under Red Cross or other neutral supervision.[15]

Regarding the problem of sanctuaries for Jews, the Emergency Conference recommended urging neutral countries to grant temporary asylum on the understanding that the United Nations would assist with food and arrange for removal of the refugees. In addition, all the United Nations should be pressed to take in Jews on a temporary basis. The conference concluded that the necessary transportation could be obtained without hindering the war effort. It pointed to rail and road traffic through Turkey and out to the Middle East. And it estimated that enough neutral ships were available to move 50,000 refugees at a time. Finally, the participants suggested a campaign to publicize the plight of the European Jews and build popular support for rescue action.

Before adjourning, the conference transformed itself into a new organization, the Emergency Committee to Save the Jewish People of

Europe. The driving force in the new committee was the same Bergson group that had directed the Committee for a Jewish Army.

The planners of the Emergency Conference had arranged its sessions to draw maximum attention to the European Jewish situation. The result was extensive press and radio exposure. Newspapers across the nation published reports on the meetings. Coverage in the New York daily newspapers was especially thorough. The conference also generated several editorials. The most striking, written by Max Lerner, appeared in *PM* under the title "What About the Jews, FDR?" Lerner outlined some of the conference's recommendations, charged that "the State Dept. and Downing St. avert their eyes from the slaughter," and challenged Roosevelt: "You, Mr. President, must take the lead. . . . The methods are clear. Neither conscience nor policy can afford to leave them unused. And the time is now." [16]

The new Emergency Committee soon opened a two-pronged campaign: national publicity and lobbying in Washington. During August and September, the publicity drive revolved around several dramatic newspaper advertisements conveying information about the European Jewish tragedy and urging support for a government rescue agency. The first advertisement, illustrated with a picture of huddled refugees on the move, announced, "They Are Driven To Death Daily, But They *Can* Be Saved." Another proclaimed, "The Jewish people of Europe is still caught between the hammer of the enemy's brutality and the anvil of democracy's indifference." * Next came an open letter from Pierre van Paassen calling on Roosevelt and Churchill to initiate rescue action. Still another large advertisement featured Ben Hecht's "Ballad of the Doomed Jews of Europe." [17]

The campaign to build popular pressure for rescue received substantial help from William Randolph Hearst. In late August, Hearst ordered the thirty-four newspapers in his chain to publish the first of many major editorials supporting the Emergency Committee and appealing for nationwide backing for its proposals. The August editorial included a complete reprint of the Emergency Conference's recommendations. In September, the Hearst papers carried two more editorials advocating the Emergency Committee's rescue plans. [19]

Throughout its existence, Hearst backed the Emergency Committee, giving it more editorial support than any other publisher.† His reasons are not clear. He was probably pleased to find a way to strike at the

* This advertisement commended the formation, a week before, of a government agency to save the art treasures of Europe from wartime destruction. But, it pointed out, the Jews needed an agency to save them too. [18]

† The *New York Post* was also a very strong proponent of the Emergency Committee. [21]

British, if only indirectly. He also seems to have been genuinely concerned about the terrible plight of Europe's Jews. In the editorials, he repeatedly pointed out an essential truth that very many of America's religious and secular leaders never grasped: "REMEMBER, Americans, THIS IS NOT A JEWISH PROBLEM. It is a HUMAN PROBLEM."[20]

The Emergency Committee's connections with Hearst and Hoover illustrated its policy of building the widest possible backing for rescue. The diverse support that had marked the Emergency Conference— conservative and liberal, Jew and non-Jew—carried over into the Emergency Committee. Certainly, numerous important liberals played key roles in the committee's campaigns, such people as Harold Ickes, Dean Alfange, Will Rogers, Jr., Max Lerner, and Fiorello La Guardia.

Along with the publicity drive, the Emergency Committee pressed forward with a lobbying effort in Washington. Responding to Eleanor Roosevelt's offer to "help in any way," Peter Bergson conferred with her in mid-August. The following day, Mrs. Roosevelt's syndicated "My Day" column dealt with the "hardships and persecution" of the Jews in Europe. But it fell short of calling for forceful action: "I do not know what we can do to save the Jews in Europe and to find them homes, but I know that we will be the sufferers if we let great wrongs occur without exerting ourselves to correct them." After the visit, Bergson sent Mrs. Roosevelt a copy of the "Findings and Recommendations of the Emergency Conference" along with a letter stressing again the need for a special government rescue agency. She passed these items to the President, but he was not very interested. He returned them with a note saying, "I do not think this needs any answer at this time. F.D.R."[22]

During her conversation with Bergson, Eleanor Roosevelt agreed to record a message of encouragement to the Jews of Europe for broadcast overseas by the Office of War Information. When Bergson contacted her about arrangements, she asked how long the speech should be. He suggested five to ten minutes and offered to provide whatever material she might wish to have in preparing it. Several days later, Eleanor Roosevelt drafted a comforting message, but it was very short (under two minutes). She explained the brevity in a note to her secretary: "Copy and send. Sorry too busy to write longer one."[23]

The broadcast was a valuable contribution, as the Emergency Committee gratefully acknowledged. It showed, though, that Eleanor Roosevelt had not modified her position on the rescue question. Her views continued to parallel those of the State Department. The message emphasized that "everything possible that can be done through our government" is being done, and stated that "we hope that ways may be found to save as many people as possible, but the best way to do that is

to win the war as rapidly as possible and that the allied armies throughout the world are achieving." *[24]

Emergency Committee efforts to reach the President met blank walls.
The White House refused the first advance, advising that the President's schedule was so crowded that it would be "some time" before
appointments were possible for any matters not "bearing directly on
the war effort." Another attempt, during the Roosevelt-Churchill conference at Quebec in August, also failed. Max Lerner telegraphed presidential secretary Stephen Early in Quebec asking that Roosevelt receive
Congressman Andrew Somers (Dem., N.Y.) and two others from the
Emergency Committee. Early put them off, explaining that a meeting
in Washington after the President's return would be much more pro-
ductive. But, despite numerous follow-up requests, that meeting never
took place.[26]

Approaches to the State Department were frustrating, but not entirely fruitless. In mid-August, Cordell Hull agreed to try to arrange
travel priorities for six Emergency Committee representatives to go to
Turkey, Spain, and Palestine to organize rescue efforts. But he turned
the task over to Breckinridge Long, who insisted there was no need for
these missions. The Intergovernmental Committee was now active, he
asserted; furthermore, the American government was already doing
everything possible.[27]

In the following months, despite Long, the Emergency Committee
managed to send two people overseas. The first, Arieh Ben-Eliezer, was
one of the Bergsonite inner circle. He left for Palestine in September.
Although Ben-Eliezer dealt incidentally with rescue matters, the Bergson group exploited this opportunity primarily to promote Irgun business. Ben-Eliezer found the underground army disorganized, poorly
led, and virtually inactive. He applied himself to its revitalization until
April 1944, when British authorities incarcerated him.†[28]

Long delayed the departure of the other representative for months.
He was Ira Hirschmann, a high executive at Bloomingdale's department
store. Hirschmann, who had some experience in refugee matters, was

---

* After the war, Eleanor Roosevelt's deep concern about those who survived the Holocaust was translated into strong support for the establishment of the state of Israel.[25]

† According to oral testimony, Ben-Eliezer probably carried a small amount of money
to the Irgun.

FBI records show that in March 1945 the bureau thoroughly investigated the Bergson
group in an attempt to locate evidence of an Irgun connection. They found none, but
thought there was a chance that a few hundred dollars had been sent to the Irgun.

While in Palestine, Ben-Eliezer played a key role in the selection of Menachem Begin
as the Irgun's new commander.[29]

prepared to go to Turkey. Although the American ambassador there telegraphed approval in early September, Hirschmann was not allowed to depart until late January.[30]

The Emergency Committee also approached Henry Morgenthau, Jr. Early in August, he told Bergson that he was deeply concerned to help stop the slaughter. But he declined to spearhead a drive to press the Roosevelt administration to act. Bergson wrote to Morgenthau three weeks later, distressed that Emergency Committee discussions with him, Hull, Long, Eleanor Roosevelt, and Attorney General Francis Biddle had won promises of support but no action. "Meanwhile," Bergson pointed out, "weeks pass and many more thousands of innocent Jews in Europe uselessly lose their lives." He appealed to Morgenthau to use his contacts within the government, especially to urge the establishment of a rescue agency. Morgenthau's reply was noncommittal.[31]

The Emergency Conference and the activity that grew out of it seemed to break the quiescence that had gripped the rescue cause since the Bermuda Conference. Pressures began to build again. Reinhold Niebuhr and several other intellectuals urged Roosevelt and Hull to ease the "unnecessarily rigorous restrictions [that] have practically stopped all immigration." The *New Republic* for August 30 included a fifteen-page section entitled "The Jews of Europe: How to Help Them." Its editors once more indicted the Western Allies:

> The failure of the democratic powers to make any sustained and determined effort to stay the tide of slaughter constitutes one of the major tragedies in the history of civilization; and the moral weakness which has palsied the hands of our statesmen is nowhere more vividly disclosed than in the now conventional formula, so often on their lips, that only victory will save the Jews of Europe. Will any of these Jews survive to celebrate victory?

The Church Peace Union called for pressure on Axis satellites to let the Jews go and demanded that room be made for them in the United States, Palestine, and elsewhere. The *Christian Century* also appealed for action and advocated the admission of more refugees to the United States and Palestine.[32]

In September, AFL and CIO leaders saw Hull. They urged that the United Nations take in all Jews who could get out and declare the rest legally prisoners of war. Shortly after that, the AFL annual convention resolved that the United Nations, and specifically the United States, should temporarily suspend immigration restrictions to provide havens for the Jews. This step was a major departure from the AFL's traditional restrictionist stance. In another unusual development, the National Re-

publican Club and the National Democratic Club issued a joint statement calling on Congress to admit 100,000 refugees on condition that
they return to Europe soon after the war.[33]

The renewed impulse for rescue led to another move to test the
waters in Congress. One year earlier, Emanuel Celler had responded to
the mass deportations from France by submitting legislation to set the
quotas aside for refugees fleeing Nazi terror. It got nowhere. Now, in
September 1943, Samuel Dickstein introduced a bill to allow refugees
who would not endanger the public safety to come to the United States
temporarily; they would have to leave within six months after the war.
W. Warren Barbour (Rep., N.J.) sponsored a parallel measure in the
Senate.[34]

The Emergency Committee supported this legislation, as did the
Federal Council of Churches and several leading Jewish organizations.
But the Roosevelt administration did not. The Justice Department and
the Immigration Service declined to take a position on it. And the State
Department opposed the resolution, explaining that it would not help
"the persecuted political and religious minorities" still in Nazi territory,
for they could not reach an American consul to obtain visas. On the
other hand, "the persons who have already arrived at a haven of refuge
do not require American visas to insure their safety." Furthermore, any
relaxation of controls might open the way for Nazi agents to enter the
United States. Neither Dickstein's nor Barbour's proposal ever reached
the floor of Congress.[35]

Even with administration support, this legislation would have encountered great difficulty. The intense anti-immigration feeling that
Congress had demonstrated the year before when it smashed Roosevelt's Third War Powers Bill had not lessened. Evidence of this rever-
berated in the House of Representatives again in June 1943. The issue
was legislation that would have slightly simplified the *naturalization*
procedure for aliens *already living in the United States* who had children
in the American armed forces. It had nothing to do with immigration.
Yet the mere mention of aliens set off a storm of anti-immigration
rhetoric. This mild naturalization bill was overwhelmingly defeated.[36]

Although the Emergency Committee supported the Dickstein-Bar-
bour resolution, it concentrated most of its resources during fall 1943
on an intensive struggle for a government rescue agency. The drive
began with full-page advertisements in the *New York Times* and *Washington Post* announcing a "call to action" on three fronts. One was a
plan to collect millions of signatures on a petition to the President and
Congress. It appealed for a rescue agency and for intervention with
Britain to open Palestine. Simultaneously, a request went out to Chris-

tian churches to set aside Sunday, October 10, as a Day of Intercession, a time to pray for the European Jews and to urge government action to save them. The petition campaign was reasonably successful. The call for a Christian Day of Intercession had little impact.[37]

The third step was a dramatic innovation that the Emergency Committee carried out with cooperation from the Union of Orthodox Rabbis and the Union of Grand Rabbis. On October 6, three days before Yom Kippur, 400 Orthodox rabbis arrived in Washington to participate in a pilgrimage for rescue.[38]

Early in the afternoon, the rabbis, conspicuous with their beards and long black coats, praying aloud, marched in a dignified procession from Union Station to the Capitol. They were met there by Vice-President Henry A. Wallace and a score of congressmen. Some rabbis sobbed audibly as their petition was read in Hebrew and English, then handed to Wallace. It called for a rescue agency and for the nations to open their gates to the stricken Jews. "The Vice President," reported *Time* magazine, "squirmed through a diplomatically minimum answer." His cautious remarks centered on pressing forward to win the war.[39]

At the Lincoln Memorial, in mid-afternoon, the rabbis prayed for America's fighting men, for a speedy victory, and for the remaining European Jews. Afterward, they walked to the White House. There, while most prayed outside the gates, five of their number presented a copy of the petition to presidential secretary Marvin McIntyre, who received it in the President's absence. The pilgrimage then proceeded to a synagogue, where the rabbis rested and ate before departing for their homes.[40]

The Emergency Committee had tried for weeks to arrange for the President to receive the rabbis' petition personally, but the appeals were unavailing. On the day of the pilgrimage, the White House informed the press that the President could not see the rabbis "because of the pressure of other business." In reality, Roosevelt had a light schedule that day, and most of the afternoon was open. Moreover, he was aware that a delegation of rabbis hoped to visit him at four o'clock (or at any time convenient to him). Shortly before the rabbis arrived, Roosevelt slipped away to Bolling Field to observe a ceremony incorporating forty Yugoslavs into the U.S. Army Air Force and dedicating four bombers that they would fly. He then left for a five-day weekend at Hyde Park.[41]

The President's failure to meet the rabbis caused a ripple of criticism. Some observers doubted that a convocation of several hundred Protestant or Catholic clergymen would have been shunted off to a presidential secretary. It is not entirely clear why Roosevelt avoided the rabbis. But two background developments are known. Shortly before the pilgrimage, the President decided that "all requests of this kind from the leaders in Jewry" were to be referred to the secretary of state "to handle for him." Rabbis or no rabbis, rescue was a State Department matter as far as Roosevelt was concerned. Another part of the picture was continued Jewish opposition to the Bergson group. Some Jewish leaders, in cooperation with Samuel Rosenman (who frequently advised the President on Jewish issues), sought to prevent the march, then to influence Roosevelt to ignore it.* [42]

Press coverage of the pilgrimage must have disappointed the Emergency Committee. It was noticeably less than that generated by the "We Will Never Die" pageant and the Emergency Conference. The main Washington newspapers all reported the event, but only the *Post* carried it on the front page. In New York, newspaper coverage was thin. Of the major news magazines, only *Time* mentioned it at all.[44]

During October, the Emergency Committee's campaign began to pick up support in Congress. Senator Elbert D. Thomas (Dem., Utah), a former Mormon missionary to Japan and university professor, sent draft legislation for a rescue commission to Secretary Hull. He asked for an opinion on whether the same end could be accomplished by the simpler device of an executive order. The response, which came from Breckinridge Long, argued at length against the whole idea of a rescue agency.† [45]

William Langer also applied pressure. Addressing the Senate on the day of the rabbis' pilgrimage, he called for a special rescue commission and charged that "by doing nothing we have acquiesced in what has taken place over there." He again emphasized the failure at Bermuda and reminded Scott Lucas that five months had passed since he had promised an early report on the conference. "Where is this report?" asked Langer. "Has anything been done?"[47]

Something *was* done that October for Jews trapped in Europe—but not by the United States, Britain, or the Intergovernmental Committee. The 8,000 Jews in Denmark escaped to life and freedom because Danes

* Jewish congressmen tried to dissuade the rabbis from participating in the pilgrimage. But the effort went awry when Sol Bloom argued that it would be undignified for such an un-American-looking group to appear in Washington. This provoked the rabbis and reinforced their decision to take part.[43]
† Long invoked the achievements of the Evian and Bermuda conferences, claimed again that the State Department had issued half a million visas to refugees, pointed to a special committee for refugee problems that operated within the Visa Division, and stressed the work of the Intergovernmental Committee. The conclusion: a new refugee agency "would interrupt the relationships already established with the Intergovernmental Committee and might affect adversely the contribution this Government can make towards a solution of the refugee problem."[46]

were willing to risk their lives for them and the Swedish government was willing to incur Germany's wrath to give them sanctuary.[48]

The Emergency Committee was quick to underscore the lesson. In advertisements in the *New York Times* and other newspapers, it declared that Denmark and Sweden had "destroyed completely the legend that 'nothing can be done.' " If the gates of Palestine and other lands would open too, thousands more would save themselves. The Emergency Committee also sponsored a "Salute to Sweden and Denmark," a mass meeting that overflowed Carnegie Hall in New York. Speaking there, Leon Henderson, former head of the Office of Price Administration, accused the Allied governments, and especially Roosevelt and Churchill, of "moral cowardice" for failing to counter the extermination of the Jews. He charged that the problem had been "avoided, submerged, postponed, played down and resisted with all the forms of political force available to powerful governments."[49]

As Henderson spoke, the Moscow Conference of American, British, and Russian foreign ministers neared adjournment. A few days afterward, a reporter asked Roosevelt whether the conference had taken action to aid "Jewish victims of atrocities or persecution." The President replied:

> That I don't know. I won't be able to tell you that until I see Mr. Hull, because that is, as you know, that whole problem is—the heart's all right— it's a question of ways and means.

In fact, the issue of the European Jews was not on the Moscow Conference's lengthy agenda, and it did not come up in the two weeks of discussions. Even the stern war-crimes warning that emerged from the conference failed to mention the Jews. Yet it named several other peoples and threatened dire punishment for atrocities against them.* [50]

The Emergency Committee struck back with an advertisement by Ben Hecht, which it ran in several major newspapers under the title "My Uncle Abraham Reports."

> I have an Uncle who is a Ghost. . . .
> He was elected last April by the Two Million Jews who have been murdered by the Germans to be their World Delegate.

---

* In mid-November, Hull made a twenty-five minute speech to Congress on the Moscow Conference. It included a feeble attempt to rectify the omission of the Jews from the war-crimes warning. In his brief reference to the warning, he noted that the "bestial and abominable" Nazi crimes had been perpetrated "against people of all races and religions, among whom Hitler has reserved for the Jews his most brutal wrath."[51]

Wherever there are Conferences on how to make the World a Better Place, maybe, my Uncle Abraham appears and sits on the window sill and takes notes. . . .

Last night my Uncle Abraham was back in a Certain Place where the Two Million murdered Jews met. . . .

"Dishonored dead," said my Uncle Abraham, ". . . of the Moscow Conference I have this to report. The Conference made a promise that the world was going to punish the Germans for murdering all the different peoples of Europe—Czechs, Greeks, Serbs, Russians, French hostages, Polish officers, Cretan peasants. Only we were not mentioned." . . .

"In the Kremlin in Moscow, in the White House in Washington, in the Downing Street Building in London where I have sat on the window sills, I have never heard our name. The people who live in those buildings— Stalin, Roosevelt and Churchill—do not speak of us. Why, I don't know. . . ."

A Woman Ghost from the Dynamite Dumps of Odessa spoke.

"If they didn't mention the two million murdered Jews in the Conference, isn't that bad for four million who are still alive? The Germans will think that when they kill Jews, Stalin, Roosevelt and Churchill pretend nothing is happening."

And from the Two Million Ghosts came a great cry. . . .

My Uncle Abraham raised his hand.

"Little Children," my Uncle Abraham spoke: "Be patient. We will be dead a long time. Yesterday when we were killed we were changed from Nobodies to Nobodies. Today, on our Jewish tomb, there is not the Star of David, there is an Asterisk. But, who knows, maybe Tomorrow—!"

This ended the Meeting of the Jewish Underground.

My Uncle Abraham has gone to the White House in Washington. He is sitting on the window sill two feet away from Mr. Roosevelt. But he has left his notebook behind.[52]

Shortly after the Uncle Abraham advertisement appeared, the Bergsonites made their most crucial move. In the three months since the Emergency Conference, they had been pressing the need for a rescue agency on members of Congress. By November, they had won some powerful backing. On the ninth, resolutions were introduced in the Senate by Guy Gillette and eleven others and in the House by Will Rogers, Jr., and Joseph C. Baldwin. These identical measures urged the President to create "a commission of diplomatic, economic, and military experts" to act immediately to save the remaining Jews of Europe. At a press conference launching the Rescue Resolution, the Emergency Committee emphasized that the new commission should set up camps as quickly as possible in Spain, Portugal, North Africa, Switzerland, Sweden, and Turkey. That action would insure that all Jews who reached those countries would be allowed to enter. In time, they could be moved to Palestine or other United Nations territory.[53]

The next afternoon, Roosevelt told Undersecretary of State Edward R. Stettinius, Jr., that he thought more could be done for Jewish refugees.* The President suggested additional refugee camps and small offices staffed by Americans in Spain, Portugal, North Africa, Italy, and Turkey. This marked Roosevelt's first initiative to help the stricken Jews.[54]

Apparently, the Emergency Committee had forced the issue on the President. Samuel Rosenman, his chief speech writer, and Eleanor Roosevelt both noticed that the large advertisements were disturbing him. The President complained that the Uncle Abraham one in particular had hit below the belt. He was surely aware that the Rescue Resolution had significant backing in Congress. His suggestion to Stettinius was amazingly similar to the one made a day earlier by the Emergency Committee. Perhaps Roosevelt was moving at last to confront the extermination issue. Or perhaps he was maneuvering to cut the ground from under the Rescue Resolution.[55]

The day after he spoke with Stettinius, the President left for the conferences at Cairo and Tehran. In his absence, the State Department demolished his refugee plan by detouring it to the Intergovernmental Committee on Refugees. The ICR pondered it for six weeks, agreed to a truncated version, and then did not act for another four months. The final outcome was the double fiasco of Heathcote-Smith and Valentin-Smith.[56]

The State Department had nullified Roosevelt's initial response to the new round of pressure for rescue. His next move on that front would come only when events forced it on him, in January 1944. Then, however, the State Department would be powerless to sidetrack it.

---

* Stettinius had replaced Welles as undersecretary in September 1943.

|| 9 ||

THE ZIONISTS

———————

Most appeals for rescue included the call for opening the gates of Palestine. The 550,000 Jews there constituted the only society on earth willing to take in masses of Jewish refugees. But the British government, which held the mandate over Palestine, had all but closed it to Jewish immigration in 1939. Arab anger and fear, aroused by the growth of the Jewish population there since World War I, had erupted in a series of riots. To allay Arab unrest and thus protect their own long-term interests in the Middle East, the British issued a White Paper in May 1939. It restricted future Jewish immigration to 75,000, to be spread over the next five years. This would limit the Jews to one-third of Palestine's population, assuring Arabs that no Jewish state would arise there.[1]

The European war broke out soon afterward, and with it Nazi persecution of Europe's Jews intensified. This did not, however, bring any easing of White Paper restrictions. Instead, the war strengthened British determination to minimize Jewish immigration to Palestine. Unrest there or elsewhere in the Moslem world could hamper military operations, threaten supply lines, and drain off British troops to maintain order. The British realized that the Jews could not turn against them.

The Arabs might. So British policy called for appeasing the Arabs, even though that meant excluding imperiled Jews from the national home the British had promised them in the Balfour Declaration of 1917.[2]

Once the White Paper was imposed, ship after ship of desperate Jews was turned away from Palestine. Sometimes boatloads of refugees did reach shore, only to be interned indefinitely, as were 800 fugitives from Rumanian butchery who arrived on the *Darien* in March 1941. A few months before, 1,600 refugees "illegally" landed from the *Atlantic* were deported to Mauritius, 4,500 miles away in the Indian Ocean. A few of these rickety ships disappeared en route to Palestine; the *Salvador,* for instance, sank in the Sea of Marmara, dooming 200 refugees.[3]

To avoid risking Arab animosity, and to make the 75,000 openings last as long as possible, the British intentionally kept the White Paper quota undersubscribed.* By October 1943 (four and one-half years into the White Paper's five-year tenure), 31,000 places (over 40 percent) remained unused.[4]

An incident in early 1942 brought the consequences of the White Paper policy sharply to the world's attention. Crowded onto a small vessel, the *Struma,* 769 Jews fled Rumania for Palestine in December 1941. But they had no Palestine entry certificates. They soon reached Turkey and apparent safety; however, the boat's engine quit there and could not be repaired. For two months, the refugees waited off Istanbul, their fate in the balance. The Turkish government refused to let them land without assurance that they could proceed to Palestine. And British administrators, quietly determined not to encourage any more "shiploads of unwanted Jews," forbade their entry there. Despite the captain's insistence that the *Struma* was unseaworthy, Turkish authorities had it towed out of port in late February 1942. Once on the open sea, the crippled boat was torpedoed or struck a mine and broke up. Only one person survived the wreck.†[6]

The *Struma* disaster brought outraged reactions in Britain and the United States. Albert Einstein asserted that the episode "strikes at the

---

* The British tactics were similar to the State Department's visa-control methods. Groups of Jews coming from Axis-controlled territory were excluded on the grounds that they were likely to be infiltrated with enemy agents. (No such agents were ever found, nor did the British have evidence that there were any.) Moreover, Palestine entry certificates were issued only through normal channels, making it almost impossible for escapees to receive them.[5]

† It is quite possible that a Russian submarine torpedoed the *Struma.* A Soviet military report credited the sinking to the submarine Shch-213, noting that three of its crew "particularly distinguished themselves" in the action. Later the Russians insisted that the *Struma*'s passengers were Nazi agents being infiltrated into the Middle East.[7]

heart of our civilization." Eleanor Roosevelt asked why technicalities should keep such people out of Palestine when the tiny quota was not even filled; "it just seems to me cruel beyond words." Responding to widespread criticism, the British Colonial Office explained that, since the refugees had come out of Axis territory, Nazi agents might have been planted among them. It added that supplies were short in Palestine.[8]

The prominent British historian and Zionist Lewis Namier quickly pointed out that the passengers could have been interned in Palestine and checked before release. He also noted that Polish, Yugoslav, Czech, and Greek non-Jewish refugees had been admitted to Palestine from Axis territory. A confidential memorandum by the British Foreign Office more closely approached the truth concerning the exclusion of the *Struma* refugees: to bypass the system of "regularized admission" of Jews to Palestine "would involve a risk of dangerous repercussions on the non-Jewish populations of the Middle East."[9]

Secretly, however, the British decided to modify the policy and permit refugee ships that reached Palestine in the future to land. The passengers would go to detainment camps for security investigation, then be freed gradually against the quota. The order had to be kept confidential, the policymakers claimed; otherwise the Germans would send not only Nazi agents but "every kind of unwanted person" from the Balkans to Palestine. Obviously, the real reason was somewhat different: general knowledge of the new ruling would have encouraged many thousands of Jews to escape to Palestine. The British, who were constantly in fear of such an exodus, had built their refugee policy around keeping that from happening. The State Department quietly but completely supported Britain's Palestine policy.[10]

More than a year later, another special arrangement initiated by British authorities exemplified their extreme care to avoid stimulating refugee flight even as they bent a little to pressures for a more humane policy. It specified that Jews who managed to reach Turkey would be allowed into Palestine. (There they would be put through a security check and counted against the White Paper quota.) The arrangement was revealed only to the Jewish Agency for Palestine (which distributed Palestine entry certificates), the State Department, and the Turkish government. No public announcement was permitted. The modification in policy brought an end to Turkey's persistent refusal to let escaped Jews enter its territory. But the lack of publicity guaranteed that the concession would help only a very small number of refugees.[11]

American Jewish organizations fought the White Paper from the start. All groups, including those opposed to Zionism, agreed that Pal-

estine must be opened to Jewish refugees. But an acrimonious controversy divided American Jewry on the question of establishment of a
Jewish state in Palestine. And this disagreement prevented both a
united struggle against the White Paper and a combined Jewish movement to press the American government for rescue action. The cleavage
proved unbridgeable largely because Zionists insisted that the statehood issue was inseparable from either the White Paper issue or the
rescue problem.[12]

Several Zionist leaders had been in the forefront of the pre–Bermuda
Conference attempts to publicize the mass killings and to stir the government into action. Yet during those months the Zionist movement
had concentrated its main efforts on the cause of a Jewish state. The
overall strategy, initiated months before the news of extermination became known, aimed at building maximum support in the United States
—as rapidly as possible—for a postwar Jewish state in Palestine. The
haste arose from the Zionists' perception that their best opportunity for
decades to come would materialize right after the war. The fluidity in
international affairs that would emerge then would very likely reopen
the status of Palestine. The Zionist movement had to be ready to wield
all the influence it could when the postwar diplomatic settlements were
made. Other factors that had led to increased Zionist activity in 1942
and 1943 were the disturbing consequences of the White Paper and
early reports from Europe of mass atrocities against Jews.[13]

The first step toward maximizing American Zionist influence was to
persuade the several competing Zionist factions to agree on a single
policy. This was achieved at the Biltmore Conference in New York in
May 1942. The formula, known as the Biltmore Program, called for the
end of the White Paper, unlimited Jewish immigration into Palestine,
and the establishment of Palestine as a Jewish commonwealth.* [14]

Zionism at that time was still a minority movement among American
Jews. Thus, immediately after the Biltmore Conference, plans went
forward for the second step: to marshal American Jewry as a whole
behind the Zionist program. The method chosen was to call all American Jewish organizations to a conference to work out a common program for the postwar problems of world Jewry. American Jews could
then present a united front at the peace negotiations. Because non-
Zionist organizations most likely would not respond to a Zionist initiative for such a conference, Zionist leaders, headed by Chaim Weizmann

* This was the first time the American Zionist movement had explicitly advocated a
Jewish state in Palestine. It constituted a fundamental shift from the previous position,
which had accepted indefinite postponement of the statehood goal while concentrating
on building up the Jewish community in Palestine.[15]

and Stephen Wise, persuaded Henry Monsky, the president of B'nai B'rith, to issue the invitations. Monsky was popular and respected among American Jews generally, and B'nai B'rith was considered neutral on the question of political Zionism. Monsky's chances of convening the conference were thus very good, and his personal pro-Zionist views could only help the cause.* [16]

Thirty-two national Jewish organizations accepted Monsky's invitation to send representatives to a pre-conference planning meeting in Pittsburgh in January 1943. Two did not. The American Jewish Committee and the Jewish Labor Committee, suspicious of Zionist motives and determined not to aid Zionist goals, refused to participate. Weeks of negotiations and pressure from the Jewish community induced them to support the conference. But the Labor Committee joined with misgivings, and the American Jewish Committee entered only after it was agreed that resolutions voted by the conference would not be binding on constituent organizations unless they also ratified them. [18]

Toward the end of May, the official conference call was issued. It stressed the importance of "common action to deal with post-war Jewish problems" and set dates for the elections of delegates. The agenda, which had been decided at the Pittsburgh meeting, had two key items: "the rights and status of Jews in the post-war world" and "implementation of the rights of the Jewish people with respect to Palestine." Rescue was not on the program. [19]

Through the late spring and summer of 1943, much of American Jewry turned its attention to the elections and other preparations for the convocation, now named the American Jewish Conference. During this time, the rescue issue was eclipsed, partly by this rechanneling of interest and partly because these were the weeks of despair that followed the Bermuda Conference. An article in June in a Zionist periodical reflected the shift: "The world at large replies to our protests and prayers and dramatizations only with resolutions and expressions of sympathy—never with deeds." "What can the Jew do now?" asked the writer. He supplied the answer himself: Jews must unite at the American Jewish Conference and demand Jewish postwar rights, especially in Palestine. [20]

Of the conference's 500 delegates, 125 were allotted to the sixty-five

---

* The small meeting at which Monsky agreed to act as convener took place during the first burst of activity following release of the extermination news. It was held December 2, 1942, the Day of Mourning and Prayer. Against that background, an outside observer might have expected the main issue under consideration to have been rescue. It was not. The focus was on postwar problems, with the major emphasis on Palestine. [17]

national organizations that finally participated. The rest were chosen by a complex system of local elections designed to provide the conference with a broadly representative character. If any doubt existed that the conference was essentially an endeavor to prove American Jewish support for the Biltmore Program, it was dispelled by the all-out election drives mounted by the Zionist organizations. Most of them agreed on joint slates of delegates for whom Zionists voted in blocs, thus defeating candidates with less thoroughly organized support. Zionist campaign rhetoric called for election of the maximum number of Zionist candidates because the main action at the conference would occur on the Palestine statehood issue and it was essential to show that American Jews were united in supporting that goal. The Zionists were extremely successful in the elections; 80 percent of the delegates were "avowed Zionists," and few of the others were outright opponents of Zionism.[21]

Some complaints were raised about the representativeness of the elections. But more important dissension arose over the allotment of the 125 delegate slots that went to the various organizations. Both Agudath Israel of America and the Union of Orthodox Rabbis withdrew from the conference before it convened, declaring that they had been granted unfairly small numbers of delegates.[22]

Another key reason for the disenchantment of these two ultra-Orthodox, non-Zionist organizations was the American Jewish Conference's continuing failure to place rescue on the agenda. As far back as the Pittsburgh meeting, Agudath Israel had unsuccessfully urged concentration on rescue as well as on postwar issues. In its withdrawal statement, the Union of Orthodox Rabbis declared that the conference should raise a "powerful outcry over the destruction of the Jewish people and demand immediate means for the rescue of Jewish lives." Rescue was added to the agenda only in late July, a month before the conference met, and then only after persistent hammering by the Jewish Labor Committee. Even then, the conference's executive committee turned down a Labor Committee appeal to make the extermination of the European Jews the central issue.[23]

The American Jewish Conference took place at the Waldorf-Astoria Hotel in New York from August 29 through September 2, 1943. At the main sessions, audiences of up to 3,000 joined the 500 delegates. As expected, the Palestine issue dominated the proceedings. Convinced of the importance of winning united Jewish support for the conference's resolutions, Stephen Wise, Nahum Goldmann, James Heller, and a few other leading Zionists planned to press for a moderate position on Palestine. They recognized that all groups, including the influential American Jewish Committee, could agree on a demand to abolish the

White Paper and open Palestine to unlimited Jewish immigration. Though fully committed to the Biltmore Program themselves, they believed the controversial Jewish commonwealth idea could wait for a later reconvening of the conference.[24]

The first speeches by Zionists stressed unity and reflected a moderate approach to the Palestine question. Two important addresses by non-Zionists—Joseph Proskauer of the American Jewish Committee and Israel Goldberg of the Jewish Labor Committee—harmonized with the Zionists' attempts at accommodation. All these speakers emphasized their agreement on the need to end the White Paper and open the gates of Palestine.[25]

By the second evening of the conference, the compromise forces seemed to have established control. But militant Zionists managed at the last minute to add Dr. Abba Hillel Silver's name to the speakers' list for late that night. Seizing the unforeseen opportunity, Silver delivered a stirring pro-statehood address that galvanized the delegates into fervent support for the full Biltmore position. A flood of pent-up emotion, swollen by over a year of terrible news from Europe, broke loose and swept through the hall. As Silver finished, the huge crowd rose to its feet shouting and cheering. "Hatikvah," the Zionist anthem, filled the air and many wept.[26]

Silver, then fifty years old, was the rabbi of an important Reform congregation in Cleveland. He was also the chairman of the United Palestine Appeal, a co-chairman of the United Jewish Appeal, and a major force in the American Emergency Committee for Zionist Affairs. A powerful orator and astute political strategist, he was probably the most militant of the front echelon of American Zionist leaders. By the time of the conference, he was engaged in a power struggle that would eventually see him supplant Stephen Wise as the leader of American Zionism. Silver had not participated in the Jewish leadership's efforts for government rescue action.[27]

In his speech that night, Silver insisted on a Jewish commonwealth in Palestine. He scorned "the thick blanket of appeals to Jewish unity" as an attempt to hide the basic problem, Jewish national homelessness. It was Jewish homelessness, he declared, that was "the principal source of our millennial tragedy," the unbroken line of disasters from the start of the Dispersion until, now, the frightful Nazi onslaught. "The only solution is to normalize the political status of the Jewish people in the world by giving it a national basis in its national and historic home. . . . Are we forever to live a homeless people on the world's crumbs of sympathy, forever in need of defenders, forever doomed to thoughts of refugees and relief?" As for the pressing problem of rescue, Silver asserted that open immigration into Palestine would not come unless Jewish political rights to the country were recognized. "Our right to immigration in the last analysis is predicated upon the right to build the Jewish Commonwealth in Palestine. They are inter-linked and inseparable." The conclusion was evident: no solution existed, now or for the future, except through the Jewish commonwealth.[28]

The conference's Palestine Committee, responsible for recommending a resolution to the full body, first met on the day after Silver's address. A compromise proposal was put forward, but the delegates had no patience for compromise, and only a few moderates were bold enough to press for it. One of them, Robert P. Goldman, a longtime Zionist from Cincinnati, disagreed with Silver's analysis. He insisted that the Palestine issue involved both an immediate problem and a long-range problem, and the immediate problem was not Jewish homelessness.

> The immediate problem, ladies and gentlemen, is rescue; and I don't care what else you say or how you characterize it, or what you say about me for saying it, that is the immediate problem and that is the problem that we should be concerned with.

Goldman warned that the demand for a commonwealth would hurt the rescue effort because it would only harden British and Arab resistance to Jewish immigration into Palestine. And it would do nothing to save the European Jews.[29]

The Palestine Committee was not impressed by Goldman's appeal or by the few other voices that pleaded for compromise. By a vote of sixty-one to two, it recommended a strong resolution that called for the reconstitution of Palestine as the Jewish commonwealth, the immediate withdrawal of the White Paper, and the opening of Palestine to unlimited Jewish immigration under Jewish control. The next day, the full conference adopted the resolution with only four negative votes and nineteen abstentions. Again, a tumultuous demonstration broke out in the auditorium, and the delegates and the audience sang "Hatikvah" and "The Star Spangled Banner."[30]

No such interest attended the conference's second main issue, Jewish rights in the postwar world generally. Resolutions were passed calling for an international bill of political and cultural rights, international agreements outlawing anti-Semitism, and postwar relief and rehabilitation of the European Jews. But, as a leading Jewish magazine noted, most delegates looked on this area as "a rather academic matter" and "fully relied on the work done by the experts."[31]

The third main issue, rescue, received little more attention. The conference had done no preparatory work on the rescue problem. Its Rescue Committee, which was not convened until halfway through the sessions, decided it could not formulate a program on such short notice. So, instead of plans for action, it discussed the proper contents of a resolution. This, despite the admonition by a leader of the World Jewish Congress that "unless we do our job, there may be no Jews for whom a postwar scheme of things is necessary."[32]

Some committee members were disappointed and upset. A woman delegate from Minnesota expressed their frustration:

> If it is just a question of taking all the programs that have been presented on this subject before, by other groups, and by existing committees, and of taking ideas that we know already exist, and simply getting them into a draft form, there is no need to bring us here from all parts of the United States.

And a man from Chicago added:

> We are told that nothing has to be done, that everything is being done. . . . Ladies and gentlemen, the mere fact that a committee that organized this Conference was forced by pressure of Jewish public opinion to put this rescue question on the agenda speaks for itself, that the Jews of America have felt that not enough . . . was done to rescue our brethren in Europe. . . . If we leave this Conference . . . satisfied merely with a paper resolution about rescue, we will be condemned by the Jews of America.[33]

In the end, a paper resolution was what emerged. It was no more than a weaker version of the proposals the Joint Emergency Committee had sent to Bermuda. The American Jewish Conference adopted it unanimously. Before it adjourned, the conference elected an Interim Committee of fifty-five people to press for action on its resolutions, attend to other necessary business, and reconvene the full assembly within twelve months.[34]

The Zionists had triumphed. A representative assembly that included nearly all segments of American Jewry had overwhelmingly ratified the Biltmore Program. Louis Levinthal, president of the Zionist Organization of America, hailed the outcome as "the culmination of almost a half-century of Zionist activity in this country."[35]

While in session, the conference dominated the pages of the Yiddish daily papers. For the most part, they were enthusiastically favorable, especially toward the Palestine resolution. But within a week doubts surfaced. For example, Dr. Samuel Margoshes, an ardent Zionist and a conference participant, pointed in his column in the *Day* to the lack of emphasis on rescue, describing it as "the most serious sin of omission of the Conference." David Eidelsberg of the *Morning Journal,* a Zionist and a staunch supporter of the Palestine resolution, was disturbed that the Palestine issue had eclipsed the rescue problem. "After all," he wrote, "the first task should be to save the Jews for whom Palestine is needed." He asserted that "by waiting till the last moment to discuss this question and by passing stereotyped resolutions, the leaders of the conference gave a signal to the powerful [governmental] ministries that nothing can be done and that we have to wait till the war is over." [36]

Not two months after the delegates dispersed, the fragile unity of the American Jewish Conference began to crumble. The American Jewish Committee withdrew, declaring that it could not support the demand for a Jewish commonwealth. This loss was critical. The American Jewish Committee was too significant a force on the American Jewish scene for the conference to be effective without it.* B'nai B'rith and four other organizations cooperated with the conference only partially, holding back on endorsement of the Palestine statement. (Stephen Wise described B'nai B'rith as "having one foot in and one foot out" of the conference.) And the anti-Zionist Jewish Labor Committee gave only tepid support before quitting the conference altogether, in December 1944.[37]

The Zionist victory had come at a high price. It ended the possibility of cooperation with the non-Zionist, ultra-Orthodox groups. And it eliminated or weakened the involvement of other important organizations. In addition, in many local Jewish communities it reawakened old Zionist versus non-Zionist animosities that had been dormant.[39]

A Louisville rabbi asserted that the American Jewish Conference had

> wrecked Jewish unity in the United States. We were getting pretty close to harmony and genuine whole-hearted cooperation all over the country. We all wanted maximum help for Jews everywhere and were getting it. Was it imperative that just now the Jewish Commonwealth idea should have been pressed and everything else made secondary to it?

From St. Louis, a longtime Zionist who had been a delegate in New York replied to a funds appeal from the conference's headquarters,

* The American Jewish Committee lacked the broad-based organizational structure needed for many types of political action. But it had important contacts in many cities and access to high levels in the government. It could also raise considerable funds. It applied these strengths to the effort for rescue only to a small extent.[38]

"You say you are in a precarious position. So are we." Because of the Zionist action at the conference, he explained, "the American Jewish community is now split wide open. . . . I was one of the few . . . who pleaded for unity. . . . But my voice was unheeded." A prominent leader of Reform Judaism analyzed the conference's impact in mid-1944 and concluded that "American Jewry has never been more bitterly divided than it is today." He noted that many organizations were dissipating energy and funds fighting each other. These disputes had, in turn, set off strife in local communities.[40]

The conference's Interim Committee did not meet until six weeks after the delegates went home, thereby losing the interest and momentum built at the New York sessions. When it did convene, it elected three leading Zionists as its co-chairmen: Stephen Wise, Henry Monsky, and Israel Goldstein. It also put the conference on a semipermanent basis by establishing commissions on postwar Jewish rights, rescue, and Palestine. Actually, the commissions were little more than a means of affixing the prestigious label of an apparently broadly representative Jewish organization onto activities that Zionist committees already had under way.[41]

About all the Commission on Post-War Reconstruction did was issue a few statements concerning restoration of Jewish rights in Europe and a proposed international bill of rights. The statements were slightly revised versions of ones developed by the pro-Zionist World Jewish Congress and its subsidiary, the Institute of Jewish Affairs. The activities of the Commission on Rescue were essentially only a relabeling of the limited steps taken by the American Jewish Congress–World Jewish Congress partnership in the area of rescue. The Commission on Palestine was never more than a rubber stamp for the American Zionist Emergency Council, the political-action arm of the leading Zionist organizations.[42]

The conference's approach to rescue had its peculiarities. Two months elapsed between the New York meeting and the first actions related to rescue. Yet recent information from Switzerland had made Jewish leaders acutely aware, once again, of the ongoing devastation of the European Jews.* When the conference finally did address the rescue issue, two of its first steps were attacks on Bergsonite activities, and a third was elimination of the Joint Emergency Committee.

* A report, received in August from Riegner and Lichtheim, advised that the Jewish death toll had reached 4 million. Excluding those safe behind Russian lines, Riegner and Lichtheim estimated that no more than 1.5 to 2 million Jews remained alive in continental Europe. And the slaughter was continuing without letup.[43]

At the end of October, conference officials appointed a small committee to investigate the Bergson-led Emergency Committee to Save the Jewish People of Europe. The objective was to prepare a public statement exposing and condemning it. That statement was released to the press late in December, at a critical stage in the Emergency Committee's campaign for congressional action on the Rescue Resolution.[44]

During the same weeks, the American Jewish Conference interfered with the Rescue Resolution itself. First, Stephen Wise and Herman Shulman pressed leading senators to replace it with legislation more agreeable to the conference's leadership. When that failed, conference officials attempted to have an amendment concerning Palestine attached to the resolution. After that fell through, they worked behind the scenes to frustrate the legislation.[45]

In the fall of 1943, American Jewish Conference leaders also snuffed out the Joint Emergency Committee on European Jewish Affairs. A month after the Bermuda Conference, the Joint Emergency Committee had met under a cloud of despair. It had appealed one more time to Sumner Welles for rescue action; his reply was noncommittal. In the next four months, only two more meetings took place. One was held in mid-July, after Jacob Pat of the Jewish Labor Committee protested the JEC's inertia. Although several suggestions were put forward then, no action resulted. In mid-August, the shocking report from Switzerland brought the group together again. It agreed on a number of moves, including approaches to the papal legate in Washington and Archbishop Francis J. Spellman of New York, and a message to President Roosevelt urging several rescue steps. These overtures achieved nothing. The meeting also discussed a march on Washington, a mass demonstration in the streets of New York, and warnings to the Roosevelt administration of large-scale defections of Jewish voters in the 1944 election if rescue action was not initiated soon. But these "more forceful" plans were referred to a committee on programs that did not then exist and was apparently never set up.[46]

Even that late, the Joint Emergency Committee might have been revived. But it desperately needed a secretariat or some other apparatus to implement its plans. Lack of such machinery had always hobbled its efforts. An early decision to appoint an executive secretary and establish an office had never been carried out.* After the Bermuda Conference,

* One crucial reason for the failure to set up an office was interagency rivalry. The American Jewish Congress quietly discouraged the move from the start, out of concern that a fully functioning Joint Emergency Committee might be exploited by the American Jewish Committee to increase its own prestige and influence. Moreover, the Amer-

the Jewish Labor Committee pressed stubbornly for the formation of an administrative structure, but the step was continually deferred and died by default.[47]

When the Joint Emergency Committee convened again, three weeks after the American Jewish Conference's New York meeting, Zionist members tried to terminate it. They argued that the conference should now take responsibility for the united rescue effort. This first move to disband failed. At the next meeting, early in November, Stephen Wise proposed that the JEC dissolve itself and merge with the conference's Rescue Commission. Four of the JEC's eight organizations were decidedly non-Zionist. They strongly desired to continue the committee because it made cooperative efforts for rescue possible without working through the Zionist-dominated American Jewish Conference. Under normal circumstances, the vote would have been a four-to-four tie, and the motion to dissolve would have failed. But in a surprise maneuver, Hadassah—which had appealed for a place on the Joint Emergency Committee many months before and had been turned down—received voting rights and provided a fifth Zionist vote.* The JEC was eliminated. Only one of the non-Zionist organizations affiliated with the conference's Rescue Commission. The united front on rescue was finished.[49]

The Rescue Commission did not attempt actual rescue or relief work, but aimed at stimulating government action through publicity and direct contact with State Department and other officials.† Its contribution was very limited, consisting mainly of participation in projects that the World Jewish Congress and the American Jewish Congress would otherwise have carried out on their own. About all the Rescue Commission could point to in its eighteen-month existence were a mass meeting in Carnegie Hall to commemorate the first anniversary of the Warsaw ghetto revolt, and an impressive outdoor demonstration in New York

---

ican Jewish Committee might put the JEC forward as a replacement for the then-forming American Jewish Conference.[48]

* Hadassah was the women's Zionist organization. Actually, it was already represented on the JEC through the American Zionist Emergency Council, of which it was a member.

† To associate itself with overseas rescue and relief, the Rescue Commission tried to establish close ties with the American Jewish Joint Distribution Committee. But the JDC refused to be linked to the conference.[51]

Although the American Jewish Conference had no role in rescue operations, various other Zionist groups were responsible for the larger part of the rescue activity that was carried out in Europe. Among the most effective were units of the Jewish Agency for Palestine, the World Jewish Congress, and the Hechaluz (labor Zionists). The JDC and some Orthodox committees were also importantly involved in rescue efforts.

in July 1944 to demand government action to save the Hungarian Jews.[50]

The conference's Palestine Commission was headed by Abba Hillel Silver, who also directed the American Zionist Emergency Council, a political-action committee working to implement the Biltmore Program. With the support of the conference's top leadership, Silver planned only one use for the Palestine Commission: to furnish the imprimatur of the American Jewish Conference for the AZEC's activities. AZEC minutes recorded Silver's expectation that, by utilizing the American Jewish Conference, "a good deal of our propaganda for the Jewish Commonwealth can be carried on not only in our name but in the name of American Jewry." The AZEC, discussing practical applications of this approach, decided that "the work [was] to be done by the Emergency Council and turned over to the Conference when representations to [the] Government were to be made." Moreover, in general, "the Conference should be used as the vehicle for public expression and public relations."[52]

In early 1944, the Jewish Labor Committee, hoping to join the fight against the White Paper without participating in the campaign for Jewish statehood, asked the conference's Interim Committee to divide the Palestine Commission into subcommittees. One would lead a united movement against the White Paper and for unlimited refugee immigration into Palestine; the other would carry on the Zionist drive for a Jewish commonwealth. Earlier, a similar suggestion had been submitted by a nonpartisan group within the conference. The Interim Committee refused, explaining that the two issues were too closely linked to be separated. Thus an opportunity was missed to broaden the struggle to end the White Paper, a rescue step that all Jewish groups could support.[53]

The victory at the American Jewish Conference in New York had completed the Zionist campaign to commit American Jewry to the Biltmore Program. The next objective was to win the backing of the American people and their government. Starting in September 1943, American Zionists poured large amounts of energy into that struggle, and they continued to do so until the Jewish state was won. Pivotal in the movement to build non-Jewish support, both in local communities and in Washington, was the American Zionist Emergency Council.[54]

Serving as the public-relations and political-action arm of the American Zionist movement, the AZEC attained a level of effectiveness seldom surpassed in American pressure-group politics. After struggling through four years of inadequate funding and excessive interference from its parent organizations, the AZEC was revitalized in the late summer of 1943.* It was reorganized; its funding leaped from $100,000 a year to over $500,000; it changed its name (from American Emergency Committee for Zionist Affairs); and, most important, Abba Hillel Silver took the helm.[55]

A driving worker and an outstanding organizer, Silver rapidly created an efficient organization. In contrast to Wise and several other leaders, he saw little advantage in pleading with Roosevelt (whom he distrusted) and other high officials for their support. He believed in building public opinion and using it to apply pressure to both political parties without becoming committed to either.[56]

Under Silver, the AZEC developed over 400 local councils, directed by volunteer leaders. They were situated in all major American communities. While the national office coordinated their operations and supplied them with information, the locals conducted a great variety of educational and political programs. They cultivated relations with their congressmen and senators as well as with local political leaders. They organized forums, provided speakers for Jewish and non-Jewish groups, obtained favorable editorials in the local press, mounted rallies, and when necessary sent deputations to Washington.[57]

These local councils secured pro-Zionist resolutions from scores of city governments, dozens of state legislatures, large numbers of Jewish organizations, and thousands of non-Jewish groups, including churches, labor unions, business federations, and fraternal associations. On short notice from the AZEC national office, the locals were able to rain letters and telegrams on Congress, the White House, and the State Department, from non-Jews as well as Jews. Politicians expressed astonishment at the amount of public interest shown. By the fall of 1944, three-quarters of the members of both the Senate and the House were on record in support of establishment of a Jewish commonwealth.†[58]

---

* Its sponsoring organizations were the Zionist Organization of America, Hadassah, the Mizrachi Organization of America (Orthodox Zionists), and Poale Zion (labor Zionists).

† Two non-Jewish organizations worked closely with the AZEC. Both had been started and were funded by the Zionist movement. The American Palestine Committee (APC) was the main vehicle for Christian American support for the Jewish commonwealth. Its membership, even at its inception in 1941, included 3 Cabinet members, 68 senators, and about 200 congressmen. Many people prominent in religious and academic circles and the labor movement belonged to the APC. By 1946, it listed 15,000 members and 75 local committees.

The smaller partner, the Christian Council on Palestine, represented pro-Zionist Christian clergy and religious educators. Headed by Henry Atkinson of the Church Peace Union and theologian Reinhold Niebuhr, it started in late 1942 with 400 members and grew to nearly 3,000 by 1946.[59]

The American Zionist Emergency Council proved that American Jewry could build a highly capable pressure organization, attract great energies, focus them on Washington, and provide the financing for a nationwide campaign. But no comparable drive for rescue was even attempted. Had the approach so effectively developed by the AZEC been applied to the rescue issue, Roosevelt's prolonged delay in initiating a program to save Jews might have ended substantially sooner. Moreover, the President might have been impelled to provide that program, once established, with the kind of support that it needed (but never received) for optimum results.

The AZEC launched its first campaign in October 1943. The main target was the White Paper. While local committees across America enlisted popular support, national Zionist organizations held mass meetings in many cities to demand open Jewish immigration to Palestine and establishment of a Jewish commonwealth. Such prominent Americans as Wendell Willkie, Dorothy Thompson, and Governor Thomas Dewey joined in the call. It echoed for weeks in newspaper editorials and in resolutions passed by Jewish and non-Jewish groups in all parts of the nation.[60]

On November 10, the British government announced that termination of Jewish immigration into Palestine, scheduled under the White Paper for March 31, 1944, would be postponed until the 31,000 remaining unused places had been filled. The announcement, which may have been timed to undercut growing Zionist pressures, did not slow Zionist momentum in any way. Rather, the AZEC soon decided to expand its campaign and press forward to commit the U.S. Congress to the Biltmore Program.[61]

At the request of the AZEC, resolutions were introduced in the Senate and House in January 1944 urging that "the doors of Palestine shall be opened for free entry of Jews into that country . . . so that the Jewish people may ultimately reconstitute Palestine as a free and democratic Jewish commonwealth." The legislation immediately drew wide support in Congress. After four days of successful hearings in the House Foreign Affairs Committee, all signs pointed to quick and favorable action. But the War Department stepped in and asked the House and Senate committees to put the question aside. It advised that further action on the resolution would stir up the Arab world and risk upheavals that would require the Allies to transfer troops to the Middle East. This halted the resolution. Actually, the State Department, which did not want to take responsibility openly, persuaded the War Department to block the legislation. The episode reflected the State Department's low-key, but persistent, anti-Zionist stance. In this instance, the President also secretly backed the decision.[62]

Several congressional leaders informed the AZEC that a milder resolution, one deleting the demand for a Jewish commonwealth and concentrating on a humanitarian appeal for free immigration of Jews into Palestine, would most likely win approval in Congress, and probably quite quickly.* (The *New Republic* and the *New York Post* were already calling for such a modified resolution.) But even though immigration to Palestine was one of the most important keys to rescue, AZEC leaders turned the suggestion down. They reasoned that accepting it would mean the end of the commonwealth resolution, because Congress would certainly not act on more than one Palestine proposal. Worried by indications that the Bergson group was about to press for such a modified resolution, AZEC officials sought to persuade congressmen not to introduce it. They also made plans for opposing it, should it reach Congress.[63]

Despite the setback to its resolution, the AZEC prepared for the next round. In March 1944, Wise and Silver saw Roosevelt and obtained a statement favorable to their general goals. At the national political conventions that summer, Zionist leaders persuaded Republicans and Democrats alike to adopt platform planks calling for unrestricted Jewish immigration into Palestine and establishment of a commonwealth there. Then, in the heat of the election campaign, Roosevelt and the Republican challenger, Thomas Dewey, both pledged strong support for a Jewish commonwealth in Palestine. Almost simultaneously, the War Department withdrew its earlier objection to the resolution.[65]

After the election, the AZEC moved to secure a seemingly certain victory. But the State Department, at Roosevelt's instruction, persuaded the Senate Foreign Relations Committee to defer action on the resolution. Publicly committed to the Jewish state, yet afraid he would jeopardize American interests in the Middle East by alienating Arab governments, the President was stalling for time to devise a way out of his predicament. (He died without finding it.)[66]

This second failure of the resolution ignited the long-smoldering power struggle between Silver and Wise. Wise, loyal as always to Roosevelt, and believing him to be Zionism's best hope, blamed the defeat on Silver's insistence on pressing for action in the Senate committee

* The available evidence supports the accuracy of this analysis. Even Roosevelt favored the basic idea. The Jewish commonwealth issue was politically and diplomatically very explosive.[64]

despite signals from the administration to hold back. Silver acidly explained why he had not waited any longer for Roosevelt to flash the
"green light" for the Palestine resolution: "It is now clear that the
'green light' is not given except at election time."[67]

Bitter strife between the Wise and Silver factions led to Silver's resignation from the AZEC. Continued fighting disabled the Zionist movement from December 1944 until July 1945. Finally, distressed Zionists
throughout the country insisted on a reconciliation and Silver's return
to frontline leadership. The resulting truce left Silver in control of the
movement.[68]

The Palestine resolution at last reached the floor of Congress in
December 1945. President Truman resisted it, asserting that its passage
at that time would tie his hands in negotiating for admission of Jewish
survivors into Palestine. The resolution nevertheless was adopted overwhelmingly by both houses.[69]

The struggle for the Palestine resolution had forced the question of
Jewish statehood on Congress and brought it to the attention of the
American public. The long debate had solidified Jewish opinion behind
the statehood plan and had attracted considerable non-Jewish backing.
Once adopted, the resolution served as a foundation on which broad
American public support was built when Jewish statehood came before
the United Nations in 1947.*[70]

While the Zionist campaign had survived setbacks and progressed,
the American Jewish Conference had disintegrated. By mid-1944, its
ineffectiveness was obvious, and criticism of its virtual inaction rever-
berated through the Jewish press and in Jewish gatherings. The conference's leading figure, Stephen Wise, admitted that his enthusiasm of a
year ago had faded. Now, he lamented, "I rather feel as if I were . . .
saying Kaddish over the American Jewish Conference, which seems to
have no life left in it."[72]

The conference declined even more in its second year. Bickering
became commonplace among its member groups. When the delegates
reconvened in Pittsburgh in December 1944, interorganizational rivalry
and strife dominated the sessions. Weak and ineffectual, the conference
limped along until the end of 1948, then expired.[73]

What is the balance sheet on the American Jewish Conference? The
main Zionist objectives for it were achieved. The delegate elections and
the overwhelming vote on the Palestine resolution demonstrated that

---

* There is a continuing dispute among scholars and others over the extent to which
Zionist activity influenced Harry Truman's Palestine policy—and American Palestine
policy generally in the early postwar years.[71]

the Zionist position had attained majority support among American Jews. After August 1943, Zionist leaders could credibly claim in their publicity and their national and international contacts that their program represented the broad cross section of American Jewish opinion. The conference experience probably also helped prepare the ground for the postwar American Jewish unity that formed behind the cause of a Jewish state.[74]

On the debit side, Zionist insistence on committing the conference to a Jewish commonwealth in Palestine, a *postwar* objective, ended the chance for united Jewish action on the immediate issue of rescue and on the related issue of the White Paper. On those points, consensus existed and Jewish unity was possible. The American Jewish Conference might have been the instrument of that unity, but by adopting the full Zionist program it lost the opportunity.[75]

An unavoidable conclusion is that during the Holocaust the leadership of American Zionism concentrated its major force on the drive for a future Jewish state in Palestine. It consigned rescue to a distinctly secondary position. Why would Jewish leaders, deeply distressed over the agony of their people in Europe, have allowed *any* issue to take precedence over immediate rescue? No sure answers are possible. But enough evidence is available to suggest the explanation.

The Zionist leadership concluded that little hope for rescue existed. Hitler had a stranglehold on the European Jews, and the Allied powers showed themselves unwilling even to attempt rescue. A Zionist editorial in September 1943, a survey of the then-closing Jewish year of 5703, mirrored the widespread despair:

> It was during the first few months of that year that the pitiless, horrifying word "extermination" became a commonplace in our vocabulary. . . . It was in that year, too, that all our cries and pleas for life-saving action were shattered against walls of indifference until we began to stifle in the black realization that we are helpless. It was the year of our endless, bottomless helplessness.

Thirty-five years later, in entirely separate interviews, two leaders of the Jewish statehood drive of the 1940s emphasized the same feeling of helplessness, the belief that little or nothing could be done. "Utter helplessness," recalled one, a foremost Zionist. "I think the enemy was helplessness, a feeling of helplessness. It's a terrible feeling to bear." The other, a prominent Christian advocate of Zionism, explained why the Zionists did not concentrate on rescue: "They thought it was a useless gesture. . . . It's impossible to do anything right now.

And we'll be told [by government officials] to go mind our business."[76]

Although some signs of despair appeared before April 1943, it was the Bermuda Conference that destroyed hope. The early efforts for government rescue action had failed to breach Washington's "walls of indifference." During that same spring of 1943, however, prospects for the basic Zionist program were rising as the American Jewish Conference movement began to gather momentum. Moreover, it was essential to press ahead rapidly with the statehood campaign in order to be ready to exert maximum influence when the crucial postwar diplomatic decisions were made.[77]

As limited as Zionist resources were, it seemed reasonable to concentrate them on the possible rather than on what appeared to be a nearly hopeless cause. One week after the Bermuda Conference, Nahum Goldmann stressed the point at a meeting of the Zionist leadership. Too little manpower was available, he said, both to continue the mass meetings for rescue and to launch a major campaign for the Zionist program. Bermuda convinced him that the emphasis should be on Zionist goals.*[78]

Reinforcing the Zionists' choice was their view of Jewish history through the centuries of the Diaspora. Abba Hillel Silver clearly expressed the view in his speech to the American Jewish Conference. The chain of disasters that made up the history of the Dispersion, he reminded his listeners, extended far beyond Hitler and the present mass slaughter. It encompassed two thousand years of world hatred and murder of Jews. No end to "this persistent emergency in Jewish life" would come, Silver warned, until Jewish homelessness ceased. And that would occur only with the creation of a Jewish state. The state offered the only real solution to the ceaseless tragedies that dominated Jewish history.[80]

The Zionist leadership, limited in the resources it commanded, faced two momentous obligations. For the immediate need—rescue—the prospects for achievement appeared bleak. For the postwar objective—the Jewish state—the tide was running and the goal looked attainable. The Zionists made their choice. Events would show, however, that they had misread the signs concerning rescue. Substantially more was pos-

---

* A similar assessment was made in Palestine. A scholarly study based on the files of the Rescue Committee of the Jewish Agency has shown that the Zionists who controlled that body concluded in 1942 that almost no useful rescue action was possible. They decided that nearly all the limited funds available to the Jewish Agency should continue to go into the development of Palestine.[79]

sible than they recognized. Their insight into the past and their dedication to the future hampered their vision of the present.*

* Occasionally one comes across allegations that Zionists intentionally avoided rescue efforts in the belief that the greater the Jewish death toll in Europe, the stronger the case would be for a postwar Jewish state. This writer has found no evidence whatever to support such a charge. The world's realization after the war of the immensity of the Jewish tragedy did advance the cause of Jewish statehood. But by no system of logic can that be construed as evidence for the accusation.

Another inaccuracy sometimes encountered is the statement that Zionists, in order to keep maximum pressure on Palestine, failed to support—or even opposed—refugee immigration to other countries. Actually, an abundance of documentation shows that before, during, and after the war Zionists time and again backed efforts to open the United States and other areas besides Palestine to Jewish fugitives. This was not, however, central to their activities.[81]

|| 10 ||

THE CABINET WAR

During the last eight months of 1943, while the Bergsonites pressed for a government rescue agency and the Zionists consolidated their gains and opened the drive for a Palestine commonwealth, developments crucial to rescue were unfolding behind the scenes in the Roosevelt administration. The flow of events commenced in the State Department. Then, in June, the Treasury Department was drawn in. In the months that followed, as the Treasury intervened increasingly in rescue policy, relations between it and State moved closer and closer to the combustion point.* [1]

The explosion that finally resulted was set off by the Riegner plan, a promising rescue proposal that originated shortly before the Bermuda Conference. In early 1943, as has been noted, Gerhart Riegner dis-

---

* Conflict between State and Treasury was no novelty. Many foreign-affairs problems had important economic dimensions, and Morgenthau and Hull (and their subordinates) frequently disagreed on policy. Areas of contention included, among others, the China silver problem of the 1930s, lend-lease arrangements, the freezing of Argentine assets during the war, plans for postwar monetary policy, and the question of deindustrialization of Germany after the war. [2]

patched a report confirming the extermination program from new sources and summarizing the terrible situation of the European Jews, country by country. Middle-level State Department officials reacted with a telegram (number 354 of February 10) to the American legation in Bern. It ordered a halt to the forwarding of further messages of that sort. The aim was to cut off the flow of information that had been fueling public pressure for rescue action.[3]

Despite the communications barrier, Riegner managed weeks later to notify the World Jewish Congress in New York that he had additional urgent news. Stephen Wise asked Sumner Welles to look into it. Welles, who was unaware of the stop order, telegraphed Leland Harrison, the American minister in Bern, directing him to obtain Riegner's latest message and relay it to Washington. Harrison did so on April 20. He also requested that

> messages of this character should not (repeat not) be subjected to the restriction imposed by your 354, February 10, and that I be permitted to transmit messages from R [Riegner] more particularly in view of the helpful information which they may frequently contain.

Welles's affirmative reply broke the blockade on extermination news. The incident did not end there, though. The matter of telegram 354 resurfaced months later, at the height of the State-Treasury conflict.[4]

Riegner's April 20 message, the basis for the Riegner plan, outlined important new possibilities for "wide rescue action" in two countries. In Rumania, relief supplies could be obtained for the Jews in Transnistria; moreover, the children there could be removed to Palestine if funds were available. In France, where deportations continued, funds were needed to support hidden Jewish children and to finance escapes of young people to Spain. In no instance would the money move into Axis territory. Sufficient local currency could be borrowed in both Rumania and France if repayment were guaranteed by transferring funds from the United States to blocked accounts in Switzerland. The accounts would be controlled by American officials there and frozen until after the war. Funds for the plan were to come from American Jewish organizations.[5]

Shortly after receiving Riegner's message, Stephen Wise and Nahum Goldmann opened negotiations on the plan with State Department officials. For the next eleven weeks, department personnel, searching for defects in the proposal, advised each other that it was too "vaguely phrased" to permit a decision, or that it might be a World Jewish Congress scheme to transfer money for ransom purposes, or that approval might encourage other organizations to ask to send relief funds to Europe. In the meantime, the World Jewish Congress received indications that Rumanian officials, for $170,000 in Rumanian currency, might revive the earlier offer to let all 70,000 Jews in Transnistria leave for overseas.[6]

It was late June before the State Department even mentioned the Riegner plan to the Treasury Department's Foreign Funds Control Division, the agency legally charged with issuing the licenses required for transferring funds overseas during World War II. Three weeks later, when State and Treasury officials finally met to consider the proposal, R. Borden Reams argued that the funds should not be transferred because the plan was not workable.* Later in the discussion, though, Reams revealed the State Department's real objection: the proposals might actually succeed. Reams considered it unrealistic to encourage large-scale rescue because only 30,000 places remained available under the Palestine White Paper quota and he "did not know of any other areas to which the remaining Jews could be evacuated." This reasoning, though standard currency in the State Department, was not convincing to the Treasury. The next day, July 16, Treasury advised State that it was prepared to issue the license.[7]

Unaware of these developments, but anxious about the long delay, Wise discussed the Riegner plan with Roosevelt during a White House visit on July 22. The rabbi emphasized that it could not possibly interfere with the war effort, because none of the funds would be unblocked until the war ended. Roosevelt agreed to the plan, informed Morgenthau, and on August 14 signed a letter to Wise reporting that the Treasury Department had approved and all arrangements were complete except for "a further exchange of cables between the State Department and our mission in Bern regarding some of the details."[9]

But even the President's intervention failed to daunt Breckinridge Long and his group. They delayed the license another six and one-half weeks, asserting that Riegner's plan would somehow provide the enemy with foreign exchange. Within the State Department, only Herbert Feis, the adviser on international economic affairs, and Bernard Meltzer, acting chief of the Division of Foreign Funds Control, pressed for issuance of the license.†[10]

* This point was irrelevant. Hundreds of licenses for funds transfers had been issued and not used. The idea was to have the funds available for rapid action if an opportunity arose to utilize them.[8]
† Privately, Meltzer expressed amazement at the arguments raised by Long and his followers. Usually, when such questions came up, it was Meltzer's Foreign Funds Control Division that opposed issuing licenses and the others in the department who insisted that political factors outweighed such minor economic-warfare considerations.[11]

Ultimately, on September 28, the State Department telegraphed the Treasury license to Harrison in Bern. Harrison, who had been aware that the license was in the works, had already expressed his readiness to relay it to Riegner. Moreover, he had left unanswered an earlier Treasury Department message asking him to spell out any problems he foresaw in issuing the license. Yet, when he received it, he telegraphed back that he wanted a specific State Department order before delivering it to Riegner. He also mentioned that, in line with standing instructions concerning such transactions, he had discussed the license with British authorities in Switzerland and they opposed it on economic-warfare grounds.[12]

The State Department took no action on Harrison's telegram. It did not order him to issue the license, nor did it inform the Treasury of his message. When the Treasury learned of it (through informal contacts it had elsewhere in the State Department), it drafted a telegram for the State Department to send to Harrison instructing him to issue the license. Treasury officials insisted that British clearance was not necessary, because the license had been carefully drawn to safeguard it from abuse. Moreover, the British had carried out comparable relief actions without consulting American authorities.[13]

Reams resisted the Treasury demand, claiming that issuance of the license would incense the British, single out "a special group of enemy aliens" for help, and improperly bypass the Intergovernmental Committee. But Long, apparently wary of a confrontation with the Treasury, gave in. On October 26, he cabled Harrison to issue the license. Within the State Department, he justified his action on the grounds that similar transmissions of funds had been allowed in the past, the chance that this one could help the enemy was remote, and the President supported it.[14]

Harrison still did not act. Seventeen days later, the British Ministry of Economic Warfare (MEW) lodged official objections to the license through the British embassy in Washington and the British legation in Bern. Only then did Harrison reply, stating that the British in Bern had orders to withhold consent until MEW had discussed the matter with the Treasury. Before defying the British, Harrison explained, he would really need specific instructions to do so from the State Department.[15]

When Treasury officials learned of the latest complications, they drafted a letter, which Morgenthau sent to Hull. It pointed out that three and one-half months had passed since the Treasury Department had embarked on "the relatively simple matter of getting our Minister in Switzerland to issue a license." The message outlined the obstacles encountered and closed with a request for Hull's assistance. Accompanying the letter was a telegram that Morgenthau asked Hull to dispatch to John G. Winant, the American ambassador to Great Britain. It asked Winant to approach the Ministry of Economic Warfare, explain that the proposed license was fully safeguarded, and try to get the British to withdraw their objections. The telegram went out without delay.[16]

Winant complied immediately, but two more weeks passed before the British responded. Their reply, finally delivered on December 15, showed that the economic-warfare argument had been a pretext which the British now realized was not going to stop the Treasury Department. Aware that Treasury's interest in the Jewish situation went beyond the Riegner license and could lead to a serious American rescue drive, the Foreign Office had stepped in. The resulting message, described by Morgenthau as "a satanic combination of British chill and diplomatic double-talk, cold and correct and adding up to a sentence of death," revealed the real British objection to the Riegner plan. It brought into sharp focus the underlying fear that had determined the entire British policy toward rescue—a fear that had similarly shaped the State Department's response to the Holocaust. The core of the message follows:

> The Foreign Office are concerned with the difficulties of disposing of any considerable number of Jews should they be rescued from enemy occupied territory. . . . [Such operations would be] greatly hampered by the difficulties of transportation, particularly shipping, and of finding accommodation in the countries of the Near East for any but a very small number of Jewish refugees. They [the Foreign Office] foresee that it is likely to prove almost if not quite impossible to deal with anything like the number of 70,000 refugees whose rescue is envisaged by the Riegner plan. For this reason they are reluctant to agree to any approval being expressed even of the preliminary financial arrangements.* [17]

Treasury officials were shocked. The four men closest to the license battle—all of them non-Jews and tough-minded lawyers accustomed to Washington's bruising administrative politics—reacted with pain and anger:

JOSIAH E. DUBOIS, JR.: The British say condemn them to death and we say they should get out. . . . Their position is, "What could we do with them if we got them out?" Amazing, most amazing position. . . .

---

* A week later, the British position was clearly spelled out again. A. W. G. Randall, head of the Foreign Office's Refugee Department, noted in an internal communication, "Once we open the door to adult male Jews to be taken out of enemy territory, a quite unmanageable flood may result. (Hitler may facilitate it!)" [18]

RANDOLPH PAUL: I don't know how we can blame the Germans for killing them when we are doing this. The law calls [it] *para-delicto,* of equal guilt. . . .

JOHN PEHLE: The British are saying, in effect, that they don't propose to take any Jews out of these areas. . . . Now, that is the general, broad, enormous issue that has been, to some extent, flushed out. . . .

ANSEL LUXFORD [referring to the State Department]: That is a stock reply when you hit the Jewish problem. . . . You can find a million reasons why you can't get them out of Europe, but if somebody put their mind to getting them out, you can then spend the next ten years on what you are going to do with them.* [19]

The British message dissolved the smoke screen of excuses that the State Department and the Foreign Office had used throughout the preceding year to conceal their actual opposition to rescue action. Now that the real issue was out in the open, Morgenthau's staff began to press him to urge Roosevelt to remove the rescue question from the State Department. The President, they argued, had to be persuaded to form a special agency to try to save European Jews. [21]

Off and on since June 1943, Oscar Cox of the Lend-Lease Administration had tried to convince Morgenthau, and the State Department as well, that a separate rescue agency was essential. Cox suggested a board appointed by the President and based on the State Department, the Treasury Department, and the Foreign Economic Administration (because it was responsible for lend-lease funds). This "War Refugee Rescue Committee" would "attack the whole problem afresh" by formulating rescue plans, developing the necessary funding, asking the various countries to accept a fair share of refugees on an emergency basis, and pressing Europe's neutral nations to let refugees enter. In October, the State Department had rejected Cox's plan, claiming that such a commission would duplicate and interfere with the work of the

---

* The anger and bitterness were slow to recede, as the transcript of a Treasury staff meeting held weeks later shows:

HENRY MORGENTHAU, JR.: When you get through with it, the attitude to date is no different from Hitler's attitude. . . .

HERBERT GASTON: You are unfair. We don't shoot them. We let other people shoot them, and let them starve. . . .

HARRY DEXTER WHITE: It is curious how many different reasons can be thought up for not taking action.

RANDOLPH PAUL: Haven't got any water—haven't got any ships.

WHITE: Yes, didn't have any water down in North Africa.

PAUL: How the devil a lot of these people lived there before, I don't know. [20]

Intergovernmental Committee. Nor had the Treasury shown much interest in the proposal. But in mid-December, during the uproar over
the British message, Cox again pressed his plan. This time he had the
support of several of Morgenthau's staff. Moreover, he asserted, Roosevelt favored the idea.[22]

But Morgenthau still held back, convinced that polite pressure on
Hull would activate the State Department. His Foreign Funds Control
staff disagreed with this optimism. But they did not object when he
insisted that before going to Roosevelt he must at least confer with
Hull. That afternoon (Saturday, December 18), Morgenthau telephoned and made an appointment for Monday morning. State Department personnel realized what was in store, for on the preceding day
Morgenthau had sent a courteous message to Hull which spelled out
once more the many complications that had prevented the Treasury
from transmitting the license to Riegner.[23]

When Morgenthau, Pehle, and Paul arrived for the meeting with
Hull, they were amazed to learn that on Saturday, at Breckinridge
Long's initiative, the State Department had dispatched an extremely
sharp message to Ambassador Winant for delivery to the British government:

> Your telegram under reference has been read with astonishment by the
> Department and it is unable to agree with the point of view set forth. . . . It
> is desired by the Department to inform you immediately of the fact that the
> philosophy set forth in their telegram is incompatible with the policy of the
> United States Government and of previously expressed British policy as it
> had been understood by us.[24]

That was not all. That same Saturday, despite British disapproval and
Harrison's objections, Long had sent the long-sought license, authorizing an initial $25,000. He acted in such haste that, contrary to
all practice, the final version was not cleared with the Treasury. Two
days before Christmas, Harrison reported that he had personally
taken the license to Riegner. Thus, eight months after he had requested
the funds, Riegner was free to carry out his now outdated rescue
plans.[25]

During the Monday morning conference, Hull explained to Morgenthau, "The trouble is, the fellows down the line. . . . I don't get a chance
to know everything that is going on. You just sort of have to rip things
out if you want to get them done." Hull was correct that recalcitrance
and obstruction "down the line" were at the center of the problem. But
he himself, even though his wife came from a Jewish family, had paid

almost no attention to his department's policies concerning the destruction of the Jews.* [26]

Breckinridge Long, uneasy about the recent turn of events, tried to use the conference to disassociate himself from the policies of his own clique. He asked Morgenthau to talk with him alone in another room. There he said, "I just want to tell you that unfortunately the people lower down in your Department and lower down in the State Department are making a lot of trouble." He proceeded to put most of the blame on Bernard Meltzer who, he claimed, had thrown technical difficulties in the way of the license and had spread accusations of anti-Semitism.[28]

Morgenthau, aware that Meltzer and Herbert Feis had fought alone in the State Department to put the license through, turned the conversation back on Long. Later in the morning, he summarized the discussion that resulted:

> So I said, "Well, Breck, as long as you raise the question, we might be a little frank. The impression is all around that you, particularly, are anti-Semitic!" I looked him right in the eye. He said, "I know that is so. I hope that you will use your good offices to correct that impression, because I am not." I said, "I am very, very glad to know it."

Morgenthau continued:

> Well, also, since we are being so frank, you might as well know that the impression has grown in the Treasury that the feeling in the State Department is just the same as expressed in that cable from London about the Foreign Office; there is no difference.

Long protested, assured Morgenthau of his commitment to rescue, and said he hoped he and the Treasury could cooperate toward that end.[29]

Immediately following the conference, Treasury officials gathered to assess the situation. Morgenthau maintained that Hull's assistance was now assured and, consequently, there was no need for a special rescue agency. Others disagreed, arguing that cooperation by Long and his

* At a follow-up conference three weeks later, Morgenthau told Hull that he had gone carefully over the State Department's rescue record and found it "most shocking." Hull replied that "he had no doubt of that." Yet he came to that meeting completely unprepared and had no idea what the discussion was about, even though he had been given a file briefing him on the issues. Moreover, to everyone's embarrassment, he was unable to introduce four of the five State Department officials involved in refugee affairs who accompanied him to the meeting.[27]

group would disappear when the heat let up. It was evident that the State Department's biting reply to the British and its sudden issuance of the license had come only after Morgenthau had arranged to see Hull.[30]

Shortly before the meeting with Hull took place, Josiah DuBois, chief counsel for Treasury's Foreign Funds Control Division, had uncovered a sensational instance of State Department malfeasance. The earliest telegram that the Treasury Department had received from the State Department concerning the Jewish situation in Europe was a message that Harrison sent from Bern on April 20, 1943. It included a reference to State Department cable 354, dispatched to Bern on February 10. Treasury officials thought 354 might contain additional information on the Riegner plan. So they asked for a copy. The State Department refused, claiming that 354 did not concern the Treasury.[31]

Eventually, DuBois managed to see 354, but only through the cooperation of a friend in the State Department, Donald Hiss, who knowingly risked his job to help. Hiss also showed DuBois a telegram to which 354 made reference, number 482 from Bern to the State Department on January 21. The latter carried Riegner's report reconfirming the Nazi extermination plan and detailing the situation then confronting the Jews of Europe. Number 354, as previously noted, was the instrument by which the State Department had cut off the flow of information from Riegner. But 354 by itself did not specify the type of information that was to be blocked. To comprehend its real meaning, one had to read it in conjunction with 482.[32]

At the State Department conference, Morgenthau managed, offhandedly and without revealing his purpose, to get Hull to tell Long to send a copy of cable 354 to the Treasury. Long did so, that same day. But the line in the cablegram that referred to 482 had been deleted. Thus the only clue to the real meaning of 354 was missing. Only because DuBois had already seen a true copy of 354 did the Treasury realize what had happened. Morgenthau immediately sent one of his staff to look at Long's copy of 354. Noticing its reference to 482, the Treasury official told Long that Morgenthau would also want a copy of 482. The next day, 482 reached the Treasury, confirming DuBois's disclosure.[33]

Even knowledge of the scheme to silence Riegner and discovery of the deceitful attempt to cover it up did not convince Morgenthau that the rescue issue had to be taken out of the State Department. But Cox and others in the Roosevelt administration were becoming increasingly anxious about growing support in the press and on Capitol Hill for the Bergsonite legislation calling for a government rescue agency. They wanted Roosevelt to take action before it was forced on him, particularly since several supporters of the legislation were opponents of the President. During the rest of December, Cox unsuccessfully pressed Morgenthau to go to Roosevelt and emphasize the need for him to set up a rescue commission.[34]

By January 10, all of Morgenthau's staff who had been working on the rescue question agreed with Cox. They were sure that Hull could not or would not do the job and that Long's cooperation would cease when the pressures slackened. What finally convinced Morgenthau was an eighteen-page memorandum on State Department obstruction entitled "Report to the Secretary on the Acquiescence of This Government in the Murder of the Jews." Led by DuBois, the Foreign Funds Control staff prepared this searing indictment, which charged that the State Department was "guilty not only of gross procrastination and wilful failure to act, but even of wilful attempts to prevent action from being taken to rescue Jews from Hitler."[35]

The report documented the long struggle for the Riegner license and the story of cable 354 as well as the deception employed in trying to keep it secret. It also pointed to the State Department's strategy of sidetracking rescue proposals to the ineffective Intergovernmental Committee, its inordinately tight restrictions on visa issuance, and its role in the fraudulent Bermuda Conference. Morgenthau received the report on January 13. Within two days, he decided to go to Roosevelt, explain the situation, and urge him to establish a rescue agency.[36]

One passage in the "Report to the Secretary" accused State Department officials of "kicking the [rescue] matter around for over a year without producing results." The State Department's own records bear that out. While the Riegner license was bogged down in the bureaucratic morass, the State Department was holding back a parallel effort by the American Jewish Joint Distribution Committee to transfer funds to Switzerland for relief and rescue. After the breakthrough on the Riegner license, the Treasury forced the State Department to issue a license for the JDC.[37]

Another project caught in the State Department maze in 1943 was the Goldmann plan, probably the most ambitious of the wartime proposals to aid Jews inside Europe. In September, Nahum Goldmann of the World Jewish Congress asked Breckinridge Long for help in providing food and medicines to Jews still alive in Poland, Czechoslovakia, and the Balkans. The aid, to be channeled through the International Red Cross, would cost about $10 million. Goldmann stated that American Jewish organizations could furnish $2 million. He hoped the U.S.

government might supply the other $8 million. Long replied that he knew of no government funds for such a purpose, but he offered to submit the proposal to the Intergovernmental Committee on Refugees. Under the ICR's new setup, Long explained, funds for specific projects that it approved would be provided by Britain and the United States on a fifty-fifty basis.[38]

On the surface, this arrangement looked like a workable answer to Goldmann's call for help. In reality, it was another runaround. Diverting the project through the ICR meant indefinite delays and no results. Ansel Luxford of the Treasury Department described the State Department's handling of the Goldmann plan: "Long first tossed it into the waste-paper basket; namely, the Inter-Governmental Committee."[39]

By January 1944, nothing more had happened concerning the Goldmann plan. When a Jewish leader inquired about it, Long explained that the ICR had approved some of its projects, but no government funds were currently available for them. Yet, less than two months earlier, Long had told a congressional committee about the Goldmann plan, citing it as important evidence of the State Department's vigorous efforts for refugees. He stated unequivocally that "we have agreed to finance half of the cost. It would be $4 million for each government." Moreover, in January, when Long insisted that no government funds could be found, a Treasury Department inquiry confirmed that $80 million remained available in the most obvious account for such undertakings, the President's Emergency Fund. The other side of the Goldmann plan collapsed in January when it became clear that the British government had no intention of participating.* [40]

The Riegner, Joint Distribution Committee, and Goldmann proposals were not the only plans that were bottled up in the State Department. A fifty-page State Department internal memorandum of July 1943 summarized several rescue projects then under consideration. Only two ultimately succeeded, and they concerned non-Jewish refugees. One involving Jews, the refugee camp in North Africa, did provide a minor benefit, but only after a thirteen-month delay. None of the other projects advanced beyond the preliminary stages.[42]

Six months later, the State Department compiled another report on its current rescue programs. Again, the projects concerned with Jews had been pursued without enthusiasm and had achieved nothing. In

---

* The State Department's treatment of the Goldmann plan differed markedly from its quick allotment earlier in 1943 of $3 million from the President's Emergency Fund for transportation to Mexico and maintenance there of up to 28,000 non-Jewish Polish refugees.[41]

the judgment of Treasury's John Pehle, one needed only to read the memorandum to see "the way they kick this stuff around. . . . All of a sudden, right in the middle of something, they will refer [it] to the Intergovernmental Committee and nothing will happen. . . . Really, they are things that something could have been done on."[43]

Why did the State Department respond so inadequately to the Holocaust? Lack of knowledge was not the problem; it had the fullest available information. Nor was disbelief a factor. Even R. Borden Reams, the most skeptical of the officials involved, described the terrible reports as "essentially correct."[44]

The failure stemmed in part from plain bureaucratic inefficiency. Close study of State Department records leaves one with the impression of a poorly administered unit where initiative and imagination were scarce. Furthermore, the absence of any comprehensive approach to rescue meant that opportunities for action were handled in piecemeal fashion. Even then they were usually fumbled. An additional handicap was the widespread belief within the department that nothing much could be done anyway. One Jewish leader described the results: "interminable delay, miles and miles of paper work, little measures for gigantic problems and gigantic difficulties for little problems."[45]

By far the most important cause for State Department inaction was fear that sizable numbers of Jews might actually get out of Axis territory. (Sizable numbers meant more than a very few thousand.) This fear determined the State Department's entire response to the Holocaust, as it did that of the British. Behind it loomed the problem that both governments regarded as unsolvable: Where could masses of Jews be put if they did come out? It was apprehensiveness about stimulating an outflow of Jews that underlay the State Department's consistently negative approach to rescue. Its own documents reveal that the basic policy was not rescue but the avoidance of rescue.*

---

* See chapters 5 and 6.

In October 1943, a State Department adviser on political relations stressed the point again: "There are grave objections to a direct approach to the German Government to request the release to us of these people. Despite the fact that such an offer would almost certainly be refused, a counter offer on the part of the German Government to deliver a large number of refugees at a specified point would have even graver consequences. Lack of a place of temporary refuge and the impossibility of diverting the necessary shipping from the war effort would make it impossible for us to take them. The net result would be the transfer of odium from the German to Allied Governments."[46]

Closely related to the fear of a large exodus of Jews from Axis Europe were two other aspects of the State Department's response to the Holocaust. One was the visa policy that shut the United States to all but a tiny trickle of refugee immigration. The other was the department's quiet, but unwavering, support for Britain's policy of very tight limits on refugee entrance into Palestine. Thus two of the most likely havens of refuge were virtually closed. And other countries were provided with justification for their own barred doors.

Under such circumstances, large-scale removal of Jews appeared impossible; yet public pressures for action could not be kept down. The State Department's solution to that quandary was the Intergovernmental Committee. Proclaimed as the international engine of rescue, its ineffectiveness hidden behind a supposedly necessary veil of secrecy, it provided an excuse for State Department inaction. Rescue proposals could be relayed to it with confidence that nothing significant would develop, that no outflow of Jews would result.

The State Department's policies arose to some degree from the personal anti-alien, anti-immigrant attitudes that prevailed among those involved in refugee affairs. Breckinridge Long was an extreme nativist, especially with regard to eastern Europeans. His subordinates shared his anti-alienism. Their attitudes influenced not only visa policy but the department's entire response to the European Jewish catastrophe.[47]

The extent to which anti-Semitism was a factor is more problematic. The fact that few Jews held State Department posts points to a generally anti-Semitic atmosphere. But direct proof of anti-Semitism in the department is limited.*[48]

In any case, much of the top and middle-level leadership seemed little moved by the European Jewish catastrophe. Cordell Hull was uninterested in and uninformed about his department's rescue policies. (It is striking that almost nothing about refugees appears in the voluminous Hull files in the Library of Congress.) Undersecretary Sumner Welles and Assistant Secretary Adolf Berle appear to have been sym-

---

* Josiah DuBois, who had close contacts in the State Department, has maintained that several of its officials were anti-Semitic. But the research for this book turned up only two documented examples. One, in 1934, concerned a visa official who told a representative of a Catholic organization that it was a relief to have someone come to him who was not attempting to get Jews into the United States. The other instance involved an official in the department's Western European Division who reportedly denounced Morgenthau as "that damned Jew in the Treasury."

There is no doubt about the existence of anti-Semitism among American consuls overseas. It was widespread.[49]

pathetic, but neither responded effectively to the challenge. By May 1943, Berle had concluded that nothing could be done to save Jews short of defeating Hitler's forces. Welles's reaction to the Holocaust remains an enigma. On many occasions, he cooperated with Jewish leaders and seemed on the point of forcing middle-level officials to act. But he seldom followed through. Edward R. Stettinius, Jr., named undersecretary in September 1943 and secretary of state in December 1944, was genuinely concerned. Under his leadership, the department's record improved, but only slightly.[50]

The people in the State Department who were most closely associated with the rescue issue were Assistant Secretary Breckinridge Long and several middle-level officials. They included George Brandt, Long's executive assistant, James Dunn and Wallace Murray, departmental advisers on political relations, Ray Atherton, acting chief of the Division of European Affairs, Howard Travers, chief of the Visa Division, and a number of lesser officers, especially R. Borden Reams. These men were indifferent to the tragedy of the European Jews. Randolph Paul of the Treasury Department described them as an American "underground movement . . . to let the Jews be killed."[51]

Since neither Roosevelt nor Hull paid much attention to the European Jewish tragedy, the main responsibility for American rescue policy fell to Long and his subordinates. Instead of sensitivity to the human values involved, Long brought strongly nativist attitudes to the situation.* Moreover, he was difficult to work with, unless his ideas prevailed. And he was extremely suspicious, as his diary clearly reveals. He viewed himself as under persistent attack from "the Communists, extreme radicals, Jewish professional agitators, [and] refugee enthusiasts," as well as "the radical press" and "Jewish radical circles." "They all hate me," he believed. The supposed assaults came also from within, from "my colleagues in the Government." Long was certain that some of them disliked him intensely, interfered with his work, and conspired against him. Toward the end of his tenure, he even concluded that he had borne "the brunt of the worst attack made against *any* officer of this Government." With a person of such perceptions and attitudes in charge, little chance existed for a positive American response to the difficult problem of helping the Jews of Europe.[52]

* Whether Long was also anti-Semitic is not clear. The record does not show him to be overtly negative toward Jews simply because they were Jews. He appears to have had good relations with the more conservative Jewish leaders—that is, the ones who did not rankle him or openly criticize him.[53]

As 1944 opened, however, Morgenthau and the Treasury Department were about to challenge the grip that Long and his followers had on rescue policy. At the same time, the legislation calling for a special rescue agency that had been in Congress since November was nearing a showdown vote. Its prospects appeared good.[54]

‖ 11 ‖

THE RESCUE
RESOLUTION

Congressional approval of the Rescue Resolution would not in itself have created a governmental rescue agency. The measure was advisory legislation that urged the President to take that step.* Nonetheless, the Emergency Committee to Save the Jewish People of Europe initiated the proposal with the expectation that its passage would force Roosevelt to act. The State Department evidently shared that perception, to judge from Breckinridge Long's maneuvers to block the resolution. In the struggle over the legislation, which began even before it was introduced, its supporters also encountered opposition from the Zionist leadership and from the most influential Jew in Congress, Sol Bloom.

But the Emergency Committee, anticipating resistance, had waged an intensive lobbying campaign and had lined up important backing in Congress. Senator Guy Gillette (Dem., Iowa) originally sponsored the

---

* The resolution, introduced on November 9, 1943, declared that Congress "recommends and urges the creation by the President of a commission of diplomatic, economic, and military experts to formulate and effectuate a plan of immediate action designed to save the surviving Jewish people of Europe from extinction at the hands of Nazi Germany."[1]

resolution. Eleven other senators joined him in introducing it. Among them were two consistent Bergson supporters, Elbert Thomas (Dem., Utah) and Edwin Johnson (Dem., Col.). Two of the cosponsors were Republicans, Robert Taft (Ohio) and Homer Ferguson (Mich.). Six of the twelve sat on the Foreign Relations Committee, where the proposal would probably face its most critical Senate test.*[2]

In the House, Will Rogers, Jr. (Dem., Calif.) was the chief proponent of the resolution. Its cosponsor was Joseph C. Baldwin, a liberal Republican from New York City. Both congressmen were members of the Emergency Committee.[3]

Endorsement by many major newspapers across the country helped build public support. The *New York Post* was emphatically favorable. It kept the resolution in the news spotlight and printed several editorials on it. William Randolph Hearst ran a series of friendly editorials in all his newspapers. The Emergency Committee further publicized the issue through radio broadcasts. Several featured Dean Alfange, the American Labor party leader who had run a strong race for governor of New York in 1942. Alfange, an ardent New Dealer, nonetheless censured Roosevelt for his "tragic inaction" and the State Department for its inertia. He called on Roosevelt and Hull to endorse the Rescue Resolution. Petitions supporting the legislation flowed into Congress, as did individual messages from Alfred E. Smith, Wendell Willkie, Chief Rabbi Isaac Herzog of Palestine, and many others.[4]

Action on the Rescue Resolution opened in the House Foreign Affairs Committee, where five days of hearings were held. Although press accounts of the first three days emphasized the vigorous endorsements made by Willkie, Alfange, and Fiorello La Guardia, Sol Bloom, chairman of the Foreign Affairs Committee, actually used much of that time to attack the Emergency Committee and Peter Bergson.† Bloom, at one time a Yiddish-speaking vaudeville comedian, took a sharp, no-nonsense stance. On the first day, he tried to intimidate Herbert Moore, a non-Jew who was president of Transradio News Features and an officer of the Emergency Committee. Moore's offense had been the production of a radio script, broadcast two days before, that charged Bloom, along

---

* Other Senate cosponsors, all Democrats, were: Bennett Champ Clark (Mo.), Sheridan Downey (Calif.), Allen Ellender (La.), Joseph Guffey (Pa.), James Murray (Mont.), George Radcliffe (Md.), and Frederick Van Nuys (Ind.). Clark, Gillette, Guffey, Murray, Thomas, and Van Nuys were members of the Foreign Relations Committee.

† Bloom's motivation was undoubtedly related to his long-standing animosity toward the Bergson group for its widely publicized characterization of the Bermuda Conference as a "mockery." Bloom had been a delegate at Bermuda and had publicly endorsed its actions.

with "large Jewish groups," with maneuvering to undermine the Rescue Resolution. Despite Bloom's repeated demands, Moore refused to retract the accusation.[5]

Bloom also denounced a telegram recently sent by the Emergency Committee to 200 of its members asking for funds "to mobilize public opinion throughout country to force passage resolution." He made a major issue of the word *force* and seized on the telegram as grounds for several harsh attacks on the group. He even turned most of one day's hearing into an interrogation (under oath) of Peter Bergson concerning the Emergency Committee's activities and Bergson's personal affairs.[6]

Bloom's negative attitude toward the Emergency Committee extended to the Rescue Resolution as well. Although he denied that he opposed the legislation, his behavior proved he was determined to choke it off. Throughout the hearings, he claimed that the Bermuda Conference had dealt thoroughly with the problem and the United States and the revitalized Intergovernmental Committee on Refugees were already doing all that was possible for the European Jews.[7]

Bloom also implied, by underscoring the costs involved, that mass rescue was virtually impossible. On the first day of the hearings, he twice talked about the expense of rescuing 100,000 people: "You have to figure at least $2,000 a person, so that would be $200 million." At the following session, he again stressed the cost factor. It was Congressman Andrew Schiffler (Rep., W.Va.), a non-Jew, who remarked, "I do not think money is of primary importance" in these circumstances. A columnist in the New York Yiddish-language *Forward* wrote in exasperation, "It is truly difficult to understand why it is such a life and death matter for Congressman Bloom to dig up arguments against the resolution."[8]

By the third day of the hearings, pressures had built to the point that Bloom put himself on record in a telegram to *New York Post* editor Ted Thackrey: "I personally agree that the resolution should pass." Later that day, he told reporters that he was 100 percent in favor of the proposal and predicted that the full House was going to approve it. Yet, two days afterward, Bloom and the State Department collaborated in a maneuver intended to kill the resolution.[9]

On November 26, the fourth day of the hearings, Breckinridge Long testified at a closed meeting of the House Foreign Affairs Committee. He insisted on secrecy because, he claimed, the Germans might block projected refugee-aid operations if they found out what he was about to reveal. In a three and one-half hour session, Long convinced the committee that the United States and the Intergovernmental Committee were already doing everything humanly possible to save Jews. He greatly exaggerated the little that had been attempted since Hitler's rise to power, assigned most of the credit for it to the State Department, and, with a verbal magic wand, turned the inert Intergovernmental Committee into an effective mechanism for rescue.[10]

Long's words and his apparent dedication to the refugee cause greatly impressed the congressmen. Karl Mundt (Rep., S. Dak.) termed the testimony "a rather complete rejoinder" to the claims of earlier witnesses that little was being done to rescue Jews. One after another, committee members expressed their gratitude to Long for all the State Department had quietly accomplished. Some asked Long for his opinion on the Rescue Resolution. He indicated that its passage might be construed as a repudiation of the work of the State Department and the Intergovernmental Committee. But he carefully avoided going on record against the measure. When Robert Chiperfield (Rep., Ill.) raised the possibility of the committee's voting against it, Long advised, "I think it would be very dangerous to vote it down, very unwise, in a way." [11]

Several of the congressmen perceived that they were dealing with legislation that had become, in Mundt's words, a "hot poker." They began to look for a way to sidestep the resolution, with its implied criticism of the State Department and the Intergovernmental Committee, and yet avoid antagonizing American Jews. The answer, suggested by James Wadsworth (Rep., N.Y.) and encouraged by Bloom, Mundt, and Luther Johnson (Dem., Tex.), was to obtain authorization to publicize an item Long had brought to the committee's attention—the still-secret mandate of the supposedly revived Intergovernmental Committee.[12]

This document, which originated at the Bermuda Conference and appeared to confer broad new powers on the ICR, had impressed the congressmen as compelling evidence that all feasible steps were already under way. It thus offered, as Wadsworth pointed out, a basis on which the committee "could rest its case for failure to act affirmatively" on the resolution. Mundt saw the idea as "a perfect answer to the dilemma in which we all find ourselves." Long offered to move immediately to arrange for public release of the secret ICR mandate. Within four days, the British government and the Intergovernmental Committee agreed to its publication.[13]

Long's testimony crippled the Rescue Resolution in the House committee, and Bloom managed to keep it from ever reaching the House floor. But the favorable response from the congressmen, who were generally ignorant about the refugee situation, misled Long and Bloom. They concluded that release of the entire transcript of Long's remarks, rather than the ICR mandate alone, would prove even more effective in quieting Jewish pressures. Vanished was the need for strict secrecy that had supposedly been essential to safeguard the interests of the refugees. On December 10, Long's testimony was made public. Instead of the result envisioned, however, it ignited a burst of criticism.[14]

Long's testimony contained several inaccuracies, the most flagrant of which concerned the numbers of refugees who had reached the United States. Along with other erroneous statistics, Long claimed that "we have taken into this country since the beginning of the Hitler regime and the persecution of the Jews, until today, approximately 580,000 refugees." People familiar with the situation knew that not over 250,000 had come and many of them were not Jews.[15]

It was more difficult to check Long's statements about the Intergovernmental Committee, because secrecy surrounded its activities. But the Jewish Telegraphic Agency, after inquiry at the ICR's London headquarters, revealed that one of Long's key assertions about that organization was wrong. He had declared that under the new mandate ICR officials had "plenary authority to do whatever they can, within and without Germany and the occupied territories." Patrick Malin, the ICR's vice-director, flatly contradicted that claim, pointing out that his committee did not have the power to deal with Germany.[16]

Long had also misrepresented the situation regarding ocean transportation. Discussing the low rate of refugee immigration to the United States, he had explained that "demands for a wider opening cannot be justified for the time being because there just is not any transportation." While the congressmen had believed this statement, in refugee-aid circles it was commonly known that Portuguese and Spanish passenger ships, which plied the Atlantic throughout the war, were sailing to the United States less than one-fourth full.[17]

Like the Foreign Affairs Committee, most of the press assumed that Long's information was accurate. The *New York Times* reported it at the top of the front page. Headed "580,000 Refugees Admitted To United States in Decade," the story marked the first time that Holocaust-related news received such prominent notice in the *Times*. Long's misleading statements also opened the way for restrictionists to whip up suspicions that Jewish refugees were flooding the country. The *Chicago Tribune,* the most influential newspaper in the Midwest, subheaded its report: " 'Open Door' Policy Bared; Quotas Disregarded."[18]

The *New York Post* and a few other newspapers analyzed Long's testimony more carefully and raised serious questions about it. The *Post* labeled it "false and distorted." The *Nation* and the *New Republic* also refuted it. The *Nation* asserted that Long's "attempt to confuse the

issue and mislead the House Foreign Affairs Committee" only proved
the need for a special government rescue commission. Shortly afterward, news releases from the American Jewish Conference and the
World Jewish Congress, as well as a long letter in the *New York Times*
from the Yiddish Scientific Institute, thoroughly documented Long's
inaccuracies.[19]

The President's Advisory Committee on Political Refugees and the
American Jewish Committee wrote Long asking for clarification. He
replied that he had meant to say that 580,000 visas had been authorized,
not that 580,000 refugees had entered the United States. On all other
questions, he doggedly insisted that he had been correct or misinter-
preted.*[20]

The controversy echoed in the halls of Congress. Samuel Dickstein
assailed Long for having created the false impression of action. Emanuel
Celler angrily exclaimed that Long "drips with sympathy for the persecuted Jews, but the tears he sheds are crocodile." He called for Long's
resignation on the grounds that he was "woefully lacking in knowledge"
or else "he did not tell the truth." Either way, Celler asserted, he was
not fit to supervise refugee policy. A month later, Celler read into the
Congressional Record a full critique of Long's testimony as well as an
analysis of the State Department's nearly impenetrable visa-control system.[22]

Long had succeeded with the House Foreign Affairs Committee. But
the furor over his inaccurate testimony helped end his control of refugee
policy. Publicity about his remarks crested in late December, at the
same time as the Treasury Department's showdown with him over the
Riegner license. These developments played their part in a State Department reshuffling that saw Long relinquish his refugee and visa responsibilities, although he continued as an assistant secretary until he
left the department a year later.[23]

While all groups concerned about rescue deprecated Long's misstate-
ments, the Emergency Committee worked almost alone for passage of
the Rescue Resolution. Zionist leaders, acting through the American
Jewish Conference, even hampered its progress. When they first learned
that the Emergency Committee planned to introduce the resolution,
they pressed its sponsors in Congress to replace it with one closer to
their own specifications. After that failed and the Emergency Committee's proposal was introduced, they maneuvered behind the scenes for

* Long neglected to mention that the figure of 580,000 included all visas, permanent
and temporary, whether actually used or not, for people from all countries that eventually fell under German control, for all the years since Hitler came to power.[21]

addition of an amendment calling for opening Palestine to Jewish refugees. When this attempt foundered, they carried the issue to the hearing room of the House Foreign Affairs Committee.[24]

The fifth and final day of House testimony on the Rescue Resolution came on December 2. Spokesmen for the AFL and the CIO appeared and urged approval of the measure. The main witness that day, however, was Stephen Wise, representing the American Jewish Conference. Wise criticized the legislation as "inadequate" because it proposed no concrete program for rescue. Most important, he emphasized, it failed to call for immediately opening Palestine to Jewish refugees. He advocated amending it to that effect.*[25]

Will Rogers, Jr., who was a member of the Foreign Affairs Committee, doubted "the wisdom of injecting this ancient and acrimonious Palestine question into a resolution specifically involving . . . rescue." He pointed out that the Palestine issue had been intentionally omitted from the legislation because it was so controversial. (In fact, leaders of the Emergency Committee, after consultation with their friends in Congress, had purposely excluded all specific plans from the resolution because almost any particular recommendation could alienate some potential supporters. Concrete proposals could come after the battle for a commission was won. Most of all, they wanted to keep issues as politically sensitive as Palestine out of the picture. Moreover, they were certain that the commission, once established, would quickly discover for itself the crucial need for opening Palestine.)[27]

Wise had based his testimony on policy set by Zionist leaders of the American Jewish Conference. This group, which included Wise, Abba Hillel Silver, Nahum Goldmann, Herman Shulman, and Rabbi Irving Miller, had taken soundings in Congress and must have realized that pressing the Palestine issue could not help the Rescue Resolution and might jeopardize it. Whether they actually intended to undermine the legislation is not entirely clear. Minutes of their meetings show that on the eve of the resolution's introduction in Congress they definitely "did not favor" it. Two weeks later, the position had changed slightly: it "does not go far enough"—it should be broadened to include the opening of Palestine and other concrete proposals. Miller and Shulman, however, believed that the conference should support the legislation with or without the changes. Yet when Wise gave his testimony, it fell far short of endorsement.[28]

---

* Wise twice stated that the American Jewish Conference favored the resolution. But each time he immediately hedged the endorsement. The whole thrust of his testimony was opposition to the legislation unless the Palestine issue were added to it.[26]

The Emergency Committee, parts of the Jewish press, and even one prominent Zionist, Rabbi Meyer Berlin, publicly accused Zionist leaders of intentionally obstructing the Rescue Resolution. They asserted that the Zionists turned to indirect methods, such as bringing in the controversial Palestine question, because they did not dare openly to oppose a measure to rescue Jews. This view took on added cogency in late December when the American Jewish Conference, in a stinging press release, disparaged the Rescue Resolution but stopped short of outright opposition.[29]

Senator Gillette, a dedicated friend of Zionism, candidly discussed the obstruction he encountered from Zionist leaders:

> These people used every effort, every means at their disposal, to block the resolution. . . . [They] tried to defeat it by offering an amendment, insisting on an amendment to it that would raise the question, the controversial question of Zionism or anti-Zionism, . . . or anything that might stop and block the action that we were seeking.

Gillette also disclosed a comment made by one of his colleagues the day the Senate Foreign Relations Committee was to vote on the measure:

> I wish these damned Jews would make up their minds what they want. I could not get inside the committee room without being buttonholed out here in the corridor by representatives who said that the Jewish people of America did not want the passage of this resolution.[30]

Zionist leaders insisted to Gillette and others that they did not oppose the resolution but were convinced it was inadequate because "there could be no concrete and constructive approach to the problem which did not include Palestine." Yet, even if it were granted that they did not work against the Rescue Resolution, the fact would remain that they publicly criticized it very harshly and lent it no support whatever. Why?[31]

The key reason was their extreme animosity toward its sponsor, the Emergency Committee. By October 1943, Zionist hostility toward the Bergson group was already nearing the flash point, and plans were under way for a scathing public attack on the Emergency Committee. Then Zionist leaders learned that the Emergency Committee intended to introduce rescue legislation. This placed them in a dilemma. They could not openly and directly oppose a step for rescue. But it was impossible to assist, or even to refrain from interfering with, the project of a group they viewed as virtually an enemy. They recognized that success for the resolution would bring prestige, additional popular support, and more strength to the Bergsonite faction. If they could have replaced or amended the Rescue Resolution, and thus claimed it as their own, they would probably have supported it. But their attempts in that direction failed.[32]

As December passed, it became clear that neither Long's testimony, Bloom's maneuvers, nor Zionist criticisms had stopped the Rescue Resolution. Instead, it picked up additional backing in the Jewish press. And one of the seven Jews in Congress finally endorsed it. Emanuel Celler wrote to the House committee, "I am in favor of this Resolution. . . . While [it] is limited in scope, it is nevertheless a step in the right direction." In a Christmas message, eight prominent religious leaders called for rapid adoption of the proposal. And over the weeks, the Emergency Committee kept pressing the issue in large newspaper advertisements carrying such titles as "HOW WELL ARE YOU SLEEPING?" "TIME RACES DEATH—WHAT ARE WE WAITING FOR?" "ONE VICTORY FOR HITLER?" and, in Yiddish, "FROM THE NAZI VALLEY OF DEATH OUR BROTHERS AND SISTERS CALL WITH THEIR LAST STRENGTH: AMERICAN JEWS, WHY DON'T YOU SAVE US?"[33]

The Senate Foreign Relations Committee saw no need for hearings, but waited to act on the resolution until shortly before Christmas. The delay stemmed from reservations held by committee chairman Tom Connally (Dem., Tex.). When Connally was absent from a meeting, Gillette and Thomas brought the issue up, and committee members approved it unanimously. Their report to the Senate penetrated to the heart of the issue:

> The problem is essentially a humanitarian one. It is not a Jewish problem alone. It is a Christian problem and a problem for enlightened civilization. . . . We have talked; we have sympathized; we have expressed our horror; the time to act is long past due.[34]

The resolution was scheduled to come before the full Senate in January, shortly after Congress returned from the holiday recess. The *New York Post* predicted "practically no Senate opposition." Gillette forecast passage "without a dissenting vote." Thus, as 1944 closed, pressures were mounting on the White House. The Senate was poised to act on the resolution. And, although Sol Bloom had bottled it up in his committee, it could break onto the House floor at any time.[35]

Bloom's obstruction had drawn angry reactions from some constituents and the threat of a campaign to block his reelection. A bitter editorial that appeared in Anglo-Jewish newspapers assailed him as a tool of the State Department, both at the Bermuda Conference and in his recent collusion with Long. It left its sharpest thrust for last: "We would not be happy in your place, Mr. Bloom. . . . We would feel blood, Jewish blood on our hands." In mid-January, Celler tried to persuade Bloom to act on the resolution. He also asked him to publish the testimony given at the hearings. Bloom met neither request.* [36]

Sol Bloom, despite his influential position in Congress, attempted next to nothing for the Jews of Europe. True, he arranged for several individual Jewish refugees to enter the United States. And he assisted the Orthodox rescue agency, Vaad Hahatzala, in some small ways. But when possibilities for major action arose, he consistently allied himself with the State Department. He seemed most of all concerned to use his post as chairman of the Foreign Affairs Committee to win the esteem of the State Department elite. Three decades later, Celler concluded that "Sol Bloom did a great deal of harm because of his attitude. He was a mere sycophant of the State Department." [37]

In the case of the Rescue Resolution, Bloom's actions probably were also motivated by loyalty to the Roosevelt administration. If the resolution had reached the floor of the House, it could have touched off an embarrassing debate on the administration's record concerning the European Jews. In addition, Bloom's own prestige was at stake. For him to acknowledge the need for a new rescue commission would amount to repudiation of his role at Bermuda and his long-standing claim that the Bermuda Conference had exhausted all practical avenues of relief. [38]

Late in December, while the Rescue Resolution hung in the balance, the American Jewish Conference released to the press its long-planned attack on the Bergsonites. The widely distributed statement castigated the Emergency Committee as a sensationalist faction whose activities accomplished nothing of value and only interfered with the work of responsible organizations. A case in point, the press release declared, was the Rescue Resolution, which had been introduced "in complete disregard" of the rescue programs that the authorized Jewish groups were pressing in Washington. [39]

This assault may have slowed the momentum of the Rescue Resolution. But it came too late to blunt its impact, for pressures in Congress were far advanced by then. Treasury Department officials, along with Oscar Cox of the Foreign Economic Administration, were keeping a close eye on the situation. They noted that Bloom was having "to do everything he can possibly do" to prevent his committee from reporting

---

* Bloom had already released Long's remarks. He suppressed the rest of the testimony. It did not become available until 1976.

the resolution to the House floor. They were convinced that if it came before either house it would pass or, at the very least, precipitate a debate in which the State Department's record and Long's testimony would "be ripped open."[40]

Although intensely committed to the idea of a rescue commission, Cox and the group around Morgenthau worried that Roosevelt might be hurt by a congressional airing of the question. They were also anxious for the President to move before Congress approved the resolution and forced his hand. Otherwise, sponsors of the legislation who were not on his side—such men as Taft, Gillette, Van Nuys, and Ferguson—could claim credit for the rescue agency.[41]

The obvious solution was for Morgenthau to go to Roosevelt and press him to create the commission. Their strongest leverage on the President, as Morgenthau himself pointed out during a staff conference, was "the imminence of Congress doing something." Acknowledging the key importance of the Rescue Resolution, Morgenthau added:

> Really, when you get down to the point, this is a boiling pot on the Hill. You can't hold it; it is going to pop, and you have either got to move very fast, or the Congress of the United States will do it for you.[42]

On January 15, two days after his staff handed him its comprehensive "Report to the Secretary on the Acquiescence of This Government in the Murder of the Jews," Morgenthau decided to see the President.* The following day, a Sunday, he, Pehle, and Paul met with Roosevelt for twenty minutes in the early afternoon. They brought a shortened version of the "Report to the Secretary." They also had a proposed executive order, provided by Cox, that would establish a rescue commission headed by Morgenthau, Hull, and Leo Crowley, director of the Foreign Economic Administration.[43]

The President did not read the memorandum but listened attentively to an oral summary of the facts. He glanced at the executive order, suggested that Secretary of War Henry L. Stimson replace Crowley, and consented to the plan.[45]

Roosevelt's quick agreement indicates that he had already appraised the pressures in Congress and recognized that he could no longer sidestep the rescue issue. The recent negative publicity over Long's mislead-

---

* There is some evidence that Morgenthau finally agreed to press Roosevelt because Josiah DuBois threatened that if he did not do so he, DuBois, would resign from the Treasury, call a press conference in Washington, and rip the lid off the entire State Department refugee scandal.[44]

ing testimony may also have influenced his decision. Morgenthau's disclosures concerning the scandal in the State Department furnished the last push.*

At that, the President acted at the final moment. The Rescue Resolution was scheduled to go before the Senate on January 24. All signs, including a mid-January poll of both houses, pointed to ready passage. On January 22, Roosevelt issued the executive order establishing the War Refugee Board. Gillette then removed the resolution from the Senate calendar, explaining that "the President's action attained the goal we were seeking." Roosevelt, in the opinion of experienced Washington news correspondents and lobbyists, had seized the initiative and "forestalled certain action in Congress." The American government stood at last on the threshold of a genuine commitment to rescue.[47]

The War Refugee Board resulted from the convergence of two sets of developments. One revolved around the Treasury Department's persistent steps for action once it was drawn into the rescue issue. The other was the long campaign for a rescue agency waged by the Emergency Committee and, earlier, by the Committee for a Jewish Army. Several other groups, mostly Jewish, contributed vitally over the months by publicizing the extermination news and creating a limited, but crucially important, amount of public concern and political support for rescue. In the forefront were the American Jewish Congress, the World Jewish Congress, and the Joint Emergency Committee on European Jewish Affairs. Others included the Union of Orthodox Rabbis, Agudath Israel, the Jewish Labor Committee, and the American Jewish Committee.

Contrary to views expressed by many journalists and political leaders, spokesmen for the American Jewish Conference denied that the Emergency Committee or the Rescue Resolution had any connection with the President's action. Rather, they claimed, their organization's efforts had brought the War Refugee Board into existence. Actually, American Jewish Conference leaders had backed a behind-the-scenes plan for a rescue commission that was to operate under the thumb of the State Department. State Department officials and Congressman Bloom had devised it in a last attempt to undermine the Rescue Resolution.[48]

---

* Sensitivity to the Jewish vote might also have been a factor. Syndicated columnist Edgar Ansel Mowrer thought the reason for the President's sudden interest in rescue was obvious. "That's right," Mowrer reminded readers, "1944 is an election year and even Jews have votes." Ben Cohen had earlier hinted that the question of the Jewish vote would carry weight with Roosevelt on this issue. But solid evidence is lacking. It seems most unlikely that American Jews would have turned against Roosevelt in any case.[46]

The Rescue Resolution's central role in the establishment of the War Refugee Board emerges clearly from the records of private discussions among the men most closely involved. John Pehle, who became the WRB's executive director, consistently maintained that the resolution had led to the formation of the board. This view was shared by his colleagues in the Treasury's Foreign Funds Control unit. And Morgenthau agreed completely, as shown by comments he made at meetings with his staff in March 1944:

> After all, the thing that made it possible to get the President really to act on this thing—we are talking here among ourselves—was the thing that— the resolution . . . to form this kind of a War Refugee Committee. . . .

> Now we have a group together, and we are a little bit more frank, if you know about the Resolution in the House and in the Senate by which we forced the President to appoint a Committee.[49]

Why did it take fourteen months from the time Stephen Wise announced the news of extermination, in November 1942, until an American commitment to rescue was won? Three interrelated explanations stand out. First, State Department officials did what they could to choke off the growth of public pressure for rescue. This was seen, for instance, in their attempts to suppress extermination information and in their cunning use of the Bermuda Conference and the Intergovernmental Committee. Second, the indifference of most Christian leaders, secular *and* religious, along with the inadequate media coverage of Holocaust news, greatly weakened all steps to enlist American popular support. Finally, American Jewry, by failing to forge a united and sustained movement for rescue, substantially diminished the influence it might have exerted on the general public, Congress, and the Roosevelt administration.

During the last months of the struggle for an American rescue initiative, Allied military forces were advancing, slowly but steadily, on all fronts. In November 1943, the Russians took Kiev. As the new year opened, they crossed the pre-war frontier into Poland. In March, they would break into Rumania.

In Italy, winter rains and harsh terrain retarded the Allied drive north. But in January the main offensive reopened, though determined German resistance delayed the capture of Rome until early June. Two developments with important ramifications for the European Jews emerged from the Italian campaign before 1943 ended. Seizure of the

Foggia airfields, which exposed central European and Balkan targets to Allied heavy bombers, brought the Auschwitz gas chambers and railways leading to them within striking range. And small boats began ferrying thousands of Yugoslav refugees across the Adriatic to Allied-occupied Italy, opening an escape route that could conceivably be extended to reach the Jews in east central and eastern Europe.

From England, great fleets of American and British bombers were pounding Hitler's strongholds. Meanwhile, preparations went forward for the long-expected cross-channel attack. Pre-invasion air strikes on France commenced as early as January.

In the Pacific theater, the slow march toward Japan continued. Late in 1943, American forces subdued the Solomon Islands stronghold of Bougainville. In the Central Pacific, marine and army units seized vital points in the Gilbert Islands and prepared for a January invasion of Kwajalein, the key to the Marshall Islands.

The War Refugee Board was born, then, at a time when the Allies had unmistakably established predominance and the Axis satellites and bordering neutral nations recognized that Allied victory was certain. The favorable military situation brightened the prospects of the new rescue drive. It might even help offset, to a small degree, the many precious months that had been lost.

(For additional information on the conflict between the regular Zionists and the Bergsonites, see appendix B.)

· *Part Four* ·

THE WAR
REFUGEE
BOARD

|| 12 ||

"WHEN ARE THE
AMERICANS COMING?"

Launching the WRB

Executive Order 9417, which created the War Refugee Board, endowed it with great potential. It directed the State, Treasury, and War departments to provide whatever help the board needed to implement its programs, subject only to the stipulation that they be "consistent with the successful prosecution of the war." It also required all other government agencies to comply with the board's requests for assistance.* [1]

* Executive Order 9417 charged the WRB with carrying out "the policy of this Government [which is] to take all measures within its power to rescue the victims of enemy oppression who are in imminent danger of death and otherwise to afford such victims all possible relief and assistance consistent with the successful prosecution of the war." The order also specified, "It shall be the duty of the State, Treasury and War Departments, within their respective spheres, to execute at the request of the Board, the plans and programs [developed by the board]. It shall be the duty of the heads of all agencies and departments to supply or obtain for the Board such information and to extend to the Board such supplies, shipping and other specified assistance and facilities as the Board may require in carrying out the provisions of this Order."

This order, which carried the force of law, should have opened the way for a powerful rescue campaign. But the WRB did not receive the cooperation that was promised. Consequently, its capacity for rescue was always substantially less than it should have been.

Only the Treasury Department met its full responsibilities. Besides housing the WRB and providing most of its staff, the Treasury was a constant source of assistance. Moreover, Morgenthau himself kept in close touch with the board.[2]

Secretary of War Stimson believed in the WRB's mission, but could spare almost no time for it because of his other heavy duties. The job of War Department liaison with the board fell to Assistant Secretary John J. McCloy. Although he seemed concerned about the European Jews, McCloy was privately skeptical that the military should take a role in their rescue. The War Department's contribution to the work of the board was very small.[3]

Cordell Hull, who preferred a limited State Department connection with the WRB, designated Undersecretary Edward R. Stettinius, Jr., to represent him. Stettinius had enthusiastically welcomed the board's formation. But he, too, had little time for rescue matters. So George Warren of the President's Advisory Committee on Political Refugees served as the State Department's main liaison with the WRB. Despite his long service in the area of refugee aid, Warren did little to counteract the opposition to the board that prevailed among the department's middle-level officials. The way was left open for them to interfere with its activities.[4]

The War Refugee Board staff, which never numbered more than thirty, revolved around a dozen people, mostly non-Jewish and mostly veterans of the Treasury's battles with the State Department over the rescue issue. They were, as one observer remarked, "young, dynamic, bold, clear and a bit brash." They were also hindered during the board's first two weeks by unnecessary delay in the selection of its executive director.[5]

Morgenthau and the rest of the Treasury group wanted John Pehle in the post. However, attracted by the President's suggestion that they find a nationally prominent person for the job, they decided on a combined leadership. Pehle could head the actual rescue work, while a public figure in the executive director's position would be invaluable in the board's relations with high government officials, Congress, and the public.[6]

Roosevelt presented several names himself but kept putting off a decision. After thorough deliberation, Morgenthau and his staff concluded that Wendell Willkie was the ideal choice. He was nationally and internationally known and respected, and he had already demonstrated deep concern about the refugee problem. But Roosevelt rejected Willkie out of hand. Presidential secretary Grace Tully, referring to Willkie's recent global tour for the President and his resulting book, *One World,* told Morgenthau, "I think he has had all the build-up he has coming to him on that trip." That ended an unparalleled chance to develop the board into a highly visible, high-powered rescue unit.[7]

Morgenthau then recommended Frank P. Graham, a southern liberal who was president of the University of North Carolina and a member of the War Labor Board. When Roosevelt rejected him, Morgenthau pressed for the appointment of Pehle. Hull and Stimson concurred. The President agreed, but insisted on holding the news for his press conference the next morning. His interest in the issue must have evaporated overnight, however, for he made no announcement about the board at the news conference. In fact, when a reporter asked whether the director had been named yet, Roosevelt said no. The President, after delaying the choice for nearly two weeks and then insisting on releasing the news himself, had thrown away an opportunity for a valuable burst of publicity for Pehle and the fledgling board.* [8]

Meanwhile, the WRB had begun to organize for action. During February and March, it chose representatives to direct its overseas operations and assigned them to locations on the borders of Axis Europe: Turkey, Switzerland, Sweden, North Africa, Italy, and Portugal. They were granted diplomatic status as special attachés to the American missions in those countries. But efforts to place representatives in Russia, Spain, and Egypt failed. The Soviet government was unresponsive to the plan. The American ambassador to Spain, Carlton J. H. Hayes, opposed such a move. And the State Department blocked the board's attempt to send Charles R. Joy to Egypt. Joy (and his employer, the Unitarian Service Committee) had been too outspoken and too politically active to satisfy State Department standards for that appointment.[10]

From the start, the WRB solicited advice from the many private agencies involved in rescue and relief activities. Nearly a score of them submitted comprehensive suggestions for rescue.† Once in action, the

---

* No such carelessness marked Roosevelt's intervention on behalf of a former official of the discontinued National Youth Authority. The WRB placed her in one of its top staff positions.[9]

† A promising effort to develop rescue plans came from a new group, the Committee on Special Refugee Problems. This largely non-Jewish, New York–based initiative was partially funded by the board. Its three dozen members included several émigré political, educational, and labor leaders who were familiar with the European scene and had

board regularly coordinated its projects with those of the private groups. And, whenever possible, it used its status as a government body to facilitate their work. For instance, the board arranged to use the State Department's coded telegraphic communications system not only for its own purposes but also for transmission of messages between the American private agencies and their representatives overseas.[11]

Under pressure from Stettinius, the State Department furnished some valuable early help to the WRB. State sent cablegrams, drafted by the board and ordering full cooperation with it, to all American diplomatic missions abroad. Soon afterward, special instructions were dispatched to American missions in neutral nations close to Nazi territory. They were directed to urge the neutral governments to permit entry of all refugees who reached their borders and to publicize their willingness to take them in. To reinforce the message, the board immediately assured the neutral powers that it would provide maintenance for the new refugees and would arrange their evacuation as soon as possible. In another early step, the WRB offered its assistance to the International Red Cross. The State Department quickly approved the message and dispatched it via the American legation in Switzerland.[13]

But middle-level State Department officials, thrust aside in the first rush of WRB action, soon moved to reestablish their grip on diplomatic affairs. By mid-March, six urgent WRB cablegrams were stuck in the State Department awaiting clearance. Delays of a month and more hobbled such important measures as warnings to Axis satellites to refrain from collaborating in atrocities and efforts to persuade the British to set up a refugee reception camp in Libya.[14]

The problem eased somewhat by April. But the board had to press constantly to obtain State Department cooperation and even then could never count on it. Yet that cooperation was vital, both to secure the crucially important assistance of the American diplomatic missions abroad and to carry on negotiations with neutral and Allied governments. Instead of providing the nearly unlimited help promised in Executive Order 9417, the State Department often stood in the way of board operations. The same was true, less frequently, of the War Department.[15]

Another impediment was the negative response of the British. They refused to establish a parallel rescue committee to work with the WRB.

---

vital underground contacts in Axis Europe. The WRB dissolved the committee after four months, though, because the State Department and the board were worried that publicity might surface concerning the leftist political connections of a few of the members.[12]

Only grudgingly did they cooperate with the board's efforts to evacuate refugees from the Balkans through Turkey to Palestine. They attempted to restrict the activities of the WRB representative assigned to southern Italy. And they persistently tried to block the board's program of licensing private agencies to transmit money to Europe for rescue and relief projects.[16]

Probably the most crucial difficulty to confront the WRB concerned funds. From the beginning, the board acted mainly as facilitator and coordinator of projects carried out by the private organizations. Even when it initiated rescue operations itself, it usually called on the private agencies to fund them. In sum, government funding was very limited, the board's work was mainly administrative, and the predominately Jewish private agencies financed and implemented most projects. Rescue had finally become official government policy. Yet American Jews, through contributions to their own organizations, had to pay most of the costs.*[17]

Jewish leaders realized at the outset that the Jewish organizations lacked the resources needed for a comprehensive rescue program. Soon after the WRB was formed, officials of the American Jewish Joint Distribution Committee (JDC) and the United Jewish Appeal (UJA) met with the board's staff to explore the problem.† They were disheartened to hear Pehle state emphatically that the board would not look to government funds for rescue operations but would depend on the private agencies for most of the financing. The reason was not stated explicitly, but apparently the WRB feared that Congress would refuse to appropriate funds for rescue. Earlier, when a WRB inner-staff meeting had touched on the funding question, Pehle had asserted, "The last thing I think you want to do is go to Congress."[18]

For weeks, the JDC and UJA attempted to convince the board of the need for "the maximum use of Government funds." But the WRB insisted it would not seek a congressional appropriation unless and until it succeeded in developing "a largescale systematic program" of rescue. That time never came.[19]

In its sixteen months of action, the War Refugee Board spent $547,000 of government funds, drawn from $1,150,000 set aside for it

* In contrast, the United Nations Relief and Rehabilitation Administration, which aided people who were already liberated, could count without question on American government appropriations. No such support was accorded the War Refugee Board, the agency charged with saving captive people from mass murder.
† The JDC was by far the largest Jewish organization conducting overseas relief. The UJA was the major American Jewish fund-raising agency and the main source of the JDC's income.

in the President's Emergency Fund. The $547,000 went largely for salaries and other administrative expenses of the board. In addition, the President allotted the board $1,068,750 specifically to buy and ship food parcels to concentration camp inmates.* The other projects sponsored by the WRB were funded almost entirely by the Jewish organizations. The Joint Distribution Committee spent in excess of $15,000,000; the Vaad Hahatzala (Orthodox rescue committee) supplied over $1,000,000; the World Jewish Congress expended more than $300,000; and other groups provided lesser amounts.† [20]

A minor problem for the WRB in its opening weeks involved the Intergovernmental Committee on Refugees. According to Stettinius, Myron C. Taylor had been "very angry" on learning of the establishment of the WRB, partly because he feared it would eclipse the ICR's work. Taylor wanted the WRB to agree to confer with the ICR before initiating projects and to channel all its approaches to foreign governments through the ICR. Pehle rejected such time-consuming procedures and offered only to keep the ICR informed of the board's activities. [23]

To clarify the situation, the top ICR officials, Sir Herbert Emerson and Patrick Malin, came to Washington in April 1944. The resulting understanding left the WRB free to develop its programs independently. The two organizations agreed to cooperate whenever possible and to keep each other informed of their respective operations in order to prevent duplication. The WRB thus avoided a clash with the ICR; but its more critical problems remained. [24]

Several factors, then, diminished the War Refugee Board's effectiveness. Although Executive Order 9417 clearly required their full cooperation, the State and War departments offered almost as much encumbrance as help. The Russians would not participate. The British were obstructive. Roosevelt took little interest except as a source of occasional favorable publicity. Morgenthau soon realized that his influence with the President on rescue matters was very limited, and he

---

* This $1,068,750 came from the general appropriation for foreign war relief voted by Congress annually from 1940 through 1945. The total amount appropriated was $85,000,000. The American Red Cross and the International Red Cross disbursed the rest of the funds in a great variety of projects, mostly unrelated to Jewish refugees. [21]

† When drafting legal papers for the establishment of the WRB, Oscar Cox and his assistant, Milton Handler, originally planned $25,000,000 from the President's Emergency Fund for the board's expenses. This could have paid for rescue operations on a fairly large scale, as well as for administration. For reasons that are not clear, the idea was dropped before the board was formed. [22]

lessened pressures in that direction. Moreover, the funding situation weakened the board from the start.[25]

What looked at first as though it might become a potent government rescue machine turned into a valuable, but limited, collaboration between the government and the private agencies. And the relatively weak private organizations carried most of the load. Nevertheless, the WRB staff was determined to do all it could, despite the difficulty of the assignment and the handicaps under which it had to operate.

Working mainly with proposals that the Jewish organizations had long been urging, the War Refugee Board forged a wide-ranging rescue program. Its main contours included (1) evacuating Jews and other endangered people from Axis territory, (2) finding places to which they could be sent, (3) using psychological measures (especially threats of war-crimes trials) aimed at preventing deportations and atrocities, and (4) shipping relief supplies into concentration camps.[26]

As for evacuation, the obvious potential outlets were Turkey, Spain, Allied-occupied southern Italy, Sweden, and Switzerland.

Turkey

The first WRB representative to see action overseas was Ira Hirschmann, a prominent New York department-store executive who had attended the ill-fated Evian Conference of 1938 and had continued to be deeply concerned about the European Jews. His post, Turkey, offered important possibilities for rescue, for hundreds of thousands of Jews were still alive—and in danger—in the nearby Balkans. In Hirschmann's words, Turkey was "a window into the Balkans. The job, as I saw it, was to attempt to make out of the window, a door."[27]

When he reached Ankara, in mid-February 1944, Hirschmann found the movement of Jews out of the Balkans, into Turkey, and on to Palestine distressingly small. Since 1940, Chaim Barlas of the Jewish Agency had worked to open this route to safety. Finally, during 1943, he managed to evacuate as many as 1,100 Jews. Most came by railroad via Bulgaria, the rest by small boats from Greece. Hirschmann learned that Barlas had to contend with an obstacle course of restrictions, red tape, and delays devised by Rumanian, Bulgarian, Turkish, and Turkish-based British officials. Spurred by the realization that the Balkan Jews lived under constant threat of deportation, and aware that tens of thousands of them were penned in disease-ridden camps, the WRB representative focused his first efforts on widening the outlet through Bulgaria.[28]

The British agreed to permit all Jews who reached Turkey to go to Palestine. Hirschmann then persuaded the Turkish government to let 200 Jews enter from Bulgaria and continue on to Palestine every ten days. But the results were not very encouraging. Only 131 came during the first month of the arrangement, and the numbers decreased in subsequent months. Although much of the problem stemmed from a tight Bulgarian policy on the exit of Jews, Turkey also kept the influx down by insisting on advance procurement of Turkish transit visas while quietly making them practically unavailable. By the end of the summer of 1944, the WRB had brought only about 450 Jews out via Bulgaria.[29]

In the meantime, late in February, the WRB in Washington had telegraphed its basic plan for Turkey to the American ambassador there, Laurence A. Steinhardt. It called for diplomatic pressures on Ankara to relax its immigration controls and to announce publicly that all fleeing Jews would be permitted to enter the country. In return, the board would agree to maintain the refugees while in Turkey, possibly in temporary reception camps, and move them on to other havens.[30]

Hirschmann, who had received only the most meager and grudging cooperation from the Turks, advised the board that no chance whatever existed that they would assent to this plan. Drawing on the excuse that American and British policymakers had invoked so often, Ankara had already insisted that easing border controls would open the way for Axis agents to flood into Turkey and then scatter throughout the Allied world. Time and again thereafter, Turkish officials relied on this pretext to justify their nation's reluctance to serve as an escape channel.* When leaders of the World Jewish Congress in New York learned about Turkey's recalcitrance, they urged the WRB to ask President Roosevelt to raise the problem with the Turkish head of government. But nothing in the records indicates that the board did so.[31]

Hirschmann next tried to open an evacuation route across the Black Sea. His plan was to charter a good-sized passenger vessel and use it over and over again to ferry Jews directly from Rumania to Turkey. From there they would travel by rail to Palestine. The search led to the

* The argument was preposterous. Refugees could have been detained and carefully checked. In fact, those who did get through were thoroughly screened. No Axis government would have been so stupid as to send its agents into such a trap.

Incidentally, permanent Jewish residents in Turkey (nonrefugees) received such bad treatment that a small but steady flow of *them* moved to Palestine during 1944.[32]

Vatan, a privately owned Turkish ship capable of carrying 800 people. But the Turkish government, pleading a shortage of ships and the danger of mines, stood in the way of leasing it. Strong pressure by Ambassador Steinhardt forced Turkish consent, but only on condition that the United States agree to replace the vessel if it should be sunk.* The WRB in Washington obtained such a commitment from Admiral Emory S. Land of the War Shipping Administration. Land also dispatched a WSA shipping expert from Cairo to Ankara to assist Hirschmann with Black Sea shipping problems.[33]

Before arrangements for the *Vatan* were completed, Hirschmann located and shifted his attention to the *Tari,* a vessel that could hold 1,500 passengers. But weeks passed before the WRB could persuade Admiral Land to guarantee replacement of such a large ship. Even with that assurance, Steinhardt had to threaten Turkish authorities with an anti-Turkish press campaign in the United States to extract permission to lease the *Tari.*† By then, two months had elapsed since Hirschmann had begun the search for a ship. Yet one crucial problem still remained. The Turkish government would not let the *Tari* sail without safe-conduct assurances from the belligerents. Although the others agreed, Germany rebuffed all requests. Thus the plans and hopes that had grown up around the *Tari* evaporated. Concurrent efforts to borrow Swedish and other ships operating in the eastern Mediterranean failed.[35]

While the board unsuccessfully sought to open its sea route, another evacuation program was achieving some results. In late March, the Jewish Agency (with WRB support and Joint Distribution Committee funds) initiated a limited exodus from Rumania to Turkey by hiring

* In 1940 and 1941, while ambassador to Russia, Steinhardt, himself a Jew, had pressed for tighter American restrictions on refugee entry and had hindered Jewish immigration from eastern Europe to the United States. Writing in the newspaper *PM* in the fall of 1943, journalist I. F. Stone drew on government documents to expose Steinhardt's actions. Stone's article received wide attention in the Jewish press. As ambassador to Turkey in 1944, however, Steinhardt worked to facilitate rescue. On a trip to the United States in spring 1944, Hirschmann spoke with numerous Jewish opinion leaders in an effort to rehabilitate Steinhardt's reputation.[34]

† At the same time, Steinhardt was extremely critical of the Allied governments. In an acid message to Washington, he pointed out that, despite several requests from him and Hirschmann, no American or British vessel, not even a small one, had been made available for the Black Sea route. He underscored the incongruity of the American and British failure to furnish as much as a single 4,000-ton boat at the very time they were "posing as the saviors of the refugees before the rest of the world," and while "incessant U.S. propaganda" was boasting of American construction of over 1.5 million tons of shipping a month.[36]

three Bulgarian boats (at exorbitant rates). These tiny vessels, unseaworthy and overloaded, running belligerent waters without safe-conduct assurances, brought out 1,200 people. Included were a few score orphans from the Transnistria concentration camps. The *New York Times* correspondent in Istanbul described them: "The children had a scared look in their eyes. They jumped at the slightest noise and often raised their hands to protect their faces as if expecting beatings. They said they had been beaten by German and Rumanian soldiers." [37]

Returning without passengers after a mid-May trip to Turkey, one of the three boats, the *Maritza,* sank in a Black Sea gale. Fearing more ship losses, the Bulgarian government forbade further open-sea voyages by small vessels. At about the same time, the WRB and the Jewish Agency decided to redirect their attempts at Black Sea evacuation to small Turkish boats whose owners (and the Turkish government) were willing to let them sail without safe-conducts. Four vessels were located. During July and early August, they moved 1,500 refugees from Rumania to Turkey.* [38]

But disaster struck shortly after midnight on August 5. Not far off the Turkish coast, three German gunboats sank one of the tiny vessels, the *Mefkura,* then machine-gunned its passengers in the water. Of 295 refugees on board, a hundred were children. There were five survivors. Among the dead were two sisters, eleven and seven years old. The parents, who had been separated from their children and were in New York, had gone to enormous lengths to get the two girls and their two older brothers out of Rumania. The boys reached Istanbul safely in October. They, too, had been scheduled to sail on the *Mefkura,* but had been turned back at the last minute for lack of room on the boat. [40]

Almost all of the 2,700 who reached Turkey by sea between late March and August 1944 arrived without Turkish transit visas. Many had to board the boats secretly in Rumania, so they could not apply for visas. But a major difficulty was that the Turkish consulate in Rumania, undoubtedly on orders from Ankara, issued transit visas extremely sparingly. When the first boat, with 239 of these "illegal" refugees, appeared in Istanbul harbor, the Turkish authorities refused to let it land. The Turkish foreign minister maintained that to do so would "open the flood gates" to ships full of illegal refugees, including spies. Following

---

* The WRB worried about operating without safe-conduct assurances, but saw no alternative in view of German unwillingness to issue them. The Jewish Agency and the JDC agreed with the board's decision. Refugees were forewarned of the risk. In actuality, Jews were ready to sail on any kind of vessel to get out of Rumania. [39]

forceful intervention by Ambassador Steinhardt, the foreign minister, as a special exception, allowed this group to land and move on to Palestine by rail. When the pattern repeated itself with the arrival of the second boatload, it was clear that Steinhardt's pressure had broken the transit-visa roadblock. Steinhardt doubted, however, that he could prevail upon the Turks to extend the arrangement to more than 500 "illegals" per month.[41]

Another escape route, across the Aegean Sea from Greece to Turkey, saved about 900 Jews during the year before Greece's liberation in October 1944. These refugees also went on to Palestine. This project, set up by a Jewish organization before Hirschmann arrived in Turkey, relied on small fishing craft and other tiny boats. It could have been expanded if it had been possible to obtain a definite landing and re-fueling base in Turkey. Hirschmann sought Turkish permission for this, but Ankara stalled on it until the Germans left Greece. In addition, the British, who controlled the coastal area, opposed the whole project on security grounds.[42]

Hirschmann's most impressive achievement did not directly involve Turkey. In early 1943, the State Department and the British Foreign Office had brushed aside a Rumanian offer to release 70,000 Jews from terrible camps in Transnistria and turn them over to the Allies. Later, pressures from Jewish organizations persuaded the State Department to take steps to help these desperate Jews. Assisted by the International Red Cross, the State Department induced the Bucharest government late in 1943 to begin transferring them from Transnistria to Rumania proper. But after evacuating 6,400, the Rumanians gave in to German pressure and ceased the operation.[43]

The situation reached the point of extreme danger soon after the WRB came into existence. Rampant disease and starvation continued in the camps. Even worse, the German army, falling back before the Soviets, was entering Transnistria. The Jews were in the path of the retreat. The WRB used all available diplomatic channels to press the Rumanian government, but the break came through Hirschmann's personal intervention with Alexander Cretzianu, Rumania's minister to Turkey.[44]

Hirschmann told Cretzianu that America was outraged at Rumania's treatment of Jews and warned him that his nation would be well advised to turn about and help save them. Cretzianu said, "If this means so much to you in the United States, why didn't you come sooner? You could have saved more lives." He agreed to urge his government to transfer the Jews from Transnistria to the interior of Rumania. The Rumanian government responded positively and in March recommenced the evacuations. Thus the 48,000 Jews still alive in Transnistria were safeguarded. The weakening German position in the Balkans contributed importantly to this outcome, but the WRB had played a key role in the episode.* [45]

In July, Hirschmann met again with Cretzianu. He also held talks with Nicholas Balabanoff, the Bulgarian minister to Turkey. With German power close to collapse in the two Balkan countries, Hirschmann sought to play on their governments' hopes to gain American goodwill. From Rumania, he received a commitment to accept, secretly, Jews fleeing from Nazi terror in Hungary. The Rumanians also agreed to cooperate in the exit of Jews from their country.[47]

Hirschmann believed that evacuation was not the best answer for Bulgaria's 45,000 Jews, now that the threat of deportation was over. Rather, he sought an end to the persecution of Jews in Bulgaria and the extension of full rights to them. He urged these steps on Balabanoff. In late August, partly because of Hirschmann's efforts, Bulgaria abolished its anti-Jewish laws and reinstated Jewish property rights. Bulgarian Jews had the possibility of rebuilding their lives.[48]

Rumania surrendered to Russia on August 23, and two weeks later the Soviets took control of Bulgaria. Hirschmann concluded that the main WRB mission in Turkey had ended. The Jews of Rumania and Bulgaria needed aid, but they were safe. He departed for home in early October, leaving Herbert Katzki to complete the board's work.[49]

Katzki, a person of wide experience with the Joint Distribution Committee, had joined the WRB in Turkey in early summer. After Hirschmann left, Katzki tried to place JDC relief teams in Rumania and Bulgaria. But the Soviets blocked that plan.[50]

Because of the widespread destitution among Balkan Jews, the Jewish Agency reinstituted its evacuation efforts in fall 1944. With Katzki's cooperation, it soon brought out 2,000 more Jews. But the British halted this exodus, insisting that, with the Germans gone, Jews in Rumania and Bulgaria were now safe and thus not eligible for admission to Palestine. The WRB closed its office in Turkey in February 1945.[51]

In all, nearly 7,000 Jews left the Balkans and reached Palestine via Turkey under the aegis of the WRB. Hirschmann's diplomatic negotiations affected far larger numbers by breaking up the abominable Transnistrian camps and bargaining for the greatest possible protection for

* To encourage him to cooperate, Hirschmann offered Cretzianu asylum in the United States. Later, while in Washington for consultation, Hirschmann quietly arranged for immigration visas for the Rumanian diplomat and his family.[46]

Jews who were still alive in Rumania and Bulgaria. Hirschmann pointed out that the very formation of the WRB had accomplished something else of importance. Its birth, according to numerous Jews passing through Turkey, had "injected new life and hope into . . . refugees throughout the European continent." One group of fugitives explained, with obvious emotion, "For two years there has been only one phrase on everyone's lips, 'When are the Americans coming?' "[52]

Spain

After Turkey, Spain appeared to be the most important escape hatch from Axis Europe. Deportations of Jews from France to the gas chambers had continued, with interruptions, since the great roundups of the summer and fall of 1942. And they would go on until France's liberation. A rush of escapes to Spain had followed the 1942 roundups. But after early 1943 only a few hundred Jews a month managed to cross the Pyrenees. The WRB planned to change that trickle into a steady flow.[53]

Germany's occupation of Vichy France in November 1942 had sent another wave of refugees, mostly non-Jewish, into Spain. The new exodus, much larger than the earlier one, ultimately numbered about 25,000 people. They were predominantly French males of military age who hoped to reach North Africa to join the Allied forces. For military reasons, the American and British diplomatic missions in Spain acted to help them and to hasten their evacuation.[54]

Only infrequently had Spanish authorities turned refugees back. But neither had they done anything to facilitate their escape.* Rather, they discouraged it by incarcerating the fugitives—men, women, and children—in prisons and concentration camps. Conditions were wretched. An American embassy report told of the vast overcrowding and pointed out that inmates were "sleeping, despite the bitter cold of winter, without blankets on cold concrete floors, crowded together with inadequate sanitary facilities, and forced to subsist on a starvation diet." In one prison, three toilets served 1,900 men. Each man slept in a nearly airless space only one foot by five and one-half feet. A three-year-old girl

---

* Spain made it abundantly clear during World War II that it did not want to shoulder any of the refugee burden. A Quaker representative summed it up in a report from Madrid in late 1943: "The attitude here seems to be limited to the demand: 'Get out!' and 'Now!' "[56]

suffered through scarlet fever and typhoid in a prison cell with her mother.*[55]

In January 1943, under American and British pressure, Spanish authorities agreed to allow prisoners to transfer to hotels and boarding-houses, but only if their support was assured and arrangements were under way for their departure from the country. Thanks to funds provided by the American, British, and French North African diplomatic missions, the male French escapees (along with some Dutch, Belgian, and Polish nationals) left the prisons. During 1943, the Allies evacuated them to North Africa.[58]

But most of the Jewish refugees had no source of help. The Joint Distribution Committee and the American Friends Service Committee managed to place a Friends worker, David Blickenstaff, in Madrid in late January 1943. With full cooperation from the American ambassador, Carlton J. H. Hayes, Blickenstaff established the Representation in Spain of American Relief Organizations and took responsibility for these refugees. Blickenstaff's organization freed hundreds of them by supplying money for their maintenance, sent aid to those still incarcerated, and worked persistently to locate emigration possibilities for the fugitives.[59]

By the time the War Refugee Board came into existence, the American and British embassies had virtually resolved the French non-Jewish refugee crisis, and Blickenstaff had the problem of the Jewish refugees under control. Furthermore, emigration plans for the bulk of the 2,500 Jewish refugees still in Spain appeared to be falling into place. As few new fugitives were entering the country, the refugee situation had been stabilized. Hayes considered the problem solved. But the WRB saw removal of the earlier refugees as only the first step. Spain was to become a channel for bringing many more threatened people out of Axis Europe.[60]

The basic WRB plan for Spain called for the American ambassador to urge the Spanish government to relax its border restrictions and publicly announce its willingness to receive refugees. Spain should also be asked to set up three reception camps along the French border. They would remain under Spanish control, but the WRB would finance them and would see that the refugees moved promptly through them and out of Spain.[61]

The Treasury and War departments agreed to the plan, but State

---

* An inmate described conditions at the largest camp, Miranda de Ebro: "We sleep on the floor, without mattress, without pillow, tortured by innumerable flies and bedbugs. Everything is covered with a thick stratum of dust which, when raised by the wind, penetrates everywhere and especially in the food. The most terrible thing is the almost complete lack of water."[57]

Department officials resisted it at first. They claimed that any pressure on Spain would threaten the nearly completed, but very sensitive, wolfram negotiations. Wolfram (tungsten), necessary for hardening steel, was essential for production of vital war materials such as machine tools and armor plate. Germany depended on Spain and Portugal for its supply. For several months, a program of large American and British purchases of Spanish wolfram had almost foreclosed its availability to the Nazis. Hayes was now in the midst of negotiations with Spain for full stoppage of wolfram exports to Germany. In early February, he arranged a temporary embargo.[62]

With help from Stettinius, the board succeeded in mid-February in persuading the State Department to instruct Hayes to press the WRB rescue plan with the Spanish government. Hayes was expressly advised to present the refugee matter on humanitarian grounds, move it along rapidly, and keep it entirely separate from other negotiations with Spain.[63]

Hayes replied that he did not believe the plan would increase the refugee flow and that he was not presenting it to the Spanish government. He asserted that relaxation of Spain's border controls would only facilitate entry of German agents and encourage efforts to smuggle wolfram out to German purchasers. He did not explain how German agents could avoid detection in the proposed reception camps. Nor did he reveal how easing controls on the *entry* of persons would weaken restrictions on the *exit* of bulky goods.[64]

No amount of pressure could change Hayes's position. He only responded with additional unsubstantiated arguments against the plan. It would somehow jeopardize Blickenstaff's work. It would hinder the escape from France of downed Allied airmen. It would antagonize the Spanish government.[65]

Hayes's reaction to the rescue plan was only one part of his noncooperation. Immediately after the WRB was formed, the State Department ordered all its diplomatic missions to inform their host governments of the new American rescue policy and to ask them to specify ways in which they would be willing to help. Hayes refused. He explained that he had regularly kept the Spanish government informed of American refugee policy, so special action on that part of the instructions was unnecessary. As to requesting Spanish cooperation, the time was inopportune because of "the present crisis in our relations with Spain." He promised to take it up some other time, "when a better opportunity presents itself." He did, after a fashion, five months later.[66]

Hayes also kept the board from placing a representative in Spain. Blickenstaff seemed the appropriate choice, and his sponsoring group, the American Friends Service Committee, stated that it could find a replacement for him. But Hayes, insisting that Blickenstaff could not be spared from his current assignment, consented to accept him as WRB representative only if he held both posts. The board replied that it needed a full-time person and offered to send James J. Saxon, a Treasury officer then in French Africa. Hayes answered that he saw no need for a full-time representative in Spain, that there was nothing the WRB could accomplish there that he and Blickenstaff were not already doing. If a person were appointed, though, it should be Blickenstaff— on a part-time basis. (Blickenstaff himself saw plenty of reason for a full-time WRB representative, but Hayes did not consult him on the question.) [67]

The stalemate continued until Hayes visited the United States in mid-July 1944. He then admitted to Pehle that more could have been done for rescue in Spain, and he reluctantly agreed to accept the WRB's James H. Mann as representative—for a two-month trial period. A month later, the State Department approved Mann. But by then the Allies were far along in the reconquest of France. The chance for important rescue work through Spain had passed.[68]

Hayes also tried to keep funds for rescue from going into Spain. In March, the WRB approved a license authorizing the Joint Distribution Committee to send $100,000 for evacuation of refugees, mostly children, from France to Spain. Part of the money was to hire border guides to smuggle the fugitives through the Pyrenees. Hayes refused to transmit the license to the JDC's agent, Samuel Sequerra. If a private agency sponsored such clandestine operations, he claimed, the Spanish government might close down all refugee-relief work, including Blickenstaff's program. In addition, Sequerra's activities might help German agents posing as refugees to penetrate Spain and move on to Allied territories. (In fact, Germany had no trouble infiltrating agents into Spain.) Furthermore, the ambassador asserted, Sequerra's loyalty to the Allies was doubtful. (WRB investigations found this charge entirely without basis.) Fortunately for the few hundred brought out with the funds, the license took effect despite Hayes's opposition.* [69]

---

* The WRB was not alone in clashing with Hayes. The Office of Strategic Services and the Office of War Information had trouble keeping agents in Spain because of conflicts with the American embassy there. On the basis of experience in Lisbon, a Unitarian Service Committee official advised the board as early as February that opening Spain as an escape channel would be nearly impossible unless Hayes was replaced or the Franco government fell. A little later, Myron C. Taylor informed Morgenthau that he and the Intergovernmental Committee "have not been able to do anything in Spain, thanks to Mr. Hayes." [70]

The board tried, but failed, to budge Hayes. Pehle persuaded Eleanor Roosevelt to seek the President's help. She reported, "I spoke to Franklin & asked if perhaps a change might be advisable & Franklin said wearily 'well the complaints are mounting.'" Morgenthau approached Roosevelt directly, asking that he send Wendell Willkie to set Hayes straight on this and other American problems in Spain. FDR, who could readily have brought Hayes into line if he had cared to, shunted Morgenthau off to Hull. In June 1944, the WRB sent James Mann to Spain to confer with Hayes. Mann made virtually no progress. The following month, while Hayes was in Washington, Pehle saw him twice, but failed to gain any cooperation apart from the acceptance of Mann as the WRB representative in Spain on a trial basis.[71]

Hayes's behavior remains a riddle. He was not entirely insensitive toward Jewish refugees, or he would not have supported Blickenstaff's work so strongly. Nor can he be considered anti-Semitic; his service as a co-chairman of the National Conference of Christians and Jews continued even while he was ambassador to Spain. Furthermore, Hayes interceded with the Spanish government on two rescue matters. In 1943 and 1944, he encouraged Spain to furnish safe haven for a few hundred Sephardic Jews, descendants of Jews expelled from Spain five centuries earlier. And when the Hungarian Jews were confronted with terror and death, his approaches in Madrid helped stimulate efforts to protect Jews by the Spanish legation in Budapest.[72]

Hayes's failure to cooperate with the WRB apparently stemmed from his view of his mission in Spain. In April 1942, just before taking up his post, Hayes told a small gathering of Americans involved in rescue and relief work that he had accepted the assignment in order to expedite the winning of the war. His main goal was going to be to stop Spanish sales of strategic materials to Germany. He also intended gradually to swing Spain away from the Axis and toward the Allies.[73]

Hayes's official communications regarding rescue and the WRB reveal an undertone of anxiety that a diplomatic misstep on his part might antagonize the Spanish government and impede progress toward his main objectives. To get French men of military age out of Spain to North Africa, he would run this risk. That would contribute to his cardinal aim, victory over the Axis. He would even approach the Spanish authorities on behalf of other imprisoned refugees, for that pointed toward their emigration from Spain, a goal ardently desired by the Spanish government. But to press for cooperation in bringing about an influx of new Jewish refugees would, in Hayes's view, provoke the Spanish government and jeopardize his central policy.[74]

In reality, Hayes was too timid. During early 1943, caution might have been necessary. But after the Axis surrendered in North Africa in May 1943 (and even more by January 1944, when the WRB emerged), Spain knew who would win the war and acted accordingly. Moreover, by December 1943, Hayes had achieved virtually all his prime objectives. As he reported to the State Department that month, Spain had rechanneled most sales of strategic materials (including wolfram) away from Germany and to the Allies, had withdrawn its Blue Division from the Russian front, and was cooperating in numerous other ways. Final agreement on a total stoppage of the small remaining flow of wolfram to Germany was incomplete. But by the time the WRB's requests reached Hayes, a temporary embargo was in effect. Its continuation was virtually guaranteed—not by Hayes's restrained diplomacy, but by an American threat to sever Spain's oil lifeline.[75]

Hayes nonetheless concluded that diplomatic pressures for the WRB's programs might interfere with the final steps of his wolfram negotiations. He apparently considered the board's work of too little significance to justify any risk. To Carlton Hayes, a renowned historian, the battle over Spanish wolfram, a battle that was already won, loomed far larger than the genocide of the Jews.[76]

It is impossible to determine what the WRB might have accomplished in Spain with Hayes's cooperation. With minimal outside help, a handful of people working in Spain for the World Jewish Congress, the Jewish Agency, and the Joint Distribution Committee proved that escapes from France were still possible. But their isolated and usually secret operations had no support services, no WRB coordination, and no diplomatic backing. Only a few score refugees came through each month—probably not many more than 1,000 altogether between the beginning of 1944 and late August, when the need for flight to Spain ended.[77]

The main refugee action in Spain in 1944 involved the evacuation of stateless escapees who had arrived there in 1943 and earlier. Although the WRB facilitated it somewhat, this movement was not a board project. It represented the fruition of plans that Blickenstaff and others had worked on for over a year. One ship sailed for Palestine in January and another in October. They carried a total of 875 refugees to permanent haven. In the spring, Canada took 220 others. And in May, a small refugee camp near Casablanca, the only achievement of the Bermuda Conference, finally opened its gates. During the next two months, it received 630 people from Spain. Adding the handful who managed to obtain U.S. visas and the few others who went to England and Latin America raises the total evacuated in 1944 to 1,800. A thousand others remained in Spain at the start of 1945. The WRB had visualized Spain as a conveyor belt, moving thousands and thousands to freedom. That hope was dashed utterly.[78]

In contrast, the WRB encountered no difficulties in the other Iberian nation, Portugal. The American minister there, R. Henry Norweb, co-operated fully. On the WRB's assurance that the United States would move them to other places, the Portuguese government agreed to open its doors to all refugees coming through from Spain. The board's representative, Robert C. Dexter of the Unitarian Service Committee, had long experience in refugee work and was thoroughly familiar with Lisbon. Dexter arrived in April and began preparations for the expected flow of refugees. But very few arrived, for the conduit through Spain never opened. Dexter occupied himself with a variety of minor projects, but for the most part he waited in Lisbon for a task that failed to materialize.[79]

Southern Italy

Allied advances in Italy following the invasion of September 1943 opened another escape route from Axis Europe. By November, refugees were streaming across the Adriatic Sea from Yugoslavia to southern Italy. Most of this exodus was organized by the Tito-led Yugoslav resistance movement.[80]

Until March 1944, the Allied military cooperated fully with the Yugoslav evacuation. The British navy transported thousands of refugees across the Adriatic. Thousands more came in small partisan boats. (Later, some were flown out in Allied aircraft.) The British army sheltered and fed the fugitives in Italy and, using two troopships, transferred them to camps at El Shatt and Khatatba, in Egypt. Nearly all of these refugees were Yugoslav civilians. Few were Jewish. (The Nazis had exterminated most Yugoslav Jews.) The Jews among them (500 of the first 15,000) remained in Italy because the British camp administration in Egypt opposed bringing Jews there.[81]

By spring 1944, El Shatt and Khatatba were three-fourths full, and refugees were still entering Italy at the rate of 1,800 per week. Concerned that the camps in Egypt would reach capacity and the escapees then pile up in Italy and overburden Allied facilities there, the military authorities issued orders to discourage further refugee movement across the Adriatic. The instructions did not stop Yugoslavs from sailing to Italy. But the absence of Allied assistance cut the influx by two-thirds.[82]

Even before the military moved to stem the refugee flow, the War Refugee Board began to look into the situation in Italy. In March, a

Treasury Department agent based in Africa made an exploratory trip. Soon afterward, Leonard E. Ackermann, the WRB's representative in North Africa, was appointed its representative in Italy as well. The board's inquiries found the Tito forces willing to try to open an escape route through partisan areas of Yugoslavia and out to the Adriatic for the gravely endangered Jews of Hungary. But the Yugoslavs themselves were hampered by insufficient boats, funds, and supplies.[83]

While seeking solutions to those problems, Ackermann learned of the military's order to slow the refugee flow into Italy. He and the board in Washington recognized that a crisis had arisen. Additional temporary havens were essential to keep the Adriatic route open. If it closed, the chance for an outlet from Hungary would also disappear. At that time, May 1944, Eichmann and his henchmen were concentrating massive numbers of Hungarian Jews for deportation. The long, crowded death trains had already started to wind through the Slovakian mountains to Auschwitz.[84]

In Washington, Morgenthau called the situation to Roosevelt's attention at a Cabinet meeting. The President responded instantaneously that under no circumstances should the refugee flow across the Adriatic be hindered. Directly afterward, instructions went to the military in Italy to lift the restriction discouraging the influx. To help relieve the pressure, the President agreed to a WRB proposal to move a thousand refugees from Italy to an emergency internment camp in the United States. He also ordered an intensive search for havens in the Mediterranean area, including in Italy itself.[85]

One brief statement in a Cabinet meeting rapidly dissolved the problem in Italy. Allied military authorities quickly found that they could accommodate many more refugees in Italy than previously estimated. They also initiated steps to open a camp at Philippeville, in French North Africa, to harbor up to 7,000 people. And UNRRA, which had recently taken over the Egyptian camps, increased their capacity from 30,000 to 40,000. The refugee movement across the Adriatic recommenced in June and continued through the summer. By late August, though, the Nazi threat to Yugoslav civilians had virtually ended. When the exodus stopped, in September 1944, over 36,000 Yugoslavs, nearly all non-Jews, had escaped to Italy. About 28,000 of them had moved on to the camps in Egypt; the rest remained in Italy until they were repatriated.* [86]

---

* In 1944, over 4,000 Jewish refugees were in southern Italy. Most were there before the Allied invasion. Some came with the Yugoslavs. In May, 571 left for Palestine; in July, 874 sailed for the internment camp in the United States. Most of the rest eventually went to Palestine.[87]

Little came of the hopes for opening an escape route out of Hungary. Tito's forces wanted to help. But the only partisan-held territory close to the Hungarian border, an area along the Drava River, was tightly guarded on the Hungarian side. Furthermore, the partisans in that sector were nearly isolated and were too hard pressed themselves to initiate rescue operations. They did take in and protect the few Jews who managed to get through.[88]

With WRB support, an attempt was made, through the Pope, to save the Jews in German-occupied northern Italy. In August 1944, Sir Clifford Heathcote-Smith, the Intergovernmental Committee's delegate in Italy, and Myron C. Taylor, Roosevelt's personal representative to the Vatican, spoke with the Pope. They asked him to urge the German government to stop the deportations from Italy and to release the Jews to the Allied-held part of the country.*[89]

The Pope agreed unhesitatingly. He told Heathcote-Smith that neither his conscience nor history would forgive him if he did not make the effort. But his approach, made through the nuncio in Berlin, brought nothing but an evasive response.[91]

Sweden

In Sweden, determined work by the WRB representative, Iver C. Olsen, brought disappointingly limited results. Olsen, previously the American legation's financial attaché, received close cooperation from the American minister in Sweden, Herschel V. Johnson. The Swedish government was also helpful. But the WRB came too late; comparatively few Jews remained alive in the northern tier of Axis Europe by 1944. And the obstacles to reaching them and getting them out of Axis territory were immense.[92]

Olsen organized and funded committees that sent rescue teams across the Baltic Sea into Estonia, Latvia, and Lithuania to bring out Jews and non-Jewish political refugees. These units developed underground contacts and obtained fast cabin cruisers, fuel, supplies, and false identification papers. But although the program operated throughout the summer of 1944, it rescued only 1,200 people, none of them Jews. Most Jews still alive in the Baltic states were in hiding and afraid

---

* The British objected to the plan, claiming that southern Italy could not accommodate more refugees. Later, after learning from the military in Italy that room was available, the Foreign Office yielded.[90]

to come out. Non-Jewish escapees reported that many Jews could have fled on WRB boats, but they suspected a German trap and would not take the risk.[93]

Plain bad luck also plagued the Baltic Sea rescue effort. Action did not get under way until mid-June, and by then the short summer nights hindered operations. The Lithuanian program suffered from the start because Olsen's key agent did not return from a preliminary trip to make rescue arrangements. In time, the Germans captured five of the boats running to Lithuania. One launch used in the Latvian project was caught by the Nazis, who threw its crew and fifty refugees into a concentration camp. Eight others who worked in the Latvian rescue effort were killed or disappeared. At the end of September, Olsen called off the Baltic operations. As the Russians advanced, military action in that region made further rescue attempts impossible.* [94]

Olsen transferred the Baltic Sea boats to another operation that was already ferrying endangered Norwegians to Sweden. This project, financed from America and sponsored by the AFL and the CIO, moved several thousands to safety. Evacuations from Norway, both across the land border and by sea in the south, proved to be the WRB's main achievement in Sweden. Ultimately, the board helped bring 15,000 refugees out of Norway. Again, none were Jews.[96]

Rescue efforts could not count on much help from the small, but comfortably situated, Swedish Jewish community of about 7,000. The main Jewish communal organization was not very interested in rescue. Olsen believed the Swedish Jews feared that an influx of refugees would put a financial burden on them. They also worried that anti-Semitism, not then a problem, would develop if more Jews came in. Olsen reported that the Swedish Jews had been "most apathetic" to the rescue of the Danish Jews in October 1943. They had done nothing for the Norwegian Jews who managed to flee to Sweden. And even when thirty Jewish orphans reached Sweden from Central Europe in 1943, the Swedish Jews "did not want to be bothered." The children went into Christian homes.[97]

Several difficulties, then, impeded Olsen's plans. But the WRB's Swedish effort did accomplish a little for Jewish refugees. With Minister

* Because Olsen's main projects developed in the summer of 1944, a serious, if ludicrous, handicap to his work was the near sanctity in Sweden of the summer vacation. Especially in July, he found it extremely difficult to transact business in Stockholm. "There was," he reported, "scarcely a brain left in town." One Swedish Jewish leader departed on schedule for his month's vacation the very next day after Olsen gave him the $10,000 he needed to proceed with a rescue assignment he had agreed to carry out. The man's financial integrity was unimpeachable.[95]

Johnson's assistance, Olsen persuaded the Swedish government to bring in the 150 Jewish refugees in Finland. This was a precaution against possible danger in that Axis nation. Together, Johnson and Olsen developed an aid program for needy refugees in Sweden, three-fourths of whom were Jewish.* They also organized a relief system for thousands of anti-Nazis in Norway. Despite its illegality, it operated with the full cooperation of the Swedish Foreign Office and the Swedish diplomatic mission in Oslo.[98]

Near the end of the war in Europe, Olsen and Johnson lent their support to a series of secret negotiations that led in April 1945 to the transfer of two groups of concentration camp inmates to Sweden. First to come out were 425 Jews whom the Nazis had deported from Denmark. Soon afterward, 7,000 women, half of them Jews, arrived in Sweden from the wretched Ravensbrück camp. This resulted from talks between SS Chief Heinrich Himmler; Felix Kersten, Himmler's doctor and confidant; Hillel Storch and Norbert Masur of the Swedish section of the World Jewish Congress; and Count Folke Bernadotte, representing the Swedish Red Cross.[100]

Because the WRB's Swedish operations helped few Jews, Olsen was sharply criticized in some quarters. But a representative of the Joint Distribution Committee who went to Sweden in the fall of 1944 looked carefully into the situation and concluded that Olsen had done all that anyone could have. The WRB leadership in Washington was also convinced that he did the best job possible under the circumstances.[101]

Switzerland

The WRB accomplished more in Switzerland than it was able to in Spain, Italy, or Sweden. Because of its location close to much of Nazi Europe, the small mountain nation became the nerve center of the board's overseas work. It was the best corridor for sending funds into Europe. It served as a vital relay point for communications into and out of Axis territory. And the Swiss government, which maintained relations with the Axis nations, provided a channel for diplomatic contacts with Germany and its satellites.[102]

The WRB was fortunate to find a person already in Switzerland who

---

* From January 1944 until April 1945, Jewish refugees in Sweden numbered about 12,000: roughly 8,000 from Denmark, 1,000 from Norway, and 3,000 who had come from Central Europe before the war.[99]

was highly qualified to serve as its representative. Roswell McClelland, director of the American Friends Service Committee's refugee-relief program there, brought to the WRB post a thorough knowledge of refugee matters and experience in dealing with high government officials. He also enjoyed good relations with several rescue and relief organizations. Many of them had underground connections and communications networks reaching into Nazi Europe. These contacts would become essential to much of his activity.[103]

From a discretionary fund of $250,000 supplied by the Joint Distribution Committee, McClelland financed numerous undercover programs: relief operations in Axis territory, production of false documents, an underground courier service, and escape projects. (The escape work required small-scale bribery of border officials and police as well as payments to "passeurs" who guided refugees through the mountains and across the Swiss border.) Financial transactions often involved what McClelland called "dime store" goods. Pocket knives, bars of soap, razor blades, cheap Swiss watches, and other small commodities were far more valuable than money, because of their scarcity in Axis countries. They were smuggled out of Switzerland in secondhand suitcases under the averted eyes of "a sterling Swiss customs guard." Conducted for the most part by already existing underground and resistance groups, board operations extended into France, Germany, Italy, Czechoslovakia, and Hungary. They enabled thousands of endangered people in Axis Europe to survive and other thousands to escape.[104]

In France, Jews and anti-Nazis who were in hiding received essential supplies, money, and forged documents (identification cards, work permits, birth and baptismal certificates, ration cards). The WRB also furnished badly needed supplies to French resistance workers and their families in return for their help in protecting Jews. Similarly, McClelland sent funds to non-Jewish resistance groups located along the French-Spanish frontier who assisted Jews trying to cross the Pyrenees.[105]

The nearly 8,000 Jewish orphans who were hidden in France in Christian homes, schools, and convents were a matter of deep concern to the WRB. It sent funds from Switzerland to contribute to their maintenance. When the Nazis unleashed a campaign to track them down for deportation, WRB money helped persuade minor officials and local authorities to cooperate in keeping the hunters off the trail.[106]

The WRB was anxious to move the most endangered of the children to Switzerland. But the Swiss government would not accept them unless a responsible government guaranteed to remove them when the war ended. The British refused, insisting that they could not reserve Palestine certificates for after the war. The State Department also declined, claiming that it could not bind a future administration to issue visas. But WRB pressure induced State to authorize postwar immigration of up to 4,000 of the children, and the program went forward. By August 1944, when the threat had passed in France, 650 of the orphans had reached Switzerland and about 600 other Jewish children had entered with their parents or relatives.[107]

In German-occupied northern Italy, resistance forces and religious leaders used funds supplied by McClelland to conceal and care for Jews and other endangered people. WRB money enabled Hechaluz, a Swiss-based Zionist underground organization, to arrange the escape of 2,000 Jews from Hungary into Rumania and of a few hundred others into Yugoslavia. The facilities of Swiss, Swedish, and Turkish diplomatic couriers and even the papal nunciature's pouch were made available to smuggle the Hechaluz funds into Axis territory.[108]

In general, WRB efforts to help Jews escape to Switzerland had limited success. Yet several thousand did reach Swiss territory during 1944 and 1945. Besides the 1,250 children, more than 3,000 Jewish adults entered from France before that country became safe for Jews, in the late summer of 1944. Attempts to bring refugees in from northern Italy were mostly ineffective because of tight German controls along that frontier. In August 1944, during the Hungarian Jewish crisis, the American and British governments guaranteed refuge for all Jews allowed to leave Hungary. With that assurance, the Swiss government agreed to ease its immigration restrictions to let in up to 13,000 additional Jews on a temporary basis. Complex negotiations between Swiss Jewish leaders and Nazi officials led to the release from Nazi concentration camps and delivery to Switzerland of nearly 3,000 Jews. Finally, in April 1945, another 1,400 camp inmates, mostly non-Jewish French women, reached Switzerland.[109]

Until August 1944, the refugee question was the focus of a heated dispute between the Swiss government, which restricted the entry of Jews, and influential segments of the Swiss public, which objected strongly to that policy. Social-welfare organizations, Christian church groups, newspapers, and some political leaders argued on humanitarian grounds for opening the borders to all fleeing Jews. They were incensed that their government turned many Jews away at the frontier, leaving them to the mercy of the Gestapo or the French police, and even expelled some who had succeeded in entering the country secretly.[110]

Exact figures are not available, but in relation to its size Switzerland was unquestionably more generous in taking in refugees than any other country except Palestine. At the end of 1944, some 27,000 Jewish refugees were safe in Switzerland—so were approximately 20,000 non-Jewish refugees and about 40,000 interned military personnel. What upset many people, however, was the basic Swiss policy. The country's borders were wide open to all who were in danger because of their political beliefs, to escaped prisoners of war, and to military deserters. Usually, the following categories of Jews were also allowed to enter: young children (and their parents if accompanying them), pregnant women, the sick, the aged, and close relatives of Swiss citizens. All other Jews who managed to reach Switzerland were liable to be turned back at the border and left more exposed to peril than if they had not attempted to escape.[111]

That the Swiss authorities turned back many Jews is indisputable. Moreover, whenever significant numbers of Jews began to arrive at the borders, as at the time of the great deportations from France in 1942, the Swiss government tightened its controls on Jewish immigration. The purpose, Swiss officials explained, was to discourage more from coming, because the country could not absorb everyone who wanted asylum. Actually, Switzerland had the capacity to take in many more Jews than it did, according to an authority on Swiss policy, Edgar Bonjour. In his view, the stringent policy was caused by the government's fear of antagonizing Germany (a compelling problem, given Switzerland's economic and military vulnerability) and by the anti-Semitism that was widespread in Swiss society. If the policy had really been unacceptable, he maintains, the people could have overturned it. Like that of other countries, the general population of Switzerland was not disposed to sacrifice very much to help Jews.*[112]

The number of Jews turned back will never be known. Also unknown is the number who, aware of Switzerland's policy, were deterred from risking flight and ultimately fell to the Nazis.[114]

During its sixteen months of active service, the War Refugee Board encountered an endless procession of difficult problems. But it never confronted any greater challenge than the Nazi campaign to annihilate the 760,000 Jews in Hungary. The Hungarian crisis began when the board was only eight weeks old. It lasted nearly a year.[115]

* Government concern about the postwar situation was also a factor. Jewish refugees, most of whom were stateless, might very well not be repatriated or otherwise removed. Almost all other fugitives would.[113]

|| 13 ||

HUNGARY

Until 1944, despite severe anti-Semitic restrictions, Hungary had permitted its large Jewish population to live in a semblance of peace. It had even served as a refuge for several thousand Jews from Poland and Slovakia. But on March 19, 1944, fearing that Hungary would defect to the Allies and angry at its failure to deport the Jews into Nazi hands, Hitler sent occupying forces into that nation. The arch-organizer of deportation, Adolf Eichmann, arrived in Budapest soon afterward and, drawing on extensive Hungarian collaboration, set his operation in motion. In mid-April, concentration of Jews into central locations began. On May 15, mass deportations to Auschwitz commenced.[1]

Eichmann had divided Hungary into six geographical zones. He planned to dispatch the Jews to Auschwitz, zone by zone, until the provincial areas were cleared. Then Budapest, the last zone, would be emptied of Jews, thus completing the "final solution" in that country.[2]

The concentration process was utterly inhumane and the suffering on the death trains worse yet. Jews were crowded, with little food or water, into ghettos, brickyards, and tobacco sheds, where they remained for two to four weeks. Conditions everywhere resembled those of the

235

15,000 Jews in a brickyard at Kosice. One of them smuggled out a letter:

> I am afraid I cannot stand it for long, for we are suffering beyond description. We lie in the dust, have neither straw-mattresses nor covers, and will freeze to death. The place is sealed, I do not see any way out. . . . We are so neglected, that we do not look human any more. There is no possibility for cleaning anything. We have not taken off our clothes since coming here. Best greetings to you all, pray for us that we shall die soon.[3]

If the writer of that letter did not perish in the brickyard, he encountered a hell even worse on the deportation train. A report smuggled to Switzerland by the Jewish underground revealed that in mid-May four trains began leaving Hungary daily for Auschwitz. Each carried about 3,000 Jews closely packed in sealed freight cars. During the two-to-three-day trip, the victims were pressed together, standing, without water or sanitary facilities. Hundreds died on the way.[4]

Convinced that accounts he was hearing were exaggerated, the first secretary of the Swedish legation in Budapest looked for himself. In one brick factory, he found 10,000 Jews herded into an area so small they had to stand, pushed closely together, old and young alike, with no sanitary facilities. Many died standing up. He also witnessed Jews being loaded into boxcars, eighty to a car, and the doors being nailed shut.[5]

Fully detailed reports took a few weeks to get to the Allied world. But the basic information came out almost immediately. At the start of April, even before concentration began, Gerhart Riegner of the World Jewish Congress in Geneva telegraphed Stephen Wise that he had reliable reports that the Germans planned to exterminate the Jews of Hungary. Registration of Jews and yellow-star identification were under way. After these typical preliminary steps, Riegner warned, concentration and deportation would surely follow. In late April, a United Press report from Zurich disclosed that 300,000 Jews had been concentrated in collection centers in Hungary. On May 10, a *New York Times* story from Istanbul, derived from neutral diplomatic sources in Budapest, revealed that the Hungarian government "is now preparing for the annihilation of Hungarian Jews."[6]

On May 18, only three days after the mass deportations began, the *Times* reported that the first transports of Jews had left the Carpathian provinces for "murder camps in Poland." At the same time, the War Refugee Board received essentially the same information via London

from the Jewish Agency for Palestine. WRB inquiries to neutral governments with diplomatic missions in Hungary soon confirmed the news.
Less than six weeks later, McClelland telegraphed the board that "at
least 335,000 Jews already have been deported." He had "little doubt"
that the destination was the extermination camp at Auschwitz.[7]

Because of the extreme difficulty of direct rescue from Hungary,
surrounded as it was by Axis territory, the WRB had to rely heavily on
psychological approaches. In April, when it first learned of the impending danger, the board sent stern warnings to Hungary through neutral
channels. Directly after the deportations started, it urged the five neutrals, the Vatican, and the International Red Cross (IRC) to assign
additional diplomatic personnel to Hungary. The presence of a larger
number of foreign observers might act as a restraining influence. Sweden and the Vatican soon complied; the IRC did eventually. Spain,
Portugal, Switzerland, and Turkey did not. The WRB also appealed to
the neutrals to grant protective citizenship documents to Hungarian
Jews who had family or business ties to their countries. Turkey did not
participate, but the cooperation of the other four ultimately contributed
to the safekeeping of thousands of Jews.[8]

From Washington, the WRB launched an intensive propaganda campaign to persuade the Hungarian government to stop the deportations.
For many weeks, a barrage of threats and warnings buffeted the country. At the board's urging, several prominent Americans put the Hungarian people and their government on notice that sure retribution
would follow if persecution of the Jews continued. Others aimed their
words at the Hungarian conscience.[9]

President Roosevelt condemned the Nazi atrocities and promised
that "none who participate in these acts of savagery shall go unpunished." Secretary of State Hull reemphasized Roosevelt's warning twice
in a three-week period. The Senate Foreign Relations Committee and
the House Foreign Affairs Committee, in highly unusual actions, directed strong statements at the Hungarians. So did Alfred E. Smith.
His message was cosigned by seventy-one prominent Christians, including nearly a score of governors and four Nobel Prize winners. Hungarian-American leaders castigated the Budapest government for betraying
"every Hungarian tradition" and urged their former countrymen to
"redeem Hungary's honor" by helping the Jews. Archbishop Francis J.
Spellman of New York recorded a message for broadcast to the heavily
Catholic country. He emphasized that persecution of the Jews was "in
direct contradiction" to Catholic doctrine.[10]

For weeks, the Office of War Information and the BBC broadcast these messages to Hungary and other parts of Europe. The OWI had them publicized throughout the neutral European press and radio. And Allied aircraft dropped them into Hungary in pamphlet form.[11]

In parallel with its propaganda drive, the WRB pressed the neutral nations, the International Red Cross, and the Vatican to urge the Hungarian government to stop the deportations. On June 25, Pope Pius XII telegraphed a personal appeal to the Hungarian head of state, Regent Miklós Horthy. Shortly afterward, the king of Sweden, Gustav V, also sent a personal plea to Horthy, asking him, "in the name of humanity," to save the remaining Jews. But the International Red Cross, fearful that it might antagonize Germany and find itself excluded from its important work for war prisoners, hesitated to intervene.[12]

Continued pressure from the board and discussions in late June between Red Cross leaders, the Czech minister to Switzerland, and spokesmen for the World Jewish Congress finally persuaded the IRC to act. The spur was a shocking, detailed report on Auschwitz that the WJC and the Czech minister had recently received.[13]

IRC president Max Huber dispatched a handwritten letter to Horthy that summarized the new revelations about Auschwitz and requested detailed information on what was happening to the deported Jews and where they were now. The IRC offered to send a mission to Hungary to be present at the deportations, help with food and medicine, and assist the deportees at their destination.[14]

Huber's message raised extremely sensitive issues in Hungary and kept the heat on the Horthy government. But by July 6, the day it was sent, the earlier pressures, along with Germany's declining military situation, had already induced Horthy to stand up to the Nazis at last and insist that the deportations halt. By then, the Hungarian provinces had been cleared. Almost 440,000 Jews were gone. But most of Budapest's 230,000 Jews were still in the capital. The appeals from the Pope and the king of Sweden, stimulated in part by the WRB, had been especially important in stopping the deportations. So had a very sharp warning that the WRB had dispatched through Swiss government channels on June 26. The board's other diplomatic efforts and its propaganda campaign had also played a significant part in the change of policy.[15]

But Horthy's control of the situation was shaky. The deportations might resume at any time. On July 18, however, hopes rose for the Jews in Budapest. In a startling reply to the International Red Cross, Horthy offered to permit emigration of all Jewish children under ten who possessed visas to other countries and all Jews of any age who had Palestine certificates. He also invited the Red Cross to provide relief to the Jews in Hungary.[16]

Horthy's overture put the pressure squarely on the United States and Britain. Within ten days, the WRB was prepared to assure that the United States would find havens for all Jews let out of Hungary. But because Horthy had directed his proposal to both the Western Allies, the board did not want to act alone. On July 29, it informed the British that it would wait until August 7 for them to join in accepting Horthy's offer.[17]

August 7 passed with no decision from London, but the board decided to wait a few more days. The British were searching for a way out of their dilemma. They were alarmed at the pressure that acceptance of Horthy's proposal would place on their Palestine policy, yet they were unwilling to bear the onus of rejecting the offer. As usual where Jews were concerned, the British leadership was far more impressed with "the practical difficulties of dealing with a large flow of refugees" than with the alternative—their annihilation in Nazi killing centers.[18]

One British solution, to hand the Horthy proposal over to the Intergovernmental Committee, offered the obvious advantage of indefinite delay. But the WRB rejected that. The British next proposed a joint statement in which they would pledge, "to the extent of their resources," to cooperate with the United States in caring for the Jews who got out of Hungary. The WRB saw this as hardly any commitment. It asked Morgenthau and Josiah DuBois, then in London on other business, to try to bring the British around. Morgenthau talked with Churchill and Eden. DuBois and John Winant, the American ambassador, held long discussions with members of the Foreign Office. These steps finally brought results. On August 17, thirty days after Horthy had made his overture, and almost three weeks after the WRB had begun to press the British, the two governments publicly issued a statement accepting responsibility for finding havens for all the Jews allowed out of Hungary.* [19]

Fleetingly, it looked as though mass evacuation from Budapest might take place. The WRB, guaranteeing financial help and prompt removal of the refugees, urged the neutral states to open their borders. Switzerland offered to take 13,000 Jews on a temporary basis. Sweden was ready to accept 10,000 children. The State Department agreed to issue 5,000 visas for children. Hirschmann and Steinhardt cleared the way

---

* To obtain British approval, Winant had to endorse a secret subsidiary statement that protected Britain's Palestine position in case large numbers of Jews should actually get out of Hungary. In it, the United States agreed "not to face the British Government with a practical impossibility" in regard to taking in refugees. In short, the United States accepted most of the responsibility for finding places of refuge.[20]

for a large flow through the Balkans to Palestine by obtaining transit permission from the Rumanian, Bulgarian, and Turkish governments.[21]

But no Jews ever left Hungary under the Horthy proposal. While the Americans and British had been negotiating, the Nazis had barred the doors. It soon became clear that the Germans, who controlled Hungary's borders, had determined to prevent Jewish emigration.* [22]

Although it could not be implemented, the American-British guarantee to accept responsibility for relocating the Hungarian Jews constituted a major breakthrough in the Allied response to the Holocaust. But it came very, very late. The same assurances might have significantly altered the course of the Holocaust had they been made during 1942, or when Rumania offered to release 70,000 Jews in early 1943, or at the Bermuda Conference, or even in April 1944, when the danger signals arose in Hungary. But by August 1944 most possibilities for rescue by evacuation had passed.

As for the Horthy offer itself, quick Allied action might have caught the Nazis off balance and succeeded in bringing numbers of Jews out to safety. But no matter what the outcome might have been, the month's delay in responding remains unconscionable. The outside world had clear knowledge of the peril that hung over the remaining Hungarian Jews.

Even though the emigration proposal collapsed, Horthy had opened the possibility of survival for the more than 200,000 Jews in Budapest. The deportations had stopped. The Red Cross accepted the invitation to bring in relief supplies. And neutral diplomats and the papal nuncio devised ways to safeguard tens of thousands of Jews from the Nazis and Hungarian fascists. Palestine visas offered some protection. Thousands of them came in through Catholic diplomatic couriers and the nunciature. Baptismal certificates were issued. The Swedish, Swiss, Spanish, and Portuguese legations provided thousands of protective documents and visas. (Zionist youth groups forged thousands of additional papers.) The neutral legations, the church, and the Red Cross also protected thousands of Jews by keeping them in buildings that they placed under their extraterritorial jurisdiction.[24]

The Swiss and especially the Swedish legations led in this unusual venture in mass preservation of Jewish lives. At the center of the effort was Raoul Wallenberg, one of the main heroes in the entire struggle to

---

* A few thousand Jews did escape to Rumania, and a few hundred others to Yugoslavia. A small Jewish underground operation kept an outlet to Rumania open until mid-September. By then, though, the Russians had advanced the battle zone into eastern Hungary, and access to Rumania had been cut off.[23]

counter the Holocaust. The thirty-one-year-old architect and business-man, member of a leading Swedish diplomatic and banking family, met with the WRB's Iver Olsen in Stockholm in June 1944. He offered to go to Hungary to do what he could for the Jews there. At Olsen's suggestion, the Swedish government appointed him an attaché to its Budapest legation. In practice, though, Wallenberg served as the WRB's representative in Hungary. Through Olsen and the Swedish Foreign Office, the board sent him suggestions for action and the funds for his mission.[25]

Working with a staff of over 300 people, largely volunteers, Wallen-berg developed relief projects, but threw most of his efforts into plans to bring Jews under Swedish protection. Soon after arriving in Buda-pest, he rented a building, applied Swedish extraterritorial status to it, and used it as a safe haven for several hundred Jewish religious leaders. He also persuaded the Swedish government to allow the legation to issue special protective passports to Hungarian Jews. With time, he brought several additional buildings under Swedish extraterritoriality and expanded the passport scheme. By these means, Wallenberg ulti-mately saved at least 20,000 Jews.[26]

For three precarious months after Horthy terminated the deporta-tions, conditions for the Budapest Jews, though bad, remained surviv-able. Then, in mid-October, with the Russians only one hundred miles east of the capital, Horthy moved for an armistice with the Allies. Reacting swiftly, the Nazis forced him to resign as head of state by threatening to kill his son. They then installed a puppet regime under Ferenc Szalasi and the fascist Arrow Cross party. Almost immediately, the fervidly anti-Semitic Arrow Cross loosed a reign of terror against the Budapest Jews, slaughtering thousands. Throughout that fall and winter, beating, plundering, and murdering continually broke out. Dur-ing the final two months before the Red Army conquered the city, the Arrow Cross killed more than 10,000 Jews and left them in the streets or in the Danube's freezing waters.[27]

The most barbaric episode during the Szalasi regime took place in November. Deportations began again, but not to Auschwitz. (The rail systems had collapsed, and the Auschwitz killing operations were soon to be shut down.) The Nazis needed labor 120 miles to the west, across the Austrian border. So they drove approximately 40,000 Jews on foot, through bone-chilling rains, toward Austria. On the march, 15 to 20 percent either died or fell out from exhaustion and exposure and were shot. Those who reached Austria but were judged unfit for hard labor were pushed back across the border into Hungary and driven into the woods to die of starvation, exposure, and disease. The horrible consequences of the marches, especially the high death rate among the women, finally became too much even for Szalasi. On November 21, he stopped the deportations.[28]

The Szalasi period put Raoul Wallenberg to his severest tests. The day after the Arrow Cross came to power, his mostly Jewish relief staff completely disappeared. The next day, he located them, one by one, and moved them to safer locations. At about the same time, the Szalasi regime declared all the protective passports void. Wallenberg managed to get that ruling retracted. Once, an armed patrol entered an area of Swedish protected houses and began to seize Jews. Wallenberg appeared and shouted, "This is Swedish territory. . . . If you want to take them you will have to shoot me first." The Jews were released. Again, when he learned that eleven people with Swedish passports had been put on a train for Austria, Wallenberg pursued it by automobile, caught it at the last stop before the border, and took the eleven off. At the time of the ghastly marches to Austria, he carried food and other supplies to the victims. And he succeeded, by various pretexts, in removing hundreds of Jews from the columns and returning them to protected houses in Budapest.[29]

During the Szalasi government's four months of terror, tens of thousands of Budapest Jews perished. When the Russians finally captured the city, in mid-February 1945, about 120,000 Jews remained alive. The Budapest Jews had suffered disastrously at the hands of the Arrow Cross. Nevertheless, the survival of 120,000 was a significant accomplishment under the circumstances. All were on the brink of extermination in July, and throughout the fall and winter they were trapped by a murderous government. The forces from the outside world that had pressured Horthy in the spring and the later protective measures inside Budapest were crucial in saving those 120,000. The War Refugee Board had been a decisive factor in both efforts.[30]

How much of this was Raoul Wallenberg's work? He was directly responsible for rescuing the 20,000 Jews housed in Swedish buildings and protected by Swedish papers. Similar measures by the Swiss, Spanish, and Portuguese legations, the nuncio, and the Red Cross helped save numbers estimated at from 11,000 to 30,000. Wallenberg was indirectly responsible for much of that achievement, for his example had influenced the others to expand their operations. Another 70,000 Jews who survived were huddled in the Budapest ghetto. For them, too, Wallenberg's actions were critical. Besides providing what food he could, he forestalled several Arrow Cross attacks on the ghetto. Finally, as the city was about to fall, plans were under way for the last-minute destruction of the ghetto and its inhabitants. Wallenberg's threat of sure postwar punishment in a confrontation with the SS commander of Budapest may have been the decisive factor in stopping that scheme.[31]

In the end, Wallenberg fared worse than the miserable Jews he saw through the devastation. He incurred the wrath of Eichmann as well as the Arrow Cross, and in the final weeks the Germans and the Hungarian fascists tried to hunt him down. The young Swede evaded them by hiding in different houses from night to night. But what the Nazis dared not or could not do, the Soviets did.[32]

On January 17, 1945, Wallenberg left the city for Russian occupation headquarters at Debrecen, apparently to request emergency relief assistance for the Budapest Jews. He was never heard from again. In June, responding to a Swedish government inquiry, Moscow advised that its last information, dated January 18, reported Wallenberg under the protection of Soviet troops. Continued inquiries finally, in 1957, elicited an official Soviet statement that he had died of a heart attack in a Russian prison in 1947. But in the years since, reports have persistently surfaced indicating that he has been seen alive, in the Soviet prison system.*[33]

Why the Russians seized Wallenberg is a mystery. It may be that his American connection aroused Soviet suspicion that he had been planted in Budapest as a spy. Perhaps the Russians were also aware that the WRB representative in Sweden, Iver Olsen, who was in regular contact with Wallenberg, was an OSS operative, and from this they inferred a Wallenberg tie to the OSS.[35]

Another sequence of events that arose out of the Hungarian Jewish tragedy also left an enigmatic trail. On May 19, 1944, four days after the mass deportations to Auschwitz started, a small German aircraft touched down at Istanbul and discharged two Hungarian Jews. One, Joel Brand, was a leader of the Relief and Rescue Committee, a Hungarian Zionist organization involved in refugee aid and small-scale escape projects. The other, Andor ("Bandi") Grosz, a convert to Christianity, made his living as a small-time secret agent.[36]

Grosz's orders, which emanated from the SS, were to arrange for a meeting between high Nazi officials and upper-level American and British officers to discuss a separate peace between Germany and the Western Allies. The real objective of Brand's mission is still unclear. But recent scholarship indicates that it, too, was an attempt by SS Chief Heinrich Himmler to bypass Hitler and, using the Zionist leadership as

---

* The most convincing of these accounts appeared in 1979. It pointed to the possibility that Wallenberg was alive and in reasonably good condition as late as 1975.[34]

a channel, to contact the Western Allies concerning the possibility of a separate peace.[37]

The proposal that Brand carried to the Zionists of the outside world was given to him in Budapest by Adolf Eichmann. On its face, it was fantastic. Eichmann offered to release one million Jews in return for 10,000 trucks (to be used, he stated, only on the eastern front) and sizable amounts of coffee, tea, cocoa, and soap. He also mentioned the possibility of an indefinite amount of foreign currency. Eichmann told Brand that he would let an initial group of several thousand Jews leave Hungary as soon as the Allies agreed to send the trucks.[38]

None of Eichmann's requirements were hard-and-fast, however. This convinced Brand that further negotiations could—and must—be pursued. In his view, the only way to stop the death trains was for him to return to Budapest within a very few weeks with some indication that the Allies did not reject the scheme. He believed that trucks were not essential, that the deportations might be halted if Britain and America expressed an interest in further negotiations.[39]

Brand left Turkey for Syria, where he was to meet Moshe Shertok, political secretary of the Jewish Agency. He reached Aleppo on June 7, only to be arrested by British authorities. After allowing him to confer with Shertok, the British took Brand to Cairo and held him there for more than three months. They also picked up Grosz. They kept him in detention in Cairo, too, and his mission ended at that point. But Brand's ordeal was far from over. Convinced that his lengthening absence from Budapest was angering the Gestapo, he became increasingly distraught about the fate of his family and the continuing deportation of Hungarian Jewry.[40]

Jewish leaders in Palestine recognized that Eichmann's conditions could not be met, but hoped that something useful might come out of the Nazi overture. During June and July, they pressed the British to keep the negotiations going and to send Brand back to Budapest so the Nazis would not conclude that the proposal had been rejected. Hirschmann, who interviewed Brand in Cairo on orders from the War Refugee Board, took the same position—as did Steinhardt. In Washington, Morgenthau and Pehle, with the express concurrence of President Roosevelt, strongly supported continuing negotiations in the hope that Eichmann's offer might be the forerunner of other proposals.[41]

In Britain, however, the proposition drew implacable opposition. Within the Cabinet Committee on Refugees, fear surfaced that negotiations might "lead to an offer to unload an even greater number of Jews on to our hands." The Foreign Office took the position that the scheme was either blackmail or an attempt to disrupt the war effort by sending out a flood of refugees. Accordingly, it should not be pursued any further.[42]

Then, in mid-June, the Soviet government, which had been informed of the Eichmann offer by the British and Americans, declared that it was absolutely impermissible "to carry on any conversations whatsoever with the German Government" on this question. The Russian reply, along with an order from Churchill on July 7 that there should be no negotiations at all with the Germans, ended any chance of an official American or British follow-up. In mid-July, that conclusion was reinforced when the British interrogation of Grosz in Cairo indicated that Himmler's real objective in the affair had been to extend feelers regarding a separate peace. The British saw it as a trap, an attempt to split the Western Allies from the highly suspicious Soviets. The Foreign Office, to scuttle the entire risky business, leaked the story to the press.[43]

The Brand affair produced two concrete results. Not long after Brand left Hungary, Dr. Rudolf Kasztner, a leading Hungarian Zionist, informed Eichmann that a report from Turkey indicated Allied acceptance in principle of the German offer. Now, said Kasztner, the Nazis should provide evidence of their seriousness. At the end of June, after extracting a sizable ransom from the Hungarian Jews themselves, Eichmann permitted a special transport of almost 1,700 Jews to leave Hungary. Supposedly bound for Spain and freedom, the train instead delivered its passengers to Bergen-Belsen. The second ransom transaction to emerge from the Kasztner-Eichmann negotiations involved some 18,000 Hungarian Jews scheduled for deportation to Auschwitz. They were diverted to labor projects near Strasshof, Austria. About 75 percent of them survived the war.[44]

Unlike the British government, the War Refugee Board was unwilling to break entirely clear of the Eichmann-Brand overture. In August 1944, responding to a German initiative, the board decided to pursue the matter indirectly, through sixty-two-year-old Saly Mayer, the Joint Distribution Committee's representative in Switzerland.[45]

Communicating through McClelland, the WRB emphasized to Mayer that no ransom arrangements were permissible and he must act only as a Swiss Jewish leader—not as a representative of any American organization (including the WRB and the JDC). Mayer thus operated from an extremely weak position; he had almost no authority and could not agree to provide the Germans with what he knew they would insist on.[46]

Mayer's tactic was to deceive the SS negotiators into believing they would eventually get, if not strategic goods, at least monetary gain. With this bait, he sought to persuade them to stop the slaughter of the Jews and specifically to halt further deportations from Hungary. The WRB objective was for Mayer "to draw out the negotiations and gain as much time as possible." Meanwhile, it was hoped, the remaining Jews would be permitted to live, and Allied military advances would put an end to the extermination process.[47]

Mayer's opening thrust brought quick results. Before he would negotiate at all, he insisted on delivery to Switzerland of an initial installment of 500 of the 1,700 Hungarian Jews who had been sent to Bergen-Belsen. The discussions commenced on August 21, at St. Margarethen, on the Swiss-Austrian border. That very day, 318 Jews arrived from Bergen-Belsen.[48]

At that first meeting, Kurt Becher, a high SS officer who represented Himmler, demanded 10,000 trucks in exchange for the million Jews supposedly still alive in Nazi Europe. Mayer replied that he saw no chance of providing trucks. He suggested instead that the Germans prepare a list of scarce, but nonmilitary, materials that the United States might allow to go to Germany from neutral countries.[49]

In a series of follow-up meetings extending over six months, Mayer ingeniously stretched out the negotiations, while still keeping the Germans interested. After the first meeting, he asked the WRB through McClelland (with whom he was in constant touch) to provide him with a substantial sum to use in leading the Nazis on. The board agreed, but stipulated that none of the money could be promised to the Germans without approval from Washington. Well before any funds were actually transferred, Mayer convinced the Nazis that he controlled at least 5 million Swiss francs ($1.25 million). He also shifted the discussions away from trucks to an offer to open an account in Switzerland on which the Germans could draw to buy nonstrategic goods. More time elapsed while the Nazis visited Switzerland to find out what might be available. Aware that the WRB would not permit any actual financial transactions, Mayer and McClelland recognized by late November that the ransom ruse had been played for all it was worth.[50]

In a bold stroke that was helped by the worsening German military situation, Mayer managed to turn the talks in another direction. He offered, in exchange for an end to the exterminations, to send food into German-held territory for the International Red Cross to distribute to the surviving Jews. The Nazi negotiators, who had been claiming that the Jews were a drain on German resources, were willing to discuss the plan. McClelland backed it and endorsed Mayer's plea to the WRB to send $5 million to strengthen his bargaining position. The money arrived three weeks later, in early January. But the project did not materialize.[51]

What did Saly Mayer achieve? In August 1944, he succeeded in bringing out 318 of the Hungarian Jews held in Bergen-Belsen. In early December, the other 1,368 people in the original transport from Hungary also reached Switzerland. Apparently, Mayer's repeated insistence that their continued internment was impeding the discussions finally persuaded the Germans to let them go. Beyond that, the negotiations had little or no practical effect. But despite the limited results, Mayer's endeavors touched on the heroic. He had almost nothing to work with, he received little support from the WRB, yet he invested tremendous effort in an almost hopeless cause. It was a gamble that he believed had to be taken.*[52]

While Mayer's negotiations were unfolding, another Swiss-based rescue attempt secretly involved Orthodox rabbis in the United States in activities that led straight to Himmler. This scheme grew out of the rescue work of Isaac Sternbuch, his wife, Recha, and other Orthodox Jews, whose committee, HIJEFS, was the Swiss affiliate of Vaad Hahatzala. Vaad Hahatzala was a New York–based rescue committee sponsored by the Union of Orthodox Rabbis.

In the spring and summer of 1944, well before the Mayer negotiations began, Sternbuch and his associates were drawn into a plan to buy Jews out of Hungary by supplying Swiss-built tractors to the Nazis. This scheme originated with an Orthodox group in Hungary that had agreed with the Germans to exchange one hundred tractors for 1,200 rabbis and other leading Orthodox Jews.† But the Hungarians could not raise enough money for the deal and turned to Sternbuch for help.[54]

McClelland found out about the plan and opposed it, on the grounds that it would aid the German war effort. But Sternbuch went ahead anyway, and in July he secretly bought the first ten tractors, paying

* Mayer and others have since credited the negotiations with several achievements. The talks possibly played some small part in Himmler's decision in the fall of 1944 to bring the extermination program to a halt. But solid evidence is lacking. The discussions did not put any brake on deportations. Although it is true that Eichmann never got the trains moving from Hungary again after Horthy stopped them in July, there is no proof that the Mayer negotiations influenced that situation. Nor did they impede the deportations to Auschwitz from many parts of Europe that went right on through the summer and into the fall of 1944.[53]

† The available documentation does not make clear whether this was an independent project or whether it represented part of the payment (or a confirmation payment) for the deal that sent the 1,700 Jews to Bergen-Belsen and eventually to Switzerland.[55]

170,000 Swiss francs.* In September, he obtained 260,000 francs from Saly Mayer (from his JDC funds), which also went for tractors. Over the next few months, Mayer passed about 310,000 additional francs to Sternbuch for the same purpose. At least twelve and possibly as many as forty-three tractors were shipped into Axis territory without Mc-Clelland's knowledge.[56]

While the tractor project was still under way, Sternbuch's group opened up a connection with Himmler that had the potential for a major breakthrough. The key figure in this episode was sixty-eight-year-old Jean-Marie Musy, formerly president of Switzerland and member of the Swiss Federal Council. In fall 1944, Sternbuch asked Musy, who had turned strongly pro-Nazi in the 1930s, to intercede with Himmler for release of the Jews in Nazi concentration camps. Musy agreed, perhaps in hopes of rehabilitating his political reputation in Switzerland. Or perhaps he thought this step might open the way for a Nazi accommodation with the West, which he saw as the only chance to avoid a Russian takeover of Germany.[58]

For Sternbuch's committee, the advantages in working through Musy —and they were of utmost importance—were his past acquaintance with Himmler, his ability to gain direct access to him, and his status as a pro-Nazi neutral. Only Musy or someone like him could have confronted Himmler face-to-face on the Jewish issue and steered him toward release of the Jews. But there was an important disadvantage in proceeding through Musy. Sternbuch anticipated that McClelland would not be cooperative and might even oppose rescue efforts that included Musy, whom he distrusted, especially if they appeared to involve ransom.[59]

Sternbuch kept the plan secret from McClelland as long as possible. Communications about it between Sternbuch and Vaad Hahatzala were transmitted through Polish diplomatic cable facilities, thus circumventing the censors, the State Department, the WRB, and McClelland. (In New York, Vaad Hahatzala kept the secret correspondence in special files marked "Incoming—Illegal—Sternbuch" and "Outgoing—Illegal Cables.")[60]

In early November, through the intervention of Walter Schellenberg,

---

* Sternbuch explained to Vaad Hahatzala headquarters, "We need part of the money for bribes to save people. But we cannot tell about it McClelland." (I.e., we cannot tell McClelland about it.) The message bypassed American censorship through the cooperation of Polish diplomats in Bern and New York.

Historians have credited Saly Mayer with bringing the 318 Hungarian Jews out of Bergen-Belsen in August 1944. But Sternbuch persistently claimed that the tractor deal he completed in July was at least partly responsible for freeing that group.[57]

a high SS official, Musy talked at length with Himmler. From Sternbuch, he brought an offer of one million Swiss francs "and perhaps more" in return for the release of the remaining Jews, whose number Himmler estimated at 600,000. Himmler said that he could free the Jews but that he needed goods, particularly trucks, rather than money. The meeting ended without a decision.[61]

During November, further negotiations led to an agreement to release the Jews in exchange for several million Swiss francs. Without revealing details of the plan, Sternbuch asked McClelland to request ten to twenty million francs from the WRB to get the Jews out. Instead, McClelland advised the board not to back the scheme, because it was vague and unreliable and because the disreputable Musy was mixed up in it.[62]

In the meantime, Sternbuch had spelled out the new plan in a secret message to Vaad Hahatzala. It called for the release of 300,000 Jews in exchange for $5 million (20 million Swiss francs), or approximately $17 per person. The Jews would come out at the rate of 15,000 per month in return for monthly installments of $250,000. Aware that the proposition involved outright ransom, the people at Vaad Hahatzala nevertheless agreed to it and immediately launched a fund-raising campaign. Two weeks later, on December 5, they dispatched their first receipts, $107,000, to Sternbuch. By mid-January, they had sent nearly $150,000 more.*[63]

The WRB did not learn of the scheme to ransom 300,000 Jews until January 24, when George Warren, the State Department's liaison with the board, reported that a representative of the Vaad had told him about the plan. The board promptly instructed McClelland to look into it.[65]

Meanwhile, in mid-January, Musy met with Himmler again. On February 1, back in Switzerland, he told Sternbuch what had been accomplished, again with Schellenberg's help. Himmler had lowered his requirements drastically. He would release virtually all the Jews, in weekly trainloads of about 1,200, if a token payment of 5 million Swiss francs ($1.25 million) were placed in a Swiss bank in Musy's name. Musy said the funds would not go to Germany—they would most likely be transferred, later on, to the International Red Cross. As proof of

---

* On December 6, Sternbuch informed the Vaad that as a result of these negotiations a train with 1,400 Jews from Bergen-Belsen would soon reach Switzerland. The transport, carrying 1,368 Hungarian Jews, arrived that night. Historians have generally agreed with Saly Mayer's assertion that his negotiations brought this convoy out. But Sternbuch's work, possibly the tractor deliveries, might have been a factor.[64]

Himmler's seriousness, Musy reported, the first train would soon leave for Switzerland.[66]

Sternbuch told McClelland about the new development on February 6. McClelland thought the board would approve the deal, provided the money went into a double account that Musy could not touch without American approval. The next day, a train arrived at the Swiss border carrying 1,210 Jews from Theresienstadt. McClelland reported the apparent breakthrough to the WRB. Both he and Sternbuch suspected that Himmler's motive was to find a way to extend peace overtures to the United States.[67]

The next move was up to the WRB. But Vaad Hahatzala did not leave it at that. Sternbuch had warned the Vaad that additional trains would not come out unless he received $937,000, the amount needed to fill out the $1.25 million that Himmler had specified. Unremitting pressure by Vaad leaders won WRB approval to transmit the money, on condition that it could not under any circumstances be used for ransom and that it be placed in an account jointly controlled by Sternbuch, McClelland, and the WRB. On March 1, a license was issued. The Vaad then obtained $937,000 from the JDC and dispatched it to Switzerland.[68]

Although it agreed to the transfer of funds, the WRB was very uneasy about this plan. Morgenthau, especially, feared that word of the Orthodox rabbis' covert activities might reach the press, along with the impression that the American government was paying ransom to the Nazis to free Jews. There was also some concern about Vaad Hahatzala's illegal use of Polish communication lines, a practice that was now fully clear to the Treasury Department. Pehle and others had known about it for some time but had not blocked it. Pehle explained to Morgenthau:

> We have never wanted to stop it, because they get results. Is it risky? Sure it is risky; this whole thing is risky; it is fraught with difficulty. . . . It is easy to stop, but it is a serious responsibility.

In the end, the board kept its hands off the Polish communication arrangement.[69]

In the meantime, in mid-February, Musy received word from Himmler's headquarters that the project would be halted unless articles appeared in the Swiss and American press giving credit to the Germans for releasing the Jews who had come out of Theresienstadt. Such reports were published. But if Himmler's purpose was to cultivate American opinion in preparation for a peace approach, his tactic backfired. The press reports came to Hitler's attention, and he snuffed out the project, ordering that not one more Jew was to leave German territory. More Jews did get out, but the Sternbuch-Musy-Himmler agreement was dead despite several weeks of determined effort by Musy to revive it.[70]

The Brand, Mayer, and Sternbuch-Musy episodes all raised the troubling problem of ransom. The WRB adamantly opposed paying the Nazis to let Jews out. The primary reason, of course, was that the compensation could aid the Axis war effort. The board was also concerned about public reaction in the United States if news spread that materials or money were going to the enemy to ransom Jews. WRB policy allowed bribery of lower officials and border guards on the grounds that saving lives outweighed any tiny advantage the Nazis might gain from those transactions. But that was quite different from payments of millions of dollars or strategically important goods.[71]

Three Jewish rescue organizations differed, in varying degrees, with the WRB's policy against ransom. In the midst of the Joel Brand affair, the Jewish Agency informed the British Foreign Office that, if it finally came to a question of money, "we believe that the ransom should be paid." It conveyed essentially the same view to the State Department. The World Jewish Congress did not press the issue, but it opposed the WRB's ban on ransom. A month before the deportations began in Hungary, the WJC foresaw the catastrophe and called on the board "to resort even to such extraordinary methods" as large-scale ransom. Later, it sharply criticized the WRB's strict policy against ransom in the Saly Mayer negotiations.[72]

Vaad Hahatzala and the Sternbuch group not only disagreed with the WRB but pursued ransom arrangements in defiance of board policy. Sternbuch did not shy at deception or illegality. "Some activities necessary in our operations are punishable," he explained, but the "sacred cause"—saving Jews—required that they be carried on. Vaad Hahatzala responded to the Holocaust on the basis of its leaders' understanding of the requirements of Jewish law for the preservation of human life. A 1944 report by another agency correctly observed that Vaad Hahatzala was "prepared to disregard any consideration other than the rescue of the maximum possible number of Jews." The Vaad itself referred to its position as a "Stop-at-Nothing" policy. This approach created some uneasiness. For instance, the head of the Joint Distribution Committee once stated, referring to transmission of rescue funds into Nazi Europe, "As regards the methods used by the Vaad Hahatzala, the less said the better." Again, the Vaad's tactics in the Musy-Himmler affair had alarmed Morgenthau and some others. But as Pehle testified, experience showed that "they get results."[73]

The Hungarian Jewish disaster had little impact on the American nation. War news, especially the Normandy invasion and the rapid drive across France, dominated the public's attention. New York and Washington newspapers reported on the Hungarian Jews, but on inner pages. In other cities, the information reached the newsrooms, but editors printed little of it. In July, a *New Republic* editorial under the bitter heading "Getting Used to Massacres" registered the widespread apathy: "Such news is received nowadays with a shrug of the shoulders."[74]

American Zionist leaders were far from apathetic about the slaughter in Hungary. But they had committed their resources to the Palestine commonwealth resolution introduced in Congress in January 1944. Wise, Silver, and other top Zionists, seizing the opportunities offered by the national elections, worked through the summer and fall to secure Democratic and Republican support for the Palestine resolution. Responsibility for pressing the rescue issue fell to a second level of leaders in the World Jewish Congress and in the faltering American Jewish Conference. They consulted frequently with the WRB and submitted rescue plans to the Washington missions of the Vatican, the International Red Cross, and various foreign powers. Otherwise, except for one midsummer project, they took little action.[75]

To generate pressure for measures to save the Hungarian Jews, the American Jewish Conference held a mass demonstration in New York City on July 31. More than 40,000 people packed Madison Square Park and adjoining streets for two hours in oppressive late-afternoon heat. Stephen Wise, other prominent Jews, and a few non-Jews spoke for swift action to save the remnant of European Jewry. The crowd endorsed a call for immediate implementation of Horthy's offer to release the Hungarian Jews. But no one in the seats of power listened, except the War Refugee Board, which was already doing what it could.[76]

Despite a distinct decline in activity during 1944, the Bergsonite Emergency Committee continued as the leading force in building pressures for rescue. When the Hungarian crisis broke, the committee formed alliances with Christian Hungarian-American societies and clergymen. One result was that leading Christian Americans of Hungarian descent telegraphed the Pope and President Roosevelt urging action to save the Jews in Hungary. They also dispatched messages to prominent Hungarians calling for an end to mistreatment of the Jews. Their statements were beamed into Hungary by OWI radio, as were excerpts from special services in support of the Jews that were held in Hungarian-American churches.[77]

Throughout the first half of 1944, the Emergency Committee had campaigned in full-page newspaper advertisements and at public meetings for opening Palestine to Jewish refugees. With the announcement of the Horthy offer, which appeared to release all Jews who had Palestine certificates, the Bergsonites accelerated their drive. They also turned once more to Hearst, who again provided substantial editorial support. And they went to Congress with resolutions calling on the President to urge Britain to open emergency camps in Palestine, where tens of thousands of Hungarian Jews could be sheltered in safety until the war ended. They could then, if necessary, be returned to Hungary or sent elsewhere.[78]

The Bergsonites saw the shelters plan as a way to open Palestine for the immediate emergency without getting the matter entangled in the politically difficult issues of the White Paper and Jewish statehood. Those questions, they concluded, could wait until after the war. This position paralleled that of the WRB. It had earlier decided to stay away from the controversy over the Zionists' Palestine resolution, but wanted pressure put on Britain to open Palestine at least as a temporary haven.[79]

The Palestine-shelters resolution quickly picked up important bipartisan backing in Congress. The Emergency Committee generated a flow of letters to Washington and claimed 500,000 signatures on petitions of support, which were presented to Congress by a small delegation of Orthodox rabbis and an archbishop of the Greek Orthodox Church. But the proposal soon collapsed, largely because of opposition from the State Department and Zionist organizations.[80]

The State Department asserted that passage of the legislation would anger the Arabs and set off unrest in the Middle East. The Zionists persuaded key members of Congress, including Tom Connally and Sol Bloom (chairmen of the relevant Senate and House committees), not to act on it. They told the legislators that the plan was unnecessary because the few Jews who might get to Palestine from Hungary could enter under the remaining White Paper quota. Moreover, the Zionists strenuously opposed any plan to send Jews to Palestine with the understanding that they might have to leave after the war. Such a concession, legitimized by the approval of Congress, might establish a precedent that could impair the Jewish claim to Palestine.[81]

Zionist opposition to the Palestine-shelters resolution was only one point of conflict with the Bergsonites that year. Acrimony reached the fever point in mid-May 1944 when the Bergson group purchased the former Iranian embassy building in Washington and declared it the headquarters of the newly formed Hebrew Committee of National Liberation. The Hebrew Committee, made up of the small Bergsonite core group of Palestinian Jews and patterned on the French Committee of National Liberation, set itself up as the government-in-exile for the Jewish (or Hebrew) state (yet to be established) in Palestine. At the same time, the Bergsonites launched a partner organization, the American League for a Free Palestine, a mass-membership body for Americans, Jews 'and non-Jews, who wished to support the goals of the Hebrew Committee.[82]

The regular Zionist organizations attacked this Bergsonite venture with a vengeance. They saw it as an attempt to wrest the leadership of the world Zionist movement from the long-established Zionist bodies —and wreck them in the process. The Jewish press and non-Zionist Jewish groups were also outraged at the effrontery and flamboyance of the young "adventurers" from Palestine. The Bergsonites, to their own dismay, had incurred the full wrath of American Jewry.[83]

Frustrated by what they considered the ineffectiveness of the regular Zionist movement, the Bergson group had sought to form a new spearhead for Jewish nationalism. They had also hoped that the Hebrew Committee, like the French Committee, might open contacts at the world diplomatic level (foreign governments, International Red Cross, Vatican, UNRRA)—contacts that could help the rescue cause. They did create a small, rival Zionist movement that remained active until the emergence of the state of Israel. And they achieved some minor gains in the rescue area. But the main outcome was to crystallize a solid front of angry opposition all across the American Jewish community.[84]

The rush of animosity took a heavy toll on Bergsonite rescue activities. Inevitably, the barrage of attacks on the Hebrew Committee and the American League for a Free Palestine injured the older organization, the Emergency Committee. Zionist publicity, along with systematic Zionist pressure on prominent Americans to dissociate themselves from all Bergsonite enterprises, cost the Emergency Committee important support. Furthermore, the Emergency Committee, along with the two new committees, spent considerable time and energy countering the widespread and continuing assaults. The Emergency Committee did not go under. But never again was it as effective as it had been before.[85]

|| 14 ||

"LATE AND LITTLE"

Central to the War Refugee Board's work were the rescue operations conducted by its representatives overseas. At the same time, though, the board pushed forward on other fronts. It appealed to Allied leaders to issue war-crimes warnings, it searched for havens for escaping refugees, and it tried to send relief supplies into the concentration camps.

War Crimes Warnings

The WRB was convinced that explicit threats of postwar punishment for those involved in harming Jews could contribute importantly to saving lives. By 1944, with Germany clearly headed for defeat, such threats should carry substantial weight. The board believed that Axis satellites would be especially responsive to that pressure.[1]

The WRB planned to create a psychological warfare campaign around a stern new war-crimes declaration to be obtained from the President. Roosevelt and other Allied leaders had issued several statements condemning Axis atrocities and promising postwar punishment of war criminals. But only two had referred specifically to Jews, the last in December 1942. The failure to mention atrocities against Jews was especially glaring in the important war-crimes declarations proclaimed at the Quebec Conference of August 1943 and the Moscow Conference two months later. There was concern that the Nazis had concluded that the Allies did not care if they went on slaughtering Jews.[2]

The board drew up a declaration that focused on the killing of Jews. Morgenthau, Stettinius, and McCloy endorsed the draft, and it went to the White House. On March 24, 1944, the President released a weakened, though still valuable, war-crimes statement. The WRB's emphasis on Jews had been dropped from the first paragraph to the fourth. The intervening paragraphs called attention to ten other victimized peoples and to American prisoners of war murdered by the Japanese. Yet the part on the Jews was strong. It condemned their "wholesale systematic murder" as "one of the blackest crimes of all history."[3]

Nevertheless, the statement had been watered down, deliberately. Roosevelt's special counsel, Samuel Rosenman, had persuaded the President that the original placed excessive emphasis on the Jews and had to be generalized. Rosenman, who was negative toward the whole idea, believed that too pointed a reference to Jews would fuel American anti-Semitism and stir up anti-administration sentiment.[4]

Within the Treasury, disappointment was bitter. Rosenman had altered a policy statement on which three Cabinet departments had agreed and which Stettinius had personally urged on Roosevelt. Pehle feared that Rosenman would interfere with future rescue decisions that went to the President.[5]

The original WRB draft had also included an offer to accept large numbers of refugees into the United States—to be kept in camps and returned home after the war. This was to provide a starting point for dealing with the critical problem of lack of havens. The final version carried only a vague pledge that "we shall find havens of refuge" for "all victims of oppression."[6]

Despite the statement's shortcomings, the WRB staff agreed with Morgenthau that "it's so much better than nothing." In it, the President promised that "none who participate in these acts of savagery shall go unpunished. . . . That warning applies not only to the leaders but also to their functionaries and subordinates in Germany and in the satellite countries." He also assured that "in so far as the necessity of military operations permit, this Government will use all means at its command to aid the escape of all intended victims of the Nazi and Jap executioner." The British Foreign Office endorsed the statement. Attempts to obtain Soviet support for it were fruitless.[7]

The WRB spread Roosevelt's words across Axis Europe through neutral radio stations and newspapers, pamphlets sent in via underground channels, OWI broadcasts, and air-dropped leaflets. Over and over in the months that followed, WRB warnings to the Axis—both public ones and those conveyed through diplomatic channels—stressed that the President's statement was a fundamental part of American policy.[8]

Calls for another top-level warning arose in September 1944 when the Polish underground reported that the retreating Germans intended to slaughter surviving concentration-camp inmates. The WRB, convinced that a statement from General Eisenhower would carry the greatest impact, sent a proposed text to the War Department. Five weeks later, on November 7, Eisenhower warned the Germans not to "molest, harm or persecute" concentration-camp internees, "no matter what their religion or nationality may be."[9]

Efforts to persuade the Russians to issue a statement parallel to Eisenhower's failed. Not until April 1945, in the chaotic last days of the war, would the Soviets join the Americans and British in warning that anyone mistreating a prisoner of war or an internee would be "ruthlessly pursued and brought to punishment."[10]

Because the credibility of the threats depended very much on policies reached by the London-based United Nations War Crimes Commission, the WRB was alarmed to learn in the summer of 1944 that the commission had no plans for punishing people guilty of atrocities against Jews of Axis nationality. The reason: no precedent existed in international law. The catalog of war crimes did not include actions by an enemy nation (or its citizens) against its own subjects or those of its partner nations. Thus, on technical grounds, the massacres of hundreds of thousands of Jews (those of German, Hungarian, Rumanian, and other Axis nationalities) remained outside the scope of the commission.[11]

Confusion was no newcomer to the fifteen-nation War Crimes Commission. Anglo-American steps to establish a United Nations body to collect evidence of war crimes and to plan postwar punitive action began in mid-1942. But the organization first met only in December 1943. Roosevelt appointed as the American representative his old friend Herbert C. Pell, the former minister to Portugal and to Hungary.[12]

From the outset, Pell wanted the commission to be "as tough as possible." He strongly opposed the view that Axis atrocities against

Axis subjects were outside the realm of war crimes. He won some members over to his broader interpretation, but they could not act without orders from their governments. The matter bogged down because neither Pell nor Sir Cecil Hurst, the British representative and commission chairman, could get his government to take a position on it. In January 1945, after eight months without an answer, Hurst quit in disgust. When he resigned, another member of the commission openly remarked that the British government treated the delegates to the War Crimes Commission as if they were "representatives of some British colony." [13]

The State Department treated Pell even more shabbily. Despite his frequent requests for instructions on policy issues, it never gave him definite directions. Thus, while he could "lobby" other commissioners, he had no authority to take official positions himself. His lack of power was no accident. Green Hackworth, the department's legal adviser, and other State Department officials assigned to the war-crimes question intended that Pell's mission fail. Their motives are not fully clear, but they apparently did not desire real action by the War Crimes Commission, and they definitely resented the President's appointment of Pell, an independent-minded outsider. These middle-level officials even arranged to saddle him with an assistant who undercut his efforts in London, both openly (even contradicting him in commission meetings) and behind his back. [14]

In August 1944, Pell approached Josiah DuBois of the WRB, then in London on Treasury Department business. He described the situation and said that a strong request from Washington for the broader interpretation of war crimes might well convince the whole commission. Soon afterward, Pehle wrote to Stettinius asking that the State Department direct Pell to urge the War Crimes Commission to include all Axis atrocities within its scope. Otherwise, Pehle pointed out, the WRB's psychological warfare program was endangered. The department's response was inconclusive. For several months, the board pressed for a decision. It always received the same reply: the question was "under active consideration." [15]

In December 1944, Pell returned to the United States to try to clarify the problem. He made no progress with the State Department, but conferred with Roosevelt on January 9. By then, Hurst had resigned from the War Crimes Commission, and it appeared that Pell would become chairman. The President reassured him and, as he left, said, "Goodbye, Bertie. Good luck to you. Get back to London as quick as you can and get yourself elected chairman." When Pell went to the State Department to bid his formal farewell, he was astonished to hear

Stettinius say that the department had been unable to obtain the appropriation for continuing his work. The only choice was to close his office and have some regular American official represent the United States on the commission. (In fact, the State Department had made only a token effort to get the $30,000 appropriation.) [16]

Pell soon discovered that the State Department had known for more than two weeks that the appropriation had failed, but had delayed telling him until after he saw Roosevelt. Obviously, the intent had been to keep him from raising the issue with the President. Actually, Roosevelt was aware that there was no appropriation even as he encouraged his old friend to hurry back to London. [17]

Pell offered to forgo his salary, but the State Department responded that it was legally impossible for him to serve without payment. He tried over and over to see Roosevelt again, but had no success. In late January, aided by the Bergson group, Pell carried his case to the press. The resulting publicity, along with increasing pressure from the WRB and Jewish organizations, forced the State Department to clarify America's war-crimes policy at last. On February 1, 1945, Undersecretary Joseph Grew announced that perpetrators of all crimes against Jews and other minorities would definitely be punished. [18]

Pell appeared to have won his long battle for a broadened interpretation of war crimes. Actually, however, officials of the War, State, and Justice departments had been studying the question of war-crimes trials since September. During January, the three departments had agreed on an overall policy and submitted it to Roosevelt. Included among war crimes were Axis atrocities against Axis subjects. But the policymakers, especially in the War Department, wanted to keep the matter secret. Some argued that additional publicity about the punishment of war crimes would stiffen Germany's resolve and delay surrender. Others claimed that the Nazis might react by harming Allied prisoners of war. Grew's press statement came reluctantly and only because of pressures generated by the Pell episode. [19]

What Pell definitely achieved, then, was to force the administration to make its war-crimes policy public, a step the WRB greatly desired. Whether his year of effort and the WRB's added pressure influenced the policy itself cannot be determined. [20]

Pell's deputy, an Army officer, filled in as American representative to the War Crimes Commission, and the State Department found ways to fund the office and its staff. At the end of March 1945, Roosevelt sent Samuel Rosenman to London with broad authority to make agreements on war-crimes policies. A month later, the new President, Harry Truman, named Supreme Court Justice Robert H. Jackson the United

States chief counsel for the prosecution of war crimes. In August, the United States, Britain, Russia, and France agreed on the basic structure and scope of the war-crimes trials. One of the categories, crimes against humanity, included atrocities against Jews, whatever their nationality.[21]

The Search for Havens

From its inception, the War Refugee Board realized that a major obstacle to rescue was the lack of places to which Jewish refugees could go. So the board began immediately to search the world for havens. There was hope that Libya, which was controlled by the British, could become an important reception area for Jews coming out of the nearby Balkans. In April 1943, the Bermuda Conference had urged Libya as a sanctuary, but the British had failed to act. In 1944, the WRB pressed the question for months. The British continued to stall, citing "involved political problems"—meaning Arab opposition to allowing Jews into Libya, even temporarily. In June, the British finally agreed to one camp, with a capacity of 1,500, but they managed by procrastination to avoid even that token step.[22]

As it hunted for havens, the WRB assisted in the final push for the long-delayed North Africa refugee camp. The Bermuda Conference had recommended the camp in order to clear Spain of refugees. But for four months after the conference, the State Department and the British government had done almost nothing about it. Once they finally chose a site, a former American Army barracks at Fedala, near Casablanca, it took almost three more months to gain the consent of the authorities in French North Africa, the French Committee of National Liberation. At that, the French set a limit of 2,000, although the facility could hold 15,000. Then, from November 1943 until March 1944, the French continued to impede the project by requiring a time-consuming security screening. (Ultimately, one-quarter of the refugees who applied were rejected.) The French were not really worried about security; it posed no problem at a holding camp like Fedala. Their concern was that refugees unable to find permanent homes elsewhere would be left on their hands after the war. The United States guaranteed postwar removal, but the French were not convinced.[23]

At the end of March, the first group was at last ready for transfer to Fedala. But the British, who had agreed to provide sea transportation, could not locate a ship. After several weeks of failed British attempts, the WRB's Leonard Ackermann turned to the War Shipping Administration office in Algiers. The response was positive. Not long afterward, the first boatload landed in North Africa.[24]

Fedala opened in early May 1944—one year after the Bermuda Conference adjourned. During that year, 800 refugees had left Spain, most of them for Palestine. French screening kept many of the rest out of the new camp. Others were reluctant to leave a known situation in Spain for an unknown camp existence. As a result, only 630 went to Fedala. The WRB was able to obtain use of the rest of the camp's 2,000 places and thus found its first haven.[25]

In mid-1944, the Allied Mediterranean military command, seeking to relieve the refugee buildup in southern Italy, put heavy pressure on the French to agree to a second camp. French permission came promptly this time. The location was a former Allied military barracks at Philippeville, on the Mediterranean coast in Algeria. It could accommodate 2,500, expandable to 7,000 with the addition of tents. By the time Philippeville opened, however, the problem in Italy had eased and the original need for the camp had passed. So a second haven became available to the WRB. The board's third and last sanctuary, a camp for 1,000 refugees at Fort Ontario, New York, came only after months of effort.[26]

While seeking openings elsewhere, the WRB was also pressing for an American commitment. If America opened its gates partway, not only would a key haven become available, but the board would gain leverage for its attempts to persuade other nations to do the same. A major problem was strong opposition to immigration (especially to Jewish immigration) in Congress, in the State Department, and among much of the American public.[27]

The board's answer was emergency camps where refugees could be interned, like prisoners of war, and repatriated after Germany's defeat. The whole operation would take place outside the immigration system, thus avoiding any question of altering quotas or visa procedures. A precedent existed; in 1942, civilian enemy aliens interned as security risks by Latin American governments had been transferred to camps in the United States, where more adequate control was available. This move, like the entry of enemy prisoners of war, had bypassed the whole official immigration structure.[28]

An opportunity to raise the issue came in March 1944 when the President's war-crimes statement was released. It included an assurance that "we shall find havens of refuge" for the oppressed. The WRB staff proposed a follow-up message for the President to issue. It would declare that, in line with the promise to find havens of refuge, the

United States was offering temporary asylum to all who could escape Hitler. They would have to live under restrictions similar to those imposed on POWs, but they would receive humane treatment. After the war, they would be returned to their homelands.[29]

The WRB also drafted a separate memorandum for the President explaining the situation. It emphasized that no significant rescue campaign was possible unless havens were opened up, and they would not open unless the United States set the example. Once America took the step, though, the other United Nations would undoubtedly follow. Furthermore, the approaching end of the war and the long transatlantic trip made it unlikely that many refugees would actually come to the United States. The important thing, the board stressed, was to offer to receive them.[30]

Before the proposal could go to the White House, it needed the approval of the secretaries of War, State, and the Treasury. Stimson had serious doubts. His main objection had nothing to do with military affairs, but arose from his own strongly restrictionist views. He believed that, if refugees entered in this way, heavy pressure later on might induce Congress to alter the immigration laws and let them stay. And he thoroughly opposed any increase in permanent immigration or any compromise of the immigration laws. This position, he maintained, reflected that of Congress and much of the public. He was willing to endorse the proposal, though, if the President obtained the consent of Congress before acting.[31]

For a time, Morgenthau also maintained that FDR should not implement the plan without congressional approval. He was worried lest the President antagonize the lawmakers and incur political damage. On the other hand, he was sure Congress would not enact the proposal, and he wanted the camps established. With time, his staff persuaded him that Roosevelt should use his executive powers to carry out the plan.[32]

Hull, basically cool toward the havens proposal, barely involved himself with the question. Visa Chief Howard Travers warned him that the idea was likely to be unpopular with Congress and the public and could open him to criticism. George Warren, the department's liaison with the WRB, advised him to be leery of any plan for bringing in more than "a limited number" of refugees. In the end, though, Hull went along with Morgenthau.[33]

Finally, Morgenthau, Hull, and Stimson agreed to a weakened form of the proposal. The original plan would have offered temporary sanctuary in the United States "for all oppressed peoples escaping from Hitler." The new version omitted the word *all*. The recommendation went to the White House on May 8.[34]

Meanwhile, public support had been building behind the plan for emergency camps. Early in April, *New York Post* writer Samuel Grafton, whose column ran in forty newspapers with combined circulations of over four million, launched a campaign for what he termed "free ports":

> A "free port" is a small bit of land, a kind of reservation, into which foreign goods may be brought without paying customs duties. . . . Goods brought into it from overseas are destined either for transshipment to other countries, or for temporary storage.
>
> Why couldn't we have a system of free ports for refugees fleeing the Hitler terror? . . .
>
> The refugees, Jewish and other, ask only for a few fenced-in acres of the poorest land in America. They don't want to keep it. They just want to sit on it until they can go home again.

During April, Grafton wrote two more columns advocating free ports. He also publicized the plan on radio.[35]

The *New York Post* hammered away on the issue in editorials and news articles. Its reporters raised the question at Roosevelt's press conferences. The *New York Herald Tribune,* the *Times,* the *Christian Science Monitor,* and numerous other papers soon joined the call for free ports. So did the entire Hearst chain, syndicated columnist Dorothy Thompson, several radio commentators, the *New Republic,* the *Nation,* the *Commonweal,* and the *Christian Century.* The Jewish press and all important Jewish organizations backed the plan. The Bergsonite Emergency Committee dramatized it in full-page newspaper advertisements that were linked to a nationwide petition drive.[36]

Among many others to advocate the free-ports proposal were the Federal Council of Churches, the Church Peace Union, the National Board of the YWCA, the Catholic Committee for Refugees, the Friends and Unitarian service committees, the President's Advisory Committee on Political Refugees, the AFL, the CIO, and the National Farmers Union. William Green, head of the AFL, sent a personal appeal to Roosevelt. Alfred E. Smith and seventy-one other prominent non-Jewish Americans, in a statement to the President, called the establishment of temporary havens a "moral obligation." Several congressmen introduced legislation for free ports.[37]

As support grew for the camps proposal, the WRB kept silent. Pressed at a mid-April news conference, Pehle would say only that the question was under consideration. By then, interest was so high that even that vague answer drew front-page coverage in major New York newspapers. Actually, behind the scenes, the WRB was actively encouraging Jewish organizations to carry out a coordinated drive to gain support for free ports from newspaper editors, radio commentators, members of Congress, and other influential Americans.[38]

A mid-April Gallup poll, requested by presidential assistant David Niles, found 70 percent approval of emergency refugee camps in the United States. Further indication of widespread backing for the plan was seen in the large numbers of favorable letters, telegrams, and petitions that were reaching the President, Congress, and the WRB. Only a few messages of dissent turned up, forerunners of an opposition that had not yet awakened.[39]

On May 11, Pehle discussed the plan for emergency camps with Roosevelt. He showed him a book of press clippings generated by the proposal, the letters of support from organizations and important individuals, and the Gallup poll. The President was impressed. He had read one of Grafton's articles the night before, he said, and liked it very much. He appeared to Pehle to be "very, very favorably disposed toward the whole idea." Pehle told the President that he thought it was too late to go through Congress. Roosevelt said he was reluctant to bring in large numbers of refugees without congressional consent. Instead, he proposed that if a situation developed in which a specific group of 500 to 1,000 refugees needed a haven, he would take them in and, at the same time, explain his action in a message to Congress.[40]

A few days later, the WRB learned of the crisis that had arisen in southern Italy. Because of the heavy influx of Yugoslav refugees, the camps in Egypt to which they were being transferred were reaching capacity. Fearing a pile-up in southern Italy, Allied military authorities had curtailed the flow. Clearly, additional temporary havens were essential for the Adriatic escape route to remain open.[41]

Pehle sent a message to the President explaining the problem. He pointed out:

> This emergency situation is, I believe, exactly the type of situation which you had in mind. We can break this bottleneck by immediately bringing to the United States approximately 1,000 refugees from southern Italy and placing then in an unused Army camp along the Eastern seaboard, where they would remain until the end of the war.[42]

Nothing happened for a week. Then, at a May 26 Cabinet meeting, Morgenthau brought up the refugee situation in Italy. Roosevelt immediately ordered the Army to reopen the refugee flow across the Adriatic. But he still did not respond to Pehle's request. At his press conference on May 30, the President was asked about the plan for free ports. He replied, "I like the idea, and we are working on it now," but went on to say, "it is not, in my judgment, necessary to decide that we have to have a free port right here in the United States. There are lots of other places in the world where refugees conceivably could go to." When Pehle heard that news, he checked with the White House. He was told that the President had meant that free ports did not have to be limited to the United States; they could be opened elsewhere too. The question had apparently caught him off guard.[43]

Morgenthau and Pehle saw Roosevelt on June 1. He was aware of the problem in Italy. But he had forgotten most of his discussion of three weeks earlier with Pehle. Pehle repeated the main points, emphasizing the widespread support for free ports. The President then agreed to bring 1,000 refugees over from Italy.[44]

At his news conference the next day, FDR was asked to clarify what he had said about free ports at the preceding press conference. He explained that some refugees would be coming to the United States, but it was only common sense to take care of most of them overseas and thus avoid the long ocean voyages over and back. He mentioned that Pehle was looking into the possibility of using a vacant Army camp in the United States. Questioned about taking refugees in without regard to quotas and visas, Roosevelt answered, "If you have some starving and perfectly helpless people—after all, they are human beings—and we can give them the assurance of life somewhere else, it seems like it's the humanitarian thing to do."[45]

That same day, Pehle found a camp. In fact, the War Department offered a choice of two Army camps, both in northern New York, one at Oswego and the other near Watertown. On June 8, Morgenthau and Pehle saw the President again and reported that two camps were available. Roosevelt enthusiastically recommended the one at Oswego: "Fort Ontario is my camp. I know the fort very well. It goes back to before Civil War times and is a very excellent place." He carefully read and then initialed the enabling documents that Pehle handed him. The next day, at his press conference, he announced that "we are going to bring over a thousand, that's all, to this country, to go into that camp—Fort Oswego—Fort Ontario."[46]

Soon afterward, Roosevelt sent a message—prepared by the WRB—to Congress. It summarized the refugee situation in Italy, explained the urgent need for additional temporary havens, and declared that "our heritage and our ideals of liberty and justice" required the nation to "take immediate steps to share the responsibility for meeting the problem." Arrangements were therefore under way to bring 1,000 refugees from southern Italy to the United States. To counter a potential negative reaction in Congress, the statement emphasized that the refugees would be kept in a camp "under appropriate security restrictions." And it pledged that "upon the termination of the war they will be sent back to their homelands." [47]

Fort Ontario was the only American free port. While America's immigration quotas allotted to countries of occupied Europe were 91 percent unfilled (more than 55,000 unused slots that year), the nation opened its gates to 1,000 fugitives from extermination. Eight months before, Sweden had welcomed 8,000 Jews from Denmark. Sweden's population and her land area were each about one-twentieth that of the United States. Journalist I. F. Stone described the American contribution as "a kind of token payment to decency, a bargain-counter flourish in humanitarianism." [48]

The outcome of the campaign for emergency havens, one camp, only faintly resembled the WRB's original objective, an American offer of temporary refuge "for all oppressed peoples escaping from Hitler." A dramatic proposal of that dimension would have put pressure on other nations to open their doors. And, a point of signal importance, Spain and Turkey might have agreed to act as bridges to safety once they were certain that the refugees would move right through. [49]

With a generous American offer in hand, the WRB had planned to launch a bold initiative and call on Germany and its satellites to release the Jews en masse. That challenge, in combination with the havens offer and the President's war-crimes threat, would make crystal clear to the Germans, and to the world, America's determination to do all it could to stop the extermination of the Jews. [50]

It is impossible to know what the plan might have achieved. At a minimum, though, if Turkey and Spain (and Switzerland) had publicly announced their willingness to take in any Jew who reached their borders, escapes from Axis territory would have increased by the thousands. The WRB proposal might not have budged Hitler, but chances were strong that the Axis satellites would have responded positively.

Actually, middle-level State Department officials were not at all sure that Hitler was immovable. They warned Hull to be cautious about the WRB plan:

> The proposal, if carried through, would inevitably involve the risk that Hitler might take advantage of the offer to embarrass the United Nations at this time by proposing to deliver thousands of refugees at stated ports on definite days. Should the United Nations fail to provide the shipping to remove them serious embarrassment to all concerned would result.

In reality, it was not shipping that worried the State Department but the specter of a mass outflow of Jews and no place to put them. At that very time, the Allies had ample shipping available for moving refugees. This was verified by Assistant Secretary of War McCloy, and it was proven by the ongoing evacuation of thousands of Yugoslavs from Italy to Egypt.[51]

The President's limited offer annulled the WRB's basic plan. The single camp failed to open any other doors. As Charles Joy of the Unitarian Service Committee pointed out, the smallness of the offer "destroys the value of the gesture. If the United States with all its resources can take only one thousand of these people what can we expect other countries to do?"[52]

In the United States, two reactions greeted the President's decision. One was gratitude, combined with disappointment that the step had been so limited. The other was bitter anger at Roosevelt for his high-handed breaching of the immigration bulwarks. The response in favor of free ports was immediate and widespread. Endorsements of FDR's action came from major newspapers, from Christian and Jewish groups, and from hundreds of individuals who sent messages to the White House. Most expressions of support also called for many more American havens. But Roosevelt had no intention of that, as he explained in a personal reply to one of the letters: "We do not need any more free ports at the present time because of the physical problems of transportation, and we are taking care of thousands of others in North Africa and Italy."[53]

On the other side, restrictionists and anti-Semites wrote angrily to the President, members of Congress, and newspapers. None believed that the refugees would go back; many saw the thousand as the entering wedge for hundreds of thousands more, mostly Jews. The undercurrent of anti-Semitism then running through American society surfaced in several letters. A woman in New York asserted that America owed nothing to the oppressed Jews; "they are the reason for Hitler!" A Colorado man insisted that the refugees were obviously not going to be repatriated: "What country would want a Jew back?" The editors of *Life* magazine were shaken by the amount of bitterly nasty mail that came in response to a photo story on the refugees' arrival at Fort Ontario.[54]

Syndicated columnist Westbrook Pegler used the thousand refugees as a club to attack Roosevelt. He warned that "many thousands" more would be coming, including Communists and crooks. Later, he wrote that "Mr. Roosevelt may admit 500,000." Promises to send them back after the war, he insisted, were worthless. Patriotic organizations took up the cry, fearful that the first thousand might form a precedent for breaking down the immigration laws. Throughout the summer, arch-restrictionist Senator Robert R. Reynolds (Dem., N.C.) kept the issue boiling. Others in Congress were indignant at Roosevelt's use of exec-utive power to bring refugees in. After all, Congress had refused him that prerogative when it choked off the Third War Powers Bill in November 1942.[55]

The Fort Ontario Experience

The refugees first saw Fort Ontario on an August morning in 1944. A returning Army troopship carried them from Italy to New York, and a special overnight train brought them to Oswego. Help came too late for one, a baby girl who died at sea of malnutrition and pneumonia. Most of the 982 who arrived had endured years of persecution, flight, and camp life; nearly a hundred had survived Dachau or Buchenwald. They came from seventeen different nations; Yugoslavs, Austrians, Poles, Germans, and Czechs were the most numerous. Their ages ranged from three weeks to eighty years, but people in their twenties were scarce, as were men of military age. The group was 89 percent Jewish. Most of the rest were Catholic.*[56]

The refugees' arrival generated pages and pages of photographs and human-interest stories. The American press for the first time had dis-covered a Holocaust-related event worthy of featured coverage.[58]

Once at the Emergency Refugee Shelter, as the camp was officially designated, the fugitives came under the jurisdiction of the War Relo-cation Authority (WRA), then within the Department of the Interior. The WRA received the job because it was experienced in operating the camps where Japanese and Japanese-Americans were interned. Ac-tually, the WRA had earlier concluded that camp life was harmful and to be avoided if possible. Before the refugees arrived, it tried unsuc-cessfully to arrange for them to leave the shelter for a normal commu-nity life after a limited reception period.[59]

The camp was located on the shore of Lake Ontario, thirty-five miles northwest of Syracuse. Conditions were livable, but not conducive to healthy family life; and three-fourths of the refugees belonged to family

* Forty-one of the refugees (including twelve women) asked to join the American armed forces, but the War Department ruled them ineligible because of the arrangements under which they were in the United States.[57]

units. Meals were eaten in mess halls. Families lived in barracks buildings that had been partitioned into small apartments. The apartments
had only the barest furnishings and lacked individual bathroom facilities. More important, the thin walls allowed almost no privacy. Friction
among neighbors was chronic.[60]

Soon after the shelter opened, Army intelligence officials screened
the refugees for security purposes. After that, they were allowed to leave
the camp and go into the town of Oswego for up to six hours at a time,
but they had to be back by midnight. No one could travel beyond
Oswego, except for essential hospitalization. Nor could anyone take
employment outside the camp. Visitors could come into the shelter, but
not even close relatives could stay overnight. In an arrangement that
proved mutually rewarding, the Oswego public schools provided free
education for 190 refugee children. Another thirty attended the practice
school at Oswego State Teachers College free of charge.[61]

Dozens of Jewish organizations, and a few non-Jewish ones, came to
the shelter to offer help. Without them, camp life would have been
substantially more difficult. To avoid public criticism, the government
provided minimum subsistence only. For example, the medical policy
was to maintain the refugees in the same general condition in which
they arrived, despite the years of deprivation many had experienced.
No medical or dental rehabilitation was to be performed except to
counter an immediate threat to health. The government did not even
furnish vitamins for babies and children. The private agencies met those
needs, supplying corrective medical treatment, dental care and den-
tures, and even items as basic as eyeglasses. They also lent social workers to the WRA for the initial adjustment period, equipped and funded
many cultural and recreational programs, and sponsored numerous
adult education courses.[62]

After several weeks of rest and adequate nourishment, the refugees'
anxieties about basic physical needs receded. Many then became restive
about the restrictions under which they lived. In Italy, after the Allied
occupation, most had moved about freely, held jobs if they wished, and
used the camps only as a home base.[63]

Before departing for the United States, the adult refugees had signed
a form in which they agreed to reside at Fort Ontario and, after the
war, to return to their homelands. These stipulations were in line with
Roosevelt's pledges to Congress and had always been part of the WRB's
havens plan. The point on postwar repatriation had been clearly conveyed to the refugees before they left Italy, but the requirement that
they stay in the camp had not. The language in that part of the form
was ambiguous. And none of the refugees had been confronted with

the form until they had made all the arrangements to leave and were about to board the ship.[64]

Through the last months of 1944, the misunderstanding about confinement to Fort Ontario led to increasing resentment within the camp. By January 1945, that factor, combined with several others, had depressed morale to the point where one suicide had occurred and many internees were near mental breakdown.* [65]

Another cause of the very poor morale was the constant tension generated by the work situation in the shelter. The WRA expected able refugees to perform basic camp services and maintenance, such as preparing food, cleaning the mess hall, removing garbage, and distributing coal. But many resisted this work, either by evasion or by open refusal. A key reason for this was the widespread negative attitude in the group toward physical labor, especially menial jobs. In addition, many who worked believed they were taken advantage of because of the low compensation. The WRA granted all refugees $8.50 per month for incidental purchases. Regular workers received $18.00 per month, which represented a real salary of only $9.50. The reluctance to work meant that the camp administration, which was basically sympathetic, was embroiled in an unending struggle to get the refugees to perform essential services. Furthermore, much of the work was poorly done; kitchen sanitation in particular posed a chronic threat to health. Camp morale suffered another devastating blow in February 1945 when one of the most cooperative workers died in a coal-unloading accident, leaving a wife and four young children.[67]

Curt Bondy, a psychologist and an expert on camp life, visited Fort Ontario at the start of 1945. His report emphasized the high level of tension in the shelter, despite the almost complete absence of physical violence. He pointed to the work situation as the worst problem, one that was unsolvable, given the WRA's refusal to increase pay. No basis for community cohesiveness existed in the camp; in fact, nationality differences bred constant conflict. (In one instance, Austrians and Germans had stalked out of a synagogue because the rabbi delivered his sermon in a Yugoslav language.) Bondy concluded that the only real solution was to phase out the shelter as soon as possible.[68]

Bondy was not alone in believing that the Fort Ontario refugees

* Other problems included an unusually severe and snowy winter (even for that area), worsened by uneven heating; the tension of being surrounded by freedom, close enough to touch it, yet not free; uncertainty about the future; eagerness to obtain employment, become self-supporting, and begin to rebuild interrupted lives; emotional damage caused by recent European experiences, including, for many, the deaths of close relatives; and too much time available to dwell on anxieties and brood over past tragedies.[66]

needed a more normal existence. Many refugees, of course, held the same view. Backed by relatives and friends outside the camp, they had begun to press hard for release. By early 1945, they had several allies. One was the camp director, Joseph Smart. Another was the WRA leadership in Washington. It called for a furlough arrangement patterned on the system by which Japanese internees were being paroled from camps into American communities. Secretary of the Interior Ickes supported release wholeheartedly and pressed for it throughout 1945. The private refugee-aid organizations lobbied steadily for it through a special "Camp Committee" led by representatives of the National Refugee Service, the HIAS, and the American Friends Service Committee.[69]

What emerged was a widely supported plan for "sponsored leave." Under it, the private agencies would provide community and job placement for the refugees and guarantee that they would not become public charges. For supervisory purposes, the refugees would maintain monthly contact with the WRA. Supporters pointed to the tax savings that would result with the closing of the camp.[70]

But powerful opposition to sponsored leave came from Attorney General Francis Biddle, President Roosevelt, and the War Refugee Board. Biddle and Roosevelt maintained that release from the camp would probably be illegal and certainly would constitute a breach of faith with the Congress. Biddle noted that members of Congress had challenged him several times to justify the entry of the refugees and he had assured them that they were staying only temporarily and would remain in detention while here. Release, he declared, would increase the suspicion, already widespread in Congress, that the administration was trying to get around the immigration laws. For some time, the WRB also opposed sponsored leave as a violation of the pledges that it and the President had made. In March 1945, though, William O'Dwyer, who had recently replaced Pehle as WRB director, began to search for a way around Biddle's ban on sponsored leave. He was not successful.*[71]

Eleanor Roosevelt was caught between the President's position and

---

* In a discussion with Morgenthau, O'Dwyer assessed the Fort Ontario situation in this way:

Well, anybody that would be satisfied to spend six hours in the town of Oswego in the middle of winter hasn't had much fun out of life. They are strange people; it is a strange town; it is in the middle of winter. They are looking at a fence all day long, worrying about what is going to happen. They have no hope. Naturally you are going to have some of them go insane. It has actually occurred and it is expected to increase.[72]

her personal concern about the refugees—a concern deepened by a visit to the shelter. She publicly voiced her unhappiness that the refugees could not be out building their futures. But because of the President's pledge and the negative attitude in Congress, she saw no way it could be done. "The whole thing seems perfectly silly to me," she wrote to a clergyman in a city near Oswego, "but we have to realize that people in war time are not logical and Congress acts in the way that they think people at home want them to act." [73]

Until the shelter finally closed, the government insisted that essential hospitalization constituted the only grounds for leaving the camp, except for the brief visits to Oswego. Thus, a refugee whose paralyzed wife lived on Long Island could not visit her even for Christmas. An older man, deafened and his health broken by beatings in a concentration camp, had a wife and two grown daughters who had escaped from Europe earlier. They lived in California and were now American citizens. His wife, who operated a successful small business, was anxious to care for him. Only in November 1945, after the man's health had deteriorated to the point where he was almost fully paralyzed, did he qualify for medical leave. His wife then took him to California. The family was reunited briefly. The husband died two months later. [74]

During 1945, psychological deterioration continued in the camp. By mid-March, four refugees had been removed to mental institutions. Germany's surrender in May briefly raised spirits; but shortly afterward even worse depression set in as rumors ran through the shelter that the whole group would soon be shipped back to Europe. The great majority dreaded repatriation. Many felt they could not face life in former homelands that had disowned them, countries where they had passed through terrible experiences and had lost loved ones. And they feared renewed persecution in a Europe where the Nazis had cultivated anti-Semitism. [75]

In addition, more than half of the shelter's inhabitants had relatives who lived in the United States outside the camp. For over a hundred of them, repatriation would mean separation from immediate family members: husband or wife in seven cases, brothers or sisters in seventy-three others, and children in thirty-five more. Fourteen of the refugees had sons in the American armed forces.* [76]

* A sixty-year-old woman from Vienna and her husband, who died in Italy in 1942, had sent their two sons to the United States in 1938. Both were now overseas with the American Army. Their wives, who lived in California, wanted to take their mother-in-law in. Would she instead be sent back to Austria? Another refugee, in flight from the Nazis, had been separated from his wife and lost track of her. He managed to reach the United States. In 1944, he learned that she had come with the group at Fort Ontario.

As spring and summer passed, the future of the Fort Ontario refugees hung in the balance. But time made it increasingly clear that repatriation was unlikely. The plight of the millions of displaced persons in Europe was emerging as a problem of immense proportions. Food and clothing were in short supply, and destruction was everywhere. If the United States sent this thousand back, it might encourage Switzerland, Sweden, and other countries to force out the much greater numbers of refugees they had harbored, adding substantially to the chaos.[78]

By fall, compulsory repatriation had become a major issue in Europe. President Truman and the U.S. Army lined up solidly against it; they also began to press for moving DPs out of Europe. Truman specifically called on Britain to permit 100,000 Jews to go to Palestine to help relieve the situation.[79]

Against that background, it would have been ludicrous for America to insist on returning 1,000 refugees to Europe. But they could not be kept at the camp indefinitely either. Not until Christmas 1945 did the answer emerge, when Truman ruled that they could enter the United States under the barely touched immigration quotas.[80]

Truman's decision followed months of continuous pressure from several sides. Interior Secretary Ickes had pushed steadily for implementation of already existing administrative procedures that permitted the Justice and State departments to admit the refugees under the immigration quotas. At the same time, the WRA stalled moves within the administration to deport the group. The private agencies and the Jewish defense organizations pressured top State Department leaders and the President, arguing that repatriation would not only be cruel to the refugees but would also contradict American policy and worsen the DP situation in Europe. Joseph Smart resigned as shelter director in May 1945 to launch a campaign for admitting the refugees as permanent immigrants. He marshaled support from leading Oswego citizens and many prominent Americans, including John Dewey, Albert Einstein, and Eleanor Roosevelt. By June 1945, O'Dwyer and the WRB were also fighting repatriation.[81]

Samuel Dickstein, chairman of the House Immigration Committee, played a pivotal role in ending the impasse. To dramatize the difficulties involved in sending the refugees back and to demonstrate the high caliber of the group as prospective immigrants, he held hearings at the shelter in June 1945. Careful planning and Dickstein's skillful management of the sessions produced a very favorable impression on the con-

---

Now she faced return to Europe. Many others at the shelter confronted similarly anguishing prospects.[77]

gressmen present as well as in the extensive press coverage that resulted.[82]

In Washington a week later, Dickstein maneuvered a compromise through the heavily restrictionist House Immigration Committee. Tough in appearance, it called on the administration to send back without delay all whose repatriation was practicable. The rest should undergo deportation proceedings, and the camp should be closed, ending a government expense of $600,000 per year. What Dickstein counted on was the impracticability of repatriation, given the situation in Europe. Nor was deportation feasible under the circumstances. Furthermore, existing regulations permitted aliens under deportation proceedings to petition to be examined for eligibility for the immigration quotas. The Immigration Committee's action thus threw the entire responsibility into the hands of the Truman administration. Dickstein, along with Ickes, then kept prodding Truman, emphasizing the terrible conditions in Europe and reminding him that he had the power to let the refugees stay.[83]

Truman's decision came on the night of December 22, 1945. It was part of the "Truman Directive," an order issued to set an international example by expediting admission of displaced persons to the United States. For the first time since mid-1940, the U.S. immigration quotas were open for full use. Concerning the refugees at Oswego, Truman termed it "inhumane and wasteful" to make them go back to Europe, where they would almost immediately be eligible for immigration visas for the United States.[84]

The White House gave the National Refugee Service the responsibility for relocating the Fort Ontario refugees and allowed one month— January 1946—to clear the camp. Despite the short deadline, the NRS and dozens of Jewish communities across the country successfully placed the 834 Jewish refugees. The American Christian Committee for Refugees and the Catholic Committee for Refugees made arrangements for the non-Jews. Thus, eighteen months after its arrival, America's "token shipment" of refugees officially entered the United States—as permanent quota immigrants.* [85]

---

* During the preparations for departure, several refugees went through a final rush of insecurities, some connected with relocation assignments. A few who were headed for Chicago worried about stories that gangsters roamed the city. An older person bound for relatives in Kansas City considered backing out. Others in the camp had warned that the streets were full of cowboys and frontier violence. One man agreed to relocate his family in Providence, R.I. The next day his wife appeared at the placement worker's desk to complain: "My husband, the Shlemiel, he had to be the one to choose the smallest state in America."[86]

Truman's decision drew sharp fire from restrictionists. Hundreds of letters to the White House demanded its reversal. Westbrook Pegler sounded the alarm again: "The adults, men and women both, for all we know may be Communists." These outbursts were only the last crash of a hailstorm of restrictionist resentment that had lashed at the Fort Ontario refugees since before their arrival. Beneath much of that restrictionism was the widespread anti-Semitism then embedded in American society. Because it had both local and national impact, the Fort Ontario episode provided a gauge of American anti-Semitism in that era.[87]

Many Oswego citizens welcomed the refugees, sympathized with them, and recognized the advantages in associating with them. But they were a minority. Within a month of the refugees' arrival, anti-Semitism began to increase rapidly throughout the city. Oswego residents who befriended refugees encountered social ostracism. Even the successful public school experience was marred by name-calling ("you dirty Jews"; "filthy refugee"). There was some ganging up on refugee children. Malicious rumors circulated persistently, especially claims that the government furnished luxury items for the refugees and drained the area of such scarce commodities as rationed foods and cigarettes in order to pamper them. These stories spread to neighboring localities and even turned up as far away as Buffalo. A physician in Syracuse told colleagues that the refugees had steak twice a week, despite the meat shortage. (In reality, they had been served no steak at all.) * [88]

Anti-Semitism also surfaced in numerous ugly anti-refugee letters to the Oswego daily newspaper. Syracuse newspapers printed many similar communications. A rash of particularly mean-spirited letters that appeared in summer 1945 convinced the publisher of the Oswego newspaper that a campaign was afoot, probably instigated from outside the area.[90]

Anti-Semitism in Oswego, a typical small American city, was probably little greater than in much of the rest of the nation. The difference was the presence of the refugees; they drew Oswego's anti-Jewish feelings to the surface. Correspondence in the Dickstein committee's files furnishes convincing evidence that northern New York's anti-Semitism was not unusual. Dickstein's efforts to find a solution for the thousand

---

* Many in Oswego resented the way the fort had been used since its well-liked peacetime garrison had departed after the outbreak of the war. First came black troops, then illiterate soldiers sent for training. A few months after they left, the refugees arrived. Many townspeople angrily felt that Fort Ontario had become "a dumping ground for the unwanted." They had endured the "niggers and the morons," they complained, only to be afflicted with the Jews.[89]

refugees were nationally publicized. The extensive news coverage generated by the hearings at Fort Ontario brought a deluge of restrictionist protest on the congressman. Much of the outcry—and it came from across the nation—was anti-Semitic. Often, the anti-Semitism was subtle; but in numerous cases, illustrated by excerpts from three letters to Dickstein, it was blatant.

> Your attempt to keep that gang of refugees from Ft. Oswego in this country is just an opening wedge to get all of that "trash" from Europe over here. The result will be anti-Jewish race riots.
> We have too much of that crap here now. I wonder why no country in the world wants them?

> To leave that bunch of refujews in this country . . . was the game to start with by Mr. F. D. Rosenblatt who fortunately died before his louzy plan could be carried out with you and your tribe. . . . We don't propose to stand idly by and have that bunch of parasite[s] pushed down our throats over here. We fought to preserve America for Americans and our children and not for a bunch of refujews.

> You lousy sheeney, what do you mean by wanting to keep those Jews in this country. . . . You kikes are the scum of the earth.* [91]

Latin American Documents

While the WRB pressed ahead with its main projects, its staff searched continually for other rescue possibilities. One plan was to exchange German citizens living in the United States and Latin America for Jews in Axis Europe. In December 1942, shortly after the news of extermination surfaced, Jewish groups had urged this. The State Department failed to respond openly, but secretly rejected the proposal on the ground that European governments-in-exile would probably protest it as favoring Jews over their non-Jewish citizens. [93]

Britain, on the other hand, had already completed two such exchanges with Germany. Germans from Egypt, South Africa, and Palestine went to Europe in return for Jews sent to Palestine. A third exchange took place in July 1944. But only 463 Jews were in-

---

* The Fort Ontario experience also brought out, time and again, the strong anti-immigration attitudes prevalent in Congress. Most members of Congress refrained from openly voicing anti-Semitic views. But it was well understood that congressional concern centered chiefly on Jewish immigration. [92]

volved in the three transfers combined. The Nazis had 4,000 more Jews cleared to go, but the British lacked exchangeable German citizens.[94]

In spring 1944, under WRB pressure, the State Department opened negotiations with Germany concerning inclusion of Jews in the next general American-German exchange. Ultimately, in January 1945, 800 Germans interned in the United States and Latin America were exchanged for 800 American and Latin American citizens. Among the latter were 149 Jews from Bergen-Belsen who possessed Latin American passports. A key obstacle to larger exchanges was that few Germans in the Western Hemisphere would agree to repatriation.[95]

A problem related to exchanges arose shortly before the WRB was established, and engaged its attention during much of 1944. The issue centered on Latin American protective passports held by a few thousand Jews in Nazi Europe. Originally, some stateless Jews with prospects for overseas migration had procured Latin American passports to remedy their lack of basic travel documentation. Many of them failed in their emigration plans. But with time it became evident that the Nazis considered Jews who held Latin American papers a potentially useful commodity. They might be exchangeable for some of the tens of thousands of German citizens resident in Latin America. So the Nazis put these supposed Latin American Jews into special exchange camps with other interned civilians of enemy nationalities. Conditions there were livable, and, most important, the Jews seemed safe from deportation.[96]

As word spread, a sizable traffic developed in Latin American passports. In Switzerland, Portugal, Sweden, and even Japan and the United States, relatives and friends of Jews in Nazi territory obtained passports from Latin American consulates and had them smuggled into occupied Europe. Most consuls sold the documents for personal gain; a few acted out of humanitarian motives. Most of these papers were of doubtful validity. But the 5,000 to 10,000 Jews who held them enjoyed a precarious safety in Nazi exchange camps.[97]

As 1943 ended, however, danger threatened. In September, Paraguay dismissed its consul in Switzerland and annulled the unauthorized passports he had issued. Two months later, at the internment camp at Vittel, in northeastern France, the Germans took up all Paraguayan passports. Word reached Washington within days that Jews there, as well as in other exchange camps, faced deportation to Poland. The State Department persuaded the Paraguayan government to honor the passports until the war ended. Paraguay then informed the Germans that the passports were still valid. At about the same time, the State Department asked the Intergovernmental Committee on Refugees to try to stop the deportations and see what could be done to protect all holders of the dubious Latin American documents.[98]

The ICR considered the question for two months, then decided not to act. Meanwhile, during January 1944, reports reached Washington indicating that the Germans were confiscating the passports of several Latin American nations from Jews in Vittel and other exchange camps. When the newly formed WRB looked into the situation, it realized that the Swiss government had failed to protest. (Switzerland represented the interests of most belligerent Latin American nations in matters concerning Germany.) The board drafted a telegram instructing the American legation in Bern to press the Swiss to prevail upon Germany to accept Latin American documents as valid unless they were actually repudiated by the Latin American governments.[99]

Middle-level State Department officials, put off by the WRB's strident approach to diplomacy, cited the impropriety of upholding fraudulent passports and blocked the telegram for almost seven weeks. The American government had, of course, not hesitated to use forged papers for numerous purposes. What State Department officials mainly objected to was the broad scope of the WRB order. They were willing, at most, to ask the Swiss to help when the Germans raised questions in specific cases. The board recognized the futility of such a piecemeal approach—a futility magnified by the fact that the Nazis were not inquiring about the passports but were simply preparing to ship the Jews out. In this dispute, the most adamant of the State Department officials were Paul T. Culbertson, chief of the Western European Division, and James H. Keeley, Jr., chief of the Special War Problems Division.[100]

What finally shook the WRB telegram loose from the State Department was a set of events in early April. The Union of Orthodox Rabbis in New York received information that the Polish Jews in Vittel had been isolated for deportation. Three rabbis hastened to Washington. Though actively supported by the offices of Senator James Mead (Dem., N.Y.) and of House Majority Leader John McCormack, the rabbis got nowhere with the State Department. They then went to Morgenthau. Upset by the long delays, and shaken when the oldest rabbi "completely broke down and . . . wept, and wept, and wept," Morgenthau phoned Hull and persuaded him to force the issue. The next day, the State Department sent the telegram to Switzerland. In Bern, the first secretary of the American legation, George Tait, echoed objections lately raised in Washington:

I do not like this matter at all in any of its aspects. This group of persons has obtained false papers to which they have no claim and has endeavored to obtain special treatment which they would not otherwise have received. We are being placed in the position of acting as nurse-maid to persons who have no claim to our protection.

But Tait was quickly overruled.[101]

Pressing its breakthrough, the WRB succeeded in sending two important follow-up telegrams. State Department opposition had not declined, but it had to bend before the impact of Morgenthau's pressure on Hull and a new burst of heat kindled by journalist Drew Pearson. One of the rabbis, angry about the protracted delay in sending the previous telegram, carried the story to Pearson, who reported it on his Sunday evening radio program.[102]

The first of the additional telegrams instructed the American legation in Bern to inform the Germans, through the Swiss, that the United States was working with Latin American nations on plans to exchange German citizens in the Americas for people held by Germany, including Jews with Latin American passports. Largely a bluff, this statement was aimed at convincing the Germans that they had something to gain by keeping those Jews alive.[103]

The other telegram initiated negotiations with fourteen Latin American governments. It asked each to affirm the passports issued in its name and to insist to the German government that holders of its documents be protected. In return, the WRB agreed to find havens elsewhere for any of the Jews who might come out. After prolonged negotiations, which the Vatican seconded, thirteen Latin American states consented.[104]

Meanwhile, the WRB and the American legation in Bern began dispatching frequent and forceful reminders to the German authorities that Jews with Latin American documents were entitled to protection and were eligible for exchange. In May, the German Foreign Office sent formal assurance that no one then in an exchange camp would be deported. At least two violations of this pledge occurred, but for the most part the agreement appears to have been upheld. No solid data are available concerning the number of Jews thus saved, but the board's own guess of about 2,000 is reasonable.[105]

The WRB's steps came too late, however, for the Polish Jews in Vittel, whose impending deportation had first alarmed the Orthodox rabbis. At least 214 of them were deported, almost certainly to Auschwitz. If the State Department had not delayed the WRB's plans for nearly seven weeks, those 214 would probably have survived.[106]

Another rescue project had virtually run its course before the WRB was established. In March 1943, the Spanish government agreed to take in 300 Sephardic Jews whom the Germans were willing to release. The 300 were part of the thousands of descendants of Jews who had been expelled from Spain in the fifteenth century. Although Sephardic Jews had settled in several lands, Spain had continued to view them as its citizens and had claimed the right to intervene to protect them when necessary. But before 1943 it had done virtually nothing to save them from the Nazis. Even under the new policy, the Spanish authorities consented to accept only a small number and then only with assurances that they leave Spain within two months.[107]

The American ambassador, Carlton Hayes, encouraged the plan, and David Blickenstaff, head of American private relief operations in Spain, offered to work to arrange onward migration. In August, a group of only 79 arrived from France. Although they carried valid Spanish passports and citizenship certificates, the Spanish government insisted that they move on promptly. The young men, however, were ordered to remain in Spain to fulfill their military obligations.[108]

Later arrangements to bring in a few hundred Sephardic Jews from Greece stretched out over many months because Spain would not accept them until the first group had departed. Meanwhile, the Germans shipped them from Greece to Bergen-Belsen, where they were suspended between deportation to Auschwitz and acceptance into Spain. The August arrivals left Spain only in December. In February 1944, trains finally brought 367 Sephardic Jews from Bergen-Belsen to Spain.[109]

Including a few score more from France, a little over 500 Sephardic Jews escaped through the actions of the Spanish government, Hayes, and Blickenstaff. Once on the scene, the WRB worked steadily to bring out more, particularly another group of 155 held at Bergen-Belsen. Hayes cooperated, but there were no results.[110]

Food and the Blockade

The WRB devoted considerable thought to plans to send food into the ghettos and camps. The broader issue of supplying food to civilian populations starving under Nazi occupation had been contested throughout the war. Despite growing public pressure in Britain and the United States, British blockade authorities, acting under the Ministry of Economic Warfare, were virtually immovable. Food could go through the blockade only for prisoners of war and certain interned civilians. The United States adhered to British blockade policies, though not without disagreements.[111]

The blockade authorities permitted one major exception. By early 1942, starvation was claiming a terrible toll in Axis-occupied Greece. After receiving assurance from Germany that it would not confiscate Greek food, the American and British governments began in August 1942 to move large amounts of food to that country from the Western Hemisphere in ships chartered from Sweden. The Swedish government, the International Red Cross, and a commission of Swedish and Swiss citizens monitored the project. At first, eight ships were delivering wheat and some medicines. By April 1944, a fleet of fourteen was carrying cargoes that also included dried vegetables, canned milk, soup powder, cured fish, baby food, rice, sugar, and clothing. After the early months, the American Lend-Lease Administration took over most of the costs. Lend-Lease provided $11.5 million in 1943 and increased the amount to about $30.0 million for 1944. The program did not end the famine in Greece, but it substantially improved conditions for the 2.5 million Greeks it reached.[112]

During 1942, Jewish groups and other organizations speaking for various conquered European populations began to press the State Department to apply the Greek arrangement to other subject peoples. The Jews emphasized that Jewish nutritional levels were the lowest in Europe and were especially devastating in the Polish ghettos, where inhabitants were allowed about two-thirds the food that the starving Greeks had been receiving before the food shipments started.[113]

The Ministry of Economic Warfare and the State Department insisted that Greece was a special case. The food situation was unusually bad there. Since the country had few industries of value to the Germans, they had no incentive to feed the Greeks. Food sent to other countries, blockade authorities argued, would only free food for German use.[114]

In late 1942, despite British objections, the State Department modified the ban slightly. It permitted American relief agencies to send $12,000 worth of food parcels per month to specific addressees in Axis Europe. The plan required assurances, by returned postcards or other means, that the packages reached the intended recipients. And the food had to come from the small surpluses produced in neutral European nations. Problems in obtaining current addresses and the inflexibility of the entire arrangement kept the trickle of parcels far below the tiny limit set by the State Department.[115]

During 1943, a national campaign for feeding the starving populations of occupied Europe gained momentum in the United States. In the forefront was Howard Kershner, formerly a relief worker for the Quakers in Vichy France. Kershner's Temporary Council on Food for Europe's Children cooperated with Herbert Hoover and several humanitarian groups to publicize the issue. They were especially disturbed by the high death rate among children in occupied Europe. Along with the obvious humane concern, the advocates of feeding emphasized the practical consequences of allowing children to starve: tomorrow's democratic leaders were dying or suffering irreparable damage. Kershner and others urged the establishment of at least a small experimental program focused on children and based on the Greek example.[116]

The British government turned a deaf ear to all such proposals. But shortly before Christmas 1943, the Senate Foreign Relations Committee —spurred by Elbert Thomas, Guy Gillette, and Robert Taft—unanimously approved a resolution calling on the administration to extend the Greek feeding plan to other populations in occupied Europe. As 1944 opened, a ground swell of support arose in the press, the labor movement, and the churches. A Gallup poll in February reported 65 percent support for feeding children in Nazi-occupied Europe. Four days later, the Senate passed the food resolution unanimously. In mid-April, the House did the same. But the campaign to send food to occupied Europe failed. The outcome was decided in London, by Winston Churchill and the Ministry of Economic Warfare.[117]

Responding to public and congressional pressure, the State Department sought British agreement to a limited program of feeding children and pregnant and nursing women in Belgium, France, Holland, and Norway. The Joint Chiefs of Staff approved it. The President supported the plan wholeheartedly and sent a personal note to Churchill asking his "most earnest consideration" of it. The response was polite but adamant. Churchill and the Ministry of Economic Warfare maintained that the blockade must not be violated.* The State Department, hoping to relieve the political pressure in America, continued for almost a year

---

* At almost the same time, curiously enough, Eleanor Roosevelt defended the blockade policy in her "My Day" column. Commenting on the issue of feeding European children, she wrote, "This is a war question and one which the Allied Military Committee must decide. . . . Only the military authorities can determine whether feeding them today will mean a longer war. . . . War is a ruthless business. It cannot be conducted along humanitarian lines."[119]

to press the British to accept at least "some proposal." Nothing resulted.[118]

President Roosevelt had suggested feeding programs before. But whenever he had brought the question up, Churchill had imposed an absolute objection, insisting that nothing must hamper the war effort and that moving food through the blockade would help Germany. Yet the British made exceptions when it suited their purposes. They supplied food to the children on the German-occupied Channel Islands (British territory near the French coast). And during 1942, sensing diplomatic advantage, they unilaterally decided to permit temporary shipments of food to Norway and Belgium.[120]

The Treasury Department had been ready by the end of 1943 to drop its previous policy against permitting food to pass through the blockade. At a staff meeting soon after the WRB was set up, Pehle summarized the new position. "We have long since passed the time," he said, when we should have begun shipping food to children. "It no longer can, in any way, interfere with the war effort, . . . the war is going to be decided on the military side and this won't make any difference."[121]

In its attempts to develop relief programs, the WRB moved on several fronts simultaneously. It had the crippling restrictions removed from the State Department's 1942 agreement permitting American private agencies to send $12,000 worth of food parcels per month to people trapped in Axis Europe. And to encourage neutral European nations to accept larger numbers of refugees, the board prevailed on the British to let enough food through the blockade to cover their needs.[122]

The most effective means of getting food to the ghettos and camps would have been to obtain prisoner-of-war status for the Jews in Nazi Europe. A precedent of sorts existed. The United States, Britain, and the Axis powers had an informal agreement under which their citizens who were interned in enemy countries were treated practically the same as prisoners of war were under the Geneva Convention of 1929. The arrangement included the right to receive food parcels and regular camp visitations by International Red Cross personnel. The visits and the resulting reports on camp conditions provided an important measure of protection. This arrangement was called "assimilation," for the internees were partially assimilated to the Geneva Convention.[123]

The WRB asked the Red Cross to approach Germany concerning a similar status for the Jews. The IRC refused, explaining that such a move would "go far beyond the limits" of its traditional work and expose it to charges of intervening in Germany's internal affairs. Any loss of German goodwill, the IRC maintained, would threaten the "slender basis" for its war-related activities and thereby endanger them. Furthermore, the proposal had "no prospect of success" with the Germans.[124]

For similar reasons, the IRC was also unwilling to seek Germany's permission to distribute food to the unassimilated concentration-camp inmates. But in March 1944, it did obtain informal guarantees from individual camp commanders that they would relay food parcels to unassimilated internees and permit IRC representatives to visit the camps unofficially to verify their delivery. The IRC was satisfied that the arrangement, though unconventional, was safe. The WRB view was that "the amount of food which might fall into enemy hands could not affect the outcome of the war nor prolong it." But the British were dubious and delayed the project for months.[125]

In August, blockade authorities finally authorized, as a trial, the shipment of 300,000 food parcels. Roosevelt allotted $1,068,750 for the program from funds already appropriated by Congress for foreign war relief. Using supplies available in Switzerland, the WRB sent advance shipments of 25,000 parcels into concentration camps during August and September. Otherwise, the project continued at a snail's pace. Packaging, done in the United States, began only in October. The 300,000 parcels arrived in Europe in December. By then, the disruption of German rail systems made delivery to the camps extremely difficult.[126]

By February 1945, only 40,000 parcels had been sent into Axis territory, so the WRB decided to furnish its own transportation. William O'Dwyer, who replaced Pehle as director in January, pushed ahead with a plan to procure trucks in Switzerland to deliver the parcels to the camps and evacuate sick and old inmates on the return trips. McClelland located twenty-four trucks but could not find gasoline or tires. Intense pressure by O'Dwyer and Morgenthau persuaded the War Department to allocate fuel and tires from Army stocks in France.[127]

Meanwhile, the SS made three concessions to the International Red Cross. It was permitted to deliver food to all internees, to station delegates in all major camps to supervise the distribution, and to evacuate women, children, elderly, and ill persons from the camps. In early April, then, IRC personnel began driving WRB relief trucks from Switzerland to the concentration camps. Before Germany's surrender, the trucks carried 1,400 women, mostly French non-Jews, out to Switzerland. The presence of Red Cross representatives in the camps during the closing weeks of the war also helped prevent last-minute atrocities against inmates.[128]

Assessment of the WRB

By the end of the war, the WRB had played a crucial role in saving approximately 200,000 Jews. About 15,000 were evacuated from Axis territory (as were more than 20,000 non-Jews). At least 10,000, and probably thousands more, were protected within Axis Europe by WRB-financed underground activities and by the board's steps to safeguard holders of Latin American passports. WRB diplomatic pressures, backed by its program of psychological warfare, were instrumental in seeing the 48,000 Jews in Transnistria moved to safe areas of Rumania. Similar pressures helped end the Hungarian deportations. Ultimately, 120,000 Jews survived in Budapest.[129]

The results of other WRB programs, though they unquestionably contributed to the survival of thousands more, can never be quantified, even roughly. These actions include the war-crimes warnings and the shipment of thousands of food parcels into concentration camps in the last months of the war. Furthermore, news that the United States had at last embarked upon rescue must have encouraged many Jews and reinforced their determination to outlast the Nazis if at all possible.[130]

On the other hand, numerous WRB plans that might have succeeded collapsed because the rest of the government did not provide the cooperation legally required of it by Executive Order 9417. Nor could the board wield the diplomatic influence that was needed; its approaches to foreign governments and international organizations always had to be filtered through the basically negative State Department. Moreover, the President took little interest in the board and never moved to strengthen it. And it was always hobbled by the government's failure to fund it properly.

The shortcomings in the WRB's record must not, however, be allowed to overshadow the significance of its achievements. Despite many difficulties and Germany's determination to exterminate the Jews, the board helped save tens of thousands of lives. As leaders of the private agencies remarked, the WRB staff acted with "enormous drive and energy" and "a fervent sense of desire to get something accomplished." Their dedication broke America's indifference to the destruction of European Jewry, thereby helping to salvage, in some degree, the nation's conscience. After considerable reflection, Roswell McClelland concluded that the board's successes, though limited, had added "a measure of particularly precious strength" to the Allied cause.* [131]

In one respect, through a miscalculation, the WRB hampered its own work. The rapid Allied advance across France in summer 1944 set off a chain of predictions by responsible military and civilian leaders that the war with Germany would end very soon, probably by October and almost certainly by Christmas. Accordingly, in September the board began making plans to wind down its affairs. In late November, at Morgenthau's suggestion, Pehle took over the Treasury's Procurement Division, the unit responsible for disposing of surplus military property. [133]

Pehle continued to work part-time with the board, but by early January 1945 negative public reaction was building and Jewish organizations were complaining that he was not giving enough time to the WRB. It was evident that a full-time director was needed. Morgenthau and Pehle arranged through McCloy for the Army to release Brigadier General William O'Dwyer for the post. On January 27, O'Dwyer stepped in. [134]

O'Dwyer had risen to fame in 1941 when, as district attorney for Kings County, New York, he had rooted out "Murder, Inc.," a kill-for-hire gang. That same year, he challenged Fiorello La Guardia in the New York mayoralty race, but lost. He entered the Army in 1942 and two years later, as head of the economic section of the Allied military government in Italy, dealt effectively with problems of high mortality, hunger, and bad public-health conditions. While in the Army, he won uncontested reelection as Kings County district attorney. [135]

With his drive, his connections in the military, and his concern for suffering people, O'Dwyer was ideal for the WRB job. But, to the dismay of Morgenthau and Pehle, he spent only three days a week in Washington. His main base, and the source of his income, was the Kings County district attorney's office. (He accepted no salary from the WRB.) When he was available, O'Dwyer showed a quick, sure grasp of rescue problems and a capacity for forceful action. But his potential for rescue work was not realized, because he applied only a fraction of his time and talents to it. [136]

---

* Most who were in touch with the rescue situation acknowledged the importance of the WRB's achievements. But not everyone agreed. Bruce Mohler, a leader of the National Catholic Welfare Conference's Bureau of Immigration, wrote to his associate, T. F. Mulholland: "We have never seen any worthwhile results from that operation and in fact felt that it was not necessary when established in January 1944. No doubt plenty of money was wasted in the operation." Mulholland agreed, pronouncing the board's performance "wholly non-productive." [132]

By early March, Morgenthau and Pehle had concluded that O'Dwyer had taken the WRB post as a route out of the Army and into the race for mayor of New York. Soon afterward, O'Dwyer asked Morgenthau to let him get away for a time. The board's work was under control, he explained, and constant hounding by political reporters "is getting me down." At Roosevelt's request, O'Dwyer gave up that plan, but he contributed little more to the WRB. At the end of May, with the war over in Europe, he left the board.[137]

In the last analysis, the WRB's greatest weakness was that it came into existence so late. Virtually everyone close to the rescue issue thought the board could have achieved far more if it had been formed a year, or even several months, earlier. Looking back at the board's work decades afterward, the two people who were most closely involved with it stressed the costliness of the late start. Josiah DuBois believed that the WRB "did a fair amount," but he emphasized that "by that time it was too damned late to do too much." In John Pehle's view, "What we did was little enough. It was late. . . . Late and little, I would say."[138]

|| 15 ||

THE BOMBING
OF AUSCHWITZ

A recurring question since World War II has been why the United States rejected requests to bomb the gas chambers and crematoria at Auschwitz and the railroads leading to Auschwitz.

Such requests began to be numerous in spring 1944. At that time, three circumstances combined to make bombing the Auschwitz death machinery and the railways leading to it from Hungary critically important and militarily possible. In mid-April, the Nazis started concentrating the Jews of Hungary for deportation to Auschwitz. Late in April, two escapees from Auschwitz revealed full details of the mass murder taking place there, thus laying bare the fate awaiting the Hungarian Jews. And by May the American Fifteenth Air Force, which had been operating from southern Italy since December 1943, reached full strength and started pounding Axis industrial complexes in Central and East Central Europe. For the first time, Allied bombers could strike Auschwitz, located in the southwestern corner of Poland. The rail lines to Auschwitz from Hungary were also within range.[1]

The two escapees were young Slovak Jews, Rudolf Vrba and Alfred Wetzler, who fled on April 10, 1944. Toward the end of April, they reached the Jewish underground in Slovakia and sounded the alarm that preparations were under way at Auschwitz for exterminating the Hungarian Jews. They dictated a thirty-page report on what they had learned about the killing center during their two years there. It detailed the camp's geographical layout, internal conditions, and gassing and cremation techniques, and offered a statistical record of the months of systematic slaughter. The thoroughness that characterized the report is seen in this passage describing the operation of one of the four large gas chambers:

> It holds 2,000 people. . . . When everybody is inside, the heavy doors are closed. Then there is a short pause, presumably to allow the room temperature to rise to a certain level, after which SS men with gas masks climb on the roof, open the traps, and shake down a preparation in powder form out of tin cans, . . . a "cyanide" mixture of some sort which turns into gas at a certain temperature. After three minutes everyone in the chamber is dead. . . . The chamber is then opened, aired, and the "special squad" [of slave laborers] carts the bodies on flat trucks to the furnace rooms where the burning takes place.[2]

A copy of the Vrba-Wetzler statement, dispatched to the Hungarian Jewish leadership, was in Budapest by early May. By mid-June, the report had reached Switzerland, where it was passed to Roswell McClelland of the War Refugee Board. He found it consistent with earlier information that had filtered out concerning Auschwitz. It was further corroborated by the disclosures of a non-Jewish Polish military officer who had also recently escaped from the camp.[3]

During June, this information spread to the Allied governments and began to appear in the Swiss, British, and American press. By late June, then, the truth about Auschwitz, along with descriptions of its geographical location and layout, was known to the outside world.[4]

In mid-May, as deportation from the eastern provinces of Hungary started, Jewish leaders in Budapest sent out a plea for bombing the rail route to Poland. The message specified the junction cities of Kosice (Kassa) and Presov and the single-track rail line between them. It added that Kosice was also a main junction for Axis military transportation. Dispatched via the Jewish underground in Bratislava, Slovakia, the request was telegraphed in code to Isaac Sternbuch, the Vaad Hahatzala representative in Switzerland. It reached him about May 17.[5]

Sternbuch rewrote the telegram for transmission to the Union of Orthodox Rabbis in New York and submitted it to the military attaché of the American legation in Bern, requesting that it be telegraphed to the United States through diplomatic lines. A week later a similar, but more urgent, telegram arrived from Bratislava. That appeal also went to the military attaché for delivery to New York. Additional pleas came, and Sternbuch relayed them to the American legation. Yet, by June 22, he had received neither reply nor acknowledgment from New York. For unknown reasons, the messages had been blocked, either in Bern or in Washington.[6]

In Jerusalem, Jewish leaders had received appeals similar to those that had reached Sternbuch. On June 2, Yitzchak Gruenbaum, chairman of the Jewish Agency's rescue committee, arranged through the American consul general in Jerusalem to telegraph a message to the War Refugee Board in Washington. His request for bombing the deportation railroads reached the WRB, but nothing came of it.[7]

Meanwhile, during the third week of May, Rabbi Michael Weissmandel and Mrs. Gisi Fleischmann, leaders of the Slovak Jewish underground, wrote a long letter pleading with the outside world for help. They described the first deportations from Hungary and stressed the fate awaiting the deportees on their arrival at Auschwitz. Their message appealed for immediate bombing of the main deportation routes, especially the Kosice–Presov railway. The two also cried to the outside world to "bombard the death halls in Auschwitz." Writing in anguish, they asked, "And you, our brothers in all free countries; and you, governments of all free lands, where are you? What are you doing to hinder the carnage that is now going on?" Smuggled out of Slovakia, the plea, accompanied by copies of the Auschwitz escapees' reports, reached Switzerland, but not until late June.[8]

Some days earlier, about June 13, other copies of the escapees' reports had come via the Slovak underground to Jaromir Kopecky, a Czechoslovak diplomat in Geneva. He immediately showed them to Gerhart Riegner of the World Jewish Congress. Riegner summarized them for delivery to the American and British governments and the Czech exile government in London. To the summaries, Kopecky and Riegner added appeals for bombing the gas chambers and the rail lines from Hungary to Auschwitz.[9]

Shortly afterward, one of Sternbuch's pleas for railway bombing, transmitted illegally through Polish diplomatic channels, circumvented American censorship and broke through to American Jewish circles. On June 18, Jacob Rosenheim of the New York office of Agudath Israel World Organization addressed letters to high American government officials, informing them of the ongoing deportations. He submitted that paralysis of the rail traffic from Hungary to Poland could at least slow the annihilation process, and implored them to take immediate action to bomb the rail junctions of Kosice and Presov.[10]

Rosenheim's appeals were relayed to the WRB. On June 21, Pehle transmitted the request to the War Department. Three days later, he discussed it with McCloy. Pehle himself expressed doubts about the proposal, but asked that the War Department explore the idea. McCloy agreed to look into it.[11]

In fact, the War Department had started to process the matter the day before, and on Saturday afternoon, June 24, it arrived at the Operations Division (OPD), the arm of the War Department charged with strategic planning and direction of operations. On Monday, OPD ruled against the proposed bombing, stating that the suggestion was "impracticable" because "it could be executed only by diversion of considerable air support essential to the success of our forces now engaged in decisive operations." Actually, the decision was not based on any analysis of current Air Force operations. The War Department did not consult Air Force commanders in Europe. Rather, the rejection was based on a confidential War Department policy determined in Washington nearly five months before.[12]

In late January 1944, in one of its first steps, the WRB had requested British help in carrying out its program of rescue. The British government was reluctant to cooperate, partly because the presence of the secretary of war on the board implied that the armed forces would be used in rescuing refugees. The War Department, moving to reassure the British on this count, set down the following policy:

> It is not contemplated that units of the armed forces will be employed for the purpose of rescuing victims of enemy oppression unless such rescues are the direct result of military operations conducted with the objective of defeating the armed forces of the enemy.

This policy effectively removed the War Department from participation in rescue efforts, except as they might arise incidental to regularly planned military operations.[13]

Another of the WRB's earliest moves was to try to arrange for a degree of cooperation from U.S. military commanders in the war theaters. In late January 1944, the board proposed through McCloy that the War Department send a message to war-theater commanders instructing them to do what was possible, consistent with the successful prosecution of the war, to assist the government's policy of rescue.[14]

Although such cooperation was specifically mandated by the executive order that established the WRB, the military leadership in Washington balked at dispatching the message. McCloy referred the proposal to the Office of the Chief of Staff after jotting on it, "I am very chary of getting the Army involved in this while the war is on." The War Department's decision crystallized in February in an internal memorandum that maintained:

> We must constantly bear in mind, however, that the most effective relief which can be given victims of enemy persecution is to insure the speedy defeat of the Axis.

In concrete terms, this meant that the military had decided to avoid rescue or relief activities.* [15]

In late June, when the Operations Division received Rosenheim's proposal to bomb rail points between Hungary and Auschwitz, it drew these two earlier pronouncements from the files and used them as the basis for its decision:

> The War Department is of the opinion that the suggested air operation is impracticable for the reason that it could be executed only by diversion of considerable air support essential to the success of our forces now engaged in decisive operations.
>
> The War Department fully appreciates the humanitarian importance of the suggested operation. However, after due consideration of the problem, it is considered that the most effective relief to victims of enemy persecution is the early defeat of the Axis, an undertaking to which we must devote every resource at our disposal. [17]

Thus two confidential policy statements, generated several months earlier, were used to rule out the proposal to bomb the Kosice–Presov railroad. That decision then served as a precedent for rejecting all subsequent requests. The War Department simply claimed it had already considered such operations and found them infeasible.

Back in February, while forming its basic policy on rescue, the War Department had knowingly set aside the executive order that established the War Refugee Board. The record of a crucial meeting of

* The War Department finally sent a message to theater commanders in early March, but all it did was inform them of the WRB's general mission. In April, the WRB learned that American military authorities in Italy were unaware even of the board's existence. That same month, a WRB representative spoke with General Benjamin Caffey at Allied headquarters in Algiers and found him adamant that military forces in the Mediterranean theater would not assist with any WRB plans. [16]

middle-level War Department officials shows that Colonel Harrison Gerhardt, McCloy's executive assistant, advised Colonel Thomas Davis of OPD's Logistics Group to "read from the executive order, in which it is stated that the War, State and Treasury Departments will cooperate to the fullest extent." Davis responded, "I cannot see why the Army has anything to do with it whatsoever." Later in the meeting, he insisted, "We are over there to win the war and not to take care of refugees." Gerhardt replied, "The President doesn't think so. He thinks relief is a part of winning the war." At the end of the discussion, Davis crystallized the problem and its solution:

> The hook in the executive order is in paragraph 3 [the section that charged the War, State, and Treasury departments with executing WRB programs]. Obviously there will be continuing pressure from some quarters to enlarge the sphere of this thing. I think that we should make our position fairly inelastic.

Davis's view prevailed.[18]

In fact, the position of the military had been inelastic all along. When the Bermuda Conference had originally recommended a refugee camp in North Africa, the War Department and the Joint Chiefs of Staff had resisted the plan, largely because they thought it might lead to more such requests. They claimed that shipping could not be spared, food supplies in North Africa were inadequate, and an influx of Jews might anger the Arab population and "necessitate military action to maintain order." Yet General Eisenhower, who was on the scene, saw no problem about keeping order; and at that very time the Allies were transporting thousands of non-Jewish refugees to camps in Africa and providing for them there.[19]

Months later, the Allied invasion of Italy opened new opportunities to rescue Jews; but again the military was negative. In fall 1943, Yugoslav partisans freed 4,000 people, mostly Jews, from Nazi internment and moved them to the Adriatic island of Rab. Because the Germans seemed likely to capture the island, the State Department, at the request of the World Jewish Congress, asked the military to help get the refugees to Italy. The Joint Chiefs of Staff replied that Allied forces in Italy were already overloaded with refugees to care for and action to aid those on Rab "might create a precedent which would lead to other demands and an influx of additional refugees."[20]

Even the State Department was taken aback. Stettinius warned Hull that if the response to the Rab situation accurately reflected military policy, the United States might as well "shut up shop" on the effort to rescue any more people from Axis Europe. He thought the President should inform the military that rescue was "extremely important . . . in fact sufficiently important to require unusual effort on their part and to be set aside only for important military operational reasons."*[21]

No such thing happened. Soon afterward, the War Refugee Board was formed and, as has already been noted, the War Department unilaterally decided against involving the military in rescue. It was this policy—never disclosed to the WRB—that extinguished Rosenheim's plea for railroad bombing.

Before McCloy could advise Pehle of the decision on Rosenheim's proposal, another request reached the WRB. A cablegram from McClelland on June 24 summarized the information that had arrived in Switzerland concerning the Hungarian deportations. It also listed the five main railroad deportation routes and pointed out:

> It is urged by all sources of this information in Slovakia and Hungary that vital sections of these lines especially bridges along ONE [the Csap, Kosice, Presov route] be bombed as the only possible means of slowing down or stopping future deportations.[23]

Pehle, not aware that the War Department had already ruled against Rosenheim's request, relayed McClelland's cablegram to McCloy on June 29, along with a note emphasizing its reference to bombing deportation railroads. The chance for approval of a proposal to bomb five rail systems was minute; indeed, it received no separate consideration. Gerhardt, McCloy's executive assistant, drafted a reponse to Pehle and forwarded it, with McClelland's cablegram and Pehle's covering note, to his chief. He also included this two-sentence memorandum:

> I know you told me to "kill" this but since those instructions, we have received the attached letter from Mr. Pehle.
> I suggest that the attached reply be sent.

The reply simply adapted the Operations Division's language rejecting the earlier Rosenheim proposal to fit the new, expanded bombing request. McCloy signed it on July 4.[24]

Calls for bombing the deportation rail lines continued to come to Washington. But starting early in July, appeals for Air Force action to impede the mass murders increasingly centered on destruction of the

* A few weeks later, the WRB sought War Department help in transmitting funds to the Jews on Rab so they could hire private boats to reach Italy. The military did not cooperate.[22]

Auschwitz gas chambers. Even before the first of these proposals reached Washington, Benjamin Akzin of the WRB staff was arguing for strikes on Auschwitz. He held that destruction of the killing installations would, at least for a time, appreciably slow the slaughter. He also pointed out that Auschwitz could be bombed in conjunction with an attack on Katowice, an important industrial center only seventeen miles from the death camp.[25]

Shortly afterward, the London-based Czech government forwarded to Washington the summary of the Vrba-Wetzler report that Riegner and Kopecky had sent out of Switzerland two weeks before. Riegner and Kopecky's accompanying plea for bombing the Auschwitz gas chambers stimulated further WRB discussion of that possibility. By mid-July, Pehle and the board decided to press the military on the question. But a careful plan to do so apparently went awry, for no formal approach took place, though Pehle and McCloy did discuss the issue sometime during the summer of 1944. That conversation must have dampened Pehle's interest in the project, because he informed Morgenthau in September that the board had decided not to refer the proposal to the War Department.[26]

Late in July, the Emergency Committee to Save the Jewish People of Europe wrote President Roosevelt calling for bombing the deportation railways and the gas chambers. The letter emphasized that the railroads were also used for military traffic and that an attack on Auschwitz could open the way for inmates to escape and join the resistance forces. Both proposed actions would thus assist, not hamper, the war effort. Nothing at all came of this overture.* [27]

The next proposal issued from the World Jewish Congress in New York and went directly to the War Department. On August 9, A. Leon Kubowitzki sent McCloy a message recently received from Ernest Frischer, a member of the Czech government-in-exile. It called for bombing the Auschwitz gas chambers and crematoria to halt the mass killings. It also proposed bombing the railways.[29]

The reply, drawn up in McCloy's office and approved by Gerhardt, was dated August 14. It followed a familiar pattern:

---

* At the same time, the Emergency Committee pointed to the use of poison gas at Auschwitz and stressed the President's earlier threat that "full and swift retaliation in kind" would follow "any use of gas by any Axis power." The committee called on Roosevelt to warn the Nazis that the continued use of gas to kill Jews would bring poison-gas attacks on the German people. This appeal was relayed to the State Department, then to the WRB, which answered that it was a military matter and thus outside its jurisdiction. In September, the proposal reached the Joint Chiefs of Staff, who ruled that it was not "within their cognizance."[28]

Dear Mr. Kubowitzki:

I refer to your letter of August 9 in which you request consideration of a proposal made by Mr. Ernest Frischer that certain installations and railroad centers be bombed.

The War Department has been approached by the War Refugee Board, which raised the question of the practicability of this suggestion. After a study it became apparent that such an operation could be executed only by the diversion of considerable air support essential to the success of our forces now engaged in decisive operations elsewhere and would in any case be of such doubtful efficacy that it would not warrant the use of our resources. There has been considerable opinion to the effect that such an effort, even if practicable, might provoke even more vindictive action by the Germans.

The War Department fully appreciates the humanitarian motives which prompted the suggested operation, but for the reasons stated above, it has not been felt that it can or should be undertaken, at least at this time.

Sincerely,
John J. McCloy[30]

In early September, pressure built once more for bombing the railroads, this time the lines between Auschwitz and Budapest, where the last large enclave of Hungarian Jews was threatened with deportation. Entreaties came from Vaad Hahatzala, the Orthodox rescue committee. Rabbi Abraham Kalmanowitz, anxious for the appeal to reach the WRB as soon as possible, telephoned Benjamin Akzin, even though it was the Sabbath. Kalmanowitz offered to travel to Washington immediately. When Akzin relayed the plea to Pehle, he took the opportunity to spell out, in polite terms, his dissatisfaction with the War Department's inaction regarding the bombing requests. He maintained that the WRB had been "created precisely in order to overcome the inertia and—in some cases—the insufficient interest of the old-established agencies" concerning the rescue of Jews. Pointing to the Allies' current air superiority, he pressed for a direct approach to the President to seek orders for immediate bombing of the deportation rail lines. But the board did not move on the appeal.[31]

On the other crucial bombing issue, the question of air strikes on Auschwitz, the WRB did act, but with hesitation. Near the end of September, members of the Polish exile government and British Jewish groups came to James Mann, the WRB representative in London, with information that the Nazis were increasing the pace of extermination. They urged the board to explore again the possibility of bombing the killing chambers. Mann cabled their plea to Washington. Other messages then reaching the board were reporting Nazi threats to exterminate thousands of camp inmates as the Germans were forced back across Poland by the Red Army. Pehle decided to raise the issue once more, though not forcibly. He transmitted the substance of Mann's dispatch to McCloy "for such consideration as it may be worth."[32]

McCloy's office thought it worth too little consideration to trouble the Operations Division with it, or even to write a reply to the WRB. Gerhardt recommended that "no action be taken on this, since the matter has been fully presented several times previously."[33]

McCloy let the recommendation stand, and the matter was dropped. Meanwhile, Mann's dispatch had independently caught the attention of the Operations Division, which discussed it briefly with the Air Force Operational Plans Division. The Air Force radioed a message to England to General Carl Spaatz, commander in chief of the U.S. Strategic Air Forces in Europe. It asked him to consult Mann's original dispatch and informed him that "this is entirely your affair," but pointedly advised that military necessity was the basic requirement. The next day, Spaatz's headquarters turned the proposal down.[34]

The last attempt to persuade the War Department to bomb Auschwitz came in November. The full text of the Auschwitz escapees' reports finally reached Washington on November 1. The detailed chronicle of horror jolted the board. Shocked, Pehle wrote a strong letter to McCloy urging destruction of the killing installations. He also pointed out the military advantages in simultaneously bombing industrial sites at Auschwitz.[35]

Pehle's appeal went from McCloy's office to the Operations Division. It rejected the proposal on the grounds that air power should not be diverted from vital "industrial target systems" and Auschwitz was "not a part of these target systems." In reality, Auschwitz was definitely a part of those target systems. OPD was either uninformed or untruthful.[36]

OPD also explained that destruction of the killing facilities would require heavy bombers, or medium bombers, or low-flying or dive-bombing airplanes. It then made two misleading statements which indicated that the mission was either technically impossible or inordinately risky:

> The target [Auschwitz] is beyond the maximum range of medium bombardment, dive bombers and fighter bombers located in United Kingdom, France or Italy.

Use of heavy bombardment from United Kingdom bases would necessitate a round trip flight unescorted of approximately 2000 miles over enemy territory.

The first statement was inaccurate; Mitchell medium bombers and Lightning dive-bombers had sufficient range to strike Auschwitz from Italy, as did British Mosquito fighter-bombers. The second statement was apparently an attempt to muddle the issue. Why else omit the airfields in Italy? Heavy bombers flying from Italy could reach Auschwitz with no unusual difficulties. The bases in the United Kingdom, however, were substantially farther from Auschwitz and not relevant to the mission under consideration.[37]

No further requests were made for bombing Auschwitz or the rail lines to it. Unknown to the outside world, Himmler in late November ordered the killing machinery destroyed. On January 27, 1945, the Russian army captured the camp.[38]

Thus the proposals to bomb Auschwitz and the rail lines leading to it were consistently turned down by the War Department. The chief military reason given was that such proposals were "impracticable" because they would require the "diversion of considerable air support essential to the success of our forces now engaged in decisive operations elsewhere." Was this reason valid? The answer is no.

From March 1944 on, the Allies controlled the skies of Europe. Official U.S. Air Force historians have stated that "by 1 April 1944 the GAF [German air force] was a defeated force." Allied air power had "wrecked Hitler's fighter [plane] force by the spring of 1944. After this . . . U.S. bombers were never deterred from bombing a target because of probable losses."[39]

From early May on, the Fifteenth Air Force, based in Italy, had the range and capability to strike the relevant targets. In fact, during the same late June days that the War Department was refusing the first requests to bomb railways, a fleet of Fifteenth Air Force bombers was waiting for proper flying conditions to attack oil refineries near Auschwitz. This mission, which took place on July 7, saw 452 bombers travel along and across two of the five deportation railroads. On June 26, 71 Flying Fortresses on another bombing run passed by the other three railroads, crossing one and flying within thirty miles of the other two.[40]

As for Auschwitz, as early as January 1944, Allied bombing strategists were analyzing it as a potential target because of the synthetic oil and rubber installations connected to the camp. Two months later, the huge Blechhammer oil-refining complex, forty-seven miles from Auschwitz, came under careful study. Then, in late April, U.S. Strategic Air Force headquarters in England wrote to General Ira C. Eaker, commander of Allied air forces in Italy, inquiring about the feasibility of a Fifteenth Air Force attack on Blechhammer. Eaker replied on May 8 that not only were strikes on Blechhammer possible, but war industries at Auschwitz and Odertal "might also be attacked simultaneously."[41]

By May 1944, the Fifteenth Air Force had indeed turned its primary attention to oil targets. Throughout the summer, as their involvement with the invasion of France lessened, the British-based U.S. Eighth Air Force and the Royal Air Force increasingly joined the Fifteenth in fighting the "oil war." Most observers, then and now, have agreed that the high attention given to oil in 1944 and 1945 was one of the most decisive factors in Germany's defeat. Loss of oil gradually strangled the Third Reich's military operations.[42]

In late June, the "oil war" was about to move into Upper Silesia, where Germany had created a major synthetic-oil industry based on the vast Silesian coal resources. Eight important oil plants were clustered there within a rough half-circle, thirty-five miles in radius, with Auschwitz near the northeast end of the arc and Blechhammer near the northwest. Blechhammer was the main target—fleets of from 102 to 357 heavy bombers hit it on ten occasions between July 7 and November 20 —but it was not the only one. All eight plants shook under the impact of tons of high explosives. Among them was the industrial section of Auschwitz itself.[43]

On Sunday, August 20, late in the morning, 127 Flying Fortresses, escorted by 100 Mustang fighters, dropped 1,336 500-pound high-explosive bombs on the factory areas of Auschwitz, *less than five miles* to the east of the gas chambers. Conditions were nearly ideal for accurate visual bombing. The weather was excellent. Anti-aircraft fire and the 19 German fighter planes there were ineffective. Only one American bomber went down; no Mustangs were hit. All five bomber groups reported success in striking the target area.[44]

Again, on September 13, a force of heavy bombers rained destruction on the factory areas of Auschwitz. The 96 Liberators encountered no German aircraft, but ground fire was heavy and brought three of them down. As before, no attempt was made to strike the killing installations, though two stray bombs hit nearby. One of them damaged the rail spur leading to the gas chambers.*[45]

---

* Both the August 20 and the September 13 air raids on Auschwitz were briefly reported in the *New York Times* and other American newspapers. Evidently the WRB did not monitor such information.[46]

On December 18 and also on December 26, American bombers again pounded the Auschwitz industries.[47]

Beginning in early July, then, air strikes in the area were extensive. For example, two days after the first raid on Auschwitz, 261 Flying Fortresses and Liberators bombed the Blechhammer and Odertal oil refineries. Many of them passed within forty miles of Auschwitz soon after leaving their targets. On August 27, another 350 heavy bombers struck Blechhammer. Two days after that, 218 hit Moravska Ostrava and Oderberg (Bohumin), both within forty-five miles of Auschwitz. Not long before, on August 7, heavy bombers had carried out attacks on both sides of Auschwitz on the same day: 357 had bombed Blechhammer, and 55 had hit Trzebinia, only thirteen miles northeast of Auschwitz.[48]

It would be no exaggeration, therefore, to characterize the area around Auschwitz, including Auschwitz itself, as a hotbed of American bombing activity from August 7 to August 29. Yet, on August 14, the War Department could write that bombing Auschwitz would be possible only by diversion of airpower from "decisive operations elsewhere."

But a further question remains: Would the proposed bombing raids have been, as the War Department maintained, of "doubtful efficacy"?

In the case of railroad lines, the answer is not clear-cut. Railroad bombing had its problems and was the subject of long-lasting disputes within the Allied military. Successful cutting of railways necessitated close observation of the severed lines and frequent rebombing, since repairs took only a few days. Even bridges, which were costly to hit, were often back in operation in three or four days.[49]

Nonetheless, bridge bombing was pressed throughout the war. And bombing of both rail lines and railroad bridges constituted a significant part of the Fifteenth Air Force's efforts, especially during September and October 1944, when it assisted the Russian advance into Hungary by cutting and recutting railways running from Budapest to the southeastern front. Railroad bombing could be very effective, then, for targets assigned a continuing commitment of airpower. But in the midst of the war, no one expected diversion of that kind of military force for rescue purposes.[50]

It might also be argued that railroad bombing would not have helped after July 8, 1944—the day on which the last mass deportations from Hungary to Auschwitz took place. The argument is convincing with regard to the three deportation railways farthest from Budapest, because most Jews outside the capital were gone by then. But more than

200,000 Jews remained in Budapest. And they faced constant danger because the transports to Auschwitz might be resumed. This threat meant that the other two deportation railways, which would have been used to carry Jews from Budapest to Auschwitz, remained critically important.

Deportation of the Budapest Jews would have taken roughly three weeks, in addition to several days of preparations. An alarm would have reached the outside world in time for cuts in those railroads to have been of some help, even if the bombing had to be sporadic. In this situation, the United States could readily have demonstrated concern for the Jews. Without risking more than minute cost to the war effort, the War Department could have agreed to stand ready, if deportations had resumed, to spare some bomb tonnage for those two railroads, provided bombers were already scheduled to fly near them on regular war missions. As it happened, on ten different days from July through October, a total of 2,700 bombers traveled along or within easy reach of both rail lines on the way to targets in the Blechhammer-Auschwitz region.[51]

In fact, deportations from Budapest appeared imminent in late August, and another appeal for railroad bombing was sent to Washington through Sternbuch in Switzerland. On September 13, the answer came back to Bern: the War Department considered the operation impossible. Yet on that very day, 324 American heavy bombers flew from Italy to the Silesian targets. En route, they passed within six miles of one of the railways. On the way back, they rendezvoused directly above the other. As they regrouped, some of them dropped leftover bombs on the freight yard below and cut the main rail line.[52]

While the ending of mass deportations from Hungary on July 8 has some bearing on the question of railroad bombing, it has little relevance to the issue of bombing Auschwitz. There is no doubt that destruction of the gas chambers and crematoria would have saved many lives. Mass murder continued at Auschwitz until the gas chambers closed down in November. Throughout the summer and fall, transports kept coming from many parts of Europe, carrying tens of thousands of Jews to their deaths.[53]

Could the death factories have been located from the air? The four huge gassing-cremation installations stood in two pairs, spaced along the westernmost edge of the Auschwitz complex, just outside the Birkenau section of the camp. Two of the extermination buildings were 340 feet long, the others two-thirds that length. Chimneys towered over them. Descriptions of the structures and of the camp's layout, supplied by escapees, were in Washington by early July 1944. Beginning in April 1944, detailed aerial reconnaissance photographs of Auschwitz-Birkenau were available at Air Force headquarters in Italy.*[54]

Could aerial bombing have been precise enough to knock out the mass-murder buildings? Definitely yes. The main obstacles to accurate bombing were clouds, smoke, extreme altitudes, enemy fighter opposition, and flak.[56]

Weather conditions in the Auschwitz region were excellent for air operations throughout August and most of September; October was a time of poor weather. The August attack on Auschwitz ran into no smoke screening. The September strike encountered some. But because the industrial area was five miles from the killing installations, it is unlikely the latter would have been enveloped in smoke anyway. (It was not during the September raid.) Unusually high altitude flight was not a problem; the missions into Upper Silesia operated at normal bombing altitudes. Enemy fighter opposition was negligible. Flak resistance at Auschwitz was moderate and ineffective on August 20, but intense and accurate on September 13.[57]

In sum, the only real obstacle to precision bombing of the death machinery would have been flak. Auschwitz had little flak defense until after the August raid. Only then were heavy guns added. In any case, the most likely operation would have combined a strike on the gas chambers with a regular attack on the industries. In that situation, the German guns would have concentrated on the aircraft over the factory area, five miles away from the planes assigned to the death installations.[58]

One procedure would have been to arrange for some of the heavy bombers on one of the large Auschwitz strikes to swing over to the Birkenau side and blast the killing facilities. Heavy bombers flying at their normal altitude of 20,000 to 26,000 feet could have destroyed the buildings. But complete accuracy was rarely possible from such heights. Some of the bombs probably would have struck nearby Birkenau, itself a heavily populated concentration camp.†

---

* Officials in Washington had data on the Auschwitz killing installations, their location, and their purpose. But they relayed none of this information to the Air Force command in Italy. In Italy, Air Force personnel had aerial photographs of the extermination buildings, but no inkling of what they were and no reason to examine them closely. Their attention was focused on the industrial areas five miles distant.[55]

† Jewish leaders in Europe and the United States, assuming the use of heavy bombers and the consequent death of some inmates, wrestled with the moral problem involved. Most concluded that loss of life under the circumstances was justifiable. They were aware that about 90 percent of the Jews were gassed on arrival at Auschwitz. They also

Heavy bombers were not, however, the only choice. A small number of Mitchell medium bombers, which hit with surer accuracy from lower altitudes, could have flown with one of the missions to Auschwitz. The Mitchell had sufficient range to attack Auschwitz, since refueling was available on the Adriatic island of Vis, 110 miles closer than home base back in Italy.[60]

An even more precise alternative would have been dive-bombing. A few Lightning (P-38) dive-bombers could have knocked out the murder buildings without danger to the inmates at Birkenau. P-38's proved they were capable of such a distant assignment on June 10, 1944, when they dive-bombed oil refineries at Ploesti, making a 1,255-mile round trip from their bases in Italy. The distance to Auschwitz and back was 1,240 miles, and stopping at Vis shortened that to 1,130. Furthermore, in an emergency, Lightnings returning from Auschwitz could have landed at partisan-held airfields in Yugoslavia.*[61]

The most effective means of all for destroying the killing installations would have been to dispatch about twenty British Mosquitoes to Auschwitz, a project that should have been possible to arrange with the RAF. This fast fighter-bomber had ample range for the mission, and its technique of bombing at very low altitudes had proven extremely precise. In February 1944, for instance, nineteen Mosquitoes set out to break open a prison at Amiens to free members of the French resistance held there for execution. The first two waves of the attack struck with such accuracy, smashing the main wall and shattering the guardhouses, that the last six planes did not bomb.[63]

Mosquitoes knocked out individual buildings on numerous occa-

---

realized that most who were spared for the work camps struggled daily through a hellish, famished existence as slave laborers and were worn out in a matter of weeks. Once unfit for hard labor, they were dispatched to the gas chambers. The bombing might kill some of them, but it could halt or slow the mass production of murder.

Although those who appealed for the bombing did not know it, many Auschwitz prisoners shared their viewpoint. Olga Lengyel, a Birkenau survivor, recalled after the war that she and the inmates she knew hoped for an air raid: "If the Allies could blow up the crematory ovens! The pace of the extermination would at least be slowed." Two sisters, Hungarian Jews who were in Birkenau when the Auschwitz industrial areas were hit, told of the prisoners in their section praying for the bombers to blast the gas chambers. They were more than ready to die for that.[59]

* The England-Russia-Italy shuttle bases system (code-named FRANTIC) became available in early June 1944. But flights that left Italy and returned directly to the bases in Italy could reach both Auschwitz and the deportation rail lines more effectively than shuttle missions could. Referring to plans to attack oil targets at Blechhammer and Auschwitz, General Eaker stated, "Return to our own bases is preferable to a shuttle operation."[62]

sions. Gestapo records centers were frequent targets, as in an April 1944 mission to The Hague. Six Mosquitoes, flying at fifty feet, blew up the structure and the German barracks behind it. In his November appeal for bombing the Auschwitz murder buildings, Pehle pointed out the similarity to the Amiens mission. But the War Department denied that any parallel existed. Actually, the Amiens attack required greater precision. And in order to strike before the executions took place, it had to be carried out in very bad winter weather.[64]

Opportunities for bombing the gas chambers were not limited to the August 20 and September 13 raids on Auschwitz. Aircraft assigned to smash the death factory could have flown with any of the many missions to the nearby Silesian targets. Auschwitz could also have been scheduled as an alternative objective when poor bombing conditions were encountered at other targets.[65]

If the killing installations had been destroyed at this stage of the war, it would have been practically impossible for the hard-pressed Germans to rebuild them. At the very least, the death machinery could not have operated for many months. (The original construction, carried out in a time of more readily available labor, transportation, and materials, had taken eight months.)[66]

Without gas chambers and crematoria, the Nazis would have been forced to reassess the extermination program in light of the need to commit new and virtually nonexistent manpower resources to mass killing. Gas was a far more efficient means of mass murder than shooting, and it caused much less of a psychological problem to the killers. Operation of the gas chambers, which killed 2,000 people in less than half an hour, required only a limited number of SS men. Killing tens of thousands by gunfire would have tied down a military force. The Nazis would also have again faced the body-disposal problem, an obstacle that had caused serious difficulty until the huge crematoria were built.[67]

Available figures indicate that 100,000 Jews were gassed at Auschwitz in the weeks after the August 20 air raid on the camp's industrial sector. If the date is set back to July 7, the time of the first attack on Blechhammer, the number increases by some 50,000. Requests for bombing Auschwitz did not arrive in Washington until July. If, instead, the earliest pleas for bombing the gas chambers had moved swiftly to the United States, and if they had drawn a positive and rapid response, the movement of the 437,000 Jews who were deported from Hungary to Auschwitz would most likely have been broken off and additional lives numbering in the hundreds of thousands might have been saved.

More significant, though, than attempts to calculate particular numbers is the fact that no one could tell during the summer of 1944 how many hundreds of thousands more would die at Auschwitz before the Nazis ceased their mass murder.* [68]

The basic principle behind the War Department's rejection of the bombing proposals was that military resources could not be diverted to nonmilitary objectives. The logic of this position was extremely forceful in a world at war. But it should be emphasized that the policy was not as ironbound as the War Department indicated in its replies to the bombing requests. Exceptions occurred quite often, many of them for humanitarian purposes. For instance, the Allied military moved 100,000 non-Jewish Polish, Yugoslav, and Greek civilians to camps in Africa and the Middle East and maintained them there. Again, the American and British armies in Italy supplied thousands of refugees with food, shelter, and medical care. [70]

The war effort could be deflected for other decent purposes as well, such as art or loyalty to defeated allies. Kyoto, the ancient capital of Japan and a center of culture and art, was on the Air Force target list. In spring 1945, Secretary of War Stimson asked McCloy, "Would you consider me a sentimental old man if I removed Kyoto from the target cities for our bombers?" McCloy encouraged him to do so. The Air Force command argued against the decision but adhered to it. On another occasion, McCloy himself prevented the planned bombing of Rothenburg, a German town known for its medieval architecture. [71]

As Soviet forces neared Warsaw at the beginning of August 1944, the Polish Home Army rose against the Germans. (The Home Army was a non-Communist resistance force linked to the Polish government in London.) The Russian advance suddenly stopped, however, and the Red Army remained about ten kilometers from Warsaw for weeks while the Nazis decimated the unaided and poorly supplied Polish fighters. [72]

Polish officials in London put intense pressure on the British government to do something about the situation. Although Air Marshal Sir

---

* Incidentally, if the gas chambers had been destroyed on August 20 or earlier, Anne Frank might possibly have survived. Arrested on August 4, she and her family were deported to Auschwitz from a camp in Holland on September 2. They went on the last deportation train from Holland. Later, Anne and her sister were transferred to Bergen-Belsen, where both died of typhus, Anne in March 1945. If the Auschwitz mass-killing machinery had been destroyed by August 20, the train very likely would not have left Holland, because most of its passengers were bound for the Auschwitz gas chambers. [69]

John Slessor, the RAF commander in Italy, argued that supply flights to Warsaw from Italy would result in a "prohibitive rate of loss" and "could not possibly affect the issue of the war one way or another," the British government ordered the missions run. Volunteers flew twenty-two night operations from Italy during August and September. Of the 181 bombers sent, 31 did not come back. Slessor concluded that the effort had "achieved practically nothing." [73]

The United States did not participate in the Italy-based missions to Warsaw. But Roosevelt, under heavy pressure from Churchill, ordered American bombers in Britain to join the effort. On September 18, 107 Flying Fortresses dropped 1,284 containers of arms and supplies on Warsaw and continued on to bases in Russia. At most, 288 containers reached the Home Army. The Germans took the rest. [74]

The cost of the mission was low in numbers of aircraft lost, but extremely high in the amount of airpower kept out of regular operations. To deliver 288 (or fewer) containers to a military force known to be defeated, more than a hundred heavy bombers were tied up for nine days. For four days, the Fortresses sat in England, loaded with supplies, waiting for the right weather conditions. After the mission, four more days elapsed before the planes reached home, via Italy. (Prevailing wind patterns made the long trip directly from Russia to England unsafe for Flying Fortresses.) The bombers did strike a rail target in Hungary on the way from Russia to Italy, but carried out no other bombing operations in the entire nine days. [75]

The director of intelligence for the U.S. Strategic Air Forces summarized American involvement in the Warsaw airdrops. His report acknowledged that, even before the September 18 flight, the President, the War Department, and the Air Force realized that "the Partisan fight was a losing one" and that "large numbers of planes would be tied up for long periods of time and lost to the main strategic effort against Germany." Still, all those involved concurred in the decision to go forward, "despite the lack of a firm commitment" to the Polish government by the United States. [76]

Why did the United States divert a large amount of bombing capacity during a crucial phase of the oil campaign? The report's closing paragraph dealt with that question:

> Despite the tangible cost which far outweighed the tangible results achieved, it is concluded that this mission was amply justified. . . . America kept faith with its Ally. One thing stands out, from the President down to the airmen who flew the planes, America wanted to, tried, and did help within her means and possibilities.

The Warsaw airdrop was executed only by diversion of considerable airpower to an impracticable project. But the United States had demonstrated its deep concern for the plight of a devastated friend.* [77]

If, when the first bombing request reached it, the Operations Division had inquired of the air command overseas, it would have found the Fifteenth Air Force on the verge of a major bombing campaign in the region around Auschwitz. Instead, OPD never looked into the possibilities. From July through November 1944, more than 2,800 bombers struck Blechhammer and other targets close to Auschwitz. The industrial area of Auschwitz itself was hit twice. Yet the War Department persisted in rejecting each new proposal to bomb the railroads or the death camp on the basis of its initial, perfunctory answer—that the plan was "impracticable" because it would require "diversion of considerable air support." [79]

It is evident that the diversion explanation was no more than an excuse. The real reason the proposals were refused was the War Department's prior decision that rescue was not part of its mission—the President's order establishing the War Refugee Board notwithstanding. To the American military, Europe's Jews represented an extraneous problem and an unwanted burden.

In the fall of 1944, Jewish women who worked at a munitions factory inside Auschwitz managed to smuggle small amounts of explosives to members of the camp underground. The material was relayed to male prisoners who worked in the gassing-cremation area. Those few wretched Jews then attempted what the Allied powers, with their vast might, would not. On October 7, in a suicidal uprising, they blew up one of the crematorium buildings. [80]

* Roosevelt's role in the effort for the Warsaw Poles is clearly documented. But evidence is lacking as to whether he was ever consulted on the question of bombing Auschwitz and the railroads to it. [78]

·*Part Five*·

CONCLUSION

|| 16 ||

RESPONSIBILITY

America's response to the Holocaust was the result of action and inaction on the part of many people. In the forefront was Franklin D. Roosevelt, whose steps to aid Europe's Jews were very limited. If he had wanted to, he could have aroused substantial public backing for a vital rescue effort by speaking out on the issue. If nothing else, a few forceful statements by the President would have brought the extermination news out of obscurity and into the headlines. But he had little to say about the problem and gave no priority at all to rescue.[1]

In December 1942, the President reluctantly agreed to talk with Jewish leaders about the recently confirmed news of extermination. Thereafter, he refused Jewish requests to discuss the problem; he even left the White House to avoid the Orthodox rabbis' pilgrimage of October 1943. He took almost no interest in the Bermuda Conference. He dragged his feet on opening refugee camps in North Africa. He declined to question the State Department's arbitrary shutdown of refugee immigration to the United States, even when pressed by the seven Jews in Congress.[2]

In November 1943, on the eve of Roosevelt's departure for Cairo and

Tehran, stirrings in Congress briefly drew his attention to the rescue question. When he returned six weeks later, he faced the prospect of an explosive debate in Congress on administration rescue policies and the probable passage of legislation calling on him to form a rescue agency. Not long afterward, he established the War Refugee Board. His hand had been forced by the pressure on Capitol Hill and by the danger that a major scandal would break over the State Department's persistent obstruction of rescue.

After creating the board, the President took little interest in it. He never acted to strengthen it or provide it with adequate funding. He impeded its initial momentum by delaying the selection of a director and hindered its long-term effectiveness by ruining the plan to appoint a prominent public figure to the post. When the board needed help with the recalcitrant American ambassador to Spain, Roosevelt kept hands off. At the urging of the WRB, the President did issue a strong war-crimes warning in March 1944. But he first diluted its emphasis on Jews. His subsequent handling of the UN War Crimes Commission and his treatment of Herbert Pell were hardly to his credit.

Even when interested in rescue action, Roosevelt was unwilling to run a political risk for it, as his response to the free-ports plan showed. The WRB's original rescue strategy depended on America's setting an example to other nations by offering to open several temporary havens. The President, by agreeing to only one American camp, signaled that little was expected of any country. A more extensive free-ports program would probably have strained relations with Congress. It might also have cost votes, and 1944 was an election year.

It appears that Roosevelt's overall response to the Holocaust was deeply affected by political expediency. Most Jews supported him un-waveringly, so an active rescue policy offered little political advantage. A pro-Jewish stance, however, could lose votes. American Jewry's great loyalty to the President thus weakened the leverage it might have ex-erted on him to save European Jews.[3]

The main justification for Roosevelt's conduct in the face of the Holocaust is that he was absorbed in waging a global war. He lived in a maelstrom of overpowering events that gripped his attention, to the exclusion of most other matters. Decades later, Dean Alfange doubted that he actually realized what the abandonment of the European Jews meant: "He may not have weighed the implications of it to human values, to history, to a moral climate without which a democracy can't really thrive."[4]

Roosevelt's personal feelings about the Holocaust cannot be deter-mined. He seldom committed his inner thoughts to paper. And he did not confide in anyone concerning the plight of Europe's Jews except, infrequently, Henry Morgenthau. There are indications that he was concerned about Jewish problems. But he gave little attention to them, did not keep informed about them, and instructed his staff to divert Jewish questions to the State Department.* Years later, Emanuel Celler charged that Roosevelt, instead of providing even "some spark of cou-rageous leadership," had been "silent, indifferent, and insensitive to the plight of the Jews." In the end, the era's most prominent symbol of humanitarianism turned away from one of history's most compelling moral challenges.[5]

The situation was much the same throughout the executive branch. Only the Treasury reacted effectively. Oscar Cox and a few others in the Foreign Economic Administration did what they could. But their impact was minor. Secretary Ickes and a small group in the Interior Department were greatly concerned; however, they were not in a posi-tion to do much. The War Shipping Administration assisted the WRB with a few transportation problems. The record of the rest of the Roo-sevelt administration was barren.[7]

Callousness prevailed in the State Department. Its officers, mostly old-stock Protestants, tended strongly toward nativism. Little sympathy was wasted on East Europeans, especially Jews.[8]

Secretary Hull did issue public statements decrying Nazi persecution of Jews. Otherwise he showed minimal interest in the European Jewish tragedy and assigned no priority to it. Ignorant of his department's activities in that area, and even unacquainted with most of the policy-makers, he abandoned refugee and rescue matters to his friend Breck-inridge Long. Long and his co-workers specialized in obstruction.[9]

Even after Sumner Welles confirmed the accounts of genocide, State Department officials insisted the data had not been authenticated. They sought to silence Stephen Wise and other Jewish leaders. They tried to weaken the United Nations declaration of December 1942. In early

---

* Roosevelt's grasp of Jewish issues tended to be superficial. To note but one example, during the Casablanca Conference he spoke for keeping the number of Jewish profes-sionals in North Africa proportional to the Jewish population there. This, he stated, would avoid the "understandable complaints which the Germans bore towards the Jews in Germany, namely, that while they represented a small part of the population, over fifty percent of the lawyers, doctors, school teachers, college professors, etc., in Germany were Jews." (Quotation from the clerk's summary of the discussion.)

In reality, Jews had composed 1 to 2 percent of Germany's population. They had occupied 2.3 percent of professional positions. In the extreme cases, lawyers and med-ical doctors, Jews made up 16.3 and 10.9 percent respectively. They held 2.6 percent of the professorships and 0.5 percent of the schoolteacher positions.[6]

1943, in order to stifle pressures for action, they cut off the flow of information from Jewish sources in Switzerland.

These people brushed aside the Rumanian offer to free 70,000 Jews. With the British, they arranged the Bermuda fiasco, another move to dampen pressures for action. Rescue plans submitted to the State Department were strangled by intentional delays. Or they were sidetracked to the moribund Intergovernmental Committee on Refugees.

The State Department closed the United States as an asylum by tightening immigration procedures, and it influenced Latin American governments to do the same. When calls for a special rescue agency arose in Congress, Long countered them with deceptive secret testimony before a House committee. After the WRB was formed, the State Department cooperated to a degree, but the obstructive pattern recurred frequently. It is clear that the State Department was not interested in rescuing Jews.

The War Department did next to nothing for rescue. Secretary Stimson's personal opposition to immigration was no help. Far more important, however, was the War Department's secret decision that the military was to take no part in rescue—a policy that knowingly contradicted the executive order establishing the WRB.

On the basis of available evidence, the Office of Strategic Services took minimal interest in the extermination of the Jews. Its information about the Holocaust was frequently out-of-date and did not lead to countermeasures. In April 1944, the OSS obtained the first detailed account to reach the West of the mass murder of Jews at Auschwitz. Prepared eight months earlier by Polish underground sources, the document in many ways foreshadowed the Vrba-Wetzler report. The OSS did nothing with it.[10]

When the Vrba-Wetzler account first arrived in Switzerland, in June 1944, part of it was delivered to Allen W. Dulles of the OSS with a plea that he immediately urge Washington to take action. Dulles instead passed the material to the WRB in Bern, noting that it "seems more in your line." Nearly a year later, the OSS received a copy of the Vrba-Wetzler report that had reached Italy. By then, the document had been widely publicized in the West for many months. Yet the OSS treated it as new information![11]

In general, the OSS was unwilling to cooperate with the WRB. At first, at OSS initiative, there was some collaboration overseas between the two agencies. Before long, however, top OSS officials issued orders against further assistance to the board, apparently following intervention by the State Department. Once more, the executive order that set up the WRB was contravened.[12]

The Office of War Information, for the most part, also turned away from the Holocaust. It evidently considered Jewish problems too controversial to include in its informational campaigns aimed at the American public. Its director, Elmer Davis, stopped at least two plans for the OWI to circulate the extermination news to the American people. During the last year of the war, the OWI did disseminate war-crimes warnings in Europe for the WRB. But Davis was cool even toward that. And in late 1944, when the board released the Vrba-Wetzler report to the press without prior approval by his agency, Davis protested angrily.[13]

The President's Advisory Committee on Political Refugees (PAC) was a quasi-governmental group of eleven prominent Americans appointed by Roosevelt in 1938 to assist in developing refugee policies. Reflecting the inclinations of James G. McDonald, its chairman, and George L. Warren, its executive secretary, the PAC worked cautiously behind the scenes. Almost without access to Roosevelt, it dealt mainly with the State Department, to which its leadership usually deferred.[14]

The PAC was instrumental in persuading the Roosevelt administration to make visas available for 5,000 Jewish children in France whose parents had been sent to Poland in the mass deportations of 1942. The Nazis never permitted them to leave, however. After that, the committee was virtually inoperative, although it did apply tempered pressure for modification of the stringent visa policies and it endorsed the free-ports plan.[15]

One reason for the PAC's weakness was its uncertain financing. It was a presidential committee, yet it received no government funds. The American Jewish Joint Distribution Committee furnished most of its tiny budget of about $15,000 per year. For a time, Zionist organizations paid half the costs, but they stopped contributing in 1941. The American Catholic and Protestant refugee-aid committees each provided a total of $500 during the PAC's seven years.[16]

Important individuals who had access to the President and might have pressed the rescue issue with him did little in that direction. Vice President Wallace kept aloof from the problem. His closest encounter took place on the Capitol steps in October 1943 when he delivered a brief, noncommittal speech to the pilgrimage of Orthodox rabbis.

Eleanor Roosevelt cared deeply about the tragedy of Europe's Jews and took some limited steps to help. But she never urged vigorous government action. She saw almost no prospects for rescue and believed that winning the war as quickly as possible was the only answer.[17]

Except for Morgenthau, Jews who were close to the President did very little to encourage rescue action. David Niles, a presidential assistant, briefly intervened in support of free ports. The others attempted

less. Bernard Baruch—influential with Roosevelt, Congress, the wartime bureaucracy, and the public—stayed away from the rescue issue.
So did Herbert Lehman, director of UNRRA. Supreme Court Justice
Felix Frankfurter had regular access to Roosevelt during the war, and
he exercised a quiet but powerful influence in many sectors of the
administration. Although he used his contacts to press numerous policies and plans, rescue was not among them.[18]

As special counsel to the President, Samuel Rosenman had frequent
contact with Roosevelt, who relied heavily on him for advice on Jewish
matters. But Rosenman considered the rescue issue politically sensitive,
so he consistently tried to insulate Roosevelt from it. For instance, when
Morgenthau was getting ready to urge the President to form a rescue
agency, Rosenman objected. He did not want FDR involved in refugee
matters, although he admitted that no one else could deal effectively
with the problem. Rosenman also argued that government aid to European Jews might increase anti-Semitism in the United States.[19]

The President, his administration, and his advisers were not the only
ones responsible for America's reaction to the Holocaust. Few in Congress, whether liberals or conservatives, showed much interest in saving
European Jews. Beyond that, restrictionism, especially opposition to
the entry of Jews, was strong on Capitol Hill.[20]

Congressional attitudes influenced the administration's policies on
rescue. One reason the State Department kept the quotas 90 percent
unfilled was fear of antagonizing Congress. It was well known to private
refugee-aid agencies that some congressional circles were sharply critical of the administration's supposed "generosity" in issuing visas. The
State Department was sufficiently worried about this that, when it
agreed to the entry of 5,000 Jewish children from France, it forbade all
publicity about the plan. As a leader of one private agency pointed out,
"Officials are extremely anxious to avoid producing a debate in Congress on the wisdom of bringing large groups of children to the United
States." Yet the immigration quotas to which the 5,000 visas would
have been charged were undersubscribed by 55,000 that year.[21]

Except for a weak and insignificant resolution condemning Nazi mass
murder, Congress took no official action concerning the Holocaust. The
only congressional debate to touch at all on the question was little more
than an outburst by Senator Scott Lucas against the Committee for
a Jewish Army for its public denunciation of the Bermuda Conference.

Late in 1943, the Bergsonite Emergency Committee persuaded a
dozen influential members of Congress to endorse a resolution calling
for a government rescue agency. The connections and prestige of these

legislators attracted substantial additional backing. Public interest in the issue was also rising. The resulting pressure figured crucially in Roosevelt's decision to establish the War Refugee Board. But even then, the newly formed board, assessing the climate on Capitol Hill, concluded that congressional indifference toward the European Jews ruled out the possibility of appropriations for rescue programs. The WRB turned instead to private sources for funding.

Of the seven Jews in Congress, only Emanuel Celler persistently urged government rescue action. Samuel Dickstein joined the struggle from time to time. Four others seldom raised the issue. Sol Bloom sided with the State Department throughout.

One reason for the government's limited action was the indifference of much of the non-Jewish public. It must be recognized, though, that many Christian Americans were deeply concerned about the murder of European Jewry and realized that it was a momentous tragedy for Christians as well as for Jews. In the words of an official of the Federal Council of Churches, "This is not a Jewish affair. It is a colossal, universal degradation in which all humanity shares." The message appeared in secular circles as well. Hearst, for instance, stressed more than once in his newspapers, "This is not a Christian or a Jewish question. It is a human question and concerns men and women of all creeds."[22]

Support for rescue arose in several non-Jewish quarters. And it came from leading public figures such as Wendell Willkie, Alfred E. Smith, Herbert Hoover, Fiorello La Guardia, Harold Ickes, Dean Alfange, and many more. But most non-Jewish Americans were either unaware of the European Jewish catastrophe or did not consider it important.

America's Christian churches were almost inert in the face of the Holocaust and nearly silent too. No major denomination spoke out on the issue. Few of the many Christian publications cried out for aid to the Jews. Few even reported the news of extermination, except infrequently and incidentally.

On the Protestant side, Quakers and Unitarians responded to the moral challenge through their service committees. But both denominations were tiny. An even smaller organization, the Church Peace Union, persistently but vainly pressed the churches to take a stand and urged the government to act. Mercedes Randall of the Women's International League for Peace and Freedom published *The Voice of Thy Brother's Blood,* a booklet calling for action on "one of the most urgent matters of our time." The only comprehensive discussion of the European Jewish disaster issued by an American Christian source during the Holocaust, Randall's essay closed with a clear warning:

If we fail to feel, to speak, to act, it bespeaks a tragedy more fateful than the tragedy of the Jews. . . . We have passed by on the other side. . . . Shall we have to live out our lives with that terrible cry upon our lips, "Am I my brother's keeper?"

(The Women's International League had to turn to Jewish sources for financial help to print 50,000 copies and distribute them to newspaper editors, radio commentators, and other opinion leaders.)[23]

The Federal Council of Churches compiled a mediocre record, yet it stood in the forefront of the Protestant effort to help. Besides several public calls for rescue, it sponsored the only nationwide attempt at Christian action, the Day of Compassion of May 1943. But even that event, which most local churches ignored, took place only because Jews urged it on the council and Jewish organizations did much of the necessary work.[24]

The *Christian Century*, a highly influential Protestant weekly, reacted to the first news of extermination by charging that Stephen Wise's statistics were exaggerated. (His estimates were actually far too low.) Thereafter, it reported on the Jewish catastrophe only occasionally, and only rarely did it speak out for rescue action. Such social-action-oriented periodicals as the *Churchman* and Reinhold Niebuhr's *Christianity and Crisis* published even less on the Jewish tragedy. Yet these three journals carried more news on the issue than most Christian periodicals. The bulk of the Protestant press was silent, or nearly so. And few cries for action arose from the pages of any part of Protestantism's print media.[25]

Indicative of the feeble Christian response to the Holocaust was the plight of two American committees established to assist Christian refugees, most of whom were of Jewish descent. Neither organization could rely on its vast parent church to fund its tiny program. The Protestant agency, the American Committee for Christian Refugees (ACCR), leaned heavily on the Jewish Joint Distribution Committee for financial support from 1934 through 1940. When those funds dried up, the ACCR survived by severely reducing its already limited services. It regained a semblance of effectiveness only in mid-1943 with an infusion of money from the National War Fund.* [26]

The Catholic Committee for Refugees (CCR) was organized in 1937

---

* The National War Fund, formed under government supervision in 1943, established a united nationwide campaign for private fund appeals related to the war effort. Among the groups it benefited were government-approved private war-relief agencies. This large-scale, broad-based fund-raising system proved a bonanza to small, foundering agencies.[27]

by the American Catholic bishops. But the church did not adequately support this very modest operation, either with funds or by lending its prestige to the committee. In its first years, the CCR needed financial help from the Joint Distribution Committee. Even so, it was all but ineffective until mid-1943, when the National War Fund assumed virtually all of its expenses.[28]

Two important Catholic periodicals, *America* and *Commonweal,* did speak out from time to time on the extermination of the Jews and called for action to help them. But the rest of the Catholic press was almost silent on the issue, as was the American church itself. No Catholic pressures developed for a government rescue effort. The National Catholic Welfare Conference (NCWC), which acted for the American bishops in social and civic matters, was America's leading organization for Catholic social welfare. It might have led a Catholic drive for rescue action. But it made no move in that direction. Instead, as can be seen in the records of its Bureau of Immigration and in the reactions of its general secretary, Msgr. Michael J. Ready, the NCWC was consistently negative toward immigration of Jewish refugees.[29]

The Bureau of Immigration was responsible for helping Catholic refugees come to the United States. The correspondence of its personnel shows little sympathy for European Jews. It also reveals a distrust of Jews generally and a particular suspicion of American Jewish organizations. They were viewed as too aggressive in assisting Jewish refugees and too little concerned about persecuted Catholics. The Bureau of Immigration was the only refugee-aid organization that encountered no problems with the State Department concerning visa issuance and visa policies.[30]

Until the end of 1943, Catholic refugees passing through Spain and Portugal, or stranded there, turned to American non-Catholic organizations for aid. Jewish, Unitarian, and Quaker agencies provided support funds and ship passage to needy Catholics, whether of Jewish descent or not. After two years' of requests that they share the burden, American Catholic leaders investigated the situation in late 1943. By then the American bishops, in order to channel National War Fund money into Catholic relief projects, had established a new branch of the National Catholic Welfare Conference, the War Relief Services. When those funds became available, the War Relief Services–NCWC started to send money to Portugal. Soon afterward, it opened its own office in Lisbon to assist Catholic refugees. The NCWC also began to contribute to the Representation in Spain of American Relief Organizations, a Jewish-Protestant venture that for over a year had been caring for Catholics along with other refugees.[31]

At the heart of Christianity is the commitment to help the helpless. Yet, for the most part, America's Christian churches looked away while the European Jews perished. So did another part of the public that might have been expected to cry out for action, American liberals. The *Nation* and the *New Republic* did speak, throughout the war, warning of what was happening and pressing for rescue. From time to time, some prominent individual liberals also urged action. But rescue never became an important objective for New Dealers or other American liberals. Even as thoroughly liberal an institution as the New York newspaper *PM,* though it did call for rescue, did not make it a major issue.[32]

The AFL and the CIO frequently endorsed Jewish organizations' appeals for rescue. In a notable change in labor's traditional restrictionism, both unions began in 1943 to urge at least temporary suspension of immigration laws to open the doors for Jewish refugees. But there was no movement to arouse the rank and file, to build active support for rescue on that broad base.[33]

Most American intellectuals were indifferent to the struggle for rescue. Dorothy Thompson and Reinhold Niebuhr were exceptions, as were those who helped the Bergsonite Emergency Committee. Overall, Jewish intellectuals remained as uninvolved as non-Jews. To note one example among many, Walter Lippmann, a highly influential news columnist who dealt with practically every major topic of the day, wrote nothing about the Holocaust.[34]

American Communists contributed virtually nothing to the rescue cause. In the wake of the Bermuda Conference, they publicly agreed with the diplomats: "It would be foolhardy to negotiate with Axis satellites for the release of Hitler's captives." They insisted throughout the war that the only answer for European Jewry was the swiftest possible Allied victory. Nor would they tolerate criticism of the President for his limited rescue steps. "Roosevelt," they argued, "represents the forces most determined on victory"; those concerned about the Jews should "speak helpfully" about him or keep silent. This, of course, coincided with the Communists' view of what was best for Soviet Russia.[35]

An organization formed in early 1944 by the American Jewish Conference seemed to open the way for effective action by prominent non-Jews. The National Committee Against Nazi Persecution and Extermination of the Jews, with Supreme Court Justice Frank Murphy as chairman, included such distinguished Americans as Wendell Willkie and Henry Wallace and other political, religious, and business leaders. But this all-Christian committee failed to attract adequate funding and amounted to little more than a paper organization. Moreover, it did almost nothing to advance its main objective, "to rally the full force of the public conscience in America" against the extermination of the Jews and for vigorous rescue action. Instead, the Murphy committee channeled its meager resources into what it announced as its second priority, combating anti-Semitism in the United States. Murphy and others contributed, in speeches and in print, to the battle against American anti-Semitism. But the rescue issue fell by the wayside.[36]

One reason ordinary Americans were not more responsive to the plight of the European Jews was that very many (probably a majority) were unaware of Hitler's extermination program until well into 1944 or later. The information was not readily available to the public, because the mass media treated the systematic murder of millions of Jews as though it were minor news.

Most newspapers printed very little about the Holocaust, even though extensive information on it reached their desks from the news services (AP, UP, and others) and from their own correspondents. In New York, the Jewish-owned *Post* reported extermination news and rescue matters fairly adequately. *PM*'s coverage was also more complete than that of most American papers. The *Times,* Jewish-owned but anxious not to be seen as Jewish-oriented, was the premier American newspaper of the era. It printed a substantial amount of information on Holocaust-related events but almost always buried it on inner pages.* The *Herald Tribune* published a moderate amount of news concerning the Holocaust but seldom placed it where it would attract attention. Coverage in other New York City newspapers ranged from poor to almost nonexistent.[37]

The Jewish-owned *Washington Post* printed a few editorials advocating rescue, but only infrequently carried news reports on the European Jewish situation. Yet, in October 1944, it gave front-page space for four days to a series attacking the Bergson group. (Inaccuracies soon forced a retraction.) Nothing else connected with the Holocaust even approached comparable prominence in the *Post.* The other Washington newspapers provided similarly limited information on the mass murder of European Jewry.[38]

Outside New York and Washington, press coverage was even thin-

---

* To note one typical example, the *Times* on July 2, 1944, published "authoritative information" that 400,000 Hungarian Jews had been deported to their deaths so far and 350,000 more were to be killed in the next three weeks. This news (which was basically accurate) received four column-inches on page 12. The *Times* found room on the front page that day to analyze the problem of New York holiday crowds on the move.

ner. All major newspapers carried some Holocaust-related news, but it appeared infrequently and almost always in small items located on inside pages.[39]

American mass-circulation magazines all but ignored the Holocaust. Aside from a few paragraphs touching on the subject, silence prevailed in the major news magazines, *Time, Newsweek,* and *Life*. The *Reader's Digest, American Mercury,* and *Collier's* released a small flurry of information in February 1943, not long after the extermination news was first revealed. From then until late in the war, little more appeared. Finally, in fall 1944, *Collier's* and *American Mercury* published vivid accounts of the ordeal of Polish Jewry written by Jan Karski, a courier sent to Britain and America by the Polish resistance. Karski described what he himself saw in late 1942 at the Belzec killing center and in the Warsaw ghetto.* Except for these and a few other articles, the major American magazines permitted one of the most momentous events of the modern era to pass without comment.[40]

Radio coverage of Holocaust news was sparse. Those who wrote the newscasts and commentary programs seem hardly to have noticed the slaughter of the Jews. Proponents of rescue managed to put a little information on the air, mainly in Washington and New York. Access to a nationwide audience was very infrequent. The WRB even had difficulty persuading stations to broadcast programs it produced.[42]

American filmmakers avoided the subject of the Jewish catastrophe. During the war, Hollywood released numerous feature films on refugees and on Nazi atrocities. None dealt with the Holocaust. Despite extensive Jewish influence in the movie industry, the American Jewish Congress was unable to persuade anyone to produce even a short film on the mass killing of the Jews. The very popular *March of Time* news series did not touch the extermination issue, nor did the official U.S. war films in the *Why We Fight* series.[43]

There is no clear explanation for the mass media's failure to publicize the Holocaust. Conflicting details and inconsistent numbers in the different reports from Europe may have made editors cautious. But no one could have expected full accuracy in data compiled under the difficulties encountered in underground work.

Another problem was the fabricated atrocity stories of World War I. This time, editors were very skeptical. Yet, well before word of the "final solution" filtered out, numerous confirmed reports of Nazi crimes

* In July 1943, Karski saw Roosevelt, told him what he had witnessed at Belzec, and informed him that the Germans unquestionably intended to exterminate all the Jews in Europe and were well on the way to doing so.[41]

against civilian populations had broken down much of that barrier to belief.[44]

The way war news flooded and dominated the mass media may have been a factor. Holocaust events merged into and became lost in the big events of the world conflict. For example, information on the destruction of the Hungarian Jews was overwhelmed by news about preparations for the cross-channel invasion, the invasion itself, and the dramatic reconquest of France that summer.

It is possible that editors took a cue from the *New York Times*. Other newspapers recognized the *Times*'s superior reporting resources abroad and looked to it for guidance in foreign news policy. A perception that the Jewish-owned *Times* did not think the massive killing of Jews was worth emphasizing could have influenced other newspapers. Again, Roosevelt's failure until March 1944 to mention the extermination of the Jews in his press conferences may have led editors to conclude that the issue was not a major one.[45]

The mass media's response to the Holocaust undoubtedly was also affected by the complicated problem of credibility. Publishers and broadcasters feared accusations of sensationalism and exaggeration. They may also have had difficulty themselves in believing the reports. Annihilation of an entire people was a concept that went well beyond previous experience. Moreover, extermination of the Jews made no sense, because it served no practical purpose. The German explanation that Jews were being deported to labor centers seemed more plausible.* [46]

The problem of disbelief may be illustrated by a conversation in December 1944 between A. Leon Kubowitzki of the World Jewish Congress and Assistant Secretary of War John McCloy. Kubowitzki recorded the episode:

> "We are alone," he [McCloy] said to me. "Tell me the truth. Do you really believe that all those horrible things happened?"
> His sources of information, needless to say, were better than mine. But he could not grasp the terrible destruction.[48]

On a broader level, the enigma was reflected in the way that military leaders, government officials, newsmen, and members of Congress re-

* On the other hand, many observers had no real difficulty believing the extermination information. To name only a few of them: the Jewish leadership, editors of the Catholic periodicals *Commonweal* and *America,* the foremost British church leaders, Treasury Department officials, and even State Department policymakers.[47]

acted to what was found when American and British forces liberated German concentration camps in spring 1945. They were stunned. Yet most had been exposed for a long time to information about the camps and the extermination of the Jews—information augmented by two striking disclosures released as recently as August and November 1944.

In August, a month after the Red Army captured the Majdanek killing center, near Lublin, Soviet authorities permitted American reporters to inspect the still-intact murder camp—gas chambers, crematoria, mounds of ashes, and the rest. One American voiced the reaction of all who viewed Majdanek: "I am now prepared to believe any story of German atrocities, no matter how savage, cruel and depraved."[49]

The newsmen sent back detailed accounts, which were widely published in American newspapers and magazines, in many cases on the front pages. A few reports pointed out that Jews were the main victims, but most mentioned them only as part of a list of the different peoples murdered there. And none of the correspondents or their editors connected Majdanek with the extensive information available by then about the systematic extermination of European Jewry. Author Arthur Koestler had tried to explain the phenomenon earlier that year. People, he wrote, can be convinced for a while of the reality of such a crime, but then "their mental self-defense begins to work." In a week, "incredulity has returned like a reflex temporarily weakened by a shock."[50]

The second disclosure, released to the press by the War Refugee Board in November, was the Vrba-Wetzler report of mass murder at Auschwitz. It had reached McClelland in Switzerland in June. He soon telegraphed a condensation to the WRB in Washington, but was unable to forward the complete text until mid-October.*[51]

The full Auschwitz report—officially issued by a government agency—received prominent notice throughout the country, including Sunday front-page coverage in many newspapers. News accounts were long and graphic; many newspapers followed up with editorials. Radio also spread the information.†[53]

---

* The delay apparently resulted from the low priority the American legation in Bern gave to WRB matters. The long wait may have been costly. The full report hit with much more force than the telegraphed summary had. It convinced Pehle for the first time that he should put strong pressure on the War Department to bomb the Auschwitz gas chambers. If it had arrived earlier, it might have heightened the urgency of rescue efforts.[52]

† Shortly before the document was available to the press, the editors of the Army magazine *Yank* asked the WRB for material for an article on atrocities. The board supplied a copy of the Auschwitz report. *Yank*'s editors decided not to use it. It was

Despite the reports on Majdanek and Auschwitz (and numerous other accounts of extermination), many well-informed Americans failed to comprehend what was happening. This explains, in part, the wave of amazement that resulted when German concentration camps were opened in April 1945. Military men were appalled and astonished at what they saw. Hardened war correspondents found the horror "too great for the human mind to believe." General Eisenhower called the "barbarous treatment" inflicted on inmates "almost unbelievable."[55]

To dispel any doubts about the accuracy of reporters' accounts, Eisenhower requested that a dozen congressmen and a delegation of American editors fly to Germany to look at the camps. The legislators emerged from Buchenwald "shocked almost beyond belief." Editors, expecting to find that correspondents had overstated the situation, came away convinced that "exaggeration, in fact, would be difficult."[56]

Failure to grasp the earlier information about Nazi camps was the key cause for this astonishment. Another reason was that camp conditions, ordinarily deplorable, sank to appalling depths during the last part of the war. As the Third Reich crumbled, administration systems broke down. Transportation of food and supplies failed. And as they retreated, the Germans shifted thousands of inmates from outlying camps to the already overloaded ones in the interior of Germany. Conditions were abysmal: massive starvation, unchecked disease, terrible crowding, thousands of unburied corpses.[57]

Ironically, these camps (Buchenwald, Belsen, Dachau, and so on) were not among the most destructive. They were not extermination camps. The horrors that took place within their confines were on a different plane from the millions of murders committed at Auschwitz, Majdanek, and the four other killing centers, all situated in Poland.

The American press, which for so long had barely whispered of mass murder and extermination, exploded with news of the German camps. For over a month, stories ran in all the newspapers and news magazines, frequently on the front pages, accompanied by shocking photographs. And newsreels, made by Hollywood studios from Army Signal Corps footage, confronted millions of American moviegoers with stark scenes of the carnage.[58]

During spring 1945, American newspaper editors blamed the false atrocity stories of World War I for their earlier skepticism about Nazi war crimes. One of the congressmen who saw the camps explained that "it was always a question whether the reports were propaganda and

"too Semitic." They wanted "a less Jewish story," one that would not stir up the "latent anti-Semitism in the Army."[54]

now they can be confirmed." In fact, after the Nazis obliterated the Czech village of Lidice, in mid-1942, the press had not hesitated to publicize German atrocities against occupied populations. But it had consistently pushed information about Europe's Jews into the inner pages, or omitted it entirely. This minimized a substantial body of evidence that pointed to a hard-to-believe fact—the systematic extermination of a whole people.* [59]

In the last analysis, it is impossible to know how many Americans were aware of the Holocaust during the war years. Starting in late 1942, enough information appeared that careful followers of the daily news, as well as people especially alert to humanitarian issues or to Jewish problems, understood the situation. Probably millions more had at least a vague idea that terrible things were happening to the European Jews. Most likely, though, they were a minority of the American public. Only three opinion polls (all by Gallup) asked Americans whether they believed the reports about German atrocities, and only one of them dealt directly with Jews. The first survey, in January 1943, specifically referred to news reports of the killing of two million Jews. Forty-seven percent thought the reports were true. (Twenty-nine percent did not, and 24 percent gave no opinion.) [61]

Late in the war, in mid-November 1944 and again in May 1945, the pollsters asked whether reports that the Germans had murdered "many people in concentration camps" were true. The November poll indicated that 76 percent believed the information was accurate. By early May, following three weeks of steady news about the liberated concentration camps in Germany, the figure had risen to 84 percent. On the face of it, public knowledge of Nazi atrocities had reached a high level by November 1944. But the last two polls furnish no real evidence about awareness of the extermination of the Jews, because Jews were not mentioned in either of them. [62]

Throughout the war, most of the mass media, whether from disbelief or fear of accusations of sensationalism or for some other reason, played

* To some extent, the pattern continued during spring 1945. News reports about the liberated camps mentioned Jews among the various types of victims, but the fact that they were the main victim did not come across clearly.

The crowning irony occurred in May, when the Soviets released an official report on their investigations at Auschwitz. The long summaries sent from Moscow by American reporters did not mention Jews, although most of those killed at Auschwitz were Jews. One reason was probably Soviet unwillingness to distinguish Jews from other citizens. Also, apparently, the American correspondents were unaware of or disbelieved earlier reports on Auschwitz, including the much publicized one released by the WRB the preceding November. [60]

down the information about the Jewish tragedy. As a result, a large part of the American public remained unaware of the plight of European Jewry. Hesitation about giving full credence to reports of the systematic extermination of an entire people may be understandable. But those who edited the news surely realized, at the very least, that European Jews were being murdered in vast numbers. That was important news. But it was not brought clearly into public view.

Popular concern for Europe's Jews could not develop without widespread knowledge of what was happening to them. But the information gap, though extremely important, was not the only limiting factor. Strong currents of anti-Semitism and nativism in American society also diminished the possibilities for a sympathetic response. A quieter, more prevalent prejudice, a "passive anti-Semitism," was another major barrier to the growth of concern. It was reflected in opinion surveys taken by the Office of War Information. They showed that the impact of atrocity information on the average American was seven times stronger when it involved atrocities in general than when it referred specifically to atrocities against Jews. A Christian clergyman with extensive connections in Protestant circles reached a similar conclusion: "Not only were Christians insensitive and callous [about rescue]; . . . there was an anti-Semitism there, just beneath the surface." * [63]

The American government did not respond decisively to the extermination of Europe's Jews. Much of the general public was indifferent or uninformed. What about American Jews—how did they meet the challenge? †

---

* Another obstacle to American concern for the European Jews was the preoccupation of most people with the war and with their personal affairs. Public opinion research disclosed that typical Americans, still acutely aware of the Great Depression, were mainly concerned about their jobs and their job chances after the war. They also worried about their boys and men away from home. And they gave a lot of attention to such questions as how to spend and save and when they could drive their cars for fun again. These personal matters crowded out even headline issues, except for the progress of the war. [64]

† Most American Jews who maintained connections with Jewish life probably knew about the ongoing extermination. The Yiddish daily press, which reached 30 percent of American Jewish families, reported on it frequently. Many of the periodicals sponsored by the numerous Jewish organizations emphasized the terrible news. Anglo-Jewish weekly newspapers, published in most sizable cities and in all regions of the United States, provided substantial coverage (drawn mainly from Jewish press services). And information must have spread by word of mouth at synagogues and other centers of Jewish activity. Wide Jewish knowledge of the extermination is evidenced by the fact that hundreds of thousands of American Jews attended rallies and mass meetings for rescue held throughout the United States. [65]

American Jewish leaders recognized that the best hope for rescue lay
in a strong effort to induce the U.S. government to act. The obvious
approaches were two: appeals to high government officials and a national campaign to publicize the mass killings with a view to directing
public pressure on the Roosevelt administration and Congress. Jewish
leaders made progress in both directions, but their effectiveness was
severely limited by their failure to create a united Jewish movement and
by their lack of sustained action.[66]

A unified effort by the main Jewish organizations did take place for
two weeks in late 1942, coordinated by the "Temporary Committee."
For ten additional weeks, from early March to mid-May 1943, cooperative action resumed under the Joint Emergency Committee on European Jewish Affairs. During those twelve weeks, some advances were
won, but that amount of time was too brief to budge the Roosevelt
administration. Besides, none of the cooperating organizations gave top
priority to the rescue problem. And they refused the Bergsonites' requests to be included in the effort.[67]

The basis for united action existed throughout the war. All Jewish
organizations agreed on the need for rescue and the need to abolish the
White Paper and open Palestine to European Jews. But the split over
the issue of Zionism proved unbridgeable. It was the chief obstacle to
formation of a united drive for rescue.[68]

The outcome was that non-Zionist organizations (American Jewish
Committee, Jewish Labor Committee, B'nai B'rith, and the ultra-Orthodox groups) went their separate ways and accomplished little in building pressure for rescue. The Zionists, who were the best organized of
the Jewish groups, were more effective in pushing for rescue action.
But the major part of their resources went into the effort for a postwar
state in Palestine.[69]

The Bergsonite Emergency Committee tried to fill the gap in the
rescue campaign. Its work was vital in finally bringing the War Refugee
Board into existence. But the Bergsonites were too weak to generate
enough pressure after the formation of the board to force the Roosevelt
administration to give it the support that it should have had. The situation was not helped when they divided their limited energies by
launching their own statehood movement through the Hebrew Committee for National Liberation and its partner, the American League for
a Free Palestine.[70]

The fact that the tiny Bergsonite faction accomplished what it did
toward the establishment of the WRB is compelling evidence that a
major, sustained, and united Jewish effort could have obtained the
rescue board earlier and insisted on its receiving greater support than

it did. Such an effort could have drawn on substantial strengths. The Zionist groups had mass followings, organizational skills, some financial capability, a few prestigious leaders, and valuable contacts high in government. The American Jewish Committee combined wealth and important influence in high places. The Jewish Labor Committee was backed by a sizable constituency and could count on help from the American Federation of Labor. B'nai B'rith held the allegiance of a broad cross section of American Jews. Agudath Israel represented a very active element of Orthodoxy. And the Bergson group offered energy, publicity skills, fund-raising proficiency, and the capacity to win friends in Congress and elsewhere in Washington.

Along with the lack of unity, American Jewry's efforts for rescue were handicapped by a crisis in leadership. The dominant figure, Stephen Wise, was aging, increasingly beset by medical problems, and burdened with far too many responsibilities. Abba Hillel Silver's rise to the top was slowed by his rivalry with Wise and by his own tendency to create enemies. He was, nonetheless, a forceful leader; but his single-minded commitment to postwar Jewish statehood meant that he did not participate in the campaign for government rescue action. No other leaders approached the stature of these two.[71]

The scarcity of fresh, innovative leadership aroused concern at the time. In 1944, the editor of the Brooklyn *Jewish Examiner* asserted that "not a new personality with the possible exception of Henry Monsky has come to the fore in the past decade." As evidence he listed the leading Jewish spokesmen of 1933 and pointed out that, except for two who had died, "the names today are the same; there are no new ones." A tendency among second- and third-generation American Jews to minimize their Jewishness may have hindered the emergence of strong new leadership during the 1930s and 1940s.[72]

An additional problem was the inability of American Jewish leaders to break out of a business-as-usual pattern. Too few schedules were rearranged. Vacations were seldom sacrificed. Too few projects of lesser significance were put aside. An important American Zionist remarked years later that the terrible crisis failed to arouse the "unquenchable sense of urgency" that was needed. Even from afar, this inability to adapt was painfully clear. In late 1942, Jewish leaders in Warsaw entrusted a message to Jan Karski, the Polish underground agent who was about to leave for Britain and the United States. It called on Jews in the free nations to turn to unprecedented measures to persuade their governments to act. But the Polish Jews had no illusions. Before Karski departed, one of them warned him:

Jewish leaders abroad won't be interested. At 11 in the morning you will
begin telling them about the anguish of the Jews in Poland, but at 1 o'clock
they will ask you to halt the narrative so they can have lunch. That is a
difference which cannot be bridged. They will go on lunching at the regular
hour at their favorite restaurant. So they cannot understand what is happening in Poland.* [73]

Despite the obstacles and failures, American Jews were responsible
for some important achievements. Finding the mass media largely indifferent, they devised ways to spread the extermination news and create
limited but crucial support among non-Jews. This, combined with pressures from the American Jewish community, helped bring the War
Refugee Board into existence.

American Jewish organizations also carried out valuable rescue and
relief work overseas. During World War II, the American Jewish Joint
Distribution Committee provided more aid to European Jews than all
the world's governments combined. In doing so, it paid for nearly 85
percent of the work of the War Refugee Board. The Hebrew Sheltering
and Immigrant Aid Society dealt effectively with migration and ocean
transportation problems. The World Jewish Congress, though chroni-
cally short of funds, undertook important rescue projects in collaboration with overseas Zionist organizations and anti-Nazi underground
movements. Vaad Hahatzala, grounded in the requirements of Jewish
law for the preservation of human life, turned to all available rescue
tactics, however unconventional. Other American Jewish organizations
contributed, though on a smaller scale. [74]

In the end, American Jewish groups and their overseas affiliates were
central to most of the WRB's direct-action projects. This fact, while
reflecting great credit on American Jewry, must cast a shadow over the
rest of the nation. Voluntary contributions from American Jews—in
the millions of dollars—funded these organizations and thus most of
the limited help that America extended to Europe's Jews.

* To some extent, the anti-Semitism of the time was another factor limiting American
Jewish action for rescue. It undoubtedly put Jews on the defensive and kept some from
speaking out. It should not be overemphasized, however. Many thousands of Jews were
publicly vocal on a variety of controversial issues.

What Might Have Been Done

What could the American government have achieved if it had really committed itself to rescue? The possibilities were narrowed by the Nazis' determination to wipe out the Jews. War conditions themselves also made rescue difficult. And by mid-1942, when clear news of the systematic murder reached the West, two million Jews had already been massacred and the killing was going forward at a rapid rate. Most likely, it would not have been possible to rescue millions. But without impeding the war effort, additional tens of thousands—probably hundreds of thousands—could have been saved. What follows is a selection of twelve programs that could have been tried. All of them, and others, were proposed during the Holocaust.[75]

(1) Most important, the War Refugee Board should have been established in 1942. And it should have received adequate government funding and much broader powers.

(2) The U.S. government, working through neutral governments or the Vatican, could have pressed Germany to release the Jews. If nothing else, this would have demonstrated to the Nazis—and to the world—that America was committed to saving the European Jews. It is worth recalling that until late summer 1944, when the Germans blocked the Horthy offer, it was far from clear to the Allies that Germany would not let the Jews out. On the contrary, until then the State Department and the British Foreign Office feared that Hitler might confront the Allies with an exodus of Jews, a possibility that they assiduously sought to avoid.[76]

In a related area, ransom overtures might have been much more thoroughly investigated. The use of blocked funds for this purpose would not have compromised the war effort. Nor, by early 1944, would payments of limited amounts of currency have hurt the progress of the war. In particular, the Sternbuch-Musy negotiations could have received fuller American backing.[77]

(3) The United States could have applied constant pressure on Axis satellites to release their Jews. By spring 1943, the State Department knew that some satellites, convinced that the war was lost, were seeking favorable peace terms. Stern threats of punishment for mistreating Jews or allowing their deportation, coupled with indications that permitting them to leave for safety would earn Allied goodwill, could have opened the way to the rescue of large numbers from Rumania, Bulgaria, Hungary, and perhaps Slovakia. Before the Germans took control of Italy,

in September 1943, similar pressures might have persuaded the Italian government to allow its Jews to flee, as well as those in Italian-occupied areas of Greece, Yugoslavia, and France.[78]

(4) Success in setting off an exodus of Jews would have posed the problem of where they could go. Strong pressure needed to be applied to neutral countries near the Axis (Spain, Portugal, Turkey, Switzerland, and Sweden) to take Jews in. To bypass time-consuming immigration procedures, these nations could have been urged to set up reception camps near the borders. In return, the Allies should have offered to fund the operations, supply food, and guarantee removal of the refugees. At the same time, havens of refuge outside Europe were essential to accommodate a steady movement of Jews out of the neutral countries. Thus the routes would have remained open and a continuing flow of fugitives could have left Axis territory.

(5) Locating enough outside havens, places beyond continental Europe where refugees could safely await postwar resettlement, would have presented difficulties. The problems encountered in finding havens for the limited numbers of Jews who did get out during the war pointed up the callousness of the Western world. But an American government deeply concerned about the Jews and willing to share the burden could have used its prestige and power to open doors. If a camp existence was all that was offered, that was still far preferable to deportation and death.

Ample room for camps was available in North Africa. In the United States, the immigration quotas were almost untouched; in addition, a government committed to rescue would have provided several camps besides Fort Ontario. A generous response by the United States would have put strong pressure on the Latin American nations, Canada, the British dominions, and Palestine. Instead, other countries used American stinginess as an excuse for not accepting Jews. For instance, in Jerusalem on his 1942 trip around the world, Wendell Willkie confronted the British leadership with the need to admit large numbers of Jews into Palestine. The British high commissioner replied that since the United States was not taking Jews in even up to the quota limits, Americans were hardly in a position to criticize.[79]

(6) Shipping was needed to transfer Jews from neutral countries to outside havens. Abundant evidence (summarized later in this chapter) proves that it could have been provided without interfering with the war effort.

The preceding steps, vigorously pursued, might have saved scores or even hundreds of thousands. Instead, important opportunities were lost by default. Early in 1943, the United States turned its back on the

Rumanian proposal to release 70,000 Jews. It was a pivotal failure; seizure of that chance might have led to other overtures by Axis satellites.[80]

At the same time, Switzerland was willing to accept thousands of children from France if it had assurance of their postwar removal. After refusing for more than a year, the State Department furnished the guarantee. But by then the main opportunity had passed. During the summer of 1943, the way opened for evacuating 500 children from the Balkans. But a boat had to be obtained within a month. The State Department responded with bureaucratic delays. Allied actions, instead of encouraging neutral countries to welcome fleeing Jews, influenced them to do the opposite. For instance, it took more than a year to move a few hundred refugees out of Spain to the long-promised camp in North Africa. With a determined American effort, these failures, and others, could have been successes.[81]

(7) A campaign to stimulate and assist escapes would have led to a sizable outflow of Jews. Once the neutral nations had agreed to open their borders, that information could have been publicized throughout Europe by radio, airdropped leaflets, and underground communications channels. Local currencies could have been purchased in occupied countries, often with blocked foreign accounts. These funds could have financed escape systems, false documentation, and bribery of lower-level officials. Underground movements were willing to cooperate. (The WRB, in fact, carried out such operations on a small scale.) Even without help, and despite closed borders, tens of thousands of Jews attempted to escape to Switzerland, Spain, Palestine, and other places. Thousands succeeded. With assistance, and assurance of acceptance into neutral nations, those thousands could have been scores of thousands.

(8) Much larger sums of money should have been transferred to Europe. After the WRB was formed, the earlier, tiny trickle of funds from the United States was increased. But the amounts were still inadequate. Besides facilitating escapes, money would have helped in hiding Jews, supplying food and other essentials, strengthening Jewish undergrounds, and gaining the assistance of non-Jewish forces.[82]

(9) Much more effort should have gone into finding ways to send in food and medical supplies. The American government should have approached the problem far sooner than it did. And it should have put heavy pressure on the International Red Cross and British blockade authorities on this issue.

(10) Drawing on its great prestige and influence, the United States could have applied much more pressure than it did on neutral govern-

ments, the Vatican, and the International Red Cross to induce them to take earlier and more vigorous action. By expanding their diplomatic missions in Axis countries, they would have increased the numbers of outside observers on the scene and perhaps inhibited actions against Jews. More important, the measures taken by Raoul Wallenberg in Budapest should have been implemented by all neutral diplomatic missions and repeated in city after city throughout Axis Europe. And they should have begun long before the summer of 1944.[83]

The United States could also have pressed its two great allies to help. The Soviet Union turned away all requests for cooperation, including those from the WRB. An American government that was serious about rescue might have extracted some assistance from the Russians.[84]

Britain, though more responsive, still compiled an abysmal record. Until 1944, Roosevelt and the State Department let the British lead in setting policy regarding European Jews. Even when the United States finally took the initiative, Roosevelt did not press for British cooperation. British officials resented the WRB, dismissed it as an election-year tactic, and tried to obstruct its work. The situation did not have to develop that way. An American president strongly committed to rescue could have insisted on a more helpful British response.[85]

(11) Some military assistance was possible. The Air Force could have eliminated the Auschwitz killing installations. Some bombing of deportation railroads was feasible. The military could have aided in other ways without impeding the war effort. It was, in fact, legally required to do so by the executive order that established the WRB.[86]

(12) Much more publicity about the extermination of the Jews should have been disseminated through Europe. Allied radio could have beamed the information for weeks at a time, on all possible wavelengths, as the Germans did regarding the alleged Russian massacre of Polish officers at the Katyn forest. This might have influenced three groups: the Christian populations, the Nazis, and the Jews. Western leaders and, especially, the Pope could have appealed to Christians not to cooperate in any way with the anti-Jewish programs, and to hide and to aid Jews whenever possible.[87]

Roosevelt, Churchill, and the Pope might have made clear to the Nazis their full awareness of the mass-murder program and their severe condemnation of it. If, in addition, Roosevelt and Churchill had threatened punishment for these crimes and offered asylum to the Jews, the Nazis at least would have ceased to believe that the West did not care what they were doing to the Jews. That might possibly have slowed the killing. And it might have hastened the decision of the SS, ultimately taken in late 1944, to end the extermination. Even if top Nazis had brushed the threats aside, their subordinates might have been given pause.[88]

The European Jews themselves should have been repeatedly warned of what was happening and told what the deportation trains really meant. (With good reason, the Nazis employed numerous precautions and ruses to keep this information from their victims.) Decades later, Rudolf Vrba, one of the escapees who exposed Auschwitz to the outside world, remained angry that the Jews had not been alerted. "Would anybody get me alive to Auschwitz if I had this information?" he demanded. "Would thousands and thousands of able-bodied Jewish men send their children, wives, mothers to Auschwitz from all over Europe, if they knew?" Roosevelt, Churchill, other Western leaders, and major Jewish spokesmen should have warned Jews over and over against the steps that led to deportation and urged them to try to hide or flee or resist. To help implement these actions, the Allies could have smuggled in cadres of specially trained Jewish agents.[89]

None of these proposals guaranteed results. But all deserved serious consideration, and those that offered any chance of success should have been tried. There was a moral imperative to attempt everything possible that would not hurt the war effort. If that had been done, even if few or no lives had been saved, the moral obligation would have been fulfilled. But the outcome would not have been anything like that barren. The War Refugee Board, a very tardy, inadequately supported, partial commitment, saved several tens of thousands. A timely American rescue effort that had the wholehearted support of the government would have achieved much more.

A commitment of that caliber did not materialize. Instead, the Roosevelt administration turned aside most rescue proposals. In the process, government officials developed four main rationalizations for inaction. The most frequent excuse, the unavailability of shipping, was a fraud. When the Allies wanted to find ships for nonmilitary projects, they located them. In 1943, American naval vessels carried 1,400 non-Jewish Polish refugees from India to the American West Coast. The State and War departments arranged to move 2,000 Spanish Loyalist refugees to Mexico using military shipping. In March 1944, blaming the shipping shortage, the British backed out of an agreement to transport 630 Jewish refugees from Spain to the Fedala camp, near Casablanca. Yet at the same time, they were providing troopships to move non-Jewish refugees by the thousands from Yugoslavia to southern Italy and on to camps in Egypt.[90]

When it was a matter of transporting Jews, ships could almost never be found. This was not because shipping was unavailable but because the Allies were unwilling to take the Jews in. In November 1943, Breck-inridge Long told the House Foreign Affairs Committee that lack of transportation was the reason the State Department was issuing so few visas. "In December 1941," he explained, "most neutral shipping disappeared from the seas. . . . There just is not any transportation." In reality, ample shipping existed. Neutral vessels crossed the Atlantic throughout the war. Three Portuguese liners, with a combined capacity of 2,000 passengers, sailed regularly between Lisbon and U.S. ports. Each ship made the trip about every six weeks. Most of the time, because of the tight American visa policy, they carried only small fractions of their potential loads. Two dozen other Portuguese and Spanish passenger ships crossed the Atlantic less frequently but were available for fuller service. In addition, several score neutral cargo vessels could have been obtained and refitted to transport refugees.[91]

American troopships and lend-lease and other cargo vessels could also have carried thousands of refugees across the Atlantic, clearing neutral European countries of fugitives and opening the way for a continuing exodus from Axis territory. War and State department correspondence shows that returning military transports could have performed this mission without hampering the war effort. In fact, U.S. Army authorities in North Africa offered in 1943 to take refugees to the United States on returning military ships. But the State and War departments blocked the plan.[92]

In spring 1944, Roosevelt himself informed Pehle that the Navy could bring refugees to the United States on returning troopships. The War Shipping Administration believed that Liberty ships could also have transported refugees effectively. While the State Department was claiming that transportation for refugees was unavailable, Liberty ships were having difficulty finding ballast for the return trips from North Africa.[93]

The United States and Britain leased Swedish ships to carry food from the Western Hemisphere to Greece. Sweden readily furnished replacements and additions to this fleet. Despite repeated pleas, however, the two great Allies never managed to provide a single boat to ferry Jews from the Balkans to Turkey or to shuttle Jews across the Mediterranean to safety. Yet the War Department admitted to the War Refugee Board in spring 1944 that it had "ample shipping" available for evacuating refugees; the problem, it agreed, was to find places where they could go.[94]

Another stock excuse for inaction was the claim that Axis governments planted agents among the refugees. Although this possibility needed to be watched carefully, the problem was vastly overemphasized and could have been handled through reasonable security screening. It was significant that Army intelligence found not one suspicious person when it checked the 982 refugees who arrived at Fort Ontario. Nevertheless, potential subversion was continually used as a reason for keeping immigration to the United States very tightly restricted. Turkey, Latin American nations, Britain, and other countries used the same exaggerated argument. It played an important part in blocking the channels of rescue.[95]

A third rationalization for failing to aid European Jews took the high ground of nondiscrimination. It asserted that helping Jews would improperly single out one group for assistance when many peoples were suffering under Nazi brutality. Equating the genocide of the Jews with the oppression imposed on other Europeans was, in the words of one of the world's foremost churchmen, Willem Visser 't Hooft, "a dangerous half-truth which could only serve to distract attention from the fact that no other race was faced with the situation of having every one of its members . . . threatened by death in the gas chambers."[96]

The Roosevelt administration, the British government, and the Intergovernmental Committee on Refugees regularly refused to acknowledge that the Jews faced a special situation. One reason for this was to avoid responsibility for taking special steps to save them. Such steps, if successful, would have confronted the Allies with the difficult problem of finding places to put the rescued Jews.[97]

Another reason was the fear that special action for the Jews would stir up anti-Semitism. Some asserted that such action would even invite charges that the war was being fought for the Jews. Emanuel Celler declared years later that Roosevelt did nearly nothing for rescue because he was afraid of the label "Jew Deal"; he feared the political effects of the accusation that he was pro-Jewish. The Jews, according to artist Arthur Szyk, were a skeleton in the democracies' political closet, a matter they would rather not mention. "They treat us as a pornographical subject," he wrote, "you cannot discuss it in polite society." *[98]

The fourth well-worn excuse for rejecting rescue proposals was the claim that they would detract from the military effort and thus prolong the war. This argument, entirely valid with regard to projects that actually would have hurt the war effort, was used almost automatically to justify inaction. Virtually none of the rescue proposals involved enough infringement on the war effort to lengthen the conflict at all or to increase the number of casualties, military or civilian.[100]

Actually, the war effort was bent from time to time to meet pressing

---

* The White House even avoided mentioning Jews in a brief presidential message commemorating the first anniversary of the Warsaw ghetto uprising.[99]

humanitarian needs. In most of these instances, it was non-Jews who were helped. During 1942, 1943, and 1944, the Allies evacuated large numbers of non-Jewish Yugoslavs, Poles, and Greeks to safety in the Middle East, Africa, and elsewhere. Difficulties that constantly ruled out the rescue of Jews dissolved. Transportation somehow materialized to move 100,000 people to dozens of refugee camps that sprang into existence. The British furnished transport, supplies, much of the camp staffing, and many of the campsites. The United States contributed lend-lease materials and covered the bulk of the funding through UNRRA. Most of these refugees had been in desperate straits. None, though, were the objects of systematic annihilation.[101]

Between November 1943 and September 1944, 36,000 Yugoslavs escaped to southern Italy. Most crossed the Adriatic by boat, thousands on British naval craft. Some even came out in American troop planes. The aircraft, sent mainly to evacuate wounded partisans, in many cases returned with civilians, including hundreds of orphaned babies. Using troopships, the British moved most of the Yugoslavs from Italy to camps in Egypt.[102]

About 120,000 Poles, mostly men of military age and their dependents, came out of Russia during 1942 and passed into British-controlled camps in Iran. They were part of the remnant of a million and a half Poles the Soviets had deported to Siberia after the seizure of eastern Poland in September 1939. The Soviets released these thousands to join the British armed forces. Two-thirds of them did; the other 40,000 became refugees. Iran did not want them, supplying them was difficult, and conditions at the camps were bad. Most were moved out, mainly on British troopships, between August 1942 and August 1943. Ultimately, about 35,000 went to camps in Africa, India, Mexico, and the Middle East. The greatest numbers were placed in British colonies in East Africa, where camps were made available by shifting thousands of prisoners of war to the United States.*[103]

Despite the demands of war, the United States, with British support, extended significant help to the Greek people. Food for Greece moved freely through the blockade, and ships to carry it were located without trouble. American lend-lease funds paid for the project.[105]

The Allies also helped thousands of Greeks to flee Nazi control and

---

* In all, nearly 425,000 prisoners of war were brought to the United States during World War II. Except for rare instances such as the above-cited transfer from East Africa, America's acceptance of POWs must be regarded as part of the war effort. Thus it is not directly relevant to the question of what could or should have been done in regard to taking in refugees.[104]

provided sanctuary for them in the Middle East and Africa. By 1944, 25,000 Greeks had been evacuated. The largest numbers, reported at between 9,000 and 12,000, were taken to Palestine—most to a former army installation at Nuseirat, near Gaza. Palestine also sheltered 1,800 of the non-Jewish Polish refugees. While the British, intent on keeping the small White Paper quota from being filled, turned back endangered Jews, they generously welcomed these other victims of the storm.* [106]

In all, Britain and the United States rescued 100,000 Yugoslav, Polish, and Greek refugees from disastrous conditions. Most of them traveled by military transport to camps where the Allies maintained them at considerable cost in funds, supplies, and even military staff. In contrast, the United States (with minimal cooperation from the British) evacuated fewer than 2,000 Jews to the three camps open to *them,* the ones at Fedala, Philippeville, and Oswego. [108]

Illustrative of the different responses to Jews and non-Jews was the double standard applied regarding British East Africa. In 1942, distressed about the *Struma* disaster, Eleanor Roosevelt suggested to Sumner Welles that Jewish refugees turned away from Palestine be taken into British colonies in East Africa. Welles answered, as American and British authorities habitually did, that no facilities existed for refugees in that area and no ships were available to transport them there. The question came up a year later, at the Bermuda Conference. That time the diplomats concluded that Jewish refugees could not go to British East Africa because 21,000 non-Jewish Polish refugees were already on their way there. [109]

It was not a lack of workable plans that stood in the way of saving many thousands more European Jews. Nor was it insufficient shipping, the threat of infiltration by subversive agents, or the possibility that rescue projects would hamper the war effort. The real obstacle was the absence of a strong desire to rescue Jews. A month before the Bermuda Conference, the Committee for a Jewish Army declared:

> We, on our part, refuse to resign ourselves to the idea that our brains are powerless to find any solution. . . . In order to visualize the possibility of such a solution, imagine that the British people and the American nation had millions of residents in Europe. . . . Let us imagine that Hitler would start a process of annihilation and would slaughter not two million Englishmen or Americans, not hundreds of thousands, but, let us say, only tens of thousands. . . . It is clear that the governments of Great Britain [and] the

---

* During 1942 and 1943, approximately as many non-Jewish Greeks and Poles were accepted into Palestine as were Jewish refugees. [107]

United States would certainly find ways and means to act instantly and to act effectively.[110]

But the European Jews were not Americans and they were not English. It was their particular misfortune not only to be foreigners but also to be Jews.

APPENDIX A

Easter at Bermuda

The most intriguing document left by the Bermuda Conference was the transcript of a frank discussion held on Easter Sunday, April 25, by the full American delegation. No British were present. By then the conference had made its decisions; but not until then did the American chairman, Harold Dodds, call in all the American technical experts for a thorough airing of the issues. Finally, George Backer, who was well informed about the extermination and refugee situations, was asked for his views. "We have never seen your comments," said Dodds, "and I would like to have you take the floor and begin from the beginning." For the rest of the morning and through a special evening session, the American delegates for the first time saw beyond the confines of State Department and Foreign Office thinking.[1]

As Backer spoke, a genuine dialogue emerged. Dodds, and to a lesser extent Lucas and Bloom, began to perceive the problem in terms of people rather than bureaucratic processes. For a time, they seemed to search for solutions instead of rationalizations for inaction.* At the end of the morning session, Dodds remarked, "I have received a lot of knowledge here this morning." But it came too late. The conference's decisions were not reopened.

Backer exposed the State Department's insistence that the Jewish plight receive no special emphasis as no more than a device for avoiding the extermination issue. He pointed out that the conference's discussions about non-Jewish refugees had shown that they were already being cared for by Britain or the United States or their own governments. "In so far as this conference is concerned," Backer asserted, "it would never have been necessary to call it" to help non-Jewish refugees.

Because it ruled out all plans for mass rescue of Jews, Backer continued, the conference had dealt with little more than the 5,000 refugees in Spain. He warned that solving that comparatively small problem would not be enough to keep the conference from being judged a failure. "I would say that at least 125,000 people have got to be taken out of eastern Europe if this Conference is to yield a result." He argued for approaches to the Axis through neutral channels for the removal of at least part of the captive Jews. He was most deeply concerned about the children:

> I think whether it succeeds or fails that this step must be taken. . . . It is an act of moral force. . . . If you gentlemen can see some way . . . to try this and to receive . . . these children you have done much, more than much to justify your efforts.

In response, Lucas reverted to the State Department and Foreign Office view, arguing that a large-scale exodus of Jews posed a great danger. He revealed in confidence the British delegation's belief that if approaches to Germany to release Jews were "pressed too much that that is exactly what might happen." Lucas hypothesized that Hitler might use the opportunity to interfere with the Allied war effort by pushing 100,000 Jews across some border or by announcing to the Allies that he would deposit 100,000 at a certain port on a certain day, saying, "You bring your ships and supplies to take 100,000 away on such and such a date." If the United Nations had made approaches for the release of Jews, they would be obligated to find a way to remove

---

* When George Warren, another technical expert, evaluated the conference afterward, he remarked that he had been "shocked by the strong resistance [to rescue action] of individual members at the Conference."[2]

and care for them. To do that, declared Lucas, "you would have to stop this man's war."

Backer maintained that Hitler could not require immediate evacuation and that the Allies could manage, over time, to move the 100,000 out. Lucas then fell back on the tight shipping situation, asserting that the interference with shipping required by such a project could "prolong this war to the end that we might lose 100,000 boys." Twice more within a brief time, Lucas insisted that mass rescue could cost the lives of large numbers of American fighting men.

Lucas's arguments against any large-scale rescue were exaggerated and thin. But Backer could not rebut them effectively. The Easter sessions were doubly tragic. They injected new information and a new perspective into the conference, but only after its decisions had solidified. And when the delegates at last appeared ready for serious consideration of the Jewish leaders' proposals, those who had developed them and could have elucidated and defended them were not available for consultation. Exclusion of such men as Stephen Wise and Joseph Proskauer helped insure the failure of the Bermuda Conference.*

---

* Lucas's arguments were vulnerable on several counts:

(1) If the Allies negotiated for the release of the Jews, they could insist on a reasonably paced exodus. If Germany nevertheless pushed refugees out en masse, the Allies need do only what was practical under war conditions. The world would recognize who was at fault.

(2) Realistically, Germany was not capable of delivering 100,000 refugees to a specific border or port at one time. Had it tried, the operation would have severely strained its *own* war machine.

(3) Enough Allied and neutral shipping for a regulated exodus was definitely available without interfering with the war effort.

(4) As Lucas spoke, the Allies were well into a program of evacuating 60,000 non-Jewish Greek and Polish refugees to the Middle East and Africa. Late the same year, similar help was initiated for 36,000 non-Jewish Yugoslavs.

(5) Approaches to Axis *satellites* for the release of their Jews would have entailed no possibility whatever of disorganized mass extrusion. By April 1943, the war had turned against Germany. Several satellites were edging toward an accommodation with the Allies. In those circumstances, to antagonize the Allied powers would have been self-defeating.[3]

APPENDIX B

---

*The Conflict Between the Regular Zionists
and the Bergsonites*

The American Jewish Conference's public denunciation of the Emergency Committee in late December 1943 was only one in a string of bitter attacks on the Bergsonites by the established Zionist forces. The activities of the Committee for a Jewish Army, efforts to show the "We Will Never Die" pageant throughout America, plans for the Emergency Conference, and the Rescue Resolution all encountered Zionist opposition.

One tactic involved frequent telephone calls, letters, and personal visits to persuade supporters of the Bergsonites to abandon the group. The American Zionist Emergency Council systematized the technique. Using the Bergson organizations' letterheads and newspaper advertisements, it collected the names of hundreds of their sponsors and conducted a thorough (and partially successful) campaign to induce them to withdraw their backing.[1]

During 1944, the attacks increased and sharpened, especially after mid-May, when Bergson launched the Hebrew Committee of National Liberation and the American League for a Free Palestine. These two organizations aimed at creating a Jewish state in Palestine. The Zionists recognized the new development as a competing movement and sought to disable it. (Animosities reached a point where Stephen Wise told John Pehle of the War Refugee Board that he seriously believed the Bergson group might take his life. WRB personnel thought it more likely that Bergson would be killed.) Zionists urged the State and Justice departments to arrange to have Bergson drafted into the armed forces or deported to Palestine (and almost certain incarceration, or worse). Others who pressed for the same objective included the British embassy, the American Jewish Committee, and Sol Bloom. The State Department did what it could. Bergson was almost drafted, despite previous rejection because of stomach ulcers. And proceedings to deport him were in process during much of 1944 and 1945. Firm intervention by friends in Congress blocked both moves.[2]

Over the years, Zionist leaders advanced numerous reasons that the Bergson organizations should be spurned. The Bergsonites, they frequently asserted, had no mandate or authorization from the Jewish public, they were unrepresentative, their actions were irresponsible and sensationalist, and they misused the large funds they solicited. (In fact, thorough investigations by the Internal Revenue Service and the Federal Bureau of Investigation uncovered no financial irregularities.) Another argument held that the strident tone of their activities and newspaper advertising increased anti-Semitism.[3]

But these accusations, which were openly leveled, did not account for the high intensity of the Zionists' animosity toward the Bergsonites. Zionist records reveal that the number one concern was fear that the Bergsonites could build an effective rival Zionist organization. Zionist leaders were apprehensive not so much that such a movement could supplant theirs, but that it would draw away sorely needed funds and members and would disrupt progress toward realization of the Jewish state.[4]

Hostility toward the Bergsonites was all the more bitter because regular Zionists were painfully aware of their own weakness in the struggle to establish a Jewish state. They needed all the help they could find, not additional complications. That both movements had essentially the same goal multiplied the anguish.[5]

The Zionists were especially disturbed by the Bergsonites' unwillingness to adhere to the discipline of the established Zionist bodies, either on the world level (Jewish Agency and World Zionist Organization) or on the national level (American Zionist Emergency Council and Zionist

Organization of America). Because the Zionist movement lacked coercive power, it depended on the acceptance of organizational discipline. Without unity, the Zionists believed, little hope existed for attainment of a Jewish state. On several occasions, they and the Bergsonites tried to negotiate a formula for unified action. All attempts broke down over the issue of submitting to the control of the established Zionist movement. In the eyes of the regular Zionists, the Bergson group's insistence on retaining its autonomy destroyed the all-important principle of unity.[6]

Thus the two movements, each able to marshal considerable skills and strengths, both pursuing common goals, could not collaborate either for rescue or for a Jewish state. Nor were the regular Zionists willing for the Bergson group to go its own way without interference. For with every Bergsonite success they saw a potential increase in the group's influence and thus its threat to their own movement. That, in their view, translated into a threat to the establishment of the Jewish state.

The conflict between the Zionists and the Bergsonites was one of numerous serious disputes that riddled organized American Jewry throughout the Holocaust. To read through the archives and publications of American Jewish organizations in the period is to journey through a landscape of continual fighting. Zionist organizations regularly clashed with such non-Zionist bodies as the American Jewish Committee and the Jewish Labor Committee. Zionists feuded bitterly among themselves, even breaking their movement apart for six months after the Wise-Silver collision of December 1944. Orthodox non-Zionists quarreled with each other. Acrimony interfered with cooperation on rescue between the Joint Distribution Committee and Jewish organizations that claimed the JDC was holding back funds. Twice between 1941 and 1945, power struggles within the United Jewish Appeal nearly destroyed that combined fund-raising mechanism. Little wonder, then, that an early War Refugee Board memorandum referring to plans for cooperation with the various private organizations warned that "one of the problems is to get all the groups, particularly the Jewish groups, to work together and to stop fighting among themselves."[7]

NOTES

Abbreviations Used in Source Notes

AAF	Wesley Craven & James Cate (eds), *The Army Air Forces in World War II*, v 3 (1951).
ACB	"Confidential Bulletin" (of AZEC). In ZAL. Cited by bulletin number. All citations are in v 1.
ACCR	Am Com for Christian Refugees
Ack	Ackermann
AECZA	Am Emergency Com for Zionist Affairs
AF	Am Friends Service Com; &

Am Friends Service Com Archives. Within the Archives:

  FS = Foreign Service File
  GF = General File
  OF = Overseas File
  RS = Refugee Services File.

Certain individual folders are abbreviated as follows:

  FS 1 = Ctry Italy, Ltrs from
  FS 2 = Ctry Italy, Rpts
  FS 3 = US Govt, Wn Trips
  FS 4 = Internees Program, AF Project at ERS, FO, Oswego, NY

  GF 1 = For Serv, Refs, Genl
  GF 2 = For Serv, France, Genl

GF 3 = For Serv, France, Relief & Refs, Children's Transports
GF 4 = US Govt, SD, VD
GF 5 = C/O, JDC

RS 1 = Ctry France, Ref Programs
RS 2 = Ctry FNA, Fr Morocco
RS 3 = Ctry Portugal, Ltrs to, Admin
RS 4 = Ctry Portugal, Ltrs from
RS 5 = Ctry Spain, Rpts (Genl)
RS 6 = Ctry Spain, Corresp & Rpts
RS 7 = Migration Services, Transportation
RS 8 = Children, Corresp with USCom
RS 9 = C/O, ICR
RS 10 = C/O, JDC
RS 11 = Migration Services, US Govt Contacts, Wn Cfs.

AHS   Abba Hillel Silver Papers. Ma = Manson file.
AI   Agudath Israel; & Agudath Israel Papers.
     AI Rpt = Confidential Rpt to the Chawerim Nichbodim of the Agudas Israel World Orgzn (1st = July–Dec 1941; 2nd = Jan–June 1942; 4th = Jan–June 1943; 5th = July–Dec 1943; 6th = Jan–June 1944).
AJC   Am Jewish Com; & Am Jewish Com Archives.
AJCf   Am Jewish Conference
AJCg   Am Jewish Congress; & Am Jewish Congress Papers.
AJH   *Am Jewish History*
AJHQ   *Am Jewish Historical Quarterly*
AJHS   Am Jewish Historical Society Archives. Within the Archives:
     I-67 = AJCf papers. In it, B 3 refers to transcript of Rescue Com Sessions, 8/31–9/2/43. B 4 refers to transcript of Rescue Com Session, 12/4/44.
     I-77 = AJCg papers. In it, B 3 refers to folders of Administrative Com Mins. B 6 refers to folders of Exec Com Mins.
AJYB   *Am Jewish Year Book*
ALFP   Am League for a Free Palestine
Am   American
AM   AZEC, Mins of Mtgs, Oct 18, 1943–Apr 26, 1949. In ZAL. Cited by serial number of the minutes.
AME   AZEC, Mins of Mtgs of Exec Com, 1943–49. In ZAL. Cited by serial number of the minutes.
Anger   Per Anger, *With Raoul Wallenberg in Budapest* (1981).
Ans   *Answer*
APRR   ECSJPE, *The Am Press & the Rescue Resolution* (1944). Copy in PSC 4/14.
ASW   Assistant Secretary of War; &
     Assistant Secretary of War Files, NA, RG 107.
     Certain individual folders are abbreviated as follows:
     ASW 1 = ASW 400.38 Countries-C-D-E-F (B 151)
     ASW 2 = ASW 400.38 Countries-Germany
     ASW 3 = ASW 400.38 Jews

ASW 4 = ASW 400.38 WRB
ASW 5 = ASW 400.38 WRB (B 151).

AtM	*Atlantic Monthly*
Avni	Haim Avni, *Spain, the Jews, & Franco* (1982).
AZ	Am Zionist Emergency Council
AZEC	Am Zionist Emergency Council
B	box
BA	Yitshaq Ben-Ami File, Dept of Justice.
Bauer I	Yehuda Bauer, *Am Jewry & the Holocaust* (1981).
Bauer II	Yehuda Bauer, *The Holocaust in Historical Perspective* (1978).
Bauer III	Yehuda Bauer, "The Negotiations between Saly Mayer & the Representatives of the S.S. in 1944–1945" in *Rescue Attempts during the Holocaust: Proceedings of the Second Yad Vashem International Historical Conference—April 1974* (1977).
BC Mins	Am minutes of Bermuda Cf sessions. In BLP, B 203, Ref Cf—Bermuda Cf 1943.
BC Rpt	Rpt to the Govts of the US & the UK from their Delegates to the Cf on the Ref Problem held at Bermuda, 4/43. In same file as BC Mins.
Ber Cf	Bermuda Conference
BG	*Boston Globe*
BI	Papers of Bureau of Immigration of Natl Catholic Welfare Conf. All documents cited are from United States Catholic Conf Records, Migration & Refugee Division. The number following BI stands for the box in which the document was located. Then come the title of the relevant folder & its serial number.
BKR Rpt	Robert Bulkley, Frederick Keppel, & F. D. G. Ribble, *Report to the President: Board of Appeals on Visa Cases: Nov 9, 1942* (1942).
BLD	Breckinridge Long Diary.
BLP	Breckinridge Long Papers.
Braham I	Randolph L. Braham, *The Politics of Genocide: The Holocaust in Hungary,* v 2 (1981).
Braham II	Randolph L. Braham (ed), *The Destruction of Hungarian Jewry,* v 1 (1963).
Braham III	Randolph L. Braham (ed), *Hungarian-Jewish Studies,* v 3 (1973).
Burns	James M. Burns, *Roosevelt: The Soldier of Freedom* (1970).
Cantril	Hadley Cantril (ed), *Public Opinion: 1935–1946* (1951).
CBA	*Bulletin of Activities & Digest of the Press* (AJCf). Cited by bulletin number.
CC	*Christian Century*
CCR	Catholic Com for Refugees
CD	*Congressional Digest*
CEP Jour	Clarence E. Pickett's Journal, AF Archives.
Cf	conference
CfR	*Conference Record* (AJCf). All citations from v 1. Number is issue number within v 1.
Cf Rpt	AJCf, *Report of the Interim Committee & the Commission on Rescue, Commission on Palestine, Commission on Post-War to the Delegates of the Am Jewish Conf* (1944).
CH	Carlton J. H. Hayes Papers. All citations from the Spanish Papers.

CH 1   Makinson, Sum of Ref Work in 1943, 1/4/44, CH, B 1, Jan–Feb 1944 Dept.

CH 2   NWB, Memo on Ref Relief Activities, 7/7/44, CH, B 1, Jan–Feb 1944 Dept.

CH 3   WLB, Relief of Refs in Spain, 7/19/44, CH, B 1, Jan–Feb 1944 Dept.

Chr R   *Christian Register*

CJA   Com for a Jewish Army

CJR   *Contemporary Jewish Record*

CM   AJCf, Mins of Mtgs. In ZAL.

C/O   Committees & Organizations (file designation in AF Archives).

Com   committee

Convsn   conversation

CP   Personal files held by Sen Claiborne Pell.

CR   *Congressional Record*

CS   US 15th Air Force, Complete Summary of Operations, 1 Nov 1943–8 May 1945. In NA, RG 243.

CSM   *Christian Science Monitor*

CT   *Chicago Tribune*

Ctry   country

CW   *Congress Weekly*

DN   *Dallas News*

DO   US 15th Air Force, Daily Operations, 1944. In NA, RG 243.

DP   *Denver Post*

DSB   *Department of State Bulletin*

EC   Emergency Com to Save the Jewish People of Europe

ECSJPE   Emergency Com to Save the Jewish People of Europe

EHR   *English Historical Review,* Jan 1977 issue.

EmC   Mins of Mtg of Emerg Com on Eur Situation, 3/6/43, AJC, PEC Memoranda & Materials.

ER   Eleanor Roosevelt; & Eleanor Roosevelt Papers (citations thus: Box/File).

ERS   Emergency Refugee Shelter (at Ft Ontario)

Estb TH   Memorandum Re: Establishment of Temporary Havens of Refuge in the US, u/c Hull, Morgenthau, & Stimson to FDR, 5/8/44, FDR, OF 3186.

ET   Elbert Thomas Papers.

Evacn   evacuation

EW   State Dept decimal file 740.00116 European War 1939.

Exec   executive

Exh   exhibit

F   folder

FCC   Papers of the Federal Council of the Churches of Christ in America.

FDR   Franklin D. Roosevelt; and Franklin D. Roosevelt Papers.

FDRL   Franklin D. Roosevelt Library

FNA   French North Africa

FO   Fort Ontario

FOH   "Investigation of Problems Presented by Refugees at Fort Ontario Refugee Shelter," *Hearings before Subcom VI of the Com on Immigration & Naturalization, House of Representatives,* 79 Cong, 1 ses (June 25–26, 1945).

FO Rpts	War Relocation Authority, Emergency Refugee Shelter, Reports, Parts I, II, III. In NA, RG 210.
FO Rpt 1	WRA, Semi-Annual Rpt, July 1–Dec 31, 1944, in FO Rpts.
FO Rpt 2	Ruth Gruber, "Eight Months Later: A Rpt on the Emergency Refugee Shelter" [4/45], in FO Rpts.
FO Rpt 3	Edward Marks, Jr, Rpt of Refugee Program, 5/46, in FO Rpts.
For Serv	Foreign Service
fr	frame
Fr	France
FR	US State Dept, *Foreign Relations of the United States* series.
FSR	*Final Summary Rpt of the Exec Director, WRB* (1945).
Garlinski	Jozef Garlinski, *Fighting Auschwitz* (1975).
GCM	Governing Council Minutes, AJCg Papers.
G/E	General & Emergency (file designation in JDC Archives).
GEC	WRB, *German Extermination Camps* (1944).
Ger	Germany
Goldmann	*The Autobiography of Nahum Goldmann* (1969).
GR	Foreign Economic Administration, "A Survey of Greek Relief, Apr 1941 to Dec 1943," 3/44, copy in W 49, FEA 2.
H I	Ira Hirschmann's first report, 3/6/44, copy in JDC, Emigration Projects from the Balkans.
H II	Hirschmann's second report, 8/19/44, copy in JDC, Rescue Work.
H III	Hirschmann's third report, 10/4/44, copy in JDC, Subject Matter WRB Rpt by Hirschmann.
H IV	Hirschmann, Memo to Steinhardt on Interview with Joel Brand, 6/22/44, copy in ASW 3.
Halperin	Samuel Halperin, *The Political World of Am Zionism* (1961).
Hayes	Carlton J. H. Hayes, *Wartime Mission in Spain* (1946).
HCNL	Hebrew Committee of National Liberation
HI	Harold Ickes Papers. Citations from Secy of Interior files, unless otherwise noted.
HIAS	Hebrew Sheltering & Immigrant Aid Society
HID	Harold Ickes Diaries. Cited by page numbers only.
Hilberg	Raul Hilberg, *The Destruction of the European Jews* (1961).
Hirschmann	Ira Hirschmann, *Caution to the Winds* (1962).
Hn	Ira Hirschmann
HSD	Henry L. Stimson Diaries
HST	Harry S Truman
Hull	Cordell Hull Papers. Citations thus: Box/Folder.
Hung	Hungary
ICR	Intergovernmental Com on Refugees
IE	Ira C. Eaker Papers.
IJPS	Independent Jewish Press Service *News*
Imgn	immigration
IMS	International Migration Service; & International Migration Service Papers.
Infield	Glenn Infield, *The Poltava Affair* (1973).
INN	Isaac Neustadt-Noy, "The Unending Task: Efforts to Unite Am Jewry from the Am Jewish Congress to the Am Jewish Conference," PhD diss, Brandeis Univ, 1976.

INS	Immigration & Naturalization Service
Int Com	Interim Committee of AJCf
IR	*Interpreter Releases*
Israel	Fred Israel, *The War Diary of Breckinridge Long* (1966).
It	Italy
J	Jewish
JDC	Am Jewish Joint Distribution Com; & Am Jewish Joint Distribution Com Archives.
JEC	Joint Emergency Com on European Jewish Affairs
JF	*Jewish Frontier*
JI	Jabotinsky Institute, Tel Aviv
JLC	Jewish Labor Com; & Jewish Labor Com Archives.
JM	James G. McDonald Papers.
JMJ	*Jewish Morning Journal*
JO	*Jewish Outlook*
JPC	Joseph P. Chamberlain Papers. Each document in this collection has its own serial number.
JTA	Jewish Telegraphic Agency *Daily News Bulletin*
JV	*Jewish Veteran*
KCS	*Kansas City Star*
Kp I	Alexander Kohanski (ed), *The Am Jewish Conference: Its Organization and Proceedings of the First Session, Aug 29–Sept 2, 1943* (1944).
Kp II	Alexander Kohanski (ed), *The Am Jewish Conference: Proceedings of the Second Session, Dec 3–5, 1944* (1945).
LAT	*Los Angeles Times*
LC	Library of Congress
Legis	Legislative Branch, NA. Number given is the relevant file number.
Lester	Elenore Lester, *Wallenberg: The Man in the Iron Web* (1982).
LJ	*Liberal Judaism*
Lowrie 1	Donald Lowrie, "The Work in the Camps," 8/24/42, JDC, G/E, France 1941–43, Rpt.
Lowrie 2	Lowrie to Strong, 8/10/42, AF, GF 2.
Lowrie 3	Lowrie to Strong, 9/17/42, AF, GF, For Serv, France, Relief & Refs, Concentration camps.
LS	Laurence Steinhardt Papers. All citations from Box 44.
Ltr	letter
Mann Rpt	Mann to Pehle, 8/30/44, W 71, Rpt on Trip to Sp & Port.
MASC	Migration & Alien Status Com (of NRS)
McC	McClelland
MD	Morgenthau Diaries. Citations thus: Book/page.
Mds	*Midstream*
Mign	migration
Mins	minutes
MJ	*Menorah Journal*
Morse	Arthur Morse, *While Six Million Died* (1968).
Moscow OH	Warren Moscow Oral History, Columbia Univ Collection.
MPD	Morgenthau Presidential Diaries.
MR	*Monthly Review* (INS)

M Rpts	US 15th Air Force Mission Rpts. In A. F. Simpson Historical Research Center. Unless otherwise noted, references are to microfilm copies.
MT	Myron C. Taylor Papers. Unless otherwise noted, citations are from Box 5, Correspondence 1938–54.
Mtg	meeting
Musy	Jean-Marie Musy, "Rapport au Comité Suisse de l'Union of Orthodox Rabbis," 1945, in files of Reuven Hecht, Haifa.
Mvt	movement
NA	National Archives
NAfr	North Africa
Natl	National
NCWC	National Catholic Welfare Conference
NJM	*National Jewish Monthly*
NP	*New Palestine*
NR	*New Republic*
NRS	National Refugee Service; & National Refugee Service Papers (number is that of the relevant file).
NYHT	*New York Herald Tribune*
NYJA	*New York Journal-American*
NYP	*New York Post*
NYT	*New York Times*
NYWT	*New York World Telegram*
OC	Oscar Cox Papers. All citations from Box 101, Refugees.
O'Dwyer	Personal files of Paul O'Dwyer.
OFR	Olsen to O'Dwyer, Final Rpt, 6/15/45, W 72, Sweden, Olsen's Rpts.
Op	*Opinion*
OR	Olsen, Operations of WRB from Sweden, 11/20/44, W 72, Sweden, Olsen's Rpts.
PAC	President's Advisory Com on Political Refugees
Pal	Palestine
Pal Com	Palestine Committee
Pal Comsn	Palestine Commission
PC	Planning Committee (of AJCg/WJC)
PC/FDR	Press Conferences of President Franklin D. Roosevelt. Typed volumes at FDRL.
PEC	Proskauer Emergency Committee (a file in AJC Archives).
Pell OH	Herbert C. Pell Oral History, Columbia Univ Collection.
PFR	*Polish Fortnightly Review*
Port	Portugal
PPA	Samuel Rosenman (ed), *The Public Papers & Addresses of Franklin D. Roosevelt,* v 13 (1950).
PR	*Polish Review*
PRO	Public Record Office, London
Pr Rel	press release
PSC	Palestine Statehood Committee Papers. Citations thus: Box/Folder. S = Scrapbook.
R	State Dept decimal file 840.48 Refugees.
RD	*Reader's Digest*
Ref	refugee

RG   Record Group
RG 165(1)   NA, RG 165, OPD 383.7, Sec II, case 21.
RM   Roswell McClelland, Rpt on the Activities of the WRB . . . Switzerland,
            7/31/45, JDC, WRB.
Rpt   report
RR   US House of Representatives, *Problems of World War II & Its Aftermath:
            Part 2, The Palestine Question* (1976).
RT   Robert Taft Papers. Number is relevant box number.
RW   Robert Wagner Papers. Citations thus: Box/Folder. All citations from
            Palestine Files.
RYP   "Review of the Yiddish Press," available at AJC Library.
SB   Sol Bloom Papers.
SD   State Dept; and State Dept decimal files. Within the files:
            EW = 740.00116 European War 1939
            R = 840.48 Refugees.
Secy   Secretary
SFE   *San Francisco Examiner*
SG   *Survey Graphic*
SIB   "Special Information Bulletin" (of NRS)
Silver   Abba Hillel Silver, *Vision & Victory* (1949).
Smolen   Kazimierz Smolen, *From the History of KL-Auschwitz,* v 1 (1967).
Sp   Spain
Spz   Carl A. Spaatz Papers.
Spz 1   Spaatz Papers, B 143, Operational Planning: Attacks Against. . . .
Spz 2   Spaatz Papers, B 182, Subject File—Operations—Warsaw Dropping
            Ops.
SS   Secretary of State
ST   *Seattle Times*
Stember   Charles Stember (ed), *Jews in the Mind of America* (1966).
Stmt   statement
Sunderman   James Sunderman (ed), *World War II in the Air: Europe* (1963).
SW   Stephen Wise Papers.
TD   Treasury Dept
Teleg   telegram
TH   NA, RG 210, War Relocation Authority, Emergency Refugee Shelter,
            Temporary Havens in the U.S. Numbers refer to relevant folder
            numbers.
TS   US War Relocation Authority, *Token Shipment* [1946].
Tur   Turkey
u/c   under cover of
UJA   United Jewish Appeal
UOR   Union of Orthodox Rabbis of the US & Canada
USC   Unitarian Service Com; & Unitarian Service Com Papers.
USCCEC   US Com for the Care of European Children
v   volume
VD   Visa Division
VF   Vertical File (file designation in ZAL).
VH   Vaad Hahatzala; & Vaad Hahatzala Papers.
Voss   Carl H. Voss (ed), *Stephen S. Wise: Servant of the People* (1969).

W	WRB Records. The number following W stands for the box in which the document is located.
Wasserstein	Bernard Wasserstein, *Britain & the Jews of Europe, 1939–1945* (1979).
WC	War Crimes
WCC	War Crimes Commission
WF	Charles Webster & Noble Frankland, *The Strategic Air Offensive Against Germany, 1939–1945*, v 3 (1961).
WH	"WRB History." In WRB Records, boxes 110–111.
WIL	Women's International League for Peace & Freedom, US section; & its papers.
Wise	*Challenging Years: The Autobiography of Stephen Wise* (1949).
WJC	World Jewish Congress; & World Jewish Congress Papers.
WLB	*Wiener Library Bulletin*
Wn	Washington
WP	*Washington Post*
WRA	War Relocation Authority; & NA, RG 210, War Relocation Authority, Field Office Records, Emergency Refugee Shelter, Central Files. Number is relevant file number.
WRB	War Refugee Board
WRS-NCWC	War Relief Services–National Catholic Welfare Conference
WTH	*Washington Times-Herald*
Wyman	David Wyman, *Paper Walls: Am & the Refugee Crisis, 1938–1941* (1968).
YIVO	YIVO Institute for Jewish Research
YSH	EC, "A Year in the Service of Humanity," 8/44, PSC 5/22 & Reel 6.
YV	Yad Vashem
YVS	*Yad Vashem Studies*
Z	Zionist
ZAL	Zionist Archives & Library
Zm	Zionism
ZOA	Zionist Organization of Am
Zt	Zionist

PREFACE

[1] Eg, *In The Dispersion,* winter 1963–64, 6–7 (Nahum Goldmann); *Martyrdom & Resistance,* 11/83, 11 (Israel Goldstein); *Reconstructionist,* summer 1983, 4 (Ira Eisenstein).

CHAPTER 1.
THE SETTING: EUROPE AND AMERICA

[1] Hilberg, ch 7, esp 177, 182–3, 261; quotation is from YVS, v 6, 301.

[2] Hilberg, 196, 225, 242, 256, 767.

[3] Ibid, 257, 262; Raul Hilberg (ed), *Documents of Destruction: Germany and Jewry, 1933–1945* (1971), 88.

[4] Hilberg, 264–5; Wyman, 205; Leavitt to Aufbau, 2/27/42, JDC, G/E, Germany-Emig Gen.

[5] Hilberg, 209, 265, 309–11, 555, 561–6, 572, 767; Lucy Dawidowicz, *The War Against the Jews, 1933–1945* (1975), 181.

[6] Hilberg, 767.

[7] Ibid, 643.

[8] Ibid, 247, 284–7, 298, 311, 333–7, 377, 645–6.

[9] Wyman, vii, 35–9, 168–83, 191–205, 209.

[10] See page 136.

[11] Wyman, esp ch 1 and Conclusion.

[12] Wyman, 4–9, and see index entry Unemployment.

[13] Ibid, 10–14, and see index entries Nativism and Restrictionists.

[14] *Natl Legionnaire,* 10/42, 2; *Am Legion Magazine,* 11/43, 37; *Foreign Service* (VFW), 7/43, 30, 10/44, 13; NYT, 4/19/44, 11; IR, 7/18/44, 233–4; *Rescue* (HIAS), 2/45, 6; RD, 3/43, 44.

[15] Sources in preceding note. Also, CEP Jour, 6/18/43; MR, 12/43, 12; *Rescue,* 2/45, 6; NYT, 9/21/42, 1, 9/23/43, 13, 4/19/44, 11, 10/13/44, 8, 10/21/45, 40; NYHT, 9/26/44, 2; *Am Legion Mag-*

azine, 4/43, 2; *Foreign Service,* 12/45, 11; NYP, 4/18/44, 4; Wyman, 79.

[16] Travers to Foster, 4/6/45, SD 150.01 Bills/3–3045; IR, 6/21/43, 169–85; CEP Jour, 1/26/44; MR, 12/43, 11–13; NYT, 8/22/44, 32; *Am Vindicator,* 4/42, 1, 5/42, 7, 11/42, 3; *Natl Record,* 4/43, 1, 12/44, 6.

[17] NYT, 9/22/42, 16; CR, v 89, 7107–8, 8594.

[18] Burton to Joy, 5/7/44, USC, Sen Burton.

[19] AF Mins, For Serv Staff, 5/14/45; NYT, 3/6/44, 9; IR, 10/9/42, 342, 11/9/43, 364, 12/14/43, 391, 8/8/44, 250–8; MR, 12/43, 12–13; JTA, 1/9/44; Hull to Dickstein, 12/15/43, 12/13/43, SD 150.01 Bills/507 & 509; HR 3487, 10/18/43, copy in BLP, B 198, Legislation.

[20] AF Mins, Jt For Serv Exec Com, 3/6/44, 4/17/44, 8/21/44; Pickett to Vail, 10/21/43, Pickett to Vail & Rogers, 10/21/43, Rpt on Recommendations, 10/15/43 (with Mins of Exec Com of NRS, 10/20/43), AF, RS, NRS; RR, 63–4.

[21] Wyman, 47, 95, 210; Stember, 145, 149.

[22] Cantril, 307. Twelve percent had no opinion.

[23] Wyman, 14–26, 85–6, 94–5, 103, 111, 128, 163–5.

[24] Ibid, 14–23; Stember, 67, 84–5, 130–3, 208–10, 214; *Public Opinion Quarterly,* spr 1942, 56; NYT, 4/11/45, 21.

[25] Wyman, 14–22; AJYB, v 44, 157–60, v 46, 137–8; Charles Tull, *Father Coughlin and the New Deal* (1965), 234–7; Sander Diamond, *The Nazi Movement in the United States, 1924–1941* (1974), 345–8; NYT, 12/16/41, 31, 4/4/42, 11, 4/15/42, 1, 4/19/42, IV, 7, 7/24/42, 1, 8, 8/13/42, 6, 3/24/43, 16, 6/19/43, 1, 28.

[26] AJYB, v 44, 159–60, v 46, 133–43, v 47, 268–79; JV, 10/42, 3, 5/44, 8, 21, 8/44, 9; NJM, 5/42, 296–7; CW, 4/30/43, 9–10, 10/29/43, 2; AtM, 7/44, 49–

50; *Cross and the Flag,* 4/42, 2, 5/42, 2, 3, 3/43, 17, 9/43, 268–9, 12/43, 315, 3/44, 363, 10/44, 455, 3/45, 530.

[27] AJYB, v 46, 141; CJR, 2/44, 65, 4/44, 179; CW, 1/2/42, 3, 11/19/43, 20; NJM, 12/43, 114, 2/44, 178; JV, 6/42, 15, 12/42, 7; *Tomorrow,* 9/44, 55.

[28] NYT, 11/16/42, 21, 12/30/43, 19, 1/11/44, 1, 24; CW, 1/2/42, 3, 10/23/42, 2, 4/2/43, 2, 11/5/43, 20; JV, 12/42, 7–8; NJM, 2/44, 178; *PM,* 8/10/44, 13.

[29] CJR, 12/43, 637–8, 2/44, 65; NJM, 11/43, 82; CW, 10/29/43, 4, 7, 12/10/43, 2; AtM, 7/44, 45–52; NYT, 11/10/43, 19; *PM,* 4/30/44, 6; LJ, 9/44, 57; AJYB, v 46, 141; *Time,* 6/12/44, 81.

[30] AJYB, v 46, 141, 491; JV, 12/42, 4, 2/43, 13; Stember, 115–20; NYT, 1/11/44, 24, 4/8/44, 2; CW, 9/24/43, 20; quotation is from *Common Ground,* summer 1943, 17; and CW, 4/9/43, 9.

[31] Stember, 135; AJYB, v 47, 162–4.

[32] AJYB, v 46, 141; JV, 12/42, 4, 2/43, 13, 3/43, 8; *PM,* 12/22/42, 6; CW, 4/30/43, 9; Gilbert Cant, *America's Navy in World War II* (1943), 91; quotation is from AtM, 7/44, 50.

[33] Quotations are from G—— to Bennet, 7/10/45, A. W. Bennet Papers, B 25, F 1, J Affairs; and W 3, Anonymous File. The latter contains several such letters, as do various archives, including SW, Jewish-Christian Relations file; and Legis 17436, Com VI Incoming Corresp.

[34] See, eg, CW, 2/11/44, 4; *Sat Review of Literature,* 1/27/45, 7–9; Chr R, 2/45, 60–1, 5/45, 175, 191–2.

[35] Diary of F. Stark, 2/20/44, PRO, FO 371/40130/8902; IJPS release, 6/11/43; Am Civil Liberties Union, *In Defense of Our Liberties* (1944), 11.

[36] NJM, 9/44, 32; *Christianity & Crisis,* 2/5/45, 8.

[37] Sylvia N[eulander] to Alice, 6/9/45, JDC, Refs, Children. For other evidence of anti-Semitism in the armed forces, see page 324n; and JV, 12/42, 4, 2/43, 13.

[38] JPC 3379; Mins of MASC, 5/11/43, Mayerson, Petluck, & Kaplan drafts, NRS 326; CW, 9/24/43, 20–1.

[39] AJYB, v 46, 137, 142, v 47, 268–70, 277; CJR, 6/43, 279; CW, 4/9/43, 2, 9/24/43, 20–1; Op, 3/45, 4; NYP, 6/27/44, 20; *Am Mercury,* 7/44, 31–7; NYT, 6/5/41, 24; CR, v 89, A1471, v 90, 1418; *Time,* 2/14/44, 17; Legis 16443; IR, 5/7/45, 108.

[40] Stember, 53–62.

[41] Ibid, 120–5.

[42] RD, 9/42, 2–4; Stember, 124.

[43] Stember, 127–8.

[44] Ibid, 131–3. Support for an anti-Semitic campaign ranged from 11 to 19%; sympathy for one ranged from 20 to 31%.

CHAPTER 2.
THE NEWS FILTERS OUT

[1] Hilberg, 619, 652; Hilberg (ed), *Documents of Destruction,* 194; YVS, v 7, 52.

[2] The statement on American newspapers is based on extensive research in 10 major newspapers and less comprehensive use of many others.

[3] Alex Grobman, "Reaction of American Jewry through the American and Jewish Press 1939–1942," MA thesis, Hebrew Univ of Jerusalem (1978), 73–4, 77; CW, 1/16/42, 3; NJM, 12/41, 114; NYHT, 12/5/41, 26; NYT, 10/26/41, 6, 10/28/41, 10, 11/2/41, 24.

[4] Grobman, "Reaction of Am Jewry," 85; NJM, 1/42, 175, 2/42, 179–80; CW, 1/2/42, 16; JF, 3/42, 10–11; CJR, 6/42, 311, 8/42, 430; NYT, 4/6/42, 2, 5/19/42, 3, 5/31/42, 17, 6/26/42, 5; *Life,* 2/23/42, 26–7; *Time,* 2/23/42, 34.

[5] NYT, 3/14/42, 7; NJM, 5/42, 292; CW, 3/20/42, 3; Grobman, "Reaction of Am Jewry," 86.

[6] NYT, 3/14/42, 7; Hilberg, 460–8; Memo on Telephone Convsn with Dr. Schwartz in Lisbon, 3/12/42, JDC, Rpts, Eur Telephone Convsns.

7 NYT, 5/18/42, 4.

8 Mds, 4/68, 52.

9 Ibid, 54–8.

10 NYT, 7/2/42, 6.

11 Mds, 4/68, 52–3; BG, 6/26/42, 12; NYT, 6/27/42, 5, 6/30/42, 7; PFR, 7/15/42, 3.

12 This discussion of newspaper coverage is based on systematic study of 10 major American newspapers: *Boston Globe, Chicago Tribune, Dallas News, Denver Post, Kansas City Star, Los Angeles Times, New York Times, San Francisco Examiner, Seattle Times,* and *Washington Post.*

13 NYT, 6/27/42, 5.

14 NYT, 6/30/42, 7.

15 Eg, WP, 6/30/42, 2; CT, 6/30/42, 6; LAT, 6/30/42, 3; KCS, 6/29/42, 8. Exceptions were NYT, 6/30/42, 7; ST, 6/29/42, 1.

16 PFR, 7/15/42, 4.

17 Ibid, 8.

18 Johnson to SS, 7/16/42, SD 862.4016/2229; Biddle to SS, 8/13/42, SD, EW/527.

19 RYP, 7/8/42, 7/16/42; CW, 6/26/42, 3, 7/10/42, 3; Grobman, "Reaction of Am Jewry," 89–90; NYT, 7/22/42, 4.

20 NYT, 7/22/44, 1, 4; Op, 8/42, 4.

21 CW, 8/14/42, 1; NYT, 7/22/42, 1.

22 CW, 8/14/42, 2.

23 Ibid, 3–4; JF, 8/42, 27; NJM, 9/42, 2; Op, 8/42, 4; RYP, 7/24/42.

24 CJR, 10/42, 520; CR, v 88, 6537; AJYB, v 45, 192.

25 CW, 8/14/42, 15.

26 NYT, 7/22, 1, 4; CT, 7/22, 7, 7/23, 17, 7/24, 6; LAT, 8/5, 10, 8/7, 13, 8/9, II, 8, 8/11, II, 2, 8/12, II, 8, 8/13, II, 1. All dates in 1942.

27 *Catholic Worker,* 6/43, 1.

28 PFR, 7/15/42, 7.

29 A. J. P. Taylor, *English History, 1914–1945* (1965), 19.

30 Cantril, 383, 1070–1; H. C. Peterson, *Propaganda for War* (1939); Arthur Ponsonby, *Falsehood in War-Time* (1928); James Squires, *British Propaganda at Home and in the United States from 1914 to 1917* (1935).

31 See pages 321–2.

32 See pages 311–21, 327n.

33 Eg, NYT, 2/3/42, 10, 6/18/42, 13, 7/27/42, 3, 9/22/42, 1, 10/2/42, 3, 2/14/43, 37; WP, 6/18/42, 1, 2, 8/16/42, 2, 9/11/42, 10.

34 NYT, 4/12/42, 1, 6/11/42, 1, 6/12/42, 6; WP, 8/22/42, 1; PFR, 7/1/42, 1, 7/15/42, 3–4.

35 Jan Ciechanowski, *Defeat in Victory* (1947), 118; *Memoirs of Cordell Hull* (1948), 1184.

36 NYT, 6/13/42, 7.

37 NYT, 8/22/42, 1, 10/8/42, 1; FR 1942, v 1, 48–71; FR 1942, v 3, 772–7.

38 WP, 8/30/42, 12; SFE, 8/30/42, B; NYT, 8/6/42, 7.

39 Donald Lowrie, *The Hunted Children* (1963), chs 5–17; Lowrie 1.

40 Hilberg, 407; Michael R. Marrus and Robert O. Paxton, *Vichy France and the Jews* (1981), 233–4, 246, 305, 308–9, 325–30. Marrus and Paxton point out that the Nazis and the Vichy authorities made no definite agreement for the exemption of the French-born Jews. They also thoroughly demonstrate Vichy's complicity in the deportations.

41 Hilberg, 408; Gerald Reitlinger, *The Final Solution* (1953), 318; CW, 10/9/42, 16; NYT, 7/26/42, 16, 9/6/42, 14.

42 MD 688I/29–30; Fate of J Children in France [11/43], JDC, France, Children; Confidential mins of for serv staff mtg, 3/27/44, AF, FS.

43 MJ, 4/45, 96; Reitlinger, *Final Solution,* 319–20.

44 Hilberg, 408; Lowrie 1.

45 Lowrie 2; Lowrie 3; Schwartz to JDC-NY, 8/13/42, JDC, G/E, France, Refs.

46 NR, 12/21/42, 817; Lowrie 1.

47 Lowrie 1; Lowrie, *Hunted,* 218–9; NYT, 9/12/42, 2.

48 Lowrie 3; "Baden-Baden Report" (AF Activities in France to 11/42), 6/13/43, AF, GF, For Serv, Fr, Relief & Refs,

Genl; ltr on deportations, 9/4/42, u/c Hyman to Pickett, 11/16/42, AF, GF 2; Lowrie, *Hunted,* 226.

[49] Lowrie 3; Hilberg, 409; MJ, 4/45, 96; Reitlinger, *Final Solution,* 326.

[50] Lowrie 2; Schwartz to Leavitt, 8/13/42, Noble to Ref Div, 9/11, 9/26, & 10/12/42, all in AF, RS 1.

[51] Marcuse to Frawley, 11/11/42, AF, GF 3.

[52] Ibid; Marcuse to Frank, 11/20/42, AF, GF, German J Children's Aid (now missing).

[53] AF Mins, For Serv Section, 9/24/42.

[54] NYT, 8/27/42, 3, 9/9/42, 9; CJR, 10/42, 526, 12/42, 646.

[55] NYT, 8/6/42, 1, 8/27/42, 3, 9/3/42, 5; CJR, 10/42, 526; John Morley, *Vatican Diplomacy and the Jews During the Holocaust, 1939–1943* (1980), 56–9, 68.

[56] CJR, 12/42, 647.

[57] CJR, 10/42, 527, 12/42, 645; Lowrie 3.

[58] Lowrie to Strong, 10/7/42, AF, GF 2; NYT, 7/26/42, 16, 9/6/42, 14; WP, 9/5/42, 10; CJR, 12/42, 635; Lowrie 3.

[59] NYT, 9/9/42, 9, 9/11/42, 4, 9/18/42, 9; Lowrie 3; CJR, 12/42, 635; Dexter to Clinchy, 11/9/42, CH, B 6, Ref Orgzns; MD 688II/195; Rescue Activities for Children in France [5/24/44], The Fate of J Children in France [11/43], JDC, France, Children; WH, 56; FSR, 30–1.

[60] Lowrie, Confidential Memo, 9/19/42, CH, B 6, Ref Orgzns; Lowrie 3; CJR, 12/42, 635; NYT, 9/9/42, 9, 9/18/42, 1, 9/22/42, 5; MJ, 4/45, 95.

[61] Lowrie, *Hunted,* 204; Lowrie, Notes on Interview with Marshal Pétain, 10/19/42, AF, GF 2; Lowrie 2.

[62] FR 1942, v 1, 463–5; FR 1942, v 2, 710–2; Atherton to Welles, 9/3/42, SD, R/3080; NYT, 9/5/42, 3; CJR, 12/42, 648–9.

[63] CJR, 10/42, 519; DN, 9/16/42, 1; Hiatt, Interview with Henry-Haye, 9/18/42, AF, GF 2.

[64] Lowrie 2; Lowrie, Notes on Interview with Marshal Pétain, 10/19/42, AF, GF 2; FR 1942, v 1, 464; Lowrie, *Hunted,* 218; 55th Mtg of PAC, 9/9/42, JM, P66; MD 692/288, 694/86; JPC 655; Frawley to Hiatt, 10/2/42, AF, GF 3; Warren to PAC, 10/16/42, JM, P66; FR 1942, v 2, 713.

[65] FR 1942, v 2, 714–5.

[66] Noble, "Diary," 10/26 & 11/5/42, Noble, Notes on Cfs, 10/16/42, Mins of Mtg, 10/27/42, all in AF, RS 1.

[67] FR 1942, v 2, 715–6; Noble, "Diary," 10/26 & 11/5/42, AF, RS 1; McDonald & Warren to Welles, 12/1/42, JM, P66; MD 721/259; Warren to PAC, 2/17/43, JM, P67.

[68] This paragraph and the following one are based on analysis of the newspapers listed in source note 12 of this chapter. LAT, 8/30/42, 7.

[69] NYT, 8/6/42, 1, 9/18/42, 1.

[70] NYT, 7/26/42, 16, 7/30/42, 9, 9/12/42, 2, 9/23/42, 10; CT, 7/26/42, 9; WP, 8/7/42, 2; ST, 8/9/42, 15; Smolen, 194; Rudolf Hoess, *Commandant of Auschwitz* (1959), 208.

[71] NYT, 9/20/42, 13, 10/29/42, 2, 11/18/42, 3, 11/27/42, 3.

[72] NYT, 9/20/42, 1, 9/27/42, 9; Edward Homze, *Foreign Labor in Nazi Germany* (1967), 180–1; DP, 8/27/42, 32; ST, 9/6/42, 2.

[73] Lowrie 2; Lowrie to Strong, 10/7/42, AF, GF 2.

[74] Niles, Case Com Rpt, 10/13/42, USC, Case Com.

[75] WP, 8/16/42, 2; KCS, 8/15/42, 1; LAT, 8/16/42, 3; Hilberg, 313, 320, 323.

[76] *The Ghetto Speaks,* 8/5/42.

[77] Mds, 5/68, 62–3, 10/82, 7; JF, 9/42, 28–9.

CHAPTER 3.

THE WORST IS CONFIRMED

¹ Elting, Memorandum, 8/8/42, SD 862.4016/2234; Wise, 274; *Das Neue Israel* (Zurich), 11/68, 359; Riegner-Jarvik interview, 10/4/78. This summary follows Riegner's description of the events. Other views appear in Shlomo Derech's introduction to the Hebrew edition of Arthur Morse, *While Six Million Died* (1972), in Yehuda Bauer, *The Holocaust in Historical Perspective* (1978), 158, and in Monty Penkower, *The Jews Were Expendable* (1983), 59–63. Terrence Des Pres suggests an intriguing alternative explanation in NR, 1/31/81, 33.

Riegner and the others, at the German's request, agreed to keep his name secret forever. In 1983, however, 3 historians (Monty Penkower, Richard Breitman, and Alan Kraut) reported that they had identified the German industrialist as Eduard Schulte (NYT, 11/9/83, 2; *Commentary*, 10/83, 44–6, 1/84, 4).

² MD 690/39; Elting, Memorandum, 8/8/42, SD 862.4016/2234.

³ Elting, Memorandum, 8/8/42, Elting to SS, 8/10/42, SD 862.4016/2234.

⁴ Harrison to SS, 8/11/42, Culbertson to Wise, 8/13/42 (not sent), Hull to Bern, 8/17/42, SD 862.4016/2233; Atherton to Welles, 9/3/42, SD, R/3080.

⁵ P.T.C. to J.W.J., 8/13/42, SD 862.4016/2233; Durbrow, Memorandum, 8/13/42, SD 862.4016/2235.

⁶ Hull to Bern, 8/17/42 (unrevised version), SD 862.4016/2233.

⁷ EHR, 91–2.

⁸ EHR, 91–3; Wise, 275; Silverman to Wise, 8/28/42, SD, EW/553.

⁹ Wise to Welles, 9/2/42, SD, R/3080. In his autobiography, Wise stated that he "immediately" contacted Welles (Wise, 275). In fact, he waited 4 or 5 days before communicating with Welles.

¹⁰ A notation on Wise's letter of 9/2/42 to Welles shows that Welles

phoned Wise on 9/3/42; Voss, 249; Wise, 275.

¹¹ Barou & Easterman to Wise [9/1/42], SD 862.4016/2238.

¹² Rosenheim to FDR, 9/3/42, SD, EW/570; PR, 1977 (v 22/4), 5.

¹³ Schenkolewski & Tress to McDonald, 9/3/42, JM, P49; Rosenheim to FDR, 9/3/42, SD, EW/570; McDonald's secy to ER, 9/4/42, JM, P 43.

¹⁴ PR, 1977 (v 22/4), 5–6; *Polityka* (Warsaw), 8/9/75; Voss, 249–50.

¹⁵ Hilberg, 614, 623–4; CW, 12/4/42, 13.

¹⁶ PR, 1977 (v 22/4), 4–7; AI, Bern, to Rosenheim, 9/4/42, Hopkins Papers (FDRL): Sherwood Collection, B 313, Book 5, Atrocities Comm; PR, 1979 (v 24/1), 48; *Polityka,* 8/9/75.

¹⁷ Voss, 248–50; Justine W. Polier and James W. Wise (eds), *The Personal Letters of Stephen Wise, 1933–1949* (1956), 260–1. Walter Laqueur's *The Terrible Secret* has left the impression that American Jewish leaders were slow to believe that systematic extermination was occurring (pp. 3, 157–62, 194–5, and possibly 121–2; also, *Commentary,* 12/79, 44). That impression is inaccurate. Once aware of Riegner's report, virtually all Jewish leaders in America recognized that extermination was under way.

¹⁸ NYT, 11/24/42, 10; GCM, 11/12/42; Voss, 250; MD 688II/223Q.

¹⁹ Voss, 250–1; HID, 7053; Wyman, 112–4.

²⁰ Voss, 249–51.

²¹ HID, 7053–4; FDR to Ickes, 10/10/42, Ickes to FDR, 1/13/43, FDR, OF 3186; BLD, 258–60; GCM, 11/12/42; Wise to Frankfurter, 9/16/42, SW, Corresp, Frankfurter.

²² JMJ, 9/20/42; JTA, 10/6/42, 4.

²³ NJM, 10/42, 36–7.

²⁴ NYT, 10/30/42, 2.

²⁵ Mds, 5/68, 62, 10/82, 6–7; JF, 11/42, 3.

[26] JF, 11/42, 3.

[27] Ibid.

[28] Hull to Bern, 9/23/42, SD, EW/597A; FR 1942, v 3, 775–7; document from Taylor at Vatican City, 11/23/42, SD, EW/726.

[29] MD 688II/223Q; Harrison to SS, 9/26/42, SD, EW/599.

[30] MD 688II/223Q; Harrison to SS, 11/23/42, SD, EW/653.

[31] Squire to SS, 9/28/42, with enclosures, SD 862.4016/2242; CW, 12/4/42, 8.

[32] Date stamps on Squire to SS, 9/28/42, SD 862.4016/2242.

[33] Squire to SS, 10/29/42 (not sent), SD 862.4016/10-2942; Harrison to SS, 11/23/42, SD, EW/653; Squire to Harrison, 11/9/42, Squire's memo of 11/7/42 interview with Burckhardt, 11/9/42, both in files of Gerhart Riegner, Geneva; Morse, 18–21.

[34] NYT, 11/25/42, 10; CW, 12/4/42; Wise, 275; Gottschalk to Waldman, 11/27/42, AJC, Genl Record, Germany Nazism 42–43.

[35] Wise, 275–6; Mins of Sub-Com of Special Cf on Eur Affs, 11/30/42, AJC, JEC; MD 688II/243; Gottschalk to Waldman, 11/27/42, AJC, Genl Record, Germany Nazism 42–43.

[36] Gottschalk to Waldman, 11/27/42, is especially convincing. It is notes of Wise's meeting with other Jewish leaders on the morning following the conference with Welles.

[37] NYHT, 11/25/42, 1.

[38] NYT, 11/25/42, 10, 11/26/42, 16; Gottschalk to Waldman, 11/27/42, AJC, Genl Record, Germany Nazism 42–43; WP, 11/26/42, 19B.

[39] NYT, 11/24/42, 10, 11/25/42, 10; Smolen, 193–4.

[40] NYT, 11/25/42, 10.

[41] NYT, 11/26/42, 16, 11/28/42, 7; CW, 12/4/42, 14–5.

[42] Hilberg, 337; *Shoah,* spr 1981, 20.

[43] Hilberg, 266; also NYT, 10/1/42, 8.

[44] Yehuda Bauer in Mds, 4/68, 51–8.

[45] Eg, *Dimensions in Am Judaism,* spr 1968, 11.

[46] EHR, 93; GCM, 11/12/42.

[47] Wyman, passim.

[48] Legis 15924; Emanuel Celler, *You Never Leave Brooklyn* (1953), 90–2; Celler to FDR, 10/10/42, FDR, OF 3186.

[49] CW, 10/23/42, 4; NYT, 10/4/42, 17; *Reconstructionist,* 10/30/42, 7; J *Forum,* 10/42, 162; Celler to Dickstein, 10/21/42, Clerk to Celler, 11/10/42, Legis 15924; RYP, 10/1/42.

[50] NYT, 11/4/42, 1, 11/5/42, 1; Burns, 280–1.

[51] CD, 1/43, 10; *Newsweek,* 11/30/42, 11.

[52] NYT, 11/3/42, 1, 11.

[53] CD, 1/43, 6–9.

[54] NYT, 11/4/42, 22, 11/19/42, 1; CD, 1/43, 10; CT, 12/13/42, 1; DP, 11/29/42, 2.

[55] BLD, 270; RCA, "Question of Bringing . . . ," 1/29/43, BLP, B 212, Genl (VD); NYT, 11/22/42, 1, 20, 11/29/42, 24, 12/2/42, 1, 12/5/42, 7, 12/11/42, 48.

[56] BLD, 270.

[57] Ibid; *Newsweek,* 11/30/42, 11.

[58] Wyman, 212–3 & passim.

[59] Hilberg, 718.

CHAPTER 4.

FIRST STEPS

[1] The 19 newspapers include the 10 listed in ch 2, source note 12, along with *Atlanta Constitution, Boston Herald, Christian Science Monitor, Cleveland Plain Dealer, Miami Herald, New Orleans Times-Picayune, New York Herald Tribune, New York Post,* and *PM.* Those providing page-1 notice were *Dallas News, Denver Post, Miami Herald, NY Herald Tribune,* and *PM.* Those that did not carry the story were *Kansas City Star* and *New Orleans Times-Picayune.*

[2] Based on analysis of the 10 news-

papers listed in ch 2, source note 12. The time covered was Nov 27 through Dec 31, 1942.

³ The single first-page report appeared on 12/18/42.

⁴ PC/FDR. The brief comment made by FDR on Nov 5, 1943, touched only obliquely on the Holocaust. The first clear comment on mass killing of Jews came on March 24, 1944.

⁵ Eliyho Matzozky, unpublished study, "American Jewish Press Reaction to the Mass Killing, Nov 24, 1942 to Mar 4, 1943" (1978).

⁶ Based on a sampling of *California J Voice* (LA), *Every Friday* (Cincinnati), *Intermountain J News* (Denver), *J Examiner* (Brooklyn), *J Review* (NYC); and an unpublished study by Edward Mainzer, "The *Ohio Jewish Chronicle* [Columbus] 1941–43" (1980).

⁷ Eg, *J Forum*, 12/42, 193; CW, 12/18/42, 4.

⁸ *Nation*, 12/19/42, 668–9; NR, 12/7/42, 728.

⁹ *Am Mercury*, 2/43, 194–203; RD, 2/43, 107–10; *Time*, 12/28/42, 24; *Newsweek*, 12/28/42, 46.

¹⁰ NYT, 11/29/42, 44, 12/24/42, 6, 12/26/42, 4.

¹¹ Mtg of PC, 12/17/42, WJC, U185/3; draft of fund appeal ltr, 12/28/42, SW, AJCg, L. Shultz.

¹² PC Mtg Mins, 12/29/42, WJC, U185/2.

¹³ NYT, 12/28/42, 5, 13; PC Mtg Mins, 12/29/42, WJC, U185/2; draft of fund appeal ltr, 12/28/42, SW, AJCg, L. Shultz.

¹⁴ Wyman, 74; *Commonweal*, 12/11/42, 204–5, 12/18/42, 220.

¹⁵ CW, 1/8/43, 7. The Church Peace Union publicized the extermination situation in its *World Alliance News Letter*, especially 12/42, 9/43, 1/44, 6/44, 12/15/44.

¹⁶ Moss to Miller, 10/27/42, FCC, B 144, L. B. Moss files, Cleveland mtg, 12/42; "The Christian Church and the Jews

in Europe," 3/16/43, JM, P67; NYT, 12/21/42, 17.

¹⁷ CC to SD, 11/25/42, SD, EW/656.

¹⁸ McDermott to CC, 11/25/42, SD, EW/656.

¹⁹ CC, 1/13/43, 53.

²⁰ CC, 12/9/42, 1518–9.

²¹ CC, 12/30/42, 1611.

²² CC, 3/3/43, 253, 3/10/43, 284, 5/5/43, 533, 9/8/43, 1005, 5/24/44, 636; Voss-Wyman interview, 2/11/78; Robert Ross, *So It Was True* (1980), 5.

²³ Eg, CC, 2/11/42, 173, 6/17/42, 772, 1/13/43, 53, 4/12/44, 453; Voss, 256; NP, 6/15/45, 229.

²⁴ WP, 11/26/42, 19B.

²⁵ Gottschalk to Waldman, 11/27/42, AJC, Genl Record, Germany Nazism 42–43; NYT, 11/25/42, 10, 11/26/42, 16; *Bulletin of the WJC*, 1/43, 1; GCM, 11/12/42; *PM*, 11/26/42, 12.

²⁶ This and the following seven paragraphs are based on information in AJYB, v 45.

²⁷ *Am J Archives*, 6/55, 203–9; Wise, 216.

²⁸ Wise, 216–32.

²⁹ Ibid; Wise to Easterman, 1/25/43, WJC, U142/19.

³⁰ Voss, 251; Voss-Wyman interview, 2/11/78.

³¹ *Dimensions in Am Judaism*, fall 1968, 36; *Who's Who in Am*, v 22 (1942–43); Carl Voss, *Rabbi and Minister* (1964), 317.

³² Mins of Sub-Com of Special Cf on Eur Affs, 11/30/42, AJC, JEC; Gottschalk to Waldman, 11/27/42, AJC, Genl Record, Germany Nazism 42–43.

³³ Same as preceding note.

³⁴ Same as preceding note. Also, CW, 12/4/42, 15–6, 12/11/42, 8–11; CJR, 2/43, 34–5.

³⁵ WP, 11/30, 8, 12/1, 10, 12/2, 10, 12/5, 8, 12/15, 8, 12/18, 12 (all in 1942).

³⁶ CW, 1/8/43, 2, 13. This step seems to have been the only outcome of a plan to convene a conference of prominent American Christians to help find ways to

publicize the mass murder and press the government to act (GCM, 11/12/42).

[37] AJYB, v 45, 193; CW, 12/4/42, 16; Mins of Sub-Com of Special Cf on Eur Affs, 11/30/42, AJC, JEC.

[38] Mins of Sub-Com of Special Cf on Eur Affs, 11/30/42, AJC, JEC; JLC, Mins of Mtg, 12/2/42 (in Yiddish), JLC Archives.

[39] AJYB, v 45, 193; CW, 12/18/42, 13.

[40] DN, 12/3/42, II, 1.

[41] Several documents (11/30–12/4/42) on arranging the meeting are in FDR, OF 76C. Included is Wise's letter to FDR, 12/2/42. GCM, 11/12/42.

[42] NYT, 12/9/42, 20; CW, 12/11/42, 2. Rabbi Israel Goldstein (Synagogue Council of Am) was scheduled to attend the meeting but was unable to do so (NJM, 1/43, 146). FDR did see the seven Jewish congressmen on Apr 1, 1943. He also saw Wise alone (but Holocaust issues were involved only incidentally) on Jul 22, 1943. On four other occasions (Mar 9 & Oct 11, 1944, & Jan 22 & Mar 16, 1945), he saw Wise, alone or with Abba Hillel Silver, but the topic was the issue of Palestine statehood.

[43] Adolph Held, "Report on the Visit to the President" [12/8/42], JLC Archives, Pt 3, Sect 1 #15, Communication with the White House 1942; Wise et al to FDR, 12/8/42, FDR, OF 76C.

[44] Wise et al to FDR, 12/8/42, FDR, OF 76C.

[45] Held, "Report," JLC Archives; "Blue Print for Extermination," 12/8/42, FDR, OF 76C.

[46] Held, "Report," JLC Archives.

[47] Ibid.

[48] Ibid.

[49] MD 688II/243; WP, 12/9/42, 18; CW, 12/11/42, 1–2.

[50] Based on analysis of the 10 newspapers listed in ch 2, source note 12. Four did not mention the event; the others placed their reports well inside their issues. NYT, 12/9/42, 20; WP, 12/9/42, 18.

[51] GCM, 12/10/42; Jt Emerg Com on Eur J Affs, 9/28/43, AJC, JEC.

[52] FR 1942, v 1, 66–7; EHR, 98–103; Barou & Easterman to Perlzweig, 12/17/42, WJC, 177A/50; Easterman to Perlzweig, 1/15/43, WJC, U142/13.

[53] Eddy to Gordon, 12/7/42, SD 862.4016/2251.

[54] Reams to Hickerson & Atherton, 12/10/42, SD, EW/674; Berle, Memo of Convsn with Vahervuori, 12/8/42, SD, R/3495½.

[55] Reams to Hickerson & Atherton, 12/9/42, SD, EW/694. Concerning Reams's repeated assertions that the State Department had not confirmed the extermination reports, see the footnote on page 51.

[56] Reams to Hickerson & Atherton, 12/10/42, SD, EW/694.

[57] Ibid.

[58] Ibid; FR 1942, v 1, 68.

[59] Text in NYT, 12/18/42, 10; EHR, 82.

[60] Barou & Easterman to Perlzweig, 12/17/42, WJC, 177A/50; MD 688II/244; FR 1942, v 1, 70.

[61] Based on analysis of the 10 newspapers listed in ch 2, source note 12.

[62] NYT, 12/20/42, 23. Same sample as in preceding note.

[63] CW, 12/25/42, 3; NYT, 12/18/42, 26.

[64] NYT, 12/18/42, 26; CW, 12/25/42, 3; NYP, 12/18/42, 37.

[65] Op, 1/43, 5, 16; J Forum, 12/42, 193; CC, 1/6/43, 26.

[66] NYT, 12/5/42, 16.

[67] GCM, 12/3/42; "Proposals" [12/10/42], WJC, 264/1; Bulletin of the WJC, 1/43, 2.

[68] "Proposals" [12/10/42], WJC, 264/1; GCM, 12/10/42.

[69] Same as preceding note. Also, PC, outline of projects, 12/14/42, WJC, U186/A; Shultz, Memorandum, 12/10/42, WJC, U185/3; Activities of AJCg & WJC with Respect to Hitler Program [1/43], WJC, U185/2.

[70] PC, outline of projects, 12/14/42, WJC, U186/A; Special Com on Eur Situation, Mins, 12/14/42, Mtg of PC, 12/17/42, WJC, U185/3. For an example of OWI's unwillingness to emphasize the Jewish situation, see NYT, 2/14/43, 37.

[71] PC Mtg Mins, 12/29/42, WJC, U185/2.

[72] GCM, 1/12/43, 12/3/42, 12/10/42; Rpt of PC, 1/12/43, AJCg; Activities of AJCg & WJC [1/43], WJC, U185/2; Special Com on Eur Situation, Mins, 12/14/42, WJC, U185/3. For an insider's perspective, see Mds, 3/64, 8–9.

[73] Burns, 123–4; John H. Franklin, *From Slavery to Freedom,* 3rd edn (1969), 578–9.

[74] NYT, 11/28, 11, 11/29, 46, 11/30, 11, 12/5, 9, 12/7, 32, 12/16, 14 (all in 1942); FR 1942, v 4, 550; CW, 12/11/42, 12; NP, 1/8/43, 3, 1/22/43, 4; RW 2/23; Mds, 3/64, 5–10; *YV Bulletin,* 4/57, 4.

CHAPTER 5.
STRUGGLE FOR ACTION

[1] Cantril, 383.

[2] MD 688II/244.

[3] Mds, 3/64, 5–10; GCM, 1/12/43, 2/4/43; CW, 2/26/43, 4–7; Memo to Wise, Goldmann, et al, 1/19/43, WJC, U285/2; JF, 3/43, 15–17. The courier, who was unnamed in these reports, was Jan Karski.

[4] MD 688II/99, 223R–S; Riegner & Lichtheim to Wise, 1/19/43, WJC, 267/8.

[5] Welles to Wise, 2/9/43, WJC, 267/8.

[6] MD 688II/100, 223-T.

[7] MD 688II/207; Josiah E. DuBois, Jr., *The Devil's Chemists* (1952), 188.

[8] MD 688II/100, 223L–M, 247, 694/199–200, 813/63–8; Hull (by Welles) to Bern, 4/10/43, SD 862. 4016/2266A.

[9] Covered in ch 10.

[10] Pr Rel, 2/14/43, WJC, U222/3; NYT, 2/14/43, 37.

[11] NYT, 2/13/43, 5. Value of lei based on Hilberg, 503–6.

[12] Mins of ZOA Exec Com, 2/20/43, SW, ZOA Exec Com; MD 609/39, 610/208.

[13] Hull to Ankara, 2/17/43, SD, R/3603; MD 611/276–7.

[14] MD 611/275; Welles to Wagner, 3/10/43, RW 2/23; Welles to Davis, 3/11/43, SD, R/3608.

[15] Proposals for Relief and Evacn of Refs [7/43], BLP, B 203, Ref Mvt & Natl Groups.

[16] Hilberg, 504; Julius Fisher, *Transnistria: The Forgotten Cemetery* (1969), 130–1; Proposals for Relief [7/43] (section on Rumania), BLP, B 203, Ref Mvt & Natl Groups.

[17] In late spring 1943, overtures again came out of Rumania for the release of thousands of Jews. Again, the chance was not pursued. (AI Rpt, 4th, 4.)

[18] NYT, 2/16/43, 11; H Con Res 60, 11/28/41, Legis 15912; Ans, 2/46, 10–11; van Paassen to Daniels, 7/31/42, Josephus Daniels Papers (LC), B 816, Folder P; JV, 5/42, 5; Aaron Berman, "The HCNL and the Rescue of the European Jews," Hampshire College thesis (1975), 16. Same sources apply to following paragraph.

[19] Yehuda Bauer, *Flight and Rescue: BRICHAH* (1970), 62; Howard Sachar, *A History of Israel* (1979), 232–3; *J Affairs,* 10/41, 6.

[20] *J Affairs,* 10/41, 2–10; NYT, 2/5/42, 12, 2/11/42, 11, 3/22/42, 45, 9/20/44, 12; Sachar, *Israel,* 230–2; Yehuda Bauer, *From Diplomacy to Resistance* (1970), 202, 355; Bauer, *Flight,* 63–6, 96–101.

[21] Berman to Wise, 4/29/42, SW, Zm; NYT, 12/7/42, 15; *J Affairs,* 10/41; Ans, 2/46, 4, 11; Kook-Cohen interview, 9/26/68, 11–13, PSC 11/33.

[22] Kook-Cohen interview, 9/26/68, 11–18; Kook-Wyman interview, 5/5/73.

Wartime conditions blocked contact between the Irgun in the US and the Irgun in Palestine from late 1940 until late 1943. Even in Jan 1945, the FBI and the British Intelligence reported that no connection between the two existed. Actually, a very few contacts did take place during 1944 and 1945, and a small amount of money was sent to Palestine. (Kook-Cohen interview, 9/26/68, 15–18; Wright to Baxter, 1/31/45, Russell to Hill, 1/31/45, PRO, FO 371/45398/8385.) Also see footnote on page 149.

[23] Ans, 6/15/44, 9, 11; NYP, 7/11/44, 29; Kook-Wyman interview, 4/14/73.

[24] Bauer, *From Diplomacy,* 236, 313, 316; Sachar, *Israel,* 188; Robert Silverberg, *If I Forget Thee O Jerusalem* (1970), 207; Bergson to Wise, 5/7/41, Wise to Bergson, 6/4/41, PSC 1/5. Also see below, appendix B.

[25] Bauer, *From Diplomacy,* 14, 315, 319; Berman, "The HCNL and Rescue," 13; NYT, 2/26/44, 4, 3/5/44, 19, 8/24/44, 7, 9/29/44, 8.

[26] Ans, 3/45, 6, 20–1, 2/46, 8; Nemzer, Memo for the Files [3/1/44], PSC 3/64; Kook-Cohen interview, 9/26/68, 12, 15–8; Lubinski to Ziff, 5/20/39, 6/30/39, PSC 1/1; Bergson to Wise, 5/7/41, Bergson to Silver, 5/25/41, PSC 1/5.

[27] Ans, 2/46, 11; Merlin to Shubow, 3/20/43, AJHS, AJCg, Uncataloged Box, F:CJA.

[28] NYT, 12/5/42, 16.

[29] Ans, 6/15/44, 11; AJHQ, 9/77, 57.

[30] NYT, 2/8/43, 8; *J Review & Observer* (Cleveland), 2/19/43, PSC, Reel 18; Stmt by Sen Edwin C. Johnson, 2/24/43, PSC 4/8.

[31] NYT, 2/16/43, 11. Same source for the following two paragraphs.

[32] Op, 3/43, 14; NP, 3/5/43, 4; Mins of ZOA Exec Com, 2/20/43, 3/11/43, SW, ZOA Exec Com; *B'nai B'rith Messenger,* 4/9/43, PSC, Reel 18; JF, 3/43, 8; CW, 2/26/43, 16. The advertisement

remains, even today, a source of sharp controversy in some circles.

[33] NYHT, 2/22/43, 16. Eg, LAT, 2/22/43, 8; *Phila Inquirer,* 2/23/43, 15; NYT, 3/10/43, 10; *Phila Evening Bulletin,* 4/23/43, 12.

[34] Op, 4/43, 7; PC Mins, 12/29/42, WJC, U185/2; Smolar in *J Times* (Phila), 2/26/43, *J Times* (Baltimore), 2/12/43, *J Chronicle* (Columbus, O), 2/26/43, PSC, Reel 18; *J News* (Detroit), 3/12/43, PSC, S 13; Merlin to Ziff, 4/23/43, PSC 1/8; NYT, 2/27/43, 5.

[35] GCM, 1/12/43; PC Mins, 12/29/42, WJC, U185/2; Deutsch in *J Times* (Baltimore), 2/12/43, PSC, Reel 18.

[36] AJCg Pr Rel, 2/22/43, WJC, U222/3; NYT, 2/26/43, 14.

[37] NYT, 3/2/43, 1, 4, 39.

[38] CW, 3/5/43, 15; NYT, 3/2/43, 4; CR, v 89, 1571–6.

[39] NYT, 3/2/43, 4; CW, 3/5/43, 16.

[40] NYT, 3/3/43, 22.

[41] NYT, 12/18/42, 26, 3/3/43, 22; NYP, 3/6/43, 21; *NY Sun,* 3/3/43, 20; NYHT, 3/7/43, II, 3.

[42] L.C., Memorandum, 3/4/43, SD, R/3739; NYT, 3/4/43, 9; MD 688II/247–9; CW, 3/12/43, 3–4; FR 1943, v 1, 140–4.

[43] Wise to FDR, 3/4/43, FDR to Wise, 3/23/43, FDR, PPF 5029; Wise to Hull, 3/5/43, SD, EW/815; Wise to Dear Editor, to Dear Senator, to Dear Congressman, 3/9/43, WJC, U185/3.

[44] *Nation,* 3/13/43, 366–7.

[45] Ans, 4/43, 6, 9; *NY Sun,* 2/9/43, PSC, Reel 18; NYT, 2/25/43, 26; LJ, 6/43, 57.

[46] Rose to Niles, 2/22/43, Pringle to Hassett, 3/3/43, Early to Rose, 3/4/43, FDR, OF 76C.

[47] Hecht to Waldman, 1/26/43, Trager to Rosenblum, 2/1/43, AJC, Emerg Com file; Voss, 257.

[48] PC Mins, 12/29/42, WJC, U185/2; Merlin to Ziff, 4/23/43, PSC 1/8; Voss, 257.

[49] NYT, 3/10/43, 12, 37; *Variety,* 3/

10/43, *Radio Daily,* 3/11/43, PSC, S 13; *J Standard* (Jersey Cy), 4/16/43, PSC, Reel 18; *PM,* 3/8/43, 17.

⁵⁰ NYT, 3/10/43, 12; JTA, 3/10/43.

⁵¹ LJ, 6/43, 63; Rose to Niles, 2/22/43, FDR, OF 76C.

⁵² NYT, 3/10/43, 12, 4/13/43, 17; PSC, Folio 6, S 13 & 16, Reels 18 & 20; "We Will Never Die" (pamphlet), PSC 10/15; Ans, 5/43, 9, 2/46, 17.

⁵³ *Miami Herald,* 4/17/43, 10A.

⁵⁴ Smolar in *J Ledger* (Syracuse), 3/19/43, *J Chronicle* (Chicago), 4/2/43, PSC, Reel 18; PSC, S 13. Magazines that did not report on the pageant included CW, *J Forum,* JF, JO, JV, NJM, NP, Op.

⁵⁵ Rpt on Attempts to Stage "We Will Never Die" [early 1944], PSC 13/57; *Variety,* 3/10/43, PSC, S 13.

⁵⁶ Rpt on Attempts to Stage "We Will Never Die" [early 1944], PSC 13/57; Taslitt in *J Review & Observer,* 4/23/43, PSC, Reel 18.

⁵⁷ Eg, Smolar in *J Ledger,* 3/19/43, PSC, Reel 18; Op, 4/43, 7. Also see below, appendix B.

⁵⁸ Voss, 257; EmC; Mtg of JEC, 3/15/43, Jt Emerg Com on European J Affairs [9/28/43], Mtg of JEC, 11/5/43, AJC, JEC; AI Rpts, 4th, 5, and 5th, 10. Not affiliated, but represented by observers, were the JDC and the United Palestine Appeal (Rosenblum to Trager and Rothschild, 3/17/43, AJC, JEC).

⁵⁹ Mtg of JEC, 3/15/43, 3/22/43, Instructions for Organizing Public Mtgs [3/43], Trager to Schultz, Epstein, & Pat, 5/10/43, Proskauer to Gerstenfeld, 3/25/43, AJC, JEC.

⁶⁰ CW, 3/26/43, 13, 4/2/43, 16, 4/16/43, 16, 4/30/43, 21; CJR, 8/43, 394; CT, 4/15/43, 1; NYT, 3/31/43, 12; Trager to Schultz, Epstein, & Pat, 5/10/43, AJC, JEC.

⁶¹ Instructions for Organizing Public Mtgs [3/43], Waldman to Members of AJC, 3/25/43, Levy to Hexter, 5/5/43, Proskauer to Gerstenfeld, 3/25/43, AJC, JEC; Voss, 257.

⁶² EmC; Shultz to J. W. Wise, 1/6/43, WJC, 268/V; Activities of AJCg & WJC with Respect to Hitler Program [1/43], WJC, U185/2; Shultz to Levy, 2/24/43, RW 2/23.

⁶³ Berlin, Confidential Memorandum, 2/24/43, AHS, Ma I-62. Same source for following 2 paragraphs.

⁶⁴ NYT, 4/12/80, 30.

⁶⁵ CR, v 89, 1570–1.

⁶⁶ EmC; CR, v 89, 1723, 2184; NYT, 3/19/43, 11.

⁶⁷ NYT, 3/10/43, 12, 3/19/43, 11.

⁶⁸ EmC; Braunstein to Silver, 3/23/43, AHS, Ma I-81; Proskauer to Gerstenfeld, 3/25/43, Rosenblum to Trager & Rothschild, 3/17/43, AJC, JEC.

⁶⁹ EmC; Program (Action on Rescue by Jt Com) [3/43], Braunstein to Silver, 3/23/43, AHS, Ma I-81; Goldmann to Taylor, 3/24/43, SD, EW/959; Wise to Taylor, 3/22/43, SD, R/3860; Mtg of JEC, 3/22/43, AJC, JEC.

⁷⁰ Braunstein to Silver, 3/23/43, AHS, Ma I-81; Mtg of JEC, 3/22/43, AJC, JEC; Proskauer & Wise to Taylor, 3/22/43, SD, R/3860.

⁷¹ Min of Mtg of Jt Com, 3/29/43, AHS, Ma I-81; 58th Mtg of PAC, 3/30/43, JM, P67; AI Rpt, 4th, 5.

⁷² Min of Mtg of Jt Com, 3/29/43, AHS, Ma I-81.

⁷³ FR 1943, v 3, 38.

⁷⁴ NYT, 4/8/43, 18. The transportation issue is analyzed below, in ch 16.

⁷⁵ MD 688II/48–9; Cabinet Com on Refs, 5/31/44, PRO, CAB 95/15/32 (cited in Wasserstein, 252).

⁷⁶ FR 1941, v 2, 875–6; Alexander to Long, 5/7/43, BLP, B 203, Ref Mvt & Natl Groups.

⁷⁷ Reams to Stettinius, 10/8/43, BLP, B 202, Refs.

⁷⁸ Mtg of Steering Com of JEC, 4/2/43, Mtg of JEC, 4/10/43, AJC, JEC; Silverman to Montor, 4/7/43, AHS, Ma I-81.

⁷⁹ Mtg of JEC, 4/10/43, Mtg of Steering Com of JEC, 4/2/43, AJC, JEC;

Wise to Early, 4/9/43, Watson to SS, 4/
10/43, Hull to Wise, 4/14/43, SD, EW/
858.

⁸⁰ Rpts on phone calls from Celler, 3/
29/43 & 3/30/43, E.M.W. to Long, 4/1/
43, FDR, OF 3186; Mtg of JEC, 3/15/
43, 4/10/43, AJC, JEC.

⁸¹ E.M.W. to Long, 4/1/43, FDR, OF
3186; Mtg of JEC, 4/10/43, AJC, JEC;
AI Rpt, 4th, 15.

⁸² JF, 1/43, 4; CW, 2/5/43, 4–5.

⁸³ Goldstein to Clinchy, 3/3/43, Israel
Goldstein Archives (Jerusalem), Corresp
file, Clinchy.

⁸⁴ Clinchy to Goldstein, 3/4/43, I.
Goldstein Archives, Corresp, Clinchy.

⁸⁵ To be discussed below, in ch 16.
Examples of Christian support appear in
CW, 6/25/43, 19; "Cincinnati Church
Council," 3/11/43, Cavert to Straus, 12/
11/43, FCC, B 48 & 49, Genl Secy's
Files (Cavert); Brautigam & Sachs to
Waldman, 3/27/43, AJC, Imgn Series,
Refs—Rescue of.

⁸⁶ Proskauer to Gerstenfeld, 3/25/43,
AJC, JEC; "The Christian Church and
the Jews in Europe," 3/16/43, JM, P67;
NYT, 3/17/43, 8.

⁸⁷ *Information Service* (FCC), 4/24/43;
NYT, 4/26/43, 17; Mtg of JEC, 3/15/
43, 3/22/43, Rosenblum to Trager &
Rothschild, 3/17/43, Mtg of Steering
Com of JEC, 4/2/43, AJC, JEC; Cavert
to Rothschild, 3/17/43, Cavert to Straus,
12/11/43, FCC, B 49, Genl Secy's Files
(Cavert); Silverman to Montor, 4/7/43,
AHS, Ma I-81.

⁸⁸ Levy to Galkin, with enclosures, 5/
5/43, Levy to Hexter, 5/5/43, AJC, JEC.

⁸⁹ NYT, 5/3/43, 20; CC, 6/2/43, 669;
Voss-Wyman interview, 2/11/78; Jacob
M. Price to David Wyman, 9/21/78.

⁹⁰ Shultz, Memorandum, 12/10/42,
WJC, U185/3; Voss-Wyman interview,
2/11/78; Cavert to Rothschild, 3/17/43,
Heller to Tucker, 3/19/43, Cavert to
Straus, 12/11/43, FCC, B 48 & 49, Genl
Secy's Files (Cavert); NYT, 12/21/42,
17.

CHAPTER 6.

BERMUDA

¹ EHR, 101; *Jour of Ecclesiastical Hist,*
7/78, 357; Stmt by Shertok, 2/24/43,
RW 2/23; NYT, 12/13/42, 11, 12/18/
42, 10, 12/21/42, 17, 1/24/43, 26; CW,
1/1/43, 2, 4/2/43, 13.

² EHR, 101; CW, 2/5/43, 4, 4/2/43,
13; NYT, 12/13/42, 11, 1/24/43, 26, 1/
29/43, 9; Reams to Hickerson & Atherton, 12/10/42, SD, EW/694; Achilles to
Welles, 3/4/43, SD, EW/848; FR 1943,
v 1, 138.

³ *Parliamentary Debates, Lords,* v 126,
811–21.

⁴ FR 1943, v 1, 134–7. Same source
for following 2 paragraphs.

⁵ Long to Brandt, Travers, & Keeley,
1/25/43, SD, R/3633; FR 1943, v 1, 138–
44; BLD, 316.

⁶ FR 1943, v 1, 140–4; Wyman, 217–
9.

⁷ Memorandum on Ber Cf on the Ref
Problem (nd), W 3, Ber Cf. Re abundance: *Commonweal,* 7/28/44, 349; *PM,*
12/14/42, 1–5.

⁸ FR 1943, v 1, 143–4.

⁹ Wyman, ch 3.

¹⁰ FR 1943, v 1, 143.

¹¹ Emanuel Celler speech, 10/23/75,
at J Hist Soc of NY; Lawrence Fuchs,
The Political Behavior of American Jews
(1956), 99; Pepper-Wyman interview, 4/
10/81; Wayne Cole, *America First*
(1953, 1971), 138–9; Israel, 307.

¹² NYT, 3/4/43, 9; L.C., Memorandum, 3/4/43, SD, R/3739; FR 1943, v 1,
144–5.

¹³ FR 1943, v 1, 144–6; NYT, 3/5/43,
5; L.C., Memorandum, 3/4/43, SD, R/
3739; FR 1943, v 3, 29; Pickett to Frawley & Vail, 3/5/43, AF, GF, US Govt,
SD; Irving Abella and Harold Troper,
*None Is Too Many: Canada and the Jews
of Europe, 1933–1948* (1982), 130–7.

¹⁴ NYT, 3/7/43, 30, 3/11/43, 2, 3/28/
43, 5; BLD, 308, 310; Memo of Phone

Convsn, Long & FDR, 3/19/43, BLP, B 202, Refs; Min of Mtg of Jt Com on Eur Affairs, 3/29/43, AHS, Ma I-81.

[15] Israel, 306; Long to Welles, 3/18/43, SD 548.G1/112; FR 1943, v 1, 147; Taylor to Welles, 4/43, Taylor to Emerson, 7/28/44, MT; MD 711/260, 262, 712/5.

[16] FR 1943, v 1, 147; Roberts to FDR, 4/8/43, Hull to FDR, 4/12/43, FDR, OF 3186; Hull to Seymour, 4/10/43, SD 548.G1/20B; Seymour to Hull, 4/13/43, SD 548.G1/19; Israel, 306.

[17] FR 1943, v 1, 147, 151; BLD, 308; Memo of Phone Convsn, Long & FDR, 3/19/43, BLP, B 202, Refs.

[18] FR 1943, v 1, 176–9, 185; BLD, 334.

[19] Roberts to FDR, 4/8/43, FDR to Roberts, 4/10/43, FDR, OF 3186; WP, 4/13/43, 4.

[20] CW, 3/19/43, 3, 4/2/43, 2; NR, 4/26/43, 548.

[21] Mtg of JEC, 4/10/43, & attached rpt by Proskauer, AJC, JEC.

[22] Mtg of JEC, 4/10/43, AJC, JEC; Proskauer to Welles, 4/12/43, AJC, Proskauer File; FR 1943, v 1, 151; 58th Mtg of PAC, 3/30/43, JM, P67.

[23] CW, 6/4/43, 5; Op, 6/43, 5; Israel, 306; Celler speech, 10/23/75, at J Hist Soc of NY; IJPS, 5/21/43; Mtg of JEC, 4/10/43, 4/18/43, AJC, JEC; Proskauer to Bloom, 4/16/43, AJC, PEC.

[24] Dickstein to FDR, 4/2/43, Long, undated draft reply for Dickstein, FDR, OF 3186.

[25] Wise (for JEC) to Welles, 4/14/43, SD 548.G1/38; CW, 4/30/43, 11–14; Mtg of JEC, 4/10/43, AJC, JEC; Proskauer to Bloom, 4/16/43, AJC, PEC.

[26] Mtg of JEC, 4/18/43, AJC, JEC; NYT, 4/19/43, 4.

[27] Long to Wise, 4/20/43, AJC, JEC.

[28] McDonald & Warren to Welles, draft, 3/11/43, JM, P67.

[29] Berle to Hull & Long, 4/20/43, Brandt to Long, 4/23/43, BLP, B 202, Refs.

[30] CR, v 89, 3434; Ans, 6/5/43, 18; WP, 4/20/43, 10.

[31] Emerson, Note on Measures for Rescue of Refs, 3/24/43, BLP, B 203, Ref Cf—Ber Cf.

[32] Ibid.

[33] Proskauer rpt, attached to Mtg of JEC, 4/10/43, AJC, JEC.

[34] FR 1943, v 1, 148, 151; KCS, 4/19/43, 16; BC Mins, 4/22, AM, 4/23, AM; Jabotinsky to Johnson, 5/6/43, PSC 1/8.

[35] For Reams, see above, ch 4. Alexander to Long, 5/7/43, BLP, B 203, Ref Mvt & Natl Groups.

[36] FR 1943, v 1, 151; Kunz to Clarkson, 4/12/43, BLP, B 203, Ref Cf—Ber Cf; BC Mins, 4/20, AM; 59th Mtg of PAC, 5/17/43, JM, P67; Schauffler to Branson, 11/6/44, AF, RS, Mign Servs, US Govt Contacts; Schauffler, Re Visa Policy, 12/21/43, AF, GF 4; AJYB, v 45, 455, 470; CJR, 6/43, 277.

[37] FR 1943, v 1, 149; Jabotinsky to Johnson, 5/6/43, PSC 1/8.

[38] FR 1943, v 1, 152; Kunz to Clarkson, 4/12/43, BLP, B 203, Ref Cf—Ber Cf.

[39] Memorandum on Ber Cf on the Ref Problem (nd), W 3, Ber Cf; Views of the Govt of the US [3/43], BLP, B 203, Ref Cf—Ber Cf. Same sources for following 2 paragraphs.

[40] Fuller discussion in ch 16.

[41] BC Mins, 4/20, AM; FR 1943, v 1, 155.

[42] BC Mins, 4/20, AM; Wasserstein, 192.

[43] FR 1943, v 1, 49–133; FR 1944, v 1, 1076.

[44] BC Mins (all).

[45] BC Mins, 4/20, AM, 4/21, PM.

[46] BC Mins, 4/21, PM.

[47] BC Mins, 4/21, AM; BC Rpt; FR 1943, v 1, 157, 176.

[48] BC Mins, 4/21, AM.

[49] FR 1943, v 1, 155; BC Mins, 4/20, AM.

[50] Shown in ch 16.

51 BC Rpt.

52 BC Mins, 4/20, AM, 4/20, PM, 4/21, AM, 4/24, AM.

53 BC Mins, 4/24, AM; FR 1943, v 1, 165.

54 BC Mins, 4/24, AM; BC Rpt.

55 BC Rpt; BC Mins, 4/21, AM, 4/25, AM; FR 1943, v 1, 157–9, 295–6.

56 FR 1943, v 1, 157–61; BC Mins, 4/21, AM.

57 Israel, 309; FR 1943, v 1, 164, 176, 295–9; Long, Memorandum, 4/22/43, SD 548.G1/4–2243; Hull to Deane, 4/23/43, SD 548.G1/44; Long, Memorandum, 4/26/43, SD R/4–2643; BLD, 328.

58 BC Rpt; FR 1943, v 1, 179, 307–25, 332–5; FR 1943, *The Conferences at Washington and Quebec* (1970), 342–6. More detail is in "Proposals for Relief and Evacn of Refs" [7/43] (N Africa section), BLP, B 203, Ref Mvt & Natl Groups.

59 FR 1944, v 1, 992; Blickenstaff, Evacn of Stateless Refs to N Afr, 12/27/44, Conard, Rpt on Visit to Spain, 10/16/44, AF, RS 5.

60 BC Rpt; A Rpt Drawn Up for the Am Embassy [8/44], Conard, Rpt on Visit to Spain, 10/16/44, AF, RS 5.

61 BC Mins, 4/22, AM, 4/23, AM; BC Rpt; FR 1943, v 1, 165–6, 175–6, 184–9, 196, 214–7, 224–5, 236–7; Explanation of Changes in Proposed Message, u/c Stettinius to FDR, 6/8/44, FDR, OF 3186.

62 BC Rpt; BC Mins, 4/22, AM, 4/23, AM; FR 1943, v 1, 163, 170. From 1939 through 1943, the US had contributed a total of $70,000 to the ICR (Grew to Rayburn, 6/19/45, SD, R/6-1945).

63 FR 1943, v 1, 171, 186; BC Mins, 4/25, AM.

64 FR 1943, v 1, 177–82, 186–7, 190–5, 199–200, 213–4, 232–3, 237, 247–8.

65 BC Rpt.

66 FR 1943, v 1, 173–4.

67 Office Com Mtg, 5/7/43, WJC, U185/2.

68 Based on the 10 newspapers listed in ch 2, source note 12.

69 NYT, 4/25/43, 19.

70 CT, 4/18, 12, 4/23, 9; NYT, 4/20, 1; DP, 4/19, 3, 4/23, 7; SFE, 4/20, 10; WP, 4/30, 1; *PM,* 4/30, 8. All in 1943.

71 DP, 4/19, 3; ST, 4/19, 3; SFE, 4/22, 11; CT, 4/23, 9; NYT, 4/25, 19; WP, 4/30, 1. All in 1943.

72 AJYB, v 45, 361; CJR, 6/43, 278, 8/43, 393; NJM, 6/43, 314; JF, 5/43, 3; Op, 6/43, 5, 5/43, 4; NYT, 5/4/43, 17.

73 JO, 5/43, 6; Wise & Proskauer to Welles, 5/13/43, Mtg of JEC, 5/24/43, AJC, JEC.

74 AI Rpts, 4th, 5 & 5th, 1; Rosenheim to McDonald, 5/26/43, JM, P40; Shultz to Wise, Goldmann, et al, 6/3/43, SW, AJCg, L. Shultz; Pat to Shultz, 6/24/43, Proskauer to Held, 6/29/43, AJC, PEC.

75 NYHT, 4/28/43, 2; NYT, 4/28/43, 6; Thomas to Hull, 6/17/43, SD 548.G1/165; Niebuhr, Poling, Oxnam, et al to FDR, 8/6/43, SD, R/4164.

76 CR, v 89, A2154, A2329; Celler to Wise, 5/14/43, AJC, PEC.

77 NYT, 5/24/43, 15; Op, 6/43, 5; Celler, "Once Bitten, Twice Shy," 7/15/43, AJC, Imgn Series, Refs—Rescue of.

78 Bloom to Anathan, 6/14/43, SB, Corresp with Constituents; Celler speech, 10/23/75, at J Hist Soc of NY.

79 Morse, 63.

80 NYT, 4/29/43, 9; NYHT, 4/29/43, 8.

81 Travers to Niebuhr, 8/26/43, SD, R/4164.

82 Israel, 316; Brandt, Memorandum, 6/22/43, SD 548.G1/198; FR 1943, v 1, 310.

83 Niebuhr, Poling, Oxnam, et al to FDR, 8/6/43, SD, R/4164; NYT, 5/2/43, 17; MDW to JMP, 5/19/43, AJC, JEC.

84 NYT, 5/22/43, 4, 6/4/43, 7; NJM, 7/43, 352; CR, v 89, A3363.

85 NYT, 4/22/43, 1; WP, 4/22/43, 6.

86 JF, 6/43, 4.

CHAPTER 7.
PAPER WALLS AND PAPER PLANS

[1] Wyman, 43, 49, 168–82, 194.

[2] Ibid, 193–4, 199, 200, 204; "Quota Immigrants Admitted" (nd), NRS, 506.

[3] Wyman, 193–6, 202.

[4] Ibid, 200–1.

[5] Ibid, 201–2.

[6] Ibid, 203; Mayerson to Sapper, 12/24/41, NRS 991; Welles to McDonald, 2/17/42, JM, P50.

[7] Bernstein & Dijour to Taylor, 4/24/42, JM, P55; McDonald & Warren to Welles (draft), 3/11/43, JM, P67; NYT, 5/14/42, 6; FR 1942, v 1, 450–7; BC Mins, 4/25, AM; Office of Censorship, Daily Rpt #7000 [9/42], SD, R/3489.

[8] Cohu's ltr of 6/3/42 from Marseille, AF, RS 1. Several other examples in McClelland to Rogers, 3/14/42, AF, RS 1.

[9] Niles, Case Com Rpt, 10/13/42, USC, Case Com.

[10] The obstruction is clearly seen in the archives of AFSC, JDC, and NRS. Warren's remarks: CEP Jour, 5/5/42; JPC 3050.

[11] JPC 3274, 3379, 3436–7; Kaplan, MASC Mtg, 1/12/43, NRS 326; [1st] Draft Mins Mign & Alien Status Sub-Com, 2/17/43, NRS 325; Schauffler, Re Visa Policy, 12/21/43, AF, GF 4; Vail, Trip to Wn, 3/12/43, AF, FS 3.

[12] JPC 3340; Mins of MASC, 5/11/43, Kaplan draft, NRS 326; IR, 10/28/43, 327; Rogers to Hiatt, 10/2/42, AF, RS 3; JPC 3282.

[13] IR, 10/28/43, 309–55.

[14] CR, v 90, 666.

[15] Excerpts & Summary of Rpt on Spain from Conard, 11/20/43, AF, RS 6.

[16] Schauffler to Heath, 1/5/43, 2/12/43, Heath to Vail, 1/19/43, AF, RS 2; Heath to Wriggins, 1/18/43, AF, RS, Ctry FNA, Fr Morocco, Casa; Schauffler to Hartley, 6/18/43, AF, RS 7; Mins of Mtg on 12/30/43 with Katzki, JDC, G/E, Germany—NRS; Schauffler to Pickett, Vail, et al, 4/13/43, AF, FS, C/O, HIAS; Translation-Excerpts, 8/9/43, u/c Dijour to Schauffler, 10/7/43, AF, GF, Ctry FNA, Genl.

[17] Mayerson to Abrahamson, Monthly Rpt, 10/7/42, NRS 459; numerous individual cases in NRS 575; Schauffler to Judkyn, 11/9/43, AF, RS 3.

[18] Pickett to Warren, 5/27/42, AF, GF 1; 54th Mtg of PAC, 6/18/42, JM, P66; [1st] Draft Mins Mign and Alien Status Sub-Com, 2/17/43, NRS 325; Mins of MASC, 5/11/43, Kaplan draft, NRS 326; Rogers, Rpt, Ref Div, For Serv Section, Jan–May 1942, AF, RS, Rpts & Discussions.

[19] Rogers to Vail, 5/20/43, with enclosure, Rogers to Warren, 6/4/42, AF, GF 1; Detzer to Baer, 6/16/42, WIL, Ref Com, 1938–43, Cases, Schottlaender.

[20] JPC 3379; Chamberlain to Schauffler, 3/12/42, AF, GF, For Serv, Switz; Warren to PAC, with enclosures, 5/8/42, Warren to PAC, 5/11/42, 54th Mtg of PAC, 6/18/42, JM, P66.

[21] DSB, 9/10/44, 277–8; JPC 3379; "Keppel Study," 8/23/43, NRS 570; anon memo (probably Keppel to Berle), 8/3/42, Travers to Long, 8/4/42, BLP, B 211, Visa Bd of Appeals; JPC 3340–4.

[22] Visa Bd of Appeals, Rpt, 11/9/42, BLP, B 211, Visa Bd of Appeals.

[23] BKR Rpt, 13; Summary of Proceedings—Special Mtg NRS, 1/23/43, AF, RS, C/O, NRS (Mins); Schauffler/Rogers to Conard, 3/27/42, AF, RS, Ctry Port, Ltrs to; NYT, 9/9/43, 25.

[24] DSB, 9/10/44, 274; SIB, 6/16/44, NRS 1391; *Rescue,* 6/44, 3; IR, 7/18/44, 228–9; Petluck to Mign Staff, 8/2/44, NRS 587.

[25] Maurice Davie, *Refugees in America* (1947), 194; Loewenstein, Suggestions for a Better Verification, 9/14/42, SD, R/3179; Elisabeth A. Dexter, "Last Port of Freedom, " draft MS (1942), ch I, p 9; Chr R, 9/42, 331.

26 BKR Rpt, 14.

27 MD 694/191; Warren-Jarvik interview, 1/22/79.

28 NYT, 10/15/42, 9; Teleg No. 78 from Tangier to MILID, Wn, 2/23/43, BLP, B 195, Foreign Territories; ltr from War Dept, 5/1/43, SD, R/3805.

29 Schmidt file in AF, OF, N Afr; memo by Heath, 9/22/43, AF, RS 2; Heath to Kimberland, 5/9/44, AF, RS, Ctry FNA, Algeria, Ltrs to; Schauffler, memo re Schmidt, 11/16/43, AF, FS 3.

30 Office of Censorship, Daily Rpt #7000 [9/42], SD, R/3489. The actual facts concerning HICEM are found in Warren, memo on HIAS-ICA, u/c McDonald to Hull, 3/13/42, JM, P50. SD views concerning subversives among refugees are seen in FR 1942, v 1, 450–6.

31 Standish to Lesser, 3/27/44, W 10, Imgn Memos; NYT, 6/28/42, 1, 7/30/42, 1, 34, 7/1/42, 1, 7/10/42, 1, 12/6/42, 59, 7/26/43, 32, 7/16/44, 7, 12/31/44, 16, 3/19/45, 19, 12/8/45, 3; Louis de Jong, *The German Fifth Column in the Second World War* (1956), 215–21.

32 Greenstein, Summary of Invitation Cf, 10/18/41, AF, GF, C/O, NRS; MD 693/217–8.

33 Ch 2. Baerwald to Beckelman, 9/8/42, JDC, Refs, Children; Notes, Mtg of US Com, 9/21/42, Hyman to Levy, 10/22/42, JDC, France, Children. Even here, though, the Visa Division raised several technical difficulties (Stmt by Warren, 9/14/42, AF, GF, US Govt, PAC).

34 Schwartz to Leavitt, 12/21/42, 1/13/43, Leavitt to Hayes, 1/29/43, McDonald & Warren to Welles, 12/1/42, JDC, Refs, Children; Conard to Pickett, 11/21/42, AF, OF, Port, 1000 Group.

35 Frawley to Pickett & Vail, 12/8/42, AF, GF 3; Mtg of MASC, 12/9/42, NRS 452; JPC 3223, 3283; USCOM, Rpt of Exec Dir to Bd of Dirs, 5/12/43, AF, RS, C/O, USCCEC, Rpts; Radio Script, 5/7/43, JDC, Refs, Children.

36 Mtg of MASC, 12/9/42, NRS 452; BC Mins, 4/25, AM; Frawley to Pickett, Vail, et al, 12/24/42, AF, GF 5; SS to Lisbon, 12/26/42, W 44, Evacn of Children from France; Frawley to Pickett, Vail, et al, 1/6/43, AF, RS 10; Schwartz to Leavitt, 1/4/43, 1/18/43, JDC, Refs, Children; Frawley to Leavitt, 1/13/43, JDC, France, Children; Ben Schauffler to Lang, 1/6/43, AF, OF, Port, USC-CEC; Rpt by Escort of 21 on Serpa Pinto, 3/20/43, AF, RS 8; JDC, Loose-Leaf Memo #32, 3/22/43, NRS 1302.

37 Katzki to Leavitt, 2/27/43, Wriggins to AF, 4/2/43, 4/6/43, JDC, Refs, Children.

38 JDC, Loose-Leaf Memo #34, 5/21/43, NRS 1302; Katzki, Lisbon, to JDC, 4/28/43, AF, RS 10.

39 Memo of telephone message from Warren, 4/12/43, HW to MF, 6/10/43, Olsen to Frawley, 9/30/43, Conard to Lang [12/43], AF, RS 8; Conard to Pickett, 9/24/43, AF, RS, Children, US Com, Case Lists; Thompson to Welles, 5/20/43, ER 894/70; Welles to Thompson, 5/28/43, ER 1703/100; Katzki to Leavitt, 9/24/43, JDC, Refs, Children.

40 Olsen to JDC (Leavitt), 6/14/45, JDC, Refs, Children; Conard, Rpt to AF for Dec 1943 to Aug 1944, 8/15/44, AF, RS 4; Gallagher to Olsen, 4/25/45, AF, FS, DP Servs, Children, USCCEC; BC Mins, 4/25, AM.

41 Conard & Wriggins, AF Lisbon Office Mid-Aug Rpt, 8/13/42, along with several letters also in this file, AF, RS 4 (1942); Conard to Vail, 6/10/43, Conard to Schauffler, 8/25/43, Wriggins to Schauffler, 8/10/43, AF, RS 4 (1943).

42 Rpt of the Secy to Exec Com Mtg of JDC, 10/22/41, JDC, Rpts; Katzki to Leavitt, 2/26/43, 2/27/43, 4/14/43, JDC, Refs, Children; Schauffler to Conard, 6/22/43, AF, RS 6.

43 Schauffler to Pickett, Vail, et al, 6/11/43, AF, GF 4; Schauffler to Conard, 6/22/43, Schauffler to Rogers, 7/26/43, Rogers to Travers, 8/10/43, Excerpts &

Summary of Rpt on Spain from Conard, 11/20/43, AF, RS 6.

[44] Brandin, memo on JDC, 6/28/43, CH, B 6, Ref Orgzns.

[45] Ibid; BKR Rpt, 23.

[46] Notes on Lois Jessup's talk with Mrs. Carlton J. H. Hayes, 4/28/44, AF, FS, AF, Wn Trips.

[47] IR, 6/14/45, 154–6.

[48] Based on 26 nations with annual quotas totaling 60,888 (Status of Quotas as of 10/31/45, NRS 502). Statistics from *Annual Report of the Immigration and Naturalization Service* (1946), 72. An estimated 5,000 entered during the portion of fiscal 1942 that followed American entry into the war (Kovarsky to Levy, 7/13/42, NRS 505; IR, 2/27/42, 83). The total eligible from Pearl Harbor to V-E Day was 208,000.

[49] MR, 4/44, 13, 6/45, 158, 8/45, 189.

[50] BLD, 399.

[51] NYT, 12/30/45, IV, 10.

[52] Pell to Taylor, 3/2/41, 3/3/41, 3/7/41, MT.

[53] Pell to Taylor, 3/2/41, 3/7/41, 3/11/41, 4/5/41, MT; 57th Mtg of PAC, 4/14/41, JM, P65.

[54] Talk by Malin to AF Staff, 4/28/44, AF, RS 9; Pell to Taylor, 3/3/41, 3/7/41, 3/25/41, 1/29/42, 7/1/42, MT; Wyman, 163; 54th Mtg of PAC, 6/18/42, JM, P66.

[55] Taylor to Emerson, 5/25/43, 7/28/44, Suggestions for Reorganization of ICR, 5/17/43, Taylor to Welles, 6/11/43, 7/23/43, FDR to Taylor, 7/7/43, 7/28/43, 6/5/44, Taylor to FDR, 7/13/43, 7/14/43, 8/31/43, 5/25/44, Taylor to Hull, 8/31/43, Taylor to Winant, 3/20/44, Emerson to Randall, 4/22/44, MT; Taylor, Confidential Memo Regarding Refs 1938–47, 7/30/47, MT, B 8; FR 1943, v 1, 190; MD 712/5; McDermott to Brandt, 7/20/43, Taylor to Pell, 7/22/43, SD, R/4101; NYT, 3/16/45, 17.

[56] LEH, Memorandum, 2/22/44, W 3, Ber Cf.

[57] FR 1943, v 1, 177, 180–2, 186–7, 190–5, 199–200, 213–4; Record of Proceedings of Mtg of Exec Com of ICR, 8/4/43, BLP, B 203, Refs, Intergovt Com on; NYT, 3/16/45, 17; Taylor to Welles, 7/23/43, MT.

[58] Warren to Fuerst, 5/22/42, IMS, Appeals to NY Fndn; Travers to Bloom, 11/16/43, SB, B 45, Selected Ltrs A–J; ICR, Summary of Activities since Aug 1943, 11/23/43, MT.

[59] Suggestions for Reorganization of ICR, 5/17/43, Taylor to Emerson, 5/25/43, Taylor to Welles, 6/11/43, 7/23/43, Taylor to FDR, 3/3/44, Taylor to Hull, 4/19/44, MT; MD 700/189–90.

[60] Emerson to Taylor, 8/6/43, MT.

[61] Emerson to Taylor, 3/5/42, 8/11/42, ICR, Summary of Activities since Aug 1943, 11/23/43, MT; 55th Mtg of PAC, 9/9/42, JM, P66; *Foreign Affairs*, 1/43, 211–20.

[62] Interview with Emerson, 4/25/44, AJC, Imgn Series, Imgn 1944–40; Talk by Malin to AF Staff, 4/28/44, Marcuse to Schauffler, 5/18/44, AF, RS 9.

[63] Interview with Emerson, 4/25/44, AJC, Imgn Series, Imgn 1944–40; Emerson to Taylor, 3/5/42, MT.

[64] W. A. Visser 't Hooft, *Memoirs* (1973), 169; ICR, Summary of Activities, 11/23/43, MT; Relief & Evacn Projects, 1/27/44, W 50, SD; FR 1943, v 1, 218–23, 227, 229, 233–4; ICR, *Mins of Fourth Plenary Session* (8/44), 6; *Intl Labour Review*, 11/44, 656–7; ICR, *Rpt of Fourth Plenary Session* (8/44), 9, 26; Emerson, Memorandum, 4/18/44, MT.

[65] Ltr to Branson on Italian operations, 2/15/45, AF, FS 2; Malin to Dejean, 7/4/44, AF, RS 9.

[66] ICR, *Rpt of Fourth Plenary Session* (8/44), 5; Jones to Branson, 7/16/44, AF, FS, Ctry Italy, Ltrs to.

[67] CEP Jour, 10/26/44; Wriggins to Vail, 9/7/44, Wriggins to AF, 10/4/44, Wriggins to Branson, 10/30/44, Branson to Moore, 11/24/44, AF, FS 1; Wriggins to Branson [recd 6/8/44], AF, RS 9; Ltr to Branson on Italian operations, 2/15/

45, AF, FS 2; Ltr from A. Greenleigh, 9/7/44, JDC, G/E, Austria, ICR; Pehle to Mann, 10/31/44, 12/18/44, Mann to Pehle, 11/14/44, 12/9/44, W 16, Mann; Louise Wood, "Italy Program: 1940–1941, 1944–1962" (7/70), 14–18, AF files; ICR, *Rpt of Fourth Plenary Session* (8/44), 23.

⁶⁸ Ltr to Branson on Italian operations, 2/15/45, AF, FS 2; Wriggins to Vail, 9/7/44, AF, FS 1; Mann to Pehle, 10/23/44, 11/14/44, 12/9/44, Pehle to Mann, 10/31/44, W 16, Mann; Ltr from A. Greenleigh, 9/7/44, JDC, G/E, Austria, ICR.

⁶⁹ Kimberland to Frawley, 6/16/44, 8/29/44, AF, RS, Ctry FNA, Algeria, Ltrs from; Frawley to Pickett et al, 9/11/44, AF, RS, Ctry FNA, Genl; Biehle to Leavitt, 11/6/44, JDC, G/E, Austria, ICR.

⁷⁰ ICR, *Rpt of Fifth Plenary Session* (11/45), 22–4; Pehle to Baerwald, 7/22/44, JDC, France, Conf 36.

⁷¹ Pehle to Stettinius, 11/11/44, W 49, ICR 3; Schauffler to Branson, Jessup, et al, 11/6/44, AF, RS 11; Sumner Welles, *Where Are We Heading?* (1946), 280.

⁷² ICR, *Mins of Sixth Plenary Session* (12/46); ICR, *Mins of Seventh Plenary Session* (6/47); ICR, *Seventh Plenary Session Resolutions* (6/47).

CHAPTER 8.
THE EMERGENCY COMMITTEE

¹ CR, v 89, 4139.

² NYT, 5/4/43, 17; CR, v 89, 4044–7, 4139–41; Truman to Bergson, 5/7/43, PSC 1/8.

³ CR, v 89, 4139, 8125.

⁴ Ans, 8/43, 4.

⁵ Perlzweig to Wise, 6/16/43, SW, AJCg, Perlzweig; Tucker to Wise, 6/17/43, AJC, PEC; Welles to Taylor, 6/23/43, MT.

⁶ Bromfield to Taylor, 6/21/43, Taylor to Welles, 6/23/43, Welles to Taylor, 6/

23/43, Taylor to Bromfield, 6/24/43, MT; Hyman to Pickett, 7/13/43, AF, RS 10.

⁷ *Daily Worker,* 7/12/43, *Morning Freiheit,* 7/12/43, PSC, S 16.

⁸ Lerner to FDR, 7/14/43, Hassett to SS, 7/15/43, Hull to Lerner, 7/17/43, Berle to FDR, 7/20/43, FDR to Lerner, 7/22/43, FDR, OF 76C; Reams to Dunn, 7/15/43, SD, EW/1008; Ans, 2/12/44, 10; NYT, 7/25/43, 30.

⁹ Bromfield to ER, 6/21/43, ER to Bromfield, 6/25/43, ER 1674/100.

¹⁰ Potter to ER, 7/15/43, ER 1694/100.

¹¹ Lerner to ER, 7/17/43, ER to Lerner, 7/23/43, ER 1689/100.

¹² ER to Potter, 7/26/43, ER 1694/100.

¹³ Ans, 7/5/43, 10, 8/43, 14, 2/46, 18; NYT, 7/13/43, 12, 7/21/43, 13; NYP, 7/22/43, 6; MD 6881/66; NYHT, 7/26/43, 14.

¹⁴ MD 6881/47–67; Ans, 8/43, 6–14.

¹⁵ Ans, 8/43, 22–3. Same source for following 2 paragraphs.

¹⁶ The heavy media exposure is shown in PSC 4/10 and S 16, with a summary in *J Review & Observer,* 7/30/43, in S 16. For editorials, eg, NYP, 7/26/43, 26, 27; *Nation,* 7/31/43, 114; NR, 8/2/43, 124. Lerner: *PM,* 7/22/43, 2.

¹⁷ NYT, 8/12/43, 10, 8/30/43, 10, 9/7/43, 16, 9/14/43, 12.

¹⁸ NYT, 8/30/43, 10, 8/21/43, 9; FR 1943, v 1, 469–83.

¹⁹ Merlin to New Zionist Political Office, Jerusalem, 8/27/43, PSC 1/10; Merlin-Wyman interview, 4/19/73. Examples: NYJA, 8/24/43, 18, 9/2/43, 14, 9/4/43, 4.

²⁰ Additional random examples: SFE, 5/17/44, 9, 8/1/44, 14, 8/22/44, 14, 8/25/44, 7, 5/1/45, 14. Merlin-Wyman interviews, 4/19/73, 3/22/79. Quote from NYJA, 8/24/43, 18, 9/4/43, 4.

²¹ Ans, 2/12/44, 5; Margoshes in *Day,* 11/25/43, 1.

²² My Day, 8/13/43 release, ER, B

3148; Bergson to ER, 8/11/43, with enclosures, FDR to Thompson, 8/16/43, ER 2899/190.

23 Bergson to ER, 10/13/43, Thompson to Bergson, 10/18/43, ER 297/30.9; Bergson to Thompson, 10/19/43, Thompson to Bergson, 10/29/43, with attachment, ER 84/30.1. Mrs. Roosevelt's message was 250 words long.

24 Bergson to Thompson, 11/3/43, text of speech, ER 84/30.1.

25 Joseph Lash, *Eleanor: The Years Alone* (1972), ch. 5.

26 Lerner to FDR, 7/31/43, Watson to Lerner, 8/10/43, 8/30/43, Early to Lerner, 8/22/43, FDR, OF 76C; Lerner to Early, 8/21/43, Bergson to Early, 8/23/43, SD, R/4431 & 4433; YSH, 7–8.

27 CJR, 10/43, 503–4; Long to Brandt, 8/12/43, Long, Memo of Convsn with Bergson and Hirschmann, 9/1/43, BLP, B 202, Refs; YSH, 5–6; Ans, 11/1/43, 5; Alfange to Travers, 1/17/44, W 29, WJC 1.

28 Ans, 6/15/44, 9, 3/45, 14, 3/46, 17, 29; YSH, 6–7; Wilf to Niv, 10/26/70, PSC, Reel 11; Kook-Wyman interview, 5/5/73; Kook-Cohen interview, 9/26/68, 17, PSC 11/33; Menachem Begin, *The Revolt* (1951), 63–4; Berman, "The HCNL and Rescue," 23.

29 Kook-Cohen interview, 9/26/68, 17–18; FBI, File # 100-316012-29, Item # NY 100-61870 [3/45], pp. 6–7, 14–8, 34–5, 72–3; HCNL, 5/2/45, FBI, File # 100-316012-36; Strickland to Ladd, 3/3/45, FBI, File # 100-316012-31.

30 YSH, 6; Ans, 11/1/43, 5; Long, Memo of Convsn with Bergson and Hn, 9/1/43, BLP, B 202, Refs; Hn to Bergson, 12/1/43, PSC 1/10; Alfange to Travers, 1/17/44, W 29, WJC 1; MD 688I/77–8; Hn to Pehle, 1/25/44, W 53, Hn.

31 MD 688I/32, 35–6.

32 Niebuhr to Dear Friend, 8/10/43, Open Ltr, 8/10/43, FCC, B 49, Genl Secy's Files (Cavert); NR, 8/30/43, 304; *World Alliance News Letter,* 9/43, 1–2; CC, 9/8/43, 1004–5.

33 NYT, 9/10/43, 26, 9/25/43, 6; JF, 11/43, 10–12; Stmt to Accompany Jt Resolution, u/c Phiebig to Beck, 9/20/43, NRS 505.

34 Celler proposal: see ch 3. Dickstein/Barbour: HJ Res 154 & SJ Res 85 (printed in JF, 11/43, 9); Ans, 10/15/43, 23.

35 Ans, 10/15/43, 23; Cavert to Dickstein, 9/28/43, FCC, B 9, Genl Secy's Files (Cavert), Immig; RYP, 9/24/43; CW, 9/24/43, 4, 10/8/43, 4; NJM, 11/43, 84, 97; JF, 11/43, 3; Biddle to Dickstein, 11/4/43, Legis 16453; Stettinius to Dickstein, 10/30/43, SD, R/4490; CR, v 89, index pp. 676, 782.

36 Mohler, Memo for Record, 10/20/43, BI 83, Refs—Restrictions on Admission as Visitors, R-4; RR, 63–4; ch 3 above; IR, 6/21/43, 169–75; CR, v 89, 5837.

37 NYT, 10/5/43, 29; WP, 10/6/43, 13; YSH, 9; Kook-Wyman interview, 11/20/78.

38 Proclamations by Union of Orthodox Rabbis and by Union of Grand Rabbis [late 9/43], FDR, OF 76C; Jabotinsky to Altman, 10/12/43, PSC 1/10. The JTA estimated the number of rabbis at 300; the NYP and the EC stated 400; while several others reported 500 (WP, WTH, *Time,* and the Yiddish-language dailies *Day* and *Forward*).

39 NYT, 10/7/43, 14; WTH, 10/6/43, 25, 10/7/43, 3; JMJ, 10/7/43, 1, 2, 10/8/43, 3; *Forward,* 10/7/43, 1, 9; JTA, 10/7/43, 4; *Wn Star,* 10/7/43, 6; Ans, 11/1/43, 4, 11; *Time,* 10/18/43, 21.

40 WP, 10/6/43, 13; NYT, 10/7/43, 14; Jabotinsky to Altman, 10/12/43, PSC 1/10; Ans, 11/1/43, 4.

41 Bergson to Early, 9/20/43, AW to RR (nd), Lerner to McIntyre, 9/29/43, Levovitz to Early, 10/3/43, MHM to Watson, 10/4/43, Watson to Levovitz, 10/5/43, FDR, OF 76C; WTH, 10/7/43,

3; President's Appointment Diaries, 10/6/43, FDR, PPF 1-0(1), B 186; Diary of the President 1943, FDR, PPF 1-0(3), B 195; NG, Interview with Rosenman, 10/6/43, AHS, Ma I-93, Rosenman; WP, 10/6/43, 13; NYT, 10/7/43, 9.

[42] Ans, 11/1/43, 7–10; JMJ, 10/7/43, 2, 10/8/43, 3, 4; Watson to Gray, 10/5/43, FDR, OF 76C; William Hassett, *Off the Record with FDR* (1958), 209. For Jewish opposition to the pilgrimage, see a bitter attack in *Bitzaron* (in Hebrew), 10/43, 67–9, and negative reactions in *Am Hebrew,* 11/26/43, 9, and Op, 11/43, 4.

[43] Jabotinsky to Altman, 10/12/43, PSC 1/10.

[44] Wn newspapers for 10/7/43: WP, 1 & B1; *Star,* 6; WTH, 3; *Daily News,* 22. In NYC: NYT, 10/7/43, 14; NYP, 10/6/43, 5; NYHT and *PM* had nothing. *Time,* 10/18/43, 21.

[45] Thomas to SS, 10/1/43, Long to Thomas, 10/27/43, SD, R/4521; *Current Biography 1942* (1942), 830.

[46] Long to Thomas, 10/27/43, SD, R/4521.

[47] CR, v 89, 8125.

[48] Hilberg, 362–3; *J Comment,* 10/15/43.

[49] NYT, 10/21/43, 18, 10/26/43, 18, 11/1/43, 5; *NY Sun,* 10/19/43, 19; WP, 10/28/43; NR, 12/20/43, 866.

[50] PC/FDR, 11/5/43, 196–7; FR 1943, v 1, 513–781; Hull, *Memoirs,* 1252–1318; NYT, 11/2/43, 1, 14.

[51] NYT, 11/19/43, 4.

[52] Eg, NYT, 11/5/43, 14; NYHT, 11/7/43, II, 2; WP, 11/8/43, 9; *Chicago Times,* 11/22/43, 20.

[53] NYT, 11/10/43, 19; RR, 16.

[54] Stettinius to Long, 11/11/43, SD, R/4843.

[55] NG, Interview with Rosenman, 10/6/43, AHS, Ma I-93, Rosenman; Kook-Wyman interview, 4/14/73; ERS to The Secretary, 11/17/43, SD, R/4796.

[56] Stettinius to Long, 11/11/43, SD, R/4843; ERS to The Secretary, 11/17/43, SD, R/4796; FR 1943, v 1, 222–3, 238; Winant to SS, 12/24/43, SD, R/4900; Winant to SS, 1/10/44, SD, R/4978.

CHAPTER 9.
THE ZIONISTS

[1] CW, 4/30/43, 17; Wyman, 37.

[2] Alling to Reams, 4/14/43, W 17, Pal; Howard Sachar, *The Course of Modern Jewish History* (1958), 392, 460.

[3] Esco Fndn for Palestine, *Palestine: A Study of Jewish, Arab, and British Policies* (1947), II, 943–8; AJYB, v 43, 332–3; CJR, 9/39, 100, 6/42, 316; WLB, 4/62, 33; Rpt on S.S. Darien, 2/11/42, JM, P35; Bauer, *From Diplomacy,* 117; Wasserstein, 74, 77; AECZA, Memo on Sinking of Ref Ship, 3/42, RW 1/14; Institute of J Affairs, *Institute Anniversary Volume* (1962), 143.

[4] FR 1944, v 1, 1012; MD 763/109; CJR, 6/43, 295; Esco Fndn, *Palestine,* II, 952; AME 32; Dobkin speech, attached to AME 15; NYT, 2/14/42, 11, 11/19/42, 3, 11/11/43, 4.

[5] Dobkin speech, attached to AME 15; Wasserstein, 49–52, 147.

[6] CJR, 4/42, 199, 6/42, 316; JDC, *Aiding Jews Overseas* (1942 annual rpt), 10–11; NYT, 2/25/42, 7, 2/28/42, 2; Wasserstein, 143–53. A second passenger survived because she was in an Istanbul hospital when the tragedy occurred (Wasserstein, 156).

[7] *J Week,* 9/10/82, 12; G. I. Vaneev, *Chernomortsy v Velikoi Otechestvennoi voine* (1978), 299.

[8] NYT, 3/11/42, 7, 3/13/42, 2, 18, 3/21/42, 16; JF, 4/42, 7; ER to Welles, 3/9/42, ER 853/70; WLB, 4/62, 33; CW, 3/6/42, 2.

[9] *Time and Tide,* 3/14/42, 211; CW, 3/6/42, 2; Foreign Office, Sinking of M/S Struma, 3/14/42, MT.

[10] Winterton to Taylor, 5/28/42, MT; Wasserstein, 52–7, 60–1, 78, 145, 148–50, 156–60; Alling to Reams, 4/14/43, W 17, Pal.

[11] Wasserstein, 162; FR 1943, v 1, 350.

[12] Even the adamantly anti-Zionist American Council for Judaism opposed the White Paper (NYT, 1/12/44, 15).

[13] INN, 175, 203; Halperin, 148, 220–1, 381–3; Goldmann, 221–2; Transactions 45th Annual Convention ZOA, 10/42, 479–504, ZAL; Silver, 41, 48, 63–4; AJYB, v 45, 207.

[14] Goldmann, 221–2; Halperin, 210, 220–2, 381–2; Emanuel Neumann, *In The Arena* (1976), 168–9, 213; AJYB, v 45, 207; NP, 5/15/42, 6.

[15] AJYB, v 45, 207; Halperin, 210, 220–2.

[16] Wise to Richards, 12/10/41, SW, AJCg; *Reconstructionist,* 5/29/42, 4–5; Neumann, *Arena,* 190, 213; Halperin, 147–9, 223, 382–3; INN, 148, 175, 203, 383; Goldmann, 222; NJM, 10/43, 42; GCM, 1/12/43.

[17] INN, 175, 203, 383; Halperin, 148, 383; Goldmann, 222; Kp I, 15–6, 319, 325, 332–3; GCM, 1/12/43.

[18] Kp I, 15–6, 41, 319; Halperin, 130–2, 226; AJYB, v 45, 213; Proskauer to Gerstenfeld, 3/25/43, AJC, JEC; CBA 2.

[19] Kp I, 325, 332–3.

[20] Ibid, 47–8; RYP, 6/11/43, 6/25/43, 7/1/43, 7/9–22/43, 8/27/43; CBA 3–5, 12; LJ, 10/43, 1; NP, 9/10/43, 17; GCM, 4/27/43, 5/6/43; JO, 6/43, 12.

[21] Kp I, 44–7, 334–44; Halperin, 152, 228–32, 383; Heller to Wise, 1/28/43, SW, US Govt, Anti-Zm; NP, 5/21/43, 6/11/43, 7/16/43, 8/20/43; Hadassah Handbook on AJCf (nd), ZAL, AZEC unsorted papers; JO, 6/43, 7; JF, 6/43, 5, 29, 7/43, 3; INN, 249, 303.

[22] RYP, 7/8/43, 7/9–22/43, 8/27/43; CBA 3, 8, 10; AI Rpts, 4th, 7, 8, & 5th, 9; AJCf, *Stmt of Orgzn of Cf and Summary of Resolutions Adopted at 1st Session* [1944], 10.

[23] AI Rpt, 4th, 7; GCM, 4/27/43; RYP, 7/9–22/43, 8/27/43; Jt Mtg Exec Coms AJCg & WJC, 7/8/43, AJHS, I-77, B 6; CM, Exec Com, 7/14–15/43, 8/12/43, 10/17/43; INN, 248–50; NP, 8/20/43, 2.

[24] NYT, 8/30/43, 6; Halperin, 233–4, 237–8, 384; INN, 310–4; Neumann, *Arena,* 190–2; RYP, 9/24/43.

[25] Kp I, 57–8, 67–76, 87–98; NJM, 10/43, 44, 78–80; Op, 10/43, 8–11; INN, 315; Halperin, 233–4; CfR 3.

[26] Silver, 13–4; Neumann, *Arena,* 191; Halperin, 234–6; INN, 316–8; NP, 9/10/43, 2.

[27] AJH, 3/81, 311–21; Melvin Urofsky, "Rifts in the Movement," in Urofsky (ed), *Essays in Am Zionism: The Herzl Year Book* (1978), v 8, 196. Silver was associated with the JEC, but he had attended only one of its meetings and had not taken part in its rescue activities (Braunstein to Silver, 3/23/43, AHS, Ma I-81; mins of the several JEC mtgs, in AJC files).

[28] Silver, 14–21.

[29] Kp I, 131–4, 139–75, 356; Halperin, 239–40; INN, 319–20. Goldman's remarks: Mins of Pal Com, AJCf Sessions held Aug 31–Sep 1, 1943, 73–7, ZAL, as cited by Aaron Berman in AJH, 3/81, 327.

[30] Kp I, 139–77, 180, 279–80; *Stmt of AJCf on the Withdrawal of AJC,* 11/7/43, 13; NYT, 9/2/43, 1; CfR 4; NP, 9/10/43, 19.

[31] Kp 1, 203–6; NYT, 9/3/43, 13; CW, 9/24/43, 6.

[32] Rescue Com, esp pp 80–93, AJHS, I-67, B 3.

[33] Ibid, 148–9, 239–40.

[34] Kp I, 61, 125–9, 220–1, 370–1; CJR, 10/43, 503.

[35] NP, 9/24/43, 6.

[36] RYP, 9/3/43; NP, 9/10/43, 17; *Forward,* 9/4/43, 6; *Day,* 9/4/43, 1, 9/5/43, 1; JMJ, 9/9/43, 4.

[37] AJYB, v 46, 583–7; NYT, 10/25/

43, 17; CfR 10; Admin Com Mtg, 6/23/44, pp 158–9, AJHS, I-77, B 3; Pat to AJCf, 1/12/44, AHS, Ma II-3; Pr Rel, 1/10/45, AJHS, I-67, B 6; CBA 41, 46; CM, Admin Com, 8/24/44. Besides B'nai B'rith, the Union of Am Hebrew Congregations, Central Cf of Am Rabbis, Natl Fedn of Temple Sisterhoods, and Natl Council of Jewish Women did not endorse the Palestine statement (Halperin, 242–4; LJ, 2/44, 37).

[38] Summary of Position of AJC [11/8/43], AJC, PEC; Naomi Cohen, *Not Free to Desist: The American Jewish Committee, 1906–1966* (1972), 240–9, 536, 552, 555.

[39] AI Rpt, 5th, 10.

[40] Rauch to Wise, 2/2/44, SW, US Govt, Anti-Zm; How Do Communities Respond to Request for Funds? 3/20/44, AJHS, I-67, B 6; LJ, 7/44, 28–9. The 3 were Joseph Rauch, Julius Gordon, Maurice Eisendrath.

[41] Mins of AECZA Ex Com, 9/20/43, Mins of AECZA, 9/20/43, AHS, 4-2 AZEC; Mins of Exec Com, 10/17/43, AJHS, I-67, B 6; CM, Int Com, 10/17/43; AM 2.

[42] Kp II, 42–52; CM, Exec Com, 1/25/45, 3/1/45; GCM, 10/4/44; Rescue Com, pp 33, 90–4, AJHS, I-67, B 4; Digest of Mins of Int Com, 3/21/44, 5/12/44, AJHS, I-67, B 6; CM generally, eg, Pal Com, 3/20/45.

[43] Mtg of JEC, 8/10/43, AJC, JEC; CW, 8/20/43, 23.

[44] Exec Com Mins, 10/31/43, 11/6/43, Int Com Mtg, 11/7/43, AJHS, I-67, B 6; AM 2; NYT, 12/31/43, 10.

[45] Exec Com Mtg, 11/6/43, Digest of Mins of Int Com, 11/23/43, 12/15/43, AJHS, I-67, B 6. See ch 11 for more about developments mentioned in this and the preceding paragraph.

[46] Mtg of JEC, 5/24/43, JEC to Welles, 6/1/43, AJC, JEC; Welles to Wise, 6/24/43, WJC, 264/7; Pat to Shultz, 6/24/43, AJC, PEC; Mtg of JEC, 7/15/43,

8/10/43, 9/24/43, AJC, JEC; AI Rpts, 4th, 5 & 5th, 1; INN, 250.

[47] Mtg of JEC, 3/15/43, 7/15/43, 9/24/43, AJC, JEC; Pat to Shultz, 6/24/43, AJC, PEC.

[48] Shultz to Wise, 3/29/43, SW, AJCg, L Shultz.

[49] Mtg of JEC, 9/24/43, 11/5/43, 3/15/43, 3/22/43, AJC, JEC; AI Rpt, 5th, 10; Braunstein to Silver, 3/23/43, AHS, Ma I-81; Isaac Lewin, *Churban Europa* (1948), 78–83; *HaPardes*, 12/43, 31–2. In favor of Wise's motion: AJCg, AZEC, B'nai B'rith, Synagogue Council of Am, Hadassah. Against it: AJC, AI, JLC, UOR. (Of these, only JLC affiliated with the Rescue Commission.) Nowhere in the many listings of the organizations represented on the JEC is Hadassah ever mentioned (eg, Kp II, 215; CfR 7; CW, 11/12/43, 20).

[50] Cf Rpt, 16; Memo on Functions of AJCf, attached to CM, Digest of Mins of Int Com, 12/15/43; Kp II, 209–20; CM, Exec Com, 1/18/45, 1/25/45; Digest of Mins of Int Com, 3/21/44, AJHS, I-67, B 6; Rescue Com, pp 33, 90–4, AJHS, I-67, B 4; Hyman to Warburg, 4/6/44, JDC, Rpts; NYT, 4/20/44, 10, 8/1/44, 17; CBA 21.

[51] Cf Rpt, 40–1; Wise, Monsky, Goldstein to Hyman, 11/16/43, Baerwald to Wise, Monsky, Goldstein, 12/7/43, W 2, AJCf; Hyman to Warburg, 4/6/44, JDC, Rpts.

[52] INN, 340–4; Digest of Mins of Int Com, 12/15/43, 5/12/44, AJHS, I-67, B 6; AME 2; Mins of AECZA (#63), 9/20/43, AHS, 4-2, AZEC; Mins of AZEC (#1), 10/18/43, AHS, AZEC Mins Book. Further proof of AZEC's relationship to the Palestine Commission is in Cf Rpt, 67–8; CM, Int Com, 6/29/44, Admin Com, 7/6/44, 7/27/44, 8/10/44.

[53] Pat to AJCf, 1/12/44, AHS, Ma II-3, AJCf; CM, Exec Com, 10/17/43.

[54] Halperin, 246; *Western Political Qtrly*, 3/72, 109–24.

[55] Halperin, 268–70; Cf Rpt, 66; *Western Political Qtrly,* 3/72, 109–24; AECZ, *A Rpt of Activities 1940–46* (nd); *Annual Rpt to ZOA, 47th Annual Convention* (10/44), 59–63; ACB 4; AJHQ, 9/70, 87; Urofsky, "Rifts in the Movement," 203; AM 2; AME 32; Mins of AECZA, 9/20/43, AHS, 4-2 AZEC.

[56] Halperin, 270–1, 391; Urofsky, "Rifts in the Movement," 201.

[57] Halperin, 260, 272–7, 392; *Am Zionist,* 11/67, 18; Cf Rpt, 66.

[58] Halperin, 183–5, 260, 272–7, 392; *Am Zionist,* 11/67, 18; AJHQ, 9/70, 98–9.

[59] Halperin, 182–4; AJHQ, 9/70, 92–4; Neumann, *Arena,* 150–5; NP, 3/31/44, 339–40; Carl Hermann Voss, "The Am Christian Pal Com," in Urofsky (ed), *Essays in Am Zionism: The Herzl Year Book* (1978), v 8. APC and CCP merged in 1946 to become Am Christian Pal Com.

[60] NYT, 10/12/43, 20, 11/2/43, 19; AJYB, v 46, 172; CW, 10/29/43, 2, 11/5/43, 2.

[61] NYT, 11/11/43, 4. The British decision had been made in July 1943 (Wasserstein, 339).

[62] Silver, 55–6; Ben Halpern (intro), *The Jewish National Home in Palestine* (1944, 1970), xxiii–iv, 1–2, 505; NYT, 1/28, 10, 2/2, 25, 2/9, 14, 2/10, 16, 2/16, 10, 2/17, 11, 3/5, 1, 3/6, 1, 3/18, 4 (all in 1944); Marks to Luxford, 2/12/44, W 6, Cong Records; Stimson to Connally, 2/7/44, Legis 16433; FR 1944, v 5, 560–657; FR 1945, v 8, 668n; Hull, *Memoirs,* 1535; MD 708/44, 709/16–8; Informal Mtg at Statler Hotel, Wn, 3/9/44, SW, Zm; AM 8; HSD, v 46, 52–6.

[63] AME 18, 19, 20; AM 6, 7; Stone to Silver, 2/22/44, AHS, Ma II-21, Bloom; MD 709/18; 16-page transcript entitled "H. Res. 418" [12/5/44], p 11, Legis 16433; NR, 3/20/44, 366; NYP, 3/8/44, 23, 3/20/44, 19; Pehle to Stettinius, 3/20/44, W 17, Pal.

[64] MPD, v 5, 1339; MD 709/18; Pehle to Stettinius, 3/20/44, W 17, Pal.

[65] NYT, 3/10, 1, 6/28, 14, 7/21, 12, 10/13, 15, 10/16, 19, 11/30, 5 (all in 1944); AJYB, v 46, 174; Informal Mtg at Statler Hotel, Wn, 3/9/44, SW, Zm; Silver to Wise, 6/28/44, Wise to Silver, 6/29/44, SW, Corresp, Silver; Wise to Frankfurter, 7/26/44, 10/16/44, SW, Corresp, Frankfurter; J. Joseph Huthmacher, *Senator Robert F. Wagner* (1968), 306; FR 1944, v 5, 616; Stimson to Taft, 10/10/44, RT 819.

[66] Wise to Stettinius, 11/16/44, Stettinius to FDR, 11/17/44, FDR to Stettinius, 11/20/44, Stettinius to FDR, 12/8/44, FDR, File Memo, 12/9/44, FDR, OF 700; NYT, 12/12/44, 16, 2/21/45, 8, 3/17/45, 13, 8/28/45, 15, 10/19/45, 4; JTA, 12/12/44, 1; FR 1944, v 5, 640–6; Memo of Cf of Silver and Sack with Connally, 11/27/44, AHS, Ma II-30, Connally; AM 16; Wise to Silver, 11/15/44, Silver to Wise, 11/22/44, SW, Corresp, Silver; Wise to Stettinius, 12/1/44, SW, US Govt, SD; Neumann, *Arena,* 199–202.

[67] Neumann, *Arena,* 202–3; NYT, 12/26/44, 19; AME 33; AM 17; Wise to Frankfurter, 10/28/44, SW, Corresp, Frankfurter; Goldstein, Stmt Relating to Pal Resolution (nd), Stmt submitted by Silver to JTA, 12/29/44, SW, Zm; Mins of ZOA Exec Com, 12/19/44, Mins of Special Mtg of ZOA Exec Com, 12/26/44, SW, ZOA Exec Com; Voss, 267; NP, 1/19/45, 82–3.

[68] AZEC, *A Rpt of Activities 1940–46* (nd), 14–5; Urofsky, "Rifts in the Movement," 206–9; NYT, 6/26/45, 10.

[69] NYT, 11/30, 10, 12/2, IV, 3, 12/13, 10, 12/18, 1, 12/20, 12 (all in 1945); CR, v 91, 12138; IR, 12/31/45, 323–4; Truman to Wagner, 12/10/45, RW 2/32; Huthmacher, *Wagner,* 331–2; *J Social Studies,* 1/73, 42–72.

[70] Neumann, *Arena,* 212–3; *Am Zionist,* 11/67, 20.

[71] For several sources on this question, see *Reviews in Am History,* 3/81, 138–43. Also see sources in preceding note.

⁷² Digest of Mins of Int Com, 11/23/
43, AJHS, I-67, B 6; AME 22; CJR, 8/
44, 430–1; GCM, 6/1/44; *Day,* 6/28/44,
1; JO, 9/44, 8; LJ, 7/44, 26–32, 9/44,
56; CBA 14–17, 19–21, 27–8, 30;
Admin Com Mtg, 6/23/44, p 156,
AJHS, I-77, B 3.

⁷³ NJM, 7/44, 360–1, 1/45, 150–1,
167; INN, 347–53; NYT, 12/4/44, 15,
12/6/44, 6; Mins of Int Com, 2/25/45,
AHS, 4-2-23, AZEC-AJCf; Pr Rel, 11/
17/48, AJHS, I-67, B 6.

⁷⁴ Halperin, 249–50; Cantril, 385;
Voss-Wyman interview, 2/11/78.

⁷⁵ *Commentary,* 3/62, 264; *Reconstruc-
tionist,* 6/23/44, 32; Selig Adler, "Am
Jewry and That Explosive Statehood
Question," in B. Korn (ed), *A Bicentennial Festschrift for Jacob R. Marcus*
(1976), 12, 16–7. Adler's essay also re-
lates to several other aspects of the present chapter.

⁷⁶ CW, 9/24/43, 3; Neumann-Wyman
interview, 11/20/78; Neumann, *Arena,*
186–7; Voss-Wyman interview, 2/11/
78.

⁷⁷ Voss, 249–50; Transactions 45th
Annual Convention ZOA, 10/42, 479–
504, ZAL; Noah Lucas, *Modern History
of Israel* (1975), 187; Silver, 41, 48, 63–
4.

⁷⁸ AECZA Mins, 5/3/43, ZAL.

⁷⁹ *Yalkut Moreshet,* 6/71, 71–7, 95.

⁸⁰ Silver, 14–21, 48–52. This view is
also seen in AM 9.

⁸¹ A few examples of Zionist support
for opening other countries (besides Palestine) to Jews: Op, 1/44, 14–5, 10/44,
14; JF, 8/42, 13–16, 11/43, 3–4, 9, 12/
43, 9–10; CW, 9/24/43, 4; Wise to
Goldmann, Kubowitzki, et al, 4/16/43,
WJC, U185/2; *J Affairs,* 11/41; J Agency
to WRB, 2/20/44, W 14, J Agency for
Pal; *Bulletin* (Am Christian Pal Com),
10/46, 2–3, 4/48, 2; MD 720/293; Wise
to Pehle, 8/13/44, TH 5.

· · ·

CHAPTER 10.
THE CABINET WAR

¹ Firsthand accounts appear in Mor-
genthau's article in *Collier's,* 11/1/47,
and in DuBois, *Devil's Chemists,* ch 19.

² See, eg, John Blum, *Roosevelt and
Morgenthau* (1970), 88, 98–100, 222–3,
236, 384–5, 485–6, 564–5; Blum, *From
the Morgenthau Diaries,* v 3 (1967), 202–
6; *Pol Sci Qtrly,* 6/71, 234, 242–9, 258;
Hull, *Memoirs,* 1379–80, 1388.

³ Ch 5 above.

⁴ MD 693/220; Wise to Welles, 3/31/
43, SW to Atherton, 4/5/43, Hull to
Bern, 4/10/43, SD 862.4016/2266 &
2266A; Harrison to SS, 4/20/43, Hull to
Bern, 4/27/43, SD 862.4016/2269 &
2268; MD 688II/99–100, 142.

⁵ Harrison to SS, 4/20/43, Hull to
Bern, 5/25/43, SD 862.4016/2269; Wise
to Welles, 5/3/43, SD, R/3821; Harrison
to SS, 6/14/43, 7/3/43, 7/10/43, SD
862.4016/2274, 2276, & 2278; Meltzer,
Convsn with Goldmann, 5/12/43, SD,
R/3827; Riegner-Jarvik interview, 10/4/
78.

⁶ Convsn Welles, Wise, & Goldmann,
4/30/43, AZEC unsorted papers, ZAL;
Wise to Welles, 5/3/43, SD, R/3821;
Meltzer, Proposed Arrangement for Relief, 7/30/43, SD, R/4211; Reams to
Long, 5/17/43, SD 862.4016/2269;
Reams, draft teleg for Bern, 5/18/43,
SD, R/2269; Meltzer, Convsn with
Goldmann, 7/14/43, SD, R/4063; MD
646/68, 688I/15; Harrison to SS, 6/22/
43, SD 862.4016/2275; Reams, Memo of
7/12/43, sections on France and Rumania, BLP, B 203, Ref Mvt and Natl
Groups; Relief and Evacn Projects, 1/
27/44, p 24, W 50, SD.

⁷ MD 646/68, 649/218, 688I/11, 15–
6, 693/220; W J Hull to Meltzer &
Reams, 7/19/43, SD, R/4102; Reams to
Long, 5/17/43, SD 862.4016/2269.

⁸ MD 688II/69.

⁹ Wise to FDR, 7/23/43, FDR to

Wise, 8/14/43, FDR, OF 76C; Wise, 277–8; MD 688I/5–7.

[10] MD 688I/10, 17, 198–201; Meltzer, Proposed Arrangement for Relief, 7/30/43, Brandt to Feis, 8/3/43, SD, R/4211 & 4212; JHK to FE, Eu, et al, 9/14/43, SD, R/4502; Meltzer to Feis, Acheson, 8/2/43, SD 862.4016/2286.

[11] MD 688I/201.

[12] MD 688I/85, 88–9, 688II/66–75.

[13] MD 688I/85–6, 693/227; Long, Convsn with Pehle, 10/28/43, SD 862.4016/2292; BLD, 277.

[14] Reams to Long & Matthews, 10/25/43, Stettinius to Bern, 10/26/43, Long, Memo, 10/26/43, SD 862.4016/2292; MD 688II/70–2.

[15] Reinstein, Telephone convsn with Palin, 11/12/43, SD 862.4016/2292; Relief and Evacn Projects, 1/27/44, p 24, W 50, SD; MD 688I/109–10.

[16] MD 688I/111–8, 134–7, 140.

[17] MD 688I/166, 688II/47A, 48–9; *Collier's,* 11/1/47, 62. For this episode through British documents, see Wasserstein, 246–9.

[18] Wasserstein, 248.

[19] MD 688II/61, 82–91, 106–30.

[20] MD 693/200–1.

[21] MD 688II/85.

[22] Handler to Cox, 6/18/43, OC; MD 642/210–3, 643/278–80, 688II/117–20; Cox to Stettinius, 10/13/43, 11/27/43, Advisor on Political Relations to Stettinius, 10/18/43, SD, R/5128 & 5129.

[23] MD 688II/63–75, 82–90.

[24] MD 688II/97, 148–51, 186.

[25] MD 688II/151, 163, 224, 694/196–7; Hull to Bern, 12/18/43, SD 862.4016/2295; Relief and Evacn Projects, 1/27/44, p 24, W 50, SD.

[26] MD 688II/88, 122, 148, 163.

[27] MD 693/81, 101; *Collier's,* 11/1/47, 65.

[28] MD 688II/156, 164.

[29] MD 688II/156–7, 164–5.

[30] MD 688II/63–5, 88–90, 153–4, 163, 166–9, 173, 176, 693/221, 694/196–7.

[31] MD 688II/99–100; DuBois, *Devil's Chemists,* 187.

[32] MD 688II/99–100, 213. This effort to block the information flow was first made public by William Langer in a speech (12/19/44) on the Senate floor (CR, v 90, 9695).

[33] MD 688II/154–5, 173–4, 186–8, 200, 206–8, 694/75.

[34] MD 688II/119, 136–8, 167–8, 191–2, 249–51, 694/88, 97–8.

[35] MD 688II/240–1, 692/25, 287–92, 693/82–91, 188–229.

[36] MD 693/188–9, 196, 212–29, 694/80–110.

[37] MD 693/214; Hyman to Long, 10/6/43, SD, R/4556; Travers, Memo for File, 11/5/43, SD, R/4780; Hodel, Memo for Files, 12/8/43, Leavitt to Pehle, 12/31/43, cable to Bern, u/c Pehle to Long, 1/3/44, W 2, AJJDC (Children from France); MD 689/202, 692/18; Hull to Bern, 1/5/44, SD 862.4016/2295.

[38] Long, Convsn with Goldmann, 9/16/43, SD, R/4542.

[39] MD 693/201, 228; FR 1943, v 1, 374–6, 379, 386–7.

[40] MD 693/204, 232–6; Brenner to Luxford, 1/28/44, W 27, WRB 1; RR, 202–3; Winant to SS, 1/12/45, W 25, Situation in Germany; Hartwig, Remnant Groups, 2/23/44, W 29, WJC 1.

[41] FR 1943, v 1, 259–60; MD 688II/117, 123.

[42] MD 692/15–27; Reams, Memo of 7/12/43, BLP, B 203, Ref Mvt & Natl Groups. Eg, see Morse, 65–7, and "Children from Occupied Areas into Sweden" (nd), W 32, Sweden, 2B.

[43] Relief and Evacn Projects, 1/27/44, W 50, SD; MD 701/242–3.

[44] Reams to Stettinius, 10/8/43, BLP, B 202, Refs.

[45] MD 688II/122, 701/243; NYT, 8/4/43, 1, 8/6/43, 14; Joseph Tenenbaum, *Peace for the Jews* (1945), 64.

[46] Advisor on Political Relations to Stettinius, 10/18/43, SD, R/5129.

[47] Wyman, 146; Israel, 225–6; BLD, 245–6; Flournoy to Travers & Holmes, 3/30/45, Travers to Foster, 4/6/45, SD 150.01 Bills/3-3045; JPC 3246.

[48] Chapman to Ickes, 1/6/45, HI, SD 1945–46; MD 688I/201.

[49] DuBois-Jarvik interview, 10/23/78; Mohler to Mulholland, 9/13/34, BI 40, Jews-Jewish, J-1; MD 718/173, 222; Wyman, 157, 163–6.

[50] MD 688II/122. Hull's lengthy *Memoirs* devote 2 pages to refugees and rescue (1538–40). BG, 5/3/43, 1, 11; CJR, 8/43, 394; MD 694/192; Dorothy Detzer, *Appointment on the Hill* (1948), 230; Denny-Wyman interview, 5/11/65; JPC 3057; Stettinius to SS, 1/8/44, BLP, B 202, Refs.

[51] Israel, 308–9; MD 688II/138, 694/67–8; RR, 181.

[52] Israel, 216–7, 231–2, 243, 260, 366; BLD, 256, 262, 276–9, 283, 383, 501–5, 522.

[53] Eg, BLD, 385, 392; Israel, 269.

[54] NYP, 12/20/43, 3; SFE, 12/22/43, 12.

CHAPTER 11.
THE RESCUE RESOLUTION

[1] RR, 16.

[2] Harper to Meyer, 10/6/44, PSC 1/14; WP, 11/24/43, 12; NYT, 11/10/43, 19, 12/21/43, 10.

[3] RR, 15, 211; Baldwin to Wn EC, 1/27/44, JI, EC #48.

[4] Eg, APRR, 5–20; NYT, 11/5/42, 1, 12/10/42, 23, 11/16/43, 6, 12/17/43, 31; Ans, 1/44, 9, 12–13; NYP, eg, 11/10, 4, 11/23, 2, 8, 12/1, 8, 12/11, 1, 3, 12/13, 23 (all in 1943); Krupp to Bloom, with petition, 11/22/43, Legis 16431; Buckley to Bloom, 11/19/43, Zaritzky to Bloom, 11/20/43, Smith to Bloom [11/20/43], Legis 16432; *NY Daily Mirror,* 1/28/44, 21; JMJ, 11/24/43, 1, 11/25/43, 3; McIntyre to SS, 11/20/43, FDR, OF 76C.

[5] Hearings were held Nov 19, 23, 24, 26, and Dec 2. NYHT, 11/20/43, 5; NYP, 11/19/43, 5, 11/24/43, 4; RR, 17, 35–42, 73–87, 93–4, 149, 212–6; Bloom to McCosker, 11/20/43, Moore to Bloom, 11/22/43, Bloom to Moore, Hale & McClintock, 11/23/43, Legis 16432.

[6] RR, 35–42, 95–107, 123–5, 133; JTA, 11/24/43, 4.

[7] RR, 30–2, 57–8, 66–7, 88–91, 100, 106, 110–1, 136, 216, 236.

[8] RR, 30, 88, 132–3; *Forward,* 11/26/43, 2.

[9] NYP, 11/24/43, 4, 12/11/43, 3; Bloom to Thackrey, 11/24/43, Legis 16432; RR, 156–60.

[10] RR, 161–210, 239 (esp 161–84, 201–6).

[11] RR, 182–5, 188–91, 196–201, 204–5.

[12] RR, 184, 196, 204–8; JTA, 12/13/43, 2.

[13] FR 1943, v 1, 170, 225–7; RR, 184, 206–8.

[14] Convsn Goldmann & Shulman with Bloom, 12/8/43, AHS, Ma I-80, Bloom; JTA, 12/13/43, 2, 12/21/43, 1; NYT, 12/11/43, 1; RR, 199–201; BLD, 381–3; FR 1943, v 1, 226–7; MD 692/22, 694/97.

[15] RR, 163, 166, 171, 191; Wyman, 217–9, 258; NYT, 12/27/43, 11, 12/31/43, 14; Cf Rpt, 43; CW, 12/24/43, 16–7.

[16] JTA, 12/22/43, 1; FR 1943, v 1, 241, 244; CJR, 2/44, 63; RR, 184.

[17] RR, 169; Remarks on Testimony of Long, u/c Gottschalk to Slawson, 12/21/43, AJC, Imgn Series, Refs—Rescue of; Proskauer to Long, 12/28/43, AJC, PEC; Cf Rpt, 44; CW, 12/24/43, 16.

[18] NYT, 12/11/43, 1; CT, 12/11/43, 8.

[19] NYP, 12/11/43, 1, 3, 12/13/43, 23; NYWT, 12/13/43, 21; *PM,* 12/14/43, PSC 4/14; *PM,* 12/20/43, 1, 3; *Nation,* 12/25/43, 748; NR, 12/20/43, 867–8; NYT, 12/27/43, 11, 12/31/43, 14; CW, 12/24/43, 14–7.

[20] JPC 713, 718–9; Proskauer to Long, 12/28/43, Long to Proskauer [1/14/44], AJC, PEC; IR, 2/28/44, 64–79.

[21] IR, 2/28/44, 64–79.

[22] JTA, 12/19/43, 3; NYT, 12/12/43, 8; SFE, 12/21/43, 6; CR, v 90, 662–6.

[23] BLD, 386; Berle to Stettinius, 1/20/44, SD, R/5193; MD 694/191–2; Israel, xxiv.

[24] The EC's campaign for the Rescue Resolution was supported only by the UOR and AI (E. Silver to Bloom, 11/25/43, Legis 16432; UOR to Gillette et al, 11/14/43, VH, B 24). Part of the Zionist reaction to the resolution was discussed in ch 9. Digest of Mins of Int Com, 11/23/43, 12/15/43, AJHS, I-67, B 6; CfR 6.

[25] RR, 217–47. Wise implied that the AJCf would not itself have proposed legislation for a rescue commission (RR, 240–1). To understand Wise's testimony, one should read it in conjunction with an AJCf press release of 12/2/43 (Legis 16432), which summarized a written statement Wise distributed to the House committee (RR, 220). Much of Wise's testimony dealt with Jewish rights in Palestine. He also advocated (but said almost nothing about) rescue camps in neutral and United Nations countries, pressure on Axis satellites to release Jews, an intergovernmental rescue agency, food shipments through the blockade, and permission to send funds to Europe (RR, 220–32, 237).

[26] RR, 220–1.

[27] RR, 235, 238; NYT, 11/20/43, 6; NYHT, 11/20/43, 5; Kuppinger to Long, 11/22/43, SD, R/5029; Merlin-Wyman interview, 9/6/73; Jabotinsky to Kitty & Ted, 1/11/44, JI, EC#70.

[28] Digest of Mins of Int Com, 11/23/43, 12/15/43, Exec Com Mins, 11/6/43, AJHS, I-67, B 6.

[29] YSH, 9, 12; Ans, 2/12/44, 20, 6/15/44, 19, 21; APRR, 33, 42; LJ, 1/44, 53; AJCf Pr Rel, 12/29/43, SD, R/5025; Lewin, *Churban Europa,* 81–3. Asked in 1979 whether the Zionist leadership had tried to obstruct the resolution, Dean Alfange replied, "No doubt about it" (Alfange-Wyman interview, 3/22/79).

[30] Interview Gillette, Feuer, & Sack [1/17/44], AHS, Ma II-35, Gillette; Gillette to Levinthal, 10/30/45, PSC 1/21; Address of Sen Guy M. Gillette, 12/20/44, *The Work Is Still Ahead* [12/44], PSC 6/27; *Oakland Tribune,* 1/3/44, u/c Keane to McCrillis, 1/27/44, HI, Associations.

[31] Interview Gillette, Feuer, & Sack [1/17/44], AHS, Ma II-35, Gillette; MD 693/234–6; Gillette to Selden, 8/1/44, PSC 1/12; RR, 218–21.

[32] Exec Com Mins, 10/31/43, 11/6/43, Digest of Mins of Int Com, 11/23/43, 12/15/43, AJHS, I-67, B 6; AJCf Pr Rel, 12/29/43, SD, R/5025; CfR 6; CW, 12/10/43, 3. A few months later, hostility reached a point where Wise described Bergson as "equally as great an enemy of the Jews as Hitler" (Wilson, Convsn with Goldmann et al, 5/19/44, SD 867N.01/2347).

[33] *Day,* 12/6/43, 6, 12/10/43, 6; JMJ, 12/5/43, 4; *Daily J Courier* (Chicago), 12/7/43, 4; APRR, 21–34; Celler, *Brief in Support of Baldwin-Rogers Resolution,* 12/6/43, Legis 16432; NYT, 12/22/43, 3. For the advertisements, see, eg, NYT, 11/24/43, 13, 12/17/43, 31; NYP, 1/13/44, 20–1; JMJ, 1/11/44, 10.

[34] IR, 1/10/44, 14; MD 693/198; Gillette to Thomas, 1/24/44, ET, B 80, C-5 Congress; Kook-Wyman interview, 1/10/74; NYT, 12/21/43, 10; JTA, 12/22/43, 2; Sen Rpt No 625 (78 Cong, 1st ses), 12/20/43.

[35] SFE, 12/22/43, 12; NYP, 12/20/43, 3; Convsn Goldmann & Shulman with Bloom, 12/8/43, AHS, Ma I-80, Bloom; MD 693/198.

[36] Numerous letters in "Jewish File" in Legis 16431; RR, 222; Flegelman to Bloom, 1/25/44, Engelman to Bloom, 2/1/44, Bloom to Jacoby, 2/3/44, Legis 16433; *J Times* (Baltimore), 12/24/43,

14; Celler to Bloom, 1/14/44, Bloom to Celler, 1/14/44, Legis 16431.

[37] Eg, Bonardelli to Bloom, 3/25/40, Yarmish to Bloom, 2/3/44, SB, B 47, Misc Ltrs & Papers; Steinreich to Bloom, 12/30/43, Kalmanowitz to Bloom, 12/3/43, SB, B 46, Selected Ltrs; de Sola Pool to Bloom, 9/23/42, Goldstein to Bloom, 5/17/42, Bloom to Goldstein, 11/11/43, Halifax to Bloom, 11/26/43, SB, B 45, Selected Ltrs; *J Digest,* 7/41, 31; Celler speech, 10/23/75, at J Hist Soc of NY; Celler-Jarvik interview, 10/4/78.

[38] MD 693/198, 694/88.

[39] AJCf Pr Rel, 12/29/43, SD, R/5025; NYT, 12/31/43, 10; Kenen to Members of Int Com, 5/12/44, AJHS, I-67, B 6.

[40] MD 688II/138, 693/198, 694/88–9.

[41] MD 688II/119, 136, 191, 693/198, 694/88, 97–8, 710/194.

[42] MD 694/97.

[43] Ch 10 above; MD 694/80–110, 190, 193–202; MD 688II/191–2, 250–1. The executive order was prepared by Cox, one of his assistants, Milton Handler, and Ben Cohen, then with the Office of War Mobilization (Handler to Cox, 1/14/44 [twice], drafts of exec order, draft memo for Director of Budget [1/15/44], OC).

[44] Merlin-DuBois interview, 8/13/81; *Commentary,* 9/83, 16.

[45] MD 694/190–3.

[46] NYP, 3/9/44, 36; MD 694/97; Fuchs, *Political Behavior,* 71–5, 99–107.

[47] Detzer, *Appointment,* 242–3; WP, 1/25/44, 10; Jabotinsky to Kitty & Ted, 1/11/44, JI, EC#70; [Jabotinsky] to Ben Eliezer, 1/11/44, PSC 1/11; NYT, 1/23/44, 11; CJR, 4/44, 177; Ans, 2/12/44, 9; CSM, 1/24/44, 1, 6.

[48] WP, 1/25/44, 10; CSM, 1/24/44, 6; NYT, 1/27/44, 4; IR, 3/27/44, 126; Weadick to Lawlor, 4/4/44, 4/5/44, BI 98, WRB, W-1; Detzer, *Appointment,* 242–3; printed EC brochure, cover missing, p 9, PSC 9/69; Gillette to Thomas, 1/24/44, ET, B 80, C-5 Con-

gress; Ans, 2/12/44, 7, 11, 16, 18; CfR 7; NP, 2/4/44, 227, 235; Rescue Com, pp 14–6, 140, AJHS, I-67, B 4; MD 693/235–6, 694/59–60, 89; RGH, Jr, to Berle, 1/21/44, SD, R/5062.

[49] Wilson, Convsn with Goldmann et al, 5/19/44, SD 867N.01/2347; MD 707/220–1, 710/194, 735/24, 26, 77.

CHAPTER 12.
"WHEN ARE THE AMERICANS COMING?"

[1] *Federal Register,* 1/26/44, 935.

[2] "Action Taken," 1/18/44, W 28, WRB 3; Stewart to Pehle, 2/8/44, W 50, TD.

[3] MD 697/165, 708/43–5, 696/169; HSD, v 46, 34; McCloy's penciled note on Morgenthau to McCloy, 1/28/44, ASW 5.

[4] MD 694/191–2, 696/168–74, 701/167, 702/146, 708/42–3, 711/100; Warren to SS, 5/5/44, SD, R/5499; FR 1945, v 2, 1146–7; Schauffler to Branson, Jessup, et al, 11/6/44, AF, RS 11.

[5] FSR, 6; Stewart to Pehle, 2/25/44, W 52, Admin Matters; Hn to Steinhardt, 4/24/44, LS.

[6] MD 695/35, 696/124–5, 146, 183–219, 697/41, 699/105, 251–2, 700/108; HSD, v 46, 34; CEP Jour, 2/17/44.

[7] MD 696/171, 183–92, 225, 697/41, 159, 166; FDR to SS, 1/25/44, Hull 53/165; *Collier's,* 11/1/47, 65.

[8] MD 697/13, 16, 30, 40–1, 698/30, 699/105, 251–2, 700/12, 24, 26, 101; PC/FDR, 2/4/44, 21–2.

[9] MD 701/174–7.

[10] FSR, 62; MD 700/257–8, 722/157, 724/321, 727/214, 728/112; Standish to Friedman, 4/5/44, W 30, Reprs; Warren to Pehle, 5/17/44, SD, R/5051; Berle, Convsn with Joy, 5/23/44, SD, R/6245.

[11] Hodel, Memo of Cf, 1/19/44, W 27, WRB 1; Hodel, Memo for Files, W 7, EC; WH, 443–5; FSR, 11–12.

[12] Mtg at Harvard Club, 2/17/44,

"Afternoon Session," 2/26/44, W 9, Free World House; W 4, Com on Special Ref Probs; Biog Sketches of Members of Joy's Com (nd), W 22, Radio (Abrahamson); USC, F: Dr. Joy—Com on Spec Ref Probs; Brundage, Stmt Re USC & WRB, 5/17/44, USC, WRB; Joy to Berle, 5/26/44, SD, R/6246; MD 735/82.

¹³ MD 696/86, 697/53; FR 1944, v 1, 987–9; FSR, 7.

¹⁴ MD 709/28–9, 710/194–5, 718/224–5, 720/291; Pollak, WRB Staff Cf, 2/23/44, W 27, WRB 1; Pehle to Warren, 4/26/44, W 33, Measures Directed.

¹⁵ MD 709/28–9,722/341;SW[eadick], Memo for Record, 8/15/44, Mohler to Mulholland, 12/7/44, BI 98, WRB, W-1; Cumming to Bohlen, Matthews, & Dunn, 5/10/44, SD, R/6422; WH, 428; Hn to Steinhardt, 6/10/44, LS; Wkly Rpt, "since 2/2/44," W 28; Friedman to Stewart, 2/22/44, W 53, Standish; Ira Hirschmann, speech at Brandeis Univ, 4/17/77. Re War Dept, see ch 15 below.

¹⁶ MD 700/227, 709/23, 741/237, 763/109, 814/143–4; Hirschmann, 146–7; JWP, Memo, 4/24/44, W 30, Reprs; Draft Cable to Winant, 10/31/44, W 30, Clearance of Licensing; FR 1944, v 1, 1097–8; WH, 382–6.

¹⁷ MD 694/207, 696/150–6, 709/27, 711/136, 716/178; Pehle to Heller, Rosenwald, & Wise, 4/7/44, W 26, UJA; Montor, Mins of Mtg on WRB, 2/4/44, Mins of Mtg with Pehle, 2/10/44, JDC, WRB.

¹⁸ Lesser, Memo, 2/23/44, W 27, WRB 1; Montor, Mins of Mtg on WRB, 2/4/44, Mins of Mtg with Pehle, 2/10/44, Montor to Leavitt, 2/14/44, Beck to Leavitt, 2/17/44, translation from *Forward,* 2/26/44, Hyman to Pehle, 2/28/44, Hyman to Resnick, 2/29/44, JDC, WRB; MD 696/176. At one point, Pehle asked the UJA to pledge a set amount for WRB-supervised projects, but pointed out that the WRB could not publicly endorse the UJA, because it had to remain impartial in its relations with the private agencies. No specific UJA pledge was made. (Mins of Mtg with Pehle, 2/10/44, JDC, WRB.)

¹⁹ MD 706/131, 716/178; Heller, Rosenwald, & Wise to Pehle, 4/4/44, Pehle to Heller, Rosenwald, & Wise, 4/7/44, W 26, UJA; Hyman to Pehle, 2/28/44, Hyman to Resnick, 2/29/44, Mins of Mtg with WRB, 3/30/44, Draft of ltr to WRB from UJA, 3/31/44, Montor to Heller, Rosenwald, & Wise, 4/10/44, JDC, WRB.

²⁰ WH, 6–7; FSR, 13–15; MD 699/119, 716/178; Coons to Voorsanger, 7/10/44, JDC, WRB.

²¹ *Foreign War Relief Operations* (House Doc 262), 7/17/45, iii–vi, 1–95.

²² Draft Memo from President to Dir of Budget, 1/14/44, Handler to Cox, 1/14/44, with attached draft Memo for Dir of Budget, draft Memo for Dir of Budget [1/15/44], OC.

²³ MD 706/22, 170; DuBois, Memo for Files, W 27, WRB 1.

²⁴ WH, 412; FSR, 8, 9; Interview with Emerson, 4/25/44, AJC, Imgn Series, Imgn 1944–40.

²⁵ MD 707/220–4, 708/1–3, 709/16–18, 711/209–14, 718/172–3, 722/157, 726/33–9, 148–50, 727/214, 728/112, 732/258; FR 1944, v 1, 1037; Pehle to Harriman, 5/19/44, W 34, Hung 2 (last); MPD, v 5, 1338–41.

²⁶ Eg, MD 848II/346–7.

²⁷ Hodel, Memo for Files, 1/28/44, W 53, Hn; Hirschmann, 130; H II, 35.

²⁸ MD 702/175–6, 183, 704/92–6, 760/88; H I, 1–3; Viteles, Excerpt of Rpt on Visit to Turkey, 7/23/44, JDC, G/E, Tur Refs; Barlas, Rpt on Imgn, 12/18/43, AHS, File 4-2-19, AZEC; Resnik, Rpt on Activities [3/44], W 41, Tur 5; Hn to Cox, 3/13/44, OC; H II, 30.

²⁹ WH, 17, 32–3; MD 706/164; H I, 2–7; H II, 8, 12, 17–8, Exh L; Russell to Warren, 12/27/44, SD, R/1-545;

Friedman, War Ref Work, 5/11/44, W 41, Tur 5; Convsn Katzki & Chaoul, 8/23/44, W 37, Bulg; McCormack to Exec Dir, 2/19/[45], W 28, WRB 3; *Yalkut Moreshet,* 6/71, 81; H III, 3.

[30] MD 704/53.

[31] MD 704/96; Excerpt, Hn to Rothschild, 3/6/44, JDC, G/E, Tur Refs; H I, Appen: Observations; WH, 17; H II, 17–8; Hn to Cox, 3/13/44, OC; Transit Policy of Turkish Govt, 4/5/44, W 29, WJC 1; Admin Com Mtg, 6/23/44, pp 38–52, AJHS, I-77, B 3.

[32] H II, 26–7.

[33] [Hn] to Goldwasser, 2/14/44, W 18, Pal Certs; H I, 4; MD 703/101, 105–7, 704/51–4, 705/294; WH, 442. Land was influenced by Leo Crowley of the Foreign Econ Admn and Oscar Cox of the Lend-Lease Admn. They guaranteed funds to replace the ship. (Crowley to Land, 2/24/44, OC.)

[34] Wyman, 146, 191–2; *PM,* 10/3/43, 6; CW, 10/8/43, 2; Hn to Steinhardt, 6/10/44, LS; Resnik, Rpt on Activities [3/44], JDC, G/E, Tur Refs; Jabotinsky, Rpt to EC, 6/14/44, PSC 3/65; Hn to Steinhardt, 4/6/44, 4/24/44, 6/1/44, 7/3/44, Hn to Billikopf, 4/22/44, Allen to Steinhardt, 4/22/44, 5/12/44, Baerwald to Steinhardt, 5/4/44, LS.

[35] WH, 20–1, 24–9; MD 714/28, 717/127, 720/126–9, 319, 722/154, 366, 723/368–9, 724/95; Simond, Rpt #12, 4/24/44, Rpt #13, 5/22/44, W 59, Jews in Rum; FSR, 22; H I, 5; NYT, 3/29/44, 4.

[36] MD 720/126–9.

[37] NYT, 4/19/44, 1, 5/4/44, 6, 5/22/44, 5; Hirschmann, 140–1; FSR, 21; Norweb to SS, 4/20/44, W 17, Pal; Friedman, War Ref Work, 5/11/44, Kolb to Simond, 5/31/44, W 41, Tur 5; Resnik to Schwartz, Re: Tari, 6/18/44, JDC, Tur (Resnik's Rpt); WH, 29–30; MD 702/175, 724/122. The 3 boats were the *Milka, Maritza,* and *Bellacitta.*

[38] WH, 30, 35, 37–9; NYT, 5/31/44, 3; Steinhardt to Baerwald, 6/9/44, JDC, G/E, Balkans; Resnik to Schwartz, Re: Tari, 6/18/44, JDC, Tur (Resnik's Rpt); H II, 7, 10, 30. The 4 were the *Kazbec, Marina, Bulbul,* and *Mefkura.*

[39] Leavitt to Schwartz, 6/23/44, Leavitt to Pehle, 6/23/44, JDC, G/E, Balkans; Pehle to Leavitt, 6/20/44, JDC, Emgn Projs from Balkans; NYT, 4/11/44, 2.

[40] MD 762/212–3; Memo on Convsns with *Bulbul* Passengers [8/44], Memo beginning, "Further interrogation of captains," 8/22/44, W 40, Tur 2B; WH, 38; H II, 10; WLB, 4/62, 33; NYT, 8/17/44, 9; Hull to Bern, 7/21/44, Steinhardt to SS, 10/26/44, W 25, Schleifer; Schleifer to Steinhardt, 9/29/44, Rosenblatt to Steinhardt, 11/16/44, LS.

[41] H III, 2; WH, 29–30; MD 716/281–2, 285, 719/109, 722/367–8, 737/202; FSR, 21; Hn to Kelley, 7/31/44, W 43, Tur 11; Hn to Kelley, 8/5/44, W 72, Rum & Bulg; Katzki, Mins of Mtg, 8/21/44, W 40, Tur 2B; H I, Appen: Observations.

[42] H II, 25–6; H III, 6; FSR, 22–3; Hn to Kelley, 8/10/44, W 45, Evacns from Greece.

[43] Ch 5 above; Friedman, Evacn of Refs from Transnistria, 2/14/44, Friedman to Pehle, 4/15/44, W 43, Transnistria; MD 703/177–80; Berry to SS, 12/11/43, SD, R/4859; Jt Mtg of Governing Council & Admin Com, 1/19/44, AJCg.

[44] Friedman to Pehle, 4/15/44, W 43, Transnistria; WH, 190–1; NYT, 10/18/44, 8; FSR, 23; MD 710/278; Steinhardt to Barlas, 4/3/44, AHS, Ma II-80, Steinhardt; H III, 8.

[45] WH, 190–1; MD 710/278, 711/139, 712/126; Hirschmann, 159; "Communication Dated March 15, 1944," W 72, Rum & Bulg; FR 1944, v 1, 1045–6; McCormack to Exec Dir, 2/19/[45], W 28, WRB 3; NYP, 4/18/44, 4; NYT, 3/14/44, 4, 4/19/44, 1.

[46] Hirschmann, ch 11; Hirschmann, speech at Brandeis Univ, 4/17/77.

[47] FR 1944, v 1, 1047; H II, 4, 33; WH, 196.

[48] H II, 13, 16, 31, Exhs I & J; H III, 3; NYT, 8/23/44, 9, 8/30/44, 8, 10/18/44, 8; WH, 186.

[49] H III, 1, 8; Pehle to Leavitt, 9/29/44, JDC, Tur Genl; WH, 40.

[50] FSR, 20; MD 748/270, 820/261; WH, 42, 188, 198; SD files R/10-1944 & R/11-2144; Grew to Paris, 2/22/45, SD, R/2-2245; Berry to SS, 3/13/45, SD, R/3-1345; Stettinius to Rome, 4/12/45, SD, R/4-1245; Baruch to SS, 5/16/45, SD, R/5-1645; Pehle to Morgenthau, 1/24/45, W 36, Rum 1.

[51] Excerpt from Katzki ltr, 11/10/44, JDC, Tur Genl; WH, 40–2; Katzki to Packer, 12/8/44, W 43, Tur 11; MD 802/194; Russell to Warren, 12/27/44, SD, R/1-545; NYT, 1/9/45, 8; Wasserstein, 341.

[52] FSR, 63; WH, 42; WRB Pr Rel 18, 5/1/45, O'Dwyer; FR 1945, v 2, 1126–7; H I, Appen: Observations; Hn to Cox, 3/13/44, OC.

[53] Institute of J Affairs, *Institute Anniversary Volume*, 73; MJ, 4/45, 96; Mohler to O'Boyle, 12/22/43, CH, B 6, Ref Orgzns; FSR, 36. The total for the Jewish exodus to Spain in 1942 and 1943 was possibly as high as 6,000, but more likely it was not over 4,000 (BC Mins, 4/21, AM). Some issues dealt with in this section on Spain are discussed in detail in Avni, esp ch 4. At some points, my sources have led me to differ from Avni's analyses.

[54] Hayes to SS, 5/31/43, SD, R/3894; CH 3.

[55] Schwartz-Elizur interview, 11/29/61, 17, 20; NYT, 2/9/43, 26; WH, 121–2; Butterworth to SS, 8/2/44, SD, R/8-244; FR 1943, v 1, 275–8, 281, 288–91, 298–9; Pehle, Memo for Files, 7/17/44, W 25, Sp; Mann Rpt; MD 706/145; Hayes to SS, 5/31/43, SD, R/3894; anonymous to Blickenstaff, u/c Blicken-

staff to AF Lisbon, 5/11/44, AF, RS, Ctry Sp, Ltrs from; Conard, Rpt on Visit to Spain, 10/16/44, AF, RS 5.

[56] Excerpts & Summary of Rpt on Spain from Conard, 11/20/43, AF, RS 6. It should be noted, though, that Spain had recently come through a debilitating civil war. That drawback could have been overcome, however, by Allied shipments to Spain of food for refugees.

[57] Sequerra to AJDC Lisbon, 7/25/43, AF, RS 10.

[58] Hayes to SS, 5/31/43, SD, R/3894; Blickenstaff to Hayes, 6/23/43, CH, B 6, Ref Orgzns; CH 1; CH 2; CH 3; Avni, 107–10; Relief & Evacn Projects, 1/27/44, W 50, SD.

[59] A Short Sum of Program of Office of RSARO, 7/18/44, Conard, Rpt on Visit to Spain, 10/16/44, AF, RS 5; Blickenstaff to Brubaker, 1/16/43, AF, RS, Ctry Sp (1942); Rpt from Spain, 8/19/43, AF, RS 6; CH 2; Blickenstaff to Hayes, 1/13/45, CH, B 1, Jan–Mar 1945 Dept; NYT, 7/21/44, 5; *JDC Digest*, 6/43, 2; Chr R, 4/43, 138. Actually, Blickenstaff was with the Brethren Service Committee, on loan to AF. During 1943, the USC associated itself with RSARO. The WRS-NCWC did so in 1944.

[60] CH 1; CH 2; Relief & Evacn Projects, 1/27/44, W 50, SD; MD 717/32; Hodel, Memo of Convsn with Leavitt, 2/1/44, W 31, Sp; A Short Sum of Program of Office of RSARO, 7/18/44, AF, RS 5. Estimates of Jewish refugees still in Spain ran from 2,000 to 3,000. Hayes's summary of the refugee situation in 1942 and 1943 appears in Hayes, 111–26.

[61] Wkly Rpt, "since 2/2/44," W 28; MD 701/18–9; FR 1944, v 1, 992–4; Standish to Pehle, 3/15/44, W 31, Sp.

[62] Wkly Rpt, "since 2/2/44," W 28; MD 701/169; Discussion of Proposed Cable to Hayes, 2/14/44, W 25, Sp; NYT, 5/3/44, 1; Hayes to Hull, 12/

27/43, Hull 53/164; Walser, Convsn with Hull, 5/26/43, "Our Spanish Policy" (nd), Hull 83/373; Hayes, 181–225.

[63] Discussion of Proposed Cable to Hayes, 2/14/44, W 25, Sp; MD 702/143; FR 1944, v 1, 992–4.

[64] FR 1944, v 1, 996–9; CH 2; MD 714/217, 721/264.

[65] FR 1944, v 1, 999, 1013–5; JBF, Memo, 3/30/44, W 31, Sp; MD 712/119–20, 721/264.

[66] FR 1944, v 1, 987–9; MD 702/37, 714/217; FSR, 37; WH, 120.

[67] FSR, 36; Hodel to Pehle, 2/10/44, W 30, Reprs; Hayes to SS, 3/3/44, Hull to Madrid, 3/16/44, W 8, McDonald, Exhs; MD 709/26, 712/119–22; WH, 114, 672; Mann Rpt.

[68] WH, 124; Pehle, Memos for the Files, 7/17/44, 7/20/44, W 25, Sp; Pehle to Stettinius, 8/7/44, Pehle to Shaw, 8/17/44, Pehle to Dexter, 8/21/44, Draft cable to Hayes from Pehle, 8/23/44, W 30, Reprs.

[69] MD 714/218, 218C–D, 717/140, 721/264, 726/121, 734/299; Hull to Madrid, 3/18/44, W 8, McDonald, Exhs; WH, 113, 117–8; Memo of Matters Discussed by Leavitt in Wn, 3/29/44, JDC, Rpts; Warren, Convsn with Thorold & Vance, 6/21/44, SD, R/6-2144; 5-page anonymous WRB memo re Hayes (nd), Rains, Re Sequerra, 4/13/44, W 25, Sp; Mann Rpt; Pehle to Leavitt, 7/13/44, JDC, Emgn Projects from Balkans.

[70] Mann Rpt; MD 710/193, 714/218; "Afternoon Session," 2/26/44, W 9, Free World House.

[71] Lash, *Eleanor: The Years Alone,* 101; MD 720/281, 721/31, 212; Mann Rpt; FSR, 37; Norweb to SS, 7/8/44, Pehle, Memos for the Files, 7/17/44, 7/20/44, W 25, Sp; Pehle to Stettinius, 8/7/44, W 30, Reprs.

[72] Hayes to SS, 1/24/44, SD, R/5131; CH 2; Hayes, Memo re Baraibar, 3/18/43, CH, B 3, Jordana; MD 754/232,

778/54, 783/111, 801/37–41, 63–4, 804/197.

[73] Discussions with Carlton J. H. Hayes, 4/24/42, AF, GF, For Serv, Sp; CEP Jour, 4/23/42; The Ref Problem in Spain, 4/21/42, Memo on Genl Conditions in Spain, 4/22/42, Chamberlain note to Hayes [4/42], CH, B 6, Ref Orgzns.

[74] MD 702/37, 736/138; FR 1944, v 1, 999, 1015n; CH 2; Pehle, Memo for Files, 7/20/44, W 25, Sp; Mann Rpt.

[75] Hayes to Hull, 12/27/43, Hull 53/164; Walser, Convsn with Hull, 5/26/43, "Our Spanish Policy" (nd), Hull 83/373; Hull, *Memoirs,* 1329–34; Hayes, 181–225, 230–1.

[76] [Pehle], Memorandum [7/44] which begins, "On July 17 and again on July 20," W 25, Sp. For a different interpretation of Hayes's response to the WRB, see J. P. Willson's article in AJHQ, 12/72.

[77] Riegner to Reagan, 3/23/44, 4/28/44, W 62, WJC; Goldmann, Memo "Jews in Fr," 3/23/44, W 29, WJC 1; Lichtenstein to Mereminski, 6/17/44, SD, R/6-1944; MD 713/214, 714/63, 718/154, 722/253, 723/353, 726/118; Schwartz-Elizur interview, 11/29/61, 10; Spiegler to Pehle, 4/11/44, W 9, HIAS; RM, 8–9; A. Leon Kubowitzki, *Survey on the Rescue Activities of the WJC, 1940–1944* (1944), 43.

[78] FSR, 37, 62; Emgn Figures, u/c Cleveland to Joy, 2/7/45, USC, AF; WH, 125; Hayes to SS, 10/16/44, SD, R/10-1644.

[79] WH, 126–7; FSR, 38; NYT, 4/17/44, 25; E. Dexter to Strunsky, 4/21/44, E. Dexter to Cahill, 5/24/44, USC, Ltrs from Lisbon; Mann Rpt.

[80] Anne Dacie, *Yugoslav Refugees in Italy* (1945), 5; Saxon, Rpt to Pehle, 4/19/44, W 70, Evacn of Yugo Refs. The Allied armies found and freed 3,000 to 4,000 Jews who were already in southern Italy. Interned in camps by the Mussolini government, they included Italian

Jews along with refugees from Central and Eastern Europe. (MD 701/86; Seagrave to FATIMA, 4/14/44, W 14, It 2; WH, 96.)

[81] Malin to Emerson, 2/24/44, AF, RS 9; DSB, 6/10/44, 533; Ackermann to Pehle, 3/7/44, 11/4/44, W 1, Ack; AAF, 399, 520–3; Resnik, Rpt on Activities [3/44], W 41, Tur 5; Yugo ref camps in Egypt, 5/21/44, W 4, Camps; Pehle to Leavitt, 10/20/44, W 14, It 2.

[82] WH, 101; Ackermann to Murphy, 5/5/44, Ackermann to Pehle, 3/7/44, 11/4/44, W 1, Ack; Ackermann to Pehle, 6/8/44, Pehle to Stettinius, 6/16/44, Marks & Sargoy, Memo for Files Re Yugo Ref Situation [6/44 or 7/44], W 70, Evacn of Yugo Refs; Wilson to AGWAR, 5/24/44, W 14, It 2; FSR, 64; FR 1944, v 1, 1078–9.

[83] WH, 96–7, 100; MD 704/59, 716/198, 719/78, 725/155; FSR, 62; Saxon, Rpt to Pehle, 4/10/44, Ackermann, Memo for Files, 4/14/44, Vucinich to Langer, 4/20/44, W 70, Evacn of Yugo Refs.

[84] WH, 100–2; Ackermann to Pehle, 3/7/44, 5/7/44, Ackermann to Murphy, 5/5/44, W 1, Ack; FSR, 64.

[85] MD 732/62–4, 738/177; JBF, Memo, 5/27/44, W 70, Evacn of Yugo Refs; Ackermann to Pehle, 6/17/44, 11/4/44, W 1, Ack; FR 1944, v 1, 1053, 1059–60.

[86] Wilson to AGWAR, 6/9/44, 6/14/44, MIDEAST TO AFHQ, 8/9/44, W 14, It 2; Ackermann to Pehle, 6/17/44, 8/14/44, 11/4/44, W 1, Ack; JBF, Memo, 5/27/44, W 70, Evacn of Yugo Refs; WH, 104, 140, 229; Weatherford to Jessup, 2/20/45, AF, FS, Ctry FNA, Algeria, Ltrs from; FR 1944, v 1, 1063–4, 1080–1, 1093–4; Goldsmith to CAO, AFHQ, 9/8/44, u/c Kimberland to Vail, 9/13/44, AF, RS, Ctry FNA, Algeria, Ltrs from.

[87] MD 701/86; WH, 96; Ackermann to Pehle, 8/14/44, W 1, Ack; Malin to Emerson, 2/24/44, AF, RS 9; Pinkerton to SS, 6/5/44, W 17, Pal; TS, 13, 16.

[88] Ackermann to Pehle, 8/9/44, 11/4/44, W 1, Ack; MD 762/16, 786/207. One report from Hungary indicated that 7,000 Jews reached Yugoslav partisan territory in summer 1944; but it could not be confirmed.

[89] Hilberg, 432; FR 1944, v 1, 1123; MD 761/133, 767/42.

[90] WH, 105–6; FR 1944, v 1, 1124, 1132, 1140.

[91] MD 761/133, 767/42; FR 1944, v 1, 1123, 1149; WH, 106.

[92] Mann to Pehle, 1/13/45, Margolis to Mann, 1/12/45, W 16, Mann; FSR, 27; Olsen to Pehle, 10/12/44, W 53, Olsen; Johnson to SS, 2/13/44 (2 items), W 31, Sweden 1.

[93] FSR, 27; WH, 84–5; OR; Margolis to Mann, 1/12/45, Mann to Pehle, 1/13/45, W 16, Mann; MD 777/166.

[94] Olsen to Pehle, 6/12/44, W 72, Sweden; WH, 84–5; MD 764/78–9, 767/184, 777/166; FSR, 28; OFR.

[95] MD 767/186.

[96] MD 764/79, 777/166; FSR, 28–9; WH, 87–8; OR.

[97] OR; MD 767/185; AJYB, v 47, 638; Rpt from Laura Margolis, 11/44, W 45, Evacns to & thru Sweden.

[98] FSR, 28; WH, 80–1, 92–3; Olsen to Pehle, 10/12/44, W 53, Olsen; OR.

[99] Johnson to SS, 2/15/44, W 31, Sweden 1; Wkly Review, 12/26/44, JDC Rpts, Wkly Review; MD 724/76, 79.

[100] MD 767/187, 843/333, 847/218; Johnson to SS, 7/15/44, 9/11/44, W 70, Ger Proposals thru Sweden; WH, 94; Hilberg, 362; FSR, 29; OFR; YVS, v 6, 217–8; file on Felix Kersten, in Joseph Tenenbaum Collection, F:16 #15, YIVO; Felix Kersten, *The Kersten Memoirs, 1940–1945* (1956), 9–21, 275–90; Hugo Valentin, "Rescue Activities in Scandinavia," in *Yivo Annual of J Social Science,* v 8 (1953), 247–51.

[101] Margolis to Mann, 1/12/45, Mann to Pehle, 1/13/45, Hodel to Mann, 2/5/

45, W 16, Mann; Rpt from Laura Margolis, 11/44, W 45, Evacns to & thru Sweden.

[102] FSR, 29, 32; WH, 43; RM, 31–3.

[103] McC biography (nd), AF, GF(44), US Govt, WRB; RM, 3; McC to Dear Friends, 3/31/43, 5/29/43, McC to Olgiatti, 3/21/44, AF, FS(44), Ctry Switz, Relief Serv, Admin Ltrs from Geneva; MD 736/211, 803/182–4; FSR, 29.

[104] Pehle to Lesser, 6/6/44, W 70, Funds for . . . Switz; MD 736/211–4, 803/177–84, 850/162–77; WH, 43–4, 53–4; RM, 3, 27–30, 69, & passim; FSR, 30.

[105] FSR, 31; RM, 3–7, 11; MD 803/183.

[106] FSR, 30–1; MD 688II/195; WH, 56.

[107] WH, 56–9; MD 688II/195–6, 692/33–5, 39, 699/140, 717/20–1; Lesser, J Children in Fr, 2/11/44, Murphy, Re Children from Fr, 2/17/44, W 44, Evacn Abandoned Children from Fr; Riegner to McC, 8/28/44, W 63, WJC 1944. At the same time, the SD assured Spain and Portugal that the US would remove up to 1,000 children if they were taken into those two countries from France (WH, 59).

[108] FSR, 31; RM, 60–1; MD 767/38, 803/188.

[109] McCormack to Exec Dir, 2/19/[45], W 28, WRB 3; Refs in Switz: Convsn with SM, 7/26/44, W 64, AJJDC; RM, 16; 53, 60–1, 64; FR 1944, v 1, 1126–7; WH, 66–9; MD 768/244.

[110] FR 1942, v 1, 469; NYT, 8/21/42, 7, 8/25/42, 3, 8/30/42, 18, 9/23/42, 4, 10/7/42, 5; MD 706/159–60; Pehle to Mayer, 4/25/44, W 21, Mayer; Sternbuch to McC, 6/22/44, W 62, UOR; Freudenberg to Cavert, 1/8/43, FCC, B 29, Genl Secy's Files, Foreign Corresp. For a discussion of Swiss refugee policy, see Bauer I, 226–32.

[111] Arieh Tartakower & Kurt Grossmann, *The Jewish Refugee* (1944), 285–6, 343–4; Harrison to SS, 3/30/44, W 32, Switz; W. A. Visser 't Hooft, *Memoirs,* 171; MD 706/159; Pehle to Mayer, 4/25/44, W 21, Mayer; FR 1942, v 1, 469; FR 1943, v 1, 359; Sternbuch to McC, 6/22/44, W 62, UOR. Numerical estimates are based on Harrison to SS, 2/15/44, W 32, Switz; MD 798/315; & Jensen, Ref Prob in Switz, 2/21/44, SD, R/2-2144.

[112] Visser 't Hooft, *Memoirs,* 171; Harrison to SS, 3/30/44, W 32, Switz; Refs in Switz: Convsn with SM, 7/26/44, W 64, AJJDC; Ostrow to White, 3/18/45, W 44, Mvt of Refs from Switz 2; NYT, 8/21/42, 7, 8/30/42, 18, 9/23/42, 4; FR 1942, v 1, 469–70; Pehle to Mayer, 4/25/44, W 21, Mayer; MD 706/159–60; Edgar Bonjour, *Geschichte der schweizerischen Neutralität,* v 6 (1970), 39–44.

[113] McC, Rpt #8, 5/29/43, AF, FS, Ctry Switz, Relief Office, Ltrs from; Pehle to Mayer, 4/25/44, W 21, Mayer; Akzin, Memo, 1/26/45, W 32, Switz; MD 688II/195–6; FR 1942, v 1, 469–70.

[114] The issue of deterrence of potential escapes was raised in MD 706/159; Pehle to Mayer, 4/25/44, W 21, Mayer.

[115] Hungarian Jewish population from Braham I, 1143.

CHAPTER 13.
HUNGARY

[1] Hilberg, 511–7, 528–9, 535–9; Braham II, xiii–xviii; YVS, v 7, 127–8; WH, 142; Mario Fenyo, *Hitler, Horthy, and Hungary: German-Hungarian Relations, 1941–1944* (1972), 159, 172, 182–4; Braham I, 926–7.

[2] Braham II, xx; Hilberg, 535–6; Fenyo, *Hungary,* 183.

[3] WH, 150; Hilberg, 536–7; Harrison to SS, 6/24/44, ASW 3; H II, Exh M 1. Additional examples in PR, 1979 (v24/1), 54–5.

[4] MB & GFl, "We are sending you," 5/22/44, W 61, Extmn Camps.

[5] MD 767/189.

[6] MD 717/145; NYT, 4/28/44, 5, 5/ 10/44, 5.

[7] NYT, 5/18/44, 5; FR 1944, v 1, 1043–4; WH, 147; MD 732/258; Hull to Stockholm, 5/20/44, SD, R/6079B; Harrison to SS, 6/24/44, ASW 3. Despite some inaccuracies, the NYT report was correct on the main points.

[8] FSR, 24; FR 1944, v 1, 1027–8, 1049–50; WH, 144–50, 170–1, 296–7; Summary of Steps, 7/13/44, W 34, Hung 1; RM, 15; Anger, 59, 92.

[9] FSR, 52–5; Summary of Steps, 7/13/ 44, W 34, Hung 1.

[10] NYT, 3/25/44, 4, 6/18/44, 24, 6/ 27/44, 6, 7/10/44, 9, 7/15/44, 3; FR 1944, v 1, 1065; WP, 6/22/44, 5; MD 735/217–9, 746/297; Weinstein to Pehle, 6/29/44, W 33, Measures Directed; YSH, 35–9; FSR, 53–4; CJR, 8/ 44, 402.

[11] FSR, 52–3; Summary of Steps, 7/ 13/44, W 34, Hung 1; Marks to Friedman & Weinstein, 5/15/44, W 35, Hung 4; Weinstein to Pehle, 6/29/44, W 33, Measures Directed.

[12] Summary of Steps, 7/13/44, W 34, Hung 1; Eugene Lévai, *Black Book on the Martyrdom of Hungarian Jewry* (1948), 231–2; FR 1944, v 1, 1068–9; Braham I, 714; Johnson to SS, 7/1/44, ASW 3; handwritten note by McC re Burckhardt, stapled to 5/29/44 ltr, W 60, Swiss Relief Com; WH, 5, 417; MD 720/318, 735/238, 742/139, 753/270.

[13] MD 735/238, 753/270–1; WJC, *Unity in Dispersion: A History of the WJC* (1948), 185–6. The report originated with two Jews who escaped from Auschwitz to Slovakia in April 1944. It reached Switzerland in mid-June and several days later was publicized in the Swiss press. Some historians believe this publicity precipitated the Pope's appeal to Horthy. That is unlikely, for the publicity began only the day before the Pope acted and was not widespread until sev-eral days afterward. The report is discussed further in ch 15 below. (*Vierteljahrshefte für Zeitgeschichte*, 4/ 79, 279; Braham I, 712–5, 754, 811, 951, 978–9, 1078.)

[14] MD 753/270–1; RM, 19.

[15] Veesenmayer via Ritter to Ribbentrop, 7/6/44, RG 242, German Foreign Ministry, T-120, Roll 100, fr 110651–5 (summary in Hilberg, 548–9); Fenyo, *Hungary,* 202–4; Hilberg, 547; Braham I, 1144; WH, 307–8; FR 1944, v 1, 1068–9, 1088–9, 1099, 1116–9; Jenö Lévai, *Feher Konyv: Kulfoldi Akciok Zsidok Megmentesere* (1946), 56–9; MD 766/125–6; Summary of Steps, 7/13/44, Pehle to Morgenthau, 9/6/44, W 34, Hung 1; McC to Pehle, 11/27/44, W 57, Jews in Hung; H II, 24–5. For a discussion of the Horthy government's decision to stop the deportations, see Braham I, chs 23, 25.

[16] Braham II, xxiv–vi; Braham III, 144, 147–250 passim; MD 758/135; FR 1944, v 1, 1128; NYT, 7/19/44, 5. Some evidence indicates that Horthy had in mind the release of only those Jews who already had Palestine certificates or special Swedish passports (a total of about 7,500), along with all children under 10. But the Red Cross, the WRB, and the British definitely understood the offer to refer to several tens of thousands. (FR 1944, v 1, 1099, 1103, 1118, 1128; Braham I, 979; Cabinet Com on Refs, Mins, 8/4/44, PRO, CAB 95/15; *Rescue Attempts during the Holocaust: Proceedings of the 2nd Yad Vashem International Historical Conf* [1977], 220; Pehle to Morgenthau, 9/6/44, W 34, Hung 1.)

[17] FR 1944, v 1, 1106–8, 1120; Note by AE to Cabinet Com on Refs, 8/3/44, pp 5–6, PRO, CAB 95/15; MD 761/ 136–7, 763/33; WH, 156; Friedman, draft message to DuBois, 8/12/44, W 70, Hung/Horthy.

[18] FR 1944, v 1, 1120–1; MD 761/130, 197, 763/108; WLB, v 27, 1973/74, 44–

7; Note by AE to Cabinet Com on Refs, 8/3/44, Cabinet Com on Refs, Mins, 8/4/44, PRO, CAB 95/15; AE to War Cabinet, 8/8/44, PRO, CAB 66/53, War Cab Mins, WP(44)434. For an informed contemporary discussion of the Horthy offer, see I. F. Stone's piece in *PM*, 8/2/44, 2.

[19] Pehle to Stettinius, 7/29/44, Friedman, Memos for Files, 8/12/44, 8/14/44, Friedman, draft message to DuBois, 8/12/44, W 70, Hung/Horthy; AE to War Cabinet, 8/8/44, p 4, PRO, CAB 66/53, War Cab Mins, WP(44)434; FR 1944, v 1, 1112–5, 1125–7; MD 763/106–9, 766/125; DuBois, *Devil's Chemists*, 197–9; Josiah DuBois, speech at Brandeis Univ, 4/17/77; NYT, 8/18/44, 5.

[20] FR 1944, v 1, 1142; Winant to Eden, 8/16/44, W 70, Hung/Horthy; DuBois, *Devil's Chemists*, 197–9.

[21] MD 761/209, 762/74, 768/242–4; Cf Rpt, 58; WH, 66–7, 157.

[22] WH, 166; Pehle to Cass, 10/10/44, W 23, Cass; MD 763/109, 766/134, 767/36–7, 778/38.

[23] H II, 20; WH, 164–6; MD 762/16, 767/38, 772/298, 803/188; Ackermann to Pehle, 8/9/44, 11/4/44, W 1, Ack; RM, 28–9; Brown, Press Cf with Pehle & Hn, 10/17/44, W 41, Tur 5.

[24] WH, 155, 297; RM, 19; Reply to Questionnaire to Apostolic Delegation, 8/18/44, W 35, Hung 4; MD 762/73, 765/185; H II, 24; Hirschmann, 181–5; Braham I, 1075–6; Anger, 58–9, 92; McC to Huddle, 2/9/45, W 57, Jews in Hung; FR 1944, v 1, 1186; Bauer I, 441, 446; Lester, 93; NYT Mag, 3/30/80, 28, 5/4/80, 142. Zionist youth, esp the Hechaluz group, also arranged some escapes from Hungary and rescued Budapest Jews caught by violently anti-Semitic Arrow Cross troopers (Braham I, 928, 982, 998, 1002).

[25] Lester, 61–4; NYT, 4/26/45, 12; NYT Mag, 3/30/80, 38; Margolis to Mann, 1/12/45, W 16, Mann; MD 748/213, 750/70, 751/153–6, 756/339, 763/109. JDC provided the funds for Wallenberg's mission (WH, 90; MD 710/246). Charles Lutz, the Swiss consul general, was also crucial to the effort to protect Jews (Anger, passim; Braham I, 1079–83).

[26] NYT, 4/26/45, 12; OFR; MD 758/136, 774/34; FSR, 25; Anger, 46–50, 58–60, 67, 92; Lester, 7–8, 94, 112, & ch 7; Margolis to Mann, 1/12/45, W 16, Mann; Johnson to SS, 3/7/45, W 34, Hung 2; WH, 91.

[27] Braham II, xxiv–vi; Hilberg, 550–4; NYT, 10/17/44, 9, 12/29/44, 5; Anger, passim; WH, 172–3; MD 800/189–90; JTA, 12/27/44, 2.

[28] Hilberg, 552–3; Braham II, xxvi; WH, 172–3; MD 804/196, 805/173; JTA, 12/24/44, 1; NYT, 12/29/44, 5.

[29] Anger, 68–71, 89–93; MD 788/235; Lester, 105–10; Johnson to SS, 3/7/45, W 34, Hung 2; BG, 8/10/79, 2; FSR, 25.

[30] Braham I, 1144; NYT, 4/15/45, 12; Lévai, *Black Book*, 471.

[31] Anger, 58–60, 67, 92–3; Lester, 5–7, 88–9, 93–5, 112–4; Braham I, 847, 873–4, 1083, 1089, 1092–4, 1143–5.

[32] NYT Mag, 3/30/80, 21; BG, 8/10/79, 2; WH, 91; OFR.

[33] Johnson to SS, 4/19/45, 6/7/45, W 36, Hung 8; NYT Mag, 3/30/80, 24, 32, 35; NYT, 8/4/79, 5; BG, 8/10/79, 1–2. For more on issues raised in this paragraph, see Lester, chs 2, 10, 11, & pp 155–73; also Anger, 147, 161–2. Wallenberg was made an honorary American citizen by act of Congress in 1981.

[34] BG, 8/10/79, 1–2; NYT Mag, 3/30/80, 35; NYT, 8/4/79, 5.

[35] O'Dwyer to Penrose, 9/12/45, O'Dwyer.

[36] Bauer II, 94–9, 114–6; Bauer III, 7–9; Wasserstein, 249; Hilberg, 542; Braham I, 942. On the Brand affair generally, also see Braham I, ch 29. In my

account of the Brand episode, I have relied heavily on the work of Yehuda Bauer.

[37] Bauer II, 144–9, 153–4; Bauer III, 9; Wasserstein, 250; YVS, v 8, 15.

[38] Bauer II, 94, 109–13; Bauer III, 8; Wasserstein, 249; FR 1944, v 1, 1050; PTO, "Handed to High Commissioner," 5/26/44, W 70, J. Brandt; H IV.

[39] Bauer II, 111–2, 129–30; PTO, "Handed to High Commissioner," 5/26/44, Squires Memo, 6/4/44, u/c Steinhardt to SS, 6/8/44, W 70, J. Brandt; H IV; Wasserstein, 250.

[40] Bauer II, 119–26, 153; Bauer III, 9; Hn, Convsn with Brandt, 10/10/44, W 70, J. Brandt; H IV; Wasserstein, 255.

[41] Wasserstein, 250–1, 255; Steinhardt to SS, 6/5/44, Pinkerton to SS, 6/19/44, W 70, J. Brandt; H IV; Bauer II, 136–7; Steinhardt to SS, 6/21/44, SD, R/6364; Bauer III, 11; FR 1944, v 1, 1061–2, 1074–5, 1091; MD 741/48.

[42] Bauer II, 132; Bauer III, 10–11; Cabinet Com on Refs, 5/31/44, PRO, CAB 95/15/32 (cited in Wasserstein, 252); FR 1944, v 1, 1056–8; Wasserstein, 252–3.

[43] Hull to Moscow, 6/9/44, Copy of Teleg Received from Foreign Off dated 7/18/44, W 70, J. Brandt; FR 1944, v 1, 1074; Bauer II, 135, 141–3, 149–50; Wasserstein, 258–62; Bauer III, 11–2.

[44] Braham I, 649–53, 948, 952–4; Bauer I, 398–9; Bauer III, 9–10; Hilberg, 543–5.

[45] FSR, 40–1; Bauer III, 5, 12–13; MJM & FH, Memo for Files Re Special Negots, 1/17/45, W 71, S. Mayer; MD 823/91.

[46] Pehle to Stettinius, 8/17/44, W 70, Hung/Horthy; MJM & FH, Memo for Files Re Special Negots, 1/17/45, W 71, S. Mayer; FSR, 40–1; Bauer III, 14–6.

[47] RM, 22–4; Harrison to SS, 8/26/44, W 58, Jews in Hung; MD 762/31; Pehle to Stettinius, 8/17/44, W 70, Hung/Horthy; FSR, 40–1; AAB, Jr to Stettinius, 9/16/44, SD, R/9-1644.

[48] MD 762/31; Harrison to SS, 8/26/44, W 58, Jews in Hung; Bauer III, 5; McC to Huddle & Reagan, 10/4/44, W 64, AJJDC.

[49] Wyler to Mayer, 8/23/44, Harrison to SS, 8/26/44, McC, Personal notes [by hand] on convsn with Saly M, 8/23/44, W 58, Jews in Hung; Bauer III, 17–8.

[50] FSR, 41; Bauer III, 19–21, 29–34, 43; Harrison to SS, 8/26/44, McC, Personal notes [by hand] on convsn with Saly M, 8/23/44, W 58, Jews in Hung; MJM & FH, Memo for Files Re Special Negots, 1/17/45, W 71, S. Mayer; MD 767/151; Norweb to SS, 11/13/44, SD, R/11-1344; Harrison to SS, 11/16/44, Stettinius to Bern, 11/18/44, W 57, Jews in Hung.

[51] Huddle to SS, 12/13/44, 12/28/44, Stettinius to Bern, 12/19/44, W 57, Jews in Hung; MJM & FH, Memo for Files Re Special Negots, 1/17/45, W 71, S. Mayer; WH, 217, 885; Stettinius to Bern, 1/6/45, W 64, AJJDC; Bauer III, 37, 45.

[52] YVS, v 8, 19; Bauer III, 23, 34–5, 43; Braham I, 963; FSR, 41.

[53] Mayer, McClelland, the WRB, the JDC, and (to a lesser extent) historian Yehuda Bauer have claimed these and other achievements for the negotiations. But they do not supply convincing evidence. (Mayer, Rpt summarizing results, 12/28/44, W 57, Jews in Hung; RM, 22–6; FSR, 42; Wise to Dear Friend, 11/7/45, JDC, WRB; *NY Sunday Mirror*, 11/25/45, 4, 26; Bauer I, 433–4; Bauer III, 18–9, 43–5.) A useful assessment appears in Braham I, 967–8.

[54] Norweb to SS, 6/13/44, W 70, J. Brandt; Harrison to SS, 7/5/44, McC, Memo on whole tractor affair, 7/21–2/44, W 58, Jews in Hung; Bauer III, 25.

[55] Sources in preceding note; also Harrison to SS, 7/26/44, W 62, UOR; Braham I, 955, 958, 1016.

[56] MD 761/139–41; McC, Memo on whole tractor affair, 7/21–22/44, W 58, Jews in Hung; Harrison to SS, 7/26/44,

7/29/44, W 62, UOR; Bauer III, 26, 34, 42; PR, 1979 (v 24/1), 57–8; JDC, Saly Mayer file #21(2). When he gave Sternbuch the first sum, Mayer apparently was unaware of the tractors deal. But he relayed the subsequent funds with knowledge of their intended use.

[57] Cable from Sternbuch & Donnenbaum, 7/14/44, VH, B 20; Bauer III, 13, 17, 44; Henry Feingold, *The Politics of Rescue: The Roosevelt Administration and the Holocaust, 1938–1945* (1970), 277; Reitlinger, *Final Solution,* 438; YVS, v 8, 19; Morse, 373; VH to Morgenthau, 8/30/44, VH, B 23; Sternbuch, Declaration [11/21/45], VH, B 8; PR, 1979 (v 24/1), 57–8.

[58] *J Life,* 11/52, 35; RM, 66; Bauer III, 26; Musy, 2; McC, Rpt of interview with Sternbuch, 1/19/45, Huddle to SS, 1/28/45, W 62, UOR; Huddle to SS, 2/8/45, W 43, Mvt from Switz 1; FH, Special Negots with Gestapo, 2/28/45, W 71, Negots in Switz. I have used Musy's own accounts of events with great caution. No critical point is based on them unless it is firmly supported by other evidence.

[59] Huddle to SS, 12/9/44, McC to Abegg, 12/20/44, McC, Sternbuch–Musy–Himmler–J Affair, 2/6/45, McC, Rpt of interview with Sternbuch, 1/19/45, W 62, UOR; RM, 65–6; Musy, 3; Walter Schellenberg, *The Labyrinth* (1956), 378; Cable from Sternbuch & Donnenbaum, 7/14/44, VH, B 20; MD 761/152, 823/95.

[60] O'Dwyer to Stettinius, Morgenthau, & Stimson, 2/28/45, W 71, Negots in Switz; Sternbuch to VH, 10/31/44, 1/16/45, VH, B 10; Levine to Sternbuch, 3/8/45, VH, B 14; MD 823/102–4. On use of Polish cable, see page 46.

[61] Schellenberg, *Labyrinth,* 378; Musy, 3–5; Huddle to SS, 2/8/45, W 43, Mvt from Switz 1; Sternbuch to VH, 10/31/44, VH, B 10; Bauer III, 26.

[62] Sternbuch to VH, 11/20/44, 11/22/44, VH, B 9; Sternbuch to VH, 11/21/

44, VH, B 8; Bauer III, 32–3; Huddle to SS, 12/9/44, W 62, UOR; FH, Special Negots with Gestapo, 2/28/45, W 71, Negots in Switz.

[63] Sternbuch to VH, 11/21/44, Kotler & Kalmanowitz to Sternbuch, 12/5/44, VH, B 8; PR, 1977 (v 22/4), 17; Hodel, Memos for Files, 11/25/44, 1/11/45, 1/24/45, FH, Special Negots with Gestapo, 2/28/45, W 71, Negots in Switz; Akzin to Hodel, 1/9/45, W 27, VH; VH (Germany), *Pictorial Review* (1948), 245; Irving Bunim, oral history on VH, 12/12/76, p 11; NYHT, 12/9/45, 3.

[64] Sternbuch to VH, 12/6/44, VH, B 20; YVS, v 8, 19; Bauer III, 34–5, 44; Feingold, *Politics of Rescue,* 278–9; Morse, 373.

[65] Hodel, Memo for Files, 1/24/45, FH, Special Negots with Gestapo, 2/28/45, W 71, Negots in Switz; MD 812/238.

[66] McC, Rpt of interview with Sternbuch, 1/19/45, Huddle to SS, 1/28/45, McC, Sternbuch–Musy–Himmler–J Affair, 2/6/45, W 62, UOR; Huddle to SS, 2/8/45, W 43, Mvt from Switz 1.

[67] McC, Sternbuch–Musy–Himmler–J Affair, 2/6/45, MWA: Our informant Mr. Gassett, 2/10/45, W 62, UOR; MD 818/178; Huddle to SS, 2/8/45, W 43, Mvt from Switz 1. Felix Kersten (*Memoirs,* 204–5, 230–2, 282) also claims credit for the release of this trainload.

[68] Sternbuch to VH, 2/10/45, VH, B 9; FSR, 43; VH to Morgenthau, 2/19/45, Hodel, Memo for Files, 2/21/45, FH, Special Negots with Gestapo, 2/28/45, W 71, Negots in Switz; MD 823/95, 238–47, 824/39; FR 1945, v 2, 1131–2; VH to O'Dwyer, 3/15/45, Leavitt to VH, 5/2/45, VH, B 18.

[69] MD 818/173, 823/90–113, 238–53, 824/39, 242–4; Hodel, Memo for Files, 2/21/45, W 71, Negots in Switz; HSD, v 50, 146–7; Levine to Sternbuch, 3/8/45 (via Polish cable), VH, B 14.

[70] Sternbuch to VH, 2/13/45, VH, B 18; Sternbuch to VH, 2/17/45, VH, B

10; FH, Special Negots with Gestapo, 2/28/45, W 71, Negots in Switz; McC to Bigelow, 3/23/45, McC, Convsn with Musy, 4/9–10/45, W 62, UOR; MD 824/43; Sternbuch to VH, 4/24/45, VH, B 17; Count Folke Bernadotte, *The Curtain Falls* (1945), 47; Harrison to SS, 4/19/45, W 44, Switz/New Prog; McC, "Musys left yesterday" (handwritten note), 3/15/45, McC to O'Dwyer, 4/6/45, W 62, UOR.

[71] WH, 8–9; FSR, 19; Pehle to Stettinius, 8/17/44, W 70, Hung/Horthy; MD 823/249, 824/244; FR 1944, v 1, 1145.

[72] J Agency to Foreign Off, 7/6/44, Weizmann Archives (Israel); Shertok to Goldmann, 7/8/44, u/c Perlzweig to Pehle, 7/21/44, W 34, Hung 1; Goldmann to Stettinius, 6/7/44, SD, R/6300; MD 720/297–9; WJC, *Unity in Dispersion,* 187–8.

[73] PR, 1979 (v 24/1), 59; Council of J Federations, Budgeting Bulletin, 6/44, VH, B 17; Office Rpt to Com Members & Patrons of VH [8/45], VH, B 8; Leavitt to Stameshkin, 5/7/43, JDC, Rpts; MD 823/107.

[74] NY & Wn press from NYT, WP, & clippings in W 35, Hung 5. Other cities based on analysis from May through Aug 1944 of CT, DN, DP, KCS, LAT, SFE, & ST. NR, 7/31/44, 117.

[75] Re Palestine resolution: see ch 9 above. One leaves the Stephen Wise Papers, for instance, impressed by the amount of activity devoted in 1944 to the Palestine resolution. Cf Rpt, 24–34.

[76] NYT, 8/1/44, 17; NYHT, 8/1/44, 13; NYP, 7/28/44, 15; Cf Rpt, 35, 56–7; CBA 21; Digest of Mins of Int Com, 9/12/44, AHS, 4-2-23, AZEC-AJCf. Roosevelt sent a feeble message to the demonstration. When journalist I. F. Stone criticized it, as well as FDR's rescue record, the Communist *New Masses* denounced Stone. Communist policy then was to shield FDR from any disapproval. (FDR to Wise, 7/30/44, FDR,

PPF 5029; *PM,* 8/2/44, 2; *New Masses,* 8/15/44, 18–9.)

[77] YSH, 31–41; Wechsler to Pehle, 4/5/44, W 7, EC; Toth, Eordogh, et al to Cicognani, 6/29/44, PSC 1/12; NYT, 6/18/44, 24, 7/10/44, 9; several telegrams re Hungary to FDR in 7/44, in FDR, OF 76C; CJR, 10/44, 511; Ans, 8/29/44, 22.

[78] NYP, 2/10/44, 20–1, 4/10/44, 16, 8/9/44, 25, 9/12/44, 17; WP, 3/27/44, 7; NYT, 4/15/44, 6, 4/30/44, 24, 8/25/44, 6; CJR, 10/44, 571; copies of legislation, W 34, Hung 2 (last). Re Hearst: eg, *Chicago Herald-Am,* 7/11/44, PSC 5/20; *Boston Record,* 7/17/44, 18; *NY Mirror,* 7/30/44, 8/1/44, PSC, Folio 6 & 5/23; SFE, 8/1/44, 14. Resolutions were introduced by Sens Ferguson, Gillette, Taft, Thomas, Murray, and Reprs Baldwin, Lane, Scott, & Somers.

[79] Ans, 8/29/44, 25, 28, 11/44, 16; Smertenko to FDR, 7/24/44, FDR, OF 3186; Pehle, Memo, 2/10/44, Pehle to Stettinius, 3/20/44, W 17, Pal; JWP, Memo for Winant, 4/24/44, W 30, Reprs; FR 1944, v 1, 1007; Pehle, Memo, 3/9/44, TH 1; Berman, "The HCNL & Rescue," ch 5.

[80] Ans, 9/12/44, 2; AME 30; Wagner to Satisky, 10/12/44, RW 2/29; NYT, 8/30/44, 15.

[81] Murray to SS, 8/29/44, SD, R/8-2544; Merriam to Morin, 11/16/44, SD, R/11-1644; Hull to FDR, 8/30/44, FDR, OF 700; Cf Rpt, 28, 79; Silver & Wise to Taft, 9/8/44, RT 818; Silver & Wise to Scott, 9/8/44, AHS, 4-2-50, AZEC; Tenenbaum to Wagner, 9/1/44, RW 2/28; CM, Digest of Mins of Int Com, 9/12/44, 10/24/44; Wilson, Convsn with Goldmann et al ("Z Attitude Toward Palestine"), 9/13/44, SD, copy in PSC 3/67; Lipsky to Taft, 9/13/44, RT 819; AJH, 3/81, 322–3; AME 30.

[82] AME 30; NP, 9/15/44, 500; Ans, 6/15/44 issue; NYT, 5/19/44, 8, 5/25/44, 5, 6/17/44, 5, 7/20/44, 4; NYP, 5/19/44, 8; WP, 5/19/44, 13, 5/25/44, 7; Smertenko to Thomas, 1/14/44, with en-

closure, ET, B 85, J-3 (J Lit); CJR, 8/44, 402–3; HCNL, A Call by the Hebrew Nation, 5/17/44, Bergson to Hull, 6/19/44, FDR, OF 3186.

[83] AME 3, 27; AM 2; Cf Rpt, 78; Smolar in *Omaha J Press,* 5/26/44, PSC 5/17; NYT, 5/19/44, 8; NP, 5/19/44, 402; Op, 6/44, 6; RYP, 6/9/44; JO, 9/44, 9; CJR, 8/44, 431–2; *J Examiner* (Brooklyn), 6/30/44, *J News* (Detroit), 6/14/44, PSC 5/19.

[84] Smertenko to Thomas, 1/14/44, with enclosure, ET, B 85, J-3 (J Lit); Kook-Wyman interview, 5/5/73; HCNL, A Call by the Hebrew Nation, 5/17/44, FDR, OF 3186; Ans, 11/44, 20-2, 1/45, 23, 7/45, 21, 24; Helen to ER, 3/14/45, Thompson to Douglas, 3/21/45, ER 1756/100; ER to Tully, 3/20/45, ER 1765/100. For more on this very complex issue, see Ans, June 1944 through 1947, esp 8/29/44, 14–7; also, Berman, "The HCNL & Rescue."

[85] AME 24, 27; CBA 22; CJR, 4/44, 180–1; Biron in *J News* (Detroit), 6/16/44, PSC 5/19; *PM,* 8/9/44, 24; Shapiro to Chairmen of Local EC's, 5/11/44, AHS, Ma II-6, ALFP; Silver to Manson, 6/7/44, AHS, II, 4-2-14, AZEC; VF, ALFP generally, esp "Withdrawals & Replies," 2/8/45; Berman, "The HCNL & Rescue," ch 4; IJPS, 5/18/45, 5; Smertenko to Pepper, 5/22/45, PSC 1/18; "Wn Post a Victim," 10/44, Shapiro to [name obliterated], 10/24/44, Lewis to X, 11/29/44, PSC 13/57.

CHAPTER 14.
"LATE AND LITTLE"

[1] FSR, 46; WH, 112; MD 704/52.

[2] Pehle to Kuhn, 3/24/44, W 33, Measures Directed; NYT, 8/30/43, 3, 11/2/43, 14, 11/5/43, 14; CW, 11/12/43, 12; Kahn to Ickes, 1/5/44, HI, Associations; HID, 8522–3. The two times that reference had been made specifically to Jews were 7/21/42 (messages from FDR &

Churchill to the NYC mass meeting) & 12/17/42 (UN war-crimes declaration). Major war-crimes warnings that did not mention Jews, besides those from the Quebec and Moscow Conferences, included those of 1/13/42 (EHR, 82, 86–7), 8/21/42 (DSB, 8/22/42, 710), 10/7/42 (NYT, 10/8/42, 1), 6/30/43 (NYT, 7/1/43, 4), 7/30/43 (NYT, 7/31/43, 3).

[3] Wkly Rpt, "since 2/2/44," W 28; MD 702/142, 704/52, 706/124, 708/1–3; early draft of Declaration by the President [3/44], PSC 3/62; NYT, 3/25/44, 1, 4; PPA, 103–5.

[4] MD 707/223, 242–3, 708/1–3, 42; Stettinius to Early, 3/8/44, FDR, PSF: Refs (copy in PSC 3/62).

[5] MD 708/1–3, 42; Pehle, Memo for Files, 3/9/44, W 28, WRB 3.

[6] MD 707/219–34, 239A, 708/4; PPA, 105.

[7] MD 708/1–3; PPA, 104–5; NYT, 3/25/44, 4; FR 1944, v 1, 1033, 1037, 1069.

[8] FSR, 51; WH, 314; MD 714/21–2; FR 1944, v 1, 1088–9, 1101, 1161–3.

[9] NYT, 10/11/44, 4, 11/8/44, 21; FR 1944, v 1, 1250; Schoenfeld to SS, 9/29/44, SD, EW/9-2944; WH, 298; FSR, 55; MD 791/103–4; Lesser, "Germans," 9/27/44, Pehle to McCloy, 9/28/44, W 72, Eisenhower Stmt; Convsn ER with Rosenheim et al, 10/14/44, JM, 324 ER; SHAEF to War Dept, 10/14/44, ASW 2. A specific reference to Jewish inmates was deleted on the advice of the Psychological Warfare Division, which maintained that it would hand the Germans a "powerful propaganda line."

[10] WH, 326; FR 1944, v 1, 1174–5; FSR, 55–6; NYT, 4/24/45, 1.

[11] WH, 12; FSR, 70; MD 805/8, 11–7.

[12] NYT, 10/8/42, 1, 12/29/42, 3, 2/2/45, 6; FR 1942, v 1, 48–71; FR 1943, v 1, 402–38; EHR, 82–106; Pell to FDR, 4/12/43, SD, EW/994.

[13] Pell to Hull, 11/11/43, 6/20/44, SD, EW/1218 & 6-2044; Stettinius to Hack-

worth, 4/18/44, SD, EW/4-1844; AJHQ, 6/76, 343–5; Winant to SS, 10/6/44, W 19, Punishment; MD 805/8, 12; NYT, 1/11/45, 9; Draft by GHH for FDR to Pell, 6/13/44, SD, EW/6-1344; WH, 423; Pell to FDR, 3/5/45, SD, EW/3-1645; FR 1944, v 1, 1322, 1401–5; Mann to Pehle, 1/13/45, W 16, Mann.

[14] Winant to SS, 10/6/44, Akzin to Marks, 12/22/44, W 19, Punishment; AJHQ, 6/76, 335, 340–5; Pell to SS, 4/24/44 (#500), CP; Stettinius to Hackworth, 4/18/44, SD, EW/4-1844; FR 1943, v 1, 407; Mann to Pehle, 9/19/44, W 70, England; Pell to Hull, 6/20/44, SD, EW/6-2044; Pell to FDR, 3/5/45, SD, EW/3-1645; Pell OH, 584–7.

[15] MD 805/8–17, 27, 815/101; Stettinius to Pehle, 12/14/44, Friedman, Memo for Files Re WC, 12/16/44, Pehle to Morgenthau, 1/17/45, W 19, Punishment; WH, 424; Stettinius to FDR, 12/27/44, FDR, PSF: WCC (copy in CP).

[16] Fite, Convsn with Pell, 12/7/44, SD, EW/12-744; Pell to FDR, 3/5/45, SD, EW/3-1645; Pell's 15-page retrospective [summer 1945], CP; Hackworth, Convsn with Pell, 1/9/45, Stettinius to Pell, 1/17/45, SD, EW/1-945; NYT, 1/30/45, 3; Pell OH, 589–91; GGT to FDR, 1/9/45, FDR, OF 5152 (copy in CP); Stettinius to FDR, 12/27/44, FDR, PSF: WCC (copy in CP); WP, 1/31/45, 10; Claiborne Pell–Jarvik interview, 1/22/79. Stettinius replaced Hull as secy of state on 12/1/44.

[17] Hackworth, Convsn with Pell, 1/9/45, SD, EW/1-945; Pell to FDR, 3/5/45, SD, EW/3-1645; Stettinius to FDR, 12/27/44 (& FDR's pencil note on it), FDR, PSF: WCC (copy in CP).

[18] WH, 423; Grew, Convsn with Pell, 1/24/45, SD, EW/1-2445; Hackworth, Convsn with Stone, 2/8/45, SD, EW/2-845; Pell to FDR, 1/9/45, 1/17/45, Pell to Watson (nd), Pell to Watson, 1/15/45, Watson to Pell, 1/16/45, Tully to Pell, 1/24/45, FDR, OF 5152 (copies in CP); Pell to FDR, 3/5/45, FDR to Stet-

tinius, 3/16/45, SD, EW/3-1645; Pell to FDR, 4/5/45, FDR to Stettinius, 4/9/45, SD, EW/4-945; "The following information" (nd), PSC 1/16; Ans, 2/45, 20; Hackworth, Convsn with Pell, 1/24/45, SD, EW/1-2445; CJR, 4/45, 195; NYT, 1/27/45, 1, 5, 1/30/45, 3, 1/31/45, 20, 2/2/45, 6; WP, 1/31/45, 10; MD 805/27, 815/101–2; CW, 2/2/45, 2; NYP, 2/2/45, 18; Pehle to Morgenthau, 1/17/45, W 19, Punishment; AJCf, Pr Rel, 1/31/45, AJCf Pr Rels, ZAL; Perlzweig to Office Com, 2/1/45, SW, AJCg, Perlzweig.

[19] Grew, Convsn with FDR, 3/2/45, SD 500.CC/3-245; Henry L. Stimson & McGeorge Bundy, *On Active Service in Peace & War* (1947), 585–7; SG, 1/46, 5; Robert H. Jackson, *Rpt of Robert H. Jackson, US Representative to the Intl Cf on Military Trials* (1949), vii, 3–9; FR 1944, v 1, 1398; HSD, v 48, 188; MD 815/101–2; Ulio to Rosenberg, 9/29/44, VH, B 8.

[20] MD 815/101–2; FR 1944, v 1, 1378–80; WH, 12.

[21] NYT, 1/27/45, 5, 5/3/45, 9, 5/13/45, 8, 8/9/45, 1, 10, 11; Hackworth, Convsn with Pell, 1/24/45, SD, EW/1-2445; Pell to FDR, 3/5/45, SD, EW/3-1645; Grew to Pell, 1/29/45, CP; Grew, Convsn with FDR, 3/2/45, SD 500.CC/3-245; Winant to SS, 4/4/45, Acheson to London (for Rosenman), 4/5/45, SD, EW/4-445; Jackson, *Report,* 420–9; Robert H. Jackson, *The Nürnberg Case* (1947), v–vi, 23; Robert H. Jackson, *The Case Against the Nazi War Criminals* (1946), viii; Bradley Smith, *Reaching Judgment at Nuremberg* (1977), 60 & chs 2–3 generally.

[22] Pehle to Ernst, 4/11/44, W 7, Ernst; FR 1944, v 1, 1007–8, 1018–9, 1053, 1058–9, 1071; MD 693/101, 697/90, 705/288, 291, 707/235–6, 708/276, 712/109, 726/116; Stettinius to Morgenthau, 2/1/44, Smith to Marks, 4/29/44, W 47, Temp Havens/NAfr; FSR, 63; Russell to Warren, 12/27/44, SD, R/12-2744.

[23] Wolff to Anderson, 1/11/44,

"Camp Lyautey, Fedhala, Morocco (Near Casablanca)" (nd), Hayes to SS, 1/8/45, W 39, Evacns to Lyautey; Conard, Rpt on Visit to Spain, 10/16/44, AF, RS 5; NAfr Ref Ctr, Camp Maréchal Lyautey, 9/12/44, AF, RS, Ctry FNA, Genl; FSR, 61–2; WH, 222–4; Murphy, Relief & Evacn Projects, 2/17/44, W 28, WRB 3; Ackermann to Pehle, 3/4/44, 11/4/44, Beckelman to Anderson, 2/20/44, W 1, Ack; Hayes to SS, 2/16/44, W 8, McDonald, Exhs; MD 702/86–7; Stmt on Casablanca Ref Camp, 5/29/44, OC; Standish to Lesser [4/44], W 49, ICR 3.

²⁴ MD 716/258, 736/224; WH, 222, 442; Ackermann to Pehle, 11/4/44, W 1, Ack; Pehle to Land, 7/11/44, W 50, WSA.

²⁵ Hayes to SS, 1/8/45, Rpt on Fedhala Camp, 8/28/44, u/c Offie to SS, 9/22/44, W 39, Evacn to Lyautey; Emgn Figures, u/c Cleveland to Joy, 2/7/45, USC, AF; Blickenstaff, Evacn of Stateless Refs to N Afr, 12/27/44, u/c Blickenstaff to AF Lisbon, 12/27/44, Conard, Rpt on Visit to Spain, 10/16/44, AF, RS 5; Beckelman to Anderson, 2/20/44, W 1, Ack; FR 1944, v 1, 996–7; WH, 11, 225–8. The camp was named Maréchal Lyautey.

²⁶ FR 1944, v 1, 1064, 1080, 1093–4; Weatherford to Jessup, 2/20/45, AF, FS, Ctry FNA, Algeria, Ltrs from; WH, 140, 229; Ackermann to Pehle, 11/4/44, W 1, Ack. This camp was called Jeanne d'Arc Ref Camp. The Allied military incorrectly estimated its capacity at 10,000 to 40,000. The French hampered its use by imposing regulations making refugee exit through liberated France difficult. (Marks, Memo for Files, 4/11/45, W 16, Mann.)

²⁷ MD 707/239–40, 712/229; WH, 232; Standish to Lesser [4/44], W 49, ICR; HID, 9783; Burton to Joy, 5/7/44, USC, Sen Burton; Pehle, Memo, 4/15/44, TH 1.

²⁸ MD 707/239–40; Pehle to Ackermann, 4/13/44, W 1, Ack; JPC 1025–7; Marks & Murphy, Cfs Held in Office of Ennis [3/44], TH 1. Emergency camps in the US had been suggested at least as early as summer 1942 (eg, AI Rpt, 4th, 6, 15; NYP, 6/21/43, 23).

²⁹ MD 716/175.

³⁰ MD 716/171–3.

³¹ MD 708/43; HSD, v 46, 86, 114–5, 145, v 47, 21; Stimson to Pehle, 3/31/44, ASW 5; Pehle, Memo, 3/9/44, TH 1; Hull, Morgenthau, & Stimson to FDR, 5/8/44, FDR, OF 3186; Estb TH. Earlier discussions of the plan with the 3 secretaries are covered in MD 709/27, 712/229, 716/174, 178–9; Pehle, Memo for Files, 3/9/44, TH 1. Stimson's Diary for Mar 9, 21, & 31 clearly shows his resolute restrictionism. There is also a hint of anti-Semitism, but a broader examination of Stimson's diary and papers tends to nullify that impression (MD 708/44).

³² MD 726/33–9, 146–62.

³³ MD 726/33; HSD, v 46, 114–5, v 47, 21; Travers to Hull, 5/5/44, Warren to SS, 5/5/44, SD, R/5499; Estb TH.

³⁴ Hull, Morgenthau, & Stimson to FDR, 5/8/44, FDR, OF 3186; Estb TH; HSD, v 46, 209; MD 716/175, 178. The attorney general advised that legal justification existed for instituting the plan by executive action (Gitlin to Cooley, 4/3/44, 4/8/44, Cooley to Atty Gen, 4/10/44, Legis 17437; Estb TH).

³⁵ NYT, 6/3/44, 15; MD 717/196, 198, 741/234; NYP, 4/5/44, 24, 4/15/44, 10, 4/21/44, 4; Grafton script, 4/23/44, W 66, G–H.

³⁶ All dates in 1944. Eg, NYP, 4/20, 23, 4/22, 4, 5/15, 18-9, 5/31, 6, 6/1, 4, 19, 23, 6/2, 1, 6/5, 17, 6/10, 11; NYHT, 4/20, 22, 5/27, 10; NYT, 5/4, 18, 6/10, 14, 6/12, 21; Lesser to Sheerin, 5/1, W 25, Sheerin; *NY Daily Mirror,* 5/13, 13; Gomberg to Beck & Rosenwald, 5/16, NRS 557; BG, 5/8, 10, 6/28, 13; MD 724/108–12, 738/42; Pringle, History of the War, 4/19, Wise to Pehle, 4/3, Baer-

wald to WRB, 4/26, TH 1; NR, 5/15, 666; *Nation,* 6/10, 670–1; *Commonweal,* 5/12, 76–7, 6/9, 172; CC, 5/24, 636; Weinstein to Pehle, 4/20, W 22, Radio/Grafton; CfR 10; Kalmanowitz to Pehle, 5/8, W 68, T–V; Draft ltr to FDR, 5/9, AJC, Imgn Series, Refs—Rescue of; YSH, 28.

37 MD 721/181, 735/217–9, 738/42–3, 741/234; Frenyear to Hull, 5/12/44, Frenyear to Pehle, 5/17/44, FDR, OF 5477; WH, 231; Cavert to Smith, 5/22/44, FCC, B 100, FCC 1940–49; Ingraham to Pehle, 4/20/44, W 29, YWCA; Pickett to FDR, 4/27/44, W 66, A; Atkinson to Pehle, 5/3/44, W 66, C–D; Joy to Burton, 5/12/44, USC, Sen Burton; McDonald to FDR, 5/12/44, W 67, M–N; Green to FDR, 5/8/44, FDR, OF 3186; NYT, 5/26/44, 19, 5/30/44, 8; IR, 7/10/44, 226.

38 Pickett, Memo on Visit to Wn, 4/4/44, AF, FS, Wn Trips; MD 722/340; NYHT, 4/19/44, 1; NYT, 4/19/44, 1; Gomberg to Beck & Rosenwald, 5/8/44, 5/16/44, 5/31/44, Beck to Gomberg, 5/12/44, NRS 557; Dept Heads' Mtg, 5/2/44, NRS 734; Gomberg to Slobodin, 9/26/45, NRS 559; Lesser to Pehle, 3/21/44, TH 1; Wn EC Mins, 4/13/44, JI, EC#48.

39 MD 722/134, 726/146. The poll registered 23% disapproval & 7% "don't know." WRB files include 3½ boxes (66–69) of incoming correspondence on free ports. It was very heavily favorable (Towler to Hodel [9/44], W 52, Admin Matters).

40 Pehle, Memo, 5/11/44, TH 2; MD 732/62–3; Pehle to Hull, Morgenthau, & Stimson, 5/20/44, FDR, OF 3186.

41 Ch 12 above, Italy section; MD 732/63–4; DuBois, Memo for Files, 5/26/44, TH 2.

42 Pehle to FDR, 5/18/44, FDR, OF 3186.

43 Ch 12 above, Italy section; PC/FDR, 5/30/44, 203; MD 737/85; Gom-

berg to Beck & Rosenwald, 5/31/44, NRS 557.

44 MD 738/39–40.

45 PC/FDR, 6/2/44, 212–4.

46 McCloy to Morgenthau, 6/2/44, TH 3; MD 741/47–8; PC/FDR, 6/9/44, 233–4; NYT, 6/10/44, 1, 9.

47 Proposed Message by the President to the Congress (nd), u/c Pehle to FDR, 5/18/44, FDR, OF 3186; PPA, 168–71; NYT, 6/13/44, 1, 8.

48 See pages 136, 153–4; *PM,* 8/2/44, 2.

49 MD 712/229; Pehle, Memo, 5/11/44, TH 2; Estb TH.

50 Pehle to Steinhardt, 4/22/44, W 26, Tur; Pehle to Ackermann, 4/25/44, W 1, Ack; Estb TH; MD 741/234.

51 Warren to SS, 5/4/44, SD, R/5499; DuBois, Memo for Files, 5/26/44, TH 2; ch 12 above, Italy section.

52 Joy to Grossmann, 6/10/44, USC, F: Dr. Joy—Com on Spec Ref Probs. Pehle later informed FDR that the Ft Ontario contribution had persuaded the British to allow 1,500 refugees into Libya and the French to agree to the camp at Philippeville. Actually, the British acceded to the Libyan proposal before FDR accepted the Ft Ontario plan. And the decision on Philippeville was the result of pressure from the Allied military. (Pehle to FDR, 10/4/44, FDR, OF 4849; FR 1944, v 1, 1058, 1064, 1080, 1093–4.)

53 Pro free ports: eg, MD 743/43–6; Ans, 7/15/44, 17; NR, 6/19/44, 801; *Nation,* 8/12/44, 171; Christian Council on Pal, Pr Rel, 8/4/44; Towler to Hodel [9/44], W 52, Admin Matters; Fry to FDR, 6/14/44, AJCg (LA) to Pehle, 8/3/44, W 66, A; Detzer to Pehle, 6/26/44, W 68, Ltrs from WRB; Petitions in W 68, Admsn of Refs; NYP, 6/22/44, 10; NYT, 8/5/44, 24; WH, 234; FDR to Hn, 8/14/44, FDR, OF 3186.

54 *Watertown Daily Times* [8/27/44], u/c Speight to FDR, 8/29/44, W 68, S;

Jordan to FDR [6/44], W 67, I–J; Mann to Sirs, 6/12/44, Fast to Johnson, 6/15/44, W 68, Disapproval; Mott to Hull, 6/21/44, SD, R/6373; *NY Sun,* 7/29/44, 6; WTH, 8/19/44, Memo beginning, "Mrs. Brown, representing Life Magazine," 8/30/44, TH 5.

⁵⁵ *Miami Herald,* 6/15/44, 6A, 7/28/44, 6A, 9/28/44, 4A; *Watertown Daily Times* [8/27/44], u/c Speight to FDR, 8/29/44, W 68, S; Kinnear to Wallgren, 8/30/44, W 27, Wallgren; John Trevor, *Refugees 1944* (7/44), Wilmeth to Dickstein, 7/27/44, Hetzel to Dickstein, 7/30/44, Legis 16453; NYT, 10/13/44, 8; WH, 948; NYP, 7/3/44, 15, 8/10/44, 7; Standish to Lesser [4/44], W 49, ICR 3; HID, 9783; Joy to Burton, 5/4/44, Burton to Joy, 5/7/44, USC, Sen Burton; Pehle, Memo, 4/15/44, TH 1; Biddle to FDR, 12/29/44, FDR, OF 3186; Dubin, Rpt on discussion with Travers, 12/5/45, NRS 558; Dubin to Loeb, 5/23/45, NRS 552; *Macon Telegraph,* 8/8/44, TH 5.

⁵⁶ TS, 10–3, 17–9; FO Rpt 1, p 39; NYT, 8/5/44, 13, 8/6/44, 29; SG, 9/44, 386; IR, 9/28/44, 295–6; Probs & Recomndns (nd), u/c Marks to O'Dwyer, 3/20/45, TH 10; WH, 235; FO Statistics Memo #6, 3/19/45, u/c Rose to Larned, 4/7/45, IMS, Oswego Proj. 7% were Roman Catholic; 3%, Greek Orthodox; 1%, Protestant.

⁵⁷ TS, 22.

⁵⁸ Rpts Office Narrative Rpt for 8/44, WRA 180; MD 763/33; Newspaper clippings in TH 5; IR, 9/28/44, 293; Myer to WRB, 9/19/44, u/c Pehle to FDR, 10/4/44, FDR, OF 4849.

⁵⁹ WH, 11; US Dept of Interior, *WRA: A Story of Human Conservation* (1946), 164.

⁶⁰ FO Statistics Memo #6, 3/19/45, IMS, Oswego Proj; FO Rpt 1, p 39; Myer to WRB, 9/19/44, FDR, OF 4849; Memo beginning, "Experience proves that living in a camp" [4/20/45], NRS 552; Schuchman's rpt [8/44], NRS 557.

⁶¹ Myer to WRB, 9/19/44, FDR, OF 4849; TS, 21, 28, 36–7; FSR, 65; FO Rpt 1, p 42; IR, 9/28/44, 296; FOH, 57.

⁶² Myer to WRB, 9/19/44, FDR, OF 4849; TS, 30–3; Memo beginning, "Experience proves" [4/20/45], NRS 552; Excerpt of ltr from Smart, 9/23/44, u/c Dubin to Beck 10/30/44, Dubin to Beck, 10/11/44, Gomberg to Dubin, 11/1/44, NRS 556; Reifer, Confidential Rpt, 1/22/45, USC, WRA; JPC 1022–4, 1037–41.

⁶³ Myer to WRB, 9/19/44, FDR, OF 4849; TS, 40.

⁶⁴ JPC 1012, 1052–3; FOH, 109–10, 178–9; MD 754/225; Schuchman's rpt [8/44], Brandeis, Rpt on ERS [8/30/44], NRS 557; *PM,* 2/26/45, 10; TS, 11–2; Interview with Mrs. Reifer, 8/11/44, USC, WRA; Wolff to AF, 5/5/45, with enclosure, draft Memorial to the President & Congress [5/45], u/c Smart to Jones, 5/8/45, AF, FS 4.

⁶⁵ Bondy, Emerg Ref Shelter Ft Ont, 1/45, NRS 559; Myer to O'Dwyer, 3/16/45, with enclosures, Probs & Recomndns (nd), u/c Marks to O'Dwyer, 3/20/45, TH 10.

⁶⁶ TS, 41; Nell to ER, 12/12/44, ER 2994/190 Misc; Wolff to ER, 2/1/45, with enclosure, ER 944/70 Morgenthau; Godfrey to ER, 2/17/45, ER to Godfrey, 2/24/45, ER 1758/100; Schauffler to Jones, 2/21/45, AF, FS 4; JPC 1022–4; Holstein to Wise, 2/2/45, NRS 552; Notes on Mtg of Com on Camps, 11/14/44, USC, WRA; Myer to WRB, 9/19/44, FDR, OF 4849.

⁶⁷ Bondy, Emerg Ref Shelter Ft Ont, 1/45, NRS 559; Memo beginning, "Experience proves" [4/20/45], NRS 552; TS, 41–3; Pitts to Myer, 6/4/45, WRA 202; Powers, Final Rpt of Shelter Director, 4/18/46, pp 13–9, FO Rpts; FO Rpt 1, pp 39, 41; Gruber to Ickes, 9/24/44, WRA 220; Smart, A Message to the People of FO, 11/9/44, Pitts to All Shelter Residents, 6/20/45, WRA 005.3; Hard-

ing to Myer, 1/31/45, Rpt of Sanitary Inspection of Shelter Kitchens, 3/20/45, WRA 290; Schroeder, Final Rpt of Mess Operations Section, 2/20/46, FO Rpts; Reifer, Rpt on Work at FO, 1/22–2/22/45, USC, WRA; The Children of A——B——, u/c Myer to O'Dwyer, 3/16/45, TH 10.

[68] Bondy, Emerg Ref Shelter Ft Ont, 1/45, NRS 559; Bondy, Observations on ERS (nd), FO Rpts; Schuchman's rpt [8/44], Brandeis, Rpt on ERS [8/30/44], NRS 557; Announcement by Shelter Dir, 1/3/45, WRA 220; Smart, An Apology, 8/19/44, WRA 005.3; Interview with Mrs. Reifer, 8/11/44, USC, WRA.

[69] Wolff to ER, 2/1/45, ER 944/70 Morgenthau; Godfrey to ER, 2/17/45, ER 1758/100; Schauffler to Jones, 2/21/45, AF, FS 4; JPC 983, 1022–4, 1052–3; Myer to Ickes, 12/7/44, TH 9; FO Rpt 3, p 14; MD 825/300–3; HID, 9783, 9789, 9812; Ickes to Byrnes, 7/31/45, SD, R/7-3145; Shaughnessy to Carusi, 12/28/44, Legis 17436.

[70] MD 825/300–3; JPC 1022–4; Smart to Myer, 9/4/44, WRA 001.

[71] JPC 985, 1037–41; Biddle to FDR, 12/29/44, FDR to Atty Gen, 1/17/45, FDR, OF 3186; MD 825/299, 828I/102–3, 829II/391, 852/141; Schauffler, Bkgd of Oswego Situation, 3/28/45, MEJ, WRA: Re ERS, Oswego, 5/2/45, AF, FS 4; Cf Held in Office of Under Secy of Interior, 12/28/44, Stmts of US Govt Officials, 12/26/44, TH 9; FO Rpt 3, p 13; TS, 91–2; O'Dwyer, Memo for Files, 3/14/45, TH 10.

[72] MD 828I/103.

[73] NYWT, 9/22/44, TH 6; *PM*, 2/15/45, 20; ER to Spitzer, 3/13/45, ER to Selden-Goth, 3/5/45, ER 1764/100; ER to Godfrey, 2/24/45, ER 1758/100.

[74] Myer to Ickes, 12/7/44, TH 9; F——K——, u/c Myer to O'Dwyer, 3/16/45, TH 10; Koppelmann to Dickstein, 7/6/45, Legis 17436; TS, 71.

[75] Schauffler, Bkgd of Oswego Situation, 3/28/45, Jones to Curtis, 5/11/45, Am Chr Com for Refs et al to O'Dwyer [5/15/45], AF, FS 4; Margolies, Wkly Rpts of Welfare Section, 3/11–17/45, 4/8–14/45, 4/15–21/45, WRA 007.1; Probs & Recomndns (nd), u/c Marks to O'Dwyer, 3/20/45, TH 10; JPC 1037–41; FOH, passim; Markley, New Residents of Am: Final Study of Attitudes, 2/13/46, p 49, FO Rpts; NYHT, 3/13/45, 21.

[76] Cf Held in Office of Under Secy of Interior, 12/28/44, TH 9; IMS, Statistical Section of a Study Made at FO, 5/1/45, pp 13–4, Hutchinson to Myer, 5/16/45, IMS, Oswego Proj.

[77] Myer to O'Dwyer, 3/16/45, with enclosures, Black to ER, 3/5/45, TH 10; *PM*, 2/26/45, 10; FOH, 39–40; Myer to Ickes, 12/7/44, TH 9; TS, 71; Mins of Com on Camps, 5/11/45, AF, FS 4.

[78] CEP Jour, 12/14/45; JPC 1046–7, 1074; Robinson, Larned, et al to HST, 10/22/45, NRS 558; NYT, 8/26/45, 1, 34, 35, 9/30/45, 1, 38, 39; Sherman to Wahl, 11/16/45, Legis 17436.

[79] JPC 1065, 1074; Robinson, Larned, et al to HST, 10/22/45, NRS 558; Sherman to Wahl, 11/16/45, Legis 17436.

[80] JPC 1072.

[81] FO Rpt 3, pp 18–24; WRA, Semi-Annual Rpt, 7/1/45–12/31/45, pp 32–3, FO Rpts; HID, 10190; JPC 1037–41, 1054, 1059–63, 1066, 1073–5; Ickes to Byrnes, 7/31/45, SD, R/7-3145; Sherman to Wahl, 11/16/45, Legis 17436; Dubin to Hurwitz, 1/30/46, NRS 557; Robinson, Larned, et al to HST, 10/22/45, Levy to Dubin, 12/11/45, Dubin, Mins of Mtg held 12/12/45, NRS 558; Smart to Myer, 5/4/45, WRA 213; Friends of FO, Stmt by Sponsors Com (nd), u/c Smart to HST, 7/9/45, WRA 111; NYT, 6/3/45, 17, 6/11/45, 16, 7/16/45, 9; Vance to Halla, 8/2/45, SD, R/7-645; FOH, 8–9, 100–2.

[82] NYT, 5/17/45, 3; FOH, passim, esp ii, 1–5, 25–30, 41–96; Smart to Dick-

stein, 6/19/45, with enclosure, Legis 17436; "A. Preliminary Statement" (handwritten notes) (nd), Legis 17437; Myer to Ickes, 6/30/45, with enclosed "Rpt on the Hearing at FO," WRA 003; Memo beginning, "In accordance with an Exec Memo," 10/1/45, Dubin to Perlman, 11/20/45, NRS 558. For press coverage: Newspaper Clippings file of TH; Clippings file of Legis 17436.

[83] Memo beginning, "To be used only in the event" (nd), Resol passed by House Com on Imgn [7/3/45], Cooley, Memo for File, 7/6/45, Pr Rel [7/6/45] (not issued), Dickstein, Com on Imgn Resol, 7/6/45, Cooley to Smart, 7/9/45, Legis 17436; Notes on mtg of Camp Com, 7/10/45, USC, Am Council; FO Rpt 3, pp 19–24; WRA, Semi-Annual Rpt, 7/1/45–12/31/45, p 33, FO Rpts; NYHT, 6/27/45, 3; Myer to Ickes, 6/30/45, WRA 003; NYT, 10/5/45, 21, 10/16/45, 25; Dickstein to HST, 10/3/45, NRS 558.

[84] NYT, 12/23/45, 1, 10. For Truman's overall policy on the European DP problem, see Leonard Dinnerstein, *Am & the Survivors of the Holocaust* (1982).

[85] JPC 1087–91, 2075. Sixty-six of the refugees had already returned voluntarily to Yugoslavia (Vance et al to State, Justice, & Interior Depts, 10/24/45, TH, Paneling of Refs at FO).

[86] JPC 1091.

[87] AJC, Memo to Members, 1/14/46, AJC, Imgn Series, Refs—Rescue of; *Syracuse Post-Standard,* 1/2/46, WRA 190.

[88] Saunders to Smart, 9/20/44, Silverman to Smart, 5/14/45, Smart to Silverman, 5/18/45, WRA 130; *Oswego Palladium-Times,* 8/4/45, WRA 190; Nash to Markley, 9/7/44, Smart to Nash, 9/11/44, WRA 170; Rpts Office Narrative Rpt for 8/44, WRA 180; FO Rpt 2, p 7; Markley, New Residents of Am, 2/13/46, p 20, Markley, Prelim Rpt

2, 1/21/46, pp 4–5, Markley, Prelim Rpt 7, 1/28/46, p 3, FO Rpts; FOH, 53–77; Whitney to Jones, 9/9/44, AF, RS, Internees, AF Proj at ERS, FO; Godfrey to ER, 2/17/45, ER 1758/100; *PM,* 2/27/45, 10; NYP, 11/22/44, 8; *Time,* 8/6/45, 22.

[89] FO Rpt 2, p 8; TS, 8; Godfrey to ER, 2/17/45, ER 1758/100.

[90] Pitts to Myer, 6/12/45, WRA 007.1; numerous newspaper clippings in WRA 190; *Syracuse Post-Standard* [7/2/45], Legis 17436; Markley, Prelim Rpt 7, 1/28/46, p 1, FO Rpts.

[91] FOH, 56; FO Rpt 2, p 8; Burke to Wagner, 5/21/45, Nase to Hawkes, 5/31/45, TH, May–June 1945; Myer to Ickes, 6/30/45, with enclosed "Rpt on the Hearing at FO," WRA 003; Quinn to HST, 6/4/45, SD, R/6-445; Ltr from Litchfield, 6/10/45, SD, R/5-1045. The extensive press coverage on the hearings is reflected in TH, Newspaper Clippings file; & in Legis 17436, Clippings file; also *Time,* 8/6/45, 22, and *Newsweek* 7/16/45, 30. Correspondence to the Dickstein committee, including the 3 quotations, is in: Com VI—Incoming Corresp file in Legis 17436.

[92] Eg, Biddle to FDR, 12/29/44, FDR, OF 3186; Joy to Burton, 5/4/44, Burton to Joy, 5/7/44, USC, Sen Burton; Dubin to Loeb, 5/23/45, NRS 552; Dubin, Rpt on discussion with Travers, 12/5/45, NRS 558; Pehle, Memo, 4/15/44, TH 1; Draft ltr to Mrs. Morgenthau [10/44], TH 7; HID, 9783.

[93] Memo on Ber Cf on the Ref Prob (nd), W 3, Ber Cf.

[94] FR 1944, v 1, 1076; MD 758/71; H II, 16, Exh K; WH, 286.

[95] Clattenburg, Convsn with Schenkolewski, 5/25/44, SD, R/6406; FR 1944, v 1, 1076, 1146–7, 1175–80, 1188; WH, 284–5; RM, 56.

[96] RM, 55; FSR, 43–4; Memo Concerning Jewish Civil Internees, 5/1/44, W 56, Jews in Eur: Feb–Apr; AI Rpt,

5th, 4; Segal to Slawson, 4/20/44, AJC, Imgn Series, Refs—Rescue of. Some of the camps were at Vittel, Compiègne, Liebenau, & Tittmoning (WH, 247). On this topic, also see YVS, v 1, 125–52.

⁹⁷ FSR, 33; WH, 247, 253; BL to Travers, 12/16/43, BLP, B 202, Refs; RM, 54–5; FR 1944, v 1, 1000–1; Memo Concerning Jewish Civil Internees, 5/1/44, W 56, Jews in Eur: Feb–Apr.

⁹⁸ MD 718/224, 723/347–8; Polish Emb (Wn), Memo, 12/24/43, SD, R/5054; Travers to Tress, 1/11/44, SD, R/5053; RM, 57; JM, Memo for Files Re Paraguayan Citizens in Fr, 2/21/44, W 46, LA Passports 1; Hull to Istanbul, 12/29/43, SD, R/4969.

⁹⁹ MD 718/89–90, 224; FR 1944, v 1, 1000–1, 1023–4; WH, 247.

¹⁰⁰ MD 718/90–2, 173, 194, 222–4, 719/181; Clattenburg, Memo of Cf [4/10/44], SD, R/3-2344.

¹⁰¹ MD 718/92, 106–15, 172, 192, 225; AI Rpt, 6th, 5; FR 1944, v 1, 1023–4; Tait to Huddle, 4/19/44 (twice), JKH to Tait, 4/21/44, W 56, Jews in Eur.

¹⁰² Clattenburg, Memo of Cf [4/10/44], SD, R/3-2344; MD 719/158, 180.

¹⁰³ Clattenburg, Memo of Cf [4/10/44], SD, R/3-2344; FR 1944, v 1, 1024–5; MD 718/194.

¹⁰⁴ Clattenburg, Memo of Cf [4/10/44], SD, R/3-2344; FR 1944, v 1, 1026–7, 1086–7; WH, 252–62. Peru did not comply (WH, 261).

¹⁰⁵ WH, 262, 268–9; FR 1944, v 1, 1071–3, 1085–6, 1100–2, 1131, 1141, 1154, 1161; RM, 56–7; FSR, 34; McCormack to Exec Dir, 2/19[45], W 28, WRB (2 entries: Lat Am Passports & Exchange).

¹⁰⁶ Rosenheim to Pehle, 1/2/45, W 46, LA Passports; RM, 57; *Rescue,* 10/44, 11; Am Legation (Bern) to Swiss Div of Foreign Interests, 2/15/45, W 56, Jews in Eur; PR, 1977 (v 22/4), 12; MD 718/89–90, 759/220.

¹⁰⁷ Hayes, Memo re Baraibar, 3/18/43, CH, B 3, Jordana; Excerpts & Summary

of Rpt on Spain from Conard, 11/20/43, AF, RS 6; Avni, 131–8. More regarding the Sephardic Jews appears in Avni, ch 5.

¹⁰⁸ Hayes, Memo re Baraibar, 3/18/43, CH, B 3, Jordana; Blickenstaff to Boyer-Mas, 12/7/43, u/c Mann Rpt; Excerpts & Summary of Rpt on Spain from Conard, 11/20/43, AF, RS 6; Avni, 141–2.

¹⁰⁹ Avni, 142, 144, 147–56; Blickenstaff to Pan de Soraluce, 11/10/43, AF, FS, Ctry Sp 1943–45, Ltrs, Confid; MD 702/36; *Rescue,* 11/44, 7; NYT, 2/17/44, 7.

¹¹⁰ Avni, 162; MD 752/131, 778/54, 793/287; Hull to Madrid, 9/11/44, SD, R/9-1144; Pehle to Leavitt, 10/24/44, W 19, AJJDC 1. WH, 274, mentions the evacuation of an additional 500 Sephardic Jews in late spring or summer 1944. FR 1944, v 1, 1036, repeats it. This is an error, probably based on a misreading of MD 752/131. The correct information appears in CH 2, pp 5–6, & CH 3, p 4.

¹¹¹ Kershner to Joy, 1/31/44, USC, AF; FR 1944, v 2, 266, 271–2; MD 706/311; FSR, 55–6.

¹¹² GR, i, ii, iv, 14; Laughlin to Pehle, 3/7/44, W 9, Gr Relief Prog; FR 1943, v 4, 167–8, 172–5; Hull to Cairo, 3/23/44, SD, R/5481B; NYT, 10/6/44, 1, 4, 5, 11/1/44, 7. The depth of suffering in Greece is readily seen in NYT dispatches in early 1942 (eg, 1/19, 3, 1/28, 12, 2/7, 4, 2/15, 25, 3/1, 27). The agreement with Germany permitted the removal of surplus varieties of food from Greece, but only if they were replaced with other food (GR, i). There were several indications of German violations (eg, NYT, 9/7/43, 12, 1/9/44, 31, 8/2/44, 8, 8/3/44, 10). But other reputable reports denied violations (eg, CSM, 4/9/43, 11; NYT, 4/20/43, 22, 4/21/43, 11).

¹¹³ Hyman, Extension of Relief in Occupied Poland, 11/13/42, Baerwald to Wise, 11/27/42, JDC, G/E, Poland, Gen; AF Mins, For Serv Section (Ctr,

Ref & Relief), 5/27/43; AF Mins, Jt For Serv Exec Com (Ctr, Ref & Relief), 6/24/43; Boris Shub, *Starvation Over Europe (Made in Germany)* (1943); CW, 4/30/43, 3–8; NYT, 11/13/43, 8.

[114] NYT, 5/12/43, 4; FR 1943, v 1, 387; FR 1944, v 2, 254; FR 1945, v 5, 29.

[115] Long, Convsn with Goldmann, Wise, & Acheson, 9/29/42, Brandt, Convsn with Leavitt, Baerwald, Hyman, et al, 12/2/ 42, BLP, B 209, Special Div Relief for Jews; BLD, 261–2; Hayes to Leavitt, 8/4/42, Buchman to Hayes, 8/7/42, Leavitt to Schwartz, 12/13/42, Katzki to AJDC, 5/4/43, 6/8/43, 8/19/43, Leavitt to AJDC Lisbon, 8/2/43, JDC, G/E, Poland, Gen; CW, 5/14/43, 13–4; JF, 3/42, 4–5, 3/43, 3; FR 1943, v 1, 386–7; Lehman to Acheson, 3/16/43, BLP, B 194, For Relief & Rehab.

[116] Detzer, *Appointment,* 244–9; Kershner to ER, 6/5/42, ER 2607/170; NYT, 12/4/42, 17; NYT (1943), 1/23, 7, 3/12, 7, 5/21, 18, 11/5, 2, 11/8, 6, 11/15, 24, 11/16, 20, 12/27, 15; NYT, 3/12/44, IV, 6; Israel, 160; AF Mins, Jt For Serv Exec Com (Ctr, Ref & Relief), 6/24/43, 11/1/43; Johnson to ER, 3/30/44, ER 1729/100.

[117] NYT (1943), 7/9, 4, 11/5, 2, 11/11, 8, 11/12, 14, 11/27, 12, 12/21, 10; NYT (1944), 1/28, 19, 1/30, 36, 2/16, 34, 3/12, IV, 6, 4/18, 5, 6/5, 14; Sen Rpt No 624 (78 Cong, 1st ses), 12/20/43; SFE, 12/21/43, 9; Detzer, *Appointment,* 245–51; S Res 100, u/c Mins of Exec Com of NRS, 5/20/43, AF, RS, C/O, NRS; WP, 1/25/44, 10, 3/25/44, 10; Johnson to ER, 3/30/44, ER 1729/100. The Gallup poll recorded 22% opposed & 13% with no opinion (NYT, 2/12/44, 6).

[118] FR 1944, v 2, 252–64, 268–81, 285–300; FR 1945, v 5, 26–31; CEP Jour, 7/13/44; Stettinius, Convsn with Kershner, 8/9/44, BLP, B 202, Relief.

[119] My Day, 3/6/44 release, ER, B 3148; WP, 3/2/44, 13.

[120] CEP Jour, 1/16/43, 3/26/43, 4/12/

43, 6/15/43, 7/13/44; Long, Convsn with Pehle, 10/28/43, SD 862.4016/2292; BLD, 258, 277.

[121] MD 701/262.

[122] WH, 10, 351; FSR, 57–8; Schauffler to Branson, 4/11/44, AF, FS, Food & Feeding; Petluck to Mign Staff, 3/24/44, NRS 585; NYT, 4/15/44, 12.

[123] WH, 10, 329; FSR, 56–7. This proposal had been advocated by the UOR as early as 1942 and by the JEC in the program it sent to Bermuda in 1943 (BG, 6/25/42, 14; CW, 4/30/43, 14).

[124] WH, 329–30, 1176–8; Huber to Harrison, 5/12/44, W 47, IRC.

[125] MD 744/191, 755/290; Rpt to the President, u/c O'Dwyer to HST, 6/25/45, W 51, Food Pkgs 6; *Foreign War Relief Operations* (House Doc 262), 7/17/45, 94; Zollinger to Pehle, 7/26/44, PSC 1/12; WH, 336; RM, 45; Burckhardt, Communiqué 284b, 5/17/45, W 60, ICRC/Camps.

[126] MD 744/191; FR 1944, v 2, 267; Rpt to the President, u/c O'Dwyer to HST, 6/25/45, W 51, Food Pkgs 6; RM, 46; FSR, 14–5, 58; WH, 7, 341–2. At the end of 1944, blockade authorities authorized 300,000 additional food parcels, and Roosevelt allotted $1,125,000 more from foreign-war-relief funds. But these parcels were not ready before the war in Europe ended.

[127] FSR, 58–9; WH, 342–5; FR 1945, v 2, 1136–40; MD 826/90–4, 840/226.

[128] Harrison to SS, 3/22/45, W 60, ICRC/Camps; MD 834/172, 840/226; RM, 52–3; FSR, 59; McC to O'Dwyer, 4/13/45, W 4, Central L I; Harrison to SS, 4/27/45, 5/4/45, W 44, Switz-New Prog. Felix Kersten was probably involved in these arrangements (Kersten, *Memoirs,* 9–21, 275–80).

[129] Numbers in parentheses refer to pages in this book.

Evacuation: via Turkey, 4,000–5,000 (pages 216–20); via Spain, 1,000 (page 226); from Finland, 150 (page 231); to Switz, 4,250 (page 233); to Switz by negotiations, 2,896 (pages 246–7, 250); Hungary to Rumania, 2,000 (page 233); Hungary to Yugoslavia, some (pages 229, 233).

Protection: McClelland's fund, 8,000 & up (page 232); exchanges & Latin American document recognition, 2,000 (pages 277, 279).

Diplomatic/Psychological: Transnistria (pages 219–20); Budapest (pages 237–8, 240–3).

Non-Jews Evacuated: to Sweden, 16,200 (pages 229–30); to Switz, 1,400 (page 284); Yugoslavs (by reopening flow in spring 1944), 5,000–6,000 (pages 227–8); also Wilson to AGWAR for CCS, 5/24/44, 6/9/44, W 14, It 2).

The WRB left no final estimate of the numbers it helped save, only referring to "tens of thousands" (WH, 13). In Feb 1945, the WRB did calculate that about 126,604 (Jews & non-Jews) had been rescued since its formation (McCormack to Exec Dir, 2/19[45], W 28, WRB 3).

[130] Hn to Lubin, 4/20/44, FDR, OF 5477; Hn to Cox, 3/13/44, OC; H III, 8. Excluding Soviet Jews, about 1,000,000 Jews remained alive in Europe at the end of the war—though estimates ranged as high as 1,500,000 (FSR, 72; Pinkerton to SS, 6/23/45, SD, R/6-2345; NYT, 1/11/45, 17, 5/24/45, 7).

[131] Hyman to Warburg, 5/10/44, JDC, Rpts; CEP Jour, 4/4/44; RM, 75.

[132] WH, 1300; Pickett to Pehle, 10/18/44, AF, RS, US Govt, WRB; Kalmanowitz to Pehle, 2/1/45, W 27, VH; Mohler to Mulholland, 6/11/45, Mulholland to Mohler, 6/13/45, BI 98, WRB, W-1.

[133] AAF, 636–7, 649; NYT, 7/24/44, 1, 8/3/44, 1, 8/22/44, 1; KCS, 8/6/44, 10A, 8/25/44, 2; WP, 8/31/44, 4; Marks, Draft Exec Order, 9/12/44, W 28, WRB 3; MD 799/179–80, 800/1–6, 12, 245; NYHT, 12/1/44, 17.

[134] Pehle to Hoffman, 12/23/44, W 9, M Hoffman; MD 809/91, 812/202; Memo beginning, "The Emerg Com . . .

has noted with regret" (nd), A. W. Bennet Papers, B 25, F 1, J Affairs; Bergson to Celler, 1/8/45, PSC 1/16; NYP, 1/29/45, 4; NYT, 1/28/45, 19; Pehle to WRB, 1/27/45, W 28, WRB 3.

[135] O'Dwyer biographical data, 4/6/45, W 26, Un J Welfare Fund; FEA, Brief Review of O'Dwyer's Activities (nd), O'Dwyer; NYT, 4/7/42, 23, 6/24/44, 7, 9/5/44, 3, 11/7/45, 2.

[136] AF Mins, For Serv Staff, 3/19/45; MD 816/45–6, 823/240, 825/134, 826/14; Schauffler to Jones, 2/21/45, AF, FS 4; O'Dwyer's Press Cf, 1/31/45, W 28, WRB 3; NYT, 1/31/45, 23, 2/2/45, 4, 5/2/45, 12.

[137] MD 825/92, 134, 828I/104, 831/220–30, 839/110, 124–6A, 243, 847/31–2, 132–4; Schauffler to Jones, 2/21/45, Jones to Schauffler, 5/16/45, MEJ, Cf with Silverman, 5/2/45, AF, FS 4; NYP, 1/29/45, 4; 3 vols of press clippings on O'Dwyer & the mayoralty race, W 53, O'Dwyer; NYT, 5/30/45. 21. O'Dwyer announced his availability for the mayoralty of New York on May 31. He was elected in November by a wide margin. (NYT, 6/1/45, 1, 11/7/45, 1.)

[138] DuBois-Jarvik interview, 10/23/78; Pehle-Jarvik interview, 10/16/78. The WRB was officially disbanded by executive order on 9/14/45 (*Federal Register,* 9/15/45, 11789).

CHAPTER 15.
THE BOMBING OF AUSCHWITZ

[1] 15AF, *Historical Summary: First Year of Operations* (1944), 5, in RG 243, 58, Sec 3.

[2] Rudolf Vrba & Alan Bestic, *I Cannot Forgive* (1964), 198, 231–4, 247–9; GEC (quotation is from pp 14, 16).

[3] Vrba & Bestic, *I Cannot Forgive,* 249–50; Braham I, 1014; Livia Rotkirchen, *The Destruction of Slovak Jewry: A Documentary History* (1961), xli; Dulles to McC, 6/15/44, with enclo-

sures, McC to Pehle, 10/12/44, W 61, Extmn Camps; Gerhart Riegner to David Wyman, 5/25/77; MD 750/354–60, 751/239, 800/193; WH, 447.

4 WLB, v 27, 1973/74, 42; *Manchester Guardian,* 6/27/44, 4, 8, 6/28/44, 8; NYT, 6/20/44, 5. McClelland telegraphed an 8-page summary of the report to Washington on 7/6/44 (Harrison to SS, 7/6/44, W 56, Jews in Eur; MD 750/354–60).

5 "Explanation of wire from our friends in Slovakia" (nd), with attached telegram, W 62, UOR (Jan–June 1944).

6 "Just now a second telegramme" [5/23/44], with attached telegram, McC to de Jong, 5/25/44, with enclosure, Harrison to SS, 6/2/44, Sternbuch to McC, 6/22/44, W 62, UOR.

7 Pinkerton to SS, 6/2/44, W 34, Hung 2 (last); *Yalkut Moreshet,* 6/71, 87–8, 102.

8 MB & GFl, "We are sending you," 5/22/44, W 61, Extmn Camps; Riegner to Wyman, 5/25/77.

9 Dulles to McC, 6/15/44, with enclosures, W 61, Extmn Camps; Riegner to Wyman, 5/25/77; MD 750/184–8.

10 Paraphrase of cable [6/12/44], attached to Hilldring to OPD, 6/23/44, RG 165(1); *Polityka,* 8/9/75; PR, 1977 (v 22/4), 14; Rosenheim to Morgenthau, Hull, Stimson, 6/18/44, W 35, Hung 5.

11 Office of ASW to WRB, 6/20/44, ASW 5; Hilldring to OPD, 6/23/44, RG 165(1); Pehle, Memo for Files, 6/24/44, W 35, Hung 5.

12 Ray Cline, *Washington Command Post: The Operations Division* (1951), ix; CAD D/F (Hilldring to OPD), 6/23/44, inc date stamps, RG 165, CAD 383.7 (1) (1-21-43) Sec 2; Hull to ASW, 11/14/44, ASW 2; all of RG 165(1).

13 FR 1944, v 1, 987–90; MD 699/22; TRH, Memo for Record [6/26/44], RG 165(1); Pasco to Gailey, 2/7/44, Handy to Chief of Staff, 2/8/44, JHC, Memo for Record (nd), RG 165, OPD 334.8, WRB, Sec 1, case 1.

14 TRH, Memo for Record [6/26/44], RG 165(1); Morgenthau to McCloy, 1/28/44, ASW 5.

15 Same as preceding note; also McNarney to ASW, 2/6/44, ASW 5.

16 WH, 439, 1315; Gerhardt, Memo for Sub-com, 2/11/44, Mtg Held at 4:00, 2/11/44, ASW 5; Saxon, Rpt to Pehle, 4/10/44, Ackermann to Pehle, 5/24/44, W 70, Evacn of Yugo Refs. Five months later, Caffey remained wholly uncooperative (Ackermann to Pehle, 9/7/44, W 1, Ack). Herbert Lehman, director of UNRRA, found the military similarly unwilling to cooperate in his organization's efforts (Allan Nevins, *Herbert H. Lehman & His Era* [1963], chs 11–12).

17 OPD D/F (Hull to CAD), 6/26/44, RG 165(1).

18 Gerhardt, Memo for Sub-com, 2/11/44, Mtg Held at 4:00, 2/11/44, ASW 5.

19 FR 1943, v 1, 176, 295–9; BL, "I talked to Gen Strong," 4/22/43, SD 548.G1/4-2243; BL, Memo, 4/26/43, SD, R/4-2643. Re transport of non-Jewish refugees to Africa, see pages 338–9.

20 FR 1943, v 1, 366; Relief & Evacn Projects, 1/27/44, BLP, B 204, Refs Relief & Evacn Proj; MD 689/203–5, 693/190, 196, 200; Hilldring to ASW, 1/25/44, ASW 4; Stettinius to The Secy, 1/8/44, BLP, B 202, Refs; Mtg Held at 4:00, 2/11/44, ASW 5.

21 Stettinius to The Secy, 1/8/44, BLP, B 202, Refs.

22 MD 699/31–2, 701/165; WH, 98–9. Ultimately, most of the Jews on Rab were evacuated by Tito's partisans and survived the war. But several hundred were caught by the Germans and deported. Britain's extreme callousness toward the Rab refugees was traced by Menachem Shelach in *Yalkut Moreshet,* 4/83, 203–11.

23 Harrison to SS, 6/24/44, ASW 3.

24 Pehle to McCloy, 6/29/44, HAG to McCloy, 7/3/44, McCloy to Pehle, 7/4/44, ASW 3.

[25] Akzin to Lesser, 6/29/44, W 35, Hung 5.

[26] MD 750/184–8; Summary of Steps, 7/13/44, Pehle to Stettinius, 7/13/44, Draft memos to Secy War, to President, & to Stimson, 7/13/44, Pehle to Morgenthau, 9/6/44, W 34, Hung 1; Pehle to McCloy, 10/3/44, W 35, Hung 5.

[27] Smertenko to FDR, 7/24/44, SD, R/7-2444.

[28] Ans, 7/5/43, 6; NYT, 7/20/44, 4; FR 1943, v 1, 406–7; Smertenko to FDR, 7/24/44, SD, R/7-2444; FH, Memo for Files, 8/5/44, AA, draft ltr to Smertenko (nd), W 35, Hung 5; Bergson to Jt Chiefs of Staff, 9/16/44, JCS 180th Mtg (Retaliation for Extmn), 10/3/44, Hull, Memo for Record, 10/5/44, JCS, Memo for Record (nd), Leahy to HCNL, 10/4/44, RG 218, CCS 385.3 (9-16-44); Bergson to FDR, 10/17/44, FDR, OF 3186.

[29] Kubowitzki to McCloy, 8/9/44, ASW 1.

[30] McCloy to Kubowitzki, 8/14/44, ASW 1. No such study was ever made.

[31] Akzin to Pehle, 9/2/44, W 35, Hung 5; Kalmanowitz to Pehle, 9/11/44, W 36, Hung 6.

[32] Winant to SS, 9/29/44, Proskauer to Pehle, 9/26/44, UOR & VH to Pehle, 9/26/44, W 18, Poland 1; Lesser, "Germans," 9/27/44, Pehle to Morgenthau, 11/3/44, W 72, Eisenhower Stmt; Pehle to McCloy, 10/3/44, ASW 3.

[33] HAG to McCloy, 10/5/44, ASW 3.

[34] OPD Routing Form, 9/29/44, RG 165, OPD 383.7, Sec 2, case 26(2); Arnold to Spaatz (41089), 10/4/44, Daily Staff Mtg #4, 10/5/44, Spz, B 19, Oct 44 Official; Anderson to Spaatz (CS178EC) [10/5/44], Spz, B 37, Cables Oct 44.

[35] Mannon to Pehle, 11/16/44, Hodel, Memo, 11/2/44, Pehle to McCloy, 11/8/44, W 6, Ger Extmn Camps; Pehle-Jarvik interview, 10/16/78.

[36] OPD Routing Form, 11/8/44, RG 165, OPD 000.5, Sec 3, case 53; Hull to ASW, 11/14/44, ASW 2.

[37] Hull to ASW, 11/14/44, McCloy to Pehle, 11/18/44, ASW 2. The US Air Force's ability to reach Auschwitz is shown later in this chapter.

[38] Garlinski, 260–2.

[39] AAF, xii, 47, 66, 792–3; WF, 132–3, 136; Sunderman, 174.

[40] AAF, 283; Eaker to Spaatz (CS440IE), 5/8/44, Spz 1, Oil Tgts; Eaker to Spaatz (CS719IE), 6/27/44, Spz, B 35, Cables June 44; CS; M Rpts, reel A6465 (7/7/44), fr 1029, 1031, 1040, 1050, 1052, 1138, 1178; Infield, 166. It should be noted that neither the Normandy invasion of June 6 nor the ensuing drive across France drew on 15AF resources. The August invasion of southern France only very briefly took a small amount of 15AF power, for the tactical 12AF assumed most of that responsibility. (AAF, 174–9, 297, 420–37.)

[41] Aiming Points Rpts, Oswiecim, 1/21/44, Blechhammer N & S, 3/15/44, RG 243, Sec 4-1g (141, 142, 163); Spaatz to Eaker (586), 4/27/44, Eaker to Spaatz (CS440IE), 5/8/44, Spz 1, Oil Tgts. The Air Force made reconnaissance photographs of the Auschwitz complex on Apr 4, 1944, and had a map of it available in May (M Rpts, reel A6494, fr 1602).

[42] AAF, 177–9, 292–6, 645, 794–6; WF, 46–7, 237–40.

[43] AAF, 177–8; WF, facing 47; CS; Infield, 181; KCS, 8/21/44, 4. There actually were two major target complexes at Blechhammer, North & South.

[44] DO, 8/44; CS; Syn Oil Plant of I. G. Farben at Oswiecim (nd), RG 243, GS 5612. The all-black 332 Fighter Group piloted 57 of the Mustangs (AAF, facing 329).

[45] DO, 9/44; Syn Oil Plant of I. G. Farben at Oswiecim (nd), RG 243, GS 5612; *Hefte von Auschwitz,* v 8 (1964),

66. The Liberators attacked from the west, thus flying directly over the gas chambers.

[46] NYT, 8/21/44, 6, 9/14/44, 6; WP, 8/21/44, 3 (UP rpt); KCS, 8/21/44, 4, 9/14/44, 2 (AP rpts).

[47] DO, 12/44.

[48] DO, 8/44; CS; M Rpts, reel A6473 (8/22/44), fr 595; Infield, 181.

[49] AAF, 72–9, 149–62, 371–2, 405, 652; WF, 260; 15AF Attacks Against Bridges, 6/7/44, Spz, B 18, June 44 Official; Miller to Maxwell, 10/18/44, Spz 1, Com & Trans.

[50] AAF, 473, 655, 736, 746; Hilary Saunders, *Royal Air Force, 1939–1945,* v 3 (1954), 223–5.

[51] Braham I, 794; CS; M Rpts, reel A6465 (7/7/44), fr 1029, 1031, 1040, 1050, 1178, reel A6473 (8/20/44), fr 172–3, 178, 214, reel A6473 (8/22/44), fr 583, 595, 606, 816, reel A6474 (8/27/44), fr 730, 733, 741, 746, reel A6477 (9/13/44), fr 623, 651, reel A6481 (10/13/44), fr 740, 775, 942, 957, reel A6481 (10/14/44), fr 1412, 1441, 1446, reel A6482 (10/17/44), fr 658.

[52] Sternbuch to VH, 8/28/44, 9/13/44, VH, B 20; M Rpts, reel A6477 (9/13/44), fr 623, 651; CS; Interpretation Rpt No DB 214, 9/16/44 (Vrutky), RG 243, GS 5612.

[53] Smolen, 209–13.

[54] Jan Sehn, *German Crimes in Poland,* v 1 (1946), 84–5, 88, fig 7; GEC, 6, 7, 15, 22; Garlinski, 77, 89; Ota Kraus & Erich Kulka, *The Death Factory* (1966), 15 (fig 2); MD 750/184–8, 354–60; NYT, 2/24/79, 2; *Studies in Intelligence,* winter 1978–79, 11–29; *Military Intelligence,* 1/83, 50–5.

[55] Syn Oil Plant of I. G. Farben at Oswiecim (nd), RG 243, GS 5612; *Military Intelligence,* 1/83, 50–5.

[56] AAF, 795. Bombing accuracy was also hampered by darkness. But the missions to Upper Silesia took place in daylight. (DO, 7/44–11/44.)

[57] Eaker to Giles, 8/31/44, 10/5/44,

IE, B 22, Corresp with Giles II; Cabell to Eaker, 10/30/44, IE, B 24, MAAF II; DO, 7/44–11/44; Eaker to Spaatz (CS171IE), 9/14/44, Spz, B 36, Cables Sept 44; Robert Poirier to David Wyman, 3/8/80; Notes on Cf, Bari, 10/15/44, Spz 1, Flak Defenses; CS.

[58] M Rpts, reel A6473 (8/20/44), fr 140, reel A6477 (9/13/44), fr 628.

[59] MD 750/354–60, 184–8; Olga Lengyel, *Five Chimneys* (1947), 123, 155–6; C____ B____ interview with Wyman, 4/17/77; C____ B____ to David Wyman, 4/18/78. Similar reactions have been recorded by many survivors of Auschwitz. Eg, Pelagia Lewinska, *Twenty Months at Auschwitz* (1968), 21; Elie Wiesel, *Night* (1960), 67; *J Observer,* 1/79, 45; *Commentary,* 7/78, 9–10.

[60] Sunderman, 320–1; AAF, 376–7, 382–3, 399. If necessary, medium bombers could have landed at partisan-held airfields in Yugoslavia.

[61] AAF, 283; M Rpts, Narrative Rpt, Mission #702, 82 Fighter Group (6/10/44) (Xerox copy).

[62] Infield, 68; Eaker to Spaatz (CS440IE), 5/8/44, Spz 1, Oil Tgts.

[63] Philip Birtles, *Mosquito* (1980), 20–5, 57, 88–93, 137–8, 145–6, 183–5; Sunderman, 324–7; Saunders, *RAF,* v 3, 91, 406; NYT, 10/29/44, 7. At least 44 Mosquitoes (and probably more) were stationed at Allied air bases in Italy in June 1944 (EA Munday [Air Historical Branch, Ministry of Defence, London] to David Wyman, 3/29/83).

[64] Birtles, *Mosquito,* 90–5, 135–40; Saunders, *RAF,* v 3, 91–2; Pehle to McCloy, 11/8/44, McCloy to Pehle, 11/18/44, ASW 2.

[65] DO & M Rpts show that alternate targets were routinely assigned for each mission and that they were struck fairly often.

[66] Smolen, 22, 193–4, 200–1; GEC, 16.

[67] Hilberg, 215–9, 255, 628–9; Sehn, *German Crimes,* v 1, 85–6; Filip Friedman, *This Was Oswiecim* (1946), 54–5; GEC, part 2, 13.

[68] Hilberg, 284, 328–9, 453, 473, 547, 630–1, 727–8; Raul Hilberg to David Wyman, 5/27/77; Smolen, 209–13; Friedman, *Oswiecim,* 25; YVS, v 8, 22.

[69] Ernst Schnabel, *Anne Frank: A Portrait in Courage* (1958), 117, 135, 148–52, 160, 166, 174; Jacob Presser, *The Destruction of the Dutch Jews* (1969), 483–4.

[70] OWI Pr Rel, 6/13/44, W 4, Camps; Hilldring to McCloy, 1/25/44, ASW 4; Ackermann to Murphy, 5/5/44, Ackermann to Pehle, 5/11/44, W 1, Ack. The evacuation of 100,000 non-Jews is discussed in ch 16.

[71] *Japan Qtrly,* fall 1975, 340–5; *Harper's,* 2/47, 105; *Amherst: The College & Its Alumni,* winter 1976, 31. Stimson himself regarded Kyoto as "a target of considerable military importance" (*Harper's,* 2/47, 105).

[72] AAF, 316; Infield, ch 13; John Slessor, *The Central Blue* (1957), 612–3, 620–1; Burns, 534–5.

[73] Slessor, *Central Blue,* 614–20; *Observer* (London), 8/16/64, 9; AAF, 316.

[74] Winston Churchill, *The Second World War: Triumph & Tragedy* (1953), 128–45; AAF, 317; Warsaw Dropping Opns [10/9/44], Anderson to Kuter, 9/24/44, Spz 2. With the election at hand, concern about the Polish-American vote may have influenced FDR. He and other Democratic leaders were worried about holding this large, normally Democratic constituency. (Robert Divine, *Foreign Policy & U.S. Presidential Elections, 1940–1948* (1974), 109–12, 138–42.)

[75] Anderson to Kuter, 9/24/44, Warsaw Dropping Opns [10/9/44], Spz 2; McDonald to Dep Commanding Gen, Opns, 10/14/44, Spz, B 139, Neut & Occup Countries: Poland; Infield, 169.

[76] McDonald to Dep Commanding Gen, Opns, 10/14/44, Spz, B 139, Neut & Occup Counties: Poland.

[77] Ibid.

[78] Burns, 534–5; Churchill, *Triumph & Tragedy,* 135, 139–44; AAF, 317; Anderson to Kuter, 9/24/44, Warsaw Dropping Opns [10/9/44], Spz 2. Archives I have searched concerning FDR and the Auschwitz bombing issue include those of FDR, War Dept, WRB, Stimson, Hopkins, Rosenman, ER, Henry Morgenthau, Jr. An exhaustive search made in 1983 by *Washington Post* reporter Morton Mintz showed that the bombing proposals almost certainly did not reach Roosevelt and most likely were not discussed at all beyond OPD (WP, 4/17/83, D1–D2; telephone convsns Morton Mintz & David Wyman, 3/25/83, 3/29/83, 4/5/83).

[79] Hull to ASW, 11/14/44, ASW 2; CS; Infield, 181; M Rpts, reel A6473 (8/20/44), fr 170, 172.

[80] Hilberg, 631; Garlinski, 247–9; Yuri Suhl (ed), *They Fought Back* (1967), 219–23.

CHAPTER 16.
RESPONSIBILITY

[1] Parts of this chapter are supported by data presented in the foregoing chapters. For the most part, only new sources of information will be cited in the notes for this chapter. Wise to FDR, 3/4/45, FDR, PPF 3292, Wise.

[2] MD 701/250. In July 1943, FDR did speak briefly about the Riegner plan with Stephen Wise. But this was subsidiary to their main discussion. The President also saw the seven Jewish congressmen in April 1943. See ch 4, source note 42.

[3] Led by Stephen Wise, millions of American Jews venerated FDR (eg, Wise, ch 13; Celler to FDR, 12/15/44, PSC 3/63; Neumann, *Arena,* 184, 200,

206–7; JO, 1/42, 2; NYT, 6/29/43, 13). To note but one typical example, Louis Levinthal, president of ZOA, drew consolation in the wake of the Bermuda fiasco from his belief that "we do have genuine, loyal friends, in government and outside of government circles, and none more genuine, more loyal than our beloved President, Franklin Delano Roosevelt" (NP, 5/7/43, 15). Helen Fein provides insight into the Jewish relationship with FDR in *Patterns of Prejudice,* 9/73, 22–8. Also relevant is Fuchs, *Political Behavior,* 71–5, 99–107.

⁴ Burns, 397; Alfange-Wyman interview, 3/22/79.

⁵ MD 106/275–6, 147/375, 151/32, 155/41–2, 692/288–90, 694/191; MPD, v 5, 1200–1, 1338–41; Hull, *Memoirs,* 1530–1; Convsn ER with Rosenheim et al, 10/14/44, JM, 324 ER; NG, Interview with Rosenman, 10/6/43, AHS, Ma I-93, Rosenman; Celler speech, 10/23/75, at J Hist Soc of NY.

⁶ FR, *The Conferences at Washington, 1941–1942, & Casablanca, 1943* (1968), 608, 611; Wyman, 27, 232; Davie, *Refugees in America,* 6.

⁷ OC, B 101, Refugee file; HID, 9789, 10187, 10190; Kingdon to Ickes, 2/1/45, Ickes to Rogers, 12/9/43, HI, Associations; CW, 1/18/43, 2; Lubin to Hassett, 3/8/45, 3/12/45, FDR, OF 700.

⁸ Eg, Flournoy to Travers & Holmes, 3/30/45, SD 150.01 Bills/3-3045; Martin Weil, *A Pretty Good Club* (1978), esp ch 2.

⁹ NYT, 10/31/42, 5, 9/11/43, 8, 6/27/44, 6, 7/15/44, 3; MD 192/291, 695/31, 696/87.

¹⁰ Description of Conc Camp at Oswiecim, 8/43, u/c Belin to Langer, 4/10/44, RG 226, R & A 66059.

¹¹ Dulles to McC, 6/15/44, with enclosures, W 61, Extmn Camps; OSS R & A Field Memo 257, 5/10/45, OSS Records 1944, Hoover Institution; CJR, 10/44, 524. Visser 't Hooft (*Memoirs,* 168)

gives further evidence of Dulles's indifference. Werner Rings's account of events in Switzerland connected with the Vrba-Wetzler report, including Dulles's reaction to it, is heavily flawed (*Advokaten des Feindes* [1966], 144–6).

¹² Lesser to Pehle, 4/18/44, JBF, Memo beginning, "1. The WRB established by," 4/20/44, W 50, OSS.

¹³ Margoshes in *Day,* 3/19/43, 1; Allan Winkler, *Politics of Propaganda* (1978), index; Allan Winkler to Eliyho Matzozky, 12/28/78 (copy in Wyman files); Mannon, Memo for Files, 11/22/44, Davis to Pehle, 11/23/44, W 6, Ger Extmn Camps; Mtg of PC, 12/17/42, WJC, U185/3; WJC, *Unity in Dispersion,* 163.

¹⁴ Wyman, 48; MD 696/204, 206, 219, 697/17; Ltrs to Shad Polier, 1/39, in Memo to File re Ref Children, 5/13/75, private files of Justine Wise Polier; McDonald to Welles, 8/8/41, JM, P50; McDonald to Grew, 5/21/45, JM, P3; McDonald to Rosenheim, 2/25/43, JM, P49; McDonald to Taylor, 6/3/43, JM, P55; 57th Mtg of PAC, 3/9/43, JM, P67; Schauffler to Branson et al, 11/6/44, AF, RS 11; Schauffler, Re Visa Policy in SD, with enclosure, 12/21/43, AF, GF 4.

¹⁵ 55th Mtg of PAC, 9/9/42, Warren to PAC, 10/16/42, 56th Mtg of PAC, 12/1/42, Warren to McDonald, 2/2/42, 54th Mtg of PAC, 6/18/42, JM, P66; JPC 655–6; Warren to McDonald, 5/9/44, McDonald to FDR, 5/12/44, JM, P68. The last recorded meeting of the PAC took place in Dec 1943. It met only 10 times between Pearl Harbor and V-E Day.

¹⁶ Warren to McDonald, Wise, & Baerwald, 1/18/41, Warren to McDonald & Baerwald, 5/3/41, JM, P65; Lourie to Warren, 11/10/41, JM, P66; JDC file G/E, Austria, Intergovernmental Advisory Com 1938–43, esp Baerwald to Warren, 12/24/41, McDonald to Leavitt, 1/14/43, Buchman to Rosner,

1/19/43, Baerwald to Bressler & Hyman, 5/20/38, Morrissey to Speers, 3/19/41.

[17] Convsn ER with Rosenheim et al, 10/14/44, JM, 324 ER; McDonald to ER, 9/5/41, JM, P43; ER to Welles, 3/9/42, Boettiger to Thompson, 8/31/42, ER 853/70; FDR to Undersecy of State, 12/10/42, with note ER to FDR, FDR, OF 76C; MD 692/288, 694/86; printed EC brochure, cover missing, p 12, PSC 9/69.

[18] Niles: MD 726/146–7. Baruch: Jordan Schwarz, *The Speculator: Bernard M. Baruch in Washington* (1981), 306–8, 417–26, 437, 446–7, 457–9, 467–74, 559–66. Lehman: nothing on rescue appears in the relevant archives or in Nevins, *Lehman & His Era*. Frankfurter: MD 696/122–3; Frankfurter Papers genly; Bruce Murphy, *The Brandeis/Frankfurter Connection* (1982), chs 6–8 genly & esp pp 243–5, 252–7, 273–4, 287–96, 308–10. Laqueur's statement (*Terrible Secret,* 94) that Frankfurter raised the extermination issue with FDR in 1942 is wrong; it is apparently based on the same error by Feingold (*Politics of Rescue,* 170, 333). Cf Voss, 248–51.

[19] MD 693/205–6, 209–10, 694/190, 707/243; Stettinius to Early, 3/8/44, FDR, PSF, Refs; SIR to Watson, 3/17/44, FDR to Wise, 7/30/44, with attached note, FDR, PPF 5029; NG, Interview with Rosenman, 10/6/43, AHS, Ma I-93, Rosenman. Also see Samuel Hand, *Counsel & Advise: A Political Biography of Samuel I. Rosenman* (1979), 139–40, 233.

[20] Berlin, Confidential Memo, 2/24/43, AHS, Ma I-62; BC Mins, 4/25, AM; RR, 63–4; Travers to Foster, 4/6/45, SD 150.01 Bills/3-3045; Joy to Burton, 5/4/44, Burton to Joy, 5/7/44, USC, Sen Burton; Biddle to FDR, 12/29/44, FDR, OF 3186; Schauffler, Re Visa Policy in SD, 12/21/43, AF, GF 4; JPC 3246, 3379–80; Kaplan, MASC Mtg, 1/12/43, NRS 326; NYT, 9/22/42, 16; CR, v 89,

8594–5; Com Mtg with Shaughnessy, 11/20/44, Legis 16453; BMM, Memo for Record, 10/20/43, Mohler to Ready, 10/20/43, BI 83, Refs—Restrictions on Admission as Visitors, R-4.

[21] [1st] Draft Mins Mign & Alien Status Sub-Com, 2/17/43, NRS 325; Kaplan, MASC Mtg, 1/12/43, NRS 326; Dubin, Rpt on discussion with Travers, 12/5/45, NRS 558; JPC 3246, 3274; Frawley to Vail et al, 10/8/42, Frawley to Pickett & Vail, 12/8/42, AF, GF 3.

[22] CW, 1/8/43, 13; *NY Daily Mirror,* 12/10/43, 25; NYJA, 9/4/43, 4.

[23] Randall to Dear Friend, 7/43, Randall & Black to Swing, 5/26/44, WIL, Ref Com, 1938–43, Releases; Randall, *The Voice of Thy Brother's Blood* (1944) (quote from p 30); Randall to ER, 6/28/44, ER 2946/190 Misc; CM, Admin Com, 5/25/44; Digest of Mins of Int Com, 3/21/44, AJHS, I-67, B 6.

[24] NYT, 12/21/42, 17, 3/17/43, 8, 4/26/43, 17; Voss-Wyman interview, 2/11/78.

[25] CC, 12/9/42, 1518–9; Hilberg, 337; *Shoah,* spr 1981, 20. The general statement on the near silence of the Protestant press is based on my analysis of ten periodicals: *Christendom, Christian Century, Christian Register, Christianity and Crisis, Christianity and Society, Churchman, Federal Council Bulletin, Lutheran, Religion in Life, Religious Digest.* (The last, while not strictly a Protestant magazine, was heavily Protestant in emphasis.)

Robert Ross, in *So It Was True: The American Protestant Press and the Nazi Persecution of the Jews* (1980), asserted that "the whole story" of the Nazi extermination of the Jews was published "extensively, continuously, and often comprehensively in the American Protestant press" (p 258). A close reading of his book, however, shows that what Ross actually demonstrated regarding the extermination period (mid-1941 to spring 1945) is the following: (1) two tiny-circulation publications issued by organizations dedicated to converting Jews to Christianity provided fairly thorough (but far from extensive) coverage; (2) the *Christian Century* and a very few other mainline Protestant periodicals published occasional (and often inconspicuous) reports; and (3) some 25 other Protestant journals said even less, or nothing at all.

The major problem with Ross's assessment of the data is that he added up *all* the references to Nazi actions against Jews that appeared in some 30 periodicals, and considered that to be such extensive reporting that American Protestants in general were exposed to the whole story. For instance, he found that in 1943 over 100 references appeared in the 31 periodicals he studied. But he did not take cognizance of the fact that few Protestants were reading more than one or two of the magazines. Seen another way, his findings show that, on the average, each periodical carried only a little over three references to the Jewish catastrophe during the entire critical year of 1943 and that no publication had more than nine. Furthermore, as Ross himself noted, many of the reports were only brief items. This is hardly extensive press exposure. Moreover, as he also showed, these Protestant periodicals printed many more references in 1943 than in any of the other extermination years. (*So It Was True,* 152–284, esp 164, 169–70, 183, 188–92, 197–202, 217, 220–5, 254–9, 264, 276, 280, 284; also the source notes for these pages.)

²⁶ Mins of Mtg with Pehle, 2/10/44, JDC, WRB; Staff planning cfs, 6/14/44, 7/13/44, AF, FS, Planning Com (Policy); W S Bennet to A W Bennet, 5/10/46, A. W. Bennet Papers, B 25, F 1, J Affairs; *Newscast* (ACCR), 2/41, 5, 3/41, 5, 4/41, 2, 9–10/44, 2, 1–2/45, 2; Mohler to Mulholland, 8/5/40, BI 87, R-8; Leiper to Pickett, 4/3/40, ACCR, Rpt of

Com on Orgzn, 11/26/40, AF, GF, C/O, ACCR; AJHQ, 12/71, 125–7; Cavert to Dexter, 9/15/43, FCC, B 9, Genl Secy's Files, Foreign Corresp; CEP Jour, 3/17/42, 5/26/42.

²⁷ NCWC, *Progress Rpt 1943: WRS—NCWC* (1943), 1; Chr R, 5/43, 179.

²⁸ J. F. Rummel, *Tenth Annual Rpt of the Catholic Com for Refs* [1946], 27; Staff planning cfs, 6/14/44, 7/13/44, AF, FS, Planning Com (Policy); Mulholland to Mohler, 1/22/37, Mohler to Mulholland, 2/13/37, 11/9/37, BI 80, Refs-CCR 1937, R-1; Mohler to Mulholland, 8/5/40, BI 87, R-8; AJHQ, 12/71, 127; SW to Mohler, 6/5/41, Mankiewicz to Dear Sir, 6/11/41, Burger to Mohler, 8/22/41, BMM, Memo for Record, 9/10/41, BI 80, Refs-CCR 1941, R-1; J. F. Rummel, *Seventh Annual Rpt of the Catholic Com for Refs* [1943], 13, 24. In 1944, the Natl War Fund supplied 90% of CCR's expenses and 77% of ACCR's (J. F. Rummel, *Eighth Annual Rpt of the Catholic Com for Refs* [1944], 25; J. F. Rummel, *Ninth Annual Rpt of the Catholic Com for Refs* [1945], 26; *Newscast,* 1–2/45, 2).

²⁹ *America:* eg, 9/19/42, 654–5, 658, 3/13/43, 630, 6/12/43, 266, 9/9/44, 550, 10/7/44, 10–1, 5/26/45, 145; *Commonweal:* eg, 12/11/42, 204–5, 12/18/42, 220, 2/19/43, 435, 6/4/43, 181–8, 5/12/44, 76–7, 6/9/44, 172, 3/23/45, 558. Other Catholic publications analyzed were *Catholic Action, Catholic Digest, Catholic Mind, Catholic Worker, Catholic World,* & *Review of Politics.* The *Catholic Mind* printed 2 or 3 inconspicuous references to the mass murder of European Jews (2/44, 120, 8/44, 450, 11/44, 664). The *Catholic Worker* published 2 articles calling for rescue (5/43, 1, 6/43, 1, 9). Regarding the National Catholic Welfare Conference and its Bureau of Immigration: BMM, "Summarization of correspondence . . . to Archbishop Rummel," 2/25/41, BI 82, Ref Problems, R–3; Mohler to Ready, 9/

8/44, BMM, Memo for Record, 9/6/44, BI 98, WRB, W-1; Mulholland to Mohler, 9/7/34, BI 40, Jews-Jewish, J–1; Mulholland to Mohler, 3/26/38, BI 80, Refs-CCR 1938, R-1; Mohler to Mulholland, 5/3/38, BI 82, Refs, German-Austrian 1938, R-3; Mohler to Ready, 10/20/43, BI 83, Refs, Restrictions on Admsn, R-4; Mohler to Mulholland, 11/29/44, BI 81, Refs, Child, USCCEC, R-2; Carroll to Pehle, 3/22/44, W 17, NCWC; Haim Genizi, "The Attitude of American Catholics toward Catholic Refugees from Nazism: 1933–1935," in *Proceedings of the Seventh World Congress of Jewish Studies Holocaust Research* (1980), 27–9, 37–8.

³⁰ Mulholland to Mohler, 8/31/44, 3/13/45, Mohler to Mulholland, 9/6/44, 12/7/44, 4/28/45, 6/11/45, BI 98, WRB, W-1; Mulholland to Mohler, 7/25/39, BI 79, Quotas, Q-1; Mohler to Mulholland, 5/25/34, Mulholland to Mohler, 4/6/37, 3/16/39, Mohler to Mulholland & Calleros, 4/12/38, BI 82, Refs, German, R-3; Buckley to Mohler, 8/4/41, BI 6, Religious; Mohler to Mulholland, 6/7/43, BI 84, R-5; Mohler to Ready, 9/22/41, BI 83, Refs, Eur, PAC, R-4; Mohler to O'Boyle, 3/7/45, BI 35, IMS, I-5.

³¹ Richie to Rogers, 5/28/42, Wriggins to Schauffler, 7/17/42, Wriggins to Rogers, 4/9/43, 6/3/43, Conard, Rpt to AF, 8/15/44, AF, RS 4; Jessup, Cf with Swanstrom, O'Conner, & Amiel, 2/9/44, A Short Sum of Program of Office of RSARO, 7/18/44, Conard, Rpt on Visit to Spain, 10/16/44, AF, RS 5; USC, Catholic Orgzns folder; Brandt, Convsn with Swanstrom, 10/7/43, BLP, B 202, Refs; Mohler to O'Boyle, 12/22/43, CH, B 6, Ref Orgzns; Egan & Amiel to O'Boyle, 3/28/44, Amiel to O'Boyle, 5/23/44, W 17, NCWC; Catholic Refs in Lisbon (nd), BI 84, R-5; NCWC, *Progress Rpt 1943: WRS—NCWC* (1943), 1, 3, 6, 8–9; NCWC, *Rpt to Board of Trustees WRS-NCWC: Aug 1943–Sept 1944* (1944), 13–4, 26.

³² *PM's* news coverage of Holocaust-related developments was relatively thorough from November 1942 through the Bermuda Conference. After that it was sporadic. For instance, it had almost nothing on the Oct 1943 Washington pilgrimage of 400 rabbis, on the Rescue Resolution hearings, or on the emergence of the WRB.

³³ Eg, Schoenberg & Gallo to Bloom, 11/19/43, Legis 16432; Robertson to FDR, 5/26/43, FDR, OF 76C; JTA, 12/16/43, 4; JF, 4/43, 3, 11/43, 10–2; Held et al to FDR, 5/4/44, Green to FDR, 5/8/44, FDR, OF 3186; N. A., Notes on Informal Cf, 6/24/43, JDC, Refs, Gen.

³⁴ Ans, 8/43, 6, 12, 15, 11/44, 18; *The Work Is Still Ahead* [12/44], pp 6–7, PSC 6/27; CW, 2/5/43, 5; Ronald Steel, *Walter Lippmann & the American Century* (1980), 330–3, 373; Roger Manvell, *Films & the Second World War* (1974), 196–9; CC, 12/29/43, 1545; *Commonweal,* 9/24/43, 563.

³⁵ *Daily Worker,* 7/12/43, *Morning Freiheit,* 7/12/43, PSC, S 16; *New Masses,* 5/11/43, 3–4, 11/30/43, 4, 8/15/44, 18–9.

³⁶ Mins of Exec Com, 11/6/43, Digest of Mins of Int Com, 11/23/43, 3/21/44, AJHS, I-67, B 6; CfR 7; NYT, 1/31/44, 5, 8/13/44, 19; LAT, 5/31/44, II, 3; SFE, 8/18/44, 7, 8/30/44, 3; Peterson to Proskauer, 5/24/44, AJC, PEC; MD 707/220; CW, 1/21/44, 20, 1/28/44, 16; J. Woodford Howard, Jr., *Mr. Justice Murphy: A Political Biography* (1968), 353; Scott to Smith, 5/22/44, TH 2; NJM, 6/44, 321; CJR, 12/44, 630; *Liberty,* 1/6/45, 15ff; Chr R, 8/44, 281–3.

³⁷ Based on extensive sampling of the NYC daily press.

³⁸ Based on a thorough analysis of WP & a sampling of other Washington newspapers. Specific references: WP, Oct 3–6 & 8, 1944, &10/13/44, 16.

³⁹ Based on a thorough survey of BG, CT, DN, DP, KCS, LAT, SFE, and ST;

and a sampling of many other newspapers.

[40] *Life* had almost nothing; *Time* and *Newsweek* had only a few, mostly minor, items (eg, *Life,* 10/11/43, 93, 8/28/44, 34, 9/18/44, 17–8; *Time,* 12/28/42, 24, 3/1/43, 30, 3/8/43, 29–30, 5/31/43, 24, 9/6/43, 26, 1/10/44, 78, 9/11/44, 36; *Newsweek,* 12/14/42, 104, 12/28/42, 46, 3/8/43, 48, 3/15/43, 36, 5/24/43, 54, 9/13/43, 40, 12/6/43, 22, 9/11/44, 64, 67, 12/4/44, 59). RD, 2/43, 107–10; *Am Mercury,* 2/43, 194–203, 11/44, 567–75; *Collier's,* 2/20/43, 17ff, 2/27/43, 29ff, 8/28/43, 62, 4/22/44, 30, 10/14/44, 18ff; *Saturday Evening Post,* 6/12/43, 16ff, 10/28/44, 18ff; NP, 3/19/43, 21, 7/16/43, 15. Karski's articles were adapted from *Story of a Secret State,* his book on the Polish underground, published in fall 1944 for the Book-of-the-Month Club (Scherman to Pehle, 12/13/44, W 6, Ger Extmn Camps).

[41] Ciechanowski, *Defeat in Victory,* 180, 182.

[42] Eg, 1943 Radio Scripts, JM, Manuscripts & Speeches file; PC Mtg Mins, 12/29/42, WJC, U185/2; Murphy to Weinstein, 4/4/44, W 22, Radio/Misc; Pehle to Green, 4/7/44, W 22, Radio/A. Green.

[43] Manvell, *Films & the Second World War,* 167–83; CC, 5/19/43, 622, 10/6/43, 1150, 1/5/44, 31, 3/8/44, 319, 5/31/44, 679; Shultz to J W Wise, 1/6/43, WJC, 268/V; Activities of AJCg & WJC with Respect to Hitler Program [1/43], WJC, U185/2; Suid-Wyman interview, 11/15/78; CW, 11/20/42, 5; Raymond Fielding, *The March of Time, 1933–1951* (1978), index; David Culbert to David Wyman, 10/31/78. Feature films dealing with refugees and/or Nazi atrocities included *Watch on the Rhine, Hangmen Also Die, North Star, The Last Chance, None Shall Escape, The Seventh Cross, Diary of a Nazi, Edge of Darkness, The Hitler Gang.* In the last, the narrator did speak, near the end, of the extermination of whole peoples: the Jews, the Poles.

[44] Ch 2 above.

[45] This is discussed by Robert Weintraub in *J Week,* 10/26/80, 32. Several newspapers used NYT copyrighted articles on events overseas.

[46] Arthur Koestler published a penetrating essay on this problem in NYT, 1/9/44, VI, 5. Other useful discussions include those in YVS, v 7, 53–5 (by Louis de Jong), & in Walter Laqueur's *The Terrible Secret,* esp 2–3, 199–206.

[47] *Commonweal,* 10/16/42, 604, 12/11/42, 204–5, 12/18/42, 220, 2/19/43, 435, 3/26/43, 566, 6/4/43, 181–8, 11/12/43, 93; *America,* 9/19/42, 654–5, 658, 3/13/43, 630, 6/12/43, 266, 5/26/45, 145; chs 2, 3, 6, 10 above; Berle, Memo of Convsn with Vahervuori, 12/8/42, SD, R/3495½; BG, 5/3/43, 1, 11; Reams to Stettinius, 10/8/43, BLP, B 202, Refs.

[48] *YV Bulletin,* #6/7, 1960, 25–6.

[49] NYT, 8/30/44, 9.

[50] Eg (all on 8/30/44): NYT, 1, 9; WP, 2; SFE, 1, 6; DN, 1; LAT, 4; CT, 6. Also, *Time,* 8/21/44, 36, 38, 9/11/44, 36; *Newsweek,* 9/11/44, 64, 67; *Life,* 8/28/44, 34, 9/18/44, 17–8; *Sat Eve Post,* 10/28/44, 18ff. *Newsweek*'s report did state that about half of the 1,500,000 killed at Majdanek were Jews. And *Life* reported that most of the victims were Jews. In his book *Six Presidents, Too Many Wars* (1972), Bill Lawrence mentioned that his report (to the NYT) had specified that most of the Majdanek victims were Jews, but the Russian censors had cut that part out (p 100). Unlike the press, State Department officials recognized the connection of Majdanek with the Holocaust (NYT, 9/11/44, 10). Koestler: NYT, 1/9/44, VI, 5.

[51] GEC; McC to Pehle, 10/12/44, W 61, Extmn Camps; MD 750/354–60, 751/239. The version released by the WRB also included the report of a Polish military officer who had escaped

from Auschwitz. A summary of the data appeared in some US newspapers in July 1944, but it attracted little notice. (NYT, 7/3/44, 3, 7/6/44, 6; *Wn Star,* 7/3/44, 2; ST, 7/3/44, 2; KCS, 7/3/44, 12.).

[52] Roswell McClelland to David Wyman, 9/18/80; Pehle to McCloy, 11/8/44, W 6, Ger Extmn Camps; MD 790/135–6.

[53] MD 799/231–6, 802/254; W 5, Ger Extmn Camps, Newspaper Clippings folders. Eg, NYT, 11/26/44, 1, 24; WP, 11/26/44, 1, 11; *Collier's,* 1/6/45, 62.

[54] Mannon to Pehle, 11/16/44, W 6, Ger Extmn Camps.

[55] All in 1945: SFE, 5/2, 8; LAT, 4/21, 1; KCS, 4/23, 6; ST, 4/25, 1; DP, 4/25, 24; NYT, 4/22, 13, 4/27, 3.

[56] All in 1945: NYT, 4/21, 5, 4/23, 5; DP, 4/23, 22, 5/15, 1; LAT, 4/22, 1, 2, 4/27, 7, 4/28, 1, 5/15, II, 1, 5/16, II, 4, 5/18, II, 1; KCS, 5/13, 1; CT, 4/23, 4, 4/29, 20; SFE, 4/29, 1, 5/16, 7; DN, 5/10, 2, 5/16, 1.

[57] Hilberg, 632–3.

[58] Eg, NYT, 4/25/45, 3; CT, 4/26/45, 3; DN, 4/26/45, II, 10, 5/2/45, 11.

[59] Based on analysis of the 10 newspapers listed in ch 2, source note 12. Quotation is from SFE, 4/22/45, 4.

[60] *1st para:* eg, NYT, 4/18, 8, 4/23, 5, 4/28, 6; WP, 4/10, 1–3, 4/16, 1, 4, 4/18, 1, 2, 4/21, 1, 3, 4/24, 1, 7, 4/28, 1; *Collier's,* 6/16, 14, 28, 6/23, 16ff (all in 1945). *2nd para:* NYT, 5/8/45, 12; LAT, 5/8/45, 4; WP, 5/8/45, 3; NYT, 8/4/79, 2; *J Advocate* (Boston), 9/28/78, II, 23.

[61] Cantril, 383.

[62] Cantril, 1070–1; WP, 12/3/44, 1. In the November poll, 12% thought the information was not true, and 12% had no opinion. In May, 9% thought the reports partly true but exaggerated, 3% considered them untrue, and 3% did not answer. Those who said they believed the reports were asked for their "best guess" as to how many had been murdered. In November, the most typical answer was 100,000. In May, it was 1,000,000.

[63] Ch 1 above; ch 14 above, section on Ft Ontario; Mtg of PC, 12/17/42, WJC, U185/3; Voss-Wyman interview, 2/11/78.

[64] NYT, 5/14/44, VI, 9.

[65] See pages 62–3; IR, 10/13/43, 291, 297; *N. W. Ayre & Son's Directory of Newspapers & Periodicals* (1943); Matzozky, "Am J Press Reaction"; RYP genly; AJYB, v 46, 473–81. Mass meetings were covered in chs 2 and 5 and elsewhere above. Also, many thousands of Jews sent letters and telegrams to Washington concerning rescue. (Seen in FDR Papers, WRB Papers, and elsewhere. Also, MPD, v 5, 1340.)

[66] Ch 4 above.

[67] Chs 4–6 above.

[68] Ch 9 above; Adler, "American Jewry & That Explosive Statehood Question," 12, 16–7; AJYB, v 44, 476–7.

[69] Ch 9 above; Adler, "American Jewry," 7.

[70] Chs 8 & 11 above.

[71] Ch 9 above; Voss-Wyman interview, 2/11/78; AJH, 3/81, 310–30.

[72] Mds, 3/64, 9; *Reconstructionist,* 1/21/44, 3–4; *J Examiner,* 1/14/44, 4.

[73] Mds, 3/64, 9; Neumann, *Arena,* 189; GCM, 11/12/42, 12/3/42; Meltzer, Convsn with Goldmann, 7/14/43, SD, R/4063; Lesser, Memo for Files, 7/21/44, W 70, J. Brandt; *In the Dispersion,* winter 1963–64, 6–7; *Reconstructionist,* summer 1983, 4; *Martyrdom & Resistance,* 11/83, 11; *YV Bulletin,* 4/57, 4; *PM,* 5/18/43, 9; JF, 6/43, 3.

[74] JDC's share of funding is based on data on pages 213–4.

[75] Sources for these rescue proposals include: NYT, 2/25/43, 10; Proposed Action, 2/19/43, Shultz to Levy, 2/24/43, RW 2/23; CW, 3/5/43, 16, 4/30/43, 11–4; Ans, 8/43, 22–3, 3/10/44, 8–9; Asofsky to Pehle, 2/10/44, W 9, HIAS;

Mtg at Harvard Club, 2/17/44, "Afternoon Session," 2/26/44, W 9, Free World House; Memo from Exec of J Agency to WRB via Hn, 2/20/44, W 14, J Ag for Pal; AF to Pehle, 2/25/44, AF, RS, US Govt, WRB, AF Proposal; Baerwald to Pehle, 2/28/44, W 2, AJJDC (Misc); Silver to Pehle, 2/29/44, W 1, AI of Am; Comsn on Rescue of AJCf to WRB [3/1/44], W 2, AJCf; Kalmanowitz & Kotler to Pehle, 3/7/44, W 26, UOR; Welt to Pehle, 3/7/44, W 17, Natl Council of J Women; Digest of Suggestions [4/44], W 50, Measures Proposed; Pehle, Memo for Winant, 4/24/44, W 30, Reprs; Cf Rpt, 17–8, 57.

[76] Warren to SS, 5/4/44, SD, R/5499; Wasserstein, 252–3.

[77] MD 697/190, 720/297–9; WH, 8–9; FSR, 19; Shertok to Goldmann, 7/8/44, u/c Perlzweig to Pehle, 7/21/44, W 34, Hung 1; Goldmann to Stettinius, 6/7/44, SD, R/6300; WJC, *Unity in Dispersion,* 187–8; PR, 1979 (v24/1), 59; Office Rpt to Com Members & Patrons of VH [8/45], VH, B 8.

[78] CW, 5/28/43, 14; Berle to Hull & Long, 4/20/43, BLP, B 202, Refs; Marrus & Paxton, *Vichy France & the Jews,* 320.

[79] FR 1943, v 1, 179; Rosenblatt to Silver, 1/28/44, AHS, 4-2-16 AZEC.

[80] Ch 5 above.

[81] Mtg of Steering Com of JEC, 4/2/43, AJC, JEC; MD 692/33–4; Katzki to Leavitt, 7/13/43, Leavitt to Brandt, 8/20/43, Brandt to Leavitt, 8/24/43, JDC, Bulgaria Genl.

[82] A few of the many possibilities can be seen in Riegner to Reagan, 3/23/44, W 62, WJC; Sternbuch to VH, 6/1/44, VH, B 5; Sternbuch & Donnenbaum to VH, 7/14/44, VH, B 20; & the Riegner & Goldmann plans, discussed in ch 10 above.

[83] FSR, 24; FR 1944, v 1, 1049–50; WH, 147–50, 296–7; Anger, 11–3.

[84] WH, 188, 198; MD 706/125, 727/214, 728/112, 732/258, 734/10; FR 1943, v 1, 167; FR 1944, v 1, 1008–11, 1016–7, 1037, 1069–70, 1074; Garlinski, 250–1; Baruch to SS, 5/16/45, SD, R/5-1645; Pehle to Harriman, 5/19/44, W 34, Hung 2 (last).

[85] Wasserstein, 252, 323–9; Mins of Mtg of Jt Com, 3/29/43, Silver to Shulman, 4/9/43, AHS, Ma I-81; *Daily Telegraph & Morning Post* (London), 1/6/43, 4; Ans, 10/15/43, 4–6, 3/10/44, 15–6; MD 692/289–90, 699/22, 741/237; Reams to Dunn & Matthews, 2/3/44, BLP, B 202, Refs; WLB, v 27, 1973/74, 43; Bauer II, 131, 140; FR 1944, v 1, 1005.

[86] Ch 15 above.

[87] MB & GFl, "We are sending you," 5/22/44, W 61, Extmn Camps; *Call* (Workmen's Circle), 10/43, 15; Wasserstein, 295–303.

[88] Elie Wiesel, *Legends of Our Time* (1968), 164–5, 186–9; Braham I, 962. Goebbels, for instance, believed that the British and Americans "are happy that we are exterminating the Jewish riffraff" (Louis Lochner [ed], *The Goebbels Diaries* [1948], 241).

[89] Wiesel, *Legends,* 166–7, 187–9; MD 717/145; WJC, *Unity in Dispersion,* 184; Hilberg, 618–24, 628–9, 647–53; Rudolf Vrba to David Wyman, 2/17/77; Kalmanowitz to Berle [5/44], W 34, Hung 1. The Jewish agents who were finally parachuted into Axis territory were too few, very late, burdened with unrelated tasks required by the British, and poorly supported (Marie Syrkin, *Blessed Is the Match* [1947], 13–76; Dorothy & Pesach Bar-Adon, *Seven Who Fell* [1947], 9–23; Wasserstein, 288–95).

[90] Hull to Am Consul Karachi, 8/16/43, Tellier to Johnson, 1/5/44, W 18, Polish Ref Proj; FR 1943, v 1, 322; Blocker to SS, 11/4/43, SD, R/4751; Yost to de Anzorena, 5/25/43, SD, R/3830A; Hilldring to ASW, 1/25/44,

ASW 4; ch 14 above, section on Search for Havens; ch 12 above, section on Italy.

⁹¹ RR, 169; Wriggins to Schauffler, 8/10/43, AF, RS 4; Memos on Telephone Convsns between Schwartz & Leavitt, 4/17/42, 4/28/42, 5/12/42, JDC, Rpts, Eur Telephone Convsns; Memo on Findings of Emerg Cf, 8/43, Legis 16431; Proskauer to Long, 12/28/43, AJC, PEC; CW, 6/4/43, 14, 12/24/43, 16; CR, v 90, 663; *Rescue,* 9/44, 2, 2/45, 5; CJR, 4/43, 171; AF Lisbon Office, Mid-Aug Rpt, 8/13/42, AF, GF, For Serv, Port; AF Lisbon Office, Mid-Oct Rpt [10/10/42], AF, RS 4; *NRS Community Bulletin,* 11–12/42, 4; Rpt of Exec Dir to Exec Com, 9/20/43, NRS 269; List of ship arrivals, 2/24/42, NRS 505; Petluck to Mign Staff, 7/12/44, NRS 586; Petluck to Mign Staff, 12/18/44, NRS 590; NYT, 3/21/42, 18, 11/3/42, 11. The 3 Portuguese ships were the *Serpa Pinto, Nyassa,* & *Guine.* Jewish organizations chartered Portuguese liners without trouble the few times there were enough refugees with US visas to justify that step (eg, Schauffler to Pickett et al, 5/12/42, AF, GF 1).

⁹² NYT, 12/19/43, 4; Bennet to Pehle, 5/11/44, TH 2; Long, Convsn with Strong, 2/12/43, Long to Strong, 2/22/43, BL to Atherton, 3/11/43, BLP, B 212, Genl (VD); Vail, Trip to Wn, 3/12/43, AF, FS 3; Heath to Vail, 1/19/43, Schauffler to Heath, 2/12/43, AF, RS 2; Heath to Wriggins, 1/18/43, AF, RS, Ctry FNA, Fr Morocco, Casa.

⁹³ Pehle, Memo, 5/11/44, TH 2; Lubin to Hassett, 3/8/45, FDR, OF 700; Algiers to War Dept, 2/17/43, BLP, B 195, Foreign Territories; CSM, 4/9/43, 9.

⁹⁴ MD 717/201; Pickett to Cary et al, 12/16/43, AF, FS, Ctry Sweden; Heath to Jessup, 3/31/44, AF, FS, Ctry Sweden, Genl; NYP, 4/23/43, 13; DuBois, Memo for Files, 5/26/44, TH 2.

⁹⁵ See pages 130–3; Probs & Rec-

omndns (nd), u/c Marks to O'Dwyer, 3/20/45, TH 10; Standish to Lesser, 3/27/44, W 10, Imgn Memos; FR 1942, v 1, 454–6; MD 692/291; Wasserstein, 49, 51, 145, 355–6. When SD officials wished, however, even suspicious persons received quick permission to enter the US. One case involved the servant of a US diplomat. (BL to Welles, 5/14/42, BLP, B 212, VD, Indiv Cases 1941.)

⁹⁶ See pages 105, 107; Visser 't Hooft, *Memoirs,* ch 23, esp p 167.

⁹⁷ Ans, 2/12/44, 9; MD 707/223; Drafts for Pr Rel on Exec Order establishing WRB, 1/22/44, FDR, OF 5477; Stettinius to Early, 3/8/44, FDR, PSF: Refs; Kp I, 119; Special Com on Eur Situation, Mins, 12/14/42, WJC, U185/3; "Afternoon Session," 2/26/44, W 9, Free World House; Wasserstein, 184, 190, 353; Visser 't Hooft, *Memoirs,* 169.

⁹⁸ *YV Bulletin,* 4/57, 4; HID, 9374; Israel, 307; CW, 5/7/43, 3–4, 6/4/43, 15; *PM,* 7/22/43, 2; NYP, 7/22/43, 26; NR, 8/30/43, 305; Pepper-Wyman interview, 4/10/81; Celler speech, 10/23/75, at J Hist Soc of NY; Celler-Jarvik interview, 10/4/78; CJR, 6/43, 312.

In public announcements, American and British officials used numerous euphemisms to avoid mentioning Jews; eg, persecuted peoples, unfortunate people, political refugees, persecuted minorities, racial and political refugees, oppressed minorities.

A prime example of insinuation that the war was fought for the Jews appeared in *NY Daily News,* 10/3/45, 4.

⁹⁹ Draft for FDR to Teller, u/c Bohlen to Early, 3/27/44, FDR, OF 76C.

¹⁰⁰ Eg, appendix A; ch 15 above; Smertenko to FDR, 7/24/44, FDR, OF 3186.

¹⁰¹ Howard to Cox, 7/3/43, OC; Jones to Sub-Com on Balkans, For Serv Staff, 4/27/45, AF, FS, Balkans; SG, 9/44, 389; NYT, 2/27/44, 8, 3/8/44, 3, 4/11/45, 15; Nuseirat Camp, 5/10/44, Aleppo Camps, 5/10/44, W 4, Camps; FR 1942,

v 1, 462; FR 1943, v 1, 381; Memo concerning maintenance of Greek refs, 2/6/43, BLP, B 199, Near Eastern Affairs; Hertha Kraus, *International Relief in Action, 1914–1943* (1944), 228. Much of the British military's assistance was nominally credited to the British government's Middle East Relief and Refugee Administration.

[102] Ch 12 above, section on Italy; Scattergood, Jugoslav Ref Camp–El Shatt, 4/21/44, AF, RS, Ctry FNA, Algeria, Ltrs from; NYT, 7/24/44, 12; AAF, 339, 520–3; Dacie, *Yugoslav Refugees,* 14–5; Akzin & McCormack to Hodel, 2/2/45, W 48, UNRRA (Rpt On) 2.

[103] NYT, 1/12/42, 5, 1/14/42, 6, 8/29/42, 2, 11/5/42, 14, 1/25/43, 4, 8/23/43, 8, 12/12/43, 41, 3/23/44, 8; IR, 9/28/44, 294; Survey of Recent Activities of HMG, 6/29/44, PRO, CAB 95/15; RR, 164; MD 650/68; Translation of Memo from Polish Minister, 2/10/44, W 17, MERRA; Goldsmith, Rpt on Visits to UNRRA-MERRA Camps, 8/14/44, W 4, Camps. Among the Poles were 1,228 Jews (NYT, 2/20/43, 6).

[104] NYT, 12/7/44, 16, 4/5/45, 25, 9/4/45, 9.

[105] Ch 14 above, Food/Blockade section; GR, 14; RR, 209.

[106] NYT, 8/17/42, 4; Wriggins to Tibbetts, 12/4/43, AF, FS, Ctry Egypt, Ltrs; MD 704/68–9; War Refs [12/44], Translation of Polish Minister Delegate's Rpt [early 1944], W 17, MERRA; Akzin & McCormack to Hodel, 2/2/45, W 48, UNRRA (Rpt On) 2; Nuseirat Camp, 5/10/44, Goldsmith, Rpt on Visits to UNRRA-MERRA Camps, 8/14/44, W 4, Camps; Barratt-Brown, Notes on Ref Camps in Middle East, 8/43, AF, RS, Refs, Intl Sanctuaries for; Survey of Recent Activities of HMG, 6/29/44, PRO, CAB 95/15; NCWC, *Rpt to Board of Trustees WRS–NCWC: Aug 1943–Sept 1944* (1944), 7–11. The 25,000 figure is the most reasonable estimate based on available data.

[107] Esco Fndn, *Palestine,* II, 953.

[108] Goldsmith, Rpt on Visits to UNRRA-MERRA Camps, 8/14/44, W 4, Camps; Akzin & McCormack to Hodel, 2/2/45, W 48, UNRRA (Rpt On) 2; Jones to Sub-Com on Balkans, For Serv Staff, 4/27/45, AF, FS, Balkans; DSB, 6/10/44, 533–4; NYT, 4/11/45, 15; Rpt on Fedala Camp, 8/28/44, u/c Offie to SS, 9/22/44, W 39, Evacn to Lyautey; WH, 226–9; Weatherford to Jessup, 2/20/45, AF, FS, Ctry FNA, Algeria, Ltrs from.

[109] ER to Welles, 3/9/42, Welles to ER, 3/14/42, ER 853/70; BC Mins, 4/20, PM.

[110] Merlin to Shubow, 3/20/43, AJHS, AJCg, Uncataloged Box, F: CJA.

APPENDIX A.
EASTER AT BERMUDA

[1] All of this appendix is based on BC Mins, 4/25, AM.

[2] Mins of MASC, 5/11/43, Kaplan draft, NRS 326.

[3] Points 3 and 4 are covered in ch 16.

APPENDIX B.
THE CONFLICT BETWEEN THE REGULAR ZIONISTS AND THE BERGSONITES

[1] Eg, IJPS, 2/28/44, 8; Bromfield to Bridges, 9/16/44, PSC 1/13; Bridges to Cavert, 3/10/45, PSC 1/17; Cavert to Smith, 5/22/44, FCC, B 100, Genl; Voss-Wyman interview, 2/11/78; Kook-Wyman interview, 5/5/73; Alfange-Wyman interview, 3/22/79; Wilson, Convsn with Goldmann et al, 5/19/44, SD 867N.01/2347; *The Work Is Still Ahead* [12/44], p 21, PSC 6/27; *PM,* 8/9/44, 24; Gillette to Shapiro, 1/13/44, PSC 1/11; AME 24; HID, 8498, 8519, 8559; Wise to Ickes, 12/23/43, Frank to

Ickes, 4/20/44, HI, Associations. System-atization: eg, Shapiro to Horwitt, 11/29/44, AZEC to Adler, 11/29/44, PSC 13/57; "Withdrawals and Replies," 2/8/45, VF, ALFP; VF, ALFP, generally; Levinthal to Szold, 12/18/42, RW 2/20; Drazin, Feuer, & Gordis to Rosenberg, 5/18/44, Shapiro to Lindey, 7/6/44, Shapiro to [name obliterated], 10/24/44, PSC 13/57.

² Eg, Stmt by AZEC on ALFP, 1/10/44, Legis 16431; card distributed by J Welfare Fund of Chicago, 10/11/44, Rabinoff to Hyman, 10/20/44, W 15, JWF of Chicago; Wilson, Convsn with Goldmann et al, 5/19/44, SD 867N.01/2347; Silver to Taft, 6/15/44, AHS, Ma II-84, Taft; MD 735/60, 77; *Meyer Weisgal . . . So Far: An Autobiography* (1971), 188; Merriam to Nemzer, 6/1/44, BA #21; Murray to Stettinius, 5/31/44, SD 867N.01/2352; Murray to Stettinius, 6/1/44, 6/2/44, SD 867N.01/6-144; Wilson, Convsn with Goldmann et al ("Zt Attitude Toward Palestine"), 9/13/44, SD, copy in PSC 3/67; Memo on Efforts to Deport Bergson, 7/26/44, and other material in PSC 10/9; Frank to Guthman, 5/19/45, PSC, 1/18; Gillette to Byrnes, 10/11/45, Stern to Byrnes, 10/16/45, Stern to Russell, 10/16/45, PSC 1/21; Halifax to FO, 5/24/44, PRO, FO 371/40131; Balfour to Jerusalem, 8/9/45, Chancery (Wn) to Eastern Dept, 8/6/45, PRO, FO 371/45399; NYP, 7/14/44, 16, 11/5/45, 11, 11/9/45, 33; NYHT, 5/23/44, 7; Wilson, Convsn with Waldman et al, 1/10/44, BLP, B 200, Pal; Thomas to Finucane, 7/3/44, ET, B 85, Jus-4 Imgn.

³ Eg, ACB 6; Kook-Wyman interview, 4/19/73; anonymous to Ruth & Dick, 6/21/49, PSC 3/58; EC, *Save Human Lives*

[3/44], p 22, PSC 5/16; Harper to Meyer, 10/6/44, PSC 1/14; Selden to Kampelman, 12/22/59, PSC 13/59; FBI file 100-316012; Alfange-Wyman interview, 3/22/79; Budgeting Bulletin, B-3, 1/12/44, VF, EC.

⁴ MD 735/77; Neumann to Wise, 10/7/42, SW, World Affairs, I. Goldstein; Levinthal to Szold, 12/18/42, RW 2/20; Cf Rpt, 78; AM 2; AME 3, 6–8, 10, 22–5, 27, 30; Alfange-Wyman interview, 3/22/79; Wilson, Convsn with Goldmann et al, 5/19/44, SD 867N.01/2347; Mins of Mtg with Pehle, 2/10/44, AHS, Ma II 90, WRB; Weisgal, *So Far,* 188.

⁵ Arthur Goren to David Wyman, 1/19/74; NP, 1/21/44, 205.

⁶ Levison to Kobacker, 12/23/40, PSC 1/4; "To Whose Tune Are You Dancing?" (nd), PSC 13/59; Goldmann to Bergson, 8/27/43, PSC 1/9; Neumann-Wyman interview, 11/20/78; Merlin-Wyman interview, 4/19/73; Goren to Wyman, 1/19/74; AME 7. Re negotiations: PSC, B 1, folders 5–10; Bauer, *From Diplomacy,* 236.

⁷ Numerous examples appear in SW, esp the Zm 1940–43 file. A few other examples: CW, 1/22/43, 9; JF, 1/43, 8–9; Voss, 266; Rosenheim to Steinhardt, 8/16/44, Schenkolewski to Steinhardt, 8/16/44, LS; Wise to Korn, 5/16/44, SW, Corresp, Korn; Extension of Relief in Occupied Poland, 11/13/42, 11/17/42, JDC, G/E, Poland; FRA[dlerstein], "WJC," 1/30/42, JJS[chwartz] to JDC, 3/17/44, Leavitt to Stameshkin, 5/7/43, JDC, Rpts; JDC files on UJA for 1941 & 1945; AJYB, v 44, 476–7, v 47, 260, 333; NYT, 6/4/45, 32; Akzin to Hodel, 1/9/45, W 27, VH; MD 699/142; Adler, "Am Jewry and That Explosive Statehood Question," 5–21.

BIBLIOGRAPHY

Archival Materials

Abbreviations: FDRL = Franklin D. Roosevelt Library (Hyde Park, NY)
LC = Library of Congress (Washington)

Agudath Israel of America Papers (NYC)
American Friends Service Committee Archives (Phila)
American Jewish Committee Archives (NYC)
American Jewish Congress Papers (partial) (NYC)
American Jewish Historical Society Archives (Waltham, Mass)
  American Jewish Conference Papers (partial)
  American Jewish Congress Papers (partial)
American Jewish Joint Distribution Committee Archives (NYC)
Yitshaq Ben-Ami (personal file, from Dept of Justice)
Augustus W. Bennet Papers (Syracuse Univ)
William S. Bennet Papers (Syracuse Univ)
Sol Bloom Papers (NY Public Library)
Irving Bunim Oral History (Yeshiva Univ)
Emanuel Celler Papers (LC)
Joseph P. Chamberlain Papers (YIVO Institute, NYC)

Columbia University Oral History Collection: Joseph C. Baldwin, William S. Bennet, Samuel Dickstein, Warren Moscow, William O'Dwyer, Herbert C. Pell, Joseph M. Proskauer, George Rublee
Oscar Cox Papers (FDRL)
Ira C. Eaker Papers (LC)
Federal Bureau of Investigation (selected files on Bergson organizations)
Federal Council of Churches of Christ in America Papers (Phila)
Felix Frankfurter Papers (LC)
Carlton J. H. Hayes Papers (Rare Book & Manuscript Library, Columbia Univ)
Cordell Hull Papers (LC)
Harold L. Ickes Diary (LC)
Harold L. Ickes Papers (LC)
International Migration Service Papers (originals at Univ of Minnesota; copies at Travelers Aid International Social Service of America, NYC)
Jabotinsky Institute (Tel Aviv)
Jewish Labor Committee Archives (NYC)
Breckinridge Long Diary (LC)
Breckinridge Long Papers (LC)
James G. McDonald Papers (Columbia Univ)
Morgenthau Diaries (FDRL)
Morgenthau Presidential Diaries (FDRL)
National Archives (Washington)
   RG 107 Secretary of War
       165 War Dept General & Special Staffs
       210 War Relocation Authority, Emergency Refugee Shelter, Reports
       210 War Relocation Authority, Emergency Refugee Shelter, Temporary Havens in the US
       210 War Relocation Authority, Field Office Records, Emergency Refugee Shelter, Central Files
       218 US Joint Chiefs of Staff
       226 Office of Strategic Services
       243 US Strategic Bombing Survey
   Legislative Branch
   State Dept decimal files: 150.01 Bills; 548.G1 (Bermuda Conf); 740.00116 European War; 840.48 Refugees; 862.4016 (Germany—Race Problems); 867N.01 (Near East)
National Catholic Welfare Conference, Bureau of Immigration Papers (United States Catholic Conference Records, Migration & Refugee Division; housed at Center for Migration Studies, Staten Island)
National Refugee Service Papers (YIVO Institute, NYC)
Paul O'Dwyer (personal files)
Palestine Statehood Committee Papers (Yale Univ)
Claiborne Pell (personal files)
Public Record Office (London): CAB 65, 66, 95; FO 371
Eleanor Roosevelt Papers (FDRL)
Franklin D. Roosevelt Papers; & Press Conferences of President Franklin D. Roosevelt (FDRL)
Abba Hillel Silver Papers (The Temple, Cleveland)
Albert F. Simpson Historical Research Center (Maxwell AFB, Ala)

Carl A. Spaatz Papers (LC)
Laurence Steinhardt Papers (LC)
Henry L. Stimson Diaries (Yale Univ)
Henry L. Stimson Papers (Yale Univ)
Robert Taft Papers (LC)
Myron C. Taylor Papers (FDRL)
Joseph Tenenbaum Collection (YIVO Institute, NYC)
Elbert Thomas Papers (FDRL)
Unitarian Universalist Service Committee Papers (Tufts Univ)
Vaad Hahatzala Papers (Yeshiva Univ Archives)
Robert Wagner Papers (Georgetown Univ)
War Refugee Board Records (FDRL)
Stephen S. Wise Papers (American Jewish Historical Society)
Women's International League for Peace & Freedom Papers (Swarthmore Col)
World Jewish Congress Papers (NYC)
Zionist Archives & Library (NYC)
  American Jewish Conference Papers (partial)
  American Zionist Emergency Council: Minutes & Executive Committee Minutes
  "Vertical Files" (on Bergson organizations)

Interviews

Dean Alfange by David Wyman, 3/22/79
Emanuel Celler by Wyman, 3/23/79
Dorothy Detzer Denny by Wyman, 5/11/65
Josiah E. DuBois, Jr., by Laurence Jarvik, 10/23/78
Eileen Egan by Wyman, 3/23/79
Samuel Grafton by Wyman, 3/23/79
Hillel Kook by Natan Cohen, 9/26/68 (transcript in PSC 11/33)
Hillel Kook by Wyman, 4/14 & 19/73, 5/5/73, 1/10/74, 11/20/78
Samuel Merlin by Wyman, 4/19/73, 9/6/73, 3/22/79
Emanuel Neumann by Wyman, 11/20/78
John Pehle by Jarvik, 10/16/78
Claiborne Pell by Jarvik, 1/22/79
Claude Pepper by Wyman, 4/10/81
Justine Wise Polier by Wyman, 3/21/79
Gerhart Riegner by Jarvik, 10/4/78
Dore Schary by Wyman, 3/21/79
Joseph Schwartz by Judith Elizur, 11/29/61 (item 291, Oral History Division, Institute
    for Contemporary Jewry, Hebrew Univ, Jerusalem)
Lawrence Suid by Wyman, 11/15/78
Ted Thackrey by Wyman, 11/20/78, 3/22/79
Carl Hermann Voss by Wyman, 2/11/78
George L. Warren by Jarvik, 1/22/79

Published Documents

Bulkley, Robert, Frederick Keppel, & F. D. G. Ribble. *Report to the President: Board of Appeals on Visa Cases: Nov 9, 1942* (1942).

Foreign War Relief Operations. House Doc 262, 79 Cong, 1 ses (July 17, 1945).

Halpern, Ben (ed). *The Jewish National Home in Palestine* (1944, 1970).

Intergovernmental Committee on Refugees. *Minutes of Fourth Plenary Session* (1944).

———. *Report of Fourth Plenary Session* (1944).

———. *Report of Fifth Plenary Session* (1945).

———. *Minutes of Sixth Plenary Session* (1946).

———. *Minutes of Seventh Plenary Session* (1947).

———. *Seventh Plenary Session Resolutions* (1947).

"Investigation of Problems Presented by Refugees at Fort Ontario Refugee Shelter," *Hearings before Subcommittee VI of the Committee on Immigration & Naturalization, House of Representatives,* 79 Cong, 1 ses (June 25–26, 1945).

US Dept of State. *Foreign Relations of the United States,* volumes for 1941–1945.

US House of Representatives. *Problems of World War II & Its Aftermath: Part 2, The Palestine Question* (1976).

US Immigration & Naturalization Service. *Annual Reports, 1941–1946.*

Newspapers, General

Atlanta Constitution
Boston Globe
Boston Herald
Boston Record
Chicago Tribune
Christian Science Monitor
Cleveland Plain Dealer
Dallas News
Denver Post
Kansas City Star
Los Angeles Times
Miami Herald
New Orleans Times-Picayune
New York Daily Mirror
New York Daily News

New York Herald Tribune
New York Journal-American
New York Post
New York Sun
New York Times
New York World Telegram
Oswego Palladium-Times
PM (NYC)
San Francisco Examiner
Seattle Times
Syracuse Post-Standard
Washington Daily News
Washington Post
Washington Star
Washington Times-Herald

Newspapers, Jewish

YIDDISH-LANGUAGE

Day (NYC)
Forward (NYC)
Jewish Morning Journal (NYC)

ENGLISH-LANGUAGE

California Jewish Voice (LA)
Every Friday (Cincinnati)
Independent Jewish Press Service *News*
Jewish Advocate (Boston)
Jewish Chronicle (Columbus, O)

Jewish Examiner (Bklyn)
Jewish Exponent (Phila)
Jewish Ledger (Rochester, NY)
Jewish News (Detroit)
Jewish Review (NYC)
Jewish Review & Observer (Cleveland)
Jewish Standard (Jersey City)
Jewish Telegraphic Agency
    Daily News Bulletin
Jewish Times (Baltimore)
Jewish Times (Phila)
Jewish Week (NYC)

Periodicals & Serials

America
American Hebrew
American Jewish Archives
American Jewish Historical Quarterly
American Jewish History
American Jewish Year Book
American Legion Magazine
American Mercury
American Vindicator
Answer
Atlantic Monthly
Bulletin of Activities & Digest of the Press
    (AJCf)
Bulletin of the World Jewish Congress
Call (Workmen's Circle)
Catholic Action
Catholic Digest
Catholic Mind
Catholic Worker
Catholic World
Central Conference of American
    Rabbis Yearbook
Christendom
Christian Century
Christianity and Crisis
Christianity and Society
Christian Register
Churchman

Collier's
Commentary
Commonweal
Conference Record
"Confidential Bulletin" (AZEC)
Congressional Digest
Congressional Record
Congress Weekly
Contemporary Jewish Record
Cross and the Flag
Defender Magazine
Dept of State Bulletin
Federal Council Bulletin
Foreign Affairs
Foreign Service (VFW)
Galilean Magazine
The Ghetto Speaks
Information Bulletin (Am Council for
    Judaism)
Information Service (Federal Council of
    Churches)
International Labour Review
Interpreter Releases
JDC Digest
Jewish Affairs
Jewish Comment
Jewish Digest
Jewish Forum

Jewish Frontier
Jewish Outlook
Jewish Social Studies
Jewish Veteran
Liberal Judaism
Life
Lutheran
Menorah Journal
Midstream
Monthly Review (US Imgn & Naturalization Service)
Nation
National Jewish Monthly
National Legionnaire
National Record
New Masses
New Palestine
New Republic
Newscast (ACCR)
Newsweek
NRS Community Bulletin
Opinion
Palestine (AZEC)

Parliamentary Debates
Polish Fortnightly Review
Polish Review
Public Opinion Quarterly
Reader's Digest
Reconstructionist
Religion in Life
Religious Digest
Rescue (HIAS)
Rescue and Refuge (USCCEC)
"Review of the Yiddish Press"
Saturday Evening Post
Social Justice
"Special Information Bulletin" (NRS)
Survey Graphic
Time
Wiener Library Bulletin
World Alliance News Letter
Yad Vashem Bulletin
Yad Vashem Studies
YIVO Annual of Jewish Social Science
Zionews

Books

Abella, Irving, and Harold Troper. *None Is Too Many* (1982).

Anger, Per. *With Raoul Wallenberg in Budapest* (1981).

Avni, Haim. *Spain, the Jews, and Franco* (1982).

Bauer, Yehuda. *American Jewry and the Holocaust* (1981).

―――. *Flight and Rescue: BRICHAH* (1970).

―――. *From Diplomacy to Resistance* (1970).

―――. *The Holocaust in Historical Perspective* (1978).

Ben-Ami, Yitshaq. *Years of Wrath, Days of Glory* (1982).

Birtles, Philip. *Mosquito: A Pictorial History of the DH98* (1980).

Blum, John M. *From the Morgenthau Diaries*, v 3 (1967).

―――. *Roosevelt and Morgenthau* (1970).

Bonjour, Edgar. *Geschichte der schweizerischen Neutralität*, v 6 (1970).

Braham, Randolph L. (ed). *The Destruction of Hungarian Jewry: A Documentary Account*, v 1 (1963).

―――. *Eichmann and the Destruction of Hungarian Jewry* (1961).

――― (ed). *Hungarian-Jewish Studies*, v 2 & 3 (1969, 1973).

―――. *The Politics of Genocide: The Holocaust in Hungary*, 2 vols (1981).

Buchanan, A. Russell. *The United States and World War II*, 2 vols (1964).

Burns, James M. *Roosevelt: The Soldier of Freedom* (1970).

Cantril, Hadley (ed). *Public Opinion: 1935–1946* (1951).

Celler, Emanuel. *You Never Leave Brooklyn* (1953).

Ciechanowski, Jan. *Defeat in Victory* (1947).

Cohen, Naomi. *Not Free to Desist: The American Jewish Committee, 1906–1966* (1972).

Craven, Wesley F., & James L. Cate (eds). *The Army Air Forces in World War II,* v 3 (1951).

Dallek, Robert. *Franklin D. Roosevelt and American Foreign Policy* (1979).

Davie, Maurice R. *Refugees in America* (1947).

Dawidowicz, Lucy S. *The War Against the Jews* (1975).

de Jong, Louis, *The German Fifth Column in the Second World War* (1956).

Detzer, Dorothy. *Appointment on the Hill* (1948).

Diamond, Sander. *The Nazi Movement in the United States* (1974).

Dinnerstein, Leonard. *America and the Survivors of the Holocaust* (1982).

Divine, Robert A. *Foreign Policy and U.S. Presidential Elections, 1940–1948* (1974).

DuBois, Josiah E., Jr. *The Devil's Chemists* (1952).

Esco Foundation for Palestine. *Palestine: A Study of Jewish, Arab, and British Policies,* v 2 (1947).

Fein, Helen. *Accounting for Genocide* (1979).

Feingold, Henry L. *The Politics of Rescue* (1970).

Fielding, Raymond. *The March of Time, 1933–1951* (1978).

Fisher, Julius S. *Transnistria: The Forgotten Cemetery* (1969).

Friedman, Filip. *This Was Oswiecim* (1946).

Fuchs, Lawrence H. *The Political Behavior of American Jews* (1956).

Garlinski, Jozef. *Fighting Auschwitz* (1975).

Gilbert, Martin. *Auschwitz and the Allies* (1981).

Goldmann, Nahum. *The Autobiography of Nahum Goldmann* (1969).

Gutman, Yisrael, & Efraim Zuroff (eds). *Rescue Attempts during the Holocaust: Proceedings of the Second Yad Vashem International Historical Conference* (1977).

Halperin, Samuel. *The Political World of American Zionism* (1961).

Hand, Samuel. *Counsel and Advise: A Political Biography of Samuel I. Rosenman* (1979).

Hassett, William D. *Off the Record with FDR* (1958).

Hayes, Carlton J. H. *Wartime Mission in Spain, 1942–1945* (1946).

Hilberg, Raul. *The Destruction of the European Jews* (1961).

Hirschmann, Ira. *Caution to the Winds* (1962).

Howard, J. Woodford, Jr. *Mr. Justice Murphy: A Political Biography* (1968).

Hull, Cordell. *Memoirs* (1948).

Huthmacher, J. Joseph. *Senator Robert F. Wagner and the Rise of Urban Liberalism* (1968).

Infield, Glenn. *The Poltava Affair* (1973).

Institute of Jewish Affairs. *The Institute Anniversary Volume* (1962).

International Committee of the Red Cross. *Inter Arma Caritas: The Work of the ICRC during the Second World War* (1947).

———. *Report of the ICRC on Its Activities during the Second World War,* 3 vols (1948).

Israel, Fred. *The War Diary of Breckinridge Long* (1966).

Karski, Jan. *Story of a Secret State* (1944).

Kersten, Felix. *The Kersten Memoirs* (1956).

Kohanski, Alexander (ed). *The American Jewish Conference: Its Organization and Proceedings of the First Session, August 29–September 2, 1943* (1944).

——— (ed). *The American Jewish Conference: Proceedings of the Second Session, December 3–5, 1944* (1945).

Kraus, Ota, & Erich Kulka. *The Death Factory* (1966).

Laqueur, Walter. *The Terrible Secret* (1980).

Lash, Joseph. *Eleanor: The Years Alone* (1972).

Lester, Elenore. *Wallenberg: The Man in the Iron Web* (1982).

Lévai, Jenö (Eugene). *Black Book on the Martyrdom of Hungarian Jewry* (1948).

———. *Eichmann in Hungary* (1961).

Lewin, Isaac. *Churban Europa* (1948).

Lowrie, Donald A. *The Hunted Children* (1963).

Manvell, Roger. *Films and the Second World War* (1974).

Marrus, Michael R., & Robert O. Paxton. *Vichy France and the Jews* (1981).

Morley, John F. *Vatican Diplomacy and the Jews During the Holocaust* (1980).

Morse, Arthur D. *While Six Million Died* (1968).

Murphy, Bruce. *The Brandeis/Frankfurter Connection* (1982).

Neumann, Emanuel. *In The Arena* (1976).

Nevins, Allan. *Herbert H. Lehman and His Era* (1963).

Office of Strategic Services. *The Overseas Targets: War Report of the OSS* (1976).

Panstwowe Muzeum w Oswiecimiu. *Hefte von Auschwitz,* v 8 (1964).

Penkower, Monty. *The Jews Were Expendable* (1983).

Pickett, Clarence E. *For More Than Bread* (1953).

Polier, Justine Wise, & James W. Wise (eds). *The Personal Letters of Stephen Wise* (1956).

Reitlinger, Gerald. *The Final Solution* (1953).

Rosenman, Samuel I. (ed). *The Public Papers and Addresses of Franklin D. Roosevelt,* v 13 (1950).

Ross, Robert W. *So It Was True* (1980).

Rotkirchen, Livia. *The Destruction of Slovak Jewry: A Documentary History* (1961).

Sachar, Howard M. *A History of Israel* (1979).

Schellenberg, Walter. *The Labyrinth* (1956).

Schwarz, Jordan A. *The Speculator: Bernard M. Baruch in Washington* (1981).

Sehn, Jan. *German Crimes in Poland,* v 1 (1946).

Sherwood, Robert E. *Roosevelt and Hopkins* (1948).

Shub, Boris. *Starvation Over Euorpe* (1943).

Silver, Abba Hillel. *Vision and Victory* (1949).

Silver, Daniel J. (ed). *In the Time of Harvest: Essays in Honor of Abba Hillel Silver* (1963).

Silverberg, Robert. *If I Forget Thee O Jerusalem* (1970).

Smith, Bradley. *Reaching Judgment at Nuremberg* (1977).

Smith, R. Harris. *OSS: The Secret History* (1972).

Smolen, Kazimierz. *From the History of KL-Auschwitz,* v 1 (1967).

Steel, Ronald. *Walter Lippmann and the American Century* (1980).

Stember, Charles (ed). *Jews in the Mind of America* (1966).

Stimson, Henry L., & McGeorge Bundy. *On Active Service in Peace and War* (1947).

Sunderman, James (ed). *World War II in the Air: Europe* (1963).

Syrkin, Marie. *Blessed Is the Match* (1947).

Tartakower, Arieh, & Kurt Grossmann. *The Jewish Refugee* (1944).

Tull, Charles. *Father Coughlin and the New Deal* (1965).

Urofsky, Melvin I. (ed). *Essays in American Zionism 1917–1948* (1978).

———. *A Voice That Spoke for Justice* (1982).

Visser 't Hooft, W. A. *Memoirs* (1973).

Voss, Carl Hermann. *Rabbi and Minister: The Friendship of Stephen S. Wise and John Haynes Holmes* (1964).

——— (ed). *Stephen S. Wise: Servant of the People* (1969).

Vrba, Rudolf, & Alan Bestic. *I Cannot Forgive* (1964).

Wasserstein, Bernard. *Britain and the Jews of Europe, 1939–1945* (1979).

Webster, Charles, & Noble Frankland. *The Strategic Air Offensive Against Germany, 1939–1945,* v 3 (1961).

Weisgal, Meyer. *Autobiography* (1971).

Weizmann, Chaim. *Trial and Error* (1949).

Wiesel, Elie. *Legends of Our Time* (1968).

———. *Night* (1960).

Winkler, Allan M. *The Politics of Propaganda: The Office of War Information* (1978).

Wischnitzer, Mark. *Visas to Freedom: The History of HIAS* (1956).

Wise, Stephen S. *Challenging Years: The Autobiography of Stephen Wise* (1949).

World Jewish Congress. *Unity in Dispersion: A History of the WJC* (1948).

Wyman, David. *Paper Walls: America and the Refugee Crisis* (1968).

Pamphlets and Booklets

American Jewish Committee. *Statement on Withdrawal from the American Jewish Conference* (1943).

American Jewish Conference. *Report of the Interim Committee and the Commission on Rescue, Commission on Palestine, Commission on Post-War* (1944).

———. *Statement of Organization of Conference and Summary of Resolutions Adopted at First Session* [1944].

———. *Statement on the Withdrawal of the American Jewish Committee* (1943).

American Jewish Joint Distribution Committee. *Aiding Jews Overseas* (1942).

American Zionist Emergency Council. *A Report of Activities, 1940–1946* [1946].

Berlin, Isaiah. *Zionist Politics in Wartime Washington* (1972).

Celler, Emanuel. *Brief in Support of Baldwin-Rogers Resolution* (1943).

Dacie, Anne. *Yugoslav Refugees in Italy* (1945).

Emergency Committee to Save the Jewish People of Europe. *The American Press and the Rescue Resolution* (1944).

———. *The Work Is Still Ahead* [1944].

Ginzberg, Eli. *Report to American Jews* (1942).

Kubowitzki, A. Leon. *Survey on the Rescue Activities of the World Jewish Congress, 1940–1944* (1944).

National Catholic Welfare Conference. *Progress Report 1943: WRS–NCWC* (1943).

———. *Report to the Board of Trustees WRS–NCWC: August 1943–September 1944* (1944).

Pickett, Clarence E. *A Summary of Activities 1943* (1944).

Randall, Mercedes. *The Voice of Thy Brother's Blood* (1944).

Rummel, Joseph F. *Seventh Annual Report of the Catholic Committee for Refugees* [1943]; *Eighth* . . . [1944]; *Ninth* . . . [1945]; *Tenth* . . . [1946].

Trevor, John. *Refugees 1944* (1944).

US 15th Air Force. *Historical Summary: First Year of Operations* (1944).

US War Relocation Authority. *Token Shipment: The Story of America's War Refugee Shelter* [1946].
War Refugee Board. *Final Summary Report of the Executive Director* (1945).
———. *German Extermination Camps* (1944).
Zionist Organization of America. *Annual Report to ZOA, 47th Annual Convention* (1944).

Articles

Abbreviations: AJHQ = *American Jewish Historical Quarterly;* J = Jewish; YVS = *Yad Vashem Studies.*

American Jewish History has several relevant articles in its issues of March 1979, March 1981, and June 1983.
Annals of the American Academy of Political and Social Science has several relevant articles in its July 1980 issue.
Adler, Selig. "American Jewry and That Explosive Statehood Question, 1933–1945," in Bertram Korn (ed), *A Bicentennial Festschrift for Jacob Rader Marcus* (1976).
Bauer, Yehuda. "The Negotiations between Saly Mayer and the Representatives of the S.S. in 1944–1945," in Gutman & Zuroff (eds), *Rescue Attempts during the Holocaust* (1977).
———. "When Did They Know?" *Midstream* (4/68).
Berman, Aaron. "American Zionism and the Rescue of European Jewry: An Ideological Perspective," *Am J Hist* (3/81).
Bernays, Murray C. "Legal Basis of the Nuremberg Trials," *Survey Graphic* (1/46).
Bierbrier, Doreen. "The American Zionist Emergency Council: An Analysis of a Pressure Group," AJHQ (9/70).
Blayney, Michael S. "Herbert Pell, War Crimes, and the Jews," AJHQ (6/76).
Brugioni, Dino A. "Auschwitz-Birkenau," *Military Intelligence* (1/83).
Brugioni, Dino A., & Robert G. Poirier. "The Holocaust Revisited: A Retrospective Analysis of the Auschwitz-Birkenau Extermination Complex," *Studies in Intelligence* (winter 1978–79).
Cary, Otis. "The Sparing of Kyoto," *Japan Qtrly* (fall 1975).
Conway, John S. "Between Apprehension and Indifference: Allied Attitudes to the Destruction of Hungarian Jewry," *Wiener Library Bulletin,* v 27 (1973–74), ns #30/31.
———. "Frühe Augenzeugenberichte aus Auschwitz," *Vierteljahrshefte für Zeitgeschichte* (4/79).
de Jong, Louis. "The Netherlands and Auschwitz," YVS, v 7 (1968).
"Doomed Ships: Refugee Ordeals on the High Seas," *Wiener Library Bulletin* (4/62).
Eck, Nathan. "The Rescue of Jews with the Aid of Passports and Citizenship Papers of Latin American States," YVS, v 1 (1957).
Emerson, Herbert. "Postwar Problems of Refugees," *Foreign Affairs* (1/43).
Fein, Helen. "Reviewing the Toll: Jewish Dead, Losses and Victims of the Holocaust," *Shoah* (spring 1981).
———. "Toleration of Genocide," *Patterns of Prejudice* (9/73).

Feuer, Leon I. "Abba Hillel Silver: A Personal Memoir," *Am J Archives* (11/67). Also see 11/68 issue, pp 127–8.

———. "The Forgotten Year," *Am Zionist* (11/67).

Fox, John P. "The Jewish Factor in British War Crimes Policy in 1942," *English Hist Review* (1/77).

Fry, Varian. "The Massacre of the Jews," *New Republic* (12/21/42).

———. "Our Consuls at Work," *Nation* (5/2/42).

Genizi, Haim. "American Interfaith Cooperation on Behalf of Refugees from Nazism, 1933–1945," *Am J Hist* (3/81).

———. "The Attitude of American Catholics toward Catholic Refugees from Nazism: 1933–1945," in *Proceedings of the Seventh World Congress of Jewish Studies Holocaust Research* (1980).

———. "James McDonald and the Roosevelt Administration," *Bar-Ilan Studies in History* (1978).

Greenberg, Hayim. "Bankrupt," *Midstream* (3/64).

Grossmann, Kurt R. "Refugees, DP's, and Migrants," in Institute of Jewish Affairs, *The Institute Anniversary Volume* (1962).

Gutman, Yisrael, & Efraim Zuroff (eds). *Rescue Attempts during the Holocaust* (1977). This book contains several relevant articles.

Hirschmann, Ira A. "Palestine—as a Refuge from Fascism," *Survey Graphic* (5/45).

Huff, Earl. "A Study of a Successful Interest Group," *Western Political Qtrly* (3/72).

Jacoby, Gerhard. "The Jewish Catastrophe and Its Aftermath," in Institute of Jewish Affairs, *The Institute Anniversary Volume* (1962).

Kimball, Warren F. "Lend-Lease and the Open Door," *Political Science Qtrly* (6/71).

Koestler, Arthur. "The Nightmare That Is a Reality," *NY Times,* 1/9/44, VI, 5.

Lester, Elenore, & Frederick E. Werbell. "The Lost Hero of the Holocaust," *NY Times Magazine,* 3/30/80.

Lewin, Isaac. "Attempts at Rescuing European Jews with the Help of Polish Diplomatic Missions during World War II," parts I, II, & III, *Polish Review,* v 22, #4 (1977), v 24, #1 (1979), v 27, #1–2 (1982).

———. "Telegrams from Hell," *Polityka* (Warsaw) (8/9/75).

Ludlow, Peter W. "The International Protestant Community in the Second World War," *Jour of Ecclesiastical Hist* (7/78).

Mervis, Leonard. "The Social Justice Movement and the American Reform Rabbi," *Am J Archives* (6/55).

Morgenstern, Aryeh. "The United Rescue Committee of the Jewish Agency and Its Activities during the Years 1943–1945," *Yalkut Moreshet* (6/71). (In Hebrew.)

Morgenthau, Henry, Jr. "The Refugee Run-Around," *Collier's* (11/1/47).

Perkins, Bradford. "Reluctant Midwife: America and the Birth of Israel," *Reviews in Am Hist* (3/81).

Rothkirchen, Livia. "The 'Final Solution' in Its Last Stages," YVS, v 8 (1970).

———. "Hungary—an Asylum for the Refugees of Europe," YVS, v 7 (1968).

Shafir, Shlomo. "Taylor and McDonald: Two Diverging Views on Zionism and the Emerging Jewish State," *J Social Studies* (fall 1977).

Syrkin, Marie. Letter, *Midstream* (5/68).

———. "What American Jews Did During the Holocaust," *Midstream* (10/82).

Szajkowski, Zosa. "The Attitude of American Jews to Refugees from Germany in the 1930s," AJHQ (12/71).

Tenenbaum, Joseph. "The Contribution of American Jewry towards Rescue in the Hitler Period," *Yad Vashem Bulletin* (4/57).

"Testimony of Herman F. Graebe, Given in Israel," YVS, v 6 (1967).

Urofsky, Melvin I. (ed). *Essays in American Zionism 1917–1948* (1978). This book includes several relevant articles.

———. "Rifts in the Movement: Zionist Fissures, 1942–1945," in Urofsky (ed), *Essays in American Zionism 1917–1948* (1978).

Vago, Bela. "The British Government and the Fate of Hungarian Jewry in 1944," in Gutman & Zuroff (eds), *Rescue Attempts during the Holocaust* (1977).

Voss, Carl Hermann. "The American Christian Palestine Committee," in Urofsky (ed), *Essays in American Zionism 1917–1948* (1978).

Willson, John P. "Carlton J. H. Hayes, Spain, and the Refugee Crisis, 1942–1945," AJHQ (12/72).

Yahil, Leni. "Scandinavian Countries to the Rescue of Concentration Camp Prisoners," YVS, v 6 (1967).

Unpublished Works

Berman, Aaron. "The Hebrew Committee of National Liberation and the Rescue of the European Jews." Thesis, Hampshire Col (1975).

Dexter, Elisabeth A. "Last Port of Freedom." Manuscript (1942).

Grobman, Alex. "Reaction of American Jewry through the American and Jewish Press, 1939–1942." MA thesis, Hebrew Univ of Jerusalem (1978).

Mainzer, Edward. "The *Ohio Jewish Chronicle* 1941–1943." Manuscript (1980).

Matzozky, Eliyho. "American Jewish Press Reaction to the Mass Killing, November 24, 1942, to March 4, 1943." Manuscript (1978).

———. "The Response of American Jewry and Its Representative Organizations between November 24, 1942, and April 19, 1943, to Mass Killing of Jews in Europe." MA thesis, Yeshiva Univ (1979).

Musy, Jean-Marie. "Rapport au Comité Suisse de l'Union of Orthodox Rabbis." Manuscript (1945).

Neustadt-Noy, Isaac. "The Unending Task: Efforts to Unite American Jewry from the American Jewish Congress to the American Jewish Conference." PhD dissertation, Brandeis Univ (1976).

US Foreign Economic Administration. "A Survey of Greek Relief, April 1941 to December 1943." Mimeographed (1944).

Wood, Louise H. "Italy Program: 1940–1941, 1944–1962." Mimeographed by American Friends Service Committee (1970).

INDEX

ABOUT THE AUTHOR

David S. Wyman was born in Weymouth, Massachusetts, in 1929, the grandson of two Protestant ministers. He graduated from Boston University in 1951 with an A.B. in history, from Plymouth (N.H.) State College in 1961 with an M.Ed., and from Harvard University in 1966 with a Ph.D. in history. At Harvard, his studies were assisted by a Woodrow Wilson Fellowship. Since 1966 he has taught at the University of Massachusetts, Amherst, where he is a professor of history and has twice been chairman of the Judaic studies program. He has also worked as a parts shipper, a milkman, a printer, and a sixth-grade and high school teacher.

David Wyman is a special adviser to the United States Holocaust Memorial Council and a member of the Academic Advisory Board of the Simon Wiesenthal Center. He is the author of *Paper Walls: America and the Refugee Crisis, 1938–1941.*